BIRD HA
of Great Brita

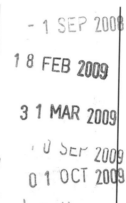

by the same author
BRITISH BUTTERFLIES
(Jarrold Publications)

BIRD HABITATS
OF GREAT BRITAIN AND IRELAND

A New Approach to Birdwatching
FOREWORD BY
SIR PETER SCOTT

Paul Morrison

A MERMAID BOOK

TITLE PAGE PICTURES:
Above left: Pied Flycatcher (page 26)
Below right: Wheatear (page 105)
Right: Nuthatch (page 33)

MICHAEL JOSEPH LTD

Published by the Penguin Group
27 Wrights Lane, London W8 5TZ, England
Viking Penguin Inc., 375 Hudson Street, New York, New York 10014, USA
Penguin Books Australia Ltd, Ringwood, Victoria, Australia
Penguin Books Canada Ltd, 10 Alcorn Avenue, Suite 300, Toronto, Ontario, Canada M4V 3B2
Penguin Books (NZ) Ltd, 182–190 Wairau Road, Auckland 10, New Zealand

Penguin Books Ltd, Registered Offices, Harmondsworth, Middlesex, England

First published in Great Britain 1989
First published in Mermaid Books 1992

Text copyright © Paul Morrison 1989
Illustrations copyright © Natural Selection

Typeset by Goodfellow & Egan, Cambridge
Colour reproduction by Anglia Graphics, Bedford
Printed and bound in Singapore by Kyodo Printing Co.

ISBN 0 7181 3183 5

A CIP catalogue record for this book is available
from the British Library

CONTENTS

ACKNOWLEDGEMENTS

Natural history, especially birds, has been a consuming passion all my life. Even so, it would be impossible for one person to be totally authoritative on all the species and habitats covered in this book. In writing it, I have drawn widely on the experience of many experts without whose generous help and specialist knowledge this book would not have been possible. I should like to thank Robert Fuller of British Trust for Ornithology for allowing me to quote from his own classic publication and Dr O'Connor (formerly BTO), Mike Shrubb and Chris Feare (MAFF) for their information on farmland birds. Steve Carter of BTO was also very helpful in providing research papers and specialist publications at short notice.

Numerous staff of the RSPB have been helpful with information and literature, including Chris Harbard for keeping me up to date with the ospreys at Loch Garten, Richard Porter for allowing me to quote from one of his articles, Chris Sargeant in the Photographic Library, Ian Dawson in the Reference Library and Anne Smith in the Conservation Department. Richard Nairn and Maggie Kelgh of the Irish Wildbird Conservancy were very helpful, together with Clive Hutchinson and Richard Mills, for information on Irish sites and species which is not readily available. Dr J.T.R. and Mrs Sharrock (British Birds) kindly gave permission to use Irish site details from their publication. I should also like to thank John Hayward and Robin Pay of Aylesbury W.P.C. Works for their time and advice.

The photographs in this book represent a lifetime's work and special thanks are due to Jimmy Young for his tireless enthusiasm and dedication to bird photography and whose skill has largely enabled this book to materialise. Chris Knights spent considerable time locating and helping me photograph the stone curlew for which I am grateful and Sid Clarkson should be thanked and congratulated for his attempts to cross open moorland by jeep in pursuit of red grouse.

My inspiration has come from many sources, but I should like to pay tribute to Eric Hosking who, through his photographic books, motivated me as a schoolboy and gave me 'an eye for a bird'; and to Percy Edwards whose legendary imitations of birds encouraged me to use my ears and learn their calls in the wild. I shall always remember the late Geoffrey Kinns for the field knowledge he taught me. Dorothy Herlihy should be thanked for her enthusiasm and encouragement and Alison, who for seventeen years tried to understand what birds meant to me and encouraged me to realise my ambition.

Knowledge of birds is insufficient to produce a book and without the editorial skills of Jenny Dereham and Anne Askwith, and the ability of Penny Mills to design it, this book would never have progressed. I am particularly grateful for their help and patience.

Finally, the administration of any book is vast and my sincere thanks go to my mother, Priscilla Morrison, for her devotion to typing my handwritten scripts often at short notice, and for checking the manuscript, and to Hilary for her typing assistance and encouragement.

BIBLIOGRAPHY

Allaby, Michael, *Book of British Woodlands*, David & Charles, 1986.

Andrews, John and Smart, Nicholas, *Farm Woodlands and Birds*, RSPB Conservation Advisory Section, 1986.

Angel, Heather, *The Natural History of Britain and Ireland*, Michael Joseph, 1981.

Arvill, Robert, *Man and Environment*, Penguin Books, 1967.

Barnes, Richard, *Coasts and Estuaries*, Hodder & Stoughton, 1979.

Batten *et al*, *Birdwatchers' Year*, T. & A. D. Poyser, 1973.

Bellamy, David, *Discovering the Countryside with David Bellamy: Coastal Walks*, Hamlyn, 1982.
Grassland Walks, Country Life, 1983.
Woodland Walks, Hamlyn, 1982.

Bennett, Linda and Everett, Michael, *The Guinness Book of Sea and Shore Birds*, Guideway Publishing Ltd, 1982.

Bere, Rennie, *The Nature of Cornwall*, Barracuda Books, 1982.

Bird Study: Volume 21 (4), 1974; Volume 27, Sept 1980.

Bishop, O. N., *Natural Communities*, John Murray, 1973.

Blunden, John and Turner, Graham, *Critical Countryside*, BBC, 1985.

British Birds: Volume 71, June 1978; Volume 73, No 2, Feb 1980.

Bromhall, Derek, *Devil Birds: The Life of the Swift*, Hutchinson, 1980.

Brooks, Alan and Agate, Elizabeth, *Hedging*, British Trust for Conservation Volunteers, 1975.

Brough, Peter; Gibbons, Bob; Pope, Colin, *The Nature of Hampshire and the Isle of Wight*, Barracuda Books, 1986.

Burton, John, *The Naturalist in London*, David & Charles, 1974.

Bury, Pam, *Agriculture and Countryside Conservation*, Farm Business Unit of Wye College of Agriculture, University of London, March 1985.

Chinery, Michael, *The Natural History of the Garden*, Collins, 1977.

Colebourn, Phil and Gibbons, Bob, *Britain's Natural Heritage*, Blandford Press, 1987.

Condry, William, M. *The Natural History of Wales*, Collins, 1982.
Woodlands, Collins, 1974.

Corke, David, *The Nature of Essex*, Barracuda Books, 1984.

Darlington, Arnold, *Mountains and Moorlands*, Hodder & Stoughton, 1978.

De Buitlear, Eamon, *Wild Ireland*, Amach Faoin Aer Publishing, 1984.

Diamond, Anthony W.; Schreiber, Rudolf L.; Attenborough, David; Prestt, Ian, *Save the Birds*, Cambridge University Press, 1987.

Dony, J. G.; Jury, S. L.; Perring. F. H., *English Names of Wild Flowers*, Edition 2, Botanical Society of the British Isles, 1986.

Dowdeswell, W. H., *Hedgerows and Verges*, Allen & Unwin, 1987.

Duffey, E. *et al*, *Grassland Ecology and Wildlife Management*, Chapman and Hall, 1974.

Edlin, H. L., *Trees, Woods and Man*, Collins, 1978.

Everett, Michael, *The Guinness Book of Woodland Birds*, Guideway Publishing Ltd, 1980.

Farming and Wildlife Trust Ltd, *Managing Change*, RSPB, 1986.

Feare, Christopher, *The Starling*, Oxford University Press, 1984.

Fitter, R. S. R., *London's Natural History*, Collins, 1946.

Flegg, Jim, *The British Ornithologists' Guide to Bird Life*, Blandford Press, 1980.
In Search of Birds – Their Haunts and Habitats, Blandford Press, 1983.

Freethy, Ron, *The Making of the British Countryside*, David & Charles, 1981.
The Natural History of Rivers, Terence Dalton Ltd, 1986.
The Naturalist's Guide to the British Coastline, David & Charles, 1983.
Wildlife in Towns (British Naturalists' Association Guide), Crowood Press, 1986.

Fuller, R. J., *Bird Habitats in Britain*, T. & A. D. Poyser, 1982.

Fuller, R. J. and Glue, D. E., *Biology Conservation 17*, Applied Science Publishers Ltd, 1980.
Effluent and Water Treatment Journal, Jan 1981.

Godwin, H., *History of the British Flora*, Cambridge University Press, 1983.

Goode, David, *Wild in London*, Michael Joseph, 1986.

Greenoak, Francesca, *God's Acre*, Orbis Publishing, 1985.

Hammond, Nicholas, *RSPB Nature Reserves*, RSPB, 1983.

Harley, J. L. and Lewis, D. H., *The Flora Vegetation of Britain: Origins and Changes – The Facts and Their Interpretation*, Academic Press, 1985.

Hepburn, Ian, *Flowers of the Coast*, Collins, 1952.

Hervey, Canon G. A. K. and Barnes, J. A. G., *Natural History of the Lake District*, Frederick Warne, 1970.

Hutchinson, Clive, *Ireland's Wetlands and their Birds*, Irish Wildbird Conservancy, 1979.
Watching Birds in Ireland, Country House, 1986.

The Living Countryside, 15-volume Partwork, Eaglemoss Publications Ltd, 1981.

Lloyd, Clare, *Birdwatching on Estuaries, Coast and Sea*, Severn House Publishers Ltd, 1981.

Mabey, Richard, *The Flowering of Britain*, Hutchinson, 1980.

Macan, T. T. and Worthington, E. B., *Life in Lakes and Rivers*, Collins, 1951.

Macmillan *Guide to Britain's Nature Reserves*, 1984

Marsden, David, *Nature Watcher's Directory*, Hamlyn, 1984.

Mellanby, K., *Farming and Wildlife*, Collins, 1981.

Mitchell, W. R., *Birdwatch around Scotland*, Robert Hale, 1983.

Mockler, Mike, *Birds in the Garden*, Blandford Press, 1982.

Moore, N. W., *The Bird of Time*, Cambridge University Press, 1987.

Morris, Pat, *Natural History of the British Isles*, Country Life (Hamlyn), 1979.

Morrison, Paul, *British Butterflies*, Jarrold Colour Publications, 1987.

Nature Conservancy Council, *Chalk Grassland – Its Conservation and Management*, 1984.
Nature Conservation in Great Britain, 1984.

Nethersole-Thompson, Desmond and Maimie, *Waders – Their Breeding, Haunts and Watchers*, T. & A. D. Poyser, 1986.

Newton, Ian, *The Sparrowhawk*, Shire Publications, 1987.

O'Connor, Raymond J. and Shrubb, Michael, *Farming and Birds*, Cambridge University Press, 1986.

Ogilvie, M. A., *Birdwatching on Inland Fresh Waters*, Severn House Publishers Ltd, 1981.
The Birdwatcher's Guide to the Wetlands of Britain, B. T. Batsford, 1979.

Owen, Dennis, *Towns and Gardens*, Hodder & Stoughton, 1978.

Pearsall, W. H., *Mountains and Moorlands*, Collins, 1950.

Pemberton, John E., *The Birdwatcher's Yearbook and Diary 1988*, Buckingham Press, 1987.

Pennington, W., *The History of British Vegetation*, English University Press, 1974.

Peterken, George, *Woodland Conservation and Management*, Chapman and Hall, 1981.

Pollard, E.; Hooper, M. D.; Moore, N. W., *Hedges*, Collins, 1974.

Prater, A. J., *Estuary Birds of Britain and Ireland*, T. & A. D. Poyser, 1981.

Prestt, Ian, *British Birds – Lifestyles and Habitats*, B. T. Batsford Ltd, 1982.

Pye-Smith, Charlie and Rose, Chris, *Crisis and Conservation – Conflict in the British Countryside*, Penguin, 1984.

Rackham, Oliver, *Trees and Woodland in the British Landscape*, J. M. Dent and Sons Ltd, 1976.
Ancient Woodland, Edward Arnold, 1980.

Ratcliffe, D. A., *A Nature Conservation Review*, Volumes 1 & 2, Cambridge University Press, 1977.

Redman, Nigel and Harrap, Simon, *Birdwatching in Britain – a Site by Site Guide*, Christopher Helm Publishers, 1987.

RSPB, *Forestry in the Flows of Caithness and Sutherland*, June 1987.
Hill Farming and Birds – A Survival Plan, July 1984.
Reclamation and Afforestation of Moorland in Mid-Wales, Dec, 1986.
RSPB Conservation Review, 1987.

Russell, Valerie, *A Tour of British Bird Reserves*, Crowood Press, 1986.

Saunders, David, *The Nature of West Wales*, Barracuda Books, 1986.

Scott, Bob, *The Atlas of British Birdlife*, Country Life, 1987.

Simms, Eric, *Birds of Town and Suburb*, Collins, 1975.
Woodland Birds, Collins, 1971.

Sitwell, Nigel, *The Shell Guide to Britain's Threatened Wildlife*, Collins, 1984.

Smart, Nicholas and Andrews, John, *Birds and Broadleaves Handbook*, RSPB, 1985.

Smyth, Bob, *City Wildspace*, Hilary Shipman Ltd, 1987.

Sturrock, F. G. and Caithie, J., *Farm Modernisation and the Countryside*, Dept of Land Economy, Cambridge University, 1980.

Tansley, A. G., *Britain's Green Mantle*, Allen & Unwin, 1968.

Tubbs, Colin, R., *The New Forest*, Collins, 1986.

Webb, Nigel, *Heathlands*, Collins, 1986.

Weightman, Gavin and Birkhead, Mike, *City Safari – Wildlife in London*, Sidgwick & Jackson, 1986.

Whitton, Brian, *Rivers, Lakes and Marshes*, Hodder & Stoughton, 1979.

Wilkinson, Gerald, *A History of Britain's Trees*, Hutchinson, 1981.
Trees in the Wild, Stephen Hope Books, 1973.

Wilson, Ron, *The Hedgerow Book*, David & Charles, 1979.

Yapp, W. B., *Birds and Woods*, Oxford University Press, 1962.

FOREWORD by Sir Peter Scott CH CBE DSC FRS

It is more than sixty years since I first fell under the spell of wild geese. As an artist, as a naturalist and as a conservationist I find that they have remained a kind of obsession for me. Wild geese, and their close relatives wild swans, have a special magic for many reasons. They make long and still incompletely understood migrations. Their wild musical calls are immensely evocative. Their society is based on a permanent pair bond and the young stay with their parents for most of the first year of their lives. Often they gather in vast aggregations which constitute some of the finest wildlife spectacles still to be seen in the world. My continuing delight and joy in their wildness and beauty has been the inspiration for my paintings and drawings, for my ornithological research and also for many years of effort in the cause of wildlife conservation.

Wildfowl, and indeed all birds, have enriched my life in countless ways, but their survival cannot be taken for granted. In the world as a whole as many as one in nine bird species are in danger of extinction, and many more are declining in numbers. In Britain, three species are now on the list of birds threatened with global extinction (the corncrake, red kite and white-tailed sea eagle), while another one in every seven species are declining in this country.

Long ago, I realised that the most important element in conservation was habitat, as most species cannot survive without the environment in which they evolved. Some birds are able to adapt to new habitats, such as the starlings, pigeons and house martins which are flourishing in our twentieth-century cities. Many more species, however, have declined in numbers because of man-made changes to their habitats.

We have been altering natural habitats in Britain ever since we first became farmers sometime around 5,000 years ago. In fact, apart from the steepest cliffs and highest mountain tops, there is scarcely a square yard of Britain that has not been modified in some way by our ancestors. But the pace of change has escalated catastrophically in the last forty years. The statistics need repeating as they help to explain only too clearly why so many of our birds are in danger. Since the end of the Second World War, changes in agricultural practice have led to the destruction of 95 per cent of flower-rich meadows and 80 per cent of chalk and limestone grasslands, the habitat of the corncrake, stone curlew, grey partridge and many others. In the last forty years half of the surviving ancient woodlands have been cleared for alien conifer plantations or cereal fields, leading to the decline of the pied flycatcher, wood warbler, honey buzzard, red kite and many others. The drainage of wetland areas has destroyed 50 per cent of lowland fens and wet valleys, the habitat of the marsh harrier and bittern. Thirty per cent of our upland grasslands and heaths has been afforested or ploughed up, leading to the decline of the golden eagle, hen harrier, merlin and greenshank.

Paul Morrison describes our present situation exactly, when he says in Chapter 13, "nationally and internationally, we sit on the knife-edge of unalterable change". An uncomfortable position indeed, and one which cannot be maintained for long. Birds are not only fascinating in themselves: they are also valuable indicators of the state of our environment. When they are in trouble, so are we. Perhaps when this is understood we will collectively be able to change our ways in time to see the return to their former numbers of harriers, nightingales and kingfishers, and of all the other birds now being squeezed out of existence by our thoughtless destruction of their habitat. Perhaps . . .

Peter Scott

Slimbridge
September 1988

INTRODUCTION

During the late 1950s and early 1960s when I was a young schoolboy and the BBC Natural History Unit was in its infancy, I regularly watched a mesmerising weekly television series called *Look*. Narrated by Sir Peter Scott, one of the pioneers of natural-history television, the series reached its peak for me when it devoted an entire programme to the RSPB reserve, at Minsmere in Suffolk. My enthusiasm for birdwatching was fired. It was hard to believe that somewhere in Britain a place existed where marsh harrier, bearded tit, bittern and avocet all bred, the latter nesting in 1947 after an absence from Britain of more than 100 years. Here was a birdwatcher's paradise: a variety of habitats, creating a haven covering 631 ha/1,560 acres, where birds sought refuge at all seasons and where, during early summer, more than 100 species could be seen in a single day. I vowed that I would one day explore Minsmere, and today I consider myself lucky to have visited it and seen the birds with my own eyes. Now world famous, the reserve is a mosaic of marshland, reedbeds, brackish lagoons with mud banks, meres, dunes, heathland, rough pasture and scrubland and mixed woodland. For birdwatchers, it is an inspiration, and a wonderful place to learn about the relationship between birds and the environment which they inhabit.

Britain has many such reserves, which protect a variety of habitats which are home to a wealth of different bird species and other wild life. But outside them all these different habitats are under threat of destruction, or have already been completely destroyed by man.

Britain's countryside has survived ice ages, one of the northern hemisphere's most unpredictable climates and even two world wars. With the huge increase in human population and the growth of towns and cities the countryside became fragmented but still remained rich and diverse. For centuries man lived in harmony with the countryside; the necessary evolution of farming practice gradually altered, but rarely threatened the framework within which human beings and wildlife co-existed. Even the development of canals, railways and motorways left only minor scars across the land. However, in the last hundred years everything has changed. Since the Second World War destruction of the countryside has taken place on an enormous scale and escalated to disastrous levels. Most people would accept that the revolutions in agriculture and forestry, exempt from usual planning controls, are responsible for much of the havoc and the deterioration in the landscape value of the countryside.

Even the Sites of Special Scientific Interest (SSSIs), areas designated by the Nature Conservancy Council as being of value because of their flora, fauna or geological or physiographical features, have been ravaged. Between 1937 and 1971, 47 per cent of Wiltshire's downland was ploughed up and in Devon between 1950 and 1972, 20 per cent of all the broad-leaf woods were felled for agricultural development or conifer plantations. The amount of Dorset heathlands has declined by over 40 per cent since 1960 and 75 per cent of all Suffolk's coastal heathland has been converted to arable land since the 1920s. Nearly 50 per cent of Britain's ancient woods, managed since the Middle Ages and comprising oak, ash and beech, have been felled since 1947 and combined with the effects of the natural

1

2

1 Regularly hunting across farmland, this kestrel has nested inside a barn, storing straw bales.

2 Masonry ledges and cavities in the brickwork frequently attract kestrels to nest close to man.

3 Female kestrel with her chicks on a moorland rocky ledge site.

4 An alternative nest site for the kestrel: an old crow's nest in a woodland habitat.

disaster of the hurricane in October 1987 when 15 million trees were destroyed, by the year 2025, unless something is done to prevent habitat destruction, all deciduous woods will be gone apart from those forming nature reserves.

To guarantee the future of many species in Britain there must be some radical land reforms, changing the way land is used by powerful sections of the community such as property developers, water authorities, the chemical industry, farmers and foresters. It is already too late to save much of the countryside that existed only ten years ago; conservationists, since the Second World War, have been virtually powerless to save our natural heritage and have in many respects lost the fight for Britain's countryside. Today, however, there are over 3 million conservationists, belonging to a number of societies, with over 500,000 belonging to the Royal Society for the Protection of Birds. These members and the millions of other people sharing an interest in the countryside agree that a new phase of conservation development has arrived to save what-ever is left of the countryside. What is already gone cannot be brought back, but future generations should not be deprived of the chance, where it is still possible, to see wild birds in their open habitats. Conservationists must all become active and campaign against the activities of the small, influential min-ority who exploit the countryside for purely financial goals. No longer is there room for gutless, armchair conservation, where people sit around and talk about what should be done to preserve the environment. Since Nicholas Ridley, the Secretary of State for the Environment, is so obviously anti-conservation, any new campaigns to protect Britain's heritage will need to be radical in their aims and methods.

An awareness of the need to conserve what is left of our countryside is vital for birdlovers. With their range of colourful plumage, frequently inquisitive behaviour, range of attractive songs and ability to master the air, birds add both magic and mystery to open countryside, giving pleasure to many. There are more birdwatchers in Britain than in any other country in the world. Some pursue the hobby so seriously that their intensity of study and positive identification has led them to be called 'birders' rather than mere birdwatchers. Others have become fanatical and totally consumed by travelling anywhere around the country to see a rare or unusual bird, and are referred to as 'twitchers', because they twitch with excitement when the bird is seen. But the majority do not profess to be experts and simply enjoy watching birds occasionally in natural surroundings.

This book looks at all the habitats in Britain and describes the birds found in each one. Its aim is to create public awareness of a diversity of landscape unrivalled anywhere in the world, at a time when exploitation of the countryside is intense. Each chapter looks at how the habitat evolved, how it was shaped by natural forces and changed by man, and how birds, which recognise no boundaries, adapt to colonise any habitat available. So severe is man's alteration of the country-side that he has become the major factor in the future survival of birds. Those species which are highly flexible survive because they can adapt to habitat changes caused by man; they evolve to colonise semi-natural environments and concrete jungles. But the future of other species, with more specialised feeding and habitat requirements which have evolved through millions of years, is threatened by the destruction of their habitat because they cannot adapt fast enough.

This book is not intended to be a substitute for one of the numerous field guides available on bird identification. In fact I would recommend that it should be used in conjunction with such a guide, which covers certain aspects of birds in greater depth. I have, however, attempted to go beyond the normal identification field guide and to encourage all those with an interest in birds to investigate the habitats of Britain and discover the birds found in each one; understand why they are there, how they co-exist with each other and adapt to their environment. By understanding more about the behaviour and secret lifestyle of each species, the birdwatcher will better appreciate the delicate balance between birds and their habitat. I hope also to create an awareness that every species is unique, with its own intricate personality, which makes birdwatching all the more fascinating and rewarding. If 'birders' and 'twitchers' benefit to any extent from this book, it will have served a purpose well beyond my expectations, since my aim is to share with ordinary birdwatchers' the knowledge and experi-ences gained over years of watching birds closely through binoculars and camera lenses.

The photographs throughout have been carefully chosen to show the birds' shape, plumage and beak details, because these are important in a book acting as a guide to birds found in particular habitats. They are identification records, rather than a series of behavioural, action photographs, where fine details are sometimes missed at the expense of capturing a dramatic shot. Occasionally such photographs have been included, wherever I felt they contributed to the species and text, without presenting recognition problems for the reader. Unfortunately the problem of publishing a book on such a vast subject in one volume is that it forces selection and therefore some species could not be illustrated.

Close observations and patience are fundamental to suc-cessful birdwatching, but it is equally important to learn to associate certain birds with a particular habitat because of their physical appearance, so as to understand the relationship and dependence between birds and their environment. Large num-bers of insects rising over ponds and rivers regularly attract aerodynamically shaped swifts, swallows and house martins to feed across their surfaces, whereas waders with their long thin legs and elongated bill have perfectly evolved to feed along the coastline in deep water or mud. Some species have even evolved to colonise farmland once their original habitat became overpopulated and so long as open fields are mixed with hedgerows, scrubland and spinneys, numerous birds take up residence and breed.

The reader will, of course, soon appreciate that because of their supreme mobility, birds are not confined to a single habitat even though they may be characteristic of one in particular. All the habitats covered in this book are categorised for the convenience of man and any habitat is normally a mixture of several others; thus deciduous woods may contain areas of coniferous underplanting and a river may meander along one of the boundaries. In such an environment the overlap of bird species is to be expected. Further variation of species within a habitat occurs because of geographical loca-tion and altitude or with the season of the year and this book attempts to explain fully the importance of both breeding and overwintering grounds for many resident and migratory birds. Likewise habitats such as wasteland, rubbish tips, sewage farms, railway tracks and the back garden demonstrate the versatility of birds. The kestrel, now firmly associated with motorway verges (page 236), also colonises moorland, wood-land, farmland and suburbia, as shown by the illustrated series of nest sites (1,2,3,4). The birdwatcher should always be prepared, too, for the species which behaves unexpectedly, like the pair of Mediterranean black-winged stilts which turned up at Holme Dune Nature Reserve, Norfolk, in 1987, and bred for the first time in over forty years.

It is important to be aware that birds select and change their habitats with great care. A male chaffinch singing from a bush in a suburban park is claiming a territory, chosen after a thorough investigation of the resources available within the habitat. The choice of the correct habitat is a matter of life or death not only for himself, but also for his mate and potential brood. The chaffinch does not sing purely for enjoyment; the song indicates that his chosen habitat provides sufficient protective cover, an adequate supply of food and ideal climatic conditions. It is worth learning how to translate and respect birdsong, since it suggests an acceptable environmental quality which man needs to preserve.

We need to realise that birds are extremely clever in adapting to habitat changes forced upon them by man, but more importantly we need to be aware of the maximum level of disturbance and changes to a habitat which birds accept. Birds thus educate man about his environment, although knowledge of a wide range of species is necessary, because continued interference with different habitats will result in the few common adaptable species replacing the more widespread and specialised birds of habitats like heath, estuary and moorland.

Sir Peter Scott once wrote, 'I believe the *Look* television series helps people to grasp what we stand to lose if our modern civilisation sweeps all the wildlife away.' It is a poor reflection on our society that insufficient numbers of influential people heed that potential loss. Today birdwatchers, conservationists, politicians, farmers, industrialists and ordinary people must be aware that we have lost much of the countryside in the last 40 years and must now do something to protect what remains. An awareness of habitats, from the point of view of the wildlife, is at the heart of conservation.

If wild birds have a range of habitats according to their needs, a supply of unpolluted food and a sympathetic public, they and other forms of wildlife may be assured of a place in a world now totally dominated by man.

Paul Morrison, 1988

Note on the paperback edition

Since this book was first published, there have been major changes in the nation's political and environmental realms.

Under the Wildlife and Countryside Act 1981, the NCC was responsible for advising the Government on all conservation issues. Normally its advice was confidential but it opted to speak out whenever it believed it was in the public interest. In 1987 it published a book, *Birds, Bogs and Forestry*, which pleaded for the retention of the Scottish peat bogs as important conservation sites. This precipitated a campaign to save the Flow Country of Caithness and Sutherland (see pp. 111–113) and the Forestry Commission and private forestry industry were exposed as damaging a valuable eco-system purely for commercial gain. In 1987 the NCC successfully called for a moratorium on conifer planting to save the Flow Country's wildlife. The outcome embarrassed the Government and further annoyed the forestry developers and Scottish landowners who, influential with the Government and the Forestry Commission, were instrumental in the NCC's dismemberment.

Despite many protests, in 1988 Nicholas Ridley, then Secretary of State for the Environment, proposed splitting the NCC into three separate conservation agencies: in England, English Nature; in Wales, the Countryside Council; and in Scotland, the Nature Conservancy Council for Scotland, an interim body until the Countryside Commission for Scotland amalgamates with NCCS to form Scottish Natural Heritage in spring 1992. All three were born on 1 April 1991. It is too early to assess whether they have similar policies, or whether these policies can be co-ordinated and, when necessary, lobbied with the same vigour and effectiveness as was achieved by the NCC.

In July 1989, Christopher Patten became Environment Secretary and he was responsible for the publication in autumn 1990 of the White Paper entitled *This Common Inheritance*. This appeared to be lightweight in its content. It contained little about new environmental policies and placed no emphasis on the unique habitats found in the UK. It gave insignificant recognition to the value of our internationally important wildlife sites, such as estuaries, and no firm commitment to conserve them, nor to extend or create new Environmentally Sensitive Areas (see p. 91), despite evidence that significant conservation benefits resulted from the scheme.

When John Major became Prime Minister in November 1990, Michael Heseltine became Environment Secretary. Just how 'green' he is has been difficult to assess. He saved part of Dorset's Canford Heath by refusing Poole Council planning permission for new houses. However, during his office, Britain has for the first time lost an entire SSSI – an area of marshy grassland called Hog's Hole in Northamptonshire. The site dried out because its natural water supply had to be diverted to protect a residential area, built too close, from flooding.

In July 1991 proposals were accepted for a charcoal company to extract peat for charcoal conversion from the environmentally sensitive Flow Country. The Treasury also refused to find funds to purchase the environmentally significant Mar Lodge Estate in the Cairngorms in spring 1991. In July 1991 Colin Moynihan, Energy Minister, accepted proposals for oil and gas exploration off Bempton Cliffs (see pp. 173–4). As a scientific site, the cliffs are protected under EC law and visited by over 100,000 birdwatchers each year; now the seabirds face threats from test rigs, oil leaks and helicopters. There is thus little confidence that the Government – which finds it politically expedient to persuade Third World countries to preserve their non-renewable habitats – has a laudable conservation policy for Britain's own equally valuable habitats.

There is also a lack of confidence in the Government's reorganisation of Britain's nature protection. In July 1991 Sir Frederick Halliday, the Chairman of the Joint Nature Conservation Committee, resigned, because of a House of Lords' decision to set up a second committee in Scotland to query decisions on SSSIs. This meant that any site receiving such protected status could effectively be deregulated by the secondary body, thus dismantling the effectiveness of the SSSI system in Scotland and the protection of valuable habitats.

Before he died in 1989, Sir Peter Scott wrote about Antarctica, 'We should have the wisdom to know when to leave a place alone.' This maxim should be considered by Mr Heseltine for the increasingly threatened habitats of Great Britain and Ireland. He must raise the profile of bird habitat conservation on political agendas and safeguard any sites qualifying for protection under the Ramsar Convention and European Birds Directive. The future of our wildlife depends on the effectiveness of Britain's three new conservation agencies and on his environmental wisdom.

Paul Morrison, 1991

CHAPTER 1

BRITISH WOODLAND

THE HISTORY OF WOODLAND IN BRITAIN

Pre-Boreal	10,000–9,500 years ago
Boreal	9,500–7,500 years ago
Atlantic	7,500–5,000 years ago
Sub-Boreal	5,000–2,500 years ago
Sub-Atlantic	2,500–today

It would be impossible to begin a detailed study of birdlife in one woodland community, such as oakwoods, without first understanding how woodland in general developed in Britain.

For many hundreds of years Britain has been one of the least wooded countries in Europe: woodland covers less than 5 per cent of the land. However, not all regions of Britain are equally poor in woodland, and, as the subsequent chapters explain, neither are regions poorly wooded for exactly the same reasons.

In order to appreciate the evolution of woodland and its establishment as a habitat in Britain today, we need to look at trees and woodland as a type of vegetation, common to most of Europe, and to investigate how and why the vegetation of Europe changed over the centuries.

Our knowledge of European vegetation goes back to the Tertiary period (from 65 million to about 2 million years ago) and, although information is extremely fragmentary, fossil records show that plants from this period resembled palms. The fact that palms were growing in Europe indicates that at that time the climates were tropical and sub-tropical. In the cooler climates that followed, the palm-like vegetation did not survive. Fossil evidence from Poland reveals that in the late Tertiary period Asiatic species like hornbeam, wing-nut and tulip-tree colonised parts of Europe, but these too became extinct, as the climate changed further throughout Europe at the end of the Tertiary period.

The Quaternary period began about one to two million years ago and fossil records again show us that it began with a temperate climate and corresponding vegetation. There were mixed deciduous and coniferous woods throughout much of Europe, including oak, alder, pine and spruce. When the temperatures cooled during this period, some heathland evolved with its typical heath-like vegetation. It was an era of extreme climatic fluctuation. In the warmest periods oak, ash, elm and hazel formed the main woodlands, whereas tundra communities of willow and birch evolved during colder, glacial phases.

The one significant factor which has influenced and determined the distribution of plants and animals in Europe is glaciation. There were numerous Ice Ages during the Quaternary period, the last of which began about 110,000 years ago, lasting to about 10,000 years ago with its maximum coverage 20,000 years ago. This period is referred to as the Great Ice Age.

At this time, northern Germany was virtually covered in ice sheet, but the Netherlands escaped. In the Alps, huge glaciers thrust south to Munich and Grenoble in the European plain. Britain was not totally affected: the eastern side, north of the Thames, suffered worst, but in parts of Scotland and Ireland there were ice-free areas.

As the ice eventually retreated, the climate improved and slowly plants and animals recolonised over the post-glacial years, which are conveniently divided into

PRE-BOREAL – During this period the melting ice caused the sea levels to rise and the North Sea became flooded, separating Britain from Ireland. In Europe the colonisation of juniper increased, quickly followed by dwarf birch, willow and some pine. Birds such as redpoll and willow warbler would have been the first species to colonise the resulting environment.

BOREAL – Towards the end of the Boreal period, about 7,500 years ago, more melting ice caused extensive flooding, forming the English Channel and separating Britain from the rest of continental Europe. The climate continued to get warmer and deciduous trees such as oak, elm and hazel became common in north-west Europe; and, during the early part of this climatic period, birch and pine forests became established. The latter became colonised by crossbill, capercaillie and crested tit.

ATLANTIC – This was the mildest, most humid post-glacial period. The climate encouraged the growth of wych elm and oak which formed large forests. Alder now became established, having colonised Ireland just before the country was isolated by rising sea levels. Lime was the next tree to colonise and it had its widest distribution in England at this time, although it never really established itself beyond the lowlands of England.

With the arrival of lime, a period of ecological stability began with various tree species attempting to colonise regions by natural succession: the natural replacement of one species of plant by another, during the colonisation of a habitat, forming what is called a climax forest. In much of Britain the natural climax is the oakwood, although it is replaced by beech on chalkland and ash on limestone. From this time the history of woodland becomes more accurate.

SUB-BOREAL – During this period there was a rapid decrease in the abundance of elm in northern Europe, although ash and birch increased. The virgin forests which were by then covering most of Britain began for the first time to be affected by the activities of Neolithic and early Bronze Age man.

SUB-ATLANTIC – The Sub-Atlantic period virtually coincides with the Iron Age in Europe, when ash- and limewoods were destroyed, creating large open fields. Trees were pollarded, branches being cut off to provide fodder for domestic animals. Climatically, this period was wetter and cooler than the Sub-Boreal and bogs and fens began to replace forests over much of northern Europe and Britain. This was undoubtedly the period of the broad-leaf woodland and there was probably an 'optimum climate' condition then, which caused broad-leaf woods to emerge as the dominant habitat in Britain. Oak, elm, ash, lime and hazel were all plenteous, with hawthorn, blackthorn, willow, rowan, cherry, aspen and holly forming a secondary shrub growth. It is likely that all the species of woodland birds became established during the Sub-Atlantic period.

MAN'S INFLUENCE ON TODAY'S WOODLAND HABITATS

Woodpecker, nuthatch, marsh tit and wood warbler are some of the pioneer woodland colonisers which still survive in the same habitat today. This is remarkable since during the last 2,000 years man has interfered extensively with the woodland habitats of Britain. This interference began with Neolithic man who, with the aid of his stone axe, felled large areas of forest for cultivation and agricultural development.

The decline of the elm is attributed to Neolithic man around 3100–2900 BC. At this time arable and grazing land was scarce and man fed his cattle on leaves and shoots pollarded from trees and in particular from the elm. The frequent cutting of the leafy shoots meant that many elms were unable to flower or shed pollen, and therefore the lifecycle of the tree was incomplete.

Throughout the Neolithic and Bronze Ages, land cultivation increased. Neolithic man cleared beech, ash and yew from the dry chalk and limestone uplands, where he began to graze livestock. On the light, easily worked soils of the East Anglian

5 Our ancestors changed the face of Britain by converting acres of natural forest into farmland. Within the last century man has accelerated his destruction of the countryside.

5

Breckland, the large Neolithic populations felled the native forests which were never allowed to regrow.

Later, Bronze Age man (1700–500 BC) extended the forest clearance further, into higher regions of land. Bronze Age man was responsible for the large-scale decline of lime in many parts of Britain, including Essex, Norfolk and Lincolnshire, where it was dominant, and it was never allowed to recover.

From about 400 BC, the Celts ploughed fields with their iron tools and effective ploughs. The Iron Age caused additional pressure on woodland because huge quantities of wood were required for smelting, especially in the industrial smelting areas of Sussex, the Kentish Weald and the Forest of Dean.

Our ancestors changed the face of Britain by converting acres of natural forest into farmland, by felling or burning or else by browsing: sheep and cattle chewing new sucker growth finally killed the stumps. Forest clearance remained permanent because livestock was allowed to roam the habitat, eating any seedlings which attempted to recolonise, and treeless grassland eventually evolved.

In the centuries following the birth of Christ there was significant development of the countryside in Britain. Much of today's landscape was shaped by AD 1200: small villages were established and areas of the countryside were allocated for farmland, leaving moors and wooded areas elsewhere. The woods were managed by a coppice rotation method which provided a succession of growth, protected by fences from the browsing livestock

We know that when the Romans occupied England, they inherited a land with an established agriculture; they developed it further into one of the major agricultural countries of the classical civilisation. The agricultural development involved most of the south-east and the Midlands and included the heavy soils of Suffolk and the waterlogged Fens.

When the Anglo-Saxons settled, they gradually exploited any forests left untouched by the Romans. The Anglo-Saxons were skilled carpenters and timber was their favourite building material. Many of the earliest Anglo-Saxon buildings were centred around posts set into the ground. These posts soon rotted and required regular replacement, which put demands on local woodland for timber. Consequently they cleared many of the lowland forests, considering pastures and grazing land more important than woodland, and turning England from a forest-covered country into an agricultural one.

By the end of the Anglo-Saxon period, there had been felling of ancient wildwood in Britain for 3,500 years. Domesday records of around AD 1086 provide us with some information about the woodlands remaining in eleventh-century England. Although the Norman Conquest of 1066 had little effect on English woodland, the Normans introduced 'forest laws' and an official feudal system requiring records and documentation. Royal forests were claimed and put outside the common law: in 1228 some twenty-three English counties had royal forests which included Windsor Forest, the New Forest, the Forest of Dean, Sherwood Forest and Arden Forest. They were exclusive hunting grounds for the rich and noble, and their restricted access suggests that quality woodland was already scarce.

In 1086, although coppice woodlands were common, the majority of woodlands were used for cattle pasture and grazing but the increase in pasturing animals in the manorial and royal forests and the demand for timber for building and fuel eventually caused the decline and destruction of Norman forests. In time the pasture woodlands were converted to farmland, or areas were felled to provide grazing scrubland for farm stock. Between 1250 and 1350 the amount of sheep-grazing increased dramatically and, due to successful exportation, corn-growing became important; both activities required the felling of more woodland. Inevitably timber for building became scarce and management of woodland finally became necessary.

The shortage of building material meant that timber had to be produced by the coppice method. Most medieval woods were managed by the 'coppice with standards' system, which was practised in 1086 but did not become widespread until 1251. Coppice with standards was usually carried out on a 10–15-year cycle. In any wood, selected trees were felled to allow more light to penetrate through the wood, and so promote growth. Some of the remaining trees were allowed to grow normally – termed 'standards' – while others were coppiced, i.e. cut just above ground level every decade or so.

Trees such as oak, ash, hazel, sweet chestnut and hornbeam, cut in this way, produce shoots from the base or bole of the tree. The shoots grow in a cluster and are pole-shaped, never reaching the diameter of the mature tree, but ideally suitable for fenceposts, poles or firewood.

The standards would be left to grow for 100 years or a period at least equal to five cuttings of the coppice. As well as providing timber for building houses and ships, they were ideal living stores of large timber. During the period immediately following a coppice rotation, when the shrub layer had not yet recolonised, many nesting birds would disappear until the habitat became suitable with the development of a healthy shrub layer offering shelter and nesting sites. Today coppiced woods, with their healthy shrub layer, are the main haunts of nightingale, garden warbler and blackcap.

Pollarding trees was another popular medieval woodland practice. Trees would be decapitated 1.8 m/6 ft above ground level, and a crown of small shoots would develop at a manageable height, which were cut for fencestakes, poles, basketry and firewood. Since all new shoots were well above ground level, they were not browsed by farm animals and pollarding was practised even in woodlands used for common grazing. Today the pollarded trees of Burnham Beeches and the hornbeam of Epping Forest provide nesting sites for jackdaw, redstart, tree sparrow and stock dove.

There were many historical and natural events between 1400 and 1750 which affected woodland and its management. In the sixteenth and seventeenth centuries all counties lost woodland to farmland; in Norfolk 75 per cent of medieval woodland had disappeared by 1790. In the seventeenth century forestry plantations became established on a small scale. Originally they consisted of deciduous trees, such as oak, beech and ash, planted together, and were managed with a coppicing system; however, there was a trend beginning in this century to grow trees purely for timber, for which purpose conifers were planted.

Trade between continents expanded in the eighteenth century with a corresponding increase in merchant shipping fleets. In addition, naval fleets were required and each war demanded bigger and more ships; the greatest amount of shipbuilding took place between 1800 and 1860, when half of all the timber vessels ever built in Britain were launched. The majority of these ships were built of English oak, with a corresponding demand on woodland.

During the nineteenth century the practice of coppicing declined and between 1870 and 1900 fewer woods were expertly managed, especially as demand for firewood declined when coal became available with the development of railways between 1840 and 1870.

In the nineteenth century timber was easily obtained by felling and shipping from Europe, but by the twentieth century this was no longer politically or socially acceptable, and so conifer plantations were encouraged throughout the country. Vast quantities of timber were required for the two world wars and the First World War severely hindered imports. In 1919 the Forestry Commission was founded and given the task of making Britain self-sufficient in trees. Commercial forestry managers today have a responsibility to grow timber, and so they do not view forests in the same way as the ancient woodsmen of Britain.

The woodland left in the British Isles today is fragmentary. Man has destroyed as much woodland in the past forty years as our ancestors did in the previous four hundred; and Britain is now one of the least wooded areas of Europe. But the woodlands we have left offer great variety and are frequently changing.

It is possible to find fragments of ancient wildwood within the countryside mosaic, even though these relics have been altered by man. There are the natural pinewoods of Glen Affric and Strathfarrar in the southern Highlands, where crossbill, capercaillie and black grouse breed; in Co. Clare, Eire, one can find hazelwoods that are probably part of the wildwood of Ireland; and the patchwork of oak and birch trees around Loch Maree originates from 7000 BC. There is something mysterious and unique about birdwatching in these pieces of woodland, which are likely descendants from the ancient wildwood; and across Britain and Ireland there are many more to be investigated.

Some of the finest woods are those clinging to the gorge of the Lower Wye Valley – one of the most significant woodland regions in Britain. The deep gorge has been cut by the river through carboniferous limestone and sandstone and the woods below Tintern Abbey, although at one time coppiced, resemble ancient woodland. More than 60 species of our native shrubs and trees grow in natural groupings. On the sandstone, oak and beech thrive, but since much of the woodland is on mixed soil, a walk through the wood reveals wych elm, ash and hazel with alder at the river bank. There are beech, small-leaved lime and yew on the higher slopes, intermixed with wild cherry. The limestone areas of these Wye Valley woods offer field maple, large-leaved lime, several rare whitebeams and the rarer wild service tree, which is a genuine indicator of ancient woodland: these areas are as close to the original wildwood as possible. Further up the gorge, north of Tintern, stand plantations of present-century conifer; thus, in a relatively short journey down the Wye, you can travel through 5,000 years of woodland history.

Our ancestors destroyed, managed and replanted woodland in such a manner that today we have inherited woods which are extremely diverse. Every county has unique features – dells, spinneys and copses. For instance, there are the famous Chiltern beeches and oaks of Sherwood and Savernake. All contribute to making the British Isles known for beautiful woodlands. Indeed, perhaps the conflicting management techniques and felling by our ancestors has produced a greater variety of woodland life than nature would have otherwise provided.

Today some 60 per cent of terrestrial birds breeding in Britain require tree cover. More butterflies are found in woodland than in any other habitat and 15 per cent of our wild flowers are woodland species. All remaining woodland, whether artificial or natural, is significantly important for native wildlife.

CHAPTER 2

DECIDUOUS WOODLAND

OAKWOODS

In any woodland, naturalists tend to become preoccupied with a certain zone of the habitat. Botanists, for example, are inclined to study with amazing detail the ground layer where all the woodland flowers and inconspicuous mosses and liverworts grow. The ornithologist, however, should be aware of the structure of the complete community because woodland birds are affected not only by the trees but also by the bushes and other smaller plants that surround them.

In most of southern England and much of the Midlands, oak is the dominant woodland. There are two native oak species: the pedunculate or common oak and the sessile or durmast oak. The pedunculate oak is the species commonly found in the woods and hedges of the Midlands and southern counties, whereas the sessile oak typically thrives on the non-calcareous soils of the west and north of England and Wales. As the name suggests, the pedunculate oak bears its acorns on long slender stalks, whilst its leaves have very short stalks. The acorns of sessile oak have short stalks or even none at all, but the leaves are borne on reasonably long stalks, which makes identification easy.

The oakwood, like other types of wood, shows a distinct four-layered structure: the *trees*, including the canopy; the *shrubs*, usually less than 5–6 m/16–19 ft in height; the *field layer* which consists of herbs, less than 1 m/3¼ ft tall; and the *ground layer* containing all the smallest flowers. Bird populations in the wood vary enormously, depending on the presence or absence of the shrub layer and the height and density of the field layer. Therefore the ornithologist with a knowledge of the botanical structure of the oakwood has certain advantages over his less experienced colleague.

Natural oakwoods grow in close canopy with the more vigorous individual trees becoming taller than their neighbours, finally killing them by shading them out. The crowns of the successful trees gradually spread out so that they meet and any gaps between the leaves are small: consequently no significant light reaches the lower woodland layers. In southern England mature pedunculate oakwood has 60–100 trees per acre with an average height of 21–4 m/69–78 ft.

With their dense canopy, mature oakwoods are not productive habitats for birdwatchers and experience will tell you to spend more time in the coppiced oakwood. Although only rarely maintained today, since the Middle Ages oakwoods have been managed by coppicing: the oaks were felled to a density of twelve per acre, making the tree canopy less dense and allowing individual trees to grow to a height of 12–15 m/39–49 ft. The cutting used to be managed on a fifteen-year cycle and because plants in the lower woodland layers were not always in dense shade, there was a rotation of luxuriant field-layer growth, followed by a dying back as the shade increased with the growth of shrubs.

Ornithologists will observe in their favourite pedunculate oakwoods that there are other species of tree growing as well.

Typically these are ash and birch, but in Epping Forest hornbeam is also common. You will see that the shrub layer is very dense, chiefly of hazel, hawthorn, blackthorn and wild rose.

In some areas the shrub is so dense that it can be penetrated only with difficulty, but in the summer months it provides excellent nesting and roosting cover for many birds. Ivy and honeysuckle are ubiquitous, and the ground layer from March to early June offers a succession of floral delights, with lesser celandine, wood anemone, wood sorrel, bluebell and wood spurge.

The sessile oakwood is very different from the pedunculate wood. There is a close canopy, but the trees do not exceed 12–15 m/39–49 ft in height and the shrub layer is poor. The soil is generally acidic where sessile oaks grow, and consequently the field layer is made up of species associated with heathland such as heather or bilberry.

The sessile oakwoods of west Wales are a perfect example of the habitat: for instance, Pengelli Forest in Dyfed, which is a managed reserve and the largest sessile oakwood left in south-west Wales. In the forest are two distinct zones: birch, rowan and holly mix with the oak in the drier regions and ash and alder mix with the oak in the damper zones. Only 5 km/3 miles south-west of Pengelli Forest is Tycanol Wood, which overgrows several rocky tors. Again, on the upper drier slopes of the wood, birch, hazel and holly intermingle with the sessile oak and here the ground flora is poor – mainly wavy-hair grass.

During May and June typical Welsh sessile oakwoods such as these act as amphitheatres for the song of redstart, pied flycatcher, tree pipit, wood warbler, coal tit and great tit, all found in any of the sessile oakwoods in Britain. Most of our sessile oakwoods grow on hillsides from 300–380 m/984–1,246 ft above sea level. As altitudes get higher, the trees become more stunted – those surviving on crags are less than 3 m/10 ft high.

Only isolated fragments of natural oakwoods survive in Britain but many semi-natural woods are predominantly oak. The established southern oakwoods, with open canopies, following a period of coppicing, offer old trees and a healthy shrub layer and are richer in birdlife than many other broad-leaf woods.

In spring and early summer there are few habitats more emotive than a pedunculate oakwood. During March and April, before the leaf canopy is fully open and sunlight readily reaches the woodland floor, early flowering dog's mercury and other flowers bloom, and the air is filled with a varied chorus of birds.

Seven species of birds dominate the pedunculate oakwood during summer: the chaffinch, robin, blue tit, great tit,

6 Rich in birdlife, the oakwood is the most typical woodland of southern Britain.

willow warbler, wren and blackbird. The blue tit and great tit sometimes compete with each other for territory, nest sites and food, but the remaining five species manage to live harmoniously together throughout the breeding season.

Another pedunculate oakwood bird, seen most frequently during the spring, is the **woodcock**. As it is a wader, closely resembling the snipe, this bird seems totally misplaced: most wading birds are seen on the coast feeding on mud flats and saltmarshes, but the woodcock prefers the woodland habitat throughout the year. It especially likes pedunculate oakwoods where the canopy is not too dense so that brambles, bracken and shrub growth are well established and the leaf litter forms a deep layer. Earthworms form the main part of the woodcock's diet, so the ideal wood must have regions that are permanently damp where the bird can probe for worms and insects with its sensitive beak. Other parts of the wood must be dry, providing nesting sites for the woodcock, which lays its eggs directly on to the ground.

Apart from Shetland, Orkney, the Outer Hebrides, the extreme south-west of England and parts of west Wales, the woodcock is widely distributed throughout the British Isles, but because the bird is secretive and perfectly camouflaged it goes undetected by many birdwatchers. Oakwoods are by far the woodcock's favourite habitat in southern England, but in Scotland birch-woods are its favourite nesting haunt. When sitting tight on the nest, the mottled russet-brown plumage, streaked with dark brown and black, breaks up the shape of the bird and camouflages it so well against the dead leaves and bracken that it remains invisible, even if only a few metres away (**7**). Its eyes are positioned high up on the side of its head, allowing 360° vision; consequently even a sitting bird can spot any danger approaching from the rear. It crouches and freezes as you get within 30.5 cm/1 ft of the nest and then it takes off or runs in a zig-zag fashion into the undergrowth.

Early spring is one of the best times to glimpse this elusive bird. During February and March the male woodcock flies slowly and purposefully around the boundaries of its woodland territory across the open glades, usually at dusk or sometimes in the early morning. The male's aim is to attract a ground-based female who will call him down to mate. This display flight is called 'roding' and many other ground-nesting birds such as lapwing and snipe make such a flight at dusk over their own habitat.

The nest is built in early March and is little more than a scrape, lined with leaves and frequently positioned under bramble or at the base of a tree. Since the woodcock is an early-nesting bird, in unfavourable springs snow might be falling even whilst the bird is incubating eggs, but this does not seem to affect the breeding cycle: **9** shows the female woodcock incubating eggs in a snow-hole.

Because the shrub layer of a sessile oakwood is generally not as dense as that of a pedunculate wood, sessile oakwoods rarely support populations of jay, garden warbler, blackcap, hedge sparrow or long-tail tit, all of which favour a rich shrub layer. However, despite a poor shrub layer, sessile oakwoods can still support a varied bird population, because many of the species nest in holes in the trees – for instance, the redstart, pied flycatcher, wren and coal tit – and others, such as the tree pipit, wood warbler and willow warbler, nest on the ground. These species, together with the chaffinch, robin and coal tit, are the dominant species in sessile oakwood.

Although during the winter months we observe most of our chaffinches feeding on arable land, during the breeding season chaffinches are typically a woodland species, favouring oak-woods. Chaffinches inhabit both sessile and pedunculate oak-woods and, because they are hardy and very adaptable to each habitat and individual habitat change, they are one of the most widely distributed of all woodland birds, breeding in every county: only in some of the northern oakwoods in Scotland does the chaffinch become outnumbered by the willow warbler.

Another species to look out for in both types of oakwood is the robin, which is also an adaptable bird. Robin populations are affected more by adverse winter conditions than by habitat and vegetation factors.

The robin's flexibility towards the woodland habitat enables it to nest in holes or near the woodland floor. It is indifferent towards shrub-layer cover and prefers a high vantage point, such as a bush, to use as a song-post. In the oakwood, the robin perches on low twigs and branches to watch for prey. It darts to the ground, seizes the insect, spider or seed and returns to the same observation perch to eat it.

On any day of the year in an oakwood, the song of the wren can be heard. Lasting only about five seconds, the shrill warble is one of the highest pitched of all birdsongs, about one octave above the highest note on the piano. The exuberant, ear-shattering song, which carries for incredible distances, is at its peak from March to early June.

Due to their diminutive size, wrens are difficult birds to observe in a vast oakwood. You are most likely to see them feeding on insects in the shrub and field layers of both pedunculate and sessile habitats. Should you see a wren, you will recognise it by its characteristically cocked tail, which gives it its rounded appearance. It is always active, darting through scrub, dense grass tussocks and bramble patches looking for food. Occasionally, when it appears in the open, the wren will hop and then take off for a brief low-level flight with whirring wings.

One of the highlights of the birdwatching year is the arrival of our summer visitors, beginning at the end of March with the return of the chiff-chaff, the first of the warblers. The vast majority of the migrant warblers spend the winter in the tropics and arrive in Britain in time to benefit from the explosion of summer insects and later hedgerow and woodland fruit. Warblers, because of their slender, pointed beaks, are considered insectivorous birds.

The willow warbler is one of the warblers best suited to the woodland habitat and being adaptable can be found in most woods apart from those in Shetland. More than three million pairs nest throughout Britain, but the highest populations are in pedunculate oakwoods which have open rides and glades and dense shrubby ground cover. They also have a preference for birch trees and they are extremely common where oaks are mixed with silver birch and downy birch. They are 'canopy feeders', picking insects from the underside of leaves – hence the alternative generic name of 'leaf warbler'.

During April, when the willow warblers become established, they immediately indicate their presence with their plaintive, soothing liquid trill making a crescendo towards the end of the song. Each individual willow warbler within the oakwood sings more musically as the season progresses. Male birds develop their songs upon arrival, and gradually produce a repertoire with increasing sophistication.

Chiff-chaffs (196) also inhabit pedunculate oakwoods. Visually indistinguishable from the willow warbler, they both have olive-green upper plumage and are yellow-buff on the underparts. It is the song of the willow warbler and chiff-chaff which enables the oakwood birdwatcher to distinguish between these two birds. The monotonous name-giving song of the chiff-chaff is quite different from the willow warbler's musical song, with a repeated double note 'chiff-chaff, chiff-chaff', usually sung from a song-post high in the trees. The enthusiastic bird-watcher really needs to master the recognition of birds by their song alone, because in so many habitats a bird is often heard before it is seen.

The chiff-chaff prefers older deciduous woods with tall trees and rough herbage for nesting. It is an agile bird and feeds in the high foliage, plucking insects and larvae from the leaves and twig crevices or sometimes catching prey in mid-air with a flycatcher-like performance.

The most widely distributed of all the tits in Britain is the blue tit (**11**). Although it haunts all broad-leaf woods, the pedunculate oak is its favourite. This familiar bird feeds in the canopy alongside the willow warbler and chiff-chaff on the diverse invertebrate fauna. The blue tit exploits this abundant supply of food with alacrity and its breeding season suitably coincides with the peak larval abundance of the green oak tortrix moth, the mottled umber and the winter moth.

The blue tit is well known because of its azure blue head, blue-green back and yellow breast. Apart from deciduous woodland and suburban gardens it is seen in any habitat where there are trees, bushes, shrubs, or hedges: over five million pairs breed in the British Isles.

The great tit sometimes competes with the blue tit for breeding territory within the oakwood, since both birds nest in holes. Their feeding territories are completely different zones of the wood: the great tit prefers to feed in the shrub layer and the majority of their feeding centres around the trunks, lower branches and ground at the base of the oak.

Although the great tit is easily identifiable by plumage, it is a great deceiver with its song. Males begin to sing each January with a simple spirited song, bringing excitement to the oakwood in the New Year. The familiar call is the clear, two-tone ringing note sounding like 'teacher-teacher, teacher-teacher'. However, the great tit is a versatile songster with a wide variation of phrases to its repertoire: in the oakwood during spring, any unfamiliar bird call is likely to be that of the experimenting great tit.

All three species of woodpecker are dependent on the woodland habitat because the trees provide a ready supply of food and ideal nest sites, but the **green woodpecker** prefers open gladed woodland, particularly oakwoods, and the bird is rarely seen in coniferous woods. Whereas the lesser spotted and great spotted woodpeckers frequently announce their presence by drumming on branches and trunks of large trees, the green woodpecker rarely drums but is extremely vocal, uttering a loud 'keu-keu-keu' laughing call as it flies away through the trees.

As its name suggests, the green woodpecker is greenish, with a bright red head and yellow-green rump. At 32 cm/12½ in, it is our largest woodpecker. Although the characteristic call-note is as familiar a sound of the countryside as that of the cuckoo, the green woodpecker can be very silent at times and its plumage blends in perfectly with the green haze of the oakwood. To get close to this bird, you need to understand its behaviour and approach quietly whilst it is feeding.

Under the branches of the canopy you might see the green woodpecker fly in an undulating movement and suddenly land on the trunk of a dead oak tree. It makes no sound in flight and only the click as its claws make contact with the dry wood gives the bird away. Through binoculars the dark eye, rimmed with a white ring, is clearly visible in a black facial patch. In the male bird the black eye patch extends into a moustache with crimson centre below the eye, whereas in the female this moustachial stripe is all black (**8**).

The bird remains motionless for minutes on the trunk, like a lizard – an ability which is a behavioural pattern of the species; and with the strange half-cocked angle of its head, the bird's profile resembles a prehistoric reptile. It moves up the trunk of the dead oak in slow jerks and with scratching claws. As you approach, it usually scuttles around the back of the tree trunk or slips behind the branch for protection, cautiously sticking its beak and head into view only once it is convinced you have gone.

You will get the best views when the woodpecker is settling down to explore a tree trunk for food. Its powerful, long grey-white bill extends forwards from a bullet-shaped head on a muscular, flexible neck. The feet of all woodpeckers are interesting: as the bird grips the bark, two toes point forwards and two point backwards, perfectly adapted for climbing. Unless they are webbed or flanged, the majority of other birds' feet have three claws pointing forwards and one hind claw pointing backwards to complete the grip in perching. The woodpecker's foot, known as a zygodactyl foot, is ideal for climbing vertical trunks and makes the bird adept at spiralling round the tree trunk as it climbs, or moving laterally along a bough before flying off.

Careful observation of the feeding woodpecker reveals that the tail is also used as a climbing aid. Once the curved sharp claws have gripped the bark the bird slightly fans its tail and wedges it against the trunk. Particularly strong feather shafts help prop the woodpecker in position as it hammers at the bark and digs into the crevices with rapid stabbing movements, looking for insects and larvae which it removes with its extremely long, flexible and barbed tongue. The green woodpecker frequently feeds on ants on the ground in the clearings and open glades of the oakwood; suburban birdwatchers will have seen this behaviour on the lawns of gardens and parks, golf courses and recreational playing fields, since it regularly returns to productive ants' nests. The prehensile tongue can only be kept inside the head when coiled, but when probing into the holes of an ants' nest it extends 10 cm/4 in beyond the tip of the bill and, covered in sticky saliva, it catches the ants and eggs, drawing them out of the nest chambers. During June and July the adults take fledgling green woodpeckers – which are less brightly coloured and spotted with black streaks on their undersides – to an ants' nest and break it open to expose the prey and give lessons in feeding.

Green woodpeckers breed from the end of April to the end of June. Each year, both male and female birds excavate a new nest hole, which consists of an entrance tunnel 7 cm/3 in long, ending in a chamber 30–40cm/12–16 in deep and about 15 cm/6 in wide. The nest hole is some 3–5m/10–16 ft above the ground and is usually excavated in decaying trees or in large dead boughs of a living tree and only the wood chippings line the nest. Starlings, which frequently nest in woodland as well as closer to man, favour woodpecker holes for their own nests, occupying many old nest sites in successive years.

Woodpeckers lay 5–7 white eggs in late April, and the parents share both the incubation of their eggs and the feeding of the nestlings on a regurgitated, paste-like mixture of insects and saliva. When the young are well grown, they squeal and

7

wheeze for food, attracting the attention not only of any birdwatcher near by but also of predatory weasels which are easily able to reach the lower nest holes. After three weeks they leave the nest.

Only in the last thirty years has the green woodpecker bred in Scotland, beginning in the Lowlands and today continuing to spread northwards although still absent from the Highlands. It is generally a sedentary bird, rarely flying more than a few kilometres at a time to colonise new areas, which is probably the reason why the green woodpecker is still not found in Ireland.

The thrush family is represented in oakwoods by birds such as the blackbird and song thrush. Of these two, the blackbird is the more common in the oakwood, feeding in the glades where grass survives and among the leaf litter. Since the blackbird prefers a rich field layer, the pedunculate oakwoods of southern Britain, such as the Forest of Dean and the New Forest, are ideal haunts. However, it is less common in the woods on poorer soil, so the blackbird is never a dominant species in the sessile woods of England, Scotland and Wales. In the Welsh sessile woods of Gwenffrwd and Dinas there are many species of bird more abundant than the blackbird,

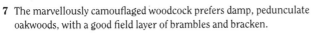

7 The marvellously camouflaged woodcock prefers damp, pedunculate oakwoods, with a good field layer of brambles and bracken.

8 Male green woodpecker showing red moustache. The female is similar, with a black moustache. The stiff tail acts as a prop whilst climbing.

9 In April, when snowfall is still possible, the woodcock continues to incubate its four eggs in a snow hole.

10 The wood warbler is a dominant species of sessile oakwoods, where it nests on the ground, but feeds high in the canopy, hidden by foliage.

11 The blue tit is a regular canopy feeder in all broadleaf woods, especially the pedunculate oak.

although it can still be seen and heard.

We expect the confident blackbird of our back garden to typify the behaviour of all its kind, but in fact in thick, isolated woodland the blackbird is both wary and shy. Often it is the well-known, mellow song which gives the bird's presence away. It is usually delivered from a high tree perch around 4.30 a.m. during the dawn chorus or at dusk before all light fades.

The smaller, more vulnerable **song thrush** also favours oakwoods with a rich shrub layer; again it is uncommon in the sessile oakwoods of England and Wales, but it is more abun-dant in those of Scotland and Ireland. Part of the thrush's staple diet are snails, and since they require calcium for shell formation, the song thrush is more commonly found in oakwoods growing on calcareous soils.

The British breeding population of the song thrush is estimated at three and a half million pairs. It is very common in some of the birchwoods in Scotland, but not so common in English or Welsh birchwoods and less frequent in most beech- and ashwoods. Because the song thrush regularly frequents gardens, it is one of the best-known British birds, and although it lacks bright colours, its plumage is attractive with warm brown underparts and cream-buff breast covered in dark spots.

All members of the thrush family have memorable songs and the clear, musical notes of the song thrush are some of the most beautiful. It sings at dawn and during the daytime, but the song is probably at its best in the evening, as the sun goes down, during spring and early summer. Accompanied by the robin, the song thrush is one of the last voices of the twilight and the arresting flutey song continues for over an hour after sundown; most birdwatchers cherish the sound – especially in suburbia when it echoes from television aerials. The song-thrush melody is vigorous yet repetitive: the bird utters the same notes up to six times, as if practising a phrase, but it has a large repertoire, skilfully interspersed with numerous notes and phrases frequently copied from other birds.

Unlike other members of the family the song thrush is a solitary bird. When not singing, it is quiet, feeding in the clearings of the oakwood using a hop-and-run technique and pausing with its head cocked on one side to listen for prey moving or danger approaching. It mainly eats insects, worms and snails, although in the winter it will join blackbird, fieldfare and redwing stripping the berries from the hedgerows. Many song thrushes breeding in northern Britain migrate to Ireland for the winter.

The nesting habits of the song thrush are interesting because it is unique among European birds for plastering the inside of its nest with a lining of mud, dung or wood fragments, mixed with saliva. The main body of the nest, built by the female, is made from coarse grasses and twigs. During April, 4–5 beautiful pale blue eggs with black specks are laid.

Just as pedunculate woodland has its dominant warblers, so the sessile oakwood has its specialities, including the migrant **wood warbler** (10). Uncommon in pedunculate woods, the wood warbler is a dominant species in sessile oakwoods because it prefers a field layer with a low density of shrubs. It uses exposed boughs as observation perches or song-posts, when the birdwatcher has a chance to distinguish the wood warbler from the chiff-chaff and willow warbler. The wood warbler is far greener on the upperparts and its underparts are white, except for the yellow breast; and close observation reveals a distinct yellowish eye-stripe. Also, at 12 cm/5 in it is larger than the other two species.

The breeding pairs of wood warbler are widely dispersed throughout Britain, most being found in the established sessile oakwoods of western Britain, even in the stunted fellwoods which grow above 335 m/1,100 ft. In many Welsh woods, the wood warbler is one of the most common singing birds, alongside redstart and pied flycatcher. The majority of the sessile oakwoods of Gwynedd for instance contain wood warblers. Where the trees are tall, wood warblers feed mostly in the canopy, but the bird is not restricted by tree height and is just as common in habitats where the trees barely reach 7 m/23 ft high.

To see a wood warbler birdwatchers need to recognise the type of oak woodland they are in. Look out for mature hillside forest or even stunted oak on damp upland slopes, where there is a closed canopy preventing a luxuriant shrub-layer. This is the preferred habitat of the wood warbler, which is why the bird is absent from eastern Britain where this habitat does not exist. In Deeside the oakwoods near Ballater are well known for wood warblers. Dinnet Oakwood, a Nature Conservancy Council (NCC) reserve, and a semi-natural pedunculate and sessile wood, is comparatively small, covering only 13 ha/32 acres, but contains breeding wood warblers every year, illustrating the fact that if habitat conditions suit, the warbler will colonise. It also breeds in open-canopy birchwoods in the north and west of Britain and among beech and chestnut with little undergrowth, wherever these occur in the south-east. In Ireland it is very rare, confined to isolated areas in the north-west and extreme east. Throughout its range it is the least widespread of the leaf warblers: for every pair of wood warblers there are 100 pairs of willow warbler and 10 pairs of chiff-chaff.

The speed at which the wood warblers find and take up territories is impressive: of the three leaf warblers they arrive last, towards late April and mid-May, yet within a few weeks they have formed territories, mated, built a nest and begun to incubate. Males generally arrive first to stake their claim on the most suitable woods, proclaiming their territories by singing from a series of song-posts within the wood. The song is an enthusiastic trill which carries throughout the wood; if you are fortunate enough to track down a singing male, you will observe that he tilts his head backwards and delivers his song with such zeal that his entire body is vibrating. There is an additional, less familiar 'zeep-zeep' note, which birdwatchers must remember belongs to this brightly coloured warbler.

Sessile oakwood is the main habitat for the redstart and coal tit. They are hole-nesting birds and coal tits prefer small natural holes close to the ground, which is where they are best observed. The **redstart** arrives from West Africa in April and sings beautifully at dusk from a series of song-perches high in the trees. The male bird executes to perfection a rich pure warble so emotively associated with sessile woods. The 'whoo-eet' call rings clearly through the oakwood and is similar to that of the willow warbler, but the redstart also has a robin-like 'twick' alarm note; this can be confusing, since at a distance the redstart not only looks like a robin but behaves like one too. The male is one of the most attractive woodland birds (12). His chestnut underparts compliment the fiery red tail, contrasting with the grey upperparts and crown, and black face and throat; above the eye is a white flash resembling a huge eyebrow. Females, with an overall duller plumage of grey-brown and russet-buff tones, are not as striking.

Originally the redstarts visiting Britain probably occupied sandy heaths with pines, but today they colonise a variety of wooded habitats: the mature sessile oakwoods of Wales, the Lake District and Scotland, are the favourite sites, although the bird is virtually absent from Ireland. In northern Scotland, birchwoods and the Caledonian pinewoods remain a stronghold for the redstart, but it has adapted well to the loss of ancient woodland, establishing itself in parks where ancient trees remain, and mature gardens and hedgerows with old trees: these old trees provide the ideal nest holes in their trunks, branches or stumps. Sessile oakwoods contain the highest density of redstarts as they require woodland with little shrub growth, and space between the canopy and ground level. Uncluttered song- and feeding-perches are important together with open space to perform the chasing courtship flight and display.

Throughout much of its range the redstart nests in natural holes in trees, but it occupies other dry cavities such as those in stone walls and buildings in northern Britain. Only the female builds the nest, which is of grass and strips of bark lined with feathers and hair. The adults and fledged young leave their breeding territory during August and begin the flight south to winter in West Africa. During the autumn migration redstarts supplement their insectivorous diet and feed on energy-giving hedgerow fruits and berries to provide stamina for the long flight.

Another summer visitor arriving in Britain during April and leaving in late August and September is the **tree pipit**. It is a slim bird with a long tail which it periodically flicks, and a fine pointed beak designed for catching insects and spiders on or near the ground.

Nearly all pipits have similar markings: brown backs and cream underparts and streaked around the throat, breast and flanks. In Britain the tree pipit is easily confused with the meadow and rock pipits, although their habitats and behaviour are different. The tree pipit is yellower than the meadow pipit and lighter in colour than the rock pipit; and through binoculars the tree pipit's legs are pink, whereas those of the meadow pipit are brown and the rock pipit's are grey.

Tree pipits prefer remote, undisturbed woodland chiefly in the uplands or on hillsides, where there is a reduced shrub layer; sessile oakwoods are therefore favourite haunts, as well as Scots pine and ashwoods, and in mature Scottish birchwoods the tree pipit is one of the most common birds alongside the chaffinch and willow warbler. Although it is absent from Ireland and the Outer Hebrides, up to 100,000 pairs nest in Britain and colonise woods wherever there are tall trees with open ground beneath for feeding.

The song and song flight makes the tree pipit unmistakable. The bird rarely stays still whilst it sings, parachuting down from the trees on arched wings with tail spread before alighting on a resting-perch. The song carries far into the wood and begins as the male flies upwards from a perch at an acute angle, reaching a height of 30 m/98½ ft before gliding back down, singing all the time and warning other males that this particular territory is occupied. The males arrive from Africa in April and from their arrival until the end of July is the best time to hear the memorable song throughout our sessile oakwoods.

No bird study of a sessile wood could be complete without mentioning the **pied flycatcher**. The black and white breeding plumage of the cock bird (14) is as familiar in these oakwoods as the robin is in the back garden. Females are greyish brown on the upperparts and white beneath but both adults take on this appearance in the autumn. Although it is not found in Ireland, in population density the pied flycatcher is second only to the chaffinch in many of the sessile woods of England and Wales. Its ideal habitat is a hillside wood with mature trees and a reduced shrub layer which offers adequate cover, with some high song-perches available, together with natural nest holes in the older trees.

Since this habitat description is critical for breeding, the pied flycatcher is not found in East Anglia, south and south-east England, but is restricted to the areas offering upland sessile oak near to water, which provides much of the insect food during April and May. The real strongholds are the sessile oakwoods of Wales and northern England; in southern Scotland and north Devon the pied flycatcher is only locally abundant. Apart from oak, it is worth looking out for this species in birch, rowan, alder and some beechwoods, although not those of south-east England because the shrub layer is too dense and unsuitable for the bird's behaviour.

Pied flycatchers are about the size of a great tit. They frequently evict resident blue tits from their nesting holes but find the great tits too aggressive to evict. It is worth investigating sessile oakwoods early in spring, because male pied flycatchers arrive at their breeding territories during mid-April

and the females follow on only about four days later. Pairing takes place quickly and once territories are claimed, both birds begin building the nest with strips of soft bark frequently stripped from honeysuckle, completing it in less than two days. Once the young have left the nest they are difficult to see, but if located can confuse the birdwatcher, because with their brown speckled plumage they resemble juvenile spotted flycatchers or robins.

As their name suggests these birds feed on insects. Whilst in the nest the young are fed mainly on insect larvae. To watch the adults feed is particularly exciting, because they specialise in taking flying insects on the wing. Perching on a suitable branch overlooking the lower sparse shrub layer, the pied flycatcher darts out, catches a fly and rapidly returns to a different branch where it continues to look for other passing insects.

Perhaps the real prize bird of the hanging sessile oakwoods, found only in mid-Wales, is the **red kite** (**17**). It is a large bird with a 1.5-m/5-ft wingspan and instantly recognised by its deep-forked chestnut tail and long wings held at an angle as it soars in wide circles searching for prey. Unlike most raptors the red kite twists and turns at speed during flight, beneath the canopy of the wood as well as above it. The agile flight is particularly useful when robbing other birds of their food: during the red kite's breeding season from April until July, it is often seen chasing buzzard, eagle, heron or crow, harrassing them and out-manoeuvring all evasive action, until they drop their food. The kite then swoops to catch it before it hits the ground.

The red kite is also one of the rarest birds in Britain and strictly protected to guarantee the minimum of disturbance. Only last century the red kite was found in England and Scotland, but persecution by gamekeepers, Victorian egg-collectors and taxidermists caused the bird to become almost extinct by the beginning of this century. Egg-collecting is still illegally practised today, but human disturbance from recreation and tourism is a more serious threat to the remaining wardened nest sites. For many years a dedicated group of ornithologists called the Kite Committee was responsible for protecting the few breeding birds; they informed and involved the local farmers, landowners, immediate residents and police who joined together to prevent nest raids. Today the Royal Society for the Protection of Birds (RSPB) and the local Naturalists' Trust are also involved and by the 1970s, despite occasional setbacks, the numbers of red kites had reached twenty-three pairs.

In 1986 there were forty-eight pairs of red kites in Wales, but despite the best breeding year ever, only half of these managed to fledge young successfully, and seven nest sites were plundered by egg thieves. Even greater protection is needed to maintain the population of this bird in Britain.

One of the most famous small birds of oakwoods is the **nightingale**, which belongs to the thrush family. Most nightingales arrive in Britain during April to colonise woodland south of an imaginary line from the Severn to the Humber. The nightingale has a distinctly restricted geographical range: it is absent from Cornwall, rare in Devon and the 10,000 or so pairs which breed in Britain prefer lowland pedunculate oakwoods which have been coppiced and underplanted with hazel, growing over a dense undergrowth of bramble and nettles, suitable to the bird's skulking behaviour.

In Somerset, although the nightingale breeds on restricted-

12

14

13

12 Redstarts arrive from Africa during April and the male is one of the most striking of our woodland birds.

13 The jay is one of the wariest of all Britain's birds and is more often heard than seen.

14 The male pied flycatcher is a typical bird of sessile oakwoods and in the last fifty years has extended its range as a breeding bird from Wales to upland England and Scotland.

15 Male blackcap at woodland pool. This warbler breeds successfully in deciduous woodland, coppices, hedgerows, scrubland, parks and mature gardens.

16 In winter, treecreepers frequently fly with mixed flocks of tits, whilst searching for insects.

17 The rare red kite usually nests in Welsh hanging sessile oakwoods, although it is more frequently seen soaring and hunting over open moorland. It may be identified by its long, deeply forked tail.

18 The skulking behaviour of the nightingale means that it is rarely seen. The chestnut tail is the only striking feature of the bird, apart from its song.

16

18

access reserves, the area represents the very extreme edge of the bird's range and populations fluctuate annually. At the north-west fringe, it favours river valleys, especially where mature pedunculate oaks mingle with pockets of young ash over bramble thickets.

Because the nightingale spends most of the time in dense undergrowth, it is rarely seen: with its chestnut-brown upperparts and greyish-brown underparts, it is well camouflaged. Equally well hidden is the nest, which is built either on the ground or in low-growing vegetation, from a mixture of dead leaves and grasses, lined with finer grass and hair. Up to 5 brown eggs are laid in May but because the nightingales leave their breeding territories towards the end of July, there is only time for one brood.

As **18** shows, the strong pointed beak is perfect for catching invertebrates in the soil and leaf litter, including worms and insects. During the latter part of the summer the nightingale, like the redstart (which is also a member of the thrush family), feeds on the berries which are ripening in the countryside. These berries provide a source of carbohydrate used as a supply of food during the southerly migration to West Africa, which commences in September.

Unfortunately, across all Europe, the nightingale is contracting its range, as a result of habitat destruction and interference, where deciduous woods are underplanted with conifer. In Britain, a 12–15-year coppice management system of the remaining strongholds is important, because if the oak canopy becomes too dense, light cannot penetrate down to the undergrowth which, in time, dies back, causing the nightingale to move on. The densest populations of nightingales generally occur where the coppiced layer is 5–8 years old.

Nightingale watching requires patience and you will have to conceal yourself within the bird's territory. The bird sings only from the middle of May and throughout June, but if you are lucky a male might perch directly in your line of vision, throw its head backwards and deliver its powerful versatile song. Although the nightingale does sing during the day my view is that you cannot claim to be a serious ornithologist until you have heard the song of the nightingale on a warm, still night. Alfred Lord Tennyson's words, 'the music of the moon/Sleeps in the plain eggs of the nightingale,' hint at the exquisite joy of experiencing one of the most perfect of all birdsongs on a moonlit summer night.

Of all the birds attempting to rival the nightingale for purity of song, the **blackcap** is perhaps the only serious contender. Uttered from the branches of tall trees in the pedunculate oakwood, the beautiful clear warble, skilfully executed in wild and free, nicely rounded phrases without any harsh notes, is pure musical brilliance. The song is similar to that of the garden warbler and often confused with it but to a trained ear the blackcap is superior: a tireless vocalist at its best early on a May morning.

Although you might have heard blackcaps singing in early March, these are likely to be some of the few which overwinter in Britain each year, whereas the majority arrive from Africa during April. Nearly every county in England and Wales supports breeding blackcaps, although they become local in Lowland Scotland and increasingly scarce further north. They are absent from the northern islands and Isle of Man, but localised fluctuating populations occur in Ireland, increasing in the north-east.

The male blackcap (**15**) is easily identified by its grey-brown back, ashy-grey underparts, and distinctive black crown and forehead; the female is similar, apart from having a reddish-brown cap. Nearly 200,000 pairs breed in the British Isles, and although the type of tree is not delimiting, many blackcaps favour pedunculate oakwoods with a mature shrub layer and growth of bramble, where the nests are commonly built. Blackcaps do not breed in sessile oakwoods with little or no undergrowth or beechwoods where the dense canopy shades out 80 per cent of the light restricting plant growth on the woodland floor. However mature hedgerows, parks, gardens or hawthorn scrubland all provide suitable habitats for this warbler, providing tall trees are present from which the males can proclaim their territory.

Ivy and honeysuckle bushes are also popular nesting sites but the nest is rarely more than 1 m/3¼ ft off the ground and generally built by the female from rootlets and grass, and lined with finer grass and hair.

Blackcaps are essentially insectivorous birds but like the nightingale and redstart begin to eat hedgerow fruits during the late summer and autumn before departing in September to the Mediterranean or Africa.

The deep crevices of the bark of both pedunculate and sessile oak contain insects, spiders and larvae which form the staple diet of the **treecreeper** (**16**). This is a diminutive resident bird, and easily overlooked, but is best seen in early spring before leaf-break prevents good views.

Between February and April, the bird becomes very vocal and utters a faint, metallic, high-pitched note, which slowly increases in tempo, ending with a loud clear 'tsee' call. In springtime, treecreepers perform their courtship display with mating chases up and down tree trunks and branches, interspersed with quivering of the wings.

Treecreepers always move in jerks up tree trunks, probing the crevices with their long, pointed, scimitar-shaped beaks. They are dull brown with buff streaks and white underparts and with their fluffy exterior they resemble mice. Once it has thoroughly examined a tree, the treecreeper flies in an undulating motion to the base of another tree, to begin its foraging climb. During the rapid, spurting ascent the tail is pressed against the rough bark in the manner of a woodpecker.

Apart from the Outer Hebrides, the northern islands and areas such as the Fens, where there are no trees, the treecreeper is found throughout the British Isles; and outside oakwoods it colonises all types of deciduous woodland with rough, deeply creviced bark such as chestnut, pollarded willow and alder carr, but it is very scarce in coniferous woods.

If you see a treecreeper with a beak full of insects, follow it up the trunk because this is the only sure way of locating the nest site. Treecreepers do not excavate a nest chamber but rely on a loose flap of bark in a decaying tree, behind which they can squeeze and form a nest chamber on a base of fine twigs lined with bark and feathers; alternatively, they build a nest where ivy forms a screen over a natural crevice or hollow in the tree trunk providing one of the best camouflaged and protected of all woodland birds' nests.

For most of the year treecreepers are solitary or will be seen in pairs, but towards high summer and into autumn, small family groups feed together in the trees, and as winter approaches, it is common to see treecreepers moving through the trees in mixed flocks, with tits.

June marks the end of the breeding season in oakwoods and the familiar birdsong fades away. There is now a period of quiescence as adult birds moult and young birds wander and finally disperse throughout the habitat. From October, the oakwoods are in their winter aspect and birds move about in mixed flocks, most commonly of tits and goldcrests. Blue tits are still the most common tit in the pedunculate wood but flocks are augmented by coal tits and long-tailed tits; the latter begin winter feeding on the hawthorn bushes of the hedgerow, but from December until April search the twigs of oak trees for hibernating insects.

Sessile oakwoods are poor habitats for birds during winter and most species desert them after the breeding season. Yellowhammers and chaffinches leave and do not return until March or April; whereas fieldfares and redwings both plunder the sessile habitat in severe weather and rooks and woodpigeons frequently fly in to gorge on the acorn crop – but they fly several kilometres from other habitats in order to do so.

The **woodpigeon** at 41 cm/16 in is the largest pigeon found in Britain and it inhabits both types of oakwood, especially in the autumn when the acorns are ripe. Walking through the oakwood you are likely to disturb the woodpigeon feeding, causing it to rise sharply from the leaf litter on heavily beating wings and fly purposefully away in a direct flight path. Its overall colour is light grey with diagnostic white neck patches and white wing bars; and with a solid rounded body, small head and short legs which just about support the bird as it bobs from front to back with each step, the woodpigeon looks slightly comical.

In most woodlands and certainly both types of oakwood, crows are scarce because they are opportunists: they have evolved to survive along the margins of woods and have expanded their range into other habitats. The **jay** (13), our most attractive crow, is an exception because its diet includes acorns, and the European distribution of the jay corresponds to the established oakwoods. But although the oakwood is the preferred habitat, it is also found in other deciduous woodlands, mixed woods and conifer plantations, and it feeds on the woodland floor on sweet chestnuts, hazelnuts, beechnuts and pine seeds. They have also learned that orchards are worth plundering for plums, cherries and pears and from May to early July steal eggs and nestlings from the nests of woodland birds.

As a resident, the bird nests throughout the British Isles except the Highlands and western Ireland, wherever there is suitable woodland; the woods must offer glades and clearings with a healthy shrub layer and well-developed undergrowth because jays prefer to build their nest low in bushes such as holly and laurel or deep in dense ivy which surrounds a tree trunk, generally only 3–6 m/10–20 ft from the ground.

Jays are nervous, shy birds and very difficult to approach but if you get a good view, you will appreciate their beautiful plumage. Most of the body is a delicate pinkish-brown with a black tail, white rump and black and white spotted crest. In flight, further colours are revealed: the primary feathers are black and grey with white wing patches and the wing coverts are striking with pale blue and black-barred feathers.

You must remember to spend some time looking up in the canopy for jays, because they fly silently from tree to tree and hop nimbly from branch to branch, well above head height. Once on the ground jays hop and never walk or run but at the first sign of danger they will immediately take to the air screaming their raucous alarm.

Without doubt acorns are the jay's favourite food and during September and October it is common to see it searching for them beneath the oak trees. It is fascinating watching the jay burying surplus acorns in its own emergency larder to eat when food is scarce in the winter, either in woodland clearings under leaves and roots or buried in moss. Even when snow covers the ground the jay remembers where it has buried the food, although a percentage of acorns are forgotten and survive to germinate into oak seedlings; as it carries the acorns 1–3 km/½–2 miles away from where they were originally found, the jay is partly responsible for the dispersal of the oak tree.

Birds such as sparrowhawk, tawny owl and nightjar can all be found in oakwoods during the summer, but these species also favour other habitats and are therefore covered elsewhere in this book. Woodpigeon, kestrel and crow hunt and feed along the margins of oakwoods, but these margins usually border on to arable land, representing a separate habitat. In southern England almost 90 per cent of the farmland passerine birds originate from woodland habitat.

The keen birdwatcher should always be aware of species and habitat overlap. No single habitat contains an exclusive checklist of birds found nowhere else; in fact, as habitats change, birds are obliged to adapt, and many species have become so flexible that they colonise a variety of habitats. It is possible for some of the pedunculate oak species to colonise scrubland rather than a tree habitat, and other birds inhabiting sessile oakwoods are also typical species of heaths or open moors, such as the yellowhammer, meadow pipit and wheatear: it is the overall structure of the wood that is more significant to the bird than the dominant oak species.

BEECHWOODS

While the oakwood is the most typical of Britain's native woodland, beech can claim to be one of our most beautiful, because for the all-year-round birdwatcher there is never a season when the tall, well-proportioned tree fails to enhance the countryside.

In winter, when all the leaves are on the woodland floor forming a deep leaf litter, the majestic silver-grey trunks stand out against the seasonally subdued colours and each twig is tipped with a slender brown bud. Frequently, only the beech tree withstands the gales of November and fights to retain its dead leaves well into January; and in late spring the brown buds swell and burst and every branch is laden with fresh, emerald green leaves, soon to be dusted with pollen from the bunches of yellow male flowers. During late April and May the beechwood is a delight to walk through, as the spring sunshine filters through the aerial green screen and dances on the woodland floor where the shrivelled fruit or beech mast rests. In a clearing caused by a fallen tree, wood anemone, wood sorrel and sanicle grow in the natural sunny glade but in high summer when the leaves have become a much darker green, very little shrub- or plantlife grows on the woodland floor, as the fully opened leaves cast a dense shade, allowing only 20 per cent of the natural light through into the wood. Look upwards and marvel at the way the leaves create a beautiful green filter to the sunlight, with every leaf fitting almost perfectly into the space between the leaves above it.

Inside a beechwood during summer, the absence of a shrub and ground layer gives a feeling of size and open space, and even on the hottest day it is appreciably cool. With the straight, smooth, unbranched trunks reaching upwards to the lofty, arching latticed canopy, and the striking quietness, the atmosphere of the beechwood is unique.

For the majority of us, the beechwood is at its most impressive during autumn, when the leaves slowly turn from dark green to yellow and brown and finally to a golden copper in a blaze of ever-changing glory. As the autumn mists filter through the beechwood in early morning or late afternoon and the watery sun lances through the shedding canopy, the beechwood has a moving beauty.

There are beechwoods throughout most of Britain. During the seventeenth century the tree was introduced to Ireland, where it is commonly seen in hedgerows; because of this introduction and the planting of beech widely throughout the British Isles there is confusion as to where beech grows as a genuine native tree. We have already seen in Ch. 1 that after the last Ice Age the climate slowly improved and during the Boreal and Pre-Boreal periods large areas of Britain were covered by birch and pine forests. Between 7,500 and 7,000 years ago, the climate became milder, with temperatures up to 2.5°C higher than today, but it was also wetter; alder, lime, elm and oak began to dominate over birch and pine, but beech was also colonising these early deciduous forests, although only on a limited scale and never as a dominant species. During the Atlantic period (7,500–5,000 years ago) beech became established, but only in southern England and south-east Wales did beech really establish itself as pure or almost pure forest.

Elsewhere in the country the beechwoods have all been planted, including many of the beechwoods in southern England. Some of the best-known and largest woods are found on the Chiltern Hills of Buckinghamshire and Oxfordshire;

19

20

there are other established beechwoods in Kent, Sussex, Hampshire and Surrey, and in the south-west Cotswolds where they grow on calcareous soils. In woods within the complex of the New Forest such as Mark Ash and Denny Wood, and in the Forest of Dean, mature, frequently pollarded beeches grow; these were planted after the natural oaks had been felled, because beech will not dominate over oak and colonise an area within an ancient oak forest. The majority of beechwoods found in Britain do not date back beyond 500 BC and they have been widely planted during the last three hundred years.

Beech trees within their native range of southern England and Wales grow on both calcareous and acidic soils and are very types of soil, beechwoods occur throughout the British Isles in many different combinations, either as acidic sessile oak-beech, acidic pedunculate oak-beech, acidic pedunculate oak-ash-beech, calcareous pedunculate oak-ash-beech or sessile oak-ash-beech mixtures: in fact, very few beechwoods are pure. The beechwoods of Epping Forest (covering 2,430 ha/6,004½ acres) are particularly well worth visiting because the beech is mixed with oak and hornbeam, a tree which thrives on the heavy wet Essex clay.

The shy, elusive **hawfinch** (**19**) favours lowland mixed deciduous woods. Throughout the summer, until the end of winter, its favourite food is the fruit of beech and hornbeam, so that wherever these two trees grow together – as, for example, in Epping Forest – you have a good chance of seeing our largest resident finch which, at 18 cm/7 in, is marginally smaller than a starling.

Hawfinches are most common on the chalklands running from East Anglia south-west to Berkshire but are localised in northern England, the Midlands and Wales, rare in southern Scotland and absent from Ireland. Because they are so secretive and wary of approach any birdwatcher managing to obtain good views of the hawfinch is to be congratulated and, as with other birds, the only way to guarantee views of a bird is first to get familiar with its call or song; gradually, through experience, you will acquire an understanding of the species. The hawfinch makes its contact call both in flight and when at rest, so birdwatchers must look up in the canopy and down on the woodland floor where they may be feeding. Listen out for a pronounced explosive clicking 'tick' call resembling that of the robin during autumn, or a faint whistling 'tzeeip' which will help to locate this attractive bird. During spring and early summer the hawfinch actually sings but it is so indistinct that frequently it is overlooked or confused with goldfinches.

Since initially you are more likely to see the hawfinch in flight, any bird with an undulating glide like a flying woodpecker is worth a second look through binoculars. The stumpy appearance with large head and massive beak is immediately obvious, and white wing bars and flashes bordering the tail help to confirm the indentification. If it is feeding on the ground, you will see its beautiful plumage of rich brown back, buff belly and flanks, offset with a lighter grey collar, black bib and mask around the beak and dark brown-black wings with a white wing bar. The stout, triangular beak is silvery blue in summer, fading to yellow in late autumn and winter. Juvenile birds are altogether more yellow with a corn-coloured beak and underparts speckled before their first autumn moult.

The nest resembles an over-sized bullfinch nest. It is built during April from twigs, roots and grass and constructed where a horizontal branch butts up to the trunk or towards the end of the branches for added protection. Even during the breeding cycle the adults are very shy; they make little noise near the nest and always feed well away from it, as a pair, to keep predators at a distance.

Apart from beech mast and hornbeam nuts, the hawfinch also eats sloes, wild cherries and raids orchards for plums. It eats the kernel, so it has to strip or crack the hard outer nut. Extremely powerful jaw muscles operate the beak like a pair of nutcrackers and the edges of the mandibles have grooves which help hold the nut whilst it exerts crushing pressure.

19 Mixed deciduous woodland, especially hornbeam and beech, attracts hawfinches to feed in small parties.

20 Bramblings often flock with greenfinches and chaffinches during winter, feeding in beechwoods or around the farmyard on spilt grain.

21 The vociferous great tit begins singing each January and the great variation of its song often confuses birdwatchers.

adaptable, but dislike extremes of wet and dry conditions. Many beechwoods of the Chilterns, North and South Downs, Cotswolds and South Wales grow on chalk or limestone, but some of the Chiltern beechwoods grow on highly acidic soils, including the well-known Burnham Beeches which are on acid sands.

Beechwoods on the side of a steep hill are called beech hangers; one of the most famous is Selborne Hanger in Hampshire at the western end of the South Downs. Here semi-natural beech grows with oak and ash which is one of the most common combination of trees wherever beech occurs. However, since pedunculate and sessile oaks grow on different

Beech trees do not produce vast quantities of fruit every year, and climatic conditions probably control the amount of fruit produced. Generally seeds are produced in large quantities once every three years, which seems to coincide with warm summers. These successful crops are referred to as 'mast years' and in the autumn and winter, when the beech mast or fruit is ripe and falls to the ground, flocks of birds fly in to gorge on the crop. Great tit, blue tit, marsh tit, woodpigeon and chaffinch all congregate on the woodland floor taking advantage of this infrequent supply of food.

A good mast year is always recognised by the arrival from northern Scandinavia and Russia of the winter-visiting **brambling (20)**. Although their numbers vary from year to year they seem to know when Britain will enjoy a good crop of mast and arrive during October and November in large flocks, probably motivated by the quantity of beech mast in other parts of Europe.

Bramblings feed alongside chaffinches and appear very similar, so that careful observation is required to identify this bird beneath the beech trees, where its muted plumage blends in with the leaf litter. Away from the beechwood, bramblings can also be seen around the farmyard and on arable land, feeding again in the company of chaffinch, greenfinch, yellowhammer and corn bunting. If you can get a good view you will see the orange breast and black-brown head and, in the case of the male, the beautiful chestnut shoulders (which of course the chaffinch does not have). However, like the chaffinch, the brambling has white wing bars which are not clearly visible whilst feeding but are shown once the bird flies away; as is the diagnostic white rump. Towards the end of winter the brown mantle and head of the male darkens to a glossy black, marking the beginning of the change into breeding plumage; this is rarely seen in Britain since bramblings leave during March and return to their breeding grounds in northern Scandinavia and Russia where they mainly inhabit birch woodland and the margins of coniferous forests. The brambling has bred in Scotland where there are up to ten pairs in habitats resembling their traditional willow and birch scrub.

Where beech grows large and outgrows ash, hazel and rowan, the resulting shade prevents the growth of the shrub and field layers and therefore the breeding population and variety of birds is much poorer than that of oakwoods and the chaffinch still remains the most common species. But abundant leaves support a rich supply of invertebrate food and in this respect beech is more productive for birds than ash. The dense canopy and sparse shrub layer suits the wood warbler, which is reasonably common in southern beechwoods. Because of its association with close-canopy sessile oakwoods, the redstart also breeds in mature beechwoods such as the New Forest and Ashridge Woods in Hertfordshire. Research shows that although the great tit is common in pedunculate oak it is also one of the most common birds of the English beechwood and not just in the autumn when it is seen feeding on the mast.

An estimated three million pairs of **great tit** nest in the British Isles except Orkney and Shetland. It is easy to identify by its black cap, white cheeks and yellow underparts with distinctive black stripe down the middle of the chest **(21)**. Compared to the blue tit, the tail is proportionally much longer and the back is an attractive olive green with blue-grey wings. The sexes are almost identical but if the chest stripe is noticeably broad and the markings are particularly striking, then the bird is likely to be a male. Because of its size (14 cm/5½ in), the great tit cannot be confused with any of the smaller tits and although it is as agile as the smaller members of the family, it prefers to feed away from the canopy. It enjoys feeding on acorns, beech mast and other nuts, which it pins to a branch by one foot and attacks with hammer blows like a woodpecker.

By scanning the tree trunks about 7m/23 ft above the ground you will discover natural holes which are used by the great tit as nest sites. From mid-April up to as late as July, up to twelve eggs are laid in a nest of moss lined with fur or hair. The whole nesting behaviour is a deciding factor in whether the woodland is suitable for the great tit or not. The older beechwoods with rotting trees are more frequently colonised.

If all the young great tits from each clutch were to survive, the countryside would soon be overrun by great tits. The reality is that predation contributes to a high mortality rate so that very few young great tits live to see the following spring.

Within the beechwood, **great spotted woodpeckers (23)** have learnt that holes in trees contain eggs or juvenile birds and they can often be seen using their powerful beaks to break open a chamber and rob the nest of eggs. They have even evolved another, shrewder method of catching the young great tits inside the nest hole, which must have been learnt initially by closely watching adult great tits feeding their young. When the juvenile great tits are nearly fledged, they scrabble to the nest hole every time an adult returns and the youngster reaching the hole first is usually rewarded with the food. The great spotted woodpecker exploits this behaviour by casting a shadow across the nest hole with its own body: as the head of a fledgling appears, the woodpecker grabs it and pulls the bird out of the nest.

The boldly marked, somewhat aggressive great spotted woodpecker is the most common and widely distributed of our three woodpeckers, colonising most of Britain except the northern Scottish islands; nor is it found in Ireland, which is difficult to explain, because plenty of ideal woodland habitat exists and the woodpecker has very catholic tastes. It is found in secluded parks and gardens wherever mature trees grow, in coniferous woods and deciduous woods, including oak, birch, sweet chestnut and hornbeam as well as beech. Its only requirement is a supply of old, dead or decaying trees where it can perform its drumming or excavate nest holes. About 40,000 pairs breed in Britain.

In early spring, usually before the end of February, males begin to drum on a hollow, resonating dead trunk or branch and the machine-gun-like rattle carries far into the wood, announcing to female woodpeckers that a mate is around and to other males that this woodland is occupied. The drumming is performed until early June and it is incredible that this sound is made by rapid blows of the beak, up to eight to ten strikes per second, against the timber. Both adults drum and you can watch the woodpecker flying through the beechwood from one favourite drumming post to another, marking the boundaries of its territory with an explosive clatter.

Similar to the green woodpecker in its movements, the great spotted woodpecker clings to the beech bark with zygodactyl claws, freezes for a few seconds and then spirals up the trunk with abrupt, jerky movements. Both sexes are very attractive birds and are 23 cm/9 in from beak to tail, similar in size to a blackbird. Contrasting with a plain black back, the striking white underparts terminate in bright scarlet under-tail coverts; and the male has a matching scarlet nape patch which shows clearly in a black crown. When the bird climbs the trunk of a

22

23

22 The attractively marked nuthatch resembles a small woodpecker in shape, but unlike the woodpecker, it can scuttle down tree trunks head first in search of insects and grubs during the summer. In winter fruits and nuts become its main source of food.

23 The great spotted woodpecker is the most widespread of the British woodpeckers with over 40,000 breeding pairs. Each spring the bird's drumming sounds echo through woodland as it claims territories, using resonant decaying trees as sounding boards.

tree, you can see its folded wings, which boast a white patch on the shoulders; the primaries are barred black and white, making the bird look stunning as it flies away uttering its explosive 'tchick' alarm call.

The pointed beak is perfect for probing and chiselling into bark and the great spotted woodpecker feeds mainly on the trunks, major limbs and large branches of the tree, winkling invertebrates from the crevices or tearing off insecure pieces of bark to feed on wood-boring larvae beneath. The bird seems to

listen for scratching or chewing noises in tunnels beneath the bark. A few frenzied blows from the beak expose the tunnel and the long, sticky and barbed tongue probes several inches into the wood until it hooks the grub on the barbs, draws it out of the tunnel and eats it.

After the male claimed the territory by the drumming ritual both birds excavate a nest chamber in April in the trunk or bough of the beech tree, usually at least 4.5 m/15 ft from the ground. The young woodpeckers are noisy and you will easily be able to locate an active nest site by following the constant call for food.

Resembling a miniature woodpecker, but in no way related, is the **nuthatch (22)**, a sparrow-sized, tree-creeping bird with blue-grey upperparts and lovely cinnamon-tinted breast, edged by chestnut-coloured flanks which are more obvious in the male. Both adults have a bold black eye-stripe which starts at the base of the dagger-like beak and runs backwards to the nape.

Nuthatches do inhabit oakwoods but not exclusively as has been claimed in the past: they favour old trees and will inhabit mature gardens and are common in established parks or along quiet suburban roads lined by avenues of lime trees. Beech-woods are as popular as oakwoods but the distribution of nuthatch is mostly confined to central and southern England and Wales, south of a line from Merseyside to Humberside with localised populations in Yorkshire and Northumberland. Of all our woodland birds the nuthatch is perhaps the most seden-tary, probably staying within 1.6 km/1 mile of its birthplace; consequently they have failed to colonise Ireland, the Isle of Man and the Isle of Wight and are very rare in southern Scotland. During the last century many of the London parks and wooded gardens had populations of nuthatch, but as air pollution worsened the bird left and it was not until the late fifties when Clean Air Acts were more strictly imposed that the nuthatch returned to breed.

If you are out in the beechwoods during winter looking for bramblings and hawfinches, it is likely that you will hear or spot the nuthatch first. It is very noisy in late winter and extremely vocal from early March onwards when territory mating display and nest-hole searching begins. Listen for the loud, clear whistle ringing through the beeches or the equally loud metallic-sounding 'chwit-chwit'. The piping 'twee-twee-twee' call is similar to that of the lesser spotted woodpecker which can occupy the same habitat, but the appearance of each bird is so distinctive that there will be no confusion once you have seen them.

Watching the nuthatch move up and down the tree trunks and along horizontal boughs, it is obvious that, like woodpeck-ers, they are perfectly evolved woodland birds; but the claws which so effectively grip the bark are not designed like the woodpeckers': they are the same as all other passerine birds, with three claws pointing forwards and one hind claw pointing backwards. Even so, the nuthatch climbs the smooth beech bark without difficulty, scuttling up and down vertical trunks, investigating every crevice, nook and cranny for hibernating insects and larvae which it removes with its beak because it does not possess a woodpecker-like tongue. During the summer invertebrates form the main diet but in winter, chestnuts, acorns, hazelnuts and beech mast become the main source of food when insects are scarce.

At the base of a particularly large beech tree a nuthatch is turning over the beech mast. The temperature has been low for a few weeks and even in the shelter of the beechwood the ground has become hard and the leaves and mast are frozen together so that the nuthatch is working hard to find a suitable beech fruit to eat. Finally, it discovers a large fruit and, gripping it firmly, it wrenches it from the leaves and takes it to an overhanging branch to eat. Wedging the hard fruit into a split in the bark, it attacks the outer casing with accurate blows from the pointed beak until the kernel is exposed. It treats all types of nut in this way and none of them resist the hammering and hatchet-like blows which give the bird its name. Even

during the spring and summer any hard food is treated similarly and the slow, laboured hammering echoes through the wood for considerable distances.

A few minutes spent watching the nuthatch crevice-foraging in the trees reveals a fundamental behavioural difference between the nuthatch and any woodpecker. You might have already seen green and great spotted woodpeckers climbing trees where they move up and down the trunk, with their heads always held upright and with their tail used as a prop. The nuthatch climbs nimbly in random fashion, either with head held upwards, moving horizontally across the trunk, or more commonly, held towards the ground as it climbs down the tree head first, relying totally on its claws for a secure grip whatever the angle of the climb.

When winter conditions are very harsh, the nuthatch is forced to leave the woodland and move closer to man, prefer-ring village and country gardens where it feeds from the birdtable on traditional scraps. In spring it returns to the wood to mate, sometimes even when the spring temperatures are still quite low. With his plumage in pristine condition, the male puffs out his feathers and flies around the edge of the wood announcing his territory with the 'twee-twee' call.

Late March is the best time to look out for the pair of nuthatches searching for nest holes. These may be natural crevices and deep fissures in the bark or old woodpecker holes; but whatever the choice, the nest site is rarely higher than 10 m/33 ft from the ground. The size of the nest-hole entrance does not bother the nuthatch because it is unique among British birds and tailormakes the entrance hole to the right size by plastering mud around it to form a collar. The birds also modify the shape of the cavity by using mud just as a builder would cement, darting backwards and forwards with their beaks full of mud, which they apply with the skill of a master plasterer until the entrance hole and internal nest chamber are to their liking. Ornithologists have recorded over 3.2 kg/7 lb of mud from inside the chamber of a nuthatch nest, which is an amazing feat for a bird only 14 cm/ 5½ in long.

With the arrival of April both birds become less vocal and as May approaches the nest chamber has been lined with wood chippings and bark. Only the female incubates and she rarely leaves the nest chamber; you can watch the male bringing food for his mate and taking it inside the nest hole for her.

The young are fed on insects and caterpillars and leave the nest after three weeks, but they never fly far away, spending the whole of their lives within the woodland they were born in.

Many of the birds covered in this chapter will remain elusive to all but the keenest of birdwatchers, and one species rarely seen is the **tawny owl (24)**. It is probably among the best known of all British birds, with an eerie triple-hoot call familiar to people living in towns or countryside. It is our most common owl, with 50,000–90,000 pairs breeding mainly in deciduous woods, but it is absent from the Isle of Man, Orkney, Shetland, the Outer Hebrides and Ireland.

As dusk falls over the beechwood the nocturnal hunters leave their roosts to hunt for prey. In the half light it is difficult to pick out the shape of the tawny owl perched on a low branch, but the deep 'hoo-hooo-hooo' belongs to no other bird. It may be regularly heard between October and November, when male owls are claiming territories, but is at its peak in January and February, when paired owls answer each other through the wood. The hooting calls are immediately followed by an abrupt 'kee-wick' note and then silence, before the next series of contact hoots begins. The sex of the owl can be determined by the call during the breeding season: the often quoted 'tu-whit tu-whoo' call is made by two birds calling to each other. Listen out for the male calling 'tu-whit' only to be answered by the female somewhere else in the wood calling 'tu-whoo' a few seconds later.

Since the tawny owl is rarely seen during the daytime, the rich tawny-brown upper plumage with softer buff underparts is not often appreciated. Dark brown and black streaks cover the plumage, together with white patches on the shoulders and wing coverts, and the facial disc is brown, offsetting the pair of huge black eyes, quite different from the bright yellow or orange orbital rings of the short-eared owl (104) and long-eared owl (46). The sexes are similar in their markings and the tawny owl is the largest British species, measuring 38 cm/15 in from beak to the tip of its tail.

Unlike most other British owls, the tawny owl is not really a mobile hunter and prefers to sit and wait, dropping from a low branch on to unsuspecting prey such as the wood mouse and bank vole, which form the main part of the diet and are supplemented with small birds, frogs, moles, beetles and earthworms. Its method of hunting and its need for hollow trees for roosting and nesting mean that mature deciduous woodland is the main habitat for the tawny owl; but it also breeds in the Caledonian pine forests and newer plantations around Speyside. They have become the most urban of the owls, taking up breeding territories in large wooded gardens, town parks, churchyards and cemeteries, golf courses and school playing fields, surrounded by trees. In London, there are over fifty pairs nesting within a twenty-mile radius of St Paul's Cathedral.

Old dead or decaying trees are an important feature of the beechwood because these are the favourite nest sites of the tawny owl, especially where a bough has broken away leaving a natural hole or deep crack with a nesting cavity. Frequently it uses grey squirrel dreys, or old nests of sparrowhawk, jay, magpie or carrion crow and in suburbia the tawny owl has been encouraged to use nestboxes made from wooden boxes with a single open end, fixed high in trees close to the main trunk. In southern England breeding begins in mid-March. The number of eggs actually laid each season depends on the availability of food and the adult tawny owl seems to have the ability to predict in early spring what the supply of prey will be like during the owlet feeding period. The number of eggs reaches its maximum (up to five) when mice, voles and rabbits are plentiful but usually the owl is single-brooded and it will even miss a season if prey is short. The eggs are laid at two-day intervals. Incubation by both adults begins once the first egg is in the nest and each egg takes about a month to hatch. This means that earlier eggs are already developing by the time the last is laid and consequently the owlets in the nest are all different sizes.

Tawny owls defend their nests vigorously against intrusion from humans, using their needle-sharp claws with devastating effect. Although the owlets look attractive, if not comical, with their grey-white down and pale blue eyes, I suggest that you do not try to get close views of the owlets in the nest; photography requires specialist knowledge, protective eye goggles, and a serious approach, often requiring the use of scaffolding equipment to reach the nest site which can be as dangerous to the inexperienced as approaching the owls themselves.

The first-born owlet usually dominates and receives the most food as the parents regularly arrive with prey. As long as the food supply is healthy, then all the owlets are fed and grow rapidly, remaining in the nest for up to five weeks. If the supply of prey fails, survival of the fittest takes over: the smallest owlet is eaten until only the largest remains. This is nature's way of making sure that at least one owlet survives rather than all four dying of starvation.

Once out of the nest, the young tawny owls are still dependent on their parents for between three and five weeks, and receive food brought to regular spots throughout the beechwood. However, as August approaches the parents begin to re-establish their territories and those juveniles which have not already left to find their own habitats are driven out by defending adults. During the first few months of independent life many young tawny owls die of starvation because, when left to hunt for themselves, some are too inexperienced to catch regular supplies of food, and others become one of a large number of road casualties.

A characteristic, but not necessarily common, bird of beechwoods is the **stock dove**, which is superficially similar to the woodpigeon, but not nearly as well known. At 33 cm/12¾ in, this dove is slightly smaller than the tawny owl but like the owl it likes to nest in natural holes and cracks in old trees, although in other habitats it nests in rabbit burrows, crevices in cliff faces and cavities in old farm buildings.

The blue-grey plumage is darker than that of a woodpigeon and its tail is much shorter. When the stock dove flies overhead, before landing at the nest hole, dark trailing wing margins are clearly visible, contrasting with the pale grey of the main wing area, and there are iridescent green patches on both sides of the neck. Within the last fifteen years, since certain toxic agricultural chemicals have been withdrawn, the population of stock doves has increased, but they do not nearly reach the numbers of the woodpigeon, which is over thirty times more abundant throughout the range, which includes everywhere except southern Ireland and the Highlands and the northern islands of Scotland.

The limitation of the population is due largely to the feeding habits of the bird. The stock dove has a slender, narrow beak designed to pick up seeds from the ground, and during the late summer and beginning of autumn it may be commonly seen gleaning the spilt grain and eating weed seeds in stubble fields. Before the frosts arrive the food supply is plentiful but as winter begins the cereal grain supply becomes exhausted, leaving nothing but wild seeds to provide the main diet when food intake is critical. The food supply is never sufficient to carry large populations through the winter, so the numbers are naturally controlled.

In early March, stock doves take up their breeding territories. The male proclaims his patch by a monotonous double-noted 'ooo-woo' uttered in the morning and again in the early evening. Two white eggs are laid in the hollow tree and both adults share the incubation which lasts about seventeen days, but the female tends to do the night shift and the male incubates during the day. When the eggs hatch the ugly chicks, called 'squabs', are initially fed on an adult crop secretion called 'pigeon milk' which is highly nutritious, containing vitamins, fats and protein. After about four days the diet is changed to adult-regurgitated seeds and after twenty-three days the young leave the nest. Frequently up to three broods are raised during the season and sometimes the female stock dove lays eggs in a new nest hole before her first brood have flown. Apart from beechwoods, the dove colonises mixed woods and parklands wherever there is mature timber, so it is worth looking out for the bird in oak, ash or even willow trees, especially those which have been pollarded.

24 The tawny owl colonises woodland, parks and large urban gardens wherever there are hollow trees for it to nest in.

25 Female mandarin duck outside the entrance to her nest hole in a hollow tree.

Although most of the British ducks and other aquatic birds belong to other habitats, some duck species are frequently associated with woodland as a nesting habitat. Teal, for instance, nest in Highland birch and juniper woods and the red-breasted merganser is sometimes a woodland-fringe-nesting bird. The goosander (page 150) is a definite woodland-nesting species using holes in trees growing close to the water's edge.

The duck most commonly found in beechwoods is the Chinese **mandarin duck (25)**. During the last fifty years, feral populations have established in Surrey and Berkshire and the most northerly wild breeding populations occur in Perth city on Tayside. The Surrey stronghold is Virginia Water, where a wild breeding population has originated from pinioned birds initially introduced in the nineteen hundreds as ornamental ducks for the lakes of private estates.

Mandarin ducks are native to the agricultural, north-eastern province of China, called Manchuria, and were introduced to London Zoo as long ago as 1830. Today the Chinese population is dwindling and the feral Surrey birds are a significant and valuable colony of a species which is becoming rarer elsewhere in the wild. The total British population is estimated at 300–1,000 pairs with the majority in south and south-east England, and it is likely that there are now more wild mandarin ducks in Britain than in native China.

The brightly coloured drake with orange wing sails and facial side whiskers is a familiar bird, but the female is less familiar with a grey-crested head, olive-brown upperparts and grey flanks with cream spots. When the males moult they resemble the females and partly because of this subtle plumage the ducks can go undetected in woodland where they spend long periods perched high in the branches, allowing the dappled sunlight to camouflage them. In the wild, mandarins spend hours away from the water, preferring to skulk in dense vegetation and feeding on beech mast, acorns, seeds and invertebrates. Partly because of their preferred diet and partly because beech and oak are the dominant trees in Berkshire and Surrey it is best to look for mandarins in these habitats. Flying at speed through the beechwoods mixed with sweet chestnuts, the mandarin duck resembles a sparrowhawk, making the same turns and executing each move with grace and precision until it reaches the nest hole, where it brakes, using fanned tail and splayed wings, and drops neatly into the nest hole, which can be up to 12 m/40 ft above the ground and 1.6 km/1 mile away from the nearest stretch of water. The young show tremendous agility, dropping from the nest hole within twenty-four hours of hatching and following the female to water where she looks after them until they are fledged.

Even though the beechwood with its dense mosaic-like canopy appears dark, silent and still during summer, there is still activity inside the wood throughout the year. The fact that birds have minds of their own and a strong streak of independence and adaptability makes birdwatching in a beechwood even more enthralling, for nobody can predict what they may see or what species may decide to colonise.

ASHWOODS

Throughout many of the deciduous woods of Britain, ash and hazel are common trees (and they are also regularly seen in hedgerow and scrubland habitats). Ash colonised Britain quite late compared with other deciduous trees and was only established during the mid- and late Boreal period (8,500–7,500 years ago). However, once established ash always grows and spreads rapidly, so that by the end of the Atlantic period (7,500–5,000 years ago) it was to be found throughout Britain, particularly in northern England, although it was scarce in Ireland. Today, ash is still not widely distributed in Ireland, but it occurs as a frequent road-verge tree, and on the upland limestone in Co. Galway and Co. Clare numerous small ash-woods are found.

When Neolithic man caused the decline of elm the ash tree became more dominant, probably because it was the most rapid coloniser of the newly cleared areas, especially if these were on calcareous soils which ash favours. If you want to enjoy the few native ashwoods left in Britain, you will need to visit the limestone regions of the north and west or the chalk downlands of south-east England.

During the last 1,000 years man has favoured oak as a woodland species because it was the most valuable as building material, but from the seventeenth century ash was allowed to grow within oakwoods and mixed woodlands because of its tough and flexible qualities, which made it perfect for the axles and shafts of carts, tool and weapon handles and even for the frames of manorhouses. As a result of its commercial value, after oak, ash has been the second most recorded tree through history, and today very few ashwoods are pure, the most common mixture being the oak-ashwood.

Apart from the most acid soils, ash will grow in all soil conditions. On base-rich soils which contain high quantities of calcium, iron, magnesium or potassium mineral salts, ash grows with hazel, wych elm and maple; on slightly calcareous or neutral soils, it grows with hazel and maple; and on the more impoverished soils it grows with hazel only. It is possible

26 Rassal Ashwood in Wester Ross is the most northerly genuine ashwood in Britain.

26

to deduce the nature of the soil by the association of other trees with ash within the wood. The finest ashwoods are found in the north, where only hazel grows alongside ash with some sessile oak: they include Gait Barrows in Lancashire, Rassal Ashwood in Wester Ross (26) and Colt Park Wood near Ribblesdale in Yorkshire – all of which grow in limestone where the soil is not rich enough for wych elm or maple and in some cases outside the natural range of these trees.

In many of Britain's ancient woodlands, the delicate green of ash may be seen, but unlike beechwood, ash trees cast a very light shade and demand a great deal of light themselves if they are to survive. Like the oak, the ash tree comes into leaf very late in the spring and it is often not until May that you can look upwards in the wood and absorb the beauty of sunlight filtering through the unfolding, bright-green, pinnate leaves, with 4–6 pairs of smaller leaflets branching from the central stem. Consequently light is able to reach the woodland floor and the ashwood resembles an open-style pedunculate oakwood, with well-developed and varied shrub, field and ground layers, which, during spring and early summer, will mesmerise even the most single-minded birdwatcher. Depending on the locality and type of soil, dogwood, spindle and wild privet grow under the ash and in southern woods traveller's joy also survives: since all these shrubs either produce berries or large seed heads, they attract thrushes and finches in autumn.

The trunk of the ash is slender and covered with cracked grey bark. Seeds from the pods or ash-keys remain on the trees all winter and are raided in spring by wandering bullfinches. Every year large quantities of seeds are produced from purplish-green flowers which burst from dark buds early in April, long before the leaves emerge. The flowers hang like tassels from the twigs and are wind pollinated, but many fail to survive because each spring woodpigeons visit ashwoods in large numbers and greedily devour the succulent flower heads.

It is most likely that in ancient Britain pure ashwoods colonised the richer lowland soils and that in the ancient oakwoods ash was a more common species than it is in oakwoods today. Originally the oak-ashwood was probably an ash coppice with pedunculate oak standards; when coppicing and management ceased, the coppiced ash trees grew, together with natural regeneration by seed. The seedlings matured and eventually, by natural selection, the strongest cast shade over the weaker trees which died, leaving the healthy ash trees to grow and outnumber the oak standards. Rigsby Wood in Lincolnshire and King's Wood in Northamptonshire show this type of development; both are nature reserves, where woodcock, redpoll and numerous other woodland birds colonise.

Wherever oak and ash grow together, the woodland is generally permanently moist and the soil rich in lime. Oak competes favourably with ash on damp loams, which is a soil rich in humus, containing all the mineral salts; but increased lime content in a soil favours ash which gradually dominates over the oak. Mixed oak-ashwoods phase into ashwoods towards the north and west of Britain as an alternative to beech which is mostly confined to southern England. Since ashwoods are better established in Britain than anywhere else in Europe, our woods represent habitats of international importance. The greatest threat to ashwoods is heavy grazing by sheep and cattle, which trample and browse the rich ground and field layers, removing the unique plant growth and preventing ash saplings from developing.

The purest ashwoods occur in four main regions of Britain. Apart from an impressive ashwood growing out of the moss-covered limestone at Tokavaig on Skye, they are all on mainland Britain, in the Mendips, Glamorgan, the Derbyshire Dales and the northern Pennines of Yorkshire – all growing on carboniferous limestone. Here the ash grows unchallenged by other species, since it is the best adapted to survive in the shallow, alkaline soils covering the limestone – even sessile oak cannot challenge for supremacy; but one of the first things you will notice about the ash trees in these areas is that they are not magnificent specimens, and are frequently withered and stunted, unlike the tall ashes reaching over 30.5 m/100 ft on the richer lowlands.

At an altitude of 350 m/1,115 ft on the northern Pennines near Ingleborough is Colt Park Wood, which, although covering only 8.5 ha/21 acres, is recognised as being perhaps the best ashwood in Britain, and is a National Nature Reserve. The trees actually grow on limestone pavement which is a flat platform of rock covered with cracks called grikes – some of which are over 1.8 m/6 ft deep – in which the ash trees are rooted. Inside the smaller cracks a profusion of flowers bloom in spring.

Compared with oak- and beech leaves, relatively few insects or their larvae feed on ash leaves, and of the forty species of caterpillar which feed on ash trees, very few are actually dependent on it. Because of the lack of invertebrate fauna, the ashwoods do not attract large numbers of breeding birds, and at any season, ashwood birdlife is far from remarkable; but due to the open canopy and airy nature of the wood, species which survive in pedunculate oak- and birchwoods also inhabit the ashwood. Wherever the ashwood is mixed with a few oak and birch trees, pied flycatcher, wood warbler and redstart breed, and the ashwoods at Kilbeggan, Ireland, have healthy populations of robin, blackbird, chaffinch and willow warbler. This warbler is also one of the most common birds in the English ashwoods.

The most northerly true ashwood in Britain is Rassal Wood in Wester Ross, covering 85 ha/210 acres, on Durness limestone. Some of the trees are spaced well apart and generally they are large, with a shrub layer composed of downy birch and hazel which grow over primroses, bluebells and wood anemone in spring.

The **wren** (27) is common in Rassal Wood and many other of the Scottish ashwoods, and although we have already met the bird in the oakwoods, its scientific name, *Troglodytes troglodytes*, which means 'a cave dweller', is more appropriate for the ashwood because the wren exploits the crevices, grikes and recesses of the limestone, frequently building its nest in their shelter. From the middle of April onwards the wren begins to breed, with the male singing loudly even whilst carrying nesting material for one of several nests which he builds alone. There is never a shortage of ideal nest sites in the ashwood, because if none of the natural cavities is suitable, the wren constructs a domed nest of grass, moss, leaves and bracken low down in the dense field layer, where there is plenty of vegetation to choose from.

The cock wren then tempts the female to inspect the nests and she flits from one site to another, visiting each nest several times before making a decision. She lines the nest of her choice with feathers before laying the eggs. Although the male builds the nest he plays no part in incubation, and when the eggs hatch, the hen always seems to do most of the feeding. Whenever food is abundant and the weather is favourable, the wren rears two broods. Up to 10 million pairs breed in Britain, provided a severe winter has not reduced the overall population.

During extremely cold weather, wrens set up communal roosts which, in urban habitats, are frequently nestboxes, but in the ashwood are in natural tree holes or limestone fissures. Up to forty individual birds fly in and roost together, producing a warm feathery bundle, each bird giving body heat, which a small bird can lose so rapidly on a cold night, to its neighbour.

The **marsh tit** is one of the most common of its family in ashwoods since it thrives in the well-developed shrub and field layers of the habitat, but because its breeding range in Scotland is restricted to Berwick, and it does not occur in Ireland, the ashwoods of Derbyshire and southern England are the best sites to see this species. The bird prefers deciduous woodland with open canopies, so pedunculate oakwoods are popular, but it rarely inhabits sessile oakwoods; they also breed in birchwoods, where they are easily mistaken for the similarly marked willow tit. The marsh tit is really misnamed because it prefers the drier habitats and it is the willow tit which is seen in alder carr, marsh scrubland and along river banks, feeding on insects and seeds from the alder catkins.

In autumn and winter the marsh tits, which pair for life, join flocks of tits and finches, which are moving through their territory. Whereas the other species move on to neighbouring woods once they have finished feeding, the marsh tits desert the mixed flock and continue to hunt for food within their own territory, which extends to about 6 ha/15 acres and is larger than that occupied by most other species of tit. By February and March the male marsh tit has claimed his breeding territory for the season and throughout summer you will be able to watch the pugnacious cock bird chasing blue tits and even great tits away. Because marsh tits use natural holes in trees for their nest sites (**29**), they are always in competition with other hole-nesting birds, and often fierce vocal and sometimes physical battles occur between a marsh tit and another bird claiming the same nest hole. Marsh tits also select nest holes in grassy banks or stone walls and the limestone rocks associated with so many of our ashwoods provide ideal nesting sites.

Ash does not survive where it is overshaded by other trees, for which reason ash very often occurs as a transitional species before another species eventually outgrows it and dominates. The chalk and lime-rich areas of southern England, such as the South Downs and Cotswolds, provide ideal conditions for ash, but it grows in competition with beech, which casts a dense shade; therefore the ash dominance is short-lived and it survives as isolated clumps or forms an intermediary habitat from scrub to climax beechwood.

It is interesting that despite its dislike for shade, ash grows in many of the sessile oakwoods of Britain, which form a dense canopy. However, many of our sessile oakwoods occupy the sides of steep hills, ravines and gorges, through which run rivers and streams, providing a natural break between the trees, with an open canopy above; here ribbons of ash grow and become established. The other factor which makes these watery clearings ideal for ash is the variety of mineral salts carried down the hillside by natural percolation and filtration, towards the river-bed. Even the slightest amount of lime which accumulates in the soil at the bottom of the slopes is sufficient to stimulate the growth of ash trees which gradually give way to sessile oak further up the hillside.

The association of ash with sessile oak means that it is not unusual to find **buzzards** nesting in ash trees (**28**). This familiar raptor is even regularly seen in the purest ashwoods, since they generally grow in upland regions, with moorland near by, which is a favourite hunting ground for the bird. In the Middle Ages when forest clearance was extensive the buzzard benefited because for hunting it likes open countryside and small fields, bordered by trees and studded throughout with copses for shelter: during the fifteenth century the buzzard was probably the most common bird of prey. But the preservation of game and the ruthless interference by man soon caused a huge decline in the buzzard population: persecution began in the eighteenth century, intensified during the nineteenth century, and by the First World War the buzzard was very rare, absent from southern England, apart from a lingering population in the New Forest, and found only in the remote, upland regions of western Britain. Persecution ceased during the Second World War and the buzzard was able to increase its range and re-establish in some of its old haunts so that today the bird is found in Wales, south-west England, the Lake District and Scotland, although it is still absent from much of southern England and only occurs in small numbers in the north of Ireland. Wales and parts of Devon are the real strongholds, where pairs breed within a 1.6 km/1 mile radius of each other. The densest population of buzzards ever recorded is from Skomer Island where eight pairs nested within the 294 ha/762 acres of the island.

Despite the fact that the buzzard is protected by law, it is still illegally killed, and this contributes to the restriction of the bird's range in certain parts of Britain. The main problem is the fact that farmers and gamekeepers still put down poisoned bait to control foxes and crows which they claim are a pest during lambing or when gamebird chicks are being reared, and, since the buzzard likes to feed on dead carcasses (carrion), many are killed, together with eagle, red-kite, hen harrier and raven, who also feed on the poisoned bait. The British Trust for Ornithology, who surveyed the buzzard population as recently as 1983, found that of all the dead buzzards retrieved, over 33 per cent had died from poisoning or had been shot or trapped, using illegal snares.

High above your head in the ashwood, you might hear an all-familiar loud, but plaintive mewing call. The 'pee-yow pee-yow' cry causes you to look up and see through the loose canopy of the ash trees a pair of buzzards soaring and gliding on the thermals. On a warm day, during sunshine, buzzards like to spend hours in the sky, wheeling and circling on broad-fingered, slightly upturned wings, with their characteristic short tail fanned out behind, and through binoculars the pale, mottled and blotched underparts are visible against the sky. Apparently just passing the time of day, the buzzards are watching, ready for the slightest twitch or rustle which exposes the presence of a field vole or young rabbit crouching on the grassy slopes bordering the wood; and if you are lucky you will see the kill, made by a swoop and positive strike.

Rabbits are a major part of the buzzard's diet, but part of the recolonisation success of the buzzard, since its decline in the mid-1950s when myxomatosis depleted the wild rabbits, is due to the wide range of prey which it takes. Voles, shrews, mice, lizards and frogs are all very popular, and an early morning walk around the perimeter of an ashwood may reward you with the sighting of a buzzard walking through the dewy grass and eating worms, beetles and other insects every few steps.

Perhaps one of the best opportunities for seeing a buzzard is when a solitary bird sits on a tree, fencepost or telegraph pole, watching for prey. They are large birds, 55 cm/22 in from beak to tail, and the females are always largest; as she sits upright on

27 The wren's small size and sombre plumage make the ever-active bird hard to see.

28 Buzzards colonise upland ashwoods, close to mountain and moor.

the post you will appreciate her stocky, compact shape. Only now can the dark brown upperparts and wings be seen which, as you will learn from experience, vary in colour from black-brown to a rufous tawny in different birds. The legs are feathered right down to the toes which are bright yellow, ending in black curved claws which match the colour of the beak.

The buzzard takes off quietly for a large bird and it rises on powerful wing beats. Its large nest is built in the top of one of the ash trees, close to the main trunk. Twigs, small branches, and heather, are used for the main construction which is then lined with green foliage before egg-laying begins. Typically, the clutch is three eggs laid towards the end of April and early May, and both adults incubate for up to thirty-five days. The juvenile buzzards remain in the nest for nearly eight weeks, with the male doing most of the hunting, allowing the female to feed them the prey he has caught.

The **lesser spotted woodpecker (30)** is the smallest (14.5 cm/ 5¾ in) and rarest of our woodpeckers and is an elusive species, preferring to stay well up in the tree tops and only locatable by the occasional high-frequency 'pee-pee-pee' call. If you bird-watch in parts of central and eastern England, you will eventually see this bird nesting in the roadside ashes only 6 m/20 ft from the ground, but the lesser spotted woodpecker favours open woodland such as pedunculate oak and birch, parks with mature trees and neglected orchards where the trees are decaying. Rarely bold enough to venture right into suburban habitats, it avoids the smaller gardens and remains on the perimeter in the roadside trees, quiet avenues lined with trees or churchyards with good tree cover.

Ashwoods and alder carr are popular haunts, because they grow in remoter areas, which suit the woodpecker. It can be seen clinging to the uppermost branches searching for insects. Even in the highest canopy it is possible to sex the woodpecker,

30

29 Unlike the similarly marked willow tit, the marsh tit uses natural holes in walls or trees, rather than excavate its own nest hole.

30 Regularly seen in ashwoods, the secretive lesser spotted woodpecker is found in deciduous woods, wooded gardens, old orchards and parkland.

which has the similar black and white barred markings of the great spotted woodpecker, but not the crimson under-tail covert; the males show an attractive crimson crown which is black in the female, contrasting with her white forehead.

Only about 10,000 pairs of lesser spotted woodpecker breed in Britain. It has a wide distribution in England and Wales, has not yet colonised Scotland, and is absent from Ireland. If you are fortunate enough to locate a breeding pair, listen for the springtime drumming which, because of the size of the bird, is far higher pitched than that of the great spotted woodpecker, but each drumming session lasts much longer than that of the larger bird. When you see a small bird floating through the trees like a butterfly, follow it through the wood because this is the courtship display flight, and will probably lead to where the

nest is being excavated by both birds on the underside of a dead or decaying bough. Squeezing through the 4-cm/1½-in-diameter entrance hole, the woodpeckers line the nest cavity with fine wood chippings; then during May the eggs are laid which are incubated by both birds for fourteen days.

As autumn approaches, even though the ash leaves are still quite green, they begin to drop to the woodland floor; because they were one of the last leaves to burst in the spring yet fall the earliest, they have a very short summer growing cycle. Some of the upper leaves that catch the first night frost of autumn turn a pale yellow, but they are so sensitive to cold that by the next frost all the leaves drop without any colour spectacle, leaving only the clusters of ash fruits or samaras bulging with seeds to be of some winter value to the birds.

ALDERWOODS

One of the most varied and fascinating regions of Scotland is Argyll, with scenery ranging from the breathtaking wild highland peaks of Glencoe and the desolate peat expanse of Rannoch Moor to the indented jagged western coastline over 1,609 m/1,000 miles long. Here numerous sea lochs cut deep into the landscape, giving protection from the Atlantic rollers and some, such as Loch Sunart and Loch Etive are favourite haunts of waders, divers and gannets. Lying off the west coast are the Inner Hebrides offering magical seascapes and unspoiled beaches. Indeed, Argyll contains a greater and richer variety of flora and fauna than any other region of Scotland.

Some of the plants, animals and habitats of Scotland are rare or unique. One example is Carnach Wood, Glencoe, which is a hanging ash-alderwood, covering 110 ha/271¾ acres and growing on the north face of a very steep slope where heavy rainfall is regular. The base rocks are calcareous schists and limestones containing the mineral salts favourable for ash trees, and the soil is a clay-loam which retains much of the water from precipitation. Alder grows where the soil is wet, allowing the roots to be regularly immersed in water from which they can absorb the rich mineral salts. In this rare example of an ash-alderwood, the two species of tree grow as a mixture with some hawthorn and hazel forming the shrub layer. Glasdrum Wood is another fascinating alderwood in Argyll, growing away from typical valley sites, high up on steep slopes.

Alderwoods are different throughout the rest of Britain but as a tree the alder is very widespread, usually growing with a mixture of other deciduous trees rather than as a dominant species. Alder trees frequently grow in the wettest parts of pedunculate oakwoods, and like ash trees, the alder is common in upland sessile oakwoods where they form a pure band at the lowest, wettest part of the hillside, usually where a river runs through or into the oakwood: this type of woodland occurs at Coedydd Aber, Gwynedd in Wales, at Lodore in Cumbria and in many other localities.

Only the common or black alder is native to Britain: all other species have been introduced as ornamental trees. Although today alder quickly colonises any new appropriate site, with copious seeds being dispersed by wind and water, after the last Ice Age alder was rather slow in colonising Britain, not reaching its complete range until the beginning of the Atlantic period. The Atlantic period was a warm and wet phase which caused pine to retreat in range but which presented ideal conditions for the alder to spread around swamps and bogs, fens and lake margins; today these are the familiar habitats where the tree is commonly seen throughout Britain, but it is less common in northern Scotland and Ireland. During and ever since Neolithic times the tree has been allowed to maintain its range and has not been over-exploited by man, probably because of the habitats which it colonises and the fact that it is not a highly commercial timber: it never grows very large, burns badly and rots quickly.

Alder is not an indicator of any particular type of soil; it is indifferent to acidity and seems to thrive on even the most infertile soils, although not on these exclusively. It is commonly seen as a non-woodland tree, but the one thing alder does indicate is that the soil is always wet and susceptible to flooding. It grows along the banks of rivers, streams and canals or, deeper into the cities, out of the cracks of concrete retaining walls such as those found in London's dockland.

In Britain distinct alder woodlands form specific habitats. In the valley alderwoods the alder grows along the margins of water courses as a fringe between the water and the dominant tree (which is frequently sessile oak). If the fringe is not pure alder, then be prepared for it to be mixed with ash, wych elm and willow; and whilst looking for dipper or grey wagtail, perched on the stones of these woodland streams, look at the eroded embankment, because here the filamentous red rootlets of the alder are clearly visible, wafting in the current. In upland Britain, especially in north-west Scotland and throughout Wales, wherever the terrain levels out, alder forms plateau woods, usually intermingled with ash, birch and sessile oak, and only rarely pure alder. There is also fen alder carr which, because fens are characteristic of flat, low-lying ground, are frequently swamped by the floodwaters from rivers and streams. The fens are too wet for the majority of other trees to survive, and these extensive familiar areas are largely confined to eastern England, where alder dominates over all other trees.

The Norfolk Broadland carrs are so dense in vegetation and surrounded by water that they are impenetrable and resemble tropical jungles. Here alder, which has been present for thousands of years, still predominates, with sallow as a secondary growth and birch, hawthorn and ash wherever the ground becomes drier. The thick field layer consists largely of blackberry or bramble, stinging nettles and *Carex paniculata*, a tussocky sedge. In winter these carrs become flooded by about 0.6 m/2 ft of water, so that the following spring the ground is thick, black, oozing mud. There is restricted access into these Norfolk carrs. Bure Marshes is a Nature Conservancy Council reserve, covering 412 ha/1,018 acres, where the habitat includes sedge and reedbeds, together with alder woodland, and is a classic example of its type, restricted by permit access only. Another part of these marshes is referred to as the Hoveton Great Broad Nature Trail on Hoveton Broad and access is possible only by boat. The whole area of peat is surrounded by alder carr and a trail is provided on duckboards so that birdwatching can be enjoyed with safety; purpose-built hides are provided, which are reached by walking through the alder and willow carr. On the open water, mallard and great crested grebe may be seen and you might spot a heron, perfectly poised in the shallows by the roots of the alder, waiting to spear a luckless fish. Overhead, swallows, swifts and house martins hawk the numerous insects and you might enjoy the graceful flight of common terns nesting near by.

The species of bird found in alderwoods varies according to season and whether the wood is alongside a loch, lake or river, or on an upland plateau. Alderwoods do not contain distinctive breeding birds. Norfolk alder carr is frequently the habitat of typical woodland and marshland birds attracted by the abundance of insects and encouraged to remain because of the dense, protective vegetation; and the regular occurrence of dead timber is useful for hole-nesting birds and those who feed on wood-boring insect larvae. Sedge and grasshopper warbler, blue tit, marsh tit, willow tit and woodcock all nest alongside many other species of woodland bird. In Scotland the redwing is a localised coloniser of birchwoods, but in certain alderwoods around Scottish lakes it can also be found nesting in limited numbers.

Alder is unique because it is the only British deciduous tree to produce miniature cones like those of coniferous trees; they are formed from the fertilised female catkins. Since the seeds of these cones are significant to birds in winter, it is interesting for the birdwatcher to know how they are formed.

If you wander into alder carr in spring, especially during March and April, before the leaves have burst, catkins are clearly visible. The alder produces two types of catkin on the same tree. The male catkins, which in winter are deep red, consist of a small finger-like column of compact stamens and in spring double their length to about 5 cm/2 in, causing the stamens to separate and dangle in the breeze. Masses of pollen can be seen drifting on the air currents as a shaft of sunlight illuminates the wood and some of these pollen grains settle on the female catkins. Looking carefully at the branches you will see that these female catkins are dark purple-brown in colour, club-shaped and only about 9 mm/⅓ inch long. Once they have become pollinated they turn green and swell, producing the rounded cone which protects the unripe seeds.

Throughout the summer and into autumn the seed-bearing cones develop to form the hard, beer-barrel-shaped cone which is a familiar sight in alderwoods in winter. Eventually the cones dry, the scales split apart and thousands of small winged seeds are released to be dispersed on the wind. Many alders over-hanging rivers shed their seeds directly into the water where the wings act as buoyancy tanks and the seeds drift down-stream eventually forming valley alderwoods. Many of the floating seeds are also greedily eaten by aquatic birds such as the teal and mallard and never get the chance to germinate.

It is the availability of food which causes birds to visit a particular type of woodland: because of the copious supply of seeds, in winter you are more than likely to see flocks of redpoll and siskin moving through the bare branches, raiding the seeds from the cones. These attractive birds are visitors from Scandinavia, who move south for the winter. Alder seeds are vital for their ability to survive the cold weather.

In eastern England, where many areas are without wood-land, alder carrs are important roosting sites. Birdwatchers spending a day watching and listening to Cetti's warbler at Stodmarsh in Kent can marvel at the evening throng of rooks and jackdaws which arrive at dusk to roost in the nearby alder carrs.

The New Forest is always a rich habitat for the naturalist and alder trees are common around the margins of many of the bogs and streams, although they would be more abundant if grazing were not so widespread. Once established, the trees grow quickly, and isolated clumps of alder carr give shelter to many plants including bog myrtle and opposite-leaved golden saxifrage. Further south-west, in Devon, Somerset and Corn-wall, alder is not so common, but it occurs as a declining habitat called the tidal alderwood. Land reclamation and coastal defence work has largely destroyed this fascinating habitat, but an outstanding example is the River Fal estuary in Cornwall, where saltmarsh stabilises to form sallow scrubland, which eventually gives way to alder woodland bordering the climax community of birch and oak. During storms and the highest annual tides, the alder woodland is washed in salt water, but this temporary immersion does not appear to harm the trees.

The largest expanse of alderwood in the British Isles is estuarine and found on land which was originally tidal, but is now reclaimed behind a sea embankment at the Mound on the east coast of Sutherland. Last century a rail and road embank-ment was built across Loch Fleet, which today isolates an area of saltmarsh from the sea. Behind the man-made barrier fresh water accumulated and the water levels increased, allowing alder to colonise and spread rapidly, so that now 267 ha/659 acres of alderwood form a nationally important reserve, which is extremely difficult to penetrate because of the dangerous swamps. The bird, insect and plantlife are particularly varied as there is virtually no interference from man and the area is of tremendous interest to the birdwatcher because of neighbour-ing Loch Fleet. In summer redshank, oystercatcher and shel-duck all feed on the mud flats at low tide, and the autumn passage of knot, curlew and golden plover is an exciting scene to witness. During winter countless ducks form huge rafts, including mallard, wigeon, teal, common scoter, goldeneye and red-breasted merganser, moving between the loch and open sea depending on the tidal conditions, all within the shadow of our largest alderwood.

Alderwoods are widespread, but in some parts of Britain the habitat is declining because its preferred soil is a highly fertile one. Man has discovered that if he drains the land where alders grow and removes the trees, he is frequently left with extremely fertile farmland; even Neolithic man found that some of his richest soil was where the valley alderwoods grew. Since the Second World War man has increasingly interfered with the natural marshy habitats of Britain, with the result that as land has been drained, the delicate balance of the habitat has been destroyed: what was a stable ecosystem is suddenly changed with a loss of vegetation, including the alder. Alder carr has developed by natural succession from marshland over hundreds of years, but if the ground becomes drier, through whatever cause, the climax vegetation gradually changes: the purple-brown female catkins which bring a sheen of colour to the alderwoods in March, and enable siskins and redpolls to survive the winter, may slowly disappear and remain only in nature reserves or inaccessible upland sites. Each species of tree is in direct competition with one another for habitat dominance and survival, and the nature of the soil and amount of shade is critical. Certain trees such as the alder survive where the soil is almost permanently wet, where other species struggle to gain a foothold. Once drainage begins, conditions deteriorate for the alder and the balance is tipped in favour of either the oak, ash or birch.

BIRCHWOODS

Birch trees, with their slim, silvery trunks and delicate wispy branches, bearing small, fine-toothed leaves, are amongst the best known of all trees. So graceful is their appearance that they are frequently used to landscape housing estates and industrial sites, where they break up the stark outlines of urban architecture; and since they are ornamental in appearance, birch trees are popular for planting in gardens and suburban parkland.

The elegant, fragile appearance of birch trees, however, is deceptive because they are among the world's hardiest trees. They grow in forests throughout the northern hemisphere and in Europe they grow closer to the Arctic than any other species, surviving some of the most severe frosts in the world.

We have already seen in Ch. 1 how birch was one of the earliest trees to colonise Britain, around 10,000 years ago when the Ice Ages came to an end. Dwarf birch was the first species to colonise the boulder-strewn soil, followed by the much taller silver birch and downy birch; and of the 40 or so world species of birch, these are the only three native to the British Isles. The dwarf birch is a shrubby, truly Arctic species which survives locally on Scottish mountains such as the Grampians around Glen Clova. Downy birch is more hardy than silver birch and is more dominant in the colder upland regions of the British Isles, whereas silver birch colonises the drier acidic soils of southern and eastern England. Frequently the silver and downy birch grow together: in the eastern Highlands silver birch is a common dominant species – as at the Craigellachie birchwood near Aviemore – whereas on wetter soils in southern England there are some woods in which downy birch dominates.

The twigs of the downy birch are covered with fine hairs, giving a downy appearance, whereas the twigs of silver birch are smooth, but the surest way of distinguishing the two species at a distance is by the trunk bark. The silver birch has white bark and that of the downy birch ranges from brown to silver grey. At the base of mature silver birch trees the characteristic smooth white bark is replaced by rough black bark but in the case of downy birch the bark remains constant right down to the ground.

During April, the leaves break from small pointed buds and at first they are bright green, triangular in shape and borne on long stalks so that the slightest breeze causes them to quiver. Birchwoods are extremely beautiful in autumn when the leaves turn bright yellow before falling in October and early November, and flocks of siskin and redpoll move in to feed on the numerous seeds in the catkins which form a large part of their winter diet.

Throughout the British Isles birch is in competition with other trees and although it sheds thousands of seeds and is a vigorous coloniser of sandy heaths, commons, felled woodland and dry grassland, birch is only a temporary coloniser of many habitats, occupying the transitional stage before oak, beech or

33 Typical birchwood in early autumn.

31 The few pairs of redwing which breed in Highland Scotland prefer birch, alder or pinewoods, although rhododendrons are used in some gardens.

32 The ubiquitous willow warbler fills the woodland with its beautiful wistful song each spring and darts among foliage looking for insects.

mixed species grow up and shade it out. Even in natural birchwoods the wood is rarely pure and many other trees grow amongst the dominant birch, including oak, ash and rowan, with hawthorn as a shrub.

The largest natural birchwoods are found in Highland Scotland, where climatically conditions are too harsh for other tree species, apart from Scots pine, to compete with them. Silver birch prefers the slopes of the glens, especially in the east, where drainage is rapid; and downy birch survives in the wetter sites or up to 600 m/2,000 ft on the mountainside, where few other trees apart from rowan or mountain ash grow.

One of the best examples of a sub-alpine birchwood similar to those of Scandinavia is Morrone Birkwood (birk is Scots for birch) near Braemar. Here, growing on slopes 380–600m/ 1,250–2,000 ft is a wood of pure downy birch, with a shrub layer of juniper growing on basic soils. Further south, beyond the southern Grampians, is Aberfeldy where on the surrounding hills after the ice had retreated 10,000 years ago, an arctic, tundra-like habitat was left. These hillsides have become famous for birch trees, which were the dominant species of the Caledonian forests which covered this area after the Ice Age. In most other areas Scots pine was the dominant species of the Caledonian forest. It still remains a mystery why birch trees dominated over pine in this area, but the birks of Aberfeldy are now recognised as a Site of Special Scientific Interest (SSSI) and a small relic of a once vast forest.

Very few natural relic birchwoods exist and most Scottish birchwoods are remnants of pine or other types of woodland after felling has been completed over the centuries. At Aberfeldy the birches average 15 m/50 ft high and are around sixty years old. Some of the best specimens are found along the banks of Urlar Burn which cuts deep into the hillside; here the trees have escaped removal by felling because of their inaccessibility, and the steep slopes covered in glacial debris provide drained soil, ideal for silver birch. Downy birch also grows along the ravine, but silver birch is the most common and is responsible for giving the area its name. Throughout the wood, even where the birches grow at their most dense, the atmosphere is light and airy because the leaves are small and sunlight filters through the canopy.

Because birch has survived for thousands of years, many insects have evolved to lay their eggs on the trees. Larvae of the birch sawfly spend all their lives defoliating the trees and because their numbers are so large, a great variety of birds have learnt that invertebrate food is readily available. There are no British species of bird specific to birchwoods and most of the birds feeding in the canopy are common to other types of open woodland, although birds such as willow tit and tree pipit are exceptionally abundant in birchwoods; other common birds you will almost certainly see include willow warbler, chaffinch, robin, redstart, coal tit, blue tit and long-tailed tit.

Although **willow warblers (32)** are common in oakwoods, they colonise any wooded or shrub area where the canopy is not dense and of all the warblers visiting us each summer, the willow warbler penetrates furthest north into the uplands, where it colonises the birchwoods in large numbers. In some areas willow warblers seem to prefer birch to oakwoods.

In appearance, willow warblers are olive green on the upperparts with yellow-buff underparts. Their song usually gives their presence away.

The beautiful domed nest is usually on or near the ground, but is marvellously concealed. It is built entirely by the female of grass and moss, lined with feathers. During May up to seven eggs are laid and the young are fed by both adults for an additional fourteen days before they leave the nest. Willow warblers arrive in Britain very early compared with other summer visitors, but they are among the first to leave. Even so, second broods are regular before they begin to migrate south towards the end of July.

Damp woodland is a popular habitat for the **willow tit** and as the name suggests, willow trees along river and stream banks are one of their favourite nesting sites. The willow tit will colonise and breed wherever there are moss-covered stumps, and it frequently uses alder and birch. Like the crested tit the willow tits excavate their nest chamber with hammer and chisel blows, resembling miniature woodpeckers, but they carry all the wood chippings away from the nest site, whereas woodpeckers leave a conspicuous pile of debris beneath the tree, which is one of the surest ways of locating their nests.

The nest chamber of the willow tit is up to 30 cm/12 in deep and the nest is constructed of a grass and root base with a feather-lined cup. Since the nest chamber is excavated in living, dying or rotten timber, the neck muscles of the willow tit need to be well developed and the thick neck of the bird is the best way of distinguishing it from the similar marsh tit which also inhabits birchwoods but prefers oak, beech and ashwoods. Both willow and marsh tit have distinct black caps and beige-brown plumage and apart from the size of the neck, the song is the only way to distinguish the two species; indeed, it was not until 1900 that the birds were recognised as distinct species. The willow tit utters a high thin 'zee-zee-zee' note frequently followed by a longer 'chay-chay' sound similar to a squeaky gate hinge, whereas the marsh tit utters a loud forced 'pitchow' note and little else. Both the birds are found in the birchwoods of England and Wales, but neither are located in Ireland; in Scotland the marsh tit reaches just into the borders whereas the willow tit is found throughout south-west Scotland and colonises some of the northern birchwoods.

Since most of the birchwoods of the British Isles are mixed with oak, ash, alder, rowan, aspen, hawthorn, holly and hazel, and wherever they are pure the wood shows an open-style canopy, many of the resident bird species are similar to those of oakwoods, where the canopy is also not too dense. In many hillside oakwoods, birch grows as a fringe tree and even colonises the clearings within the wood before the oak canopy closes over.

In southern England birch is commonly found on sandy, dry heaths and after heathland fires birch scrub is one of the earliest colonisers; but if gorse and heather are too dense birch is choked out in the early stages of growth, resulting in the typical scattering of birch trees, familiar on many heaths and commons. Most of the southern birchwoods are visited by blue tit, coal tit and bullfinch from autumn to the spring, when they extract the seeds from the catkins and search for insects in the bark crevices. All these species can be seen at Holme Fen, Huntingdonshire, which is an NCC reserve covering 263 ha/649¾ acres; it is one of the best lowland birchwoods in the country with trees of variable age.

Spring is a beautiful time of year in the birchwood with the cascading branches bearing fresh green leaves and blue tits flying through the open canopy inspecting the branches and crevices, undisturbed by a great spotted woodpecker drumming on a neighbouring glistening white trunk. Sunlight filtering through the leaves reaches the woodland floor in one of the numerous glades which the woodcock, commonly a bird of oakwoods, favours for its display flights; in Scotland where oak is scarce they nest in birchwoods in good numbers since the habitat is an ideal substitute.

Redwing (31) have nested in Scotland since 1925, although this Scandinavian thrush is most commonly seen as a winter visitor, feeding in the hedgerows on berries and other fruits. But throughout the 1960s there was an upsurge in the number of redwings remaining to breed in Britain: by 1968 20 pairs were recorded in Wester Ross and by 1988 over 300 pairs had colonised, although the numbers fluctuate annually. The majority of the breeding redwings are found in Scotland, and although their habitat selection is varied, birchwoods and birch and willow scrub are most commonly used.

The complicated migrational habits of the redwing are probably responsible for the initial pairs colonising Scotland. Before severe winter weather sets in, redwings, accompanied by fieldfares, migrate south from Scandinavia to Britain and Ireland in large numbers. During the initial southerly migration, vast populations of birds reach eastern Britain, where they stop to feed before dispersing throughout the British Isles, reaching the West Country and Ireland for late autumn and winter. Some of the birds overwintering in the British Isles spend the next winter in southern Europe; overwintering European birds might choose Britain on alternate years, so there is always a varied movement of birds between different countries. It is very likely that during a particularly large autumn migration, some Scandinavian birds overwintering in Britain decided to remain and breed here in the spring. Alternatively, some of those birds which overwintered in southern Europe flying north in the spring might have been blown off course to the west, landing in Britain rather than reaching Scandinavia, where they would have bred in the birch and pine forests. Finding suitable birch- and oakwoods in Britain, the redwings bred successfully and have continued to do so ever since.

The redwing's nest is very similar to that of the song thrush, built of rough grasses with a mud lining, but whereas the song thrush lays its eggs directly into the mud-lined nest, the redwing further lines the mud-cup with fine grass and then lays the eggs during May.

Although birch trees are short-lived, they produce more seeds than many other species and grow easily from seed. Birch is quick to possess any land cleared of other shrubs or trees and has become one of the most ubiquitous species in Britain, both in ancient woodlands and in secondary woods recolonising fens, heaths, commons, conifer plantations and waste or derelict land. Since the seeds are wind-dispersed and extremely light, they travel on the air currents to habitats where there is little competition. This is one of the reasons why birch is a successful coloniser of the uplands of Britain, where birch scrub phases into open moorland without a clear transitional boundary.

It is obvious that certain birds are specific to one type of woodland because of the density of the canopy, the structure of the wood, or the amount of food available within the wood. Other species are more ubiquitous – as abundant in the pedunculate oakwood as they are in the beechwood or birchwood – and most of these species have also successfully adapted to thrive in parks, gardens and on farmland. Such birds as blackbird, song thrush, robin, chaffinch, wren, great tit and blue tit, although typically woodland birds, are certainly not confined to this habitat, but woodland is important to them, especially each summer, when these birds return there to breed.

Woodland habitat is of significance to nearly half the birds which breed in this country, and yet ever since Stone Age man began clearing the forests that covered Britain, man's assault on this habitat has been continuous. Today, woodland covers only about 1,780,000 ha/4½ million acres. Much of it is still under threat from agricultural and urban development, with government policies and public money supporting the destruction, so it is important that birdwatchers should be aware of the special significance of woodland conservation. The habitat and the wildlife it contains represent our original natural environment and the most important woodlands are the remnants of our ancient natural forests which have been part of the countryside for hundreds of years. Many of these are now nature reserves, but there are numerous other secondary woods which should be designated nature reserves, because of their ornithological interest, but which local Naturalists' Trusts and Conservation Societies are unable to purchase, due to lack of funds. Further, once purchased, woodland needs regular management, according to the traditional methods of coppicing and pasturing, where rides and clearings are made and maintained to allow regular penetration of sunlight, which, in turn, encourages flower growth, insect abundance and ideal conditions for numerous birds. This management costs money and conservation societies have to accept that they are financially unable to purchase all valuable woods, make them into nature reserves and still afford to maintain them. Woodland nature conservation, more pertinent since the vast hurricane damage of October 1987, will have to be achieved in the long-term by an education process and by the allocation of sufficient government funds to landowners with important woods on their estates to persuade them to include nature conservation in their overall use and management of the land. Only by such measures will we be able to make sure that woodland birds will have somewhere they can continue to breed and where, in winter, birdwatchers can see flocks of tits and bramblings feeding, as they have done for centuries before.

CHAPTER 3

CONIFEROUS WOODLAND

Although oak is the dominant broad-leaf tree in southern England today, birch was the first tree to colonise the British Isles after the Ice Ages, during the Pre-Boreal and Boreal periods. It was quickly followed by Scots pine which gradually dominated over birch scrub by casting dense shade over it and colonised the semi-tundra-like habitats which were exposed as the ice sheets retreated.

For several thousand years after the last Ice Age, the climate of Britain remained cool, which suited trees such as Scots pine, yew and the shrub juniper and all three species covered large areas of lowland and upland Britain.

During the Atlantic phase the climate improved and temperatures rose so that conditions became favourable for broad-leaf trees such as oak and elm which began to dominate in southern England, forcing the pines and conifers further north. Today the southern Highlands form a natural frontier for Scots pine: north of this region yew, juniper and Scots pine flourish whereas in the ancient Black Wood of Rannoch (**34**) in the southern Highlands birch trees grow among the pines and south of Loch Rannoch, oaks and other broad-leaf trees occur.

The Highlands were once covered by the ancient Caledonian pine forests, which at their greatest extent dominated 1.22 million ha/3 million acres. Today only 8,094 ha/20,000 acres of natural pine woodland remain and as through the ages man felled the trees, he also killed the wild animals; the last wolf was killed in Inverness-shire in 1743.

Conifer trees are planted throughout the British Isles but only three conifers are native: the Scots pine, yew and juniper. Scots pine, because of its ability to grow quickly, even in poor soils, has been planted in many parts of Britain, such as Breckland (page 66) but only in Scotland has the species grown continuously, since the end of the last Ice Age.

Yew commonly grows on chalk and limestone, where it frequently gives way to beech trees or remains as part of a mixed wood interspersed with ash and whitebeam. There are good examples of mixed yew-woods in Wiltshire, Hampshire and West Sussex, where in early spring the white undersides of

34 Ancient Scots pine survives in Black Wood of Rannoch, a remnant of the Caledonian pine forests.

35 The talons of the osprey are perfectly designed to grip slippery fish.

36 Since the RSPB repaired the vandalised nest at Loch Garten, ospreys have returned to breed successfully.

37 The female capercaillie is perfectly camouflaged on the nest even though it is a large bird.

38 Displaying male capercaillies can be very aggressive, threatening sheep, deer and even humans.

35

36

37

38

the newly opened whitebeam leaves contrast with the dark green leaves of the yew. One of the finest yew-woods in Europe is that at Kingley Vale, West Sussex, covering an area of 114 ha/281½ acres, on a south-facing chalk escarpment. Some of the trees are over five hundred years old and cast a shade so dense that nothing grows on the woodland floor of this strange, dark and mysterious forest. Birds colonise the wood: jay, turtle dove, willow warbler and chiff-chaff are seen or heard. An equally sinister, extensive yew wood is Great Yews near Salisbury; yew trees also grow on Box Hill in Surrey and Old Winchester Hill.

The finest example of juniper forest in Britain is the Tynron juniperwood in the valley of the Shinnel Water, 25 km/15 miles north-west of Dumfries. The steep south-east-facing slope of the valley is covered with 5 ha/12 acres of juniper with an astonishing density of up to 5,000 shrubs per hectare. This is an unusually high density for Scotland, where juniper usually occurs as isolated bushes on sheep-grazed hillsides or forms the shrub layer of Scots pine and birch forests. The oldest junipers in Tynron forest are 150 years old, but the majority vary from 80 to 120 years old. Buzzards and sparrowhawks are frequently seen flying and hunting near the forest and siskin, goldcrest, hedge sparrow, willow tit and coal tit all nest in the dense juniper.

Since yew- and juniperwoods are scarce in Britain they are not regarded as particularly rich in birdlife, especially since most birds favour a well-developed shrub layer in a woodland which the dense shade of both these species prevents.

Pinewoods have a reputation for being dark and devoid of plantlife; certainly, the majority of pine plantations over 15–20 years old are little more than ranks of straight, bare trunks, with a dense canopy preventing light from penetrating, and the atmosphere is cool, dark and quiet; there are no flowers and none of the rich songbird call associated with the broad-leaf woods, but a few coal tit, siskin and redpoll feed in the upper branches and chaffinch occupy the rides.

However, the ancient Caledonian and mature Scots pine forest is different from the recently planted conifer plantations because, like many natural woods, the remnant tracts of Caledonian forest are mixed. Some of the trees grow straight and tall for 27.4 m/90 ft, whereas others are stunted and bent. Three-hundred-year-old trees, gnarled with cracks and fissures in their trunks, are attractive to hole-nesting birds and there are wide sunny glades where downy birch trees grow and heather covers the forest floor. In these glades, which act as glorious sun-spots, the liquid song of a willow warbler may be heard and meadow pipit and whinchat feed. Unlike forestry plantations planted throughout upland Britain these woods are rich in birdlife.

The most impressive relic pinewoods occur in the central Highlands. They survived from Boreal times because of their remoteness and inaccessibility. They occupy the well-drained, poorer, mineral-deficient soils, forming scattered and fragmented tracts, many of which are within a 19-km/12-mile radius of Aviemore. The ancient Boreal forests covered much of Scotland, stretching from Glencoe in the west, across to the Forest of Mar on Deeside in the east, and from Loch Lyon, through Rannoch and north to Strathspey. The old trees are covered with grey outer bark arranged in large, armour-like plates, beneath which is a characteristic orange-pink colour.

Around Aviemore the Scots pine forests occupy slopes varying in altitude from 210 m/689 ft to 610m/2,000 ft, although the highest treeline in Britain occurs on Creag Fhiaclach at 640 m/2,099 ft. At Glen Feshie, 19 km/12 miles south-west of Aviemore, within the Cairngorms National Nature Reserve (NNR) four hundred years ago Mary Queen of Scots stood on a knoll, still called the Queen's Nose, and watched the Caledonian pinewoods of Glen Feshie being set ablaze. She was observing the beginning of man's destruction of the Caledonian forests, which accelerated during the eighteenth century when timber was required for iron-smelting furnaces. A variety of demands during the two world wars put the requirement for timber at its highest and felling was widespread.

The main Caledonian pine forests are north of Glen Feshie: Inshriach Forest, Invereshie Forest, Rothiemurchus Forest, Glenmore Forest and Abernethy Forest on Speyside. Rothiemurchus lies mostly on gentle slopes and the trees are large; and Abernethy Forest, covering 4,250 ha/10,501 acres, is the largest area of Scots pine on Speyside, lying predominantly on gentle sloping terrain. In 1988, the RSPB successfully purchased 1619 ha/4,000 acres of old native pine within the Abernethy Forest Estate and have now secured the future of this vast remaining area of the ancient Forest of Caledon, together with its rare and specialised wildlife. A greater variety of birds will colonise Abernethy Forest providing felling management generates a habitat with pockets of trees at different ages and stages of growth, together with glades offering a healthy shrub and field layer.

Another RSPB reserve within Abernethy Forest is called Loch Garten, and it has an important place on the ornithological map because of the ospreys which have returned to breed each April since 1959. The reserve covers 891.5 ha/2,203 acres and, apart from the loch and pine forests, moorland and bog habitat are abundant so birdwatching can be both rich and varied: Scottish crossbill, siskin, crested tit, capercaillie, buzzard, sparrowhawk, golden eagle, merlin, teal, wigeon, goosander and black-headed gull can all be seen. Within the reserve 144 species of bird have been recorded, 73 of which have bred.

The **osprey (35)** is a specialised fish-eating bird requiring an expanse of water where it can feed on pike, perch, salmon, trout or carp. It is only in Britain that breeding ospreys have preferred to nest in the upper branches of Scots pine; in other parts of the world they nest on cliffs, rock stacks and even cart wheels on top of tall poles, forming a platform. The British breeding birds mostly fly from Africa and although up to 33 pairs breed in the Scottish Highlands, the pairs on Loch Garten Loch of Lowes remain the most well known and easily seen.

Ospreys are magnificent birds with a 1.5-m/5-ft wingspan, rich brown upper plumage and striking white underparts. You may spend a fascinating time at Loch Garten observing the ospreys fishing in the loch. Generally they catch small fish of 1–2.2 kg/½–1 lb, but they are capable of carrying fish over 4.4 kg/2 lb in weight. The osprey circles the loch on slow flapping wings, looking out for surface-feeding or basking fish. When it has found one, the bird makes a spiral turn and hovers before beginning the dive which is sometimes a vertical plunge from up to 16 m/50 ft, or more frequently, a long, slowly descending approach ending in a low-level strike when it thrusts its talons forwards to grasp the fish as it enters the water. It rarely dives deeper than 1 m/3 ft below the surface and always holds its wings high above its body on impact, ready to gain lift as quickly as possible. Once up from the water the osprey manoeuvres the fish in its claws until the head faces the direction of flight and maintains a firm grip fore and aft of the prey as it flies to a nearby Scots pine to feed, or takes the fish back to the nest.

Because ospreys are exclusively fish-eaters, they were persecuted by gamekeepers in the past who believed they reduced the stocks of salmon and trout. However, the breeding population is so low today that fish farmers have become tolerant of the few fish poached from their hatcheries and honour the strict protection of the species under the 1981 Wildlife and Countryside Act which makes them Schedule I birds.

Over 1¼ million people have visited Loch Garten to view the osprey. Every April the birds return from their overwintering grounds in Africa, beginning the long flight north shortly after pairing. The male usually arrives at the traditional site a few days before the female and surveys the old nest and surrounding terrain to make sure the entire area is suitable. When the female arrives, he is already adding new twigs to the nest and in a bid to welcome her, he begins his spectacular soaring display flight before mating occurs, usually several days after the female has arrived. Up to three chocolate-flecked, rich brown eggs are laid, and the juveniles are in the nest for seven to eight weeks before they can fly. The surviving birds remain in their wintering quarters until they are three years old and ready to breed. During the incubation period the ospreys are still vulnerable to egg thieves and despite sophisticated electronic alarm systems, raids have been made on several of the Scottish sites and in earlier years, nest-robbing was sadly responsible for failed breeding seasons.

Nest-robbing is not the only threat. As was well publicised, in January 1986 at Loch Garten, someone armed with a chainsaw tried to fell an entire Scots pine tree with a nest in the uppermost branches. When they failed on the main tree trunk, they concentrated the attack on the upper branches, which they succeeded in cutting and, together with the nest, the boughs fell to the ground. Still not satisfied, the chainsaw operator attacked neighbouring pines where ospreys had nested between 1959 and 1979. To date, nobody has been charged with this mindless vandalism, which has persisted as recently as December 1990 when an unknown arsonist completely destroyed the osprey site reception buildings, including £40,000 of stock, and further damaged one of the public hides.

At the time the chainsaw damage occurred, the ospreys which use Loch Garten were already on their way to Scotland, flying along the sand-dunes on the west coast of Africa. The RSPB, with specialist tree surgeons, quickly had to repair the tree, supporting branches with artificial braces, and rebuild the nest. As **37** shows the operation was successful, and in late March, 1986, the ospreys returned. On this occasion a female arrived first, immediately adopted the man-made nest and began adding twigs to it. Eventually a male bird arrived and began courting the female, but he was a young male and although he brought branches to the nest, he ate most of the fish he caught himself, leaving the mature female calling for food in what is supposed to be part of the courtship ritual. Affection didn't last very long and the young bird left, to be replaced by another male, but he arrived too late in the season for breeding to take place.

In 1987 the ospreys returned again to Loch Garten and the repaired tree was still intact. Three eggs were laid and incubation began successfully, but unfortunately two eggs cracked, probably because the female was young and inexperienced. The RSPB decided to put the remaining egg in an incubator and placed three dummy eggs in the nest for the bird to continue incubating herself. The female osprey accepted the false eggs, settled on them and began incubating as normal, closely monitored by wardens. Because she returned to regular periods of incubation it was decided to replace the one true egg, which was developing in the artificial incubator, exchang-

ing it for a false egg from the nest. Initially everything went according to plan with the female happily incubating one real egg and two imitation eggs, but then, quite unexpectedly, the male osprey ejected the genuine egg from the nest and so for the second year running, no ospreys have bred successfully at Loch Garten. It is quite common for young adults taking up territory for the first time to miss a year before breeding. At Loch Garten the problem has chiefly been caused by sexually mature but inexperienced birds turning up, whereas up to 1985, the site had produced 50 young. During that year, nest-experienced birds set up territory, but during the season the male bird badly dislocated a wing and was unable to hunt, so the female was forced to leave the nest and fish herself. Again circumstances forced the RSPB to transfer the eggs to an incubator. One chick hatched and was transferred to another osprey nest, and successfully reared by foster parents.

Since the ospreys returned to Scotland in the late 1950s their breeding success has been remarkable: during 1985 53 young birds fledged from 33 nesting pairs. But the birds still face disasters by natural or other means: 50 per cent of ospreys die in their first year, because they are inexperienced in catching sufficient food or cannot adequately defend themselves. After several failed seasons at Loch Garten, there was finally success in 1988. Mature and experienced ospreys returned to breed and in late July three healthy youngsters left the nest on a hesitating but impressive maiden flight.

When felling and total localised destruction of the Caledonian forests took place, the large gamebird called the **capercaillie**, which was a specialised pine-forest species, became rarer and eventually extinct around 1760. In 1837 new stock from Sweden was introduced into the Highlands where it has re-established, but it has not spread to the conifer forests of Wales and Ireland, which it also used to colonise. Today priority is given to the conservation of the old pine forests where the capercaillie survives and it can be found throughout the east and central Highlands from the Firth of Forth to the Moray Firth and with good populations in Abernethy Forest, where the variably aged trees and clearings suit its habits.

Capercaillies are exclusively birds of mountain pine forests, especially those which include river valleys, and occupy altitudes up to 487 m/1,600 ft. The forest canopy must be dense in places but open glades are important where undergrowth such as bilberry and heather grow and young juniper and birch forms the shrub layer. This type of habitat provides the capercaillie with ideal nest sites and sources of food: during winter the birds are arboreal, climbing through the branches and eating needles of Scots pine, together with buds and shoots of the younger trees. During the spring and summer months the birds feed near or on the ground on bilberries and crowberries, together with leaves, sedges and mosses supplemented with insects and spiders.

Spring is the most rewarding season in which to watch capercaillie. Towards the end of winter the males begin to display, calling from lofty pine branches, and descending towards the ground as March approaches. Early morning, well before sunrise, is when courtship activity begins and normally, as a mist hangs on the pines and the forest is haunting in its silence, a series of repetitive clicks cuts through the trees. This is the beginning of a range of incredible sounds which announce the fact that a male capercaillie is walking towards you. The clicking sounds accelerate until they combine into a continuous rattle, immediately followed by a sound like a champagne cork being freed from the bottle; this popping call is interspersed by wheezing, hissing and gurgling sounds.

From out of the undergrowth, the male capercaillie suddenly reveals itself. Resembling a turkey, it is large, weighing up to 4 kg/8½ lb and up to 94 cm/37 in long. As the bird moves closer you will see its distinctive dark green-blue plumage with a white bill and red patch of skin above each eye. The female is smaller, only about half the weight of the male and reaching 67 cm/26¼ in long. Because capercaillies are ground-nesting birds, protection on the nest is by camouflage and the female capercaillie is variably marked with chestnut breast and brown mottled and barred back with black markings (**37**).

Strutting out into a clearing beneath the pines the male bird spreads its tail feathers as an erect fan and the wings are partially opened and drooped in display. It holds its head upright, but raises bristle-like feathers at the throat as it slowly walks on to a tussock of heather (**38**). Without warning it makes the cork sound again and the bird leaps into the air, running a few paces before repeating the dance.

The sound of the calling male, together with the sight of it leaping and gliding across the glade, attracts the hen birds to perch and watch the spectacle. Other male birds within the forest also respond to the sounds and enter the clearing to begin their own displays with the aim of attracting a mate. The dominating male rounds up the females into his harem, mating with one or two of them. It appears that the capercaillie's courtship behaviour is changing. At one time, groups of rival males would congregate for communal displays called 'leks'. Upon encountering a rival the male capercaillies would try to intimidate one another by strutting towards each other with lowered wings and arching their tails over their backs. Unless one bird backed off, aggressive battles began, with birds leaping into the air, kicking claws, and pecking and stabbing with their bills. In recent years, however, each male capercaillie seems to have his own forest clearing where he displays and attracts females without competition. This behavioural change has recently been observed in another grouse, the black grouse which is well known for courtship displays (page 110): in 1986 surveys revealed that during displays, the male or blackcock was performing on his own to a gathering of females and the traditional grouping of rival males was not occurring. Ornithologists are unable to explain whether this change in both capercaillie and black grouse is due to a falling population or if it has evolved by choice; equally unknown is whether unrivalled males will be as successful at breeding as those who bred following a challenge, where at least a dominating, physically strong male passed on its genes to the next generation.

The female capercaillie lays her eggs in late April, in a hollow lined with pine needles and grass, amid the heather and low vegetation. Once hatched, the young feed themselves, but the female continues to protect them even after they can fly, whereas the male capercaillie shows no interest in any parental duty, preferring to remain solitary until the following displaying season arrives.

Most birdwatchers visit Speyside forests to see the **crested tit (39)**, because although it is widely distributed elsewhere in Europe, in Britain it is our rarest tit and virtually confined to the Scots pine forests south of the Moray Firth, spreading north of Easter Ross to the Highlands. Only about 1,000 pairs breed in Scotland, favouring mature forests with clearings and groundcover of bilberry and heather, and colonising forests growing at altitudes of up to 600 m/1,968 ft. Despite the development of new Scots pine plantations all over Scotland, expansion of the crested tit is a slow process because the bird is

39

40

41

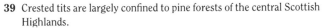

43

44

45

39 Crested tits are largely confined to pine forests of the central Scottish Highlands.

40 Siskins are rarely found far away from conifer or birchwoods. Here the male siskin feeds the young in a nest which is usually difficult to find.

41 With its neck air-sacs fully inflated the male black grouse or blackcock performs its "rookooing" display, uttering a "roo-oo-roo-oo" call.

42 The common crossbill builds its nest in coniferous trees. Only the female incubates the eggs, although both adults feed the young.

43 The diminutive goldcrest is one species that has benefited from coniferous afforestation, although it also breeds in deciduous woods and large gardens.

44 Coniferous woodlands are a popular haunt of the coal tit, but it is also found in deciduous or mixed woods, gardens, parks and orchards.

45 The firecrest prefers to nest in Norway spruce but can be found among a range of conifers and mixed woodland. It is established as one of Britain's rare breeding birds with only around 100 pairs in Southern England.

highly sedentary, rarely moving more than a few kilometres away from its birthplace and remaining in breeding pairs throughout summer and winter. If weather conditions become severe the crested tit suffers high mortality, and when food is very scarce it even takes food from available birdtables.

One relatively new pine forest which has been colonised by the crested tit is Culbin Forest, covering 2,400 ha/5,930 acres on the south shore of Moray Firth. The forest is mostly Scots pine, mixed with Corsican and lodgepole pines, and the shrub layer includes birch and willow in the damper areas. Much of the habitat is afforested sand-dune and saltmarsh and has become recognised as a top site for the crested tit, with up to 200 pairs nesting in good seasons.

The high-pitched, trilling call first announces the presence of the birds. The adults are similarly marked with broad white cheek patches trimmed with black, and the unique, pointed, black and white vertically banded crest makes the bird instantly recognisable as it flits from trunk to trunk and perches on bare branches. The branches of the upper canopy are the bird's favourite forest zone when hunting for insects among the pine needles during spring and summer. In the winter, crested tits may be seen on the forest floor, feeding on seeds and berries, but they are frequently on their own since they prefer not to form flocks with other tits.

Towards the end of April up to eight eggs are laid in a nest hole excavated by the female in a decaying Scots pine, birch or alder stump. The nest hole is often only at head height so it is possible to get good views of the female taking in moss to build the nest and hair to line it. The young are fed by both parents and remain together as a family for many weeks after leaving the nest.

The ancient Caledonian pine forests are the only forests in Britain where the **Scottish crossbill** can be seen. The common crossbill is seen in other pine forests of Britain but not Ireland. It breeds in southern conifer plantations in varying numbers and the brecklands of East Anglia are a particular stronghold; but the endemic Scottish crossbill has been isolated in the ancient Scots pine forests for centuries. It has evolved a slightly heavier bill, designed to cope with obtaining seeds from tough cones of the Scots pine. The common crossbill (**42**) has a less-developed bill, suitable for prising open the more manageable cones of spruce, larch and Corsican pine.

Scottish crossbills, despite their sedentary lifestyle, are not easy to observe, because they remain high in the trees, feeding on cones still fixed to the branches, but their loud 'chup-chup-chup' note mixed with typical finch-like twitterings identifies them to the discerning birdwatcher. They are stocky birds, 17 cm/6½ in long. The males are brick red with brown tail and wings; the females, requiring camouflage at the nest, are duller with a greenish-yellow plumage. Both birds resemble minia-ture parrots with their large heads and beaks; and it is this highly specialised beak, with upper and lower mandibles crossing over, with sharp cutting edges, which gives the bird its name. The bird inserts the beak into a cone and by twisting and prising the cone scales apart snips out the protected seeds with a scissor-like action of the mandibles. The common crossbill breeds in Lowland and eastern Scotland as well as England, so positive identification is sometimes difficult.

Apart from Speyside and Deeside, there are smaller frag-ments of Caledonian forests in Argyll, at Crannach, near Rannoch Moor. The Black Wood of Rannoch is an important pine forest on the south shore of Loch Rannoch and is mixed with birch. It probably represents the margin of the natural limits of Scots pine, because oak occurs on the north shore of the loch and increases in abundance south of it.

In Wester Ross, Loch Maree and Ben Eighe are important areas with the best examples of north-west remnant Caledo-nian pine forest spreading from the shores of the loch up into the mountains to 400 m/1,312 ft above sea level. The entire region has a humid climate, and is renowned for heavy rainfall. Since no roads enter the interior of this part of Scotland, the wild beauty and birds can be seen only by those prepared to walk – often through rough terrain in unreliable weather.

These Caledonian forests are sanctuaries, not only to their own species of pine but to the rich and specialised birdlife found within. Most birdwatchers are also familiar with other conifer forests which have become a ubiquitous feature of the British landscape this century. Between the two world wars, timber shortage was so acute that in 1919 the government founded the Forestry Commission whose sole responsibility was to build up reserves of timber for the future. The Second World War emphasised how deficient Britain was in working timber: the conifer trees planted during 1919 were too small for commercial use and deciduous woods were further plun-dered for timber to prop up bomb-damaged buildings. The government decided to initiate a huge planting scheme to grow 2.02 million ha/5 million acres of forest within a fifty-year period and the Forestry Commission was given wide-ranging powers to achieve this aim.

Conifers were favoured from the outset by the Forestry Commission because they are rapid-growing, reaching timber maturity within 50–60 years compared with 80–150 years for many deciduous trees. The conifers are able to grow on the poorest, most infertile soils, even where rainfall is high, so the Forestry Commission took over unused land in the form of the mountains and uplands of Britain, which they have been planting with conifers ever since. Recently indiscriminate planting has caused the Forestry Commission to be viewed with suspicion and it is largely responsible for the destruction of the Flow Country of Caithness and Sutherland (page 111).

In the early days of planting, the Forestry Commission favoured the native Scots pine which is found in East Anglia, Surrey and Anglesey, but larch, Norway spruce and sitka spruce have all recently become more popular. In Ireland 50 per cent of all afforestation is with sitka spruce, whereas only 3 per cent of all woodland planted in Ireland is deciduous. In Wales there are very few mountains from which conifers cannot be seen, and plantations managed by the Forestry Commission account for 70 per cent of British woodland. The Commission is one of the largest landowners in Britain, controlling 9 per cent of the countryside.

This large area of woodland represents the new forests of Britain and although when mature the plantations seem dark and forbidding, with little sign of birdlife, they are worth exploring in their earlier stages of growth. The fact that the trees are not native does not mean that birds ignore them: nature would never leave unexplored a habitat which has been planted with thousands of trees. The entire plantation in any one area can never be of exactly the same age and the trees are actually planted as a crop, so that some areas mature before others, offering blocks of variable ages which suit a wide range of birds. The felling cycle is designed on a 40–60-year rotation and upon maturity huge areas of the forest are clear-felled, often leaving younger trees on each side of the cleared area. In Breckland, the nightjar has colonised the clear-felled regions of Thetford Forest and a significant percentage of the British population breeds in this locality.

Some birds, like the hen harrier and short-eared owl, owe their survival to conifer plantations up to 10–15 years old; and the **black grouse**, which thrives where woodland borders on to moorland, has benefited during the earlier planting programmes as new plantations spread into the uplands.

Although not found in Ireland, the black grouse inhabits upland Wales and Scotland; the breeding population fluctuates but is in excess of 10,000 pairs. Second only in size to the capercaillie, the black grouse is a large bird, with a body length of 40–55 cm/16–22 in. The male or blackcock is striking, with a dark blue-black glossy plumage and red wattle over the eyes (**41**). The lyre-shaped tail is a distinguishing feature of this species, although absent in the female or grey hen, which is duller and resembles a red grouse, with brown upperparts and greyish belly, covered entirely in black bars and spots.

Black grouse are mainly vegetarian and like the capercaillie spend the winter feeding in the branches of young pine plantations or birch trees. They eat the buds and growing shoots of the young pine trees, together with pine needles and cones or catkins of birch, supplemented with heather leaves. From spring until autumn the black grouse feed on the ground, taking some insects with the main diet of bilberries and new heather shoots, but newly hatched birds feed mainly on protein-rich insects for a few days, before changing to a vegetarian diet.

The black grouse have always used the higher moorland slopes for mating and their feeding habits require coniferous woodlands near by, so when the Forestry Commission first began planting pines in the uplands, it provided the perfect mixture of open moors and woodland. The scrub vegetation growing between the rows of pine trees was ideal nesting ground for the solitary grey hens, which deserted the ground once the canopy became too dense.

There are many other aspects of forestry which provide a short-term benefit to various birds. Newly planted areas are always surrounded by a rabbit-, sheep- and deer-proof fence and the numerous wooden fenceposts provide excellent look-out posts for perching species such as whinchat and reed bunting. Protected from grazing, the grass and scrub vegetation surrounding the miniature conifers grows rapidly and soon provides nesting sites for the meadow pipit and the yellowhammer, which sings as if it is occupying its normal farmland and hedgerow habitat. Next, mammals such as shrews and voles arrive which attract predators like the short-eared owl.

In the first few years the young conifers are of little value to the birds, but eventually they grow higher than the heather and grass and become perching spots for woodland birds like the robin, blackbird, chaffinch and various warblers. In the next phase of growth the conifers thicken out and provide shelter and food amongst their branches, so that from about its eighth to its fifteenth year the conifer plantation provides ideal nesting sites for birds which are not normally associated with moorland or heathland. They leave it immediately conifer conditions become unsuitable.

When the plantations are about ten years old the **redpoll** moves in to nest in small colonies within the bushy young trees; their numbers have increased as afforestation has extended across Britain, with a total of 300,000 pairs breeding. Only in the south and south-west of England, the Hebrides, Shetland and Orkney are they rare or absent altogether.

Redpolls resemble linnets, but have a characteristic red forehead and black chin; and the males are tinged with pink, on a generally brown-streaked body. During flight, a 'chee-chee-chee' call identifies the birds moving among the upper branches of the conifers. However birchwoods are equally popular, together with alderwood, and hawthorn chalk scrubland.

Siskins (40) frequently fly in the company of redpolls during the winter, sharing the seeds of the silver birch which are found in the female catkins, at the end of wispy branches. Hanging upside down and exercising all the agility of a member of the tit family, the siskins extract the seeds throughout the autumn and winter.

In summer their staple diet is conifer seeds, especially spruce, and characteristically the siskin is associated with young plantations in Scotland, Wales and Ireland, with isolated colonies in Devon and Hampshire. Siskins have adapted better than many birds to sitka spruce plantations and as this species became more popular with forestry developers, the siskin has extended its range into southern England. The ancient Scots pine forests of the Highlands, up to 457 m/1,500 ft, are also recognised as good haunts for this small finch.

In any conifer wood they are difficult to see because, except in winter, they tend to be secretive and rarely stay still, spending much of their time in the upper canopy. At all times of the year the plumage helps the siskins blend into their habitat. In winter the male is yellow-green, with streaked markings, black cap and yellow eye-stripe. In the breeding season his plumage darkens to golden yellow and the cheeks turn bright yellow. Lacking the black cap, the female is always duller and the yellow markings tend to be more grey in tone so that throughout the year, and certainly during breeding, she is well camouflaged. During March the display flight of the male is worth watching. Making a constant, jingling, twittering song, the male launches himself from the top of a conifer and with rapidly beating wings and fanned tail, he floats down to a neighbouring tree to repeat the performance. Since the nests are small, they are almost impossible to find and usually well concealed within pine needles, towards the end of the highest branches.

Away from pine- and birchwoods most birdwatchers observe siskins during the winter feeding on peanuts in their gardens. This behaviour occurs for only a couple of months in late winter, and is a method of increasing body weight very rapidly before the breeding season begins in April.

As the trees of the conifer plantations grow taller and ever more dense, **goldcrests** colonise. This bird has really benefited from afforestation and there are over 1.5 million pairs throughout the British Isles, except the East Anglian fens and Scottish Highlands. After severe winters the population crashes, because, weighing only 5 gm/⅕ oz our smallest bird is unable to conserve sufficient body heat to survive the cold winter nights.

The goldcrest is so small that even though it is common in plantations, it is very difficult to see. Feeding high in the trees, goldcrests are constantly active, creeping along outer branches, gleaning the needles for insects and spiders, constantly flicking their wings and uttering their high-pitched 'zee-zee-zee' call, which is reasonably loud for such a small bird and probably the only way of locating a flock within a plantation. Watching goldcrests high in the tree tops, without the aid of binoculars, you might confuse them for tits, but the short tail is a diagnostic feature.

During March, both birds begin nest-building and construct

a beautiful moss basket, held together by spiders' webs, painstakingly collected from the pine needles, and lined with feathers. The whole structure is fixed hammock-style between two small branches or slung beneath a densely foliated branch, affixed to the pine needles (**43**).

The bird most likely to be confused with the goldcrest is its relative, the rarer **firecrest**. Only twenty-five years ago the firecrest was a continental bird, seen in Britain purely as a spring-passage migrant around south and east coasts. This passage migration still occurs, but in 1962 sharp-eyed ornithologists observed young fledglings in the New Forest, Hampshire, and a small colony has established itself there ever since. Other southern and eastern counties of England, such as Kent, Suffolk and Norfolk, have also been colonised and the firecrest is established as a rare breeding bird. The firecrest prefers deciduous woods with glades on the Continent, but in England it shares the coniferous plantations with the goldcrest, often engaging in territorial battles; Norway spruce is one of the most popular trees. They, too, are difficult to see as they move about, high in the evergreen branches. The firecrest's camouflaged plumage rivals that of the goldcrest, but firecrests are brighter with green and golden upperparts, bronze shoulders and a distinctive orange-yellow crest which is darker in the male bird (**45**). Between May and June listen for an accelerating 'zit-zit, zit-zit' call uttered repetitively through the tree tops.

When the conifer plantations reach fifteen years old, the canopy becomes very dense and many of the lower branches, starved of light, die quickly. In most cases birds simply desert the conifer plantations; goldcrests, however, remain.

Another conifer specialist, the **coal tit**, also continues to breed in the plantations, frequently using mouseholes between the roots as a nest site. Coal tits are slightly smaller than blue tits but are larger than goldcrests, although they can be confused with this species because of their high-pitched 'tsee-tsee-tsee' call made as they flit through the tree tops. The upperparts of the body are olive grey with buff underparts but the most obvious feature is the black head and throat with white cheek patches and triangle behind the head (**44**). The bird is widely distributed throughout the British Isles, apart from the northern islands and fenland East Anglia, although it is very scarce in parts of western Ireland. In other regions of Ireland a distinct race has evolved called *Parus ater hibernicus*; in this form the normal white neck patch and cheeks have a yellow tinge.

Afforestation throughout Britain has aided the distribution of the coal tit and its long narrow bill is perfect for probing into pine needles and small cones for insect eggs, larvae and adults. But it also feeds on fruits, seeds and nuts which it takes from birdtables in winter and pushes into crevices in tree bark, as an emergency cache during prolonged snowy weather.

Although only a few small birds remain in the plantations once they are established, these birds attract a number of predators; species such as the sparrowhawk and long-eared owl occupy the canopy where they utilise old crow and woodpigeons' nests, built when the plantation was younger and suitable for these species.

The **long-eared owl** (**46**) is, of all the five British species of owl, perhaps the most nocturnal, competing with the larger tawny owl for the title of 'true hunter of the night'. Over 3,000 pairs

46 The long-eared owl is truly nocturnal and favours coniferous forests, where it nests in deserted squirrel's dreys or old crow's nests.

47 Female sparrowhawk with young. This woodland bird of prey frequently nests in copses or along the margins of conifer plantations.

48 Goshawk in heraldic pose. It is one of the supreme predators of woodland, swift in flight, and with huge claws used to kill woodpigeons, crows, rabbits and hares.

breed in the British Isles in coniferous woods everywhere except the West Country, the Midlands, west Wales and north-east Scotland. There are large populations in Ireland, where it is by far the most common species of owl.

Birdwatching at night, or even at twilight, in a coniferous wood requires some bravado before you can settle down to enjoy the experience. The first thing you will notice is the incredible silence because inside the coniferous wood there are none of the familiar sounds of a deciduous wood, such as leaves rustling in the wind, or two boughs rubbing together and groaning in the breeze.

Throughout the year long-eared owls are normally silent, but from February to May each pair occupy a territory and call with a variety of hoots, growls and wails, made sometimes in alarm and aggression. The male announces his territory with soft but penetrating triple 'hoo-hoo-hoo' hoots, which are more extended than those of the tawny owl, each note being separated by two or three seconds, and they are like the sound made by blowing across the neck of a bottle. In June you can hear the cry of the young owls, which carries a considerable distance on a still night. The sound resembles a gate swinging on rusty hinges: a high whining metallic wheeze as the owlets demand food from their hunting parents long into the night. The contact call from the owlets can nearly always be tracked down to an old crows' nest or squirrels' drey converted by the adults into a nest.

Like the short-eared owl of upland moor, the male long-eared owl performs a display flight in which he zig-zags between the trunks of the conifers, or over the canopy, loudly clapping his wings together when near the nest site. The wingspan of 76 cm/2½ ft is impressive, particularly when you see its shadow moving at speed between the trees as the bird looks for prey. Whereas the tawny owl prefers to sit on a perch and drop on to passing prey, the long-eared owl is a mobile hunter and has catholic tastes. If it hunts within the plantation it is usually preying on birds such as goldcrest, coal tit, chaffinch or jay, which it plucks from a roosting perch without warning. Its favourite food is the short-tailed vole which lives in the grass of the plantation rides or adjacent scrubland: when hunting for voles, it systematically quarters the clearing a metre above the ground, pouncing with outstretched talons on to the prey. In Ireland, woodmice, housemice, rats and shrews are predated, the woodmouse being the most regular prey, but in Britain short-tailed voles are the priority, supplemented with bank voles, harvest mice, common shrew and some large beetles.

During the daytime, when it is easier to investigate the conifer wood, it is possible to find long-eared owls at roost, but despite their size, they are very difficult to see and usually it is the clamour of other birds which gives the owl away: when they discover it roosting, agitated chaffinches, wrens, tits and blackbirds mob the owl, shrieking their alarm calls and flying all around the sleeping bird until it wakes and is forced to float silently away to a more secluded part of the plantation. It is possible to walk right underneath a roosting owl without noticing it because the mottled grey, buff and dark brown upper plumage blends perfectly with the trunk of the conifer in which it prefers to roost, resembling just another piece of bark.

In the depths of winter many people prefer to confine their birdwatching to the back garden, where the birdtable and peanut feeders provide a welcome source of food for wild birds. The sparrows, chaffinches, blackbirds, blue tits and great tits can all be happily feeding when suddenly a large brown bird swoops across the birdtable, hits a chaffinch busily feeding and, without stopping, carries it straight over the garden hedge and out into the countryside beyond. This fleeting glimpse is a rare view of the female **sparrowhawk (47)**, which, having fought back from the poisoning effects of DDT and organochlorine pesticides in the 1960s, is now one of the commonest birds of prey in the British Isles.

The distribution of sparrowhawks is controlled by the availability of woodland suitable for roosting and nesting. They prefer large woods (over 80 ha/197 acres), but if they cannot find any they nest in small woods, copses and thick scrub patches. They nearly always favour conifers as nest trees, so coniferous plantations have become one of the best habitats to watch the hawk. As afforestation developed into the uplands the bird increased its range into new, previously uncolonised regions.

Female sparrowhawks, at 35 cm/14 in, are larger than the males which measure 30 cm/12 in from beak to tail. Both sexes have long yellow legs and streamlined bodies which are useful for weaving and twisting between tree trunks when hunting. The nest is made of twigs and, like the long-eared owl, frequently built on an already existing base formed by an old crows' nest. The male begins forming the structure and the female joins in at the lining stage, using fine twigs and bark. The entire nest is usually constructed close to the main trunk of the tree, so that it is difficult to see from the ground.

Sparrowhawks time their breeding to coincide with the availability of young songbirds. Although forest cover is essential, the sparrowhawk prefers to hunt almost exclusively for songbirds in open country with swift low-level flights at a speed of 30–40 k.p.h./20–25 m.p.h. along country lanes and hedgerows. The hedge-hopping and open-country hunting flights are the only occasions when sparrowhawks show themselves for any length of time. Seeing the bird then, many people confuse it with the kestrel. In fact, the sparrowhawk's flight is quite different from the kestrel's: although the birds are similar in size the sparrowhawk never hovers. Taking advantage of woodland and hedgerow cover, the sparrowhawk seizes its prey whilst it is still perched or just after it tries to fly away. Often it is killed by the pure impact. Usually it takes sparrow, chaffinch, starling and song thrush, but it also attacks larger birds like fieldfare and woodpigeon; in the case of larger birds the impact is not always sufficient to kill them outright. The sparrowhawk attacks the prey and fights to bring it to the ground, pinning it down with its long powerful legs, before beginning to tear at it with its sharp hooked beak. The long legs keep the body of the sparrowhawk away from the flailing wings and stabbing beak of the prey as it tries to overcome it. Once killed the prey is plucked, leaving circles of feathers often seen on the ground in the countryside. Smaller birds are taken to a favourite plucking post, usually a tree stump or branch, where the feathers disperse on the breeze more readily, leaving little sign that the sparrowhawk has fed.

The sparrowhawk is a resident bird, but after nesting, young birds move to their own future breeding territories, usually about 20–50 km/12–30 miles away from their birthplace. This guarantees that populations are evenly distributed and that young birds do not interbreed. Since sparrowhawks do not live very long, those that do survive beyond their first year must continue a healthy strain in as wide an area as possible. Nearly 70 per cent of male sparrowhawks die within twelve months of birth, the highest rate of death occurring just after they become independent, although some are killed by females because they are the right size for prey.

The sparrowhawk is a fascinating bird of prey, secretive for most of its life. In spring, however, courtship and territorial displays begin. Males establish their territory and encourage the females to enter, whereupon several may compete for his attention. Once a female is accepted and shows interest in the nest site, all other females are chased away and a wood which is occupied as a nesting territory is advertised by an exciting flight display, high above the canopy. The sparrowhawk soars into the air, then, tucking in its wings, drops like a stone towards the tree tops, but at the bottom of the dive opens its wings and soars skywards again to repeat the display in a series of U-shaped peaks and troughs. These displays are very obvious not only to birdwatchers, but to other territory-seeking sparrowhawks.

Apart from man, the sparrowhawk has few natural enemies but the rare larger **goshawk (48)** is perhaps the main predator: although the goshawk preys on small mammals such as squirrels, it attacks adult sparrowhawks and the juveniles which have recently left the nest.

The goshawk and sparrowhawk are difficult to distinguish, but the female goshawk at 50 cm/20 in is about the size of a buzzard and almost twice the size of a male sparrowhawk, whereas the largest female sparrowhawk is similar in size to the male goshawk. Both species prefer woodland habitats with little disturbance but the goshawk is highly susceptible to disturbance by man and requires a large territory, frequently exceeding 3,237 ha/8,000 acres, 25 per cent of which must be undisturbed forest.

Before 1900, when persecution by gamekeepers exterminated the last breeding goshawks from this country, the bird bred regularly in small or large deciduous and coniferous woods and hunted over open country. In 1968 the goshawk was rediscovered as a breeding bird and these individuals were probably the result of escaped falconers' birds initiating new wild stock. Today the goshawk is a very rare regular breeding bird, with around sixty pairs nesting in seven areas of Britain and confined to forested areas. Coniferous trees and mature plantations of spruce, pine and larch are its main haunts although some pairs nest in mixed woodlands where oak and beech predominate.

Goshawks claim their breeding territories very early in the year, and during April lay three to four eggs. Most of the successful breeding sites and individual nests are re-used each season and it is fortunate that some of these are in conifer plantations owned by the Forestry Commission which makes every effort to protect the goshawk, especially as they help to control populations of woodpigeon which damage newly planted trees. In East Anglia most of Thetford Forest belongs to the Forestry Commission and within this vast area of woodland the goshawk can be seen. The Thetford Forest bird trail, near Santon Downham, covers a 5.6-km/3½-mile organised route, including heathland, coniferous and mixed woodland and open country. At Mayday, right in the middle of the forest, a large clear fell area is one of the best sites to see goshawk hunting or displaying from March to April. In Scotland, the ancient Caledonian forests of Deeside and Speyside contain breeding goshawks and those of Glen Tanar, Glen Muick and Glen Tromie are some of the best forests to catch a glimpse of one of our shyest birds of prey.

The future of the remaining tracts of Britain's ancient Caledonian forests seems relatively secure. More than ever before their conservation value as wildlife sanctuaries and their intrinsic appeal as part of the landscape of Scotland has been recognised: 80 per cent of the Highlands where these forests remain are considered nationally important for nature conservation and National Nature Reserves incorporate 30 per cent of the Highlands, including significant forests such as Rothiemurchus Forest, Beinn Eighe, Glen Tanar and Glen Strathfarrar. Contrasting with the ancient Scots pine forests, the coniferous plantations represent the 'new forests', because for over 60 years the Forestry Commission has afforested much of Britain, changing the habitat of the more remote, generally upland region of the country into ranks of trees.

Public opinion towards the Forestry Commission still remains divided between those whose enjoyment of the countryside does not extend beyond the recreational or picnicking facilities of one of the 600 excellent sites and those who support conservation of the countryside and whose enjoyment comes from observing animals and flowers in their natural environment.

Conservationists are not totally against the planting of conifers, because it has to be agreed that certain areas of moorland are of limited value to wildlife and the planting of a young conifer crop at least offers a period of habitat change which will encourage birds and mammals such as pine marten and red squirrel to colonise. But where the Forestry Commission still goes wrong and causes anguish for naturalists and conservation societies is whenever they ignore requests and destroy unique or special habitats, despite an Amendment in 1985 to the 1981 Wildlife and Countryside Act which charged the Commission with a duty to 'seek a reasonable balance between timber production and wildlife conservation', in addition to the Countryside Acts of 1967 and 1968 which already obliged them to 'have regard to the desirability of conserving the natural beauty and amenity of the countryside'. Each Forestry Commission District produces its own conservation schemes which are supposed to identify sites where particular control is required to preserve the natural wildlife but if this is so, it is difficult to see how the destruction and afforestation of the Flow Country (page 111) is justified. Equally, in the last six years, the Forestry Commission has sold off many of the state-owned woods and, pressurised by the government, has even sold ancient woodland of SSSI status in order to raise the £82 million requested by 1986. Conservation bodies tried to buy many of the ancient deciduous woodlands as they came on the market, but their funds were limited and many fell into the hands of private companies and individuals for commercial development. Whereas the Forestry Commission opened many state-owned woods to the public, private owners do not have to grant public access. Thus once again the policy of the Forestry Commission has conflicted with nature conservation and amenity requirements.

To a certain extent the Forestry Commission is powerless to stop this destruction, because it is obliged to carry out the government's forestry policy, which currently appears to support upland destruction, together with its wildlife. The government also seems to support afforestation by the private sector rather than allowing the Forestry Commission to get involved in environmentally sensitive areas, and since 1982 when the Forestry Commission was forced to sell many of the woodlands it managed to the private sector, it appears that the government has engineered a rather one-sided policy which ignores wildlife and countryside conservation at the expense of tree planting and profit.

There are many birdwatchers and conservationists who want forestry policies changed but this is not to say that afforestation should cease. Afforestation must be taken away from the upland and ecologically important areas and performed elsewhere. The RSPB is right to point out that today farmers produce so much from the land that almost all cereals, dairy produce and beef are in surplus each year, and have to be sold off cheaply, destroyed or stored, all at the expense of the taxpayers, who partly financed their production anyway. To purchase, store and dispose of surplus cereals costs around £250 for each hectare grown in Britain annually, and the National Farmers' Union accepts that 150,000 ha/370,650 acres will need to be removed from production each year for the next decade if surpluses are to be controlled. This farmland is rich land which could be turned over to deciduous and coniferous timber crops, which would benefit the farmer, add variety and beauty to areas of Britain turned into prairies and be of value to wildlife, especially birds which favour lowland woods, leaving the unique uplands to the wildlife. The government must be persuaded that farm surpluses and forestry can be tackled together, so that farmers, conifers and wildlife can all survive. This may be a radical reform of rural land, but what Britain's countryside desperately needs is a government with real long-term vision and imagination so that an environmentally detrimental forestry policy can be changed to save important habitats and species of bird and other wildlife well beyond the twenty-first century.

CHAPTER 4

LOWLAND HEATH AND BRECKLANDS

LOWLAND HEATH

The birds found in each of the major habitats of the British Isles form an integral part of the overall ecosystem; each habitat is equally important and were one habitat to be endangered the whole of that ecosystem would be threatened. The most endangered of all habitats are the southern heathlands, which stretch from Dorset to Surrey, and are mostly found on areas of infertile Tertiary (up to 70 million years old) sand. At the present rate of destruction, unless something radical is achieved by the general public and conservationists, in particular by lobbying Parliament, by the year 1992 there will be little or no viable heathland left in counties such as Dorset.

So, what are heaths, where are they found and why are they so vulnerable that their entire future is in the balance? Even the most casual observer of Britain's habitats will notice that heathland is an area dominated by purple heather. The trouble is that although this observation is accurate, heather also dominates moors: although the two habitats are similar, they are not one and the same thing. Generally, moorland is found on ancient rocks with acidic peaty soils and is common in the north and west of Britain, where the rainfall is high. Heaths occupy light, sandy soils, in areas of low rainfall, mainly in lowland Britain. That they are to be found in the lowland of Britain is their most significant characteristic, and this chapter will concentrate on lowland heaths colonised by heather and gorse at altitudes below 250 m/800 ft.

In Britain the differences between moors and heaths seem to be marked by a clear distinction between north and south, upland and lowland, wet and dry, peat or sandy soils; yet it is not quite as simple as that, as some lowland heaths have extremely boggy areas lined with peat, called mires, constituting a wet heath, and some dry heaths can be found, in the uplands. So it is important not to make hard and fast distinctions between moors and heaths.

Heathlands were once thought to be natural habitats where

51 Thursley Heath, Surrey. Typical heathland plants include birch, scrub and bracken, bell heather in the foreground, and ling.

49

50

49 The long tail, reddish-brown underparts and red-rimmed eye make the rare heathland Dartford warbler unmistakable.

50 Male stonechat perched on a gorse bush. He may be paired to more than one female, each of which lays five or six eggs.

the purple heather and birch scrub was the climax vegetation of certain areas of the country. In fact, heaths are not natural at all, but have been created by the activities of civilisations over thousands of years; and it is ironic that our most endangered habitat, requiring more conservation than any other, was created by man removing and destroying the trees that once grew on the poor soils of the heath.

Typically, heathland occurs where the underlying rocks eventually formed into acidic, low-quality, frequently sandy soil, and any water drained away rapidly. Any minerals in the surface layers were leached out and deposited further down, which is one of the reasons why heaths have an ashy-coloured surface soil. Geologists call this type of soil a podsol, where vegetation has decayed on the surface in an acidic layer. Below this is the mineral-leached layer of sand and further down a layer called the hard-pan, where the minerals are deposited in a thick band, so hard that tree roots cannot penetrate it.

During the Atlantic era the climate in Britain became milder, more humid and generally wetter, which affected the rate of soil leaching and podsol formation. The pre-heath woodlands were already growing on shallow soils with poor mineral content and the chances of their survival were in delicate balance. It is likely that any clearance of trees would trigger off changes which would increase podsolisation and soil acidity and prevent future colonisation of trees.

The lowland heaths we walk on today were undoubtedly covered by the ancient wildwood of hazel, ash and oak, which Neolithic man began to clear about 5,000 years ago (page 15), although on a limited scale. We have already seen how Bronze Age man increased forest clearance and was largely responsible for the decline of tree species, such as lime, and we now know that some of our heathlands were established in the latter part of the Bronze Age.

Cleared of trees, the leached-out, poor soils did not support any growth of crops and were turned over to rough grazing, a practice which continued for years: the shared common grazing lands of medieval times frequently included heaths.

Today in the New Forest, which remains the largest area of lowland heath in Britain (12,500 ha/30,887 acres), ancient grazing rights are still maintained and horses, pigs, sheep and cattle are all seen at different times of the year; and certainly cattle and sheep are still seen on the heaths of Dorset and Cornwall. Any grazing helps to maintain the heathland habitat as the cattle quickly browse off any regenerating woodland vegetation.

Our best-known heaths are in southern England, concentrated in the London Basin, Surrey, Hampshire, Dorset and Devon. There are also heaths on the south-west coast at the Lizard and Land's End, and even in the extreme north of Scotland, at Cape Wrath. Apart from the New Forest, few large heaths are left and farming developments, urban sprawl, forestry and military exercises have fragmented the rest, even putting at risk some of the sixty nationally important heathland sites, which collectively cover only 20,000 ha/49,200 acres. One of the main reasons for the fragmentation of the heaths is that heathland occupies areas which are largely unused – at least in a commercial sense – and with the increasing shortage of space in towns and cities for development, and the need for farmers to produce more from their land, the heaths have become victims of exploitation. It is now up to the public to save what is left.

Naturalists, especially botanists and birdwatchers, find heaths very special places. The flora and fauna of the heaths largely depend on the climate and type of soil, as heaths are found on a variety of mineral bases, from the driest in eastern England to the wetter heaths in the west. Transformed by dazzling yellow gorse early in spring, heaths offer a great variety of rarities found nowhere else in Britain, including insects, reptiles and amphibians.

Along the north coast of Cornwall there is what is called maritime heath, over a base rock of carboniferous culm measures. The action of salt spray and wind make the habitat different from inland heaths. Sea pink or thrift grows alongside common heather and bell heather. A good example of maritime heath is stretches of the cliff top at Chapel Porth. Whilst birdwatching here for the usual cliff-face species, you will also see heathland birds.

The most impressive heathland in Cornwall is found on the Lizard. During Anglo-Saxon times the Lizard was already open heath, but by the thirteenth and fourteenth centuries agricultural use of the habitat had declined. The present-day appearance of the Lizard heath was probably formed by agricultural changes between the sixteenth and eighteenth centuries. Today dry and wet heaths occur separately on the downs. On the dry heath granite areas, bristle bent grass dominates, with common heather, bell heather and cross-leaved heath growing in large patches, forming what is called a 'short heath'. Where the wetter, poorly drained alkaline soils cover serpentine rock, there is another type of heath with higher plant growth, called 'tall heath'.

Most of the Devon lowland heaths lie between the estuaries of the River Exe and the River Otter. About 1,000 ha/2,460 acres of varied heathland, including Aylesbeare Common, occur on soils formed from sandstone with mixed pebble deposits where drifts of common heather and western gorse fill shallow valleys. On the dry heath, night jar breed, stonechat and linnet sing from the tops of the gorse bushes and curlew nest on the valley bogs. Aylesbeare Common (an RSPB reserve) has a healthy woodland margin and birdwatchers should keep an eye open for buzzard, raven, hobby – which in high summer hawk for dragonflies – and tree pipit, to be seen flying out from hawthorn scrub.

Whereas Cornish and Devon heaths all lie on poor acidic soils, derived from ancient Palaeozoic rocks (600–270 million years old) such as granite and old red sandstone, the Dorset heaths are derived from Tertiary rocks (70–25 million years old). These heaths are on sandy and acidic soils surrounding Poole Harbour, which also has deposits of London clay. The clay restricts drainage, so that there are mires across the tracts of heathland. Heaths that are both wet and dry include Studland Heath, Arne Moor and Hartland Moor. In the days when Thomas Hardy eulogised Egdon Heath, the heaths of Dorset stretched from Poole to Dorchester, but today mere fragments are left. Since 1750, 86 per cent of the Dorset heaths have been lost to the plough, afforestation, and urban development. Most of that was destroyed in the last thirty years: in 1950 Britain still had 64,000 ha/158,000 acres of heathland; today 40 per cent of that total has gone. In Dorset less than 5,000 ha/12,355 acres remain, one sixth of what Hardy knew.

Arne is another Dorset heath now protected by the RSPB, covering 525 ha/1,297 acres of wet and dry heathland. The area is coloured purple and yellow by heather (sometimes called ling), bell heather and dwarf gorse, which spreads across the peaty soil. Where the gorse is dense, one of Britain's rarest birds creeps amongst the spiked stems, looking for insects. The **Dartford warbler** is more common in the Mediterranean, but reaches the northern limit of its breeding range on the southern heathlands. Unlike other warblers, this species is a resident, remaining in its habitat throughout the winter and breeding during April to June.

Mild winters enable the Dartford warbler to survive, but in 1963, after two hard winters, most of the British population had died, and only eleven pairs survived. The bird is exclusively an insect-eater and hard winters kill off its natural food supply, causing certain death. By 1970 the numbers had increased to 70 pairs and there were 560 pairs by 1974, which shows the level of recovery possible if the winters remain mild. Sadly the winter of 1978–9 was harsh and the numbers of Dartford warbler plummeted so low that on neighbouring Aylesbeare Common no birds survived; following another hard winter in 1981–2 the population of this bird today is around 450 pairs.

The warbler is confined to the remaining, larger southern heathlands, where gorse, heather and cross-leaved heath provide dense cover and many small insects for food. It is a shy bird, skulking through the impenetrable vegetation and easily avoiding detection. On bright clear days in summer you may be lucky enough to see one, because sometimes the bird perches momentarily on spikes of gorse, before disappearing into another thicket with low, darting flight. The bird cannot be confused with any other because its long tail is cocked upright and the small roundish body is dark with a characteristic high forehead and pointed beak; its large red eye-ring is immediately obvious (49). The male in breeding plumage is particularly attractive, with pink-chestnut underparts, grey-brown upperparts, slate-grey head and white spots on the chin. During April the cock bird reveals itself whilst holding territory by singing from the top of a gorse bush. Ensconced on your favourite heath in spring you might be fortunate enough to see the male begin its courtship display. Rising above the heather and gorse canopy, the bird dances up and down whilst in flight, fluttering to earth on quivering wings. In behaviour and song the Dartford warbler resembles the common whitethroat, but it is more controlled in flight and the song is more mellow, with a mixture of liquid and chattering notes, uttered from deep inside the gorse.

Away from the Dorset heaths, the other main strongholds for the Dartford warbler are the heaths of the New Forest. Most of the dry heath is dominated by ling, bell heather, dwarf and common gorse, growing on the gravel and sand; but, as any visitor knows, there are large areas of wet heath in the New Forest and valley mires bordering these heaths where the peat substrate is permanently waterlogged and prevents drainage. Centuries ago the New Forest was famous for breeding populations of red-backed shrike, honey buzzard, kite, Montagu's harrier and hobby, but during the nineteenth century many of these species were hunted either to extinction or near-extinction levels; today only twenty pairs of honey buzzard breed in Britain, some of them still within the New Forest. During the last decade the New Forest has completely lost its breeding population of red-backed shrike: the last known birds nested in 1978. In 1982 no shrikes were found on the heath and the remaining few pairs are now confined to the heathlands of East Anglia, where they are wardened closely during the breeding season.

Common birds nesting on the New Forest heath include skylark, meadow pipit, whitethroat, yellowhammer, linnet, cuckoo, whinchat and stonechat. The **stonechat** is an indicator of the heathland habitat, a specialist like the Dartford warbler, with a preference for heather and gorse. Unlike the Dartford warbler, the stonechat is conspicuous, since it has a penchant for perching on the tops of gorse bushes, uttering its alarm call, which resembles two smooth pebbles being knocked together, giving a loud 'chack-chack' sound.

Like the Dartford warbler, the stonechat hunts spiders and insects but it perches on a gorse branch about 1 m/3¼ft from the sandy soil, surveying the ground beneath. As prey scurries by, the stonechat launches from its vantage point, snaps up the prey and returns to the branch to eat it. During a period of prolonged sunshine, the warm air currents carry small insects across the heath on the wafting breeze, so the stonechat moves to the tops of bushes and birch scrub, 5 m/16½ ft above the ground, and takes the inspect prey from the air as it floats by. Both birds are specialist, but stonechats are more flexible than Dartford warblers, and, as winter approaches and insect food becomes scarce or covered in snow, many of the birds fly from the heath to milder coastal wintering grounds, but must return to the heath to breed each spring.

Male stonechats are striking birds (50) with black head and back, broken by white markings on the wings and neck. You can see the distinctive white rump when the bird flies away, and its underside is chestnut on the breast fading to buff elsewhere. The female is duller, but ideally marked for camouflage on the nest with streaked brown upperparts, pale buff underparts and subdued white body markings.

The stonechat builds its nest very close to the ground, often in the shelter of a gorse thicket, but where it is still vulnerable to ground predators such as rat, weasel and stoat. Whilst the hen is brooding, the male sits on a high vantage point such as a neighbouring gorse bush. Although this is good for seeing danger approach, it also reveals to bird predators that a nest is close by. Intelligent birds such as magpie and carrion crow have learnt to watch the adults carrying food to the nest. The stonechat always perches with its beak full of insects and caterpillars before flying down to the nest, at which moment the crow launches its attack and follows the stonechat, stealing the fledglings.

Stonechats are really the sentinels of the heath. Even when danger is 100 m/328 ft or more away, they start the alarm call: every heathland birdwatcher has been the victim of this verbal assault. Sometimes it can be frustrating when, as you attempt to sneak closer to another bird for a better view, the vigilant stonechat sounds off, alerting yellowhammer, willow warbler, reed bunting and even Dartford warbler about your distant approach.

The heathlands to the north and east of the New Forest are on different types of soil, sandwiched between the North and South Downs and the Kentish Weald, which is enclosed by a belt of lower greensand. The Hampshire heaths at Bramshott, Ludshott and Woolmer Forest are on such deposits, with extensions into Surrey at Leith Hill; but the most significant Surrey heathlands are at Thursley and Hankley.

Thursley Heath (51), an NCC reserve, is one of the largest in Surrey, covering 250 ha/617 acres. It was covered in deciduous forest before early civilisations felled it for arable land. There is wet and dry heath with characteristic flora, but because the heathland is interspersed with birch woodland and strands of conifer, the birdlife is extremely rich: 65 species nest on the reserve but over 140 species have been recorded on the heath, including numerous rarities.

Thursley is recognised as a significant British site for birds of prey, which fascinate most birdwatchers. It is one of the best places to see the **hobby**, a summer visitor from the African savannas, requiring open country to hunt across and marginal

52 For aerial speed and agility the hobby has few rivals. It usually occupies an old crow's nest high in the treetops where it lays three eggs in June.

53 The nocturnal nightjar rests on the ground by day, perfectly camouflaged against its heathland background, and colour-matched to a lichen-encrusted boulder.

trees to nest in. The hobby's ideal nest site is in an isolated group of trees surrounded by a large open space such as heath. Hobbies return each May to the same area, males arriving a few days ahead of the females. Both birds have similar markings: dark grey crown, upper wings and back contrasting with a cream throat and chin. A diagnostic facial marking is the black stripe running below the eyes and forming an obvious moustache each side of the beak (52). A buff breast heavily streaked with black is highlighted by the lower belly, tail coverts and thighs, all of which are bright rust red.

High above the heath the first sight of the hobby is given away by a 'kew-kew-kew' call, as the agile bird twists and turns after dragonflies, swifts and swallows, which it catches with amazing skill. Display flights are even more breathtaking, especially when the male swoops down from aloft, streaks round a group of trees and then soars so high that it disappears from view. When the hen bird is around, the male really shows off, chasing and swooping around her and demonstrating manoeuvrability unequalled by any other falcon. Sometimes the male passes food to the hen bird mid-flight in death-defying style. The birds fly alongside each other, destined for collision at speed, but either they roll sideways so that the hen is able to grab the 'food gift' from the male's talons, or else he drops it at the last moment, allowing the female to tumble earthwards to catch it.

The hobby chooses a nest site carefully. It is most commonly an old crows' nest, which the adult hobbies flatten into a platform, but do not add to. Only three reddish-brown, spotted eggs are laid and the young leave the nest after about five weeks, when they are immediately able to catch insects on the wing, but have to be taught the skills of catching birds. Aerial agility is a matter of survival for the hobby and any amount of play helps the young birds to practise their skills until towards late summer, when they can outpace and capture skylark, meadow pipit, house martin and swift.

Undoubtedly the hobby is the most agile and elegant bird of prey seen in Britain but since only about 500 pairs breed here you will be lucky to see one. In the late afternoon and early evening the adults patrol for dragonflies, and in the summer there is a glut of the insects which provide an important part of their diet; but this is short-lived, reaching a peak between July and August, which is probably one of the reasons why the hobby migrates south soon after the insect food is exhausted.

There is something special about a day spent on a lowland heath; but there is something truly magical about dusk on the same heath during June and July, when rich golden yellow hues of broom and gorse contrast with purple drifts of heather. The air is filled with the drone of insect life, and suddenly another sound begins, completely evoking the spirit of the ancient heath: the sound of the nocturnal **nightjar**.

Like the hobby, the night jar arrives from Africa in mid-May and either claims a territory in new forestry plantations or, more regularly, shares the bracken-clad heath with the hobby and the stonechat. Usually the adult nightjars return to within a few metres of their previous year's nesting site; and one of the reasons for their drastic decline especially since 1975 is the destruction of the heathland.

Your collection of birdwatching highspots will not be complete without the memory of the sound of the nightjar. Get yourself into a suitable position as the sun begins to set: the recommended spot is an area of heath with some bracken cover interspersed with silver-birch scrub, and the occasional dead tree trunk, where the birds perch and utter their characteristic

song. The soft, vibrant, hypnotic 'churr' of the nightjar is as typical of a warm June evening on the heath as the nightingale song is characteristic of southern oakwoods. The bird makes the churring call while it lies or crouches along a branch or boulder (53) and the sound lifts as the bird turns its head or the breeze changes direction. It reaches a peak, lasting minutes, before an abrupt silence overcomes the heath.

During the day the hen night jar incubates the eggs and the soft grey-brown plumage makes her invisible to all but the keenest-eyed birdwatcher. The nest is an unlined hollow, often adjacent to pieces of dead wood. In late May or early June she lays two white-brown flecked eggs.

As dusk arrives the nightjars begin to feed, whilst on the wing, flitting like giant moths above the bracken and catching insects in their gaping beaks. The beak of the nightjar is unique and **53** clearly shows the row of bristles along the upper mandible, which point outwards and help to snare prey whilst flying.

Recent surveys reveal that a maximum of 2,000 pairs of nightjar now nest in Britain each summer. The main stronghold is the breckland of East Anglia, but the Surrey heaths are regular breeding sites and Thursley Heath is amongst the best.

To the north of the greensand heath of Thursley different soil and heaths occur on what is called the London Basin, bounded by the chalk ridges of the Chilterns in the north and North Downs to the south. It is composed of Tertiary minerals, much of which is overlaid by London clay: most of the heathland around Bagshot, Windsor, Aldershot and Farnborough are typical podsols.

The London Basin heaths are typically dry and botanically interesting with common heather, bell heather, dwarf and common gorse abundant. However, because of their proximity to London and major Thames Valley towns, most of the heaths have been developed and built upon in the last twenty-five years or used as training areas for the armed forces, making the habitat highly fragmentary. Most of the common heathland birds, like linnet, whitethroat and stonechat, can be seen on Frensham, Horsell and Chobham Commons, but the heaths are too small to encourage colonisation by species such as the Dartford warbler. Because of the high density of human population, they also suffer from recreational use which disturbs the shyer nesting birds.

The largest, most famous heathland in south-east England is Ashdown Forest. Covering 2,560 ha/5,325 acres of the Weald, it was once the royal hunting forest of Wealdon. The area offers a magnificent mosaic of wet, damp and dry heathland, with mires and river valleys, bordered with scrub and woodland, and lies on top of a mixture of Cretaceous sands and clays, and typical podsol.

As we have seen, woodlands were continuously felled from the Middle Ages onwards; and during the fifteenth century, when blast furnaces were smelting iron on a huge scale, timber was cut from Ashdown Forest to fuel the furnaces. By the eighteenth century large areas had been cleared, and as these were turned over to grazing cattle, so the heath developed.

Today, reduced grazing has resulted in the recolonisation of scrub birch and pine woodland, and where areas have been burnt, bracken has quickly invaded. Because of the adjoining woodland, blackcap, willow warbler and nightingale all occupy the scrub, whereas nightjar, kestrel, woodcock and occasionally hobby nest on the heath, making the entire habitat complex a very rewarding site for birdwatchers.

BRECKLANDS

Imagine an inland area of sand, so vast and mobile that during a raging gale in the seventeenth century sand was blown for over 10 km/6miles, completely burying a neighbouring village. Today the area has the lowest rainfall in Britain (558 mm/22 in per year); the summers can be extremely hot and dry, but the winters can be perishingly cold. Such an area is the Breckland of East Anglia, a unique mosaic of sandy heath mixed with chalk grassland and totally created by ancient man, only to be transformed by present-day man during the last sixty years.

The sand was blown from Wangford Warren (54) near Lakenheath in 1668, burying the town of Santon Downham, but today all that remains of this once vast sandy heath is a small nature reserve of 16 ha/39.5 acres called Wangford Glebe, offering the last remaining picture of what the ancient Brecklands were like. The Brecklands cover 101,175 ha/250,000 acres, forming a low-lying landscape rarely rising above 60m/197 ft and crossed by the Rivers Lark, Little Ouse, Wissey and Thet, which run towards the Fenland Basin. The sandy soils stretch from Swaffham in the north to Bury St Edmunds in the south; Garboldisham is the eastern extremity whilst the Fenland Basin forms the natural boundary in the west.

The area still has the feel of a vast wasteland, but thousands of years ago the Brecklands had a different appearance. Large settlements of Neolithic man began to clear the oak forests using axes carved from flint mined at Grimes Graves near Brandon. Slowly, clearings were made in the forests and once the trees were felled Neolithic man would have found the loose, sandy soil easy to clear. Unfortunately, he soon discovered also that the poor soil was not ideal for cultivating crops and he resorted to grazing his livestock on the cleared areas. This began a tradition which endured for thousands of years and transformed the ancient wooded Brecklands into a habitat dominated by grass and heather. Small tracts of the ancient desolate heaths can be discovered today, uncultivated since flint tools tilled the soil around 5000 BC.

Thetford and Wangford Warren are two of the many areas of Breckland named after the warrens into which the area was divided when rabbits were introduced from France as food during the Norman Conquest: thousands of rabbits were licensed to landowners, who bred them for food and fur. Combined with sheep grazing, the overgrazing and burrowing by the rabbits caused erosion of the light topsoil of the Brecklands and the prosperity of the area began to decline. By the late Middle Ages, much of the population had moved on to other areas leaving 'ghost villages' and stony, shallow soil so depleted of nourishment that crops could no longer be cultivated.

54 The small nature reserve called Wangford Warren, near Lakenheath, is all that remains of true sandy Breckland today.

54

55

57

55 Stone curlews nest on undisturbed downland, heaths and stony
    brecks and farmland, but their numbers have declined in recent
    years as habitats are destroyed or because of disturbance by
    man.

56 Male red-backed shrike. This is Britain's only breeding shrike,
    but habitat destruction and climatic changes have reduced its
    numbers to only a few pairs in East Anglia.

57 The rare woodlark resembles the more common skylark, but has
    a shorter tail. Woodlarks require short grass on which to feed,
    longer grass for nesting and trees and bushes as song posts.

56

For the next three centuries, the Brecklands were left very much to themselves, with sand constantly blowing for many kilometres. The Victorians tried to reclaim and fertilise some of the fields, but they had to plant Scots pine to anchor the shifting sand. This huge area of East Anglia never became recolonised by natural growth because anything left ungrazed by rabbits and sheep was browsed by wild deer.

In its productive heydays, Breckland was one of the most densely populated areas of Britain. Today military airbases – Lakenheath alone covers 4,451 ha/10,998 acres – and expanses of conifer plantations have obliterated large areas of prime heath and fragmented the rest. But between NATO exercise grounds and sterile forests, you can still find an ancient heath and discover the birdlife. Some of the birds are typical of any heathland in Britain, whereas other species are rare and almost confined to the Brecklands.

Skylarks, with their familiar rippling flight call, rise above the heather and the tree pipit sings from its song-post amongst the birch scrub. Both birds unwittingly confuse the inexperienced birdwatcher by their likeness to another brown mottled bird which flies across the heath. Only when the **woodlark** sings is it unmistakable and seasoned birdwatchers claim the ringing song is the finest of our resident birds' songs with beautiful contralto flutey notes mixed with clear warbles and uttered uninterrupted for twenty minutes or more. Like the tree pipit, the woodlark prefers grassy areas for feeding, taller vegetation for nesting and high vantage points such as trees and bushes for song-posts, but it often sings its musical song as it traces lazy spiralling circles in the sky, hence the visual confusion with the skylark.

It is worth spending some time on the Brecklands learning to identify the woodlark, because this bird is rare and restricted to southern Britain, one of its strongholds being on this unique habitat. Similar to the skylark, but with shorter tail, the woodlark has a longer, more pointed beak and a diagnostic brown and white patch on the leading edge of the wings (**57**).

Since the European **golden oriole** breeds only in very small numbers, the chances of seeing one of Britain's thirty pairs is slight. If you are lucky, it is an incredible sight because the thrush-size male is a bright yellow and black bird whereas the female is olive green and dark brown. Again, the birdwatcher is more likely to hear the flute-like call as the bird flies through the tree tops and on sunny days in dappled light the brightly coloured birds are actually difficult to see.

Man has planted neat rows of poplars at the western edge of the Brecklands where the orioles breed; the forest is a commercial one and the trees are regularly cut for converting to matchsticks. The rides between the trees are thick with nettles so that seeking the birds is uncomfortable at the best of times, and the risk of disturbance caused by groups of birdwatchers is a significant hazard. The golden orioles struggling to breed at the northern edge of their range arrive each spring to rear offspring in an artificial wood which, if the threat of complete felling were to materialise, would cause the birds to move elsewhere or fail to return.

We know that the future of lowland heaths is in the balance and none more so than the unique form known as the Brecklands. Birds become extinct as the habitat is destroyed and when red-backed shrikes (**56**) failed to return to the New Forest heathland in 1982, the Brecklands became the last traditional breeding site of this fascinating Continental bird. The local sands of time are running out here too: in 1987, only a couple of pairs returned to breed.

The changes in Breckland caused by the actions of man are disastrous for many species, but beneficial for a few. One bird which has expanded its breeding population is the common crossbill, not to be confused with the Scottish crossbill which, along with the red grouse, is one of Britain's two endemic birds. In the 1920s the Forestry Commission planted thousands of Scots and Corsican pines on the heaths which, together with the already established Scots pines planted by the Victorians, provided a perfect habitat for the crossbill. In 1920, a huge influx of these birds arrived from the Continent and many stayed to breed, making use of the plantation of pines which grow happily on the sandy soil and now cover 25 per cent of Breckland. Pinewoods are poor habitats compared with deciduous woodlands, but at least in East Anglia they have provided a haven for the crossbill.

Birdwatching in select spots on the Brecklands in spring and late summer promises to be a memorable experience, because Britain's largest breeding concentration of **stone curlew** (**55**) nests on the stony heaths and flinty warrens. Chalk downland such as Salisbury Plain is the favourite haunt in southern England but in East Anglia the stone curlew occupies the variable Brecklands. Since the conversion of large areas to arable land in the last forty years some have adapted to nesting in these fields. Fifty years ago, about 2,000 pairs nested in England; today only 200 pairs are known to breed.

Weeting Heath in late summer (138 ha/340 acres) is a meeting place for flocking stone curlews. The Norfolk Naturalists' Trust has provided permanent hides where up to forty birds may be seen congregating before they fly south to Spain and North Africa. They favour this site because rabbits which are very common here have grazed the turf, with the result that the stony heath is maintained, providing excellent nesting conditions for several pairs. In Suffolk a few pairs nest on the well-drained sandy heath of Staverton Park and Dunwick Heath: since stone curlews are loyal to traditional breeding sites, returning each year to the same area they have used for centuries, keen birdwatchers are sure to be rewarded with good views. Even more remarkable are the few pairs which nest close to the runway at Lakenheath airbase, defying man's developments, which have at least offered some real protection.

Imagine a day in early April spent birdwatching on the Brecklands. As afternoon gives way to early evening crossbills are feeding young in the upper branches of roadside pines. The light is rapidly fading and across the breck can be heard the strange eerie wails and high-pitched whistles made by the newly arrived stone curlews. They remain invisible in the half light but as darkness looms the birds call to each other whilst feeding on worms, beetles and woodlice. Their huge yellow eyes help them in nocturnal vision and hunting and although you cannot see them, they can pick out human shadows and if frightened take to the air with loud squeals.

Although they are the size of a pigeon on long yellow legs, they are difficult to see during the day as their streaky brown plumage blends perfectly with the grassy warrens and flinty brecks. The photograph on page 67 was taken from a distance of 4.5 m/15 ft and yet the birds are almost invisible against the background. The chicks are downy and attractive with black bands running down their backs and leave the nest within a day of hatching. When disturbed they freeze, crouching flat to the ground and depending entirely on cryptic camouflage for protection.

As the Brecklands have become increasingly fragmented by commercial development and forestry, the stone curlews have moved into the arable fields which, because they are ploughed heathlands, retain a flinty, sandy appearance and provide camouflage for the nesting birds. The dangers are those related to ploughing, spraying and seed sowing, but many farmers are co-operating in order to preserve their rare visitors by marking the nests with bamboo canes, so that the tractor drivers avoid destroying them. The British Trust for Ornithology has maintained a regular study of stone curlews and all nestlings are colour-ringed on the legs in order to help monitor their dispersal and survival as they mature. With the co-operation of the farmers there is still time perhaps to increase the numbers of this bird on the Brecklands so that its haunting calls will continue to be heard across the warrens at night for many years to come.

Sandy heaths similar to the Brecklands are found in Lincolnshire and South Humberside, especially north and south of Scunthorpe. Although no stone curlew are found on these small heaths, grasshopper warbler, redpoll, long-eared owl, night jar and kestrel all nest here, together with common birds associated with scrub vegetation on the margins of heathland. In the Midlands, Cannock Chase, appears spectacular in summer with heather covering the plateau. Although originally covered by royal forest in Norman times, by the end of the seventeenth century much of the forest had been cleared for grazing and charcoal burning, and open heathland evolved. On the boulder clay, sandstone and gravel soil, bell heather, bilberry and crowberry grow and the whole area is managed to allow recreation and nature to continue in harmony.

Because woodland remains in some areas of the Chase a mixture of heath and scrubland birds breed here. Tree pipit, whinchat and wood warbler nest and two-thirds of the Midlands' nightjar population can be heard here at night. During the spring and autumn migration, wheatear, ring ousel, merlin and hen harrier can be seen across the heath and it is one of the best places in Britain to see great grey shrike in the winter.

If we are to guarantee the future existence of heathland birds and to allow future generations to birdwatch on our heathlands, today we should be making plans to safeguard the habitat. When Neolithic, Bronze Age, Roman and Anglo-Saxon man cleared the forests for grazing and created our heathlands, little did they know that twentieth-century man would ignore the historical and ecological value of the heathlands they had created and convert them to housing and industrial estates, or replant them with acres of transitory pine trees. The ancient wildness of heathland has now almost gone from Britain and the situation is similar in Europe. Destruction of our heathland, together with unnecessary disturbance, has caused populations of nightjar to fall in the last thirty years. It would alter our summers for ever if they were silenced completely or if one day stone curlews calling loudly to each other in the dusk had nowhere to return to.

CHAPTER 5

DOWNS AND SCRUBLAND

Grassland is one of the commonest forms of vegetation found throughout the British Isles. A large percentage of the British Isles is agricultural land, over 60 per cent of which is grassland, providing a major source of food for forty-five million grazing livestock. But being variable in form, it is a habitat which causes confusion to the birdwatcher or botanist.

There are three main types of grassland. Permanent grassland is found in lowland England and Wales, and borders river valleys in upland Britain, occupying about 4.04 million ha/10 million acres of countryside. Essentially used for pasture or hay it is only considered permanent grassland if it is over seven years old. A further 1.82 million ha/4½ million acres of temporary grass is sown from a mixture of clover and grass seed, and is ploughed and reverted to arable on a rotation basis every three to five years. In agricultural terms these fields are referred to as leys. The third, most varied form of grassland is the 6.8 million ha/17 million acres of rough grazing or hilltop grassland occupying the moors of upland Britain and the open uncultivated commons. These three groups of grassland are mainly agricultural categories but as birdwatchers are aware, not all grassland is situated on farmland, and grassland in Britain can also be divided into three further groups, depending on the soil type: calcareous, neutral or acidic.

Calcareous grasslands are those which grow over rocks composed mainly of calcium carbonate, which are collectively referred to as limestones.

Neutral grasslands occur mostly on loams and clays where

58 Ancient downland like The Manger, Uffington, is threatened by farming developments.

the soils are neither particularly acidic or alkaline, and are found throughout Britain, mainly in the south and east, but the more acidic neutral grasslands are found in Wales and northern Britain; in all cases they tend to be below 300 m/984 ft. There are other neutral grasslands in lowland areas bordering rivers and streams, which temporarily flood, especially during autumn and winter, forming flood meadows. This permanent grassland is found in East Anglia, the south Midlands and Thames Valley. On slightly higher ground than flood meadows, receiving some silt deposits during flooding but escaping the water submergence, are wet alluvial meadows, which are grazed by cattle in summer and provide excellent breeding grounds for waders and ground-nesting birds such as skylark.

The most widespread of all grasslands in Britain are the acidic or siliceous grasslands, occurring on the older rocks of upland Britain, such as the Pennines, Lake District, Cheviots and much of Wales, Scotland and Ireland up to 914 m/3,000 ft. Dominant grasses include common bent grass, sheep's fescue and mat grass. Because these grasses grow on the poorer, more inaccessible soils, acid grassland is mostly used to graze sheep. Wherever grazing is not maintained, acidic grassland will change by succession to moorland in the uplands (page 96) and grass heath in the lowlands.

These various types of grassland are categorised according to their geographical location, nature of the soil, degree of wetness and most significantly, the way in which they are managed. The one thing that all grassland types have in common is that almost none of it is natural, having been created and shaped in some way by the activities of man.

We have seen how Neolithic, Bronze Age and Celtic man stamped his mark on forest-covered Britain by felling trees and cultivating land. Neolithic man began clearing the chalkhills of their tree cover, because the soil was light and easy to work. By the Bronze Age much of chalkland Britain, including Salisbury Plain, the South Downs and Yorkshire Wolds was being cultivated, and the heaths and Brecklands of East Anglia already existed in tree-felled areas (page 66).

During the fifteenth and sixteenth centuries grassland was important because the price of wool increased and landowners concentrated on rearing sheep, which constantly close-cropped the grass, maintaining traditional downland turf. The shepherds discovered that their sheep were always healthier when grazing short grass so grass downlands were exploited as sheep walks for many centuries. We know that during medieval times nearly all accessible chalk and limestone soils had been converted to downland by grazing, and some of these remain in the twentieth century. Rabbits, which arrived with the Norman Conquest and were penned and bred for fur and food, eventually became less fashionable and were released to breed freely in the countryside; since about 1750 they have had a tremendous influence on chalk downland and its structure by their incessant nibbling and grazing.

Since chalk is the softest form of limestone and permeable to water, chalk downlands are fairly dry habitats, especially those on warm, south-facing hillsides, which are covered with numerous colourful flowers in summer. However, these smooth and gently rolling hills are only maintained by continual grazing by sheep and rabbits and can be invaded by scrub vegetation very rapidly. Because this natural lawn-mowing process has been going on for centuries, a unique and valuable habitat has been created. The significance of grazing highlights how artificial downland really is.

The characteristically springy turf of downland is a pleasure to walk on whilst birdwatching, but to know whether you are on ancient downland you need some knowledge of natural signs around you. The green woodpecker may present you with the first.

Probing into the shallow turf of the down the handsome male woodpecker uses his coiled tongue to trap ants beneath the surface. Suddenly he takes off and flies a short distance to a strange plant-covered hummock which he attacks with his beak with unparalleled ferocity. If it were not for the behaviour of the woodpecker you might not have noticed this hummock but looking around you will see that there are hundreds of them, 30–60 cm/1–2 ft high, situated all across the down.

These mounds are the anthills of the yellow meadow ant. There are vast colonies of these anthills, increasing slowly over the centuries and built to catch the rays of the sun, which warm the larval brood chambers inside. The green woodpecker has learnt to exploit these mounds, but for the birdwatcher they indicate that the downland has not been ploughed or disturbed by man for years and has probably been grazed for centuries. The slightest disturbance by a plough destroys these colonies, so the anthills increase in size and multiply only if left undisturbed.

The versatile birdwatcher needs to be familiar with certain downland flowers for the second clue of antiquity, because some species growing together in good numbers suggest that the downland is very old, including early spider orchid, squinancywort, field fleawort, chalk milkwort and horseshoe vetch. These species rarely all grow together, but if you identify a number of them in reasonable quantities, it is likely that the downland has remained undisturbed for between 100–150 years.

If the downland has been disturbed within the last 50–70 years, another group of plants will be found growing together, including kidney vetch, tufted vetch, common vetch and creeping cinquefoil, all of which prefer a calcareous soil which has been recently ploughed.

Downland which was converted to arable between the twelfth and sixteenth centuries will show a formation called a lynchet which is revealed as a low grassy bank. On the downland slopes, parallel ploughing caused subsidence of the bank of the higher field edge, so that gradually the loose soil moved downhill and built up the lower edge. Eventually a series of terraces was formed, each demarcated by a lynchet bank which has become overgrown, undisturbed since it was formed. The lynchets do not disappear by natural means so any downland without lynchets and with some of the above flowers probably escaped medieval ploughing and could be several thousands of years old.

Sadly, during this century, as open grazing land and downland slopes have been reclaimed for valuable arable land, the countryside has changed. The downland soils are very shallow and are largely composed of dark grey, decaying plant and animal tissue, but ploughing brings the underlying white chalk to the surface, giving the field a sparkling white appearance. In Wiltshire, between 1937 and the early 1970s, 25,900 ha/64,000 acres of downland were ploughed up and lost for ever, even though landowners and government knew that 70 per cent of the country's open downland was found in the county. Throughout Britain the story has been the same. Today there is less than 20 per cent of the grassland there was in 1940, and in the last few decades only downland within nature reserves or on slopes too inaccessible to be reached with the plough have escaped, remaining as scattered relics of the ancient chalk downlands.

Because of the extremely short grass, few birds actually breed on the downs, but the ubiquitous skylark, which is a common breeding bird of farmland, is perhaps the most common breeding species.

In the Chilterns, where I do much of my own birdwatching, the **meadow pipit** is very common, although it is nowhere near so abundant on the downlands further south and west. Resembling a dunnock, with much longer legs, the meadow pipit is a small and slender bird with a variably brown-streaked plumage, making it extremely inconspicuous (**59**). It is widespread and by no means confined to downland: birdwatchers will regularly see it in coastal habitats, and in the uplands from 500–1,000 m/1,500–3,000 ft where it is part of the staple diet of merlin and hen harrier. On many saltmarshes they nest to a density exceeding fifty pairs per sq. km. Britain and Ireland support a breeding population of around three million pairs.

On the downland, where the grass has escaped grazing, the tussocks offer additional cover and here the meadow pipit runs after insects, snapping them up before running back into the grass. Its head, wings, tail and back are olive brown but its underparts are buff white, except for the throat, belly and under-tail coverts, which are a light brown. Dark brown and black streaks cover the underparts and continue up over the shoulders. This combination of markings, together with distinct white outer tail feathers, pointed insectivorous beak and peculiar habit of running everywhere, rather than hopping, identify the bird.

Often, only an indistinct high-pitched 'tissip-tissip' indicates that a bird is around at all. If this alarm call is drowned by the breeze, always present on the exposed faces of the downs, the first sign of the meadow pipit may be when it flies away with jerky movements and occasional flapping of wings.

During spring and early summer look out for the male meadow pipits performing their characteristic display and song flight. Usually the bird takes off and rises steeply from the down to a height 15–30 m/50–98 ft, whereupon it descends with tail fanned and wings quivering, and drifts across the sky like a parachute. Although quite similar in physical appearance to the skylark, the flight display is different: the skylark hovers during its aerial song, whereas the meadow pipit constantly descends whilst singing.

Towards the end of April, the female lays 4–7 grey-brown eggs, marked with dark brown speckles, in a nest which is built by both sexes, deep in a grass tussock. The main structure of the nest is constructed of dry, coarse grass, with finer grasses and a little animal hair lining the cup. The chicks are fed in the nest by both parents on an entirely invertebrate diet. There are normally two broods. The nest is almost impossible to find, because it is always built where there is maximum protection from the elements, commonly in a narrow depression, where dying tangled grass provides a roof over the nest, as well as secluded walls.

In Britain and Ireland, the **cuckoo** parasitises the nests of meadow pipits more frequently than those of any other bird. It is probably the high nesting densities and the behaviour of the displaying males which enable it to achieve this. During May and June watch the female cuckoo patrolling the downland and neighbouring scrubland, criss-crossing the territories of dozens of meadow pipits. The small display flight indicates to the cuckoo that somewhere on the ground, close to where the male pipit landed, a nest will be built. Although repeatedly mobbed by the adult pipits over a period of days, the cuckoo builds up an accurate picture of all the actual and potential nest sites, then perches out of sight in a nearby hawthorn bush and waits.

The female meadow pipit lays a single egg each day until the clutch is complete, and during these crucial days the cuckoo swoops down to the unattended nest, removes one of the eggs in her beak, swallows it and lays her own as a substitute. You will have to be both fortunate and quick to see all this happening, because the entire act is performed in a single visit with the cuckoo's wings still beating slightly as she lands on the nest, removes an egg, lays a replacement and leaves as quickly as she arrived.

The incubation period of the cuckoo's egg is critically selective: whereas the meadow pipits hatch around the fourteenth day after laying, the egg of the cuckoo hatches in twelve days, so the young cuckoo, although totally blind upon hatching, has up to two days to eject all the other eggs or chicks from the nest, and begins to do this when only about eight hours old.

Once hatched, the cuckoo's appetite is ferocious and it begs for food so persistently that for the next three weeks both meadow pipits are totally preoccupied with insect hunting and feeding their foster child and are even unaware of their own eggs, lying cold next to the nest cup (**61**). Around the countryside in different habitats the cuckoo uses other foster parents, such as dunnock and pied wagtail on farmland, and reed warbler in marshland (**122**), but there are always unlikely foster parents too: over fifty species of British bird have been known to fall victim to the cuckoo.

For their entire life female cuckoos lay eggs only in the nest of one particular species of bird, probably the species into whose nest she was born: thus if a female cuckoo was born in a meadow pipit's nest she will, through imprinting, only ever lay her eggs in the nest of a meadow pipit. Certain birds are definitely avoided, such as the blackcap which will desert its nest if a cuckoo egg is deposited in it.

Apart from the times when females are seen flying from one nest to another, cuckoos are shy and elusive birds. They are highly vocal once they arrive in April until the end of June but only the male utters the universally known two-note 'cuck-oo'. The pitch of the call varies between males, but up to twenty calls are normally given, each one lasting about a second and most commonly uttered when perched. The call of the female is less familiar: it is a very distinctive, fluid bubbling sound, mixed with chuckling notes on a descending scale, and lasting for about three seconds. The cuckoo is slightly larger than the male sparrowhawk of the coniferous woodland, but with its grey upperparts, long tail, barred breast and down-curved beak, the cuckoo in flight can be mistaken for the female sparrowhawk, especially as the cuckoo can inhabit woodland.

The cuckoo's flight is, however, distinctive: although it flies low like a sparrowhawk, its rapidly beating wings, held below the mid-line of the body, are distinctly pointed, whereas a sparrowhawk's are broad and rounded, and the cuckoo always glides the last few metres before alighting on a fence or branch (**60**).

The stock dove, a hole-nesting bird of the beechwood and other deciduous woods, also visits the downlands, where it occasionally nests in a disused rabbit burrow. Since its diet includes the fruits and seeds of flowers, it visits the downlands mainly to capitalise on the abundance of flower heads. It also regularly visits the shingle banks at Rye and Dungeness to feed on the seed pods of sea pea, one of their favourite foods when colonising cliffs and rock faces on the coast.

Feeding on the rich supply of insects, some wheatears arriving from Africa in March remain on the southern downlands to breed, although the largest populations fly onwards to the uplands (page 96).

Starlings and rooks visit downland, where their pointed beaks are ideal for probing into the springy turf for invertebrates, which form a large part of their diet. Elsewhere on the slopes the length of the grass largely determines the variety and population of the bird community.

One of the aspects affecting bird colonisation on the downlands is the fact they are attractive habitats for walking, picnicking, kite-flying or hang-gliding. Naturally, regular human visitors disturb the birds, which is one of the reasons, together with arable disturbance, for the decline of stone curlews, which used to breed on many of the downs in southern England. The downs are still one of the most valuable habitats for stone curlews in Britain, but they are now confined to large inaccessible sites used by the military such as parts of Salisbury Plain. In 1987, which was a frustrating nesting season with a dry spell in April and incessant rain from late May into mid-July, the stone curlews on the Brecklands, their other stronghold, raised both young and many had double broods, but those on the chalk downland in southern England were not so succesful.

Woodland is the natural climax vegetation in Britain. A climax habitat is one where the entire community is in total equilibrium with the environment. When ancient man removed the natural forests of beech covering the chalklands, he upset the natural equilibrium of the habitat and provided conditions ideal for invasion of plants and animals usually found outside a pure beechwood.

The grassland ancient man exposed was used for grazing his sheep and cattle, or for converting to arable land by the plough. Only the natural behaviour of his livestock prevented the grasses from growing much taller and the innumerable seedlings of various trees sown by wild birds from maturing and reverting the cleared land to woodland again. This natural recolonisation of cleared land by vegetation, called succession, most frequently occurs after the destruction of another community or habitat. The individual stages of plant colonisation forming the succession are called a sere, of which scrub vegetation on the chalk slopes is one example.

Downland and scrubland are so delicately balanced that regular management is necessary in order to conserve each habitat: of all habitats, downland is the most susceptible to natural succession, once grazing is removed.

Scrub vegetation and its rate of development depends on the nature of the soil, the extent of management and the regular availability of seed from nearby sources. Many of the shrubs on chalk downland are adorned with attractive berries which, in the autumn, are devoured by blackbird, song and mistle thrush, redwing and fieldfare: the birds naturally disperse the indigestible seeds as they move across the down from one area of scrub to another.

The rabbit was undoubtedly one of the most important natural influences on downland maintenance, especially during periods of history when sheep and cattle grazing was reduced in favour of arable farming. However, the arrival of the viral disease myxomatosis in 1953 virtually eliminated the rabbit in Britain within two years, and the effects on vegetation, freed from the pressure of regular grazing, was astonishing, to the extent that scrubland developed everywhere. When grazing is removed by natural or other means, the fine-leaved sheep's fescue and red fescue are replaced by coarser grasses including rough meadow grass, false brome, upright brome and meadow oat grass. These form a tussocky and matted field layer and represent the first seral change on downland.

Hawthorn, the most abundant shrub in the hedgerow, produces masses of berries in autumn which are dispersed by birds to the established coarser grasses. Eventually it will dominate as a scrubland bush, forming thickets 10 m/33 ft high. Interspersed with hawthorn are blackthorn, elder and hazel.

A rewarding time to birdwatch in scrubland is autumn, which is the best time to see migrants passing south feeding and roosting in scrub vegetation. At this time of year it is enjoyable to identify the scrub by its tints and the birds as they perch in the branches. Possibly up to twenty different species of shrub grow on chalk downland, forming a kaleidoscope of colour with golden bronze beech, flame-red and orange field maple, scarlet guelder rose, pale lemon blackthorn and violet-red dogwood. Strewn across low hawthorn bushes, old man's beard or wild clematis grows, the seed heads resembling white feather dusters as they contrast with the red haws. Other fruits, greedily eaten by birds during autumn, are the spherical black berries of the wild privet and buckthorn, found first by resident blackbird and mistle thrush, before winter-visiting redwing and fieldfare gorge what is left.

Whinchat, pied flycatcher, redstart and various warblers always visit scrubland in southern England at this time of year providing a late opportunity to see them away from their normal breeding habitats.

One of the rarest scrubland birds, usually seen anywhere east of the Isle of Wight, is the **great grey shrike** which is a winter visitor from Scandinavia, marginally larger than a blackbird (23–25 cm/9–9½ in). The shrike likes to perch towards the top of hawthorn and other bushes and, with its long black tail with white margins, black wings, black mask running through the eye and the rest of the upper body light grey, it cannot really be mistaken for any other species. The scrub offers perfect shelter during the winter months, and because the shrike feeds on small birds, voles and large insects, especially beetles, the habitat also provides a rich supply of food.

On the chalk downs and wolds, the ungrazed, open ground changes to scrub within three years and as the habitat matures, the diversity and density of birds increases. Isolated clumps of shrubs covering small areas of the down attract the tree pipit, dunnock, yellowhammer and linnet into the habitat; but as scrubland increases and begins to represent 50 per cent or more of the chalk slopes, the number of bird species taking up

59

60

61

59 Meadow pipit removing faecal sac from the nest. This is one of Britain's commonest birds often seen performing its conspicuous song flight.

60 Cuckoo perched in hawthorn with typical horizontal, wing drooping posture.

61 Young cuckoo in a meadow pipit's nest with an ejected egg remaining on the ground. The tempting, bright orange gape of the cuckoo attracts the foster parent and other passing birds to feed it.

62 A specialist finch of heathland and scrubland, the linnet is seen in flocks on farmland in winter and occurs in gardens during summer.

63 Jewelled water beadlets cover the back of this garden warbler, nesting in dense vegetation.

64 Long-tailed tits line their lichen-encrusted nests with as many as 2000 feathers.

residence becomes double that of downland with scattered bushes. Many of the birds are common to the hedgerow and farmland habitat because the increase in bushes provides sites where the birds can nest off the ground and the taller scrub is ideal for territory-proclaiming song-perches. Summer visitors include the turtle dove, willow warbler and nightingale, which give a touch of magic as they sing from the thickets and nest low down in the herbage. These birds are usually species of open woodland where there are dense shrub and field layers and clearings and rides, but individuals are evolving, showing a preference for the areas of dense scrubland with adjoining downland and rich supply of food.

The chalk scrubland is worth visiting from April to June when most birds in Britain are breeding, including the **linnet (62)**. With its informal, soft twittering song, a male linnet perches on a dogwood bush and, as it perches on an upper branch, you will clearly see its summer plumage. The most obvious features

are the crimson breast and crown, with a light grey head, but the dark brown wings and tail, both edged with white, match the white throat and also help to identify the bird. During winter identification would not be so simple, because the male linnet loses the red markings. The only constant feature, clearly visible as the bird sits on the dogwood branch, is the attractive chestnut-brown back, which remains throughout the winter, providing the only foolproof means of identification.

The bird is common throughout most of the British Isles, with a scattering of pairs in the Highlands, Shetland and the Hebrides and healthier numbers in Orkney and eastern Scotland. Elsewhere linnets are common in open lowland habitats, especially heaths, commons and farmland.

Occupying the same piece of downland scrub for a few days, the male linnet has been displaying and calling as he announces his breeding territory. The behaviour has apparently been rewarded, for low down in the bushes a female linnet is picking off insects from the twigs and has obviously

63

64

decided to mate and spend the summer with him. Her colouring is drabber but practical, for the lack of crimson markings and the distinctive streaked plumage help camouflage her on the nest.

In May the linnets feed on unripe seeds, but they are omnivorous, feeding on insects whenever they are available to supplement their diet. Scrubland with adjacent downland has good supplies of both. Wherever the food and potential nest sites are abundant, several other pairs of linnet take up territory near to each other, forming a tolerant nesting colony.

The female builds her nest low down in the bushes, skilfully weaving grasses and twigs together with a little moss and lining the structure with some wool, pulled from where a sheep browsed against a briar rose. Other females in the colony might choose grass tussocks at the margin of the scrubland for their nest sites.

Young linnets are fed on large quantities of insects, mixed with seeds, collected within the scrub and out on the open downland, but the insect supplement seems only to be given for the first few days after the young hatch, probably as a concentrated source of protein.

With the arrival of autumn, the downland scrub linnet populations decline, as some of them migrate south across the Channel to France and Spain, although plenty of linnets remain to form their winter flocks which later chase around farmland with other finches.

Walking across the down from the scattered clumps of scrub to the denser areas, you will almost certainly see a **long-tailed tit**. This elegant bird with creamy-white underparts, tinged with pink on the flanks, and upperparts which are a patchwork of black, rust brown and pink, is also seen along hedgerows and in open woodland. Through binoculars, the bird looks deceptively large, but is in fact a minute ball of fluff: since the total body length of 14 cm/5½ in is mostly tail (8 cm/3 in), it has the smallest body of all British tits.

The long-tailed tit does not belong to the family *Paridae* or true hole-nesting tits, but is the sole British member of a closely related family called the *Aegithalidae*. It builds one of the most spectacular of all birds' nests in thorn bushes to protect it from predators. Within the downland scrub, many of the bushes have thorns, but the species which attract this delightful bird most are blackthorn, hawthorn and bramble. The nest is usually built at a height of 1–3 m/3–10 ft.

Away from the scrubland of southern England, the long-tailed tit occurs throughout the British Isles except parts of Scotland and the outer islands. Although up to 150,000 pairs breed each year, large numbers die during prolonged, severe winters, so populations fluctuate regularly.

If you spot one long-tailed tit in the downland scrub, it won't be long before others appear, because they are unique in forming flocks at all times of the year, often of only three to six birds but sometimes numbering twenty or more, especially after the breeding season and during the autumn and winter, when they roost communally in 'powder-puff' balls with their tails protruding.

On a winter afternoon as the temperature drops within the scrubland, you might see a large flock of long-tailed tits pass overhead. The continuous 'zee-zee-zee' contact call keeps the flock of both sexes and mixed ages together when they fly around within a territory several hundred metres across. As purely insectivorous birds, they rarely feed on the ground but utilise the higher branches, moving quickly from one bush to another, gleaning hibernating insects from crevices with their pointed, narrow beaks.

The long-tailed tit is one of the first birds to be seen in down scrubland during the spring. The winter flocks break up immediately the days lengthen and the temperature increases. Breeding pairs are established by early February with nest-building already in progress in mid-February or early March. The pair rapidly chase each other through the scrub vegetation in their pursuit of a nest site, hovering repeatedly at likely bushes before making their final choice. Once the nest site is agreed, both birds take up to four weeks to complete the nest.

The birds are relatively easy to watch nest-building, flying backwards and forwards with moss and hair bound together with spiders' webs, to form the base. After thousands of visits and much patience, the nest becomes an oval dome-shape with a small entrance towards the top but it is not yet complete: the outside is then entirely covered in lichens, giving the nest a decorative appearance (**64**), before the inside is lined with a copious number of soft feathers to insulate the eggs and chicks.

In southern chalkland scrub, egg-laying begins in early April (with a corresponding adjustment in the colder regions of Britain) and 8–12 eggs are laid. Large numbers of eggs are taken by carrion crow, jay, magpie and weasels, who rip the nest apart in the process of stealing the clutch. The replacement nest is never so perfectly built as the first and the predation also means that egg-laying is delayed until late May.

The permanent flocking behaviour of the long-tailed tit pays dividends when the eggs hatch after sixteen days, because when they are extremely young the chicks are fed not only by their own parents, but also by other adults flying past; this assistance continues for up to a week. Young fledglings do not resemble the plumage of their parents – their tails are shorter and their feathers much drabber – but by October they become identical in appearance because of a unique moult. Throughout July, once the fledglings and adults of the territory have formed family flocks, both adults and juveniles begin to shed feathers. Whereas fledglings of other British birds only replace their body feathers, the long-tailed tit moults its entire tail and body feathers. By autumn the moult is completed and adults and young look alike, which is why it is impossible to tell whether the long-tailed tits moving restlessly through the trees in November are young or old birds.

Long-tailed tits visit mature gardens in winter but never the birdtable, and the insects which form their main diet become more scarce as the weather deteriorates. Therefore 90 per cent of the autumn population of long-tailed tits may die in severe weather because the heat loss from such a small body is rapid: one reason why so many eggs are laid each spring.

The scrubland habitat is rich in birdlife because of the wide variety of shrubs growing at different heights and densities. As succession advances, the shrubs become taller and the habitat is less open in character which suits the long-tailed tit and the chaffinch. Other finches, like the greenfinch, redpoll and winter-visiting brambling, prefer to roost in dense chalkland scrub; very often this is where the flock of brambling are flying to when they take off having spent the afternoon feeding in the neighbouring beechwood (page 30).

The Cotswolds, formed by a huge escarpment of Jurassic limestone, is an area of dramatic scenery which to the west looks out over the Severn vale. With their well-trodden pathways the slopes and rich scrubland are easily accessible for birdwatchers.

Cleeve Hill is the highest point of the Cotswolds, 6.4 km/4 miles north-east of Cheltenham, and in mid-summer a visit to the hillside is usually very rewarding. The butterflies are varied and abundant and stonechats scold from the top of gorse bushes on the common; whinchats skulk in the denser scrub and kestrels are frequently seen hovering overhead, dropping on to voles, field mice and skylarks which form their staple diet.

Suddenly an unusual, high-pitched, rapid whirring sound comes from the thick scrub, appearing to increase and fall in volume before silence returns to the patch of undergrowth. Many birdwatchers are confused by this sound and some cannot even hear it, because the reeling song, which belongs to the summer-visiting **grasshopper warbler**, is uttered at a frequency only detectable by sensitive ears. Again the sound begins, only this time the small (13 cm/5 in), normally secretive bird reveals itself by sitting on an exposed twig, where it continues to sing. If you saw the bird without hearing the song, identification would not be so easy, because with buff underparts and dark streaked, olive-brown back, the grasshopper warbler is an indeterminate species. As it sings from the upper branches, with its beak wide open, it moves its head from side to side in an arc, which is why the whirring song sounds alternatively louder and softer from deep in the undergrowth.

Although the song can be heard throughout the day, the best times are early morning or dusk; and a highlight of a day spent birdwatching in scrubland is when the grasshopper warbler builds up its song allowing it to drift across the hillside on the evening breeze at about the time pipistrelle and long-eared bats begin hawking for insects over the slopes.

The British population of warblers is estimated at around 25,000 pairs, although they do not occur in Shetland and are rare in northern Scotland. In other habitats the warbler nests low down in reed- and rush-beds, but in scrubland the bird chooses the thick undergrowth and scrubland margin.

May is a marvellous month of the year for all aspects of natural history, and early on a May morning, as the first rays of sun glint horizontally through the hillside scrub, a garden warbler begins to sing. The free, rhythmic, sweet warble is similar to that of the blackcap and since both birds also inhabit open-gladed, deciduous woods, the two birds are often confused in song but the garden warbler has lower pitch, recognised by experience.

Where the chalk scrubland is gradually maturing to a climax beechwood and some of the bushes have grown tall, there are song-perches which attract the garden warbler into the scrubland habitat. About 100,000 pairs breed in Britain, with the greatest density in England and Wales; they become rarer in Scotland and are totally absent from the Highlands and Ireland. This breeding population make it about half as common as the blackcap, which does colonise dense scrubland, but prefers the open canopy of the oakwood (page 18).

The melodious song of the **garden warbler (63)** is heard more often than the nondescript greenish-buff and brown bird is seen. The males arrive from Africa first, towards late April and May, when they set up breeding territories and begin singing from low down in the vegetation. Although the males sing throughout the summer, it is from late April to early June that they are at their most vocal. The persistent singing always pays off and as the females arrive they are attracted towards the song and then the males court and chase the birds through the undergrowth, stopping to fan their tails and quiver their wings as part of the display. Once paired, both birds build the grass, hair-lined nest, barely off the ground, in matted grass tussocks, brambles and low-growing scrubland bushes.

Another summer visitor, which prefers even taller song-posts than the garden warbler and open areas of scrub is the **lesser whitethroat**. Like the ordinary whitethroat, which also colonises scrubland but prefers the hedgerow and farmland habitat (page 78), the lesser whitethroat is a secretive and skulking bird mostly identified by its 'tacc-tacc' alarm note. Many scrubland warblers are characterised by their scratchy songs and the tuneless 'chikka-chikka-chikka-chikk' of the lesser whitethroat may frequently be heard rattling out from the scrub as the bird forages and moves about for insects.

The total British population is up to around 50,000 pairs but because Britain is the western extremity of its world range, it is not found in Ireland and is rare in Scotland, west Wales and south-west England. In the south-east of England where the breeding is most dense, it even outnumbers the common whitethroat.

Towards the middle of April, about a week before the females arrive, the male lesser whitethroat vocally claims its territory from the top of tall bush song-posts. In mature pockets of scrub on the margins of the climax vegetation the males display to the females with erect head feathers, fanned tail and shivering wings.

At a maximum of 3 m/10 ft off the ground, the male lesser whitethroat begins building the nest, using grass stems and roots and frequently hiding it in a blackthorn, hawthorn or bramble bush. When the nest is half complete the female takes over to line and finish the structure. In May five eggs are laid and incubated by both birds for ten days.

The south-facing slopes of chalk downland with their associated scrub are one of the few localities in Britain where you are likely to see the rare **cirl bunting**, but since our shores represent the northern limit of its range, the bird only nests south of Worcestershire. The bunting was first discovered nesting in 1800 in Devon and by the early 1900s had spread throughout England and Wales, reaching Cumberland in the north. Today its range has contracted and only about 500 pairs remain, inhabiting farmland, the margins of heath, woodland or quiet parkland as well as scrubland.

Change in climate is largely responsible for the decline in population, because as a Mediterranean bird it is unable to tolerate regular cold and wet summers and following those of 1986 and 1987 the numbers have been affected.

The male cirl bunting resembles a brightly coloured yellowhammer but it is plumper and has a shorter tail. Most frequently the bird is seen in flight, when it utters a thin 'sissi-sissi-sip' call, quite different to its normal rattling song which can be confused with that of a lesser whitethroat sung at fast speed. In the breeding season the male is identified by a black chin and black eye-stripe, with yellow border above and below. A distinctive green-grey band runs across the breast, the flanks are a beautiful chestnut and it has an olive rump; but in all other respects the markings resemble those of the yellowhammer. The olive rump is characteristic, especially in females and juveniles, who lack the finery of the male and are generally heavily streaked on a brown plumage.

As with the yellowhammer, the female cirl bunting is responsible for building the nest and incubating the eggs, but the male provides food for her whilst she sits, and brings food to the nest once the eggs have hatched so that she can allocate it to the chicks.

Scrubland frequently attracts local common birds to visit the habitat for food, roosting and possible breeding sites. There may well be a variety of man-made or natural habitats close to the scrubland which overflow when breeding densities become too high, which is why scrubland birdwatching can be so rewarding: up to 30 different species might have adapted to breed in the temporary habitat at any time.

Unfortunately people have different attitudes towards scrubland. To the farmer it is wasteland suitable only for grubbing out and making productive; to city folk scrubland is unattractive and a scruffy wilderness; but to many birds of Britain it is an oasis of food and shelter, vital to their survival in an otherwise alien environment. The open downland is already under threat as hill by hill it yields to the demand for agricultural land or as farmers remove sheep from the short downland turf, which becomes colonised by coarser grasses and tree seedlings.

The fact that downland and scrubland are found together cannot be disputed, but the controlled management of both habitats to create the unique mixture of short grass and dense undergrowth is more vital today than ever before. The real challenge is for naturalists, ecologists and birdwatchers to persuade farmers that they should turn an unproductive corner of their land over to scrubland for the wild birds and possible pheasant cover. If downland and scrubland are both under threat, the colonising birds are too. It is sensible to encourage some of the birds to move down the hill and colonise scrubland, provided by the farmer and protected by him, with the additional help of local birdwatchers and conservationists working in agreement with each other for the future of the birds.

CHAPTER 6

HEDGEROW AND FARMLAND

HEDGEROWS

There are many things which are not really appreciated until they begin to disappear: how true this is of the lowland hedgerows, which are accepted as a predominant feature of our landscape and yet in many counties have been severely reduced or almost totally removed. Simply defined, hedges are straight or sinuous bands of vegetation, composed mainly of different shrubs with occasional trees, which divide one area of land from another. In many cases hedges border the roadside with an associated verge; alternatively, the hedgerow runs across the middle of farmland, forming fields used for arable cultivation or grazing livestock. Although many of the fields have been extensively cultivated in the last forty years, the hedgerows often reflect what was growing in the field before it was reclaimed by man.

Hedgerows, like many other habitats, are totally created by man as a result of homestead and farming requirements. Although most of the hedges we see today date back only to the eighteenth or nineteenth centuries, some are much older, dating back to the Saxon and Norman civilisation, and a few have a history of at least two thousand years.

If you were Mesolithic man walking around the countryside of Britain in 4000 BC, four thousand years after the last Ice Age, you would have had a nomadic lifestyle, and been surrounded by dense forest or wildwood, with neither the clear land nor the knowledge to grow crops; your survival would have depended on killing deer and boar, catching fish in the rivers and eating wild fruits and seeds.

Neolithic man was a farmer rather than a hunter, felling some of the forest to build homes and creating enclosures for keeping and grazing his cattle. As he cleared the fields, he used some of the larger rocks as boundary markers; eventually wild seeds brought in by visiting birds germinated between the boulders and the first hedges, which were probably bramble, began to grow.

Iron Age and Bronze Age man continued to clear the wildwood and built hilltop fortresses, surrounding their encampments with ditches; and they increased the cultivation of cleared land with ox-drawn ploughs. By this time, low-lying banks already marked the boundaries of fields.

The Anglo-Saxons invaded the country from the fifth century onwards. As they were village dwellers, they settled in hamlets, cultivating groups of fields around them in strips. These strips were ploughed individually and separated by grassy banks; some of the strips were left fallow, marking the beginning of the crop rotation system. Crop rotation cultivation expanded as the population grew: eventually each village had a central manor surrounded by large arable fields, divided so that cereal crops would be grown in some, whilst others remained fallow. The peasants or commoners had the right to graze their livestock on the common or arable fields after the crops were harvested and this required easily erected fences to prevent straying of livestock, so the 'dead hedge' constructed from

hazel was born. Birdwatching around the countryside you will see how dead hedges are still being used in some areas. There are the typical stone walls of the Cotswolds, Wiltshire and the north of England, where wheatear and wagtail have adapted to nest between the stones; in Cornwall many of the fields and lanes are bordered by high earthen banks, faced with stones, which now resemble living structures, adorned with flowers and shrubs each spring; and in Ireland the earthen banks are modified further, faced with growing turf. Throughout the British Isles hedges are different structures; some are dead, others are living, but all are used to define a boundary or as a fence to control livestock.

The most significant periods of history which shaped the appearance of our landscape are 1460–1600 and 1740–1850. During the sixteenth century sheep farming was profitable because of the value of wool and commoners were cleared from manor lands, which were converted to fields. Between the thirteenth and seventeenth centuries extensive areas of land were enclosed with live hedges – much of it done illegally, since no laws had been passed to support this hedge-planting.

At the beginning of the seventeenth century the first Enclosure Act became law and from 1740 to 1830, with the backing of Parliament, the most extensive period of hedgerow-planting took place, much of it with hawthorn. Hedges had been planted for centuries, but it was at this time that the English landscape was transformed to the pattern we know today. Probably half the farming land in the country was enclosed by 1730, especially in north-east England, East Anglia, Kent, Surrey, Devon and Cornwall, although open fields were still common in the Midlands, Yorkshire and Wiltshire.

During the Industrial Revolution and up to 1860 the importance of wool declined and the trend in agriculture swung towards producing crops for urban populations. Arable farming became increasingly important, requiring larger fields, with the result that long before the final Enclosure Act of 1903 there was debate about the continued need for hedges to divide up fields. So a period of hedge removal began, which has continued at various paces ever since, especially during the last twenty-five years, when arable farming has become a big economic business and farmers have been expected to produce large quantities of crop. Farm machinery has become much larger so that small fields, suitable for a man and horse-drawn plough, do not suit such machines as the combine harvester, and the fields have had to be enlarged by the removal of the dividing hedgerows.

Today, it is very clear that hedges have disappeared, for a variety of reasons. Some of the removal is justified; and if careful management and control is given to the selection of which hedge to remove, then breeding birds need not suffer on our farmland.

Hedgerows are a national asset. The way in which they divide

65

our fields, making an attractive landscape, is envied by American and Australian visitors, for whom our farmland resembles parkland, compared with their own open prairies. Walk across much of the countryside of East Anglia, where many of the hedgerows have been removed, and it is easy to understand what they mean. Even on the Continent, hedges are more scarce than in Britain: in Denmark and Holland there are hedges in only a few areas, in France they tend to be restricted to the surrounds of Brittany, and in Germany they are localised in the north-west.

Hedgerow removal has been going on for over 200 years with a tremendous increase in the last few decades. During the decade from 1929 to 1939 an annual loss of about 1,600 km/1,000 miles of hedges was caused by building developments on farmland. The period between 1946 and 1974 was one of massive hedgerow removal: it is estimated that 230,000 km/

65 Woodland birds overflow from the over-populated beechwoods in the distance and colonise hedgerows bordering farmland and country lanes.

143,000 miles of hedges were totally removed. Farmers are not responsible for all hedgerow removal since the last war: 192,000 km/120,000 miles have been removed by farmers but 32,000 km/20,000 miles have been lost for non-agricultural activities. However, during the last forty years, 20 per cent of Britain's estimated 965,000 km/600,000 miles of hedgerow has been removed. Hydraulic machinery can rip out a hedge in a few hours, but it takes over twenty years for a hedge to mature and establish.

It is the mature hedge which is so important to birds and other wildlife. Before forests were cleared and hedges planted, all wildlife was adapted to woodland; most of the birds were forest species, and as the forests were increasingly felled, the birds were forced to adapt and colonise alternative habitats, which included the hedgerows. Most species inhabiting hedgerows are found in woodland too, but for birds hedgerows are second best; although they represent 20 per cent of the British countryside covered by broad-leaved trees, they are not ideal for the rarer woodland species, and only provide shelter for the more adaptable common birds, such as hedge sparrow and yellowhammer. Generally, about fifteen bird's nests are found in 1.6 km/1 mile of hedge, and as hedgerows have been removed the nesting birds have been obliged to nest closer together in whatever remains. Eventually in any one hedge a saturation level is reached, when birds are forced to move elsewhere to breed, putting an additional pressure on their tenuous survival.

Although only a few hedges are considered sufficiently ancient or special to be protected by law as nature reserves, in aggregate all hedges are important and their future requires careful investigation by conservationists and farmers alike. If we accept that our hedgerows total around 772,000 km/ 480,000 miles with an average width of 1.8 m/6 ft, the total area of hedges is 141,154 ha/348,800 acres, which is greater than all the nature reserves together. Within this ribbon of hedgerows, transecting the countryside, many species of shrub are found. The ordinary hawthorn is the most common, but other frequent species include blackthorn, field maple, hazel, and dog rose. At the base of the hedgerow amongst the moss and leaf litter, flowers such as primrose and dog violet bloom and attract insects searching for nectar, which in turn attract insectivorous birds to feed.

Growing in corners, very often at the intersection of two farmland hedges, are nettles; nearly thirty species of insect feed on this plant, many of them during their larval stages and all providing a rich source of food for foraging birds. The small tortoiseshell butterfly lays eggs on the nettle leaves in May and early July and the caterpillars feed greedily on the leaves which in turn are eaten by the hedge sparrow or dunnock.

While many birds use hedgerows to feed in, nest or roost in, but not necessarily all three, the **dunnock (66)** relies on the hedgerow in every way, although it is commonly seen in gardens and parks where there is dense cover, coppices and the margins of woodland. Dunnocks prefer hedges with a dense groundcover of nettles and brambles, where they remain secretive, skulking for insects and caterpillars.

The cock and hen birds are similarly marked with a brown ground colour with dark streaks across the back, grey throat and belly with a grey eye-stripe visible only through binoculars. Since the dunnock is shy, it is its song which first gives away its location. Especially during the spring, the treble-sounding warble rings from the top of the hedge or bush and may be heard intermittently throughout the summer, although there is a period of silence in late July and August. Courtship displays involve several males flicking their tails and shivering their wings to win the attention of a single female watching at the base of the hedgerow.

The behaviour of the dunnock typifies hedgerow birds. They rarely fly far from cover and haunt the undergrowth, feeding on insects which are plentiful in the spring and summer and supplementing these with spiders and worms when they become less common in the autumn. During the winter they change to a diet of small seeds to enable them to survive to the following spring.

Dunnocks are always nervous and alert, perching low down and flying in short bursts on blurred wings, before landing to hop and walk in search of food. Only the female incubates the four or five pale blue eggs, which are laid during April in a cup-shaped nest, deep in the hedgerow, built of grass and moss and beautifully lined with hair and wool. The young hatch after two weeks when they are fed by both parents on an insect-rich diet. Frequently two broods are reared, the second clutch being laid in late May and June; and in exceptional summers a third brood is raised during July. In most years the dunnock becomes a popular foster parent for the cuckoo, which is a mystery, since the cuckoo's egg is entirely different in colour from that of the dunnock and yet is accepted by the host.

After a few hours' birdwatching near hedgerows and farmland you will realise that most of the birds seen around the hedges may also be observed in the woodlands. Hedgerows are relatively new habitats for birds and many species still require the more dense vegetation of a woodland to survive, although they will visit the hedge to feed before returning to the wood for the breeding season.

Hedgerows are more important to birds in certain parts of the country where woodland is scarce. In East Anglia, numerous hedges were planted as a result of the Enclosure Acts, but they have subsequently been ripped out especially in the last fifty years, as this part of Britain has been converted by the landowners to prairie-style farming. Any hedgerows which remain are an important haven in what is otherwise a wildlife desert; and birds which used to nest in the ancient woodlands of East Anglia, then in the hedges bordering many of the fields 200 years ago, have declined.

Birds use the hedgerow for three main reasons. There are those species like the dunnock which feed and nest in the habitat and are seen to rely totally on the hedgerow. Some birds use the hedge to feed, but prefer to nest elsewhere; and some of the most frequent sightings of the woodland sparrowhawk are made when the adults are hunting low over a hedgerow before taking the unfortunate yellowhammer or dunnock to a plucking post in the neighbouring copse. Other birds, such as the summer-visiting turtle dove, nest in the hedgerow, but feed in other habitats.

The hedgerow-nesting species occupy definite zones within the hedge and although I wouldn't encourage you to actively seek the nests of these birds, it is possible to build up a fairly accurate picture of these zones by watching them from a discreet distance, noting the levels that different birds enter the hedge with food in their beaks.

The ground-nesting birds, hidden in the vegetation at the base of the hedgerow, include the pheasant and grey partridge; both species are familiar on open farmland. The **pheasant**, introduced hundreds of years ago by the Romans, is a native of Asia, but it has been recognised as a breeding bird in Britain since the eleventh century. In the eighteenth century other species of pheasant with white neck-collars were introduced. These have interbred with the earlier forms, so that some pheasants in the wild can be seen with white neck-bands and others without.

As **69** shows, the male is a magnificent bird, with long tail feathers and an iridescent sheen to the plumage, especially around the head. Since the pheasant has catholic tastes, it finds plenty of food in a mature, mixed hedgerow, feeding on a diet of seeds, fruits and leaves, mixed with insects and grubs, such as grasshoppers and leatherjackets (larvae of cranefly).

As dusk falls, outside the breeding season the pheasants

66

67

68

69

66 The hedge sparrow or dunnock is a typical hedgerow bird also common in gardens, copses, scrubland and woodland habitats.

67 Remaining together throughout the winter, a brace of grey partridges crouch together for warmth.

68 The colourful red-legged partridge remains remarkably concealed in open country, farmland or coastal habitats.

69 The pheasant remains Britain's most widespread game bird although it is native to Asia. The adult male is extremely colourful, but varied in plumage.

leave the farmland and hedge to roost in the nearby wood; they especially like conifer plantations, which offer dense cover. The anxious, repetitive call of the cock pheasant is well known to all nocturnal birdwatchers, who listen to the bird climbing towards the top of a tree, flying and clambering noisily from branch to branch until he reaches a favourite perch close to the central trunk.

Much smaller than pheasants, and less colourful, even in the males, is the stocky **grey partridge (67)**. It is a resident bird: about half a million pairs breed in Britain, although it is absent in the west Highlands and Welsh uplands. The hedge and field margins provide the partridge with a variety of food, although they often feed on slugs well out in the middle of open farmland, where if they are disturbed they crouch and freeze immediately, before running quickly for the shelter of the hedge if the danger lingers. The most fascinating response to watch occurs when the danger causes the partridge to take to the air: with a loud whirr, and rapidly beating wings the bird skims over ploughed fields and hedges before it glides with down-curved wings into the shelter of the rough land at the corner of the field or thick vegetation at the base of the hedge.

The female partridge selects the hedgerow vegetation to provide cover for the nest, which is a scrape or shallow hollow lined with dried grass and leaves. During April, she lays nine to twelve pale olive eggs which she incubates for over three weeks. Once they have had a chance to dry, the downy chicks leave the nest within a few hours. Unlike the pheasant, the male partridge helps to feed and chaperone the chicks, but just over a week after leaving the nest, the young partridges can flutter a few metres and quickly assume independence.

Due to changes in farming methods, numbers of the grey partridge have declined nationally since the 1950s. Part of the decline has been caused by the removal of hedges from many fields, so that shelter and nest sites have disappeared; but the other reason for the population drop is the use of crop pesticides on the farmland. To watch partridges feed, you must get up early in the morning, or stay out in the habitat at dusk, when the birds feed on the fruits and seeds of a host of plants, especially common chickweed. Young partridges, however, need a protein-rich intake of invertebrate food to support their rapid growth in the early part of their lives. The pesticide sprays have done much for the farmer in reducing the number of insects living in his crops, but the drastic result is that young partridges starve, because pesticide has drifted into the hedgerow, killing insects there too. Additionally in recent summers there have been prolonged periods of bad weather, and insects do not thrive so well in wet conditions as in dry and warm weather, with the result that insect food has been limited. If pesticides could be a little more discriminatory and leave some harmless insects in the fields and hedgerows, partridges would increase their numbers; and if farmers left a few more hedges many of the larger fields would become good partridge country.

The only other hedgerow and farmland bird likely to be confused with the grey partridge in shape and size is the more colourful **red-legged partridge**, which was introduced from France in 1790 and is more common in the drier eastern regions of Britain, such as East Anglia. During warm dry days, the red-legged partridge likes to dust bathe, squirming its body into the soil and frequently flicking its wings. As **68** shows, the bird has a bright red beak, with white cheeks and throat. With chestnut, black and white markings the rest of the body is

extremely attractive, but the bird still manages to conceal itself in the habitat. Like the grey partridge, it nests at the base of the hedgerow. The female lays two clutches and both adults incubate and rear their own brood.

Above the thick vegetation of the under-hedge are the first branches of the hedge itself; and here the **yellowhammer (70)**, one of the most typical and well known of hedgerow species, nests.

Like most hedgerow birds, yellowhammers prefer to occupy the countryside away from human disturbance. On many occasions the cock bird shows itself as a natural performer, loving to fly along the hedgerow, perching on song-post branches, uttering the familiar, repetitive, staccato notes. On warm clear days in early February the male yellowhammer begins to call and continues until autumn; the wheezy song that floats around the hedgerows is one of the emotive sounds of our countryside, reminding the birdwatcher of many things: it is associated with catkins blooming in February, it echoes throughout May when birdlife is at a nesting frenzy, and it doesn't even cease on the long, hazy days of high summer.

When walking by hedgerows and in farmland, look above your head at the telephone wires, at saplings growing from the top of hedges and at the gate- and fenceposts along the edge of the fields: these are the favourite song-perches for the yellow-hammer, and the bird sings all day whether you have entered its territory or not.

The courting yellowhammers are well worth watching. During April the cock bird is in fine breeding plumage, with bright yellow head and crest matched by the breast which has dark streaks; the back and wings are generally a darker rust brown all over. The birds chase up and down the hedgerow during courtship, the hen bird refusing many of the early advances of her suitor by twisting and diving on the wing. The final stages of courtship take place on the ground with the male bird strutting in front of the hen, spreading out both tail and wings which he repeatedly quivers. Females are still predominantly yellow, but paler, and the markings are softer with additional streaking to help camouflage them on the nest.

The hen builds the nest low in thick hedges; it is made of grass lined with hair. Adult yellowhammers have short pointed beaks, as they are seed-eaters, but they feed the nestlings on insects and caterpillars before they leave the nest.

During the late autumn and winter yellowhammers change their appearance and habits. Both male and female moult to a drab fawn ground colour with additional streaks and brown patches. Leaving the hedgerows, they congregate in flocks with sparrows and chaffinches and feed on arable land and stubble or weedy farm corners where they glean seeds and unharvested grain.

You will soon learn from experience that about fourteen species of bird breed within the hedge and all but one of these are resident birds. The exception is the **common whitethroat (75)**, a migrant insectivorous bird which arrives from West Africa late in April. The best hedges for the whitethroat are those with small trees or tall bushes along their length because males quickly take up territory upon arrival and favour singing their scratchy song for a few seconds from tall uncluttered song-posts. Any grey-headed bird, with white buff underparts and grey-brown back, seen rising to 10 m/30 ft before dropping and tumbling on outstretched wings, whilst singing, is likely to be the whitethroat.

The whitethroat's alarm call is a scolding 'tack-tack' sound accompanied by raised head feathers and, since this bird is extremely wary, it won't be too long before you are the object of alarm. Twenty years ago this bird was one of our most common summer visitors, but although in the autumn of 1968 the usual numbers of whitethroats migrated south, the following spring only about 20 per cent of the adults returned. The losses were due to severe droughts in the Sahel region of Africa, which the locals had turned into virtual desert in their desperate search for food, leaving no food for the arriving whitethroats, and they with other birds starved in their thousands. The warbler was a rare visitor to Britain for the next ten years, but has gradually built its numbers back up to over 500,000 pairs. Numbers of whitethroat still fluctuate annually and although the arrivals were poor in 1986, and worsened by one of the wettest, latest, breeding seasons for twenty years, the whitethroat came back again in 1987 in good numbers.

Two of our most attractive finches nest in the hedgerow: the bullfinch and the greenfinch. Both have a lifestyle which reflects their preference for woodland margins but they have adapted and moved out into mature hedges of farmland. The male **bullfinch** (72) has rose-pink underparts, black cap, wings and tail, contrasting with a pale grey back. Females are duller and the pink more grey. They pair for life, never venturing far from their birthplace, and although family groups exist in late summer and autumn, unlike other finches, they never form winter flocks.

Bullfinches are some of the most secretive of hedgerow birds, always remaining in good cover but sometimes giving themselves away with a piercing whistle which has a far greater volume than the normal weak, piping contact call.

The nest is built of roots and hair on a base of twigs, several metres above ground, deep in the hedge. The bullfinch uses the hedgerow to nest only if its preferred habitat of woodland margin copse or thicket is unavailable, but it collects food elsewhere since much of its diet consists of buds from fruit trees, supplemented with seeds, berries, small spiders and snails. It is unique amongst finches in eating snails, but as the bullfinch's beak is short and conical with sharp edges it can easily strip the snails of their shells before swallowing the flesh. During the breeding season, a pouch is formed under the bird's tongue, so that the collected 'porridge' of various food material can easily be transported to the young.

The behaviour of the **greenfinch** clearly illustrates that thousands of years ago it was a woodland bird. Along the hedgerow, the greenfinch prefers to nest during April, in the higher parts, about 15 m/50 ft from the ground, or better still, in the branches of hedgerow trees if they have been allowed to grow. This nesting behaviour is an inherent response to the ancient tradition of nesting in trees, rather than lower down in hedges, and although greenfinches do nest and feed in the hedges they still require trees and woodland for additional food and shelter. Now, however, it is an opportunist and whilst still found along woodland margins, it has learnt to colonise open countryside where trees, bushes and hedges provide food and protection; even parks and mature gardens are suitable.

The males are bright olive-green with yellow tail and wing bars, whereas females are more sombre in their markings. From January and into summer it gives the monotonous wheezy 'zweee' call from trees in the hedgerow; but the courtship display flights are a highlight of hedgerow bird-watching. Flying up from the song-perch to a good height the male floats down in wide circles with wings and tail out-stretched, showing off the yellow bars. It frequently utters the call until it lands on a favourite song-perch before taking off again to repeat the performance. As if the bird is motivated by the act of flying, its wheezing song becomes more varied and certain prolonged notes resemble those of a woodlark (page 68).

Clearly the greenfinch is particularly adaptable, as it also nests in large conifer plantations, which is one reason why the bird has expanded its range throughout the British Isles – except for the western Highlands where it still remains rare, and Shetland, where it doesn't exist at all. An estimated two million pairs breed in the British Isles and during autumn and winter they form large flocks mixed with tree sparrow, yellow-hammer, linnet and chaffinch. This is the best time of year to guarantee close views.

With shuddering whirring wings the birds haunt wasteland and stubble looking for grain or seeds, and in late summer they plunder fields of corn, stripping the grain from the ears of wheat. During the spring the adult and juvenile diet is strictly vegetarian and **76** clearly shows green seeds being fed to the youngsters in the nest. The seeds are commonly collected from plants such as groundsel, chickweed, dandelion and dog's mercury.

On farmland with a good supply of healthy mature hedgerows, along every 900 m/3,000 ft stretch of hedge, about twenty birds of different species can survive, although this density is not so high during the breeding season, when territories are more important.

One bird which has learnt to exploit hedgerows and their bird populations is the **magpie** (74). You will find it almost impossible in the British Isles (except in parts of Scotland) to walk through farmland and not see the large black and white bird with long wedge-shaped tail and loud machine-gun call. During spring, before the leaves break, the magpie's domed nest, built of large twigs and sticks, is clearly visible in the top of a tall hawthorn, blackthorn or isolated hedgerow tree. The magpie's diet is varied, including insects, worms, berries and small rodents: during the spring and early summer watch how, flying along in pairs, but separated by a few metres, they cleverly exploit the farmland hedge for small birds and eggs. The leading magpie flushes the sitting birds from the nest as it flies low over the hedge, so giving the hidden site away to the bird bringing up the rear, and both magpies scavenge eggs, fledglings or both. Many first clutches of hedgerow birds are lost to magpies feeding in this way, and their behaviour doesn't discriminate against pheasants and partridge, much to the annoyance of gamekeepers.

Magpies are resident throughout the year and thrive where thick unmanaged hedgerows criss-cross farmland, and where taller trees have been allowed to grow. Like greenfinches they require trees in proximity to hedges and do not colonise the prairie-style farmland or fields without trees. However, the tree cover has to be just right and those woodlands without rides and clearings are unsuitable for magpies to set up territory.

Many farmers cut their hedges to a uniform height using a mechanical flail mower, which performs its task quickly, thus saving money, but unfortunately rips at the hedge rather than cutting the branches cleanly. Indiscriminatory use of the flail removes saplings of hedgerow trees such as ash, oak and maple, which, if left to mature, would make the habitat more varied and provide potential nest sites for woodland birds. The hedgerow trees need to be old with holes in their branches and

70

71

72

73

trunks, or carry a thick growth of ivy, before the woodland birds will be induced to the hedgerow.

Both green and greater spotted woodpeckers drill holes in hedgerow trees if they are unable to find a suitable, unclaimed tree within the woodland. Old woodpecker nestholes from previous seasons are taken over by starlings, which are never far from buildings and are quite at home nesting in the hedgerow and feeding in and around the farmyard, where they exploit the insects on the manure piles and floor of the cow byres.

Woodpigeons and rooks build their nests in the uppermost or outermost branches of tall hedgerow trees. Rooks are really a mixed blessing for the farmer, because although they eat large numbers of insects and larvae, such as leatherjackets, they also boldly eat newly sown grain. But any significant loss to the crop has not so far been blamed on the rook, and in any case, such blame would have to be balanced against the control of farmland pests by this wily old bird.

Tawny owls soon colonise any tree where boughs have broken

75

70 Frequent in scrub grassland, commons and hedgerows, yellowhammers often feed around farm buildings with other buntings and finches during the winter.

71 Juvenile little owls nearly three weeks old regularly leave the shelter of the nest hole to receive food from the hunting adults.

72 A bullfinch taking a drink. Daily water is vital for all birds, especially during drought.

73 Tree sparrows raise two or three broods a year in an untidy nest built inside an old hollow tree.

74 Magpies are single brooded, but family groups remain throughout late summer and in winter small flocks occur.

75 Female whitethroat approaching its well-concealed nest which is built of dead grasses and roots, and lined with hair.

76 A male greenfinch feeding its young on green seeds which form a large part of the spring, vegetarian diet.

76

off. The most common hedgerow and farmland owl in lowland England and Wales is the **little owl**, which quickly adopts any tree with a hole in the trunk and often nests in cavities where the large roots have broken the surface at the base of the tree.

One of the reasons why the little owl is now so widespread is that it is frequently diurnally active and feeds on slugs, worms and beetles and occasionally mice, voles, rats or smaller birds. No small resident bird of prey had this lifestyle and so the little owl has been able to fill an environmental niche with no serious competition. The grey-brown, spotted bird may be seen with its gnome-like silhouette perched on fence- or gatepost, telegraph poles or the branch of a tall tree in the hedge.

If you approach closely, the owl shows the first sign of alarm by dipping and bobbing, up and down, followed by the mewing 'keeu-keeu' alarm note before finally flying away, skimming low over the ground to the shelter of the farmland scrub or a distant hedge.

At the base of the hedgerow, rabbits dig their burrows and little owls often take over a single burrow as a nest chamber, laying three to five eggs during May, which take up to a month to hatch. The owlets are in the nest for a further four weeks and the cock bird spends much of his time feeding the young, which frequently leave the confines of the nest chamber and wait patiently at the entrance (**71**) for food to arrive.

There are two species of true sparrow in Britain: the noisy, chirpy house sparrow, familiar to us all, and the less familiar **tree sparrow**, which is typically a woodland bird but may be seen along hedgerows and in parks and gardens, wherever holes occur in old trees, especially oak and lime. In East Anglia, where many of the hedgerow trees have gone, the tree sparrow has taken to colonising the pollarded willows which border farmland ditches and wetlands.

The markings of the sexes are similar and **73** clearly shows the chestnut-brown cap which distinguishes the bird from the more common grey-capped house sparrow. Tree sparrows are more common in southern and eastern England, and are scarce or totally absent in west Wales, the Highlands and Ireland. Wherever they are found, they tend to be shy, secretive birds, feeding on a mixture of insects, spiders and a variety of seeds. They form large flocks in autumn and winter, roosting together in ivy-clad hedgerow trees or large holes.

One of the fascinating things about watching herons feeding their youngsters at the nest is that shooting out from the base of the huge nests fly tree sparrows, which have learnt to breed in a perfectly made, dense hedgerow. The cavities within the heron's nest are ideal for tree sparrows to build their own untidy nests. During courtship, both adults run along the tree branches with their wings drooped and extended, tail held erect, continuously uttering the 'chip-chip-chip' call. Young herons, well grown by April and May when this noisy courtship begins, frequently look down from their nest with quizzical aloofness.

In the autumn and winter, although hedgerow and farmland look bleak and empty, there remains constant activity in the shelter of the hedgerow. The mature hedge is always a rich habitat since it frequently forms the extension of a nearby wood and attracts plants, birds and other animals from the open fields, who use it for shelter and protection.

As summer gives way to autumn and the last of the harvest is in, mists begin to hang over the farmland and the length of daylight is noticeably shorter. The birds of the hedgerow have completed their summer breeding and many have moulted into a new or winter plumage. In autumn the hedgerows provide a colourful scene of rich harvest: birds fly in to feed on glowing red berries and the black fruits of the bramble attract wasps and flies which are themselves eaten by a variety of birds. The shiny scarlet berries of black bryony and white bryony are greedily eaten by blackbirds and the red hawthorn berries (haws) on long stems are gleaned and vigorously defended by groups of mistle thrushes, which also eat the miniature plum-shaped fruits of the blackthorn bushes.

The song thrush, commonly a bird of woodland on calcareous soil and of parks and gardens, colonises the farmland hedgerow throughout the autumn and winter. Like so many birds, their presence in the habitat is determined by the abundance of food, but the song thrush is flexible and begins feeding on the hawthorn and rowan berries in the autumn, and, as supplies become exhausted, moves out into the open fields, especially of winter wheat, where it feeds on worms, and invertebrates, many of which are in overwintering pupal stages.

Garrulous starlings devour the small purple-black berries of the elder bushes and at night several thousand of them might roost in the dense hawthorn, waking early each morning to continue their plundering activities along the ready-made larder. The hedgerow shrubs produce much heavier crops of berries than their woodland counterparts because they are exposed to more light during the summer growing season.

In June and July the dog rose bloomed. Now the flowers have gone, and in their place, orange-red hips can be found between the thorny branches. Once the glut of other hedgerow berries is exhausted, many birds turn to this larger, more fibrous hip as their main source of food; indeed, if it were not for the varied supply of fruit in the hedgerow each autumn and winter, hundreds of birds would die of starvation, as the countryside becomes frozen solid, or covered in snow.

The wilder, unmanaged hedgerows that have been left to mature provide the richest harvest of all, and in these migratory fieldfares and redwings overwintering from Scandinavia and Russia may be regularly seen. During the last century hedges were universally well maintained, cut and trimmed by hand into low stock-proof barriers, which were of little value to birds, since the shelter was minimal. Today the neglected hedges which have been allowed to grow vigorously and produce their fruits offer the best wildlife sanctuary, especially for the birds.

The redwing is the smaller and more timid of the two visiting thrushes; it usually arrives during September, remaining along the hedgerows of our farmland until April. Since 1967 an increasing colony of redwings has remained to breed in Scottish birchwoods, but the vast majority are winter visitors. The redwing is slightly smaller than a song thrush but with characteristic, russet-red patches on the flanks and beneath the wings. Through binoculars, you will see the attractive diagnostic white eye-stripe, but in winter the bird never gives its true song and all that can be heard is a babbling sound made around 'chup-chup' notes.

Fieldfares, with blue-grey heads, russet backs, black tails and yellow breasts marked with black, avidly feed on hips and haws in the hedgerows (**77**), giving their ceaseless, chattering 'chak-chak-chak' call.

In the corner of the field, at the intersection of two hedges, a patch of thistles grew in summer and have now gone to seed. Teasels with their barbed stems grow in between. Here twittering flocks of linnet and goldfinch feed, during the autumn and winter months. Towards the end of the nineteenth century, when farm labour was much cheaper, these weedy field corners were regularly cut with scythes; and deprived of their winter food, goldfinches became rarer. But today their numbers have improved and the nervous twittering of goldfinches is a regular sound of farmland, especially towards the later part of the year.

FARMLAND

Seventy-five per cent of the British Isles is agricultural land, all originally reclaimed by forest clearance. Much of the land is peppered with a system of woodland and copses, interconnected by the hedgerows, which form a communication motorway network enabling birds and other animals to exploit the more open farmland and fields. The very first fields were temporary because ancient man was nomadic, moving on when areas became over exploited, but modern farmscape and farming methods have a high degree of permanence about them.

In Britain as many as forty different birds are considered farmland species, but many of these are more accurately fringe woodland or hedgerow birds. A farm without neighbouring woodland will still contain up to twenty different species as long as hedgerows are present, but without hedges the number of breeding birds drops dramatically to around eight species. Only birds like the skylark and lapwing can survive in open fields without cover from woodland or hedgerow. The blackbird and skylark are probably the two most common species on agricultural lowland, but if the hedges are removed the farmer is left with only the skylark to consume the insect pests of the open fields.

Today farming and the methods used, with huge modern combines and drilling hoppers, are remote from the days of ancient man and the hand-held antler used to dredge a seed furrow. In the last four decades, farming has progressed from a paid vocation, where systems and farming techniques were reasonably beneficial to wildlife, into a huge industry with specialised, highly skilled activities designed to remove pests which damage crops and to obtain maximum return from the land. Most of the methods used to increase soil fertility, improve yields and drain unproductive wetlands are themselves harmful to wildlife, but farmers are obliged to produce crops and they equally have a right to earn a good living from what is often a frustrating and exhausting job. It is difficult to persuade farmers that they should employ conservation techniques and strategies which protect all the wild flowers, birds and animals on their land when livestock and arable farming are more profitable wherever competition from wildlife is at a minimum. Modern cereal farming is far removed from the country saying about sowing corn: 'one for rook, one for crow, one to rot and one to grow'. Today the farmer expects each seed to grow; he uses chemical technology to restrict the effects of weeds and disease and his industry permits little scope for natural wastage. Any conservation methods the farmer wishes to employ will cost him money and rarely increase his profit; even so, throughout Britain there are some farmers who successfully farm their land and compromise on methods used so that wildlife also survives on the farmland.

Naturalists and birdwatchers must learn to compromise on their attitudes to farming too, since to encourage wildlife in a commercial piece of countryside is difficult and requires the skill and advice of conservationists working alongside the farmer wherever possible. In my view a farmer should not be expected to maintain outdated methods solely for the preservation of wildlife when he will lose money in the process; equally, the hedgerows, which are havens for many birds, sometimes cause a dilemma for the farmer when larger fields would be easier to sow and therefore less time-consuming to manage. Certainly throughout rural Britain most hedges belong to a farmer who determines their future. Since 97 per cent of the population are not farmers, and the majority of farmers are sensible and want to maintain the good will of the general public, they try to remove hedgerows in a way that continues to enhance the countryside and maintain conservation, as well as improving the layout of their land for commercial reasons.

Despite the interface since 1969 between farmers and the Farming and Wildlife Advisory Group (FWAG), little is known about the ecology of farmland birds, or how sophisticated agricultural methods affect their populations. But we do know that changes in farming methods and the associated changes in the appearance of the fields can bring about the loss of a particular species. When cereal farming developed on the Yorkshire Wolds, the populations of great bustard declined, because the vast open tracts of land, specific to their breeding requirements, were broken up by the planting of hedges which acted as crop wind-shields.

Most farmland birds exploit farming methods which provide a source of food. Two regular operations at different times of the year prove extremely rewarding: during tillage, buried seeds and invertebrates are brought to the surface, and in summer, during the harvest of grass for hay and cereals for their grain, vast areas are disturbed and cleared, revealing seeds, countless invertebrates and small rodents for birds of prey to catch.

The type of farm largely determines the extent of feeding opportunities for the birds. Mixed farms of cereal, root crop and livestock grazing provide the widest range of feeding opportunities, whereas extensive cereal farms offer the least, since there is little maintenance activity during spring and early summer, when the crops are growing and ripening. Many birds inhabiting the farmland have a roving nature and are opportunists, flying around the area looking for recent activities of man and sources of food. Flocks of black-headed gulls following the plough (78) are a common sight and although this bird is a wide-ranging inland-breeding gull, it nevertheless flies many miles from the breeding sites to the farmer's field purely to exploit the surface supply of worms, grubs and beetles.

During the tilling of soil, thrushes, blackbirds and finches invade the disturbed earth, often well away from their typical feeding zone, to feast on the available source of seed and invertebrate fauna, regardless of territorial boundaries. This sometimes brings the risk of prolonged exposure to potential predators, such as the hovering kestrel. The kestrel has learnt that men and machinery operating in a field are likely to provide a rich source of food and it is commonplace to see this falcon hovering close to a field being worked, ready to pounce on preoccupied prey such as feeding starlings, sparrows or yellowhammers. The kestrel also feeds on worms and large beetles, so exploiting a ploughed field is sensible behavioural pattern.

The seasonal work on the farm and its exploitation by birds results in the development of rigid feeding patterns, as birds definitely associate farming activity with food. The tremendous changes in the last forty years in the types and varieties of crops and the manner in which they are grown have changed the entire life pattern of many farmland birds.

For many years wheat has been sown in the autumn, and now barley, formerly a spring-sown crop, is sown in autumn

77

78

77 Fieldfares plunder the hedgerows for berries whenever invertebrate food becomes scarce during cold winters.

78 Black-headed gulls following the plough is a frequent sight on farmland.

79 Each spring rooks congregate in tall trees to build their rookeries. They are distinguished from all other crows by their bare face patch.

80 The plumage of the skylark is sombre but it is still one of Britain's best-known birds. The nest is always in a hollow, partly concealed by a grass tussock.

81 Lapwing well camouflaged on its nest, which is little more than a shallow scrape lined with straw or grass.

too, so that by spring it is already growing and in July it is ripe enough to harvest, producing large yields. The new method of growing this crop has entirely altered the farmer's routine, and has caused the birds' habits to change with the trend.

The sowing of any crop requires the field to be prepared: ploughing, harrowing and drilling are the main farm practices. These activities turn the soil and cause the invertebrates, such as worms and various larvae, to lie on the surface, providing easy food for birds such as the **rook** (**79**). Less than forty years ago much cereal sowing was done in the spring and this activity yielded a ready source of food during the rook's breeding season from March to early May. Young rooks would be in the nest in March and April and the glut of invertebrates from the ploughed fields was a perfect, easily obtained diet for adults and juvenile rooks. Now that the seed is sown in the autumn, this flush of food occurs during late August and throughout September, which from the rook's point of view is not as useful as during the breeding season.

Autumn-sown cereals ripen earlier than spring-sown crops, and the ripening barley provides a supply of food in June and July. Then invertebrate food lies deep in the dry soil and the hard surface makes digging more difficult; and fruits, seeds and nuts such as acorns are not yet ripe. So rooks have adapted; they raid the barley fields by flying in with outstretched wings, flattening the growing stems as they land. Rooks generally plunder an area of the crop already partially flattened by storm damage, where the barley heads are close to the ground and require less trampling to obtain the grain. It is essentially a change in farming methods that has caused the rook to evolve this feeding behaviour, which, coupled with the damage it does to newly sown cereals, has made it more unpopular.

At different times of the year, golden plover, lapwing, starling, jackdaw and other birds rely on a supply of invertebrates just below surface level. Some of these birds are grassland and meadow colonisers and regularly survived in the traditional hay meadows. Prior to 1940, fields were managed by a system whereby there was a rotation of grass or arable crop from one year to the next. Leys, or fields turned over to clover or grass as a commercial hay crop, alternately planted with a cereal crop, were rich in invertebrate fauna. But nowadays dressing fields with artificial fertilisers means that a cereal crop can be grown in the same field year after year. This monoculture farming technique has caused a noticeable reduction in the population and diversity of soil invertebrates, which has been mirrored by a fall in the population of jackdaws and rooks during the last forty years, which used to predate the insect fauna on the grassland during the summer.

Within a few hours a fleet of combine harvesters working a large cereal field can harvest the crop with minimum effort. Grain which is shed to the ground is a valuable source of food for farm birds who quickly discover it when seeking protection between the shallow rows of straw left on the ground. If the crop was wheat, much of the straw is burnt and stubble-burning has become an emotive subject.

Farmers claim they do it because it is cheap and quick and if they have no livestock there is no need for fodder; some farmers plough their fields within a few hours of burning, and the burnt straw returns potash to the soil which is of value to the healthy growth of autumn-sown crops.

Conservationists argue that stubble-burning pollutes the atmosphere, wastes a valuable humus supply which should be ploughed into the soil, damages hedges and threatens wildlife. Some of these claims are true, and the National Farmers' Union, aware of public opinion, have issued 'The Straw

Burning Code', which is designed to protect the environment and its wildlife.

Only a few years ago it was thought that stubble-burning did not really affect the farmland food chain too much. Because only the surface of the soil briefly reached high temperatures, only the surface invertebrates and a few foraging rodents were killed. However, recent research has shown that stubble-burning has long-term effects on bird food supply. Earthworms are chiefly affected by the burning away not just of straw but of all the organic matter, which would normally rot back into the soil and be digested by the worms. Over a period of years, earthworms have been almost exterminated from many arable fields because of stubble-burning. The flames incinerate up to 80 per cent of weed seeds fed upon by linnets which, together with the repeated use of herbicides which has also markedly reduced the number of weed seeds in the soil, has caused the number of linnets to decline over the last 15 years. The linnet has one safety valve in the situation: the increasing trend towards growing oil-seed rape as a high-yield commercial crop. Seed-eaters such as linnet and greenfinch feed heavily on this new crop and perhaps the linnet population will begin to expand.

Sowing cereal crops in autumn has resulted in new problems for the farmer to overcome. In the 1970s, farmers observed starlings digging up cereals only just sprouting after the autumn sowing: up to several thousand starlings would descend on a field to feed before retreating to the hedge and copse for their communal roost. Nationally this became a vast problem and it was a while before it was realised that farmers had brought this starling damage upon themselves by changing their farming practice. Rather than ploughing the fields after harvesting a crop, many farmers had begun to sow seeds after using a herbicide to kill weeds and fertiliser to enrich the soil. The seeds were sown by a drill which only penetrated the soil to a depth of 2.5 cm/1 in, much shallower than in previous decades, and the exact depth to which a starling's beak can probe.

Changes in methods of farming have so far produced a 'win some, lose some' situation: some bird species suffer and decrease in numbers, whilst others benefit and possibly even thrive.

The **lapwing (81)** or peewit is a familiar farmland bird. Peewit is an apt name because it reflects the sound of the bird's call, which begins in the first months of spring and continues long after dusk arrives.

Imagine that it is mid-February and snowdrops are blooming at the base of an ancient farmland hedge, which is bare at this time of year except for the hanging clusters of yellow hazel catkins. Across the brown field, which shows a haze of green as the new shoots of an autumn-sown crop appear, a male lapwing performs: a true sign of spring. Tumbling, somersaulting, reeling and corkscrewing, the lapwing is caught up in his acrobatic display flight on wings that seem out of control, yet perfectly execute each critical manoeuvre.

The male birds tend to be the first to arrive at the old nesting sites, acting as bachelor advance parties before the mixed flocks arrive a week or so later. Lapwings feed mainly on invertebrates from just below and on the surface of the soil. As they are unable to feed on ground which is frozen or snow-covered, the lapwings have a complex international migration system with distances determined by local weather conditions. Scandinavian and Norwegian birds migrate across the North Sea to overwinter in Britain, whereas our own homebred birds behave as partial migrants: either they remain close to their birthplace, perhaps moving between counties or regions; or they migrate south to France or Spain; or else they fly westwards and spend the winter in Ireland, where they have a fairly wide resident distribution.

It is difficult to say precisely whether lapwings on British farmland are resident or migratory birds because some of the individuals which overwinter here undoubtedly stay on to breed. In Britain the breeding season finishes around July, when flocks begin to congregate and build up in numbers throughout August, with some migrating from September onwards. More Scottish lapwings actually migrate than English lapwings: about 50 per cent of the southern Scottish population migrate to Ireland for the winter. During August and September some lapwings migrating from Finland and Scandinavia arrive in Britain and so the passage of birds is extremely variable.

The male lapwings arriving on the farmland in February spend a great deal of time settled on the field. They are beautiful birds with wispy, forwardly curved crests, dark bottle-green wings, white underparts and face with a black band running back from the beak. Seen in good light the green wings of the male reflect a purple sheen, and when they take off their wings are distinctly rounded as they flap slowly with a bat-like flicker in between the deliberate beats. During the day lapwings feed on worms, caterpillars, grubs, beetles and invertebrates potentially harmful to crops. They are selective and prefer to feed on ground which is well broken up and wet, and they will fly around the farmland until they locate such favourable conditions. If you see a lapwing patting the ground with one foot, watch it closely; it has learnt that this behaviour imitates rainfall and brings the worms close to the surface, ready for eating. The lapwing patters the ground and then listens, and as the worm surfaces, the entire body tilts forward to capture the prey.

These elegant, harmless birds still appear to be common across our farmlands but in fact they are becoming rarer, especially in the south and south-east of England. The British Trust for Ornithology has surveyed the species throughout south-east Britain, and results confirm that resident breeding populations are about one-third of what they were only twenty-five years ago. This drop is chiefly due to the changes in farming methods already described, and particularly the trend to autumn-crop cultivation, with practically all the wheat and half the barley in Britain sown during September and early October.

You will discover lapwings nesting in other habitats such as marshes and flood meadows, moors, heaths and wasteland, but the majority favour farmland, where they scrape out an unpretentious nest in arable field and grassland meadow.

Lapwings prefer to breed on fairly bare soil, with little plant growth, and the trouble with autumn-sown cereals is that by early spring the crop is too tall for the birds to colonise the field; they won't nest where vegetation is over 9 cm/3½ in high. The crops planted in autumn are now always sown so densely that the ideal thinner, barer patches of soil don't exist. When only a few decades ago crops were sown in spring, the disturbance to the soil provided ready supplies of invertebrate food for the lapwing during the breeding season. Today, with autumn sowing, the soil remains undisturbed in the spring.

Mixed farming has been replaced by intensive crop specialisation, and the small farms are being swallowed up by the larger ones, with the result that about one-third of our most productive land is owned by a minute 3 per cent of farmers.

Whereas two decades ago half the fields in southern England were grass meadows, today two-thirds of all fields are sown with cereals. The loss of grassland as an alternative nesting habitat has coincided with arable land being less suitable, due to the changes mentioned above. Wherever grass crops do remain, changes in farming methods have reduced their suitability too. Current trends favour cutting the grass for silage as opposed to hay, which means that the first cut takes place during May rather than late June or July. This earlier cutting threatens eggs and newly hatched chicks; and the fertilisers applied to silage-making grass cause the crop to grow too dense and high for lapwings nesting during April.

Farming methods seem destined to reduce the population of lapwings unless there are changes. The decline since the late nineteenth century has been extremely worrying; a bird that has nested on farmland for many hundreds of years relies more on the upland fields each year. Present-day farmland is not really designed or managed for large numbers of breeding lapwings and modern farming will continually threaten this inoffensive bird unless something can be done on a national scale. Birdwatchers in association with the FWAG and RSPB could, perhaps, persuade farmers to leave a few hectares of rough or marshy ground on their land, purely for the lapwing; or to take extra care to allow chicks to survive wherever grass crops are machine-harvested during May.

Every birdwatcher in a position of influence, however small, should use it to persuade farmers that the peewit, exclusively a predator on farmland pests, is his ally and one that deserves to survive, even in times of intensive, commercial farming when maximum returns are expected from each hectare of land.

There is one glimmer of hope which occurred during 1987 (around the time of the Conservative Party's run for a third term in office). A scheme was launched by the government to establish Environmentally Sensitive Areas (ESAs), with the aim of protecting wildlife from intensive farming practices. For the first time ever, the Ministry of Agriculture, Fisheries and Food agreed to provide grants to farmers in exchange for an agreement not to maximise food production. These ESAs are listed throughout Britain, some of them covering areas where the lapwing is declining; and because the farmer isn't obliged to register all his farm under the scheme, it would make sense to register certain marshy and pasture areas to be reserved for the lapwing as a breeding sanctuary.

In a way this governmental idea has come a little too late, as our wildlife has suffered so much already, but since it was instigated in the same year that the Queen's speech confirmed the government's intention to 'help farmers diversifying from agriculture', it seems time to capitalise on the beginning of a change of opinion towards farming requirements and intensive methods – for the sake of the lapwings at least, who cannot speak for themselves.

One species of bird which appears to benefit from the loss of pasture land to arable production since 1940 is the **skylark (80)**, which is about twice as common on arable land as it is on pasture land. The bird has even adapted its breeding habits to suit the nesting environment available: skylarks breeding in grassland pasture delay their egg-laying to late April and reach a peak in May, so enabling them to make maximum use of the glut of invertebrates disturbed by silage-cutting in mid- to late May. Birds nesting in the arable fields have several broods and many skylarks, who reared their first brood in grassland, move across to arable for their second after the silage has been cut.

The mid-morning song flight of the skylark, and its cease-less, bubbling rippling song, acclaimed by Shelley, is known to all birdwatchers. Even on days when a gale is blowing the male skylark proclaims his presence by rising vertically from the ground, bursting into song immediately his feet leave the ground. Hanging in the air on quivering wings, the skylark sings constantly before dropping back to the ground on upwardly inclined wings.

On the ground skylarks can easily be overlooked, because they are drab, streaky-brown birds, with long tail and short crest. Much of their day is spent feeding on the ground, but fence- and gateposts are favourite perches, so the margins of the field are a good starting point to look for this common bird.

Not so well known as the skylark is the **corn bunting**, one of the most enigmatic of farmland birds, which favours arable grass-land during the breeding season. Distribution is patchy in England; it is rarely seen in Wales or the Scottish Highlands, and is confined to coastal strips in Ireland.

The best farmland on which to begin looking for the corn bunting is where barley is grown because farmers have noticed that as they increase their barley acreage, so the corn bunting population increases. Hedgerows, fenceposts and telephone wires bordering the fields are also favourite requirements of the corn bunting. Identifying the bird is not that easy, since it resembles a slightly large, plump female house sparrow. The plumage is similar to that of a skylark: brown above and light buff below, and streaked dark brown. When the adults are perched, the dark streaks can be seen through binoculars to form a necklace-like bib, highlighting an unstreaked chin and throat.

More definite identification is possible when the corn bunt-ing flies, with characteristic dangling legs, resembling an aircraft with its undercarriage down. This is the surest way of confirming the corn bunting, especially when the flight is accompanied by the flourishing song from spring to August resembling the jingling-jangling sound of a bunch of keys.

The breeding season starts early. The territories must be reasonably large because male corn buntings are polygamous, taking three or four mates, each rearing her brood within the male's territory, which he regularly patrols. The cock bird has perimeter song-posts or look-out posts, which are used daily to remind possible intruders that the area is occupied.

Females, attracted by a displaying male, enter the territory and choose a nest site. The nests are well concealed, sometimes among the coarse grass in the headland of a field, or even concealed underneath gorse or brambles along the margins of farmland (82). More frequently the nest of grass and fine roots is built in the middle of the cereal field, secured in a hollow at the base of a large arable weed, such as a thistle or dock. The three or four brown eggs are incubated by the female for twelve days. The chicks grow rapidly and leave the nest before they can actually fly, sometimes only nine days after hatching; they may be seen fluttering around the field margins, being fed by the female for at least a further ten days. It is likely that leaving the nest early is an evolutionary adaptation to prevent the young from being killed during harvesting of early- ripening crops.

As the last of the crop is harvested the males cease to be solitary, stop their singing and group up in bachelor parties, flying around the farmland feeding on seeds and invertebrate fauna. The females join the flocks a few weeks later, once the offspring have become independent; the mixed flocks can number several hundred birds.

Corn buntings are resident and in the autumn and winter

82

83

84

82 The diet of both adult and young corn buntings consists of fruits and seeds, supplemented by insects, snails and worms.

83 The most noticeable feature of the collared dove's plumage is the narrow back half-collar round the back of the lower neck.

84 Seventeen-day-old swallows demanding food. Juvenile swallows receive about 150,000 insects before they leave the nest at twenty-one-days old.

85 The white, heart-shaped face and long legs are two of the obvious features of the barn owl when it perches between hunting forays.

they form large flocks mixed with sparrows, finches and larks. During winter they are seen roosting in reedbeds and dense scrub vegetation around the farmland ponds and ditches. The best time to observe this is as the sun begins to go down, when corn buntings and their relatives the reed buntings fly into neighbouring trees and, once they are convinced it is sufficiently dark to move unnoticed, fly down into the communal roost in the reeds.

The reed bunting has in recent years begun to move away from nesting in wet meadows into drier habitats, such as farmland. It favours the weedy margins of hedgerows and fields, but even the middle of barley fields have been used for nesting since 1970. Although this is not fully understood, ornithologists believe that the colonisation of the new habitat is due to a population expansion; rather as woodland birds competing for space were forced to move into the hedgerows, so an overcrowding of the preferred marshy fields caused some reed buntings to look further afield for nesting territories and they have remained ever since.

Farm buildings represent yet another environment for farmland birds to colonise. When you visit the farmhouse to ask the owner for permission to birdwatch on his land, take the opportunity to glance around the yard and numerous outbuildings. Within these barns and sheds many of the birds which feed on the farmland return to nest, and if a garden or orchard is near by a large number of species may be seen within the area of the farmyard.

Old farmhouses and outbuildings are better for the birds than utilitarian prefabricated structures, but wherever there are buildings, blackbird, song and mistle thrush, jackdaw, dunnock, robin, house sparrow, greenfinch and collared dove are never far away.

The **collared dove** (83) first nested near Cromer, Norfolk, in 1955, and there are over 50,000 pairs today throughout Britain. The dove is dependent on human activity and thrives anywhere near buildings, sitting on chimney pots and roof tops, and feeding on grain or occasionally fruits and berries. The collared doves' preference for buildings is thought to originate from their ancestors, which were semi-captive birds in their native Near East.

Around the farm, the collared dove feeds outside the grain store or mill, but very rarely does it feed on stubble. Sometimes flocks of collared doves invade maize fields, but more often the wary bird uses the farmyard as its dining table.

During May, many of the summer visitors arrive in Britain, and the spotted flycatcher and the **swallow** are both attracted to farm buildings by the above-average quantity of flies in the habitat. The flycatcher is typically a bird of deciduous woodland, parks and gardens, but the swallow is always seen around cultivated land, farm buildings and farm ponds. From May to September, these metallic-blue birds, with white underside and chestnut throat and forehead, twist and turn as they hunt their insect prey over the fields and farmyard.

Telegraph wires and poles, the roofs of farm buildings and even unused trailers and machinery act as perches, but with its aerodynamic slender body, the swallow spends much of its day on the wing, catching myriad insects which would otherwise damage the farmer's crops. Eighty per cent of insects eaten by swallows are flies, and cow-pats in summer pasture are perfect sources of food, although a mixture of horses, cows and pigs on the farm is the best combination for swallows, because they

find that their manure heaps are superb sources of food.

Swallows build their nests inside barns, outbuildings, sheds and cow byres on beams and rafters. Look out for the cup-shaped nest, grey in colour from the mixture of mud pellets, fine straw and saliva, lined with hair and feathers collected around the farmyard. Swallows are double brooded, and the young are fed by both adults.

Young swallows (84) are usually satisfied by a meal of a few large flies each time the adult visits the nest, and on warm, still days, fifteen to twenty meals are provided by each adult every hour. Most of this insect food is caught on the wing but the swallows will also hunt the orchard and woodland margin for a special reason. During May and June hundreds of caterpillars feed on the oak leaves, and many of them hang down on silken threads, suspended like belayed mountaineers. Swallows have learnt to exploit these larvae and the diet of first-brood nestlings includes a large percentage of caterpillars.

Most of the time adult swallows are content with finding food close to home around the farm buildings, but water is vitally important to all birds for survival. On many lowland farms, ponds have been dug as a source of water for livestock, and many species fly long distances to visit the farm pond each day. For the swallow, the pond provides water which they drink whilst skimming low over the surface, but it is also a guaranteed source of insects and on dull days the swallow can even be seen hovering around the margins, snapping up sluggish flies and beetles from the vegetation.

The weather of recent summers has been disappointing, and when conditions are damp, dull or windy, the swallow's feeding patterns are affected. Fewer insects fly when it is cold, since adults do not emerge from the pupal stage; and on overcast days, insects tend to remain hidden in vegetation, so swallows are forced to fly further afield to feed themselves and their young. They can survive the occasional day of bad weather, but prolonged wet and cold days are fatal to developing nestlings. Over 150,000 insects are required to raise a single young swallow to the fledgling stage. This number of insects takes considerable hunting by both adults and if the summers are poor then the insect food is scarce and even the adults can become exhausted trying to find sufficient food to raise their young and feed themselves.

Eventually the youngsters can be seen catching their own food and building up energy reserves for their first 6,000-mile journey to South Africa, only to return to the farm next spring, to within metres of their own birthplace.

Perhaps the most well-known bird associated with farm buildings and man is the shy, beautiful **barn owl** (85), with its ghostly white face and golden buff upperparts, sprayed with blue-grey flecks. It is one of the most widely distributed owls in the world, but those found in Scotland are at the northern limit of their range. Of all our farmland birds, the barn owl has perhaps suffered the most. At one time it was a popular target for the gun, but although for many years it has been protected by law from becoming a fireplace trophy, it has become instead a casualty of the numerous changes in agricultural practices during the last few decades. Since 1940 numbers in the British Isles have crashed from 40,000 pairs to an estimated 6,000 pairs.

Barn owls prefer to hunt over rough grassland, marshland, farmland and recently planted forestry plantations. The best time to look for them is at dawn or dusk, when they are hunting. A major cause of the population decline is the fact that the barn owl habitually hunts within a small territory of about 10.3 sq. km/4 sq. miles and although within the last twenty-five years many environmental changes have occurred within their territories, the bird has failed to adapt quickly. Hedgerows provide a favourite source of food, such as bank voles, but as intensive cereal production increased and many hedgerows were removed, the owl has been forced to range further for adequate supplies of food. During breeding, up to 25 km/15½ miles of hedgerow are required to provide sufficient food for the young; this has meant that many owls have been obliged to fly across roads and motorways, and casualties have been high.

Hedgerows with mature trees were always popular for nesting and holes in oak, ash and elm were traditional sites. When dutch elm disease created havoc with hedgerow elms, hundreds of trees were felled and barn owl nest sites with them. Other favourite nesting places included old barns, buildings and church towers, where birds nested undisturbed, but many of the old stone barns have been demolished and modern replacements with clinical steel girders, rather than beams and rafters, are not suitable for barn owls.

Today conservation-minded farmers are providing tea-chest nestboxes for barn owls, fixed into the rafters of their outbuildings. They realise the value of these birds – which pair for life – in keeping rodent populations down on their farmland. Barn owls attack prey silently, making no noise with their slowly flapping wings, as they quarter up and down hedgerows and ditches. The claws are curved and needle sharp, giving a firm grip on prey which they kill with a bite from the beak.

Throughout most of the British Isles, voles, shrews, rats and mice form the staple diet, but in Ireland and the Isle of Man, where short-tailed voles and common shrews are absent, they eat more mice.

One of the highlights of walking farmland in the winter is seeing a barn owl perched on a gate or fencepost during the daytime, sitting motionless, in upright posture on long legs, waiting for unsuspecting prey to pass beneath. In split seconds it seizes the vole and with buoyant flight interspersed with glides, it disappears to the shelter of the hedge or barn to swallow the vole in one gulp.

Barn owls are silent, except for the occasional wild, haunting shriek – unforgettable when heard in the half light of dusk. It will be a great loss to the farmer and the British countryside if the ghost-like barn owl declines even further; but at least re-introduction operations are being officially carried out in some parts of the country reducing this risk to a minimum.

Agricultural demands on the land are vast and farming methods and trends will constantly change with unavoidable effects on birds. Hedgerow and farmland birds have been forced to adapt ever since ancient man began to farm areas which were previously wildwood. Not all changes are for the worse – although some certainly have been, and farmers in retrospect would be the first to admit to them. Any future changes proposed and farming developments must be made not in isolation but with the joint knowledge, understanding, and expertise of conservationists and farmers alike. Only then will agricultural land be in harmony with the rest of the British countryside.

CHAPTER 7

MOUNTAINS AND UPLAND MOOR

Home for some of our rarest birds, the mountains and upland moors of the British Isles are among the most remote areas of our islands, offering some of the wildest, most rugged and magnificent scenery found anywhere in Europe.

Curiously, although everyone knows a mountain when they see one, it is more difficult to define where the lowland finishes and the upland begins, and where the upland habitat finally becomes mountainous. Naturalists make arbitrary decisions, based on flora and fauna colonisation, climatic conditions and the nature of the underlying soil and rocks, but it is impossible to make rigid boundaries and in all cases there is a gradual transitional stage between one habitat zone and another.

For the purposes of birdwatching, uplands may be defined in general terms as those vast areas of moor and bog found at over 240 m/787 ft above sea level and broadly speaking, mountains begin at 610 m/2,000 ft, but birdwatchers should not rely too much on classification by altitude, for they will learn from experience that species observed at 400 m/1,300 ft in Angus can be completely different from those seen at 400 m/1,300 ft in Sutherland and all could rightly be termed upland birds.

The aspects common to all mountains and moorland are their bleakness and openness. They include areas of untamed ground, the remnants of true wilderness in the British Isles, carved and shaped over millions of years by the Ice Ages. We have seen in Chapter 1 how various Ice Ages changed the shape of our planet, which around 670 million years ago was mostly covered in ice. An aerial view of Europe would have been totally different 20,000 years ago. Britain, Ireland and Europe were all joined as a single land mass and from the air the reflection from the snow and ice cap would have been dazzling. Most of Scotland and Wales was covered and only the extreme south and west of Ireland was free from ice. In England huge crushing glaciers smothered the Lake District, advancing down the Pennines and flattening the Cheshire Plain; and at the extremities of this wedge of ice was a huge lake, which today forms the River Severn. Another huge flow of ice extended down the eastern side of England to the Wash and north Norfolk coast, ending in another lake.

The ice covering Scotland and the north of England was up to 1.6 km/1 mile thick and the ice-free zones in the south resembled barren Arctic wasteland, making Britain one of the most inhospitable areas on Earth. At the end of the last Ice Age, 10,000 years ago, the total population of Britain was probably only a few hundred and conditions were still unfavourable, although improving all the time.

Today the glaciers have retreated, leaving many geological and topographical features caused by the ice, such as the gouged U-shape valleys of the Lake District and the fascinating drumlins found in southern Scotland and central Ireland. As the ice moved, its effect was tempered by variation in resistance to rock erosion, so that where the rock was easily eroded the surfaces became grooved and pock-marked with basins which filled to form corries and tarns or peat-filled hollows, leaving the more resistant rocky outcrops and hummocks and producing the worn, scraped, rough-gouged upland landscape we know today. Much of the mineral matter scraped off by the advancing glaciers was deposited as glacial debris at great

distances from the parent rock: consequently upland is a mixture of rock types completely different from the base rock beneath.

In Ireland there are over 4,100 sq. km/1,583 sq. miles of land 300–600 m/1,000–2,000 ft high and 240 sq. km/92½ sq. miles of land above 600 m/1,968 ft; this includes 45 peaks rising above 750 m/2,500 ft and 190 peaks above 600 m/2,000 ft. The highest mountain in Ireland is Carrantual (1,041 m/3,415 ft), the summit of which is covered in grass moorland. This peak is in the Kerry range called MacGillycuddy's Reeks, but very few upland birds actually breed in these mountains and there is better birdwatching elsewhere.

To the south of Dublin is the greatest upland area in Ireland, called the Wicklow Mountains, with over 530 sq. km/204½ sq. miles above 300 m/1,000 ft. The lower slopes are covered with coarse grass and gorse, whereas the upper slopes above 380 m/1,246 ft are heather moor and the peaks are blanket bogs with cotton grass predominating. In these uplands and mountains ring ousel and peregrine can be seen, especially around Glenmalure.

In west Galway, the Connemara region is desolate, wind-lashed and mountainous, comprising a mixture of lochs, bogs and the peaks of the Twelve Bens and Maam Turk mountains. The base rock is ancient eroded gneiss and the landscape is the same as that found in north-west Scotland and the Outer Hebrides. Further north, beyond Sligo Bay, are carboniferous mountains forming the peaks of Ben Bulben and rising 450–600 m/1,500–2,000 ft. Here, lower rough grassland slopes meet sheer cliffs of limestone, capped with a peat plateau; and some of the cliffs are famous for mountain flowers as well as birds.

In north-west Ireland, Co. Donegal is a region of mountains, upland moor and bog with quartz peaks ranging from 670 m/2,198 ft to over 750 m/2,500 ft. In the Derryveagh Mountains the Glenveagh National Park is an excellent birdwatching area: mountains mix with upland woods and lakes, covering an area of 1,600 ha/3,953 acres, where peregrine, merlin, raven, red grouse, ring ousel and golden plover breed, representing the true range of upland birds.

Wales is another mountainous country with the higher ground concentrated inland and nearly 40 per cent of the country ranging above 240 m/787 ft. The volcanic, glaciated mountains of North Wales rise to their highest peak at Snowdon (1,085 m/3,560 ft) but the Snowdonia National Park, covering an area of 218,455 ha/539,795 acres, includes a variety of mountainous country, upland moor, oakwoods and valleys. Breeding on the heather moors are red grouse and waders such as snipe, curlew and redshank; and it is possible to see short-eared owl, hen harrier and merlin in the more remote areas of the park. Many other areas of Wales are equally mountainous. Throughout Wales there are famous peaks such as Cader Idris 890 m/2,900 ft, Glyder Fach 978 m/3,260 ft, and Aran Fawddwy and Crib Goch both 900 m/2,952 ft. In South Wales there are the Brecon Beacons, which are the main

86 Fleetwith Pike, Crummock Water and Buttermere are typical of the upland scenery of the Lake District.

uplands of the area: made of old red sandstone, they rise to over 880 m/2,887 ft with typical moorland vegetation of heather, bilberry and crowberry. In central Wales the Cambrian mountains formed of slate and shale have been eroded forming plateaux covered in bogs and molinia grass moor.

In south-west England the only major uplands are Dartmoor and Exmoor, rising to a little over 600 m/2,000 ft and 500 m/1,640 ft. Dartmoor covers 94,500 ha/233,500 acres and stands upon a vast granite base with scattered boulders and tors as characteristic features. Heather, cross-leaved heath and purple moor grass predominate with bracken on the lower slopes. True moorland birds such as golden plover, dunlin and red grouse only occur in small numbers on Dartmoor but ring ousel, wheatear, whinchat and snipe are common.

Exmoor, dominating the north Somerset and Devon coasts, is smaller than Dartmoor, covering 68,635 ha/169,597 acres. Because it lies on sandstone and fertile sedimentary rock, much of Exmoor is now agricultural land but whilst the upland moorland has become fragmentary, the moor and heathland vegetation still remains; here raven, merlin and buzzard may be seen and, on the upland streams, dipper.

North-east from Exmoor the next upland area is the Pennines, which include the Peak District and the Yorkshire Dales. In the southern Pennines there are famous upland heather moorlands like Kinder Scout at 636 m/2,086 ft, whereas the central Pennines are famed for carboniferous limestone pavements such as at Ingleborough, over 700 m/2,300 ft above sea level. The highest spot on the northern Pennines is Cross Fell rising to 293 m/2,929 ft; the flanks of this peak are clad with heather.

The geology of the Lake District is complex, with a regional mixture of slate, volcanic rock, limestone, granite and silurian rocks. The northern area is mostly Skiddaw slate, the famous dark grey rock which splits and erodes to form the scree-sloped moor-covered mountains. South of Keswick the Borrowdale volcanic rocks break the surface and form the characteristic warped and rugged peaks. Many Lake District peaks rise above 600 m/1,968 ft and some tower over 900 m/2,952 ft, such as Scafell Pike, the highest peak in England at 978 m/3,210 ft. Further south, at Coniston and Windermere, wooded limestone slopes border the lakes whereas at Eskdale and Shap there are outcrops of granite.

Beyond the Pennines to the north-east are the Northumberland Hills and the Cheviots where peaks rise to 815 m/2,674 ft. The hills were volcanically formed and shaped by ice and are covered in grass with intense sheep-grazing. The Northumberland National Park covers an area of 113,110 ha/279,494 acres of upland moor and mountains, surrounded by farmland.

On the managed grouse moors in the Cheviots, the elusive curlew, golden plover, dunlin and merlin can all be seen and heard on the higher, more remote stretches.

The highest, bleakest and most formidable mountains of the British Isles are those of the Scottish Highlands, north of the Highland Boundary fault line running on the west coast from Helensburgh on Gare Loch, up to Stonehaven, south of Aberdeen on the east coast. Above this line lies 66 per cent of the total area of Scotland and not only is it the least-populated part of the British Isles, but much of the Torridonian and Lewisian rocks, mixed with old red sandstone and granite outcrops, that form the Highlands, are well over 1,219 m/3,998 ft. The Grampians, lying north of the Highland Boundary and south of the Great Glen faults, range in height from 600–900 m/2,000–3,000 ft, but Ben Nevis, south-east of Fort William, is the highest mountain in Britain at 1,344 m/4,406 ft. The real

mountain massifs are the Cairngorms, a ridged granite plateau covering 25,949 ha/64,119 acres between Aviemore and Braemar in Upper Deeside. The range has an almost constant height of 900 m/3,000 ft including four of the highest peaks in the British Isles, all over 1,220 m/4,000 ft, including Ben Macdui 1,310 m/4,296 ft, which is second in height only to Ben Nevis. Such peaks are inhospitable, frequently shrouded in mist or snow and littered with rocky debris and corries.

The north-central, north-west and north-east Highlands are all mountainous and moorland country, each area with a character of its own; some mountains are formed from the oldest rocks in Scotland, whereas others, made of Torridonian sandstone, provide some of the most attractive mountains in Scotland. Canisp (847 m/2,779 ft) in the north-west Highlands is capped with quartzite, rising so abruptly from surrounding low-lying moors that it looks particularly spectacular. The north-east Highlands of Sutherland and Caithness are much lower and rarely higher than 300 m/1,000 ft but where mountains such as Beinn Laoghal and Ben Hope rise from the desolate moors, they look altogether more impressive.

Low temperatures are always associated with higher altitudes and mountain ranges are seldom free from mist, cloud and rain. In upland country temperatures drop by 1.6°C to 2.8°C for every 300 m/1,000 ft climbed. Temperature changes are also very fickle: during summer the south-facing slopes can be encouragingly warm, whereas a few kilometres away on the north face or in the shade of a corrie, the temperatures are low and in sheltered spots in the Cairngorms snow pockets survive into August.

In the Highlands, the driest time of year is from March to June, when the wind changes direction from the west to the east and sunshine and daylight hours reach their zeniths together. Although it is warmer during July and August, at this time of year there is usually an increase in rain, which ceases by September, just as the first new snow of the winter arrives.

Birdwatching in the mountains and uplands, you will soon see that in the British Isles the natural tree line stands at around a maximum of 600 m/2,000 ft. This represents the altitude where the montane or mountain zone begins, below which is the sub-montane zone.

After the last Ice Age, when the climate improved, juniper, birch and pine invaded the tundras of northern Britain. There followed two thousand years of warmer, wetter weather, when many trees became waterlogged and died, and the bogs and moors were largely formed. Most of the trees covering the moors and bogs of the British Isles were felled in prehistoric and historic eras but isolated groups of trees in the more inaccessible spots escaped and remain today as ancient natural tree lines.

By 500 BC the moorlands of Dartmoor, North York Moors and the Lake District were deforested but it was not until the eighteenth century that the Scottish Highlands were affected. The Caledonian forest remained largely untouched until the late Middle Ages, when it was almost 9,000 years old; five hundred years later it was virtually destroyed by man. It is clear that today's moorlands were created by man felling upland forests, whereas the associated blanket peat bogs were formed during one of the prolonged wet spells after the Ice Age.

Raised bogs are different in structure from blanket peat bogs. One of the best examples of a raised bog is Cors Tregaran, 150 m/492 ft above sea level in Dyfed and formed within a drained preglacial lake. Raised bogs initially form in large wet depressions where drainage is poor: as peat accumulates the level of vegetation and surface of the bog rise above the surrounding water. Eventually heather colonises the raised surfaces, together with sphagnum moss, so that the entire bog resembles an up-turned saucer, higher in the middle than at the edge, and rainfall running past the roots becomes the main source of water for many plants in the raised section.

Upland vegetation includes a wide variety of plants which have colonised the lowlands and are extending into the sub-montane region. As the altitude increases so some species decrease, eventually leaving other species which indicate that the habitat is a sub-montane or upland one. These species include bilberry, crowberry and a predominance of heather. If you see ptarmigan, dotterel or snow bunting, then you have entered true mountain country, since these are the only three British birds of montane habitat. They are confined to the Highlands between 820 m/2,690 ft and 1,220 m/4,002 ft.

Birdwatching in the mountain plateaux begins in spring. Even then the biting wind whips across the face of the mountain and snow squalls swirl against the dark grey sky; but each March one of Britain's rarest breeding birds returns from the coasts to find mountain territories and breed in the Highlands. The **snow bunting (87)** is known as a winter visitor. Flocks feed along various coastlines of Britain from October until the New Year. At this time of year the birds are in their non-breeding plumage: muted brown back and wings with white underparts. The male is more boldly patterned with a brownish-red cap and in both sexes the beak changes from black to yellow-brown.

During March, the male snow buntings returning to the mountains are in spring breeding colours with black backs, distinct black and white wings and tail and pure white underparts. The bill is now black and the snow-white head accentuates the black eye. Although resembling a stocky sparrow, this handsome bird is more the size of a yellow-hammer.

As with the corn bunting of the farmland, male snow buntings arrive in bachelor parties, staking their claim on their territory either by energetically singing from rocky outcrops or by making a gliding display flight 9 m/30 ft in the air. The resident bird aggressively guards the territory and threatens intruders by flattening its body and uttering loud, short calls.

As patches of snow begin to thaw in April, the females arrive on the mountains. They are drabber than the males; their markings resemble the male's winter markings of fawn brown but they have a distinct russet head and white flashes on the wings and tail.

For a few weeks the mountain tops become an arena for the cock birds to court and display to the females. With wings and tail splayed, the cock bird runs away from the hen, showing off his black and white markings before turning and running towards her. This ritual is performed until the hen accepts her suitor but the following weeks are spent feeding together with much aerial chasing before mating takes place. After mating, the female begins to build a nest in a crevice or fissure between the rocks. It is built of grass, moss and lichen, and lined with insulating wool and feathers.

The snow bunting is careful not to breed until summer has definitely arrived, laying eggs from May onwards so that the juveniles hatch to benefit from the peak insect glut of the brief Highland summer. The young grow rapidly and leave the nest within two weeks to build up reserves of food, ready for the autumn migration southwards.

As the snow is melting in late April and early May, the first of the summer-visiting mountain birds arrive. Rounded whale-back summits and short-grassed plateaux over 900 m/2,952 ft, where cross-winds blow the snow away, are the favourite haunts of the **dotterel**, which arrives from northern Africa and the Middle East to breed.

In England, dotterels have been recorded nesting between 750–880 m/2,460–2,887 ft but the main breeding grounds are the ridges and stony ground of the Cairngorms, central and west Grampians, the Monadliaths east of Loch Ness, Cumbrian fells and the mountains of North Wales; and just over ten years ago the first pair nested in Ireland. In good years between 100–150 pairs nest amongst the peaks of the British Isles.

In breeding plumage the dotterel is a very colourful wader (**88**) and like the red-necked phalarope, the roles are reversed: the female is more colourful and leaves the male to incubate the eggs. A broad white eye-stripe meets in a V at the nape of the neck and the crown is dark brown. The throat is grey, running down into a white band which marks the beginning of the striking chestnut-red breast and ebony-black lower belly.

It's an arduous climb up to high-level dotterel country, but it's worth the effort since en route you might well see meadow pipit, wheatear and ring ousel. Above 800 m/2,625 ft the dotterel shares the pure air with ptarmigan and snow bunting. Often you'll get your first sighting of the dotterel after you reach the summit and plateaux, as it stands on a large rock bobbing up and down with the sky behind. At closer range the bird is a jewel of the mountain, on yellow legs which blur as they run in short bursts across the stony ground. Dotterel-spotting is not difficult since they are confiding birds and allow you to approach very close.

Courtship is initiated by the female who chases after and displays in front of the cock bird but once the pair bond is formed 'nest dancing' begins. In this ritual, both birds simulate the movements involved in scraping out a nest hollow with their breasts and feet, sometimes over large areas and for several days. They don't actually make a nest hollow, but the behaviour forms the bond between the two birds and they make frequent tinkling contact calls. Eventually the token nest-building movements become serious and both birds concentrate on one area, scraping out a hollow in the short vegetation which is sparsely lined with grasses, mosses and lichens. Sometimes ptarmigan droppings are collected to surround and line the nest.

Weather conditions influence the breeding of the dotterels and in milder springs egg-laying begins in late May but in late seasons nest dancing may not even begin until June. The heavily blotched brown eggs are laid over a period of several days and after the second egg is in the nest, the male assumes his incubation role for twenty-six days. Its perfect camouflage renders the bird invisible whilst sitting and very often the cock bird refuses to be flushed from the nest – you can be a few metres from a nesting bird without realising it.

The female birds form hen parties once the males are busy incubating and disperse some distance from their nesting territory. Most hen birds in the Cairngorms find a second mate while their first mates are still brooding. The advantage of this behaviour is that it guarantees twice as many offspring in what is a very short and difficult breeding season: many of the brown-black chicks die in the first few days from exposure to severe cold and rain. The chicks leave the nest after a day and many are predated by marauding hooded crows which take both eggs and chicks. Other predators are merlin and kestrel – although they rarely hunt the high plateaux – and peregrine, golden eagle and hill fox.

Man is the main cause of the decline in the dotterel,

especially in the eighteenth and nineteenth centuries, and despite strict protection today the dotterel has never completely recovered from the decline that began 200 years ago. Increased recreation and tourism in the Highlands threaten to invade even the most inaccessible summits where the dotterel has evolved to live.

Small flocks of these birds congregate in early August, ready to fly south to overwinter. During this passage migration, birdwatchers in southern and eastern England observe the birds feeding on recently ploughed farmland or open heaths. These specific feeding stations have been used for centuries, which is an important reason why these habitats should be protected.

The **ptarmigan** is a resident grouse of the mountains and of the three high-altitude birds it is the most numerous with around 10,000 pairs. It is most common in the central and west Highlands and thrives above the moorland and scree slopes in the true montane zone, from 800 m/2,625 ft to as high as 1,200 m/3,937 ft. The favoured vegetation is stunted willow and heather, where lichen and crowberry grow on stony ground, resembling an Arctic alpine heath.

The ptarmigan is one of the most hardy birds in the world, positively thriving in snow and even moulting in winter to pure white, for perfect camouflage when foraging. They rarely fly far, preferring a terrestrial lifestyle; therefore camouflage at all times of year is important, for protection against attacks from golden eagle and peregrine.

Bilberry and crowberry form part of the ptarmigan's staple diet, but young developing shoots of heather are the most important element and flocks of ptarmigan can be seen quartering the higher slopes looking for the right heather bushes. During snowstorms the birds burrow into snow and, because their feet are covered with insulating feathers down to the tips of the claws, the body-heat loss is restricted to a minimum.

Ptarmigans are seen exploiting ridges and hollows which have been blown free of snow, collecting seeds, fruits, leaves and shoots. March and April are the best months to observe the ptarmigan; they become territorial and moult from pure white to their summer plumage (**89**), which is grey-brown breast and flanks, with barring on all the feathers. Males display themselves to females from the tops of boulders and once pairing has taken place all unmated birds are driven to the perimeters of the territory, where they are more exposed to hunting foxes and birds of prey.

Small autumn family groups can be seen across the mountain tops from September onwards, but by the time these have fused into winter flocks or packs, there may be over one hundred birds scratching food from out of the snow.

Surrounding the summits and plateaux of the higher mountains are sheer rock faces with gullies, crags and ledges, forming buttresses for the main mountain peaks. In the higher more inaccessible crags the raven, peregrine and golden eagle compete for space. Wherever it is present the **golden eagle (90)** dominates the habitat. Seeing a golden eagle is more a matter of chance than design, because only 250–300 pairs breed in Britain, mostly in the Scottish Highlands, with a few in south-west Scotland and several pairs in the Lake District. Although we have more pairs than any other European country, they occupy remote rock faces and their hunting territory is enormous, covering 4,000–6,000 ha/10,000–15,000 acres of upland moor and lower mountain slopes. This territory

87

88

89

87 Male snow bunting at the nest. The first snow buntings nesting in Britain were recorded in Scotland in 1886.

88 In a reversal of roles, the male dotterel assumes all the parental duties of incubating the eggs and feeding the young.

89 Ptarmigan in summer plumage on high mountain slopes. This is the only British bird which undergoes a series of moults from pure white in winter to mottled grey-brown in summer.

90 The magnificent golden eagle with eaglets. At the rim of the nest can be seen the remains of prey.

91 The eyrie of the peregrine is typically found on remote rocky ledges of mountains and sea cliffs. It hunts over moorland and across estuaries in winter.

is about the size of an average London borough. Even though golden eagles use regular favourite nesting sites, it is impossible to know which eyrie will be selected in any given breeding season. If you do spot a golden eagle, get into a comfortable position and enjoy the spectacle.

Towards the end of March males fly across their territory, announcing the beginning of the breeding season. High in the sky the bird soars on 2.1-m/7-ft wings, moving in wide circles and watching over the entire panorama, scanning for prey all the time. Few birds have such mastery of the air. Only the splayed finger-like primaries at the end of each wing twitch occasionally, to steer and control the riding of the air currents. Barely more than 3 km/2 miles away a ptarmigan raises its head out of the heather which is sufficient to alert the eagle; and with eyes ten times keener than our own the huge bird turns towards the unaware grouse. Tucking wings into the body, the soar changes to a stoop, reaching 144 kph/90 mph as the eagle drops out of the sky towards its prey. Employing all his hunting skills the male eagle uses the contours of the rocks and moorland slopes to conceal his attack; the first stoop was purely to lose altitude so that the prey could be approached from a neighbouring gulley with low-level attack from behind. As the ptarmigan perches itself on the heather bush it fills the eagle's vision. Swooping up from the ravine and crossing the heather at speed the eagle extends its talons and crashes into the luckless bird, which is dead before the swirling feathers settle on the ground.

The golden eagle eats a wide variety of food, including mountain hare, deer, hill fox, dead sheep, red grouse and numerous upland waders. It prefers prey which can be carried away whole, but if not, will mantle the carcass and tear it into manageable portions with its vicious hooked beak and vice-gripping talons.

From autumn to the following spring, a pair of eagles – which stay together for life – repair an old nest, adding new branches, sticks and heather sprigs, until the final diameter reaches 2 m/6 ft across. The nest is generally on a ledge or in a tree and very occasionally on the ground beneath a shade-giving bush. Between March and April two large white eggs are laid, up to four days apart; although both eggs may hatch normally, only one chick may survive, because the chick of the first-laid egg grows rapidly and often attacks the new-born eaglet from the second egg, which usually dies. If it survives the onslaught and receives food from the adults, it stands a chance of fledging. Only 20 per cent of adults raise both young completely.

By autumn young eagles are independent and drift up to 160 km/100 miles away from their parents' territory, sometimes on to lower moorlands where red grouse are reared as gamebirds. Although strictly protected by law, the eagle is still persecuted by hill farmer and gamekeeper who see the bird as a threat to their livelihood.

The favourite haunts of the **peregrine (91)** are the sea cliffs of Wales, the West Country and our off-shore islands, but the upland crags with good views over steep-sloping moorland are also ideal territories. The adult male and larger female have similar markings; and the blue-black upper plumage, with grey-barred, brownish-white underparts, make the peregrine difficult to see when it is perched on a vantage point high on the rock face. They are usually seen when soaring on the thermals over the moor, rising 300 m/1,000 ft or more, on long broad-shouldered powerful wings which end in a point. Once the peregrine perches you can observe the dark head with characteristic black 'moustache' markings, immediately below huge white-rimmed eyes. Like the golden eagle, the eyes of a peregrine are incredibly perceptive and it can see the slightest movement of prey hundreds of metres away.

The peregrine is the largest British falcon and both sexes are built for speed. At rest in upright stance the birds are barrel-chested, because of their large pectoral muscles which drive the wings in rapid powerful beats, followed by a glide. The yellow legs are sturdy and muscular and partly covered with feather gaiters, ending in sharp curved talons. Nothing can outpace the hunting peregrine: its method of killing is unrivalled and very characteristic. Soaring high overhead the falcon sees, say, a stock dove flying across the moor to its nesting crevice. Dropping one wing the peregrine arcs into a breathtaking dive and with wings swept back into its body it hurtles at over 125 kph/80 mph towards the dove. Just before impact it extends its muscular legs and the sabre talons rip into the dove like a meat cleaver, killing the bird upon impact. Dropping on to prey from over 150 m/500 ft the peregrine, which weighs 1.1 kg/2½ lb, can kill even large birds the size of a carrion crow or raven.

Peregrines pair for life and require a large hunting and breeding territory. In February pair-bond displays begin, the two birds passing food in flight, and eventually a nest site is chosen – a scrape on a grass-covered ledge or a disused raven's or buzzard's nest. In April three or four eggs are laid which hatch together, so, unlike the golden eagle, there is every chance for all the brood to survive. The female feeds and guards the young, whilst the male predominately hunts, bringing prey back to the ledge and dropping it for the female, who flies off the nest, to catch it in mid-air.

Before the seventeenth century the **raven** was a bird of the lowlands, and even a regular sight in cities such as London, scavenging the streets for digestible refuse. From the seventeenth to the nineteenth centuries they were persecuted by city rat-catcher, shepherd and gamekeeper, with the result that today the bird has been forced by man to the remote moors, mountainside and deserted coastline, where it ranges over large territories, generally at altitudes of 350–450 m/1,150–1,500 ft. Ireland, Scotland, Wales, the West Country, the Pennines and the Lake District are the strongholds of this unmistakable bird.

Ravens are our largest crow (64 cm/25 in) and jet black, including the huge beak. The wedge-shaped tail and up-turned finger-like primaries when flying are diagnostic features. More often the call of the raven is heard before the bird is seen and the deep-throated croak and 'chuck-chuck' sounds echo down the ravines as it glides by. Ravens are not sexually mature until after their third season, when pairing and breeding begins as early as February. Their courtship is magical to watch because the breeding pair perform aerobatics which involve barrel-rolling, somersaulting, tumbling and diving. The male is a real exhibitionist and in level flight will suddenly roll over completely on to his back with his legs uppermost, before flicking back on to an even keel. You can regularly see this behaviour when walking remote sea cliffs and the raven even makes a point of showing off in front of birdwatchers.

Many of the raven nest sites have been used for centuries on crags or trees growing out of ravines. Those in trees become vast stacks over the years, many metres tall (**95**). Both adults add to old nests, bringing branches and large twigs to make the platform, lining the nest cup with roots and earth before adding a final layer of wool and fine grass.

It is the fact that ravens are seen pulling wool from the backs of live hill sheep that has caused farmers to shoot the birds. They also feed avidly on still-born lambs and adult sheep corpses. In the past farmers have mistakenly believed that ravens actually kill lambs, whereas in fact the birds frequent the lower sheep-rearing slopes during lambing because the major source of food for the young ravens is the placenta left by ewes after giving birth. The availability of easy food during the lambing season has caused the raven to evolve an early nesting season: eggs are always in the nest by March, even in early February. The spring-time mortality of lambs, newborn birds and carrion from rabbits, deer and fox provides the young ravens with a high-protein start in life – a life which may continue for over fifty years.

Young ravens roam the moors and mountains in flocks, until they are mature enough to breed. When they eventually pair, they aggressively defend their new territory against eagle, kestrel and peregrine, sometimes to their downfall. The most unfortunate moorland hunting raptor is the buzzard, because ravens seem to derive pleasure from mobbing this slow-moving bird; one of your earliest observations of ravens is likely to be as they harrass a buzzard on its hunting sortie.

Often seen in large numbers on the lower gently sloping moors, **carrion (92)** and **hooded crows** also haunt the crags and cliffs below the mountain summit and have been forced there by persecution from farmers and gamekeepers.

In appearance, the carrion and hooded crows suggest different species, because the carrion crow is all black, but the hooded crow has distinctive grey back and underparts, together with the main black ground colour. However, interbreeding is common and the two birds are really regional races of the same species. The hooded crow is normally associated with the uplands of Ireland, the Isle of Man and north-west Scotland, and the carrion crow fills in the remaining gaps throughout the country. The last Ice Age was probably responsible for the two races of crow, by dividing the stock population for long enough for the plumage variation to evolve, but not long enough for a separate species to develop.

Both the crows are bold in character but when scavenging across moorland slopes they are often mobbed by curlews and oystercatchers. Generally the crows are opportunists, scrounging from rubbish tips and farmyard waste or seizing a dead lamb carcass and it is this style of feeding which accounts for the large populations of both hooded and carrion crow. These birds nest in lower moorland slopes and valleys with farms near by, as well as colonising the crags with raven and peregrine.

Each spring, arriving from southern Europe and Africa at the same time as the dotterel, the **ring ousel** stakes out its territory in the uplands of Britain. In early March the first birds are seen on the moors of south-west England but this region never proves the most popular with the ring ousel: although some stay to breed, others move on and occupy territories in southern Ireland. Ring ousels reach the North Yorkshire Moors and the Lake District by April and the Scottish Highlands by May, seeking out their potential nest sites in the crags and rock faces at 350–650 m/1,150–2,132 ft and even as high as 1,000 m/3,300 ft.

The size of a blackbird (25 cms/10 in), the male ring ousel is similar in shape and appearance, but with silvery feathers on the wing margins and a distinct white band across its lower throat, resembling a vicar's dog-collar; the rest of its plumage is dark sooty black. The female is much browner and the gorget is not so distinct, but both sexes have a pale yellow bill – not a vivid yellow one as sported by the cock blackbird.

Unlike the garden blackbird, the ring ousel is a timid nervous bird, requiring the high open spaces away from habitation. With purposeful direct flight it moves quickly through the ravines and valleys, hedge-hopping the heather before perching on a boulder or isolated hawthorn. These perches are regular look-out posts, from which intruders are scolded with a loud 'tac-tac-tac' alarm note, bursting into a rattling chatter if the intruder fails to leave. The ring ousel frequently chases away crows, buzzards and humans from the crags in defence of nests and territories, which usually include a gulley with bushes and dwarf trees. The nest site varies. Bilberry, heather, grasses and bracken overhang a steep rock face and at the top of the cliff on a ledge, settled below a large boulder, the nest is built of grasses and heather shoots, directly on the ground (**93**).

The ring ousel prefers lofty rock buttresses and higher moorlands, but has a wide nesting range down the moorland slopes. As you walk down from the mountains, you will hear its regular clear piping whistle, which comes from ring ousels with their own territories much lower down.

Within a few days of arriving in the uplands, nesting begins, and by the time the heather on the higher moors begins to turn purple in August, the ring ousels begin their migration south. By early October these upland summer visitors have gone.

Between 8,000 and 16,000 pairs breed in the British Isles, but sadly some of their old haunts are now being deserted. In the last ten years a massive increase in afforestation has caused the habitat to change and the ring ousel is one of the many birds showing a decline. It is also in increasing competition with the ordinary blackbird for breeding territories because, as our climate has become milder, the blackbird has evolved and extended its range from the valleys up into the hills, where the slopes at 250–510 m/820–1,673 ft are becoming more acceptable for nesting. This is particularly so in Ireland, where there is a limited amount of high ground for the ring ousel to colonise, and during the last hundred years numbers have declined markedly. In the West Country the ring ousel has restricted its range and the decline in the stronghold of Scotland is far from encouraging.

From May onwards with the increase in temperature thousands of insects, including mosquitoes, midges, gnats and flies complete their lifecycle and emerge from the pools and sphagnum moss of the blanket bogs. The general wind, with the up-currents and thermals forming across the moors and cliff faces, sweep thousands of these insects to higher ground where birds have adapted to exploit their arrival.

The **wheatear (98)**, which arrives in Britain from Africa from March onwards, is insectivorous and benefits from the glut of insects in the uplands. When they feed on beetles, flies, midges and moths they bob up and down, flitting from rock to rock, revealing a pure white rump. The males have obvious black cheeks and pearl-grey upperparts with a buffish belly, whereas the females have brown upperparts and their cheeks are dark brown rather than black.

Wheatears dislike tall vegetation and are rare on heather moors, but their numbers increase with altitude where the vegetation becomes sparse or the surface is broken by rocky outcrops and boulders are strewn about. In most upland country the wheatear's nesting territory ranges from between 300 m/1,000 ft to over 1,000 m/3,300 ft but it is always where the vegetation is short.

92

93

94

95

92 Carrion crows are often seen feeding on pheasant or rabbit carcases and even still-born lambs.

93 The normally shy and nervous ring ousel becomes aggressive during the breeding season, vigorously defending its nest from any intruder, including humans.

94 The reddish-brown plumage of the male red grouse provides particularly effective camouflage in its usual moorland habitat. Only the red eye-wattles and white legs give the bird away.

95 Ravens usually nest on sheltered, rocky ledges or crags, but sometimes use trees, returning to the same site each season until the nest becomes huge.

96 Male golden plover incubating four eggs. It is one of our most handsome waders with gold speckled upperparts.

97 The down-curved bill of the adult curlew is diagnostic whereas that of the chick is straight. The loud clear whistles and bubbling trill of the curlew is heard on moorlands each spring and summer.

98 Wheatears are ever-active, summer visitors, which colonise upland moors, heathlands and coast. Here the male perches on a boulder.

In the British Isles the wheatear is widely distributed with about 80,000 pairs breeding each year; and, coupled with its size, the wheatear becomes ideal food for all the upland birds of prey like merlin, peregrine, short-eared owl and kestrel.

There are many upland species of bird which are scarce on the mountain tops and plateaux but more common on the lower slopes. Dunlin sometimes nest above 750 m/2,500 ft but are mostly found on high peat bogs at around 300 m/1,000 ft.

The **golden plover** is one of our few exclusively upland breeding waders and it is very likely that this bird will be seen while watching for dotterel and snow bunting on the higher mountain tops up to 1,000 m/3,300 ft. Beautifully marked with a spangled black and gold upper body, the plover is also found much lower down the moorland, nesting in the blanket bogs alongside dunlin, but frequently on the well-drained, sloping heather and grass moors at 300–450 m/1,000–1,500 ft.

The golden plover is a familiar sight to many birdwatchers in autumn and winter, when the black underparts have moulted and the bird is feeding on the marshes and lowland arable fields. In the breeding season, when up to 30,000 pairs nest, their camouflage whilst sitting on the eggs is perfect (**96**) and it takes some searching to see them. Very few pairs breed on the south-westerly uplands and in Wales the golden plover is one of the more localised waders with only about 500 pairs. Elenydd is one of the best upland areas for both dunlin and golden plover, which also breed on Plynlimon and in Doethie Mallaen. In Powys, the RSPB has one of its few upland reserves at Lake Vyrnwy where there is a mixture of habitats from upland lake, deciduous and coniferous woodland and heather moor, 300 m/1,000 ft above sea level. Golden plover nest on the reserve in small numbers alongside much larger populations of curlew.

From the Pennines, northwards, populations of golden plover increase, but even here, due to afforestation and agricultural developments, their numbers are falling annually; and as habitats change their vegetative structure, predation on these ground-nesting birds has increased. Only about 430 pairs of golden plover nest in the entire Peak District and 250 of these pairs are confined to the Derbyshire moors, which they share with dunlin and curlew.

In summer, the plaintive bell-like call of the male golden plover as it flies high over the heather is one of the most wonderful sounds of upland country. Earlier, in March, the bird claims territories on gently sloping or flat ground with short vegetation. The golden plover dislikes tall vegetation for nest grounds, and requires total visibility and open ground for the chicks to use as their playground, which is why the bird favours managed burnt grouse moors and limestone grassland in the Pennines. The chicks, which are as beautifully marked as the adults, leave the nest within a few hours of hatching, after which they are fed by both parents on invertebrates and berries until they can fly a month later.

To the majority of birdwatchers, **curlews** are most familiar as the long-legged long-billed bird probing the estuary mud during winter and uttering its long whistle, but as the largest British wader it is one of the more spectacular and common of our moorland birds, returning to the uplands from the coast each February. Curlews nest at altitudes of 300–600 m/1,000–2,000 ft in the heather, grass or blanket bog areas, although they prefer undulating grassland pasture and marshy meadows. On the higher semi-montane ground the density of breeding curlews is always lower, but up to 70,000 pairs nest on the uplands of the British Isles in good seasons.

Curlews are unmistakable birds, unless you are on the moors of Shetland where the very similar smaller whimbrel breeds. The long curved bill and streaky brown plumage are diagnostic and could not belong to any other bird (97). Curlew-spotting is a magical experience on an April morning when the air is still: then their bubbling, wild, free song carries across the moor and the males perform their territorial and courtship flights. Watch for the male flying low and deliberately over the moor, followed by a sudden vertical climb on rapidly quivering wings. At the height of its climb the curlew hovers and flutters before gliding down on extended wings, trilling, gurgling and bubbling all the way to the ground and ending with the namesake 'coo-er-leew'. This attractive flight is repeatedly performed and once pair-bonding is secured, both birds are seen gliding side by side across the heather before breeding begins.

The four blotched, variable brown-green eggs are laid in an open scoop during April and May, and although quick to leave their nests as danger approaches, both birds vigorously defend their aerial and ground territory from crows or birds of prey. Throughout the breeding period, the adults are nervous and alert and the non-sitting bird remains on guard in the territory whilst the other is brooding.

By July and early August, the breeding grounds become deserted and the adults begin to moult, congregating in flocks on the moors and dispersing to feed in the neighbouring countryside at night. While on the uplands both young and adults feed on worms, invertebrates and their larvae, fruits and seeds, whereas in the winter on estuaries, the diet is chiefly molluscs, small crabs and marine worms.

Heather moorlands have for centuries been associated with grouse shooting and, because large areas of moor are specially managed for **red grouse (94)**, the habitat remains suitable also for many other moorland plants and animals. The red grouse, which is endemic to Britain, feeds mainly on heather shoots, supplemented with crowberry and bilberry. The favourite heather shoots are those which are young and green on plants up to four years old. Red grouse prefers older, denser heather for nesting sites, and because it is so dependent on heather, landowners manage their moors by rotational burning to make sure that over half a million pairs continue to breed on the heather uplands of south-west and northern England and throughout Ireland, Wales and Scotland.

Generally red grouse occupies the moorland at 300–600 m/1,000–2,000 ft. From here to the summits the ptarmigan colonises. Although the presence of red grouse is used by many ornithologists to determine an upland moorland habitat, this is not always accurate, since the bird also nests at sea level on extensive sand-dune heaths of the Sands of Forvie National Nature Reserve, encompassing the estuary of the River Ythan in Aberdeenshire. Here, within 1,018 ha/2,515 acres of mixed habitat, red grouse selects the dune heath vegetation with heather and crowberry, next to the largest breeding eider duck population in Britain and numerous shelduck on the sand-dunes.

The red grouse is a large plump bird with a small head, short tail and rounded wings. When observed at a distance, the dark reddish-brown plumage of the cock bird, standing on a heather bush or rock for a better view, sometimes looks black, but in this position the white-feathered legs may be clearly seen.

The moors on lime-rich soils seem to be the most productive for red grouse and some of the North Yorkshire Moors are the best grouse moors in the country, wherever the heather grows away from the acidic sandstone rock. Heather on the limestone carries more pairs each spring and the broods are larger and seem to survive better. Productive grouse moors consist of a patchwork of heather which is managed by burning in strips, creating different heights of growth within a small area. The tall heather is for nest cover whereas the shorter heather provides succulent shoots.

If grouse management were to cease, then afforestation or sheep grazing would probably increase, and as the conifers and coarse moorland grasses spread, the heather and more natural moorland vegetation would decrease. The golden plover, curlew, lapwing, dunlin, merlin and hen harrier would also decline as their preferred nesting habitats became swallowed up by an alien conifer plantation or the nests were trampled by hundreds of roaming sheep. Moorland birds have learnt that the grouse-managed moors are some of the most suitable for their own breeding territories and here some of the best upland birdwatching can be enjoyed.

For the conservationist, management of the moors for red grouse guarantees the survival of this species, and also significantly improves the chances of the upland heather moor surviving as a habitat. Moorland owners are facing serious pressures from forms of commercial development, but red grouse moors are important to the overall environment and successful breeding of rare upland birds.

Poor management of the heather will contribute to population declines. Unfortunately gamekeepers do not seem to be as fully aware of this fact as they should be. Many still believe that the fall in numbers of red grouse is due to predation by birds of prey – namely the golden eagle, merlin, hen harrier and short-eared owl. These birds are natural hunters and it is true that some adult red grouse and chicks fall victim to birds of prey. However, these birds require large hunting territories and in a semi-natural environment such as a grouse moor, the ratio of the hunter to the hunted will be in balance or certainly in the favour of the grouse. The few grouse taken by a bird of prey only means that a few less grouse die of starvation, since apart from death by the gun, starvation and predation in winter are the main causes of death.

The red grouse is highly territorial and like the ptarmigan of the mountain plateaux the males set up breeding territories in the autumn, which they maintain throughout the winter and into spring when they begin their displays in February and March. Those birds failing to claim territories are banished to the marginal areas where food and cover is poor and death by starvation or predation is inevitable by natural selection. The gamekeeper should be aware that grouse falling victim to birds of prey are normally the weaker birds, who could not claim a territory and are therefore genetically not the most suitable for continued breeding.

Although protected since 1954 by the Protection of Birds Act, the large **hen harrier (101)** is today still unjustifiably and illegally persecuted by those who shoot the grouse moors. The bird has already made one recovery from near extinction in Britain, but the expansion of the hen harrier population since 1950 is meeting with a decline as a result of habitat destruction and continued shooting. Unfortunately for the bird, the hen harrier is a moorland specialist and just like the red grouse requires heather moorland where it takes young and weak birds. Research has proved that on a well-managed and -stocked grouse moor, a single pair of hen harriers reduces the number of grouse available to the huntsman by about fifteen birds, but this is not a reduction large enough to warrant any killing of the harriers, even if it were legal.

In the sixteenth century the hen harrier was a bird of open country. As forests were felled it generally increased its distribution and during the eighteenth century was actually known to nest close to towns and cities. In 1825 very few counties in the British Isles were without pairs of breeding hen harriers despite persecution since 1800. There followed in the nineteenth and early twentieth centuries a ruthless campaign by gamekeepers to control any predator. Between 1820 and 1860 the bird almost became extinct from northern England to southern Scotland, and if the account is true for two Ayrshire estates, where 351 hen harriers were killed between June 1850 and November 1854, it is easy to understand how this low level was reached.

At the beginning of the First World War the hen harrier was extinct except for two pairs in Orkney and the Uists and a few pairs in Ireland; only after the Second World War was there any sign that populations had increased and recolonised some of the old haunts, including the Highlands by 1946 and southern Scotland by 1950, when it also began to increase in Ireland. During 1962, three nests were discovered in North Wales and two aspects of the hen harrier were recognised. One was that this magnificent bird would fight back for survival and secondly that they were nomadic, wandering birds by nature, since the increase of the Orkney colony was largely responsible for the wider-ranging recolonisation. This expansion has continued, largely aided by the establishment by the Forestry Commission of conifer plantations in Scotland and northern England since 1920. Hen harriers prefer good groundcover for nesting and were quick to colonise this new habitat with its abundant supply of prey. The value of this nesting habitat is short-lived because the canopy completely covers the hunting territory as the trees mature. However since new plantations were being planted at an astonishing rate, the hen harriers soon discovered other nesting habitats.

Today 400–500 pairs breed in the British Isles, representing almost half of the European population, and in parts of north-west Britain the density is increasing, counteracted by declines in other areas, particularly in the all-time stronghold in Orkney. As moorlands are being reclaimed for upland agriculture, so the suitability of habitat and range of prey changes and because the hen harrier is at the top of the food chain, any loss of usual prey causes the harrier population to fall. In central and southern Ireland these two factors are responsible for the recent population crash in what was one of the other remaining strongholds for hen harrier. Co. Wicklow, with its many conifer plantations, still offers good nesting sites for the bird, which can frequently be seen hunting on the open moorland. In Northern Ireland's Co. Fermanagh, in the vicinity of Lough Navan Forest, hen harriers can be found – again in association with red grouse.

Towards the end of March and early April, on moorland and at the same altitude at which golden plover and red grouse prefer to breed, pairs of hen harriers circle widely looking for potential nest sites. The two birds, apart from their silhouette against the sky, are completely different in their plumage. The female at 48 cm/19 in is larger than the 43-cm/17-in male; his pale silvery-grey upperparts and black wing tips, with grey-white underparts, are very characteristic. Both sexes have an owl-like face, piercing yellow eyes and a hooked bill with black tip and long yellow legs and toes, but the female is dull brown and very buzzard-like in her markings, with broad dark bands on the tail and a distinctive white rump.

Display flights are breathtaking and completely in contrast with the usual graceful, buoyant low-level flight with abrupt changes of direction as the harrier hunts for food. In display, the male soars to over 30 m/100 ft and begins his dancing – a sky-diving routine, in which he somersaults, rolls and twists, followed by a dive to earth, pulling out at the last moment and soaring skywards again to repeat the show.

The nest site is chosen by the female and is generally in coarse heather or in thick vegetation which has been flattened by the feet of both birds.

Whilst the female is incubating the male hunts for prey, which is mainly small birds, such as meadow pipit, skylark, wheatear, ring ousel, and mammals like young rabbits, mice and voles. The male hunts by sound as well as sight; he rarely chases flying prey, but prefers to hover like a barn owl, capturing his prey by surprise before flying back to the female on the nest. As the male approaches the nest with prey in his talons the sitting female leaves the eggs and rises into the air to meet her mate. Approaching from beneath and perfectly co-ordinated, she flicks over on to her back, extends a leg and either catches the food with her claw as the male drops it, or snatches it from him, before righting herself and returning to the nest. This perfectly executed 'food pass' always takes place near the nest and helps to maintain a bond between the male and the hen bird as well as providing one of the most spectacular sights of upland birdwatching.

Hunting low over the heather moor, making short glides between deliberate wing beats, the hen harrier has a characteristic shape with long narrow tail, elongated body and broad wings. It usually floats low over the heather, methodically searching and listening; then with a skilful turn, it drops on the prey, employing its long slender legs as lethal grappling irons.

Although they are quick to colonise new conifer plantations, the increasing afforestation of Britain's moorland provides ideal shelter for only about ten seasons, and the blocks of conifer are so huge and highly concentrated today that the open hunting grounds are disappearing. Hen harriers have deserted many moorland regions and their population has become so fragmented that they are failing to colonise recently planted areas, and they are already twenty times more scarce than the buzzard in Britain.

Birdwatching is full of surprises and one of the most interesting relationships between moorland birds is that of the **merlin** and hen harrier which occupy the same heather moorland territory. Ranging from 27–33 cm/10–13 in, the smallest merlins are the size of a blackbird and they are our most diminutive raptor. On the open heather moors, pairs of nesting merlin actually nest within the same territory as hen harrier which do not attack the smaller bird of prey even though they compete for food; and the swift agile merlin will sometimes catch a meadow pipit which has been flushed by the hunting harrier. No theory has been confirmed as to why these two birds live in harmony on the moors, but it is likely that the smaller merlin obtains some protection from the arrangement. Although the merlin defends its territory vigorously, even mobbing golden eagle, buzzard and raven, it is also attacked itself by peregrine and goshawk from the lowlands visiting the moors for grouse; so perhaps merlin nesting close to a larger bird of prey like the hen harrier obtain immunity from aerial attacks.

Male merlins (105) are slate blue above, with streaked off-white underparts and red-brown flecks on the breast; the tail has broad bands and is black-tipped. Similar to a kestrel,

99

100

101

99 The elegant greenshank is a bird of bleak remote country but even here, habitat disturbance is threatening the future breeding of this species in Britain.

100 The summer plumage of the dunlin is characterised by the black belly and brown upperparts and it remains unobtrusive on the damp moorlands of upland Britain during summer.

101 Any small animal up to the size of a hare can be seized by the powerful talons of the female hen harrier.

the female and juveniles (**103**) are dark brown with a banded tail and streaked and flecked underparts. Both birds have yellow legs and toes which seem too big for the size of the body but are perfect weapons when they are hunting and flying low over heather catching meadow pipit, whinchat and ring ousel, flushed from their cover.

Like all other moorland birds of prey, the merlin has a large territory in which to find sufficient food. The hunting radius is about 4 km/2½ miles and includes the fringes of the moorland such as upland farms and small copses, where it will catch up to two birds daily for itself. For a small bird this is a large prey intake, but with high metabolic rate and large hunting territory, a great deal of energy is expended and needs to be replaced.

Those birds breeding in Britain are at the southernmost limit of their nesting range and moorland is the ideal natural

103

102 Black cock displaying or lekking with blocks of conifers in the distance which have become responsible for the birds' decline.

103 When merlin chicks are about twenty days old, they begin to tear up their own food. The female no longer having to perform this task for them, can join the male hunting for prey.

104 Unlike most other owls, the short-eared owl regularly hunts by day across rough grassland and moor.

105 When perched, the male merlin appears more compact than other falcons. The dead meadow pipit is one of the many small birds taken in low-level flight.

105

habitat. Unfortunately the merlin has been declining in numbers throughout Britain for the last fifteen years, and the total population is 350–500 pairs; the healthiest numbers are in the north-east Pennines, the grouse moors of Yorkshire and Northumbria, and north up to central and east Scotland. The southern Pennines and Dartmoor and Exmoor are almost without merlin today and in north and west Scotland it is a rare breeding bird. The most alarming decline is in Wales where once-healthy populations have crashed since 1976. The RSPB attributes this decline to habitat loss. Unlike the hen harrier the merlin only suffers minimal persecution on grouse moors but the habitat loss elsewhere is causing drastic national reductions. In mid Wales 12 per cent of all moorland has disappeared: since 1973 two-thirds has been lost to farming development and a third to afforestation. Powys (formerly Radnor and Montgomery) always used to be rich in moorland but in 1971–85, the RSPB surveyed 210,000 ha/518,910 acres and found that in certain areas the open moorland had completely disappeared along with its specialist moorland birds. As conifer plantations grow they fragment the moorland; and when this is combined with ploughing of upland grassland, breeding territories are permanently destroyed, and birds such as golden plover, curlew, red grouse, hen harrier and the merlin become threatened. The merlin lives for only about ten years, and as the number of sexually mature birds falls by natural means, younger adults are failing to maintain populations. The danger is that this will become an irreversible trend.

There is a strong case for the extension of government grants for Environmentally Sensitive Areas, which aim to preserve areas of lowland farmland where the lapwing is declining, to include the moorland farmer, because the lapwing is forsaking the lowland arable fields for the upland pastures and moors. If this habitat continues to be destroyed by local farming developments, the lapwing will have nowhere to go; and the elusive upland merlin will share the same fate. It would be far more worthwhile to subsidise upland farmers and encourage them to develop the declining habitat and preserve the wildlife so dependent on it than to produce a greater crop of cereal to add to an already bulging grain store. Only if conservation societies and birdwatchers pressurise the appropriate ministers, Forestry Commission and farmers, will the birdwatcher continue to be able to enjoy the agile flight and fearless character of the merlin on British moorlands.

The **short-eared owl** (104) is commoner and easier to see than most owls because it hunts during the daytime. Long narrow wings and bouncing, buoyant flight cause the short-eared owl to be mistaken for the female hen harrier, especially as the owl is light brown and has a streaked plumage, but the owl is typified by its large domed head. Like the hen harrier, the owl uses a glide, listen and grab technique, and hunts for voles in the young forestry plantations where up to several thousand can be caught each season, before it leaves the uplands and migrates to the coast for the winter, hunting over saltmarsh and sand-dune.

This owl is chiefly found in the north of England, Scotland and Wales. The fringes of the moors are favourite hunting grounds, including farm tracks, forest margins and upland grazing pasture, where it flies low over the ground, quartering up and down with purposeful wing beats and periodically gliding for a few metres. A popular hunting technique is to perch on a Forestry Commission fencepost and, without any movement, survey the dense vegetation with huge yellow eyes. The stout, muscular, feather-covered legs are then clearly visible, as are the long needle-sharp claws which grab the prey as the owl launches headlong from the fencepost into the thick vegetation.

The availability of field voles completely controls the population density of short-eared owls because this rodent forms their staple diet. When voles are everywhere, which happens after a peak breeding year once every four years, the owls move in from the surrounding moorland and begin hunting in organised groups. This results in extra broods of owls being reared and extra-large clutches of ten or more eggs being laid.

Nature always controls any imbalance and when the density of voles gets too high, they just stop breeding; with extra predation, the population quickly crashes, so that next season unless the surplus owls have moved to their own territory, competition for food is high and many younger birds fail to breed for a season.

During March birdwatchers will observe the short-eared owls performing their 'wing clapping' display which normally begins early on a warm spring evening. For up to fifteen minutes the male owl flies around its territory in wide circles, uttering his low 'booo-booo-booo' call. When it gets to a reasonable height it brings its wings down and claps them together several times beneath its tail, tumbling through the air as it does so and finally joining his mate in the ground vegetation.

The owl's nest is little more than a scrape in the ground and during incubation the female rarely leaves the nest and the male catches all the prey for her.

Once breeding is over the short-eared owls leave the moors and fly to the coast where their diet changes. In winter it is common to see the owl catching waders and finches from a winter flock with an impressive display of skill for such a large bird.

The peregrine, hen harrier, merlin and short-eared owl all occupy similar zones of the moorland, the peregrine preferring the higher crags. Within the habitat they compete for food, which is largely small birds nesting in the heather or amongst the rocks. On moorlands in the southern Pennines, the central and western Highlands and the north and west of Ireland these birds have an additional source of food, the **twite**. Shaped like a typical finch, the male is dark brown with a pink rump, whereas females are universally brown with a tawny throat. Damp moorland above 300 m/1,000 ft with good visibility is the twite's preferred habitat but its liking for seeds often takes it to the rough grassland of the moorland fringe.

Although the moorland birds have adapted to the declining moorland habitat, with a fluctuating degree of success, the black grouse is one bird which initially benefited from afforestation. It prefers the margins between moorland and woodland, especially young coniferous or birch woodland. This habitat is widespread but although in the last century the black cock could be found throughout Britain, a contraction of range now confines the bird to Exmoor, Wales, the Pennines and throughout Scotland, where its populations are variable.

One reason for the decline of the black grouse is that the conifer plantations have become too concentrated and densely planted. Moorland is important to this bird particularly during the mating and breeding season because the female prefers thick scrub or heather for her nest site and later accompanies her chicks to the damper moorland with bog myrtle, rushes and straggling heather bushes for cover. The male uses the moorland for lekking, the black grouse's most fascinating behaviour.

During March to April in the crepuscular hours, male black grouse move up on to the open moorland to traditional flat display areas, the 'arena', and here they display or 'lek'. Within the large arenas, the males stake their territories which may be visited by other intruding males, or by hen birds. Up to twelve cock birds may attempt to hold territories within the arena, each competing strongly against the other (102). Mating takes place within the arena and females are particularly attracted to fighting males, especially those in the centre of the arena. Black grouse do not form pair bonds and males attempt to mate with any female walking through their territory. Lekking is the seasonal opportunity for the males to display their virility and the females to select the best males for mating.

Traditional lekking sites on the moors have been used for over fifty years. Part of the reason for the bird's decline in

Scotland is that huge tracts of conifer have been planted indiscriminately across the ancient lekking sites. Afforestation helped the black grouse to increase its numbers at first, but by converting moorland into temporary forests on a massive scale, man has rapidly denied the black grouse the opportunity for its ancient courtship ritual, vital for survival, in large areas of Wales and Scotland in particular.

It is not just the rarer moorland and upland birds which are worth watching. Some of the most interesting birds are the waders; and during April a walk on the hills listening to the wild songs of lapwing and the rippling call of the redshank is memorable. The snipe, a bird of the wetter moorlands and lowland marsh, provides a highlight with a drumming display that echoes across bog and grassland. Watch the bird climb in the sky, calling continuously and then diving towards earth on winnowing wings. Held at right angles to the body, on the downward flight, are two outer tail feathers which, as air quickly passes over them, produce a resonant bleating sound referred to as drumming.

Snipe lay their dark, heavily marked eggs in a rush or grass tussock lined with dry grasses, somewhere on the upland bogs. Some of these upland bogs hardly fit into the category of uplands, yet the low rugged moors, grass and heather complex mixed with permanently waterlogged blanket bogs cover most of Caithness and Sutherland just above 300 m/1,000 ft. This vast area is called the Flow Country and, together with the coastal bogs of the Hebrides, Shetland and Orkney is an important habitat for many localised and rare breeding birds found nowhere else in Britain. Greylag goose, wigeon, common scoter, wood sandpiper, Temminck's stint, dunlin and greenshank all inhabit the blanket bogs and although the soil is generally infertile, because of the deposits of peat and excessive leaching, the waterlogged peat of Caithness and Sutherland is vital to moorland birds.

The Flow Country is an ancient habitat, thousands of years old and the largest area of this unique environment found anywhere in the world. Conservationists have acclaimed the area as being in the 'big-league' of world ecosystems, as important in its own way as the Brazilian rainforests and African Serengeti. Looking down from an aircraft, it is easier to understand how this area of Scotland received its name because the peat landscape comprises large pools and shallow lakes joined by flat moorland (**106**). The areas of water are formed in arcs radiating from a common central point and appear to flow like the tongue of an advancing glacier. The areas of water are in fact largely static, with little flowing movement, and the origin of these arcs of water is not fully understood. Currently there is national outrage over the future of this unique upland area, because since 1980 private industry, funding forestry development, together with the Forestry Commission, have drained and afforested thousands of acres of Flow Country at such a rate that it has been impossible to monitor the effect on the bird populations. By 1988, 32,600 ha/80,500 acres will have been afforested, representing 18 per cent of the total habitat.

In July 1987, the Nature Conservancy Council, the government's own official watchdog, called for an immediate ban on further forestry planting of the Flow Country. Their Chairman said, 'The peatlands already lost to forestry represents the most massive loss of important wildlife habitat in Britain since the Second World War.'

During winter in the Flow Country the mosaic of lochs, lochans, blanket bogs, rivers and heather moors are bleak, with the appearance of an Arctic habitat found further north. Red grouse brave the environment along with the wandering, hunting golden eagle or crow. In the spring, the entire habitat changes, with hundreds of waders and wildfowl flying in to breed. Golden plover, dunlin and greenshank are the main waders, all of which are ground-nesting birds.

Between 500 and 1,000 pairs of **greenshank** breed in Britain, and until forestry development occurred, 70 per cent of this population nested on the flows of Caithness and rugged moors of Sutherland. The female makes shallow nest scrapes in short heather and lichen or on slightly raised rocky ground, often with a stone or boulder behind (**99**); the nests are extremely difficult to find, partly because of the amazing camouflage of the sitting birds.

The plumage of a greenshank is ash grey but, in the breeding season, each feather on the upperparts and head has a black centre and the birds have a mottled appearance. Other characteristic features include the distinct white rump, dark wings when in flight and the light green legs that give the bird its name. Breeding in the Flow Country and elsewhere in the Highlands the greenshank nests from sea level to around 600 m/2,000 ft although the greatest density occurs below 300 m/1,000 ft; and in Caithness and Sutherland the nests are on the low-lying moors.

The male birds arrive first from Africa, usually towards the end of March and, following a courtship ritual involving aerial chases and hopping on the ground, the females lay their eggs so that they will hatch by late May. Upon hatching both adults lead the young to suitable feeding grounds where the family probes for invertebrates in shallow water.

At 18 cm/7 in the **dunlin** (**100**) is much smaller than the greenshank. It is the rarest of the common moorland waders: curlew outnumber it by ten pairs to one, and for every pair of dunlin there are up to thirty-five pairs of lapwing. Consequently many moorland regions are without breeding dunlin at all; of the 8,000 pairs nesting in Britain, 20 per cent nest within 184,000 ha/455,000 acres of the Flow Country and are semi-colonial, favouring peat pools with mossy margins.

Very few dunlin nest south of the Pennines and the few that do are confined to Dartmoor; these have become the most southerly breeding colony of this species anywhere in the world. The dunlin is an attractive wader but in the winter on the coast, when it is most commonly seen, it is in grey and white plumage and more difficult to identify positively. In spring plumage both birds are chestnut with a black area on the lower breast and black markings on the upperparts. The bill curves slightly downwards.

Our breeding population of dunlin spends the winter on English coasts, or further south in Europe or Africa. Each May they return to the breeding grounds where they begin their rise-and-fall display flights with occasional aerial chase. Typically four eggs are laid in a nest – which is little more than a delicate hollow within a grass tussock – and after three weeks the young are quickly able to feed themselves. In July the dunlin begin to leave the uplands, in order to spend autumn in a different habitat in milder climates.

The golden plover nests in the Flow Country and although one of the most common of the waders of the area, it is rare in other parts of Europe. Now its existence in the Flow Country is threatened. In 1987 the Forestry Commission authorised conifer-planting on an area of the Flows known to be the

106

breeding grounds of over 600 pairs of golden plover. Even though Forestry Commission is not primarily concerned with landscape or wildlife conservation, and its sole objective appears to be to develop afforestation to supply timber for commercial gain, under the Countryside Acts it has a responsibility to 'have regard to the desirability of conserving the natural beauty and amenity of the countryside'. It is a huge landowner, and the methods and procedures used to achieve its objectives need to be examined and reviewed; clearly, a more flexible policy is required with more sympathy towards a habitat and its wildlife. What it is partly responsible for in the Flow Country is without question counter to conservation interests and even threatens the very existence of both habitat and wildlife.

Apart from common species such as mallard that nest in the Flow Country, the not-so-common teal and even scarcer wigeon feed and nest on the waterlogged complex; as does the misnamed black diving duck, the common scoter. Other rare aquatic birds, such as black-throated diver, have some of their few British breeding sites in this habitat and their presence comprises the entire EEC's breeding population. All the moorland birds of prey breed in the Flow Country and, together with certain rarer aquatic birds, are listed as requiring special protection under the EEC Directive on the Conservation of Wild Birds. Nowhere else in Britain can this wide variety of

106 The blanket peat bogs of the Flow Country with drainage ditches destroying dubh lochans prior to afforestation.

moorland birds be found, but forestry has already destroyed the feeding, nesting and roosting grounds of 20 per cent of the nesting area of the most important wading-bird populations; and the future of other types of birds in the Flow Country seems destined to be equally threatened.

But although savaged the Flow Country is not completely lost. Societies and official bodies such as the Worldwide Fund for Nature (formerly World Wildlife Fund), the RSPB and the Nature Conservancy Council are fighting together to make sure that what remains does not succumb to conifers, which would be drastic not only for wildlife but also eventually for the local population who can gain employment only at the planting and felling stages. It is already obvious to the people campaigning for their protection that the moorlands, peat flows and lochans of Caithness and Sutherland should be designated an Environmentally Sensitive Area (ESA). The 1986 Agricultural Act states that for any area to be given ESA status it must be of tremendous conservation interest and also support farming communities. Since the Flow Country is the largest primeval habitat in Britain and one of the largest single expanses of upland blanket bog in the world, its conservation value must be undisputed; and it provides the livelihood of crofters, fishermen, moorland and sheep farmers. It thus meets both requirements of the Act.

If the Flow Country were to become an ESA, then under the grant scheme farmers and landowners would be financed to preserve and improve the environment by carrying out management for wildlife on their land. Additional grants under the Agricultural Act are offered for tourist development and since people visit the Flows for the wild scenery and its unique birdlife, there would be scope for farmers to diversify. Since the first ESAs were only designated in March 1987, they are still a new concept of preserving both a habitat and its wildlife. However, in the Flow Country, because of pressure from conservation groups, the Forestry Commission is already having to make concessions without the area being awarded ESA status. From February 1987 it has been obliged to consult with the NCC for any proposed new afforestation in the Flow Country. Once this becomes regulated, or restricted to alternative areas of Scotland, where minimum habitat damage occurs, this outstanding upland area can be left to survive. Designated an ESA, the local community, natural habitat and the wildlife could develop in harmony and the future of all interests would be guaranteed.

As remnants of the wilderness of the British Isles, the mountains and moorlands, with their associated bogs, are part of our heritage. It is surely more important to work for their long-term preservation than to destroy one more habitat for short-term gain, so extirpating an elusive, fascinating birdlife for good.

CHAPTER 8

RIVERS AND STREAMS

There is something adventurous and exciting about tracking a river down to its source. Some rivers begin as a small bubbling pool surrounded by trees, such as the official source of the Thames at Trewsbury Mead, near Cirencester; others begin in upland bog, such as the Wye and the Severn which rise beneath the Plynlymmon mountain in Wales. The vast majority of our rivers begin on high ground, perhaps as a spring filtering from a rock face or a slender, glistening, ripple of water forming on a mountainside. On their way to the sea they are fed by countless tributaries, forming ribbons of life which constantly change along their course until, flooding into the sea at the estuary, their dynamic energy is almost spent.

As the ice retreated ten thousand years ago, Britain's landscape was wet. The gouging power of the ice had bulldozed vast U-shaped valleys, changed the courses of rivers and created lakes by forming dams of ice and glacial debris. Huge quantities of water were produced from the melting ice, with the result that in upland Britain any natural hollow became filled with water, forming corries and lakes. In the south-east of England, just beyond the reach of the fingers of the glaciers, the effects were different, as mountains of ice were not melting and deep valleys had not been gouged; but with the retreat of the ice, the sea levels rose by over 90 m/300 ft and, as much of lowland England became flooded, wetlands formed.

Today freshwater is probably the most widely distributed habitat in Britain and yet it covers only 1 per cent of the land mass (although the percentage is greater in Ireland). Freshwater habitats are diverse, including lakes, ponds, gravel pits and reservoirs, all characterised by expanses of open water; rivers and streams represent the mobile part of the habitat. We have seen how habitats change by natural succession and this occurs, too, with lakes and other static or slow-moving expanses of water, where silt and organic debris builds up, especially at the margins, and willows, reeds and moisture-loving plants colonise, eventually stabilising and reclaiming the land from the water so that a wetland habitat is formed. These include reedbeds, marshland, fens and bogs and they all have a distinct bird community.

The freshwater habitats of the British Isles have been modified by man and rivers have become a vital part of our lives. Industrial and domestic water supplies are drawn from them, sewage and manufacturing effluent is poured back in and flood waters are diverted through the natural river channels. In certain parts of Britain the force of the river current is harnessed to generate electricity; and rivers also provide places for recreations such as walking, boating, angling and bird-watching. The rivers and their associated flood meadows provide a habitat for a large number of specialised birds. As our wetlands are drained and reclaimed for agricultural and industrial land – a process which began with the Romans, who drained parts of the Fens, Pevensey Levels and Romney Marshes for farmland – these birds are under a greater threat than many other species.

The fertility or mineral richness of the water partly determines the plants and animals able to live in the river and is regulated by the mineral salts leached out from the rocks and soil along the course of the river. In Britain the small rivers rising from chalk are called chalk streams. These have a higher level of dissolved calcium, nitrates and carbon dioxide in them than those rivers running over hard upland rocks which do not erode rapidly and release few minerals into the water. Chalk streams are rich in small invertebrate life, they are extremely clear and, because of their relatively fast flow, they are well aerated and free from the accumulation of silt. Any water rising from chalk or limestone is typically hard and in some cases, such as the Caher river in Co. Clare, western Ireland, the lime is redeposited on the river-bed as the river flows along its route. The quality of the river is also influenced by the rate of flow. Upland rivers and streams tumbling and crashing over rocks have a high oxygen content, since turbulence helps to aerate the water.

From source to estuary, all rivers have four distinct zones. A river starts with the headstream way up in the hills or mountains, which is frequently made of rivulets so imperceptible that several have to run together before it becomes obvious that a stream has begun its journey. Once these headstreams have joined they cut a deeper wider channel with a constant bubbling flow which, depending on the gradient, includes rapids and waterfalls where the current sweeps all but the largest stones along and prevents plantlife from rooting.

Below the headstreams are the upper reaches of the river; these are sometimes called the troutbeck because brown trout inhabit this region, although the current is still very fierce.

Further down its course, as the river reaches flatter country, the current decreases but the volume increases as countless other streams run into the main flow and form the middle or minnow reaches. Plant debris, including leaves which have fallen or blown into the river, decompose, add nutrients to the water and become digested by snails and other invertebrates which find the moderate current flow more acceptable. The banks of the river have become stabilised by the middle reaches and aquatic plants are able to colonise and help silt up pools in the slower-moving regions close to the bank.

Below the middle reaches, the current slackens even more and the volume of water continues to increase as the river widens to form the well-known slow-moving lower reaches or bream zone of the river, where silt accumulates on the bends and fills in bays, eroded by winter floods, enabling reeds and rushes to colonise. Water plants can easily tolerate the gentle current and fish are at their most dense in this region of the river.

Apart from chalk streams, most rivers at their lower reaches are cloudy, due to detritus in suspension. On the river bank the trees are well established and line the banks, which are dense with vegetation or cleared to provide grazing land on the flood meadows. Along the lower reaches of most rivers in the British Isles the landscape is one of fields with hedgerow margins mixed with spinneys and glades; but it is also the region of human colonisation, with villages and towns increasing every year. Consequently the greatest concentration of pollution enters the rivers from here down to the estuary, in the form of human, industrial and agricultural effluent, which affects the majority of the rivers in the British Isles.

Finally all rivers enter the sea. As they approach the coast,

107

107 River Itchen, Martyr Worthy, Hampshire. A good example of a fast-flowing, clear chalk stream with abundant submerged and bankside vegetation.

many meander slowly over flat ground where they begin to deposit their heavy loads of silt. The silt which the river carries down to the sea is eventually deposited, forming the mud flats or mud bars found around all our estuaries (Ch. 11).

Although generally conforming to this neat division of zones, rivers are individually different and many rise and flow through a tremendous range of countryside, passing over equally diverse types of rock, which release their minerals into the water. Consequently rivers in south-east England often lack bubbling upper reaches and have a completely different character from those of western or northern Britain.

Whereas many of the chalk streams remain high in calcium salts, despite flowing for many kilometres over non-calcareous gravel and sands, other rivers change their chemical qualities throughout the various zones as they flow down to the sea. Britain's longest river is the Severn, which has its source in acidic upland Wales. Nutrients and mineral salts from different soils enter the river as the Severn flows through the agricultural regions of eastern Wales and through the plains of Shropshire, and gradually it becomes more alkaline and richer in animal and plantlife all the way to Gloucester, where it becomes tidal.

The Severn is polluted by man, especially along its lower reaches, but the most recent threat is to the estuarine area of the river, which covers 20,000 ha/50,000 acres: a barrage is proposed across the estuary from Lavernock Point in Wales to Brean Down on the English coast. The barrage is designed to generate hydro-electric power on the ebb tide, but it would reduce the tidal range up-river by half. The intertidal mud flats are used by various wintering waders, including 12 per cent of the British population of dunlin, and the barrage and the alteration of tidal levels will affect these feeding grounds, with a completely unknown but huge impact on the habitat. The Severn Barrage is still only a proposal at the time of writing, but it is one of the biggest construction projects ever planned in Britain. Ornithologists and conservation societies need to be aware of the threat to large populations of birds requiring these mud flats as feeding stations in order to survive each winter.

Although it is difficult to imagine the magnitude of the thaw as the ice sheets melted ten thousand years ago, early spring birdwatching in mountain country, especially the Highlands, gives one the glimmer of an idea of what it must have been like, when, as winter fades, the snow begins to melt, glacial corries overflow and numerous trickles of water begin their journey to the lower valleys. The melting snow adds to the volume of water in the hillside streams which initially bubble gently, but within a few hundred metres of their precipitous journey become raging foaming torrents, carrying any loose debris in their wake down towards the larger valley rivers. This can be witnessed anywhere along the Spey Valley, which receives the melt water from the winter snow of the Cairngorms and Grampians in a series of tributaries such as the River Feshie, making the River Spey one of the largest water catchments in Scotland.

Breathlessly gushing down the mountainside, the cold, clear water of the mountain stream gives a touch of quicksilver to the dull rocky terrain. It weaves its way around large boulders and cascades over ledges where the ground has eroded to produce a waterfall. It is constantly changing through the year: during the driest weeks of summer the stream becomes a mere thread of water, but swelled by autumn and winter storms the upland stream rapidly changes character.

It is March and the upland stream rushes downhill, charged with large volumes of melt water from the hills. The bubbling call of a curlew drifts across the moor and meadow pipits continuously perform their song flights. Alder catkins hang from the bare branches of the overhanging trees. The river is ever active; and so is the plump, rounded bird with stumpy tail sitting on a boulder in the middle of the current, bobbing up and down on strong legs every few seconds: a movement which gives the **dipper** its name. It is one of the most characteristic birds of upland rivers and streams or lochs and tarns in mountainous country.

About 18 cm/7 in long, the dipper is slightly smaller than the song thrush. A resident and sedentary bird, it can be found along the rivers and streams of northern and western England, Wales, Scotland and Ireland, at altitudes of 300–600 m/1,000–2,000 ft, although some dippers occupy stretches of river at 1,000 m/3,300 ft. In certain parts of northern England and Scotland, where the uplands drop rapidly to sea level, dippers may be seen feeding on insects around the seaweed stranded at high tide; these birds nest only a few metres away from the beach. You will get the best view of the bird when the dipper perches on mid-stream boulders, but since the sexes are similar and many pairs occupy their territory throughout the winter, it is impossible to tell whether the bobbing bird is male or female.

With the foaming white water behind, the dipper's striking white bib from the throat down to the belly provides good camouflage, but the dark brown upperparts, short wings and cocked, wren-like tail help to identify the bird. In most Scottish and English breeding dippers, the white bib gives way to an attractive broad chestnut margin, which fades into the darker feathers of the lower belly and flanks (**108**). However, in the Hebrides or on Irish rivers such as the beautiful Shannon in

Galway, Little Brosna in Offaly or River Roe in the Roe Valley Country Park, Co. Derry, you will notice that the dippers have much less chestnut: this is a distinguishing characteristic of the Irish race.

Even during winter the clear warbling song of territorial dippers can be heard and it continues until the following June, when the breeding season normally ends. As spring arrives the dippers reclaim their own stretch of river, and they begin nest-building which is performed by both birds between February and late March.

The dome-shaped nest, made from grass and moss, is carefully built to make the most of the features of the habitat: it may be in the exposed roots of a streamside alder, perhaps well concealed underneath the overhang of the bank; or hidden under bridges between rocks on the bank, or woven into a thick grass tussock on a steep bank where erosion is unlikely. The most unusual and well-known nest site is behind a waterfall and the adult birds can be watched flying through the screen of falling water, to feed the chicks in the nest on a dry ledge behind.

In the lowlands, especially for those dippers on the slower-moving rivers from Dorset across to Humberside, two broods are common, but in the Highlands, where spring arrives later, only one brood is reared. Once out of the nest the young resemble their parents in shape and white bib, but the rest of the body is charcoal grey, without the brown and chestnut markings. Dippers can always be seen flying up and down the same stretch of river because they are highly territorial. The territorial stretch of water varies in length from 0.5 to 3 km/0.3 to 1.86 miles. They respect a neighbour's breeding patch and refuse to cross over the boundary line into another stretch of river.

One of the most fascinating aspects of dipper-watching is witnessing the bird feed. When it is perched on a mid-stream boulder, its strong legs, with powerful claws, allow the bird to walk under water, gripping the rocks and boulders; and, angling its wings to the current in the way that a fish uses its fins, it is able to keep itself on the river-bed. Since only a few invertebrates such as the stonefly nymph and caddis larvae can withstand the rushing currents of the upland stream, the food supply is limited, and this unique method of feeding allows the dipper to exploit it without competition. Occasionally you might see the dipper floating on the surface like a dabchick; as a proficient swimmer it can dive for food from this position or from an overhanging branch like a kingfisher.

Whenever the dipper emerges from the water, it repeatedly blinks and a distinct white eyelid, called a nictitating membrane, sweeps horizontally across the surface of the eye from beak to nape. It does this after every dive, clearing surplus water away from the eye. During submergence, this third eyelid becomes completely transparent and, like the mask of a scuba-diver, protects the dipper's eye from possible damage from mobile gravel and debris.

Sadly the bobbing dippers are becoming rarer on many of our upland streams and rivers, and on some of the rivers, where they have bred for centuries, they are now completely absent. Man is once again responsible for the decline, which is caused by water pollution over the last 200 years: in industrial areas, such as South Wales where rivers drain the mining areas, up to 60 per cent of all moving water is highly polluted. Of course man is in a position to do something about the pollution he creates and in certain areas of Wales, such as on feeder streams of the River Ebbw in Gwent, clean-up campaigns have resulted in dippers returning to breed from 1983.

But a more sinister form of pollution, responsible for the decline of dippers in rural Wales, Scotland and northern England, is now apparent, in the form of increased water acidification which is killing many forms of aquatic life in the rivers, including the stonefly and mayfly nymphs, caddis fly and blackfly larvae which form the dipper's staple diet.

Dippers are always scarce or absent on naturally acid streams because the chemical nature of the water does not suit invertebrate fauna, and as otherwise neutral or normally acid-free rivers become polluted and turn acidic, the territory available to the breeding dippers is severely reduced. Acid rain and increased afforestation of the uplands combine to make certain rivers more acidic. Pine needles on the coniferous plantation floor take a long while to decompose and the leaf litter they form is highly acidic; consequently any rivers and streams draining these plantations receive high levels of acidic salts.

In the last forty years, 25 per cent of mid-Wales has become afforested, with 12 per cent of all remaining Welsh moorland affected in the last 14 years. The conifer plantations have not only destroyed the valuable breeding grounds of rare upland birds, but the acid water run-off is polluting upland rivers and is being transported downstream to the reaches where dippers breed.

Ornithologists are monitoring the effects of increased acidic water on dippers and have found that generally they begin breeding later in the year, they lay fewer eggs and the reduced broods take longer to fledge. Calcium salts present in rivers allow snails to form shells and other arthropods to develop a carapace, and since these invertebrates are always part of the dipper's pre-breeding diet, some of the calcium is passed on to the birds at a time when the mineral is vital for egg development. When acidic water kills off the invertebrate fauna the dippers are unable to take in sufficient calcium, which probably accounts for the smaller clutches of dippers remaining on acid-polluted rivers.

The fact that dippers are so sensitive to acid streams should act as an early warning of the levels of atmospheric and water pollution caused by man, but at the moment not enough precautions are being taken. On the River Wye, one of Britain's most famous rivers, running through areas of outstanding natural beauty and providing recreation for thousands of people, the dipper populations have declined over the last twenty years, which reflects the increased acidification of certain tributaries draining afforested catchment areas and running into the Wye.

The government is aware of the fact that the estimated 30,000 pairs of dippers are declining in Britain, but it appears to ignore the effects of afforestation and attributes the cause entirely to acid rain, which is produced by the emission of sulphur dioxide and nitrogen dioxide into the air, by motor cars, factories and, most significantly, power stations which emit 66 per cent of the total.

When these gases mix with water vapour in the air, acid rain is formed. Although the government acknowledges the existence of acid rain, it appears to take no interest in doing anything about it, perhaps because not all the acid rain comes down in Britain. But acid rain has contributed to the death of wildlife in over one hundred Welsh rivers: the Llyn and Brianne catchment areas are almost fishless and the situation is similar in the catchment area of the Duddon and Esk in Cumbria. Scotland has become especially vulnerable and today there are over 57 lakes damaged, many of them polluting rivers which drain from their shores.

Only fairly recently in Britain has there been significant public awareness of the problem of acid rain and various conservation societies are working towards highlighting the effects of the continued pollution.

Sharing the same stretches of river as the dipper is the slender **grey wagtail (110)**, which has even been known to lay its eggs inside a dipper's old nest. Frequently the first indication that the wagtail is flying downstream towards you is a short but clear metallic 'tzi-tzi' call; then with bounding flight, the bird arrives in front of you on a rock and constantly flicks its long tail up and down.

Grey wagtails are elegant, beautiful birds; their slender form contrasts with that of the plump dipper. They have short legs and a streamlined body which is blue grey on the upperparts and white on the flanks. But their most noticeable markings are the vivid lemon-yellow patches on the belly and under-tail coverts. During the summer, the males sport a striking black throat patch, whereas that of the female is white. The summer months enhance the appearance of this wagtail, when the yellow belly markings frequently increase to cover the breast; and the male can be further distinguished by bright white stripes above and below the eye. As summer gives way to autumn the birds moult and male and female become very similar in appearance, with buff-white throats and dull yellow breasts, and the vivid yellow remains only around the tail coverts.

Early in spring the grey wagtails form pair bonds and claim territories along the fast-running streams. They are pugnaciously territorial and in spring you are likely to witness incredibly vocal entertaining fights between rival pairs as territories are infringed and straying birds are chased at high speed down the river.

The female builds the nest of moss and grass, and may use a variety of sites, including holes or ledges along the banks of the stream, crevices in between rocks, amongst overhanging tree roots, or between loose brickwork under bridges. The male shares in feeding the young on an invertebrate diet. It is one of the greatest thrills along the river to watch the male catching mayflies as they emerge in mid-summer and swarm in the late afternoon, or flying out across the water and, hovering like a spotted flycatcher, snapping at the myriad courting gnats.

The breeding population of the grey wagtail is slightly higher than that of the dipper, with between 25,000 and 50,000 pairs evenly distributed across Ireland, Scotland, Wales and western England; the scarceness or absence of the bird from low-lying East Anglia, the central Midlands and Lincolnshire, indicates its preference for fast-flowing water. In the lowlands the bird actively searches for the weir streams, sluices and mill races, which are most similar to its preferred upland habitat.

Although the grey wagtail occupies identical stretches of river as the dipper, it is not so drastically affected by acid rain and run-off. One of the reasons is that the wagtail is more catholic in its feeding habits and does not feed exclusively on submerged invertebrates. A large percentage of its diet is aerial insects, especially flies caught under overhanging deciduous trees; and it seems to ignore the rivers draining coniferous plantations, probably because the insect fauna is much poorer underneath these trees.

The upland river continues its journey through the upper reaches, sometimes frothing and bubbling as it runs through a steep-sided chasm cut by the water over thousands of years. At the seaward end of the chasm loose boulders, rocks and broken

108

109

110

tree branches are spewed out as the river widens into a deeper, slower-moving stretch of river.

Shingle is generally associated with the coast but in many of Britain's rivers there are large shingle beds where the river has eroded the underlying rock and transported the boulders downstream. In some cases the erosion of the shingle continues and the pebbles are further worn down to sand and eventually fine silt, but in Scotland, Wales and northern and western England the bedrock is exceptionally hard and river shingle banks and bars are common.

In the upper reaches, because the current remains strong, the shingle is randomly deposited and comprises small boulders and pebbles where the grey wagtails perch and feed. The natural slope of the river-bed allows the water to sort and shift the smaller stones and particles, carrying them further down-river until they arrive at the middle and lower reaches where the slower current allows the shingle to stabilise.

In the New Forest, Docken Water is a gravel-bedded river with small shingle banks, where the Tertiary sands slowly yield to natural weathering; and river shingle is also found on the Greensands of the Weald, the harder sandstones of Devon and South Wales and the oolite of Northamptonshire and the Cotswolds. Sometimes shingle deposits are found in lowland areas where there are no hard rocks, but this shingle is remnant glacial debris, transported by the lowland river purely because it courses through regions where the shingle was deposited ten thousand years ago by the retreating glaciers. Such glacial shingle deposits are found in the Rivers Wharfe, Ure and Swale as they run into lowland Yorkshire. Because rivers change depending on the seasons, wherever shingle beds are formed they are unstable and frequently only temporary structures. The shingle of fast-flowing upland rivers is continually moving across the river-bed and downstream, despite the fact that it is made up of large cobbles and pebbles, but further downstream fine gravel and sand begin to accumulate around the larger pebbles, eventually stabilising the shingle bank as newly arriving stones become embedded and form a resistant base. Such shingle deposits become permanent and only the heaviest flood waters will destroy them or change their shape; as they continue to grow by further deposition, they gradually alter the flow of the river. These river shingle banks are typical of many Scottish rivers such as the River Dee near Braemar and there is good river shingle at the River Tyne Gravels, a Northumberland Wildlife Trust reserve covering 5 ha/12.3 acres where goosander can be seen and dipper, grey wagtail, oystercatcher and common sandpiper breed.

Many coastal shingle nesting birds such as the oystercatcher suffer because of human disturbance (Ch. 11), but in the last 20 years the oystercatcher has adapted and today uses stable-river shingle banks as a major nesting habitat and the ringed plover has also learnt to exploit stretches of river shingle.

Early in the morning, when the atmosphere of the mountain river is at its best, the quietness is broken by a small bird with dark olive-brown back flying low over the river with down-curved wings and calling with a shrill 'tsee-wee-wee' note. Its flight is jerky and the wings have conspicuous white bars on the upper surface, clearly visible as the bird glides to land on the shingle bank.

The legs and relatively long, straight bill suggest that the bird is a wader. It is the **common sandpiper (109)** amongst the most dainty of our wading birds. Perched on the shingle bank the sandpiper is well camouflaged and because it is only 19

108 The dipper is declining in many areas of upland Britain, partly because of the increasing acidification of water courses.

109 The pebbly and shingle-strewn banks of a lake or reservoir, or the margins of upland streams, are the favourite habitats of the common sandpiper during summer.

110 Grey wagtails are gregarious in winter, but are solitary or move in pairs at other times of the year. The nest is always built close to rapidly flowing water.

111 Male kingfisher on its favourite perch from which it dives after prey and against which it stuns the fish before eating it.

cm/7.5 in long, it is difficult to see, but if you watch it land you will notice the white breast with brown markings around the throat and dark rump and tail. The common sandpiper has a distinctive feature of bobbing its head and tail up and down like the dipper and grey wagtail; but unlike these two birds, it is a summer visitor, arriving from Africa towards the end of March and early April, and returning to favourite pebble and shingle banks of clear upland rivers and streams in Scotland, Wales, northern England and western Ireland. The majority of common sandpipers nest at altitudes up to around 500 m/1,640 ft, although a few can be seen as high as 800 m/2,625 ft. During autumn the best places in which to see common sandpipers are gravel pits, rocky shorelines and mud flats, where the wader stops for food and rest before crossing the English Channel.

When the male sandpipers arrive at the breeding grounds, they immediately take up their territory: a stretch of river about 2 km/1¼ miles long with at least one stretch of shingle. Any intruding male is chased away but male sandpipers occupying a territory will try to mate with any female which arrives in or flies through his patch of river. If you see two birds standing on the shingle facing each other with raised wings and bills pointing downwards, they are males about to engage in a territory fight; they run towards each other to begin combat.

The display behaviour is even more riveting and begins on the shingle with the two birds who are trying to form a pair bond facing each other. With rapid steps the male moves towards the female, sometimes holding his wings aloft. At the same time the hen bird runs towards the male and fans her tail sideways as an encouraging sign to the male that she wants to copulate. When the two birds meet they leap into the air on quivering wings and allow their bills to touch end to end, occasionally leapfrogging over each other.

The courtship is one of the most attractive of all waders, and once paired the male takes off and begins his aerial display over the territory, rising high above the river, then descending with twists and turns on fluttering wings and singing in rhythmic trills and liquid notes. To see these display flights and hear the calls of the common sandpiper is a wonderful experience when birdwatching on upland rivers; they continue for up to fifteen minutes early in the morning, by day or late evening, sometimes even by the light of a full or new moon.

Although common sandpipers mostly feed close to the river on shingle bars and vegetated river banks, the nest can be some distance from the water. It is a simple scrape with a scanty lining of debris from the river or vegetation collected from the immediate vicinity and the favourite sites are beside large stones or boulders, in tussocky grass on the river bank or in heather.

The young common sandpipers are attractive, downy birds, essentially grey in colour, but with white throats and underparts and occasional black streaks on the upperparts. Within three hours of hatching they can leave the nest but many remain for at least the first twelve hours, after which they disperse to hide amongst the stones and vegetation. Both the adults chaperone the chicks and a prolonged 'see-eee' call is usually a good indication that a slightly anxious parent is about to lead its offspring out across the exposed shingle.

Most birdwatchers are familiar with a typical stretch of lowland river where the current sometimes runs fast, then slows down, forming deep pools, before winding through a wide valley with trees and farmland on either side.

Water is vital for all birds because they need to drink each day, so although the obvious lowland waterbirds such as mallard, heron, dabchick and grey wagtail are found near the appropriate water, because their lifestyle depends on it, other species like swift, house martin and swallow exploit the huge insect population associated with water and may always be seen skimming over the surface of lowland rivers where they drink on the wing.

Perhaps the best known of all true waterbirds in lowland country is the brilliantly coloured **kingfisher (111)**. Although its numbers can be seriously affected by severe winters, when rivers freeze over and food becomes unobtainable, it is most common on slow rivers in England, Wales and Ireland. Its other habitats include streams with steep banks, canals, ponds, lakes and flooded gravel pits: wherever there is a regular supply of sticklebacks and minnows.

On the branch of an overhanging sallow willow tree the kingfisher remains motionless, watching for small fish, water beetles and aquatic insect larvae which form its staple diet. Only 16.5 cm/5 in long, the bird has a squat body with a disproportionately large head bearing a long dagger-like beak, short tail, and legs so small that the bright red feet appear inadequate to support the body. The plumage is unquestionably beautiful and as the bird begins to shuffle on its perch the iridescent feathers change colour with every movement. The upperparts are cobalt blue one moment, flashing to emerald green the next in a rainbow of colour as the light catches the bird at different angles. As the kingfisher turns on the branch you will see a distinct pale blue patch from nape to tail, contrasting with the underparts and cheeks which are chestnut red with patches of white on the throat and each side of the neck. It is only possible to judge the sex of the kingfisher with binoculars because male and female plumage is identical, although the breast of the male is perhaps slightly more brilliant than that of the female. The lower mandible of the beak is the main distinguishing feature. If it is black, matching the colour of the upper mandible, the kingfisher is male; the female has an orange-red lower mandible, and an immature bird of either sex will have a white tip to the beak.

Without warning, the kingfisher drops from its perch straight into the water. In seconds it is back on its favourite branch holding a stickleback in its beak. It beats it against the branch until it is dead and, when the dorsal spines are flat and no longer stick in the throat, it swallows the fish head first. It swallows minnows and bullheads, which have no spines, immediately without any branch beating, but whatever the fish you will often see the kingfisher juggling with its prey to arrange the fish head first in its beak before swallowing.

The kingfisher always watches for its prey from a perch, so if there are no overhanging branches, the bird perches on bridges, fence- and gateposts, close to the rivers. Adults catch a fish nearly every other dive, but this is an acquired skill, and it is comical to watch a young kingfisher learning to fish; 90 per cent of its dives fail and sadly many young kingfishers drown by becoming waterlogged in the process of perfecting their techniques.

The severity of the winter frequently determines how early in spring the kingfisher claims its territory, but its breeding season is prolonged, extending from March to September, with the majority laying eggs between April and May. In the non-breeding months kingfishers keep to their regular stretch of river with males and females occupying different areas of river bank, but as February arrives, pair bonds are renewed when the male chases the female up and down the river.

From the initial chases, the courtship develops with the

male slowly hovering around the perched female who quivers her wings in encouragement. The male then flies off, catches a fish and returns to offer it to his partner as a gift, holding it by the tail and offering her the head so that she can swallow it immediately.

Throughout the period of courtship feeding, both birds are also constructing the nest, which is a metre-long tunnel excavated into the bank of the river. The kingfishers initially loosen the soil by flying at the steep bank and stabbing at the sandy soil with their beaks but once a foothole is secured, they use their feet as shovels and excavate the tunnel which ends in a rounded chamber, sometimes lined with fish bones. After the nest has been built, the eggs are laid and incubated by both birds for nearly three weeks. Upon hatching the young are immediately fed on fish and when the fledglings are well developed, four or five fish are taken into the chamber each hour. Occupied kingfisher nest-tunnels are easy to find because as the young birds grow, the build-up of discarded fish bones, regurgitated pellets and droppings smells strongly and the glutinous mass begins to ooze from the entrance of the tunnel creating such a mess that each time an adult emerges after feeding the young, it has to dive into the water to clean off.

As with all resident birds, harsh winters cause many kingfishers to die of cold or starvation, but an estimated 9,000 pairs nest throughout the British Isles, although they are absent from northern Scotland and only sparsely distributed in southern Scotland. The most regular threat to the survival of this attractive bird comes from water pollution and the removal of river-bank trees used by the kingfishers as perches. Additionally, as river banks are cleared and seeded with grass, to become uniform slopes, the potential nesting sites are destroyed, thus preventing the kingfisher from breeding on many of our lowland rivers.

At their richest, the tranquil reaches of Britain's lowland rivers and bordering wetland support more wildlife than any habitat on dry land. Trees abound on the river bank, which is adorned with wild flowers and thick vegetation which provides shelter for nesting birds. One of these birds is the **moorhen (112)**, which finds plenty of plant and animal food in and around the river and conceals its nest within the dense riverside vegetation. The moorhen is only 33 cm/13 in from beak to tail; it is therefore smaller than most ducks, but can be confused with the larger coot which may occupy the same habitat. Most lowland rivers have at least one pair of moorhen: with around 300,000 pairs they are one of our most common waterbirds, breeding on small ponds, lakes and woodland ditches as happily as they do on rivers and streams. They are found everywhere in the British Isles apart from the western Highlands, mid-Wales and upland regions of Ireland. With dark olive-brown plumage and white flashes down the flanks, both sexes are identically and insignificantly marked, but because of the bright red forehead and yellow tip to the bill the bird is not unattractive. Perhaps the most noticeable feature of the moorhen is the way it swims: it jerks its head backwards and forwards and holds the tail well out of the water, flicking it constantly and revealing white under-tail coverts.

Although very common, the moorhen is a secretive bird, spending much of its time skulking in the marginal reeds and overhanging vegetation of the river; but if disturbed it scutters across the water uttering a loud 'curruc' alarm call and a stammering 'kiki kiki-klk-kik-kik' trill. The first indication that a moorhen is near by is likely to be the harsh 'kaak' call from the edge of the river bank. The species is reluctant to fly,

so you will rarely see it gliding with its long legs trailing limply underneath.

Spring is the most exciting time to watch moorhens, because they are extremely territorial and defend their patch vigorously. At the boundaries, occupying males puff out their feathers, extend their necks and bodies low into the water, clearly revealing their red beaks, and erect their tails so that the under-tail coverts are visible. The two birds swim around and towards each other and, if neither of them back off, the resulting commotion wakens the entire river. Both males rear up on their tails and with feet thrashing, their breasts meet and their claws interlock. From the shelter of the undergrowth, the females appear, running across the water to the fighting males and joining in the action, which can last for several minutes.

At the beginning of the breeding season you will probably see the male moorhen building several nest platforms amongst the marginal vegetation. The female selects one of the platforms as a suitable breeding site and the male then adds vegetation to the platform and converts it into the true nest, with some help from his mate. Sometimes the nest can be totally on dry land, but wherever it is built it is always well concealed. Moorhens use reeds, leaves, sedges and floating aquatic plants to form the large deep cup. Some female moorhens behave almost like cuckoos; they swim downstream to a neighbour's unattended nest and lay several of their own eggs to be incubated by another brooding female. Occasionally a nest is found with up to twenty eggs, indicating that several roving females have played the same dirty trick, which is referred to as 'egg-dumping'.

Without exception, the best known of all lowland rivers in the British Isles is the River Thames, which meanders from its source in Gloucestershire for over 320 km/200 miles to its estuary in the North Sea. After the Severn it is Britain's longest river and during its course through towns, farmland, water meadows, arable grassland and woodland, it is joined by 2,400 km/1,500 miles of rivers and streams which unite to create a drainage basin of nearly 10,400 sq. km./4,000 square miles.

The river has been used as a highway for over 4,000 years: Bronze Age man transported animal skins and flints to distant settlements and today the Thames is one of Britain's busiest thoroughfares.

For the birdwatcher the river is both varied and interesting. Numerous birds breed on its banks and thousands of waders and wildfowl amass at the estuary. The grey heron may be seen throughout its length from the clear rippling headstream where the water is swift and shallow to the wide expanses of mud and saltmarsh at Leigh, in Essex.

River islands appear more frequently as the Thames approaches London, providing shelter for birds such as moorhen, coot and mallard which nest in the lush vegetation; and even though the course of the Thames is channelled between concrete banks as it flows through the city, scavenging black-headed, herring and common gulls are regularly seen devouring waste from the refuse barges and scraps from the pleasure cruisers.

When the Thames frees itself from London, it flows through the reclaimed marshlands of south Essex and north Kent, which attract waders and wildfowl in the autumn and winter, including pochard, shelduck, wigeon and teal. Large autumnal flocks of lapwing gather on the coarse grassland alongside the river, attracted by the marginal silt lagoons which are replenished with invertebrate food daily by the effects of the tide. Redshank and ringed plover also join in the feast.

112

113

114

112 Moorhens often feed well away from water, searching river
     banks for insects and larvae, worms, snails and fruits and seeds
     from land and aquatic plants.

113 The nest of the mute swan is an enormous pile of aquatic plants
     and can be as large as 4m/13ft across.

114 Confined to the Orkneys, Shetlands and isolated moors in the
     far north of Scotland, the whimbrel is one of Britain's rarest
     breeding waders.

115

115 River Suck from Shannonbridge. The surrounding low-lying meadows become flooded in winter forming callows and those at Shannonbridge and Muckanagh are important for wild fowl.

Of all the birds it is possible to see, the large white **mute swan** is associated with the Thames more than any other. Occupying in particular the middle and lower reaches of the Thames, the mute swan has become used to human presence; walking along the bank, every birdwatcher is familiar with the graceful swan approaching in the hope of food. The bird hardly requires description. The pure white plumage and orange bill with black base are the same in both sexes, but the male (cob) is slightly larger than the female (pen) and, especially at the beginning of the breeding season, he has a large black knob on top of the bill, near the forehead. For a bird measuring between 130–150 cm/50–60 in from beak to tail and weighing up to 20 kg/44 lb, the head is unusually small and is supported by a long curving neck, held in an S-shape as the bird swims.

Moving powerfully through the water the swan holds its wings over its back with its tail cocked. Every few moments it dips its head and neck below the surface and eats aquatic plants, worms, insects and small fish, although the swan prefers a vegetarian diet. It prefers water which is only about 45 cm/18 in deep and may submerge its head for ten seconds or more as it sifts the silt on the river-bed.

On land the swan is nowhere near so proficient, since the stocky grey legs with black webbed feet are positioned at the back of the swan's body for maximum propulsion in the water; walking on the river bank the swan's centre of gravity is hopelessly displaced and the familiar waddle is all it can manage. As one of the world's heaviest flying birds, the mute swan also finds it difficult to get airborne and the take-off approach is spectacular. Across a clear stretch of water with a runway of 100 m/300 ft the male swan runs along the surface, with outstretched neck, violently thrashing its wings to achieve lift. The momentum increases leaving a foaming wake and gradually the bird takes off. The 1.5-m/5-ft wingspan produces powerful beats, making a characteristic throbbing sound as the bird gains height. If you are watching flying swans coming in to land you will hear the rhythmic hum of their beating wings getting louder as they descend towards the river. Just as the birds are about to touch the water they spread their wings and throw their webbed feet forwards to act as water brakes; then with a series of bow waves they land and begin to swim towards the far bank, uttering trumpet-like honks.

Swans are highly territorial and once an area of river is chosen, the swans, which pair for life, will return to the same spot each year. The cob selects the nest site but allows the pen to build the nest; he passes freshly collected material to her which she piles into a platform, making no attempt to conceal the nest of reeds, sticks and waterweeds lined with down, which is built close to the water's edge and can be 4 m/13 ft across and 0.45 m/1½ ft high (113).

Within about thirty-six days the eggs hatch and the pen carefully removes all the pieces of broken eggshell before turning her attention to the cygnets. Downy grey, they are born with their eyes open and are independent enough to leave the nest during the daytime, only four days after hatching.

Every July on a stretch of the Thames from Maidenhead down to Putney Bridge, a tradition called swan-upping takes place. This census has been performed for centuries and records clearly show that the mute swan population has declined disastrously on the Thames since the late 1950s. In 1956 there were over 1,000 birds on the Thames between Putney and Henley with 200 cygnets marked, whereas by 1983 there were only 123 adult swans and 56 cygnets.

The Secretary of State for the Environment asked the Nature Conservancy Council to investigate the death of swans as long ago as 1979 and by 1981 it was known that the swan decline was due to lead poisoning from fishermen's lead weights discarded or lost in the river; research on various rivers proved that 3,300–4,000 swans were dying each year from lead poisoning. The government accepted these findings and agreed to pass legislation to ban the use of lead weights as substitutes were developed.

As part of their feeding behaviour swans swallow quantities of gravel and grit to aid digestion, because their gizzard operates like a coffee-grinder, and requires small pellets to grind the food into a paste. Unfortunately the lead shot resting on the river-bed was also being ingested with the gravel and was being broken up and absorbed into the bloodstream, bringing about paralysis of the neuromuscular system. When this happens the nerves and muscles of the swan's digestive tract begin to fail, the gullet ceases to pass food to the stomach, resulting in congestion, and the swan dies slowly of starvation.

After much publicity and persuasion by the RSPB and conservation societies, non-toxic angling weights are now manufactured and on 1 January 1987, the government made it illegal to import or supply old-style lead shot.

In parts of the British Isles where rivers run over low-lying ground there is always the risk of natural flooding, especially during the winter when heavy rainfall causes the rivers to burst their banks and swamp the adjacent fields, so forming a temporary but important bird habitat. These fields are known as flood meadows and there are many along the Thames and other rivers of East Anglia and the south Midlands. Each winter the River Shannon – the longest river in the British Isles and the most important freshwater habitat in Ireland – and its numerous tributaries overflow their banks, forming huge alluvial flood meadows or callows, so rich in invertebrates and the floating seeds of plants that hundreds of tufted duck, pochard, teal, wigeon, whooper and Bewick's swan, lapwing and golden plover congregate to spend their winter where food is abundant.

One of the less numerous winter visitors to the flood meadows of the River Shannon is the **white-fronted goose (116)**. Small parties of 600–1,000 birds congregate at several regular flood areas, arriving towards the end of September. The geese are grey-brown birds with a diagnostic white forehead which gives them their name; the under-tail coverts and lower belly are also white, but there are wide black bars on the upper belly. Both sexes are similarly marked.

The main overwintering flocks are found on the Wexford Slobs in south-east Ireland, north of Rosslare, where 5,000–7,000 white-fronted geese feed entirely on plants of the flooded pasture and meadows.

White-fronted geese winter far south from their breeding grounds in the Arctic, anywhere from north-west Russia, and Siberia to Arctic Canada, Alaska and western Greenland, but there are a number of distinct races. Those geese wintering on the Shannon and the Slobs are Greenland white-fronts (*Anser albifrons flavirostris*) and the entire world population of 16,000 birds winters in the British Isles, either in Ireland or on Islay in the Inner Hebrides. The European race, *Anser albifrons albifrons*, which breeds in western Russia, overwinters in southern and western Europe, and a few stop off in southern England and Wales. About four thousand of them feed on flooded meadows at Slimbridge on the River Severn and a few hundred can be seen on the River Towy near Carmarthen, Dyfed, the River Avon in Hampshire and on the Isle of Sheppey in Kent. In Ireland the European white-front is a rare visitor but a few occur on the Wexford Slobs each year. Both races are the same size, between 66–76 cm/26–30 in long, but the Greenland race has a yellow-orange bill and the European goose has a pink bill.

In Britain, during the last twenty years most of the remaining flood meadows and low-level river valleys have been drained to prevent winter flooding and the wetland meadows have been converted to profitable arable land, thus losing the valuable habitat. Those rivers which do still flood naturally in the winter have become favourite haunts for birdwatchers and include the Parrett and Axe in Somerset, the Avon at Ibsley, Hampshire and the Great Ouse River in Cambridgeshire.

Between the sixteenth and eighteenth centuries farmers in southern England realised that winter flooding of their meadows improved the quality of the grass and in counties like Wiltshire, Dorset and Hampshire they skilfully formed water meadows. For centuries man grazed his flocks and herds in between natural or controlled flooding and he was always rewarded with a good crop of hay together with healthy sheep. In the winter the meadows were left to fishermen and the wild birds but by the end of the eighteenth century man attempted to improve the natural water system and started to drain the flood meadows and lower the water-table so that he could convert the low-lying meadows into permanent arable land.

Undoubtedly widespread drainage by the Victorians affected the species of birds which colonised flood meadows and caused the extinction of wetland species such as ruff and black-tailed godwit. By the mid-1860s common species such as the redshank were rapidly declining in numbers the south-east and did not recover until the 1890s, after the agricultural depression caused the practice of field drainage to decline.

From 1970 to 1981, when Britain's water industry was being reorganised and the Ministry of Agriculture, Fisheries, and Food had vested interests in it, huge land draining operations caused extensive damage to flood meadows and many wild habitats where rare birds bred were lost for ever. Using public funds in the late 1970s, the Ministry implemented the drainage of 100,000 ha/250,000 acres of wetland per annum in England and Wales. The Farming and Wildlife Advisory Group revealed that of the 754,729 ha/1,864,910 acres of land drained between 1971 and 1980, nearly 10 per cent was drainage of new untouched wetland.

Lying between the Mendips and the Quantock Hills near Taunton, the Somerset Levels cover 57,000 ha/140,000 acres of low-lying wetland formed by the flood plains of the Rivers

Parrett, Brue, Cary, Axe and Huntspill. Although rainfall on the Levels and surrounding Somerset Moors is surprisingly low, their catchment area includes the southern Mendips which have a high rainfall, so precipitation flowing into the Somerset Levels is frequently high and during winter can be so great that the rivers, dykes and drainage channels are unable to contain the water and the whole area becomes flooded, especially if storms coincide with high tides.

During summer, the flooding is not so acute because in the 1800s major drainage schemes were implemented which improved the run-off from the rivers. These involved the cutting of wide, deep ditches called 'rhynes' which acted as natural barriers to grazing cattle and coped adequately with flood waters. The agricultural and draining activities from 1970 to 1981 continued to alter many of the natural flood meadows and together with peat extraction, have gradually destroyed the moors. The wildlife of this region is now largely preserved only in nature reserves such as West Sedgemoor in Somerset. Here over 140 pairs of breeding waders are found and thousands of wildfowl feed in the winter.

In January when the flood waters spread across the fields, the sky above West Sedgemoor is full of thousands of lapwing, golden plover from Scandinavia and Scotland and hundreds of snipe and dunlin, which all fly in to feed on the flood meadows where the invertebrates drown and float to the surface and the seeds of plants are easy to find. Ducks use this area of Britain as one of their winter refuges and mallard, teal, wigeon and shoveler all congregate to feed until the following spring.

With the arrival of spring the Somerset Levels remain a birdwatchers' paradise. Wintering ducks and swans depart for their summer breeding grounds and spring visitors arrive. One of the most exciting is the **whimbrel (114)**, which, on its return from winter retreats in tropical West Africa, stops off at the Somerset Levels to feed and roost. Towards the end of April and early May as many as 2,000 birds roost in Bridgwater Bay, representing the largest populations in Britain, before flying north to breed in Iceland and Shetland where about 200 pairs stay and breed on dry moorland such as on Fetlar in the Shetlands.

If you are fortunate enough to get close-up views of the bird feeding, then you will appreciate immediately its similarity to the curlew. The whimbrel is much smaller (41 cm/16 in), and has a darker brown plumage, shorter legs and less curved bill than the curlew, but the most distinctive features are the two dark brown bands running from nape to beak across the crown.

One of the most frequent sounds in the Somerset Levels is the piping call of the **redshank**, which is a variable yodelling 'tuu-oodle', but another common note is the haunting, mournful 'tuuu' or 'tu-hu-hu' call uttered when the bird is sitting on a fencepost.

The redshank feeds on estuaries during autumn and winter; the 28-cm/11-in grey and brown flecked wader is easily distinguished by its bright red legs and long dark brown bill which turns red nearer the face. However, during the summer the redshank's back changes to golden brown with black markings and the head and neck are liberally marked with black streaks; when the bird flies off, the white rump, tail and wing bars along the trailing edges are quite clear. Its flight is very quick and low to the ground; the bird twists and flicks its wings all the time it is airborne but upon landing it lifts both wings vertically above its back and momentarily bobs up and down. On the Somerset Levels redshanks may often be seen in flight because they prefer to feed a good distance from the nest,

sometimes up to 1.6 km/1 mile away where they probe along the margins of pools and dykes for insects.

In late February and March these coastal-feeding birds move inland to set up breeding territories and they prefer meadows with waterlogged areas and damp marshland such as the Somerset Levels. Once you hear the piping call you will know that the redshanks are performing their courtship displays. They build their nest in a dry grass tussock (**118**) where the leaves meet overhead to camouflage the nest from patrolling crows and gulls.

Whilst the redshank is one of the most common breeding waders of the Somerset flood meadows, the **black-tailed godwit (117)** is among the rarest in the British Isles and between 1847 and 1952 it was extinct as a breeding bird. Until the nineteenth century it was common, but drainage programmes, shooting and egg-collecting rapidly caused the bird's decline. In 1952 it was rediscovered at its alternative stronghold, the Ouse Washes in Cambridgeshire, and although it increased its numbers up to 64 pairs by 1972, in recent years there has been a gradual decline due in part to losses caused by severe spring and summer floods when the nest, eggs and chicks have been totally lost. The Ouse Washes used to accommodate 75 per cent of the breeding population in Britain, but are now home for only 35 per cent; the remainder breed in a single region of north Scotland and four other English counties.

The black-tailed godwits seen in the British Isles belong to two sub-species: one originates from continental Europe and the other, which has redder plumage and a shorter bill, comes from Iceland. In winter the European race, including some of the British nesting birds, migrates to West Africa, south of the Sahara, but the Icelandic race migrates south to winter in Britain and Ireland; about 4,000 winter in England and Wales at sites such as Langstone and Chichester harbours, the Exe estuary, Devon and the Burry Inlet, West Glamorgan, and up to 10,000 feed and roost around Wexford, Cork, Ballymacoda and Dungarvan Harbours and Clonakilty Bay in Ireland.

The black-tailed godwits arrive on the Somerset Levels to breed in March, when the winter floods have receded and the grass is lush. The male performs courtship display flights which also serve to mark territories. At this time of year he is very handsome with chestnut head, neck and upper breast, dark rump and white tail with the name-giving wide black band at the extreme margin.

The shallow cup which forms the nest is made of leaves and a scanty amount of dead grass and is sited in a tussock usually in the hollow of a meadow, which is why the species is prone to nest loss in spring floods.

By June the grass across the Somerset Level reserves is waist-deep, rippling in the wind, and stands of meadow rue, devil's bit scabious and great burnet grow from the damp, soft ground. Many waders find these soft-soil meadows ideal probing ground for food, and curlew, snipe and redshank all breed in them. However, the management of these meadows is vital for the birds in their exploration for food.

The tall, dense growth of flowers and grass is excellent cover for nesting, but probing waders find it difficult to penetrate into the soil whilst the vegetation is so tall. Therefore the meadow is cut for hay in June after the birds have nested and the adults and young have moved on to the nearby arable land to feed. Heavy grazing of some areas is necessary because wigeon require a short-cropped 'lawn' to feed on during the winter, so sheep are used to produce this effect annually.

116

117

118

116 Greenland white-fronted geese overwinter on the callows of the River Shannon and Wexford Slobs.

117 The breeding success of the few nesting pairs of black-tailed godwits has been affected by severe spring flooding which has swamped the nest sites.

118 From April onwards, redshank breed on damp meadows and marshland, nesting in a dense grass or sedge tussock.

119 Whooper swans in flight. The slow powerful wing beats of these swans make a quiet swishing sound, contrasting with the distinctive throbbing hum of the flying mute swan.

120 Bewick's swans are the smallest of the three species seen in Britain and are often observed in winter flying over the Norfolk Broads in V-formation like skeins of geese.

In mid-April a clear musical 'tsweep' call from the undrained meadow draws attention to a slim yellow bird, 16.5 cm/6½ in length with a long tail. Its appearance and behaviour is very similar to the grey wagtail of the upland river but close examination reveals that the upperparts are yellow green whereas those of the grey wagtail are distinctly blue grey. This is a **yellow wagtail**. Its name is apt because the underparts are bright canary yellow but these markings are only true of the male since the female has a much browner back and the yellow breast is pale in comparison.

The yellow wagtail likes to be near water but prefers open meadows and low-lying farmland. Large numbers breed on the Somerset Levels each year and around 25,000 pairs breed in the British Isles, mostly in England with an appreciable fall-off in northern England, Scotland, west Wales and Ireland.

Male birds arrive from Africa a few weeks ahead of the

females and begin claiming territory by singing from the rhyne banks, gateposts and bushes. Their song attracts females as they begin to arrive. Once pairing has been established the two birds regularly call to each other but mating only occurs once the male has performed his beautiful, fluttering display flight. Rising into the air, the male hovers earthwards at an angle, uttering a musical trill; but just as he reaches the ground, he ascends sharply, continuing the display for several descents before landing in front of the female and pirouetting around her. This is when the female responds, by turning round quickly on the spot before lifting her tail vertically and allowing him to mate. The female bird needs only four days to build the nest in the lush vegetation of the damp meadows with dry grass lined with fur, wool and hair, collected up to 0.8 km/½ mile away from the site.

Before yellow wagtails migrate for the winter they undergo a moult which takes place between the end of July and August and makes the birds difficult to sex, as both have a drab yellow-brown plumage. As well as moulting, they call less frequently. As many as several hundred congregate together in September, roosting in reedbeds and tall grass at night, before leaving as a flock just after dusk in late September and flying 5,000 km/3,000 miles south to West Africa.

For centuries man has been reducing the area of meadows which flood naturally. For instance, areas alongside the River Nene in Cambridgeshire have been drained and subjected to the plough, although in severe winter floods the drainage authorities have to run flood water deliberately on to the fields to prevent serious flooding elsewhere. Retaining banks have been built around certain meadows and when excess water flows down the river, threatening to breach these banks, it is run off by a network of sluice-gates into overflow meadows or washes where it is stored until the river levels return to normal.

The famous Ouse Washes represent the largest of the flood meadows; 1,900 ha/4,700 acres of small fields are divided by 141 km/88 miles of regulatory dykes and from October to April they are deliberately flooded. The artificial flooding is necessary every year because with the vast area of surrounding flat land, there is no other cost-effective way of dispersing the surplus water from the winter storms. The Ouse Washes run the length of the Old Bedford River, but flood to a width of 0.8 km/½ mile, forming one of Britain's most important wetlands. Thousands of wildfowl amass on the flood meadows to feed in the winter and in spring the meadows provide nesting grounds for waders, as important in eastern England as the Somerset Levels are in the south-west. Since the whole area has been designated of international importance by the government, any environmental changes can be made only if they are deemed of national significance. With 808 ha/1,997 acres under the control of the RSPB and appropriate areas managed by the Cambridgeshire and Isle of Ely Naturalists' Trust and Wildfowl Trust, the future of this valuable area is relatively safe.

Management of the Ouse Washes reserves is important and an entire area is grazed by sheep which crop the grass close to the ground, creating perfect feeding grounds for the stately Bewick's swan and 35,000 wigeon which arrive to feed each winter on the shallow flooded meadows. These birds are completely vegetarian and feed on soft meadow grasses such as velvet bent and marsh fox-tail which have a surge of growth during the autumn when they receive the last graze. Then the meadows are carefully flooded to allow a shallow covering of water which attracts countless teal, gadwall and pintail to glean the invertebrates flushed from the grass by the water.

In spring the flood waters disperse, leaving the saturated meadows teeming with exposed freshwater insects, molluscs and larval stages. These form the staple diet for numerous waders and rarities like the ruff and black-tailed godwit which perform their courtship displays on these meadows in between bouts of feeding.

Towards late September and throughout October the skies above the Ouse Washes are hectic with the arrival of flocks of swans which have their breeding grounds much further north in Iceland, Scandinavia and Arctic Siberia. Two different species arrive which, with their white plumage, superficially resemble the mute swan, but once on the ground can be seen to be completely different.

These are **Bewick's (120)** and **whooper swans (119)** and number 2,000 and 200 birds respectively each year on the Washes. The Bewick's swans arrive from Siberia after a journey which has taken several weeks' flying overland, stopping at regular resting places. The Bewick's swans begin to arrive in October and continue until January; their traditional wintering sites include the Nene and Ouse Washes in Cambridgeshire, the Somerset Levels, Slimbridge in Gloucestershire and the Wexford Slobs, Lough Neagh, Swilly and Foyle in Ireland.

The whooper swans arriving in the British Isles number up to 6,000 birds. They fly from Icelandic breeding grounds and their journey across the north Atlantic covers 1,300 km/800 miles in a single and unbroken stretch until they reach the coasts of Scotland and Ireland. After a period of rest and feeding the whooper swans disperse, forming large flocks, sometimes over a thousand birds in each, and they congregate at sites such as Tayside, Strathbeg and Leven Lochs in Scotland and Loughs Foyle, Gara and Erne in Ireland. As the winter progresses more of the whooper swans leave Scotland and fly to Ireland: about 33 per cent of the British population eventually overwinter in Ireland, where they become the most common wintering wild swan.

The whooper swans which fly as far south as the Ouse Washes in Cambridgeshire present an identification problem for the birdwatcher because when feeding on the submerged vegetation on the flooded meadow they are difficult to distinguish from the 2,000 Bewick's swans already on the Washes. From bill to tail the Bewick's swan is 1.2 m/4 ft whereas the whooper is larger at 1.5 m/5 ft and has a generally more bulky appearance. As the swans fly down on to the flooded meadows the call of the whooper swan is deeper and more trumpeting with a characteristic 'whooping' note while the Bewick's call is more variable. The most reliable distinguishing feature involves the head. The whooper swan has a larger head and the neck and head are also proportionally longer: any swan with an elongated neck is a whooper swan. A careful study of the bill will confirm the identification: on the whooper swan the yellow patches on the side of the bill continue well down to below the nostril region ending in a point, whereas on the Bewick's swan the yellow patches are rounded and never extend beyond the nostril area.

There are twenty species of duck which may be seen regularly in the British Isles and one of the rarest breeding species is the **pintail** with only fifty pairs scattered across northern England, Scotland, Kent and East Anglia. In most years a few pairs nest on the Ouse Washes, but the best time for birdwatchers to see this graceful 56-cm/22-in duck is when they overwinter in Britain in large numbers, arriving from September through to December. Most of these wintering birds breed in northern Russia and 25,000–30,000 birds spend the winter in the British Isles, up to 75 per cent of them on the Mersey estuary near Liverpool.

The male is particularly attractive with a chocolate-brown head and hood continuing to the lower back. White markings run down the side of the neck from just behind the eye and the upperparts are silvery grey. The duck's name comes from the male's elongated central tail feathers, but the neck is also long and thin compared to most other members of the genus. The female is far more drab. She lacks the chestnut head and long tail feathers and her plumage is a uniform mottled brown.

On the Ouse Washes, pintails nest on the wet meadows when the floods have gone. The nest and eggs are frequently hidden in a grass or sedge tussock but never far away from pools of shallow water where they 'up-end' to feed on seeds and aquatic invertebrates.

The flood meadows of Britain are continuously under threat from agricultural improvements involving drainage and reclamation; however, the prospects for wetland birds are now more encouraging than ever before. Thanks to persistent lobbying and publicity from conservation societies the public support the preservation of the remaining wetlands for both their natural beauty and wildlife appeal. The Nature Conservancy Council has increasingly utilised legislation empowering it to declare flood meadows Sites of Special Scientific Interest, worthy of protection; and, perhaps most importantly, the government has realised at last that the economic return from expensive land drainage schemes is comparatively low, compared with the extreme environmental losses when the schemes go ahead. Land-drainage capitation has been drastically cut with incentives given to landowners who diversify from farming and utilise their land in other ways. This has resulted in a drop in the number of applications to drain land and farmers are being encouraged to develop their land in sympathy with wildlife and conservation – even to the extent of the government designating Environmentally Sensitive Areas where farmers are rewarded for farming in an environmentally aware manner.

The flood meadows are a rich and colourful habitat, once a common sight throughout Britain and now almost entirely confined to the Somerset Levels, the Ouse Washes, Pevensey Marshes and Amberley Wild Brooks in Sussex and the 'Ings' of Yorkshire. The haunting calls of wild swans arriving each winter and the carefree wheeling of the lapwing will probably always continue over these low-lying meadows, but it would be both sad and irresponsible of man to restrict these experiences to only a few isolated reserves.

CHAPTER 9

MARSHLANDS, FENS AND BROADS

Marshlands, fens and broads are frequently confused because many birdwatchers believe that they are one and the same thing, but with different names. Certainly many species of birds are common to all, but this is because particular aquatic and hydrophilous (water-loving) plants colonise marshland, fens and broads and therefore provide suitable food and cover for them. The three habitats can collectively be referred to as wetlands although this generic term also includes rivers, streams, lakes, ponds and reservoirs.

Just as uplands (page 96) are defined by considering altitude, climatic and geological conditions, together with plant colonisation, so marshland and fen are simply distinguished by the nature of the soil. A swamp may be defined as any area of wet ground where the summer water-level is above the soil surface; but if this area happens to be on acidic wet peat, with a predominance of sphagnum moss, then the area is biologically more accurately referred to as a bog, as found on much of the moorland of the British Isles. Thus the nature and quality of the soil influences the naming of the habitat – as it does for marshland and fenland.

Marshland is waterlogged ground where the summer water-level remains at or near the surface and where the soil has an inorganic or mineral content such as clay or silt. The area around the edge of ponds, lakes and undrained river flood plains is frequently marshland. Fens, sometimes called mires, are waterlogged areas where the soil is organic, made from wet peat derived from plant remains which have accumulated and decayed over thousands of years. Fenland is typically alkaline, although in some areas of Britain it can be neutral or slightly acidic. As a habitat, fens have similar vegetation to marshes. They are most common in Suffolk, Norfolk, north Essex, Anglesey, the head of Esthwaite Water in the Lake District, Oxwich National Nature Reserve in South Wales and the shores of Lough Neagh in Ireland, but in the majority of these areas the fenland has become fragmented because of drainage for cultivation. The alkalinity of the fens is due to the surface water which has drained through or passed over calcareous rocks and in East Anglia, which represents the largest area of fenland in England, the calcareous rock is chalk.

The fens were formed at the end of the last Ice Age, when the sea levels rose with the melting of the ice sheets, causing flooding of the areas of Britain we call East Anglia and the Somerset Levels. Glacial debris and deposits transported by the rivers to the lowlands gradually filled in some of these low-lying, waterlogged regions of Britain and by succession, pine, birch and oak eventually colonised the flat, richly silted land.

About seven thousand years ago, a further rise in sea level flooded these low-lying forests and the trees died and sank into the mud, only to be naturally replaced with reeds and sedges which survived their normal lifespan and then died themselves. As this swamp vegetation decayed, it drifted below the water surface, where, starved of oxygen, it decayed very slowly and amassed to form an extremely deep layer of peat. During thousands of years the continuous deposition of peat caused the level of the land to rise slowly so that it became drier, and willow and alder carr (page 42) began to grow.

A large number of areas of open water such as lochs, lakes and ponds, many of which were formed after the Ice Age, are doomed to be lost eventually to the vegetation they support. Silt, washed into these basins of open water, becomes trapped by the vegetation, especially around the margins, but in time the silt shelves away into the deeper water. Over hundreds of years, as the sediment continues to be deposited, the water becomes shallower and plants begin to colonise. Fen vegetation forms a variably wide band around open water and gradually advances into the water until the edges meet in the middle and the open water disappears.

The first stage of this succession occurs in the shallow water where common reed grows within a network of dense vegetation called reed swamp. This is the vegetation used by reed, Cetti's and Savi's warbler, bittern and bearded tit. There are reed swamps at Leighton Moss (Cumbria), Stodmarsh (Kent) and Minsmere (Suffolk), which developed as poor-quality farmland was flooded, but, apart from the Norfolk Broads, there are no huge areas of reed swamp in Britain. Reed swamp generally grows on the landward side of the open water and requires a permanent depth of at least 20 cm/6 in.

It is only a matter of time before reed swamp develops by succession into fenland, providing that the water is alkaline, and fens become dominated by great fen sedge. The ground becomes more stable as the level rises, due to the build-up of peat, and fens are constantly changing because they are one of the seral phases in the transition from water to dry land. Some of the first plants to colonise the fen peat add a splash of colour to the habitat, including greater spearwort, great willowherb broad-leaved dock and the beautifully scented water mint.

Only by centuries of management and harvesting was the natural succession of the fens kept in check but in many areas today true fen has been lost to broad-leaf woods which have gradually dominated. The other main reason for the loss of the habitat is that drainage schemes have altered the delicate structure of the fens and caused the natural vegetation to die, so that eventually the peat has become reclaimed for agriculture and lost to the plough – like the flood meadows in Ch. 8 – or the peat has been commercially extracted, destroying the surface of the fenland anyway.

Although human activity destroyed most of the natural fenland of Britain, this same activity now maintains and preserves the remaining isolated pockets of fen habitat. At Woodwalton Fen (208 ha/514 acres) and Wicken Fen (272 ha/672 acres), both reserves are surrounded by drained and managed farmland, so that it is impossible for them to be subjected to natural flooding. The Nature Conservancy Council has had to install a pump system at Woodwalton to provide artificial flooding and the National Trust regularly floods Wicken Fen from a drainage dyke, using a windmill which was once used to drain the neighbouring farmland. The wardens have to spend a lot of time and effort regulating the water-levels so as to maintain the fenland species, but the efforts are certainly worth it, because at Woodwalton, where the peat is slightly acidic, common reed, purple small reed, wood small reed, common meadow-rue and the rare fen violet grow; and Wicken Fen boasts a natural wilderness of 170 fenland plants.

121

Wherever fenland vegetation exists, the habitat is rich in bird-life, because deep in the decaying peat, millions of insect larvae complete their metamorphosis, providing invertebrate food in the form of gnats, midges, alder flies, beetles and dragonflies for the smaller insectivorous birds; and the reeds and sedges provide dense cover made more secluded by the floating-mat vegetation, which prevents human disturbance.

From the dense thickets of the pale green reed swamp you might well hear a repetitive but characteristic song. The 'churr-churr-chirruc-chirruc' sound belongs to the **reed warbler (122)** which at 12.5 cm/5 in is one of the smallest birds totally dependent on common reedbeds, always close to water. It is only after late April when the bird arrives from Africa that the song or 'churrr' alarm note may be heard coming from deep vegetation. A close-up view shows that the reed warbler is a neatly designed bird with a pointed, fairly long beak, which moulds smoothly into the head. The tail is graduated with shorter outer feathers and sheathed by extra-long upper and lower tail coverts, making it look very sturdy.

Because they keep themselves well-concealed it is difficult to census this species, but it is estimated that 60,000–100,000 pairs breed in Britain, mostly confined to eastern and south-

121 Hickling Broad is the largest of the Norfolk Naturalists' Trust's reserves, with reed swamp fen and open water covering a total of 566 ha/1400 acres.

east England, where the appropriate habitat is more common. Isolated breeding colonies occur in central and south-west England, but they are rare in northern England and Wales and absent from Scotland and Ireland.

The male reed warblers begin setting up territories soon after they arrive in spring and the song flows from the reedbed for several seconds at a time. Unfortunately for the bird-watcher, the reed warbler is a great mimic and often combines the song of other wetland birds with its own methodical chatter which consists of one or two phrases repeated several times in succession, with only a change in pitch for variety.

When the females arrive at the reeds, the male performs a restricted display, which involves the raising of the crown feathers and slight fanning of the tail and wings. Eventually he secures a mate. The female builds the nest, which is cylindrical and has a deep cup to prevent the eggs or nestlings falling out; constructed of grass and reed flowers, the nest is attached to the reeds and supported only by several criss-crossed reed stems – consequently, when the reeds sway in the wind the nest moves alarmingly left and right. Experienced birds select a nest site low down in the reeds where the wind is less of a problem.

Although reed warblers set up a personal territory before nesting, they regularly nest in colonies where some birds build in the reed swamp and others in the fen vegetation, including the stems of purple loosestrife and meadowsweet. However, all breeding birds prefer to collect their insectivorous diet some distance from the nest, and during this activity, individual birds may be observed being aggressive and antagonistic towards other birds from the colony who are collecting their own food.

Reedbed warblers all tend to be very similar in appearance, but the black streaks on the ginger-brown upperparts of the **sedge warbler** easily distinguish this 13-cm/5-in bird from its smaller counterparts. The sedge warbler also has a dark crown with a clearly visible, creamy eye-stripe with black margin above the eye, and delicate yellow-buff underparts (**124**). It breeds happily in reed swamp but is equally able to colonise the drier fenland vegetation wherever the cover remains dense.

Upon arrival in early April the males become very vocal, even singing well into the night during the early part of the season, because as nocturnal migrants, they try to attract the females as soon as they arrive at night. Their song, frequently uttered from a favourite song-post, is a mixture of harsh strident 'churr's and sweeter, melodious trills rapidly joined together in a jumble of phrases, but at a higher pitch than the reed warbler and certainly less repetitive. The song flight of the sedge warbler may often be seen during the daytime: the male rises vertically from the vegetation, singing boldly as he ascends, with a series of scratchy notes, reminiscent of that of a whitethroat, before descending on outstretched wings and fanned tail. This aerial display may be seen any time from April to the middle of July.

The mating display progresses from the song flight to courtship, in which the male chases the female of his choice through the undergrowth, stopping periodically to erect his crown feathers and lower splayed wings to the ground as an act of encouragement. The bulky nest is built by the female, who uses dry grass and moss and lines the cup with hair. It is always well concealed in the dense undergrowth and frequently close to the ground, making it far more difficult to find than the hammock-slung, basket nest of the reed warbler.

Apart from the willow warbler (page 46) the sedge warbler may be seen farther north than any other European warbler and around half a million pairs breed throughout the British Isles, except Shetland – a fact which is largely due to the ability of the sedge warbler to colonise not only reed swamp and fenland, but scrubland, hedgerows and even inland arable fields.

Many of the richest fens in Britain have vast reedbeds at the transition zone between water and true fenland vegetation. These reeds are important to numerous birds, both during the breeding season and during migration. Just after the breeding season many species of birds congregate in large flocks ready for their journey south; throughout August and September hundreds of swallows, house martins and sand martins, after skimming across the open water hawking insects, fly down into reedbeds, just after dusk. The protection of the reedbeds is similarly used at night by yellow wagtails (page 126) and thousands of starlings, which are a spectacular sight at the end of an autumn or winter's day birdwatching. Of course these communal starling roosts form throughout the year, but they are swelled in numbers during autumn and winter by thousands of immigrant starlings arriving from parts of Europe such as Scandinavia. Starlings have long fascinated me: to me they are the street-wise, self-made entrepreneur of the bird world, as they strut about with confidence and disregard. Their arrival at the evening roost site is part of a well-executed itinerary of events: small flocks within a particular area all join up to converge on the roost together. As the birds converge on the roost site, the flock increases as small flocks of waiting birds take off to join the aerial throng (**180**). If you have been on the fen all day, you will hear and see these birds arriving around sunset. They do not fly straight into the reedbeds, but circle and swirl across the fen before landing in pre-roost assemblies in nearby alder and willow carr or neighbouring farmland where they collectively feed. The pre-roost assembly increases as other starlings fly in to join the many thousands of birds all engaged in preening, feeding and singing – if you can call the incessant clicking, screaming and whistling, singing. Suddenly the mass of birds takes off, and in a cloud-like, swirling, co-ordinated set of movements, the vast flock of starlings descends into the reedbed for the roost.

Roosts of starlings and other birds take place at regular times throughout the winter and other birds have learnt to patrol the fens and reed swamps for easy prey. As it moves south from our heathlands to overwinter in Africa, the hobby catches the occasional roosting wagtail or starling by flying fast and low over the reeds as the bird descends to roost. It is worth looking out for short-eared owl, hen harrier and sparrowhawk who have also learnt to hunt across this habitat during roosting activity.

The reed swamps of Britain provide nest sites for the entire breeding population of some of our rarest birds. One such fen and reedbed specialist is the **Savi's warbler** which, having become extinct for over a century, recolonised a few localities in eastern and south-east England in the 1950s. You will need to visit Stodmarsh in Kent, Minsmere in Suffolk or Hickling Broad in Norfolk for a chance of seeing this warbler, but with national populations ranging between 20 and 30 pairs, the chances of success are slight. Arriving from the Mediterranean, north Africa or the Middle East in mid-April, the bird is slightly larger than a sedge warbler, but specifically requires the dense reed- or sedgebeds for the tall stems which it uses as song-posts. The warbler likes to sing, often in full view, always close to the water and generally at dawn or dusk. The song is loud and characteristic, commencing with a series of rapid 'tick-tick' notes which increase in tempo to a reeling trill. It mimics the grasshopper warbler, but with modifications, including a slower pace than that of the grasshopper warbler, with a shorter, deeper, but louder whirring sound and sometimes a harsh chatter.

With uniform dark brown upperparts without streaks, the Savi's warbler can be confused with the reed warbler, but they may be differentiated by their songs. The underparts are off-white with the edge of the breast and flanks grading to a rich brown and the tail shows the long tail coverts and graduation of the reed warbler; if you manage to get your binoculars focused before the warbler flies low and rapidly over the top of the reeds you may see its distinctive white chin.

At Stodmarsh and Minsmere you might be fortunate enough to see not only the Savi's warbler, but also the localised **Cetti's warbler**, which first appeared in Britain during 1961. The unexpected appearance was due to a natural expansion of its European range and, having landed in Britain and found ideal breeding habitats, the Cetti's warbler has become established as a resident bird. It has bred regularly since 1972, with populations fluctuating between 100 and 300 pairs, depending on the severity of the winter. At Stodmarsh, before the cold winter of 1985–6, it was common to hear as many as eight Cetti's uttering their explosive 'chewee, chewee, pit, pit, pit' call from the dense vegetation near the official car park.

Cetti's warbler is also found at Strumpshaw Fen in Norfolk, which is an RSPB reserve covering 244 ha/602 acres of open water, reed swamp, fen vegetation and alder and willow carr. It is exactly this variety of habitat which appeals to the Cetti's warbler and enables the species to spread to wetlands which provide the seral succession from reed swamps to dense carr. As a typical aquatic warbler it prefers to conceal itself in the tangled vegetation but it is generally seen on the driest parts of the fen where the scrub and carr vegetation is established.

The Cetti's warbler is the same size as the Savi's warbler, but this difference in habitat preference should help to distinguish the two species. The upperparts are dark rufous becoming slightly paler towards the rump and upper tail coverts; and the cheeks and neck shade to light grey-brown, with off-white underparts, and dark brown-black tail. Sometimes the Cetti's warbler utters a harsh 'churr' alarm note and then takes off, moving through the reeds and carr vegetation in fast, low-level flights, but it prefers to skulk low down in sallow and alder and even on the ground, where it repeatedly flicks its rounded tail downwards.

Within a rich fenland, a wide range of bird habitats are available, both for nesting and foraging, and the extremely rare **marsh warbler** requires the zone where the wet marshland gives way to plants which cannot tolerate flooding and are interspersed to form a mosaic with scrub and carr vegetation. Marsh warblers are one of Britain's rarest breeding birds: in 1982 the population was around 50 pairs, but by 1986 it had dropped to only 10 known pairs and although a few isolated pairs have bred elsewhere, it seems that the British population is now restricted to Worcestershire, along the River Avon valley. The birds arriving in late May are on the far western extremity of their breeding range, and the Worcestershire marsh warblers have no supplement from Continental birds, so unless the European breeding population naturally expands westwards our marsh warblers are destined to remain as small groups or disappear altogether.

Imagine that it is early June and dusk has fallen along the river bank on one of those evenings when the air is beguilingly warm. In the dense vegetation along the river valley the high-pitched chirping of crickets can be heard and will continue well into the night but at the moment they punctuate the lugubrious murmur of the last of the daytime flying insects. Just as a small bat dips and flickers across the river, a bird starts singing from the undergrowth and the sounds of the night have begun. The bird you can hear has a highly developed musical song delivered with incredible vigour; but to your astonishment you also start to hear tropical African birds such as bulbuls and weaver birds, followed by the sounds of cackling house sparrow, blue tit and blackbird which experience tells you stopped singing hours ago.

This marvellous array of song is made by the marsh warbler which commonly sings early in the morning or at night and sometimes continues right through the night without stopping; which, together with the rich, diverse, flowing quality of the song, clearly separates it from the reed and sedge warblers. Research has shown that each marsh warbler can perfectly mimic about seventy-five species of bird, forty-five of which have been learnt when wintering in Africa and thirty copied from European birds.

As dawn breaks over the Worcestershire Nature Conservation Trust reserve at Eckington Bridge, the marsh warbler still occasionally breaks into song. Fortunately this site is ideal for hearing and seeing the birds without entering and disturbing the habitat. The sounds pour from dense marsh vegetation well back from the river, where stinging nettle, great willowherb and meadowsweet dominate and crack willow forms a backdrop.

Towards the end of the last century when the marsh warbler first bred in Britain, the traditional nesting sites were found in the west Midlands, southwards to the Somerset Levels. This was the region of basket-weaving where osier or withy beds were managed commercially and the new growth produced pliable wands, which were bent and fashioned into wickerwork. The marsh warbler's nest is similar to that of the reed warbler and the osier wands provided suitable stems for the attachment of the basket-nest, whilst the lush marsh vegetation gave dense seclusion.

But traditional osier beds have fallen into disuse as synthetic materials replaced the withies and the marsh warbler now weaves its nest to the stems of marsh vegetation (**125**). The nest sites are all protected by law and by the local naturalists' trusts, who manage the reserves in order to provide exactly the conditions the warbler requires. Unfortunately the numbers are still declining and although the initial sudden loss of breeding birds was probably a result of the deterioration of the osier beds, the losses in the period 1982–8 are due to a combination of other factors, including a natural contraction of the bird's breeding range and a succession of bad summers when heavy rain and flooding destroyed nests and young birds. Such destruction occurred during the June floods of 1985, and although replacement clutches were laid, these were smaller and fledged later in the season, probably with inadequate time to 'feed up' before migrating south.

Migration may also be a key factor in declining numbers: hundreds of millions of birds are killed each year as they pass over Europe and the southern Mediterranean countries to winter in Africa. The traditional migration routes pass over islands like Malta and Cyprus where there is shooting and trapping on a large scale. International Council for Bird Preservation figures reveal that 30,000 swallows and house martins, 50,000 robins, 250,000 Spanish sparrows, nearly 1,000 hobbies, 100 stone curlews and 3,000 nightjars are shot annually, and there is every chance that a few marsh warblers suffer the same fate – especially as in appearance they resemble a slightly more olive reed warbler.

It could be that only by conservationists maintaining the remaining known breeding sites and international co-operation to outlaw the use of the gun on migratory birds that this outstanding mimic and other more common but equally meritorious birds continue to breed in Britain.

However, not all birds inhabiting marshland and fens are rare and one of the most widespread is the **grey heron (126)** which, being stork-like and large, is well known in the British Isles. Most sightings of the grey-backed heron, with long white neck, are of the solitary bird standing motionless at the edge of the reed swamp in the shallow water, its neck retracted towards its body and the bayonet-shaped bill pointing towards the water as the bird waits for a fish or eel to swim too close. As prey comes into range the bird extends its neck with breathtaking speed and swallows the stabbed fish in one head-flicking gulp.

Few people see herons in their nesting colonies but because they nest in communal groups they are relatively easy to census: the heron has the longest running survey of any British bird, operated for over fifty years by the British Trust for Ornithology. Population figures show that there has been a decline of about 12 per cent since the cold weather of February 1986; there are currently about 5,000–5,500 pairs throughout Britain, with the densest populations in the south-east and east of England but the numbers are healthy in Scotland, where there are over 300 heronries.

The heron's stealthy behaviour and preference for standing still whilst food swims into range allows the birdwatcher the opportunity of securing clear views of this magnificent bird. Its total length is about 95 cm/37½ in, of which the body represents only 43 cm/17 in. The huge wingspan of 175–95 cm/69–77 in never fails to impress, as the bird flaps slowly across the reed swamp. The wings are broad and always arched in flight, revealing the black upper-wing tips and uniform grey undersurface; and with its head drawn into its body and long legs trailing well beyond the tail, the silhouette of the grey heron is unmistakable.

Adult herons show a distinct wide black stripe running from the eye to the tip of a wispy crest and an obviously yellow bill, but although young herons have the black stripe, they lack the crest and the upper mandible of their bill is brown. With few natural enemies, herons colonise a wide range of habitats such as marshes, fens, river and stream margins, lakes, ponds, reservoirs, canals, sewage farms and garden pools. Fish are always the favourite prey although you will see the heron catching eels, grass snakes, frogs, tadpoles, newts, water voles and even young birds such as moorhen chicks and mallard ducklings. The coarse, honking 'fraank' call of the heron is a familiar sound in all the above habitats, and increasingly the call is heard early in the morning in suburban areas, where herons have learned to raid local council rubbish tips: along with the gulls, they turn over the rubbish looking for chicken carcasses and edible household scraps.

The heron suffers the disadvantage of being at the top of a food chain when its feeding ground is polluted by poisoning and toxic chemicals, such as agricultural spray run-off, draining into a river. If fish have been feeding in water which is slowly being polluted, they accumulate toxins in their body; the toxins may not be sufficiently concentrated to be lethal at first, but will eventually kill them. The heron fishing a polluted river consumes over 0.45 kg/1 lb of fish each day and if each fish is slightly toxic, the poison levels in the heron increase as it consumes more fish. Most herons die in severe winters when ice prevents them from reaching their staple diet, but all birdwatchers have seen dead herons wrapped around overhead grid-cables by the neck: 8 per cent of all known deaths are caused in this way.

The nesting colony of herons at Tring in Hertfordshire is one of the few heronries on the ground in tall reedbeds, since most herons prefer to build their nests in tall deciduous or coniferous trees, sometimes 25 m/80 ft above the ground, although in Scotland herons use cliffs, islands in the middle of lochs, or dense patches of heather. Between ten and thirty nests form the average colony with exceptional cases of up to two hundred nests.

When the winter has been mild, male herons arrive at the colony towards the end of January and early February, and the

122

123

122 Reed warbler with fostered cuckoo. At sixteen days old the cuckoo dwarfs its foster parent and totally fills the nest which is attached to the reedstems.

123 Unexpectedly flushed from the cover of the reedbeds the bittern still adopts its protective frozen posture with bill pointing skywards. Normally the black, brown and gold-flecked plumage offers camouflage with the vertical lattice of the reedstems.

124 Widespread, yet elusive, the sedge warbler conceals itself in dense vegetation close to water, where it hunts for insects, occasionally breaking into song from a favourite singing post.

125 The marsh warbler is distinguished from the reed warbler by its flatter head, and its incredible song confirms this rare bird's identity.

126 Herons use the same nest every year, which eventually reaches 1m/3¼ft diameter. Up to 5,500 pairs nest in Britain with populations falling after severe winters, when ice prevents the herons from obtaining their food supply.

127 A pair of bearded tits or reedlings in their typical reed-bed habitat.

125

127

first thing the established male heron does once it has claimed last year's nest is overhaul it and add new branches to the already bulky structure. The nests so perfectly resemble a miniature hedge or thicket that other smaller birds actually build their own nests inside the base twigs. First-year breeding birds or new arrivals to the colony are forced to build their own nests at the edge of the colony, where the branches are thinner and the position altogether less secure.

Visit the heronry in the early morning, or at dusk, because these are the periods of peak activity at the nests. The males strain their necks upwards and call for a mate, then bow to the nest to encourage a female to join them. Eventually a female responds, and courtship display begins, involving preening and serious nest-building where the male collects twigs and leaves and the female arranges them into the existing structure. This mutual preening and nest-building is an important bonding ritual for the herons and is eventually followed by a prolonged mating display, accompanied by shrieks, honks and guttural noises as the birds spread their wings and raise the neck and throat feathers and their boot-lace crests. The bills are obviously a sign of sexual prowess; the usual yellow colouring becomes tinged with orange during the breeding season and pairs frequently clatter them together in sword-parrying behaviour.

Both adults incubate the blue-green eggs for up to four weeks but the males seem to carry out their stints mostly during the day. Once hatched, the young constantly demand food which in the first few weeks is regurgitated by the adults into the throats of the chicks. They grow rapidly and at twenty-five days old are able to leave the nest and clamber about the branches; then the adults regurgitate fish into the bottom of the nest and leave their offspring to feed themselves.

Occasionally the fledged herons return to the nests for night roosts, but they soon become independent, preferring a solitary existence, especially when fishing. As they are sedentary by nature the majority of herons remain within a 100-km/62-mile radius of their birthplace, but during severe weather they become nomadic, flying great distances in search of food and often locating new sewage farms, garden pools and open water, where food is more abundant. A few British herons even migrate to Europe in winter, but most remain, and their populations are swollen by the arrival of other herons from Scandinavia, unable to survive the winter in their colder climate.

Reed swamp, fenland and marshland are important habitats for common and rare species of birds and the most outstanding fenlands which still contain managed reedbeds are found in the Norfolk Broads. It is ironic that whereas much of the natural reed swamp and fenland has been destroyed by man since Roman occupation, the fens with reedbeds which remain the most valuable for birdlife today are those which were originally created by man. Stodmarsh in Kent for example, is an outstanding area of fenland for the ornithologist, occupying an area where coal mining subsidence allowed flooding of the valley of the Great Stour. The Norfolk Broads are the best example of flood-plain fens in Britain occurring in low-lying, east Norfolk, between the valleys of the Rivers Ant, Bure, Thurne, Waveney and Yare. Here over 3,300 ha/8,154 acres of reed-swamp fen and carr vegetation surround a network of more than forty Broadland lakes, the largest being Hickling Broad (**121**) with over 140 ha/350 acres of open water and reedbed, with numerous smaller lakes, not much deeper than

3–4 m/10–13 ft. At one time the Norfolk Broads were thought to be natural, but we now know that during the twelfth and thirteenth centuries peat was cut on a large scale along the river valleys of Norfolk, when the level of the land was also about 4 m/13 ft higher than it is today. Towards the end of the thirteenth century, the sea levels rose dramatically and the extensive peat excavations became flooded by river tidal changes. Eventually the peat workings were deserted and the Broads were formed.

From the air the Broads appear as acres of silver water, with fringing reedbeds giving way to alder and sallow carr as the fen becomes established. Isolated farm buildings stand where marshland has been reclaimed and the landscape is threaded with dykes and ditches linked to pumps which drain the water into one of the numerous rivers.

During the Victorian era, with the development of the railways, the Broads began to appeal to tourists: rowing, sailing, shooting and fishing were all popular forms of recreation. Today the area is still regarded as one of the most important regions of the British Isles for wildlife, but although superficially the Broads appear to be a large tract of wilderness with a wide variety of flora and fauna, the wetland is not as healthy as it was even twenty years ago.

Surrounding the Broads is reclaimed arable land and grazing marshes which flood during the winter, providing feeding sites for thousands of ducks and waders. The whole of the Broadland habitat is very diverse with a huge tourist and recreational appeal. Tourism contributes significantly to the economy of the area and man has gradually disturbed the Broads so that in some parts the extensive marginal reed swamps are dying and the thousands of cruisers available for hire cause conservation problems. The river banks have become eroded by the wash of the pleasure boats and have been unsympathetically replaced with metal reinforcements which do not suit colonisation by plants. The reedbeds, so important to birds, have become susceptible to swamping and stems are broken and nests are washed away. Man has also cleared the margins of some of the Broads, so that today only 485 ha/1,200 acres of pure reedbed remain, which is 50 per cent of what there was after the Second World War.

The reedbeds are also dying because of water pollution caused by agricultural chemicals which drain from the land into the Broadland waterways and release excessive quantities of nitrates and phosphates into the water. Traditionally the freshwater of the Broads is clear with numerous submerged aquatic plants supporting invertebrates like pondsnails, caddisfly larvae and damselfly nymphs, which provide food for fish and coot, duck, grebe and swans. But chemicals and plant nutrients cause the lower forms of plants such as algae to reproduce very rapidly in what is called an algal bloom, which dominates the habitat, restricts the growth of higher plants and gradually reduces the clarity of the water, so restricting light penetration and eventually photosynthesis of the green plants responsible for releasing oxygen into the water.

Hickling Broad, with its 113 ha/280 acres of reedbed gradually advancing into the open water, has suffered in this way and many higher plant types have totally disappeared. Treated sewage which still contains nitrates and phosphates is discharged into the Broads and the river system, contributing to the biological death of many of the lakes.

Broadland conservation is both expensive and time-consuming and is now essentially confined to those Broads which are still rich in nature reserves. The excessively nutrient-rich water can be regulated at important times of year, so that algal blooms do not occur when other plants are at their maximum period of growth or fish are breeding, although it may be that the recent control of agricultural chemical run-off into the Broads has been implemented too late to help much of this flat watery landscape. A positive development is the Broads Grazing Marshes Conservation Scheme, which is funded by the Ministry of Agriculture, Fisheries, and Food (MAFF) and the Countryside Commission, and offers cash incentives to farmers owning land on a 4,000-ha/9,884-acre important marsh area to enable them to use their land for grazing cattle, rather than arable farming; in return they are obliged to inform the conservation team of any proposal to use agricultural chemicals or plans to change the appearance and structure of their land. The Countryside Commission is the quango that advises the Government on rural conservation matters, and was partly responsible for suggesting to the Government that the Norfolk Broads be given the equivalent of National Park Status, with the result that from 1988 onwards the Broads are likely to receive more official protection and conservation that at any time previously.

Every April common terns arrive in the Broads, as they have done each year since 1949, when they first nested at Ranworth Broad. Since then, special nesting platforms have been made and these terns now breed at Ormesby, Cromer, Hickling, Martham and Hoverton Great Broads in good numbers (page 159). During the summer, the Broads are a paradise for the birdwatcher, with different warblers singing everywhere and mute swans, coot, moorhen, mallard, teal, gadwall, garganey and shoveler all breeding.

In November, the Broads attract birdwatchers from all over the country because the reclaimed fenland at Buckenham Marshes in the Yare Valley has become the only regular British site for overwintering bean geese: up to three hundred of these large birds arrive in autumn and remain until March, grazing alongside smaller numbers of white-fronted geese. The meadows at Buckenham Marshes are alive with skylark and reed bunting during summer, but in winter, apart from geese and Bewick's swan, only the occasional short-eared owl and hen harrier hunt across these low-lying wide-open fields.

For the birdwatcher, the fen vegetation and the reedbeds are the most interesting and rewarding habitats within the Broads, providing the last refuge in Britain for many rare species of bird. *Pharagmites australis* dominates the reed swamps of the Broads, together with narrow leaved reedmace, but on the open-water side of the reed swamp common club rush grows in thick impenetrable stands. All the plants of the reed swamp are characterised by their tall, slender stems and dense growth, providing excellent shelter for birds. The phragmites beds of the Broads provide the last stronghold for rare nesting birds like the bittern, bearded tit and marsh harrier. Only fleeting glimpses reward the most patient of birdwatchers and sometimes days will pass without sight or sound of these specialised reed-nesting species.

The huge expanse of common reed stretches as far as the eye can see on this flat landscape; no longer do the stems and flower heads ripple in the breeze, because on this dark January morning there has been a sharp frost and the reeds stand erect with stiffened, dead flower heads from last summer. The marsh is silent, except for your footsteps crunching through the frozen vegetation and with your breath just visible as a cloud of vapour in the darkness. What it is that makes you stumble along overgrown paths amongst the reeds is difficult to explain, but one of the rewards in early January is the sound of the

bittern beginning to exercise its oesophagus ready for the territorial season, which begins in February. The low-pitched coughs and grunts of the bittern are some of the rarest sounds of the reedbeds, always uttered when the peat-lined pools are splintered with ice.

Only the male bitterns make these noises and around dawn is the best time of day to hear the bitterns as they increase in strength and volume before reaching full voice by the first week of February. Bitterns claim their territories in late winter, occupying and defending them until July.

The bittern is a roundwinged member of the heron family, 76 cm/30 in from beak to tail, with a rich golden-brown plumage, mottled and barred with black markings which break up the shape of the bird and make it disappear into the vertical world of the reed stems. It is so secretive and perfectly camouflaged that even if you manage to get within metres of the bird it remains unseen to all but the trained eye. The crown is black, matching the long moustache each side of the powerful bill, but the underside is corn coloured with darker brown stripes and lines. These markings save the bittern whenever danger threatens. If you approach it too closely, the bird, rather than fly away, stretches its neck vertically, points its bill to the sky and the markings blend totally with the reed stems (**123**). If there is a breeze, the bittern even sways slightly to resemble the movement of the reeds and remains in this position for hours, until you retreat to a more acceptable distance.

Bitterns are solitary feeders and their diet is mainly fish and eels caught in the shallows at the margin of the reed swamp during the daytime or early evening. Like the heron they also eat frogs, water voles, the eggs and young of ducks and moorhens, molluscs, worms or insects, but only feed when the risk of disturbance is at a minimum. Much of their food is caught in disused drainage ditches which have become colonised by reeds and fenland vegetation.

It is still cold on an April morning two hours before dawn, but the mating season of the bitterns is at its peak and from the centre of the reedbed a deep, resonant, double note echoes across the marsh, resembling the 'whoomp' of a ship's foghorn; in the still air the sound carries 2–5 km/1–3 miles.

Although the booming bittern can be heard during the daytime, the hours just before dawn are the most rewarding. Nothing compares with the booming of several bitterns at opposite ends of the reedbed, just as the horizon turns neon blue, flushed with pink, as dawn breaks across the marshland. When you hear the booms for the first time, their resonance and penetrating power almost seem too great to have come from a bird, but the call is produced by a controlled rush of air passing over the vocal cords whilst inflating the muscular oesophagus which acts as a sound chamber.

In Britain the distribution of the bittern is restricted by the availability of dense reedbeds, which it needs for feeding, breeding, roosting and overwintering. Persecution caused the bitterns to decline drastically in the last century: the last breeding pair was found in 1868 and it was not until overwintering birds from Europe decided to stay and breed that the bittern once again became a regular breeding species by 1911, gradually colonising Broads such as Hickling, Horsey and Catfield, spreading to Suffolk by 1930. More widespread colonisation was achieved by 1970, with up to 70 known pairs nesting in Britain, but there has been a gradual decline in the last 18 years, with only 40 pairs remaining in 4 counties. Fortunately most are found on reserves in East Anglia, and in Lancashire, with an isolated colony in Wales.

128

129

The decline is due to several factors, including severe winters, which prevent the bittern, like the heron, from catching food. Nitrate and phosphate poisoning, which kills the invertebrate fauna, eventually has its effects on animals higher up the food chain and as the fish die, the main diet of the bittern disappears. In Norfolk an obvious decline since 1976 is linked with an increase in disturbance from pleasure boats and fishing. Even though the majority of the remaining birds are on reserves the future of bitterns in Britain is far from certain, and it is the responsibility of every birdwatcher and conservationist to make sure that the bittern is not forced to fight back from extinction for a second time in only 120 years.

Watch out also on the Broads for a rufous-backed bird, with a grey head and long tail, flying low over the reeds. One is likely to be followed by several more. These are the resident **bearded tits (127)**, also known as reedlings, and they are totally dependent like the bittern on reedbeds for survival.

The best way to track down reedlings is to listen for their bell-like 'ping' call as they fly amongst the reed stems. Their flight is characteristically weak and fluttering, and when the wind is strong, rather than risk being blown about above the reed flower heads, they keep low down and can be seen moving through the reed stems, calling as they go.

Their distribution is restricted to the large areas of fenland, where extensive reedbeds grow. 400–600 pairs nest in Britain, with the majority found in East Anglia, although breeding populations have colonised Radipole Lake in Dorset, Oxwich Nature Reserve on the Gower Peninsular and the RSPB reserve at Leighton Moss, Lancashire. The numbers are affected by severe weather and after the cruel winter of 1946–7 they became close to extinction, with only six pairs remaining in East Anglia.

During the summer months, reedlings whirr backwards and forwards carrying insect food to their young. Like the summer-visiting reedbed warblers, which they nest alongside, the reedlings feed heavily on insects, caterpillars and spiders found amongst the reed stems; but unlike warblers which migrate south in the winter and can continue feeding on insects all year round, reedlings remain in Britain throughout the winter and have to change their diet if they are to survive once the insects have gone. Winter flocks of reedlings are an attractive sight as they move from reedhead to reedhead, picking out individual seeds or searching for the occasional insect hibernating in the brown heads of the bulrushes. To accommodate the seasonal change of diet, the bird's stomach has to swell to twice its summer volume, but if snow and ice, encapsulating the previous summer's reedheads, make the seeds unobtainable, the small reedlings are unable to find sufficient food and soon die in large numbers.

Reedlings are slightly larger than long-tailed tits and the male shows distinctive long, black moustachial markings, giving the bird its other name. His head is a blue-grey lilac with a short, downwardly curved yellow bill. The female lacks the black facial markings and her head and bill are light brown. Both sexes have long brown tails with graduated feathers similar to reed warblers; the feathers are longest in the middle and shorten towards the outside of the tail.

Reedlings nest low in the reeds, close to the ground, and it is important that there should be a thick supportive understorey of sedges and fenland vegetation beneath the nest, where the adults can skulk and feed, although feeding parents habitually fly up to 100 m/300 ft away from the nest to collect invertebrate food for the five to seven youngsters. Since the breeding

128 The long legs and toes of the water-rail are adapted for walking across floating aquatic plants.

129 When weather is severe the water-rail leaves the shelter of the reedbeds in search of food, which can include carrion, like this moorhen.

130 The Montagu's harrier is one of Britain's rarest breeding birds, nesting in reed beds, sand dunes and on open moorland. Recently the species has adopted arable land and here the female settles on to her four eggs hidden in a field of oats.

131 Female snipe approaching nest, well concealed in marsh vegetation. A recently hatched chick and three eggs remain in the nest.

conditions of the reedling are specific, there are detailed management schemes on all the occupied reserves, making a network of wet areas available for feeding, together with drier fenland patches suitable for nesting each summer.

You need to choose a cold day in winter to search the reedbeds for the **water rail**. Its shy and secretive nature means that it is rarely seen, but a protracted spell of freezing weather brings the water rail out into the open, to search for food. In the summer they are most likely seen after dusk, skulking along the margins of the reedbeds and dykes, but in the winter they often become desperate and forage for food during broad daylight without any cover at all (**128**).

Only 25 cm/10 in long, this bird is slightly smaller than the familiar snipe. The underparts are bluish-grey, whereas the chestnut-brown back and flanks are cryptically streaked with black, so that the bird merges into the uniform pattern of the reed stems when feeding or incubating. The slender red bill is another striking feature, perfectly shaped to cope with a varied diet of small fish, frogs, lizards, insects, freshwater crustaceans, seeds, roots and berries, depending on the availability and time of year. Normally the water rail is not aggressive towards other birds, but when food is really scarce, it stabs reed buntings and other small roosting birds with its bill like a heron.

Like the heron and bittern, the water rail's long muscular legs trail out beyond its short tail when in flight, but the water rail only flies as a last resort; although they are partially migratory, capable of reaching Europe after the winter, they prefer to climb through the reeds rather than fly low across the tops on their stubby, rounded wings. The legs end in three slender, forwardly pointing toes and one hind toe which, with a wide tripod-like splay, are ideal for carrying the water rail across soft mud and lily-pads, acting like snow-shoes in deep snow (**129**).

Depending on the severity of the winter, the water rail population fluctuates, but around 4,000 pairs breed in the British Isles; they are particularly widespread in Ireland, but absent in north-west Scotland. Reedbeds and fenland are strongholds for the bird, but it has also colonised canals, rivers and lakes, wherever there is dense cover and soft mud occurs which can be probed wader-like for food.

For most of the year, the water rail leads a solitary life, but each spring, during the mating season, pairs vigorously defend their territory. This is also the time to listen for the vocal sounds of the bird which cannot be confused with any other species. Just as dusk falls across the reedbed, a strange, eerie pig-like squeal pierces the air, followed by grunts and clucking. Other high-pitched whistles and trills mimicking the little grebe may also be heard during the breeding season, when the male displays to the female by bowing his head and exposing the white feathers of the under-tail coverts, in between chasing his partner through the reeds.

The water rail lays 6–11 buff, grey-brown blotched eggs during April and July in a deep, cupped ground nest made from reeds, sedges and any other aquatic vegetation available. It is very difficult to find, because it is always sited in dense vegetation and frequently on moist ground which will not support human weight.

The **marsh harrier** is one of Britain's rarest birds of prey, with 20–30 pairs (1986) breeding in Britain. Your best chances of seeing this summer visitor are at the East Anglian RSPB reserves of Strumpshaw Fen, Titchwell and Minsmere which are attractive to the harrier because of the extensive, undisturbed reedbeds which are necessary for breeding.

The marsh harrier is larger than the hen harrier of the moorlands (page 106), 48–56 cm/19–22 in; it is heavier built and the wings are broader. Both sexes are mainly brown, but the males have partially grey wings with black tips and grey tails whereas the female has a golden yellow head and cream shoulder patches which often catch the sunlight. Apart from a few overwintering females, the marsh harriers arrive in April. 'Skywatching' with binoculars is a regular birdwatchers' pastime in early spring: as the dark, broad-winged birds appear on the horizon, you can hear their faint repeated calls carrying on the wind, then with intermittent wing flaps the birds spiral and glide down with wings held slightly above the horizontal, until the shelter of the reedbeds is found.

The female builds the large nest in the middle of the reeds, forming a raised platform of reeds and small twigs, where she lays 3–8 eggs over two or three days. Whilst she sits tight on the nest, the male feeds her, and food is normally given by the traditional harrier food pass. The young harriers grow rapidly and at twelve days old receive 3–4 items of prey each per day, but they do not fledge until 35–40 days old. They are easily distinguishable by their pale yellow heads as they fly across the reeds.

The Norfolk Broads and East Anglian fens remain the ideal breeding sites for the marsh harrier because the adults range widely across open country whilst hunting. They prey heavily on various aquatic birds and their young, but they also like to hunt rabbits on the neighbouring fields and heaths.

Historically, marsh harriers have always nested in dense reedbeds and the large majority still do, but recently, as the populations have slowly increased, some pairs have nested in the arable fields surrounding the reedbeds, part of the mosaic of the Broads and fens.

These birds are not the only harriers which nest in lowland Britain: the rare **Montagu's harrier**, the smallest of the three British species (41–6 cm/16–18 in), also breeds in various lowland sites. The Montagu's harrier has always been rare in Britain because it is at the northernmost edge of its range, but in the 1950s, 30 pairs nested in Britain, before illegal persecution and death by agricultural toxic chemicals removed the harrier as a breeding bird by the early 1970s. Today a few pairs are back from southern Europe and these birds, used to nesting in arable and cereal fields, have begun to colonise the same habitats in Britain. Seventeen years ago the Montagu's harriers breeding in Britain used heathland moors, reedbeds and fenland as nest sites but the majority of recently discovered nests have been on farmland, although some pairs still nest on the drier fens of East Anglia and elevated marshland. In 1986 7 pairs bred and raised 13 chicks on sites ranging from Devon commonland, open moorland, coastal heath and downland, to farmland, amongst crops (**130**). During 1987 6 pairs successfully raised 15 young.

Montagu's harriers arrive in Britain during May and are about the size of a large woodpigeon. The male is similar in appearance to the male hen harrier, with dove-grey plumage, but has diagnostic black bars on the upper wings and a grey rump. They are both very agile, hunting over flat open country with the ability to twist and turn rapidly, using their long legs to snatch prey, which is mainly small birds.

Because of the Montagu harrier's new habit of nesting in arable fields in Britain, it has been necessary for wardens to work in close co-operation with farmers to help maintain breeding pairs. The adults are fairly tolerant of machinery passing close by, but once the young have hatched, they are susceptible to agricultural sprays, and it is encouraging that, without exception, all farmers and landowners have co-operated with the wardens by controlling their use of spraying and combining machines. Their support and awareness is most important since it is likely that farmland will be the main habitat in the future for visiting nesting Montagu's harriers, but the harriers will also need the total co-operation of birdwatchers. As the harriers are strictly protected Schedule 1 birds, birdwatchers must respect them. Although most nesting sites are closely guarded secrets, others have become known sites with groups of birdwatchers eagerly awaiting their first glimpse of this nesting rarity. Frequent observation and intrusion can cause desertion and already in 1987 one pair less nested than the previous year.

We have seen how the availability of reedbeds determines the colonisation of birds like the bittern, bearded tit, marsh and Montagu's harriers, but not all reedbeds attract these specialised species. Only the sedge warbler, reed warbler, moorhen, mallard and **reed bunting** are generally widespread reed-swamp or fenland species.

In March the resident reed buntings begin to occupy their regular nest sites and the males announce their presence by perching on the tops of the reed stems where they sing and proclaim their territory. Clearly distinguished by a black head and bib, divided by pure white moustachial stripes, the 16-cm/6-in bird is robust and sparrow-like. Around the back of the neck a white collar separates the head from the rich brown, black-streaked back, but the off-white underparts are clearly visible as the bird flits from one reed head to another. The female lacks the black head but her moustachial stripes are pale buff and match the stripe above the eyes. Both sexes show distinctive white feathers along the outer edges of their tails.

When a female flies through an occupied territory, the male takes off in pursuit. A sexual chase develops and periodically the male heads off the female, encouraging her to land, whereupon he displays with partly opened wings, excitedly quivering his fanned tail. At the same time he raises his crest feathers and inflates his throat to show off the black bib to his proposed mate. If his advances are accepted, the female remains in the territory and she begins to build an untidy nest in a sedge or grass tussock, or sometimes in a small bush, always close to the ground. The nest is constructed of grass and lined with moss or the fluffy seed heads of the reeds. Upon hatching both adults feed the young and in favourable summers up to three broods are successfully reared.

After breeding, which finishes in July, most of the reed buntings of fen, marshland and reed swamp disperse and form flocks, often feeding on farmland, but a few fly to the Continent for the winter and those which remain are joined by visiting birds from northern Europe.

The reed bunting is now increasingly found in upland country too where it colonises the moors (page 96). In the last twenty-five years its range has extended to include completely dry habitats, and downland and arable land have become very popular with nests built in the middle of cereal crops, but there must always be fenceposts or hedges near by, where the male can perch and utter his territorial song.

Marsh and fenland birds have declined as their habitats have been disturbed, amongst them the **common snipe (131)**. There are 100,000 pairs nesting throughout the British Isles, but it has declined rapidly in areas where marshland has been drained, especially in the last few decades. The shy, secretive 27-cm/10½-in bird is widespread across southern England, with larger populations in the west and north where it favours damp meadows, river valleys, bogs and marshland. In the Scottish Highlands, heather moorland is the snipe's main habitat and large breeding populations are found on the Scottish islands where the St Kilda race are larger with darker markings than southern birds. The central extensive peat bogs of Ireland are a recognised stronghold of the snipe, but even here they are increasingly disturbed by commercial peat extraction and this widely distributed wader is beginning to decline in what was once the perfect undisturbed marshy wilderness. Some individuals breed on the coastal saltmarshes of Britain.

On the freshwater marshland where coarse grasses and sedges form dense tussocks, the snipe, with its golden brown, cream and black plumage is perfectly camouflaged as it crouches without the slightest movement. It sits tight until almost trodden on, when it rises sharply from the ground, uttering its alarm note, and twists and turns across the marsh before banking in rapid flight to assess the danger. It circles several times but eventually returns and lands to hide amongst the damp vegetation.

Snipe-watching is best in the evening during the summer when most feeding and flight activity take place, but in the winter, food shortage forces them to feed in daylight. They use their long straight bills to probe for invertebrate fauna – chiefly worms and snails. Winter is also the time of year when snipe form small flocks called 'whisps'. Each spring they disperse to occupy breeding territories and for the rest of the year are very solitary. Many of the birds of reedbed and marshland suffer losses during cold weather, but snipe are clever at finding unfrozen ground where large groups of up to a hundred birds often congregate. Only if the weather becomes severe and prolonged do English birds fly to Ireland, where the climate is milder because of the effects of the Gulf Stream; a few even migrate to Europe for the winter.

You may hear the evocative 'chipp-er, chipp-er' song of the snipe across the marshland each spring as the breeding season begins. It is accompanied by drumming, which is one of the highlights of marshland birdwatching.

Hidden amongst grass tussocks, sedges or small clumps of reeds, the snipe's nest is little more than a flattened scrape. In April the female lays and incubates four buff, brown-blotched eggs for around twenty days. Upon hatching, the attractive, rich chestnut, white-flecked, downy chicks leave the nest immediately and the male, who played no part in the incubation, resumes interest in the family by returning to help feed and protect them. The chicks are very independent but do not fledge for a further nineteen days, during which period the adults frequently divide them into two groups, probably to prevent total loss by attack from a predator. In good summers, or when the first clutch is lost by cattle trampling across the marshland, the snipe is double-brooded.

Over the centuries large areas of Britain's marshland have been drained and reclaimed for grazing pasture and arable land and very little of the ancient fenland and extensive reedbeds of the lowland flood plains remains. The rustling, wind-blown reeds, the sedges and the carr vegetation of the fen are unique and important to many rare and common species of bird but their future and that of these watery habitats remains in the balance, to be saved or lost by the decisions of the influential few.

CHAPTER 10

LAKES, PONDS, GRAVEL PITS

LAKES

Wetlands attract birds for three reasons: food supply, potential breeding sites and relative safety. Other habitats provide the first two requirements, but many do not offer the same degree of sanctuary as that created by a large, surrounding expanse of water, which is alien to man and, in most cases, keeps him at an acceptable distance.

Of all our areas of free-standing water the lakes are probably the best known. The Lake District in Cumbria attracts many thousands of visitors each year, and yet a tourist, visiting a number of these lakes in summer, will be surprised how each varies from the other. At their richest, lakes can support a greater number and range of animals and plants than any other habitat, but some of those in the Lake District, although aesthetically appealing with their mountainous backdrops, are almost sterile. Because of this huge variance lakes are studied in distinct categories to make it easier to understand why the flora and fauna of lakes differ so much from one to another.

Lakes fall into two broad categories: upland and lowland lakes. In the British Isles the uplands are those regions over 240 m/787 ft above sea level, and the lowlands are all the other areas. The birdwatcher should also be aware that in Ireland, lakes are called loughs, pronounced the same way as lochs, the name given to lakes in Scotland, and that lochs and sea lochs are completely different habitats.

Our upland lakes represent some of the most natural habitats in the British Isles, scooped out of the solid rock by the huge glaciers of the last Ice Age, whereas most of the lowland lakes are man-made. As a habitat, lakes are very localised and represent 1 per cent of our land surface.

Upland lakes are more common than their lowland counterparts, because of the difference in the geology and climate of the British Isles. Upland Scotland, Wales and Ireland receive heavy rainfall for many months of the year and although the soil layer is thin, the underlying rock is hard and impervious. Therefore any natural precipitation and water draining from the hills runs off as spirited mountain streams, down into the valley, where it often drains into a deep natural lake. In lowland southern England, the soil layer is deeper and lies over porous rocks like chalk, so the less frequent rain is soaked up by the soil or drains away through the permeable rock substrata. For this reason, lowland lakes are generally found on clay soils, which are impermeable to water, or where a hard-pan (page 62) is formed. Most lowland lakes are shallow and much smaller than those of upland country.

A lake in summer with fields, woods or mountains reflected in the calm surface appears idyllic, but lakes are distinguished from other still-water habitats by being large enough to be affected by the forces of the wind. A tranquil scene can quickly change when a storm rages, whipping up the surface of the lake into choppy waves which erode the margins and unprotected shores, frequently preventing the colonisation of reeds and water plants.

The changeability of lakes in mood and physical nature, together with the type of shoreline, depth, area and mineral nature of the water, limit the species of birds able to colonise them. All lakeland birds survive either on the open water or around the margins and their success depends upon how well they can adapt to regular changes of habitat conditions.

The waters of freshwater habitats have a nutritional value, depending on their acidity or alkalinity. This organic richness is called the trophic status, and determines the plants and animals able to survive in and around the water. Most of our lakes are either alkaline and therefore eutrophic, or acidic and oligotrophic. Since the type of rock over which rainwater and rivers flow influences the quality of the water, the majority of our upland lakes are oligotrophic, because these regions of the British Isles are the main areas of acidic rock; amongst these are most of the large lakes in northern and western Britain, including some of those in the Lake District, and they are usually deep with stony shores. The majority of lowland lakes, on the other hand, are eutrophic, because below 240 m/787 ft much of the rock is calcareous and alkaline; these have vegetated margins and the water is generally shallow. Experienced birdwatchers are soon able to classify a lake by a combination of its chemical and physical qualities.

Not all freshwater habitats are eutrophic or oligotrophic. Habitats where the water is more acidic than the normal oligotrophic habitat are referred to as dystrophic; and lakes and pools where the water has an alkalinity far greater than the accepted eutrophic habitat are called marls. These are usually found in limestone areas, where the name-giving, fine, white chalk deposits settle on the bottom and the water is extremely clear and blue. The Burren, an area of outstanding limestone pavement in Ireland's Co. Clare, has a fluctuating water-level, and many of the temporary lakes, called turloughs (**132**), are marl habitats.

Dystrophic pools usually occur within an acidic or oligotrophic habitat, wherever the acidic mineral salts are allowed to concentrate. The habitat is most common in the peat mires of the northern and western regions of the British Isles, and the dubh lochans and peat pools of Caithness and Sutherland are the most widespread dystrophic waters known. Loch Laidon (465 ha/1,150 acres) in Argyll is one of the largest single examples of a constantly dystrophic lake. It receives drainage water from Rannoch Moor and although it contains a few fish, the lake margins are decidedly bare of vegetation and few ducks or geese are ever seen.

Sometimes an aquatic habitat has water with qualities which fall between eutrophic and oligotrophic. These restricted type of lakes are called mesotrophic and in the British Isles are sited where uplands and lowlands meet: acidic water running from the mountains into the lake mixes with more alkaline water running over calcareous rocks, forming the low-lying end of the same lake. Loch Lomond is a well-known example of a

AND RESERVOIRS

132

partially mesotrophic lake: at its deeper northern end, where it is fed by mountain streams, the water is oligotrophic, and at the southern end, the shallower water are fed by the River Endrick, which has drained from agricultural land and is eutrophic. Where the two types of water mix within the Loch, mesotrophic conditions occur, increasing to eutrophic as the water reaches the inflow of the River Endrick. Birdwatching is far more rewarding at this southern end of the loch.

In the British Isles, pure mesotrophic waters are rare, but Hatchet Pond in the New Forest and Esthwaite Water in Cumbria are examples, the latter being one of the largest volumes of mesotrophic water in the country. It was oligotrophic at one time but, due to agricultural run-off, it has slowly become enriched so that eventually the entire lake will probably become eutrophic. Esthwaite Water is not important for wildfowl but, walking around the shores, you will see that aquatic plants are not as common as they are in a pure eutrophic lake and therefore coot, swan and dabbling duck which feed heavily on vegetation are also not so common; but the roach, rudd, perch and stone loach, easily visible in the clear water, attract a few grebe and diving ducks. Some Canada and greylag geese nest around the lake.

Since birds colonise lakes because of the food, breeding and sanctuary potential, the shallower, lowland, eutrophic lakes hold the most birdlife, because the birds rely for food on invertebrates and plants which are more abundant under eutrophic conditions. Lowland eutrophic lakes are easily recognised by the lush vegetation around their margins and deep fertile mud at the bottom. This mud is so rich in nutrients that it causes the algae in the water to reproduce quickly; and

132 Pale blue turloughs are a specialised form of Marl lake, characteristic of limestone country in Ireland.

primary producers in the food chain of the lake provide food for invertebrates, which, in turn, feed the fish which feed various species of birds. The shallow water and floating plants encourage other species which mostly stay to breed wherever the marginal cover is suitable.

Although eutrophic lakes are rich in plantlife, with corresponding advantage to the birds, one serious disadvantage is that, as the plants die and decompose, they fall into the lake and constantly add to the natural silting up of the open water. Eventually reed swamp and fen vegetation take over and stabilise the land around the lake, and alder and willow trees establish as the ground level rises. By succession of plants, the area of open water is encroached upon, and in some cases almost completely dries out, unless dredged and managed by man, removing vegetation before it becomes too established. All the areas of still water in the British Isles are also prone to evaporation, which generally exceeds the rate at which water naturally enters them. Thus many of our lakes, ponds and pools are doomed to disappear.

Out in the centre of a lowland lake, a pair of **coots** are diving. Each time they return to the surface, the water weeds they have retrieved hang down the side of their faces, resembling green moustaches. Like those of grebes and swans, the legs of the coot are positioned well back along the body and although they are adept in the water, they are comical and clumsy on land. The coot is therefore a true wetland bird inhabiting the lake for food, sanctuary and breeding. Frequently submerged for over 15 seconds, coots dive to over 3.6 m/12 ft and their ability to find submerged plants enables them to feed in the deepest lakes, rivers and reservoirs. They cannot really be mistaken for any other bird, except perhaps the smaller moorhen of rivers and streams (page 121): with their distinctive white shield on the forehead, which is larger in the male than the female, and even black plumage, coots are easily identified. At close range you can see that they lack the broad bill of ducks, and at a distance coots are distinguished by their humped appearance. This is quite different from the straight-backed shape of the ducks which they feed alongside in winter, forming huge rafts of up to 5,000 birds.

Coots are always reluctant to take off, preferring to run frantically across the water surface on their powerful feet. On the rare occasions when a coot takes off, look for the characteristic pale white wing bar along the trailing edge and faint green legs dangling beneath. Unlike most aquatic birds the coot does not have webbed feet, but broad, semi-circular skin lobes border both sides of the toes and propel it through the water.

It is only in severe winters that large numbers of coots move from the lakes to coastal waters: generally the 100,000 breeding pairs are sedentary, remaining on their breeding lakes and reservoirs all year round. For most of the year coots are gregarious, but each spring they defend their territories ferociously between groups, each pair occupying up to 0.4 ha/1 acre. The territory is chosen to provide all the food and shelter necessary for the offspring and whenever fights break out, they are usually between four birds competing for a favourable territory, with the two males fighting each other and the females creating their own *melée* with thrashing wings and flailing claws. These claws are about 2.5 cm/1 in long, inwardly curved and as effective as a cat's.

Eventually territories are claimed and both birds build the large floating nest from water plants and dead leaves, attaching it to overhanging tree branches which dangle into the water, or to the stems of reeds. It is always very concealed. The pair work as a team: the male is responsible for collecting the nest material and the female shapes it into the nest platform. In April she lays up to ten eggs, which both adults incubate for 23–25 days. Upon hatching, the male feeds the chicks, but the female broods them in the nest for the first two or three days, after which they leave and feed themselves. Adult coots are chiefly vegetarians, with some mollusc and insect intake, but young coots require invertebrate food during their first few days because of its added protein content. Small flies, gnats and mosquitoes emerging on the surface from their larval cases are the main diet, but the inexperienced young coots are not really quick enough to seize these insects as they sit on the surface film. Watching the coots darting in every direction, trying to satisfy their hunger, is both fascinating and entertaining. It is not until they are about ten days old that they master their hunting technique with speed and agility. Twenty days after hatching the feet have developed and the coots are able to dive below the surface to find submerged water plants to add to their diet. They grow more rapidly once they have mastered the technique of diving and become fully fledged at eight weeks, when they begin to resemble an adult, but have whiter underparts; the rest of the plumage is ash grey, rather than black.

By March on the lake great crested grebes are beginning to enact their elaborate, ritualistic courtship on a quiet, open stretch of water; and as April enters its second week, swallows dip across the surface, heralding their return from South Africa and the new breeding season ahead of them. Southern lakes attract the swallows as they arrive, because the first emerging insects of spring begin to leave the water in mid-April, coinciding perfectly with the swallows' need to replace energy lost during flight. When the marsh marigold is in bloom, birdwatchers can expect to hear and see the female cuckoo, looking for the nest of the reed warbler, which is the cuckoo's favourite host species in wetland habitats. As summer fades, house martins, swallows and swifts congregate over the lake to capitalise on the late summer insects and some of the swallows use the reedbeds as their evening roosting site, prior to migration; but as autumn arrives, their numbers decline as wildfowl begin to arrive from northern and eastern Europe.

Among these is the **pochard** from Russia. Pochards are slightly larger than coots, reaching a length of 46 cm/18 in. Drakes are particularly handsome. The reddish-brown head and neck, contrasting with the black breast and silvery-grey plumage, adds a touch of brightness to any lowland lake in winter, and through binoculars the diagnostic black bill with blue-grey stripe is clearly visible. This bill marking is even clearer on the female, who is less brightly coloured than her mate, but is recognised by the dark brown head, neck and breast, light grey-brown upperparts and lighter flanks. Both adults arrive in winter with this breeding plumage, which results from the summer moult and remains until the following July, when the birds become much duller as feathers are lost and gradually replaced.

Between two and three hundred pairs of pochard are resident in the British Isles, breeding on densely vegetated natural lakes and marshland, mainly in eastern England, but each winter our resident birds are joined by thousands of visitors, and the wintering population reaches 40–50,000 birds.

As a breeding bird, the pochard is rare in Ireland with as few as ten pairs, but in autumn and winter, birdwatchers are greeted with some of the largest flocks of pochard anywhere in the British Isles. As early as September huge rafts occur on Loughs Derravaragh, Neagh and Corrib with up to 20,000 birds on each lough, and on Lough Corrib they dive alongside 16,000 coots, offering a spectacular sight in the winter sunshine. The pochard, which begin to arrive at Lough Corrib in July to overwinter, reach their peak in early November, when on one occasion over 22,000 have been counted, representing 10 per cent of the entire north-west European population.

Their dispersal in the spring is equally dramatic: by January only around 2,000 remain, falling to several hundred by March. Most of the birds return to eastern Europe to breed, although a few possibly remain in Ireland or England for the summer. But although they are not common as a breeding bird, we are at least able to watch their courtship displays before they depart, because many pairs are formed during February and March, whilst they are still in their large flocks. As well as being gregarious, pochard are sociable birds and they become very tolerant of birdwatchers, so even on the London reservoirs and Thames Valley gravel pits their display behaviour is easy to observe.

A drake pochard chases a duck on to the water, where he begins to puff out his neck feathers and whistle to the duck, who responds by dipping her bill into the water. Encouraged by her response, the drake repeatedly shakes and flicks his head before throwing it right back over his shoulders uttering a 'krik-krik' call as he does so. This courtship is performed on the

133 Female goosander, one of the few species of duck that regularly nests in holes in trees.

134 Wigeon are grazing ducks and in winter can be seen feeding on the flood meadows of the Ouse Washes and Somerset Levels or on the numerous estuaries and mud flats.

135 The shy corncrake is declining everywhere because it prefers to nest in quiet grassy meadows and hayfields which have become affected by changes in farm management and grass-cutting mechanisation. It is now confined to Orkney, the Hebrides, Western Scotland and Ireland.

136 Apart from in north-west Ireland and Scotland, the common gull is not particularly common. Inland it feeds on insects and seed; on the coast, worms, molluscs and crustaceans form its main diet.

137 Every March black-headed gulls return to their breeding grounds where they nest close to one another amongst the sedges and rushes and laughingly call to each other.

open water and is often disputed by rival males, but by the time the pochards depart, many of them have paired for the summer.

The few that nest in England colonise lowland lakes or any shallow stretch of stagnant eutrophic water where the reedbeds and vegetation are particularly dense, because the nest is not built on dry land but is constructed by the duck out of leaves and reed stems, actually on the water surface or right at the margin amongst the bulrushes and reeds.

Pochards in both Britain and Europe used to nest on marshlands, but since many of these have been drained and developed within the last few decades, they were forced to move elsewhere. Whereas the tufted duck has successfully colonised reservoirs and gravel pits, pochards are not so adaptable because many reservoirs lack the necessary dense, nesting, marginal vegetation.

Lough Neagh is the largest freshwater lake in the British Isles, occupying a huge basalt depression in the centre of Northern Ireland. Because it is shallow (12–15 m/40–50 ft) and highly eutrophic, fed by at least six major rivers running through farmland, it is one of Europe's most significant wildfowl haunts. The coastline is 24 km/15 miles long and a regular haunt for birdwatchers.

As any visitor to Ireland knows, there is a lot of rain and the Lough Neagh area is no exception, with an average of 84 cm/33 in spread over the 150–175 wet days each year. Because the surrounding soil is mixed clay deposits, it is poorly drained so extensive fenland is established around the lough, providing a valuable habitat for birds.

It is early morning in December: waders probe the mud in the nearby water-logged fields and wigeon, teal, pintail and goldeneye circle across the water before coming in to land. From now on the wildfowl population peaks, with even more pochard, tufted duck, Icelandic whooper swans and Siberian Bewick's swans joining the resident mute swans on the lough. The rich supply of invertebrate food, brought in with the sediment from the feeder-rivers, provides an endless supply of food for the thousands of different birds spending the winter here.

Like so many wetland habitats in the British Isles, Lough Neagh and the surrounding fenland is under threat from drainage and agricultural schemes. In many areas the poor clay soils have been fertilised and their drainage improved, and cereal crops and potatoes are grown in the fields surrounding the lough, especially on the southern and western shores. In winter and early spring these same fields provide feeding grounds for black-tailed godwit, curlew, snipe, lapwing and redshank; only the flooded meadows of Upper Lough Erne in Co. Fermanagh hold larger populations of these species in Northern Ireland.

Birdwatching around Lough Neagh in March is particularly rewarding, because of the large colonies of great-crested grebes which nest on the lough. The Oxford Island Nature Reserve, which is a peninsular on the south-east shore, is one of the best regions to watch the grebe where reedbeds only 45 m/148 ft long conceal over a hundred occupied nests.

A few weeks later, in the fields surrounding the south-eastern shore of Lough Neagh, a great rarity may be seen. Frequently heard at night, but towards late April and throughout May in the daytime too, the loud, rasping 'krrx-krrx' of the **corncrake** carries on the breeze. The long grass and dense vegetation bordering the margins of the fields is the corncrake's favourite habitat, but even when calling it remains well hidden and as

with the water-rail a certain amount of luck is necessary to catch a sight of this declining and shy species.

At 17,000 ha/42,000 acres, Lough Corrib in Galway is the second largest lake in Ireland and one of the largest areas of eutrophic water in the British Isles. The south-eastern end is narrow, with a maximum depth of 6 m/19½ ft and the water lies on limestone, with fen habitat towards the south. The northern end of the lake is much wider, and its depth penetrates to 45 m/147 ft; the water lies over a mixture of granite sandstone and shale, although most of the shoreline shows exposed limestone, covered by a sparse bog-like vegetation. The large quantities of limestone release their minerals into the water, concentrating the calcium salts in some areas of the lake to such a degree that marl deposits are formed on the bottom. The marl conditions are unsuitable for plankton, so the water of Lough Corrib is exceptionally blue and clear.

Marl lakes are found in uplands and lowlands, wherever chalk and limestone occur. Malham Tarn in Yorkshire, and the Cotswold Water Park in Gloucestershire are two of the best-known English examples, but the most fascinating marl conditions are found in the temporary lakes of Ireland, called turloughs, meaning dry lakes. Turloughs are little more than grassy depressions in limestone regions, and are found nowhere else in the world outside Ireland. They are most common on the Burren of Co. Clare and eastern Co. Galway, where the bare, limestone pavement resembles a lunar landscape. Since limestone is permeable, any fluctuation in subterranean water-levels filters through the limestone and fills the depressions, forming marl-bottomed turloughs, with their characteristic pale blue appearance (**132**).

Their formation of turloughs depends on the volume of rainfall and the rise and fall of the water in these areas. When they do form, they are good places for birds, especially vegetarians like swan, wigeon, brent and white-fronted geese, who flock to feed in the shallows. The turloughs vary widely, from the extremely shallow, saucer-like depressions only a few metres across to large basins covering hundreds of hectares. Rahasane in eastern Galway is the largest turlough in Ireland, over 3 km/2 miles long and 1 km/½ mile wide, with a uniform depth of about 1.5 m/5 ft. Deep in the centre of the Burren, the Castletown river flows through the Carran Depression, which at 60 m/200 ft is a very impressive valley with steep, towering limestone cliffs overshadowing. Small permanently filled turloughs are found throughout this valley and they all tend to be around 1.5 m/5 ft deep. Perhaps the most dramatic aspect of many turloughs is their habit of disappearing completely. When rainfall is heaviest from November to April, water fills and flows through the subterranean passages which honeycomb the limestone rock and the turloughs become filled with water. As mid-summer arrives, the rainfall reduces, water drains away through the same channels, often within the space of a few days, and all that remains is a damp grassy depression where hundreds of birds were drinking and feeding just days before.

The clear water of a turlough appears to be lifeless but those which are permanently flooded are always richer in animal life than the basins which flood only periodically. The size, marginal vegetation and type of sediment on the bottom of the turlough are additional factors which encourage invertebrate life to colonise, and fish, especially sticklebacks, are only found where drainage is minimal. In winter flocks of curlew, golden plover, dunlin and lapwing mix with smaller groups of black-tailed godwit to probe in the shallows for the invertebrate feast.

Land reclamation and drainage schemes do not spare these

mysterious unique turloughs and in the last few years many of them have been destroyed; even Rahasane, which is in internationally important winter feeding ground for white-fronted geese from Greenland, is now under threat. The plans for drainage are totally unacceptable to conservationists because the turlough has for centuries provided sanctuary and food for up to five thousand wigeon, hundreds of mallard, shoveler, pintail, teal and tufted duck, together with regular flocks of whooper, Bewick's and mute swans.

Of particular concern is the fact that plans and schemes for draining are discussed and implemented without any thorough study of the real benefits to agriculture. Arterial drainage destroys the naturally filling turloughs and will prevent Rahasane from being the ornithologically significant site it becomes each autumn and winter. Surely its geological interest and the fact that it is the largest remaining permanent turlough in the world, make it sufficiently important to be left untouched, a protected example of a fascinating and unique habitat.

If man continues to destroy the wetland habitats of Ireland, including the extensive peat bogs, migratory and over-wintering birds will suffer. Although the River Shannon has not been extensively interfered with, other large and small rivers have been altered along their lengths by diversion and drainage schemes, which alter the natural water-level and reduce the flow of the river, preventing winter flooding of the neighbouring fields and the formation of turloughs. A significant problem is that the birds cannot be forewarned that their traditional habitats are disappearing. The Irish climate is oceanic, with a mean January temperature normally above 4°C, so lakes, ponds or turloughs rarely freeze over for long. Because of this, Ireland has always been a major overwintering area and refuge for countless species of birds forced to fly west by adverse conditions over the rest of Britain and Europe. Waders and wildfowl have used the wetlands of Ireland in winter for thousands of years, and it is the first landfall for many birds moving south from their breeding grounds in the Arctic Circle. Instinct causes the winter birds to arrive each year, but their habitats could decline to a level that will be unable to support the arriving populations.

Lough Neagh and the northern Lough Beg represent habitats considered to be 'Wetlands of International Importance', and on these large eutrophic lakes nest thousands of tufted duck, alongside red-breasted mergansers, shelduck, shoveler, teal and the rarer gadwall and garganey.

Only 500–700 pairs of **gadwall** nest in the British Isles, mostly on eutrophic lakes in East Anglia, but some nest on Loughs Beg and Neagh amongst the rush tussocks. Female gadwalls resemble female mallards with their uniform mottled brown plumage, but as they take off and fly away across the lough, their diagnostic white wing speculum distinguishes them from mallard ducks, which have a bright violet-blue speculum. Additionally the bill of the gadwall duck is slimmer than the mallard's with orange sides, and her forehead has a steeper incline when seen in profile.

Unlike most other species of duck, the drake gadwall is not strikingly marked and because it is also rare it is frequently overlooked by birdwatchers. As the drake gadwall dabbles for aquatic vegetation and the occasional mollusc at the edge of the lough, it appears brownish-grey at a distance. It is darker on the upperparts, and the neck and chest are delicately marked with black, grey and white, forming a reticulated pattern. When the drake timidly drifts closer, white markings are visible on the wings, even whilst it is at rest on the water

surface. Whenever it takes to the air, the pointed wings beat more rapidly than the mallard's, and these white markings are revealed as distinguishable patches occupying the rear half of the secondaries. In good light it is these white patches and the beautiful chestnut and black shoulder markings which identify the male gadwall.

The first official records of gadwall breeding in Britain were announced in 1850. This was a pinioned pair, released in Norfolk, whence the offspring spread across Britain and into Ireland. Each winter our small groups of resident gadwall are joined by an influx from Iceland and northern Europe, with as many as 5,000 overwintering on well-vegetated lakes, meres, ponds, quiet reservoirs and coastal brackish marshes like Cley in Norfolk.

Very few birdwatchers actually see gadwall performing their breeding and courtship displays, but gadwall nest each year on St Serfs Island in Loch Leven, Tayside, which is one of the most important wildfowl breeding sites in Britain. They can also be seen at Leighton Moss Reserve in Lancashire. Once paired, the duck builds the nest on her own in the reeds or amongst dense vegetation on the lakeside bank. It is always placed on elevated ground, but close to the water; islands in the middle of lakes are very popular, as part of a breeding territory which occupies between 10–30 ha/24–72 acres.

Although it is chiefly vegetarian, dabbling for roots, leaves, stems and seeds, the gadwall is often seen upending in shallow water, disturbing the base sediment for invertebrates like snails, worms and tadpoles.

Each April a small 38-cm/15-in duck, about the size of a pigeon, lands on the flooded coal workings of Stodmarsh in Kent, and on a few other choice shallow lakes in Kent and East Anglia, dropping on to the water after flying from south of the Sahara in West and East Africa. This rare species is the **garganey**, the only summer-visiting duck in Britain. Our shores are the extreme western edge of their breeding range, so only about 50 pairs now nest here; they are mostly confined to southern England, although a few pairs breed on the Ouse Washes in Cambridgeshire and at Leighton Moss.

More nervous than many other ducks and always restlessly swimming close to the reedbeds and marginal vegetation of the lake, the drake garganey is a handsome bird, with a distinguishable curved, white eye-stripe, which begins just in front of the eye and arches down to the nape of the neck. The reddish-brown head is elegantly marked with grey-white markings on the cheeks, extending down to the breast and flanks. The light bluish-grey upperparts are usually partially covered with beautiful sickle-shaped, pendulous grey, brown and white scapular feathers, which are prominent when the drake flies. Also revealed in flight is the stunning green speculum bordered by a white margin in front and behind. These wing markings always identify the drake garganey, and are some of the most attractive of any wildfowl.

As a pair of garganey wheel and turn across the reedbeds their swift flight resembles that of teal, but they are more acrobatic and they are marginally faster.

In Britain garganey favour lakes, meres, ditches, pools and freshwater marshes where there is variable plant growth, sedges and preferably some carr vegetation close by. During April the duck searches for a quiet, inaccessible site within the lakeside undergrowth and shuffles her way through the foliage until she finds a nest site which will not flood very easily.

Most birdwatchers see garganey during their arrival or passage in spring, or when they congregate before flying south

138

138 Truly wild breeding greylag geese are confined to the heather moors and loch margins of the north-west Scotland and the Outer Hebrides.

139 Nests of the red-throated diver are built close to the water on a small island in the middle of a loch.

to their wintering grounds from August onwards. They confine themselves to eutrophic water where they can be mistaken for a rather slender teal, dabbling for water plants which are their main diet, but sometimes supplementing these with worms, snails and insects plucked from the floating vegetation.

Because many species of gulls are always seen near the coast, some people assume that all gulls are sea birds. However, the **black-headed gull**, which really has a dark chocolate-brown head in summer and an almost white one in winter, has, since the early 1900s, become increasingly more an agricultural and terrestrial than a marine bird, and is frequently seen following the plough on farmland or squabbling for the freshly exposed worms; during winter this small 36–38-cm/14–15-in gull is common inland as well as along the coast, throughout the British Isles.

It breeds in colonies throughout the British Isles, many of which, like those on the Rye Harbour reserve and Burrowes Pits at Dungeness, are accessible to view from hides. Interestingly the southern England sites are generally near the sea, around brackish lagoons and pools, whereas in the Midlands and north the traditional colonies are around moorland tarns and lowland and upland lakes, with some coastal sites on sand-dunes, salt-marshes, and islands in estuaries. As the

black-headed gull has become more urbanised, it has also started to breed on sewage farms, gravel pits and the quieter corners of water parks.

Since the winters in northern Europe are more severe than our own, thousands of Continental black-headed gulls arrive to flock with our own resident population, so no winter bird-watcher ever has a problem finding large groups of these birds. Their appearance does not live up to their name in winter, because the characteristic head markings (**137**) shown by both sexes in the summer, are reduced to nothing more than a small grey-brown patch behind the eye in winter. Confusion can occur when, around December, some black-headed gulls begin to regrow their dark hood: the intermediary stages might suggest a different species of gull to an inexperienced bird-watcher.

During winter, the normally bright red legs, feet and beak become duller and the beak assumes a black tip, only really distinguishable through binoculars, but in the summer months the silvery-grey upperparts contrast attractively with the white neck, breast and underparts. The wing tips are black and the leading edge of the primaries are pure white, remaining as a diagnostic field characteristic throughout the winter, when most other distinguishing features have changed.

Around the margins of the Loch of Kinnordy, in Tayside,

The ability of the black-headed gull to colonise so many habitats means that its diet is equally varied. On farmland it feeds on insects, larvae and earthworms, often stealing them from the more docile lapwings feeding in the furrows; or it scavenges the fish offal from canning factories each day, alongside herring gulls (**201**). It even behaves like a starling in high summer, twisting and turning after swarming ants, which it catches on the wing, showing just how adaptable it is and why it is able to colonise and breed around upland, oligotrophic lakes and the organically richer lowland lakes and meres.

The shallow meres of Cheshire and Shropshire were formed in a variety of ways. In the last Ice Age the whole area was covered by southward-advancing glaciers, bulldozing soil and rocks along their paths so that, when the last Ice Age ended and the ice sheets retreated, some huge blocks of the glaciers became isolated and surrounded by mineral debris, forming an impermeable bank. As the ice melted, the water was unable to flow away and kettle-hole lakes were formed which have subsequently been kept full by rainfall and drainage from the surrounding hills.

In contrast, in the remote and rugged uplands of the British Isles, the power of the ice gouged deep, narrow and seemingly endless trenches through the hard rocks and particularly in western Ireland, southern Scotland, the Lake District and North Wales, dark lakes remain, filled initially by the melt water of the ice 20,000 years ago. Many of the mountain tarns and corries have been formed by the action of ice which rasped, cut, chiselled and pulverised the uplands to produce natural depressions which eventually filled with water. Some upland lakes have non-glacial origins and were formed by huge movements in the earth's crust, generally along weaknesses or fault lines, like the 38.6-km/24-mile Loch Ness on the Great Glen Fault in the Highlands.

Since upland lakes tend to be oligotrophic, and are also increasingly affected by acid rain (page 117), these lakes lack organic life such as algae and plankton and are exceptionally clear. Ennerdale Lake in Cumbria, Loch Grannoch in Galloway and Loch Fleet in the eastern Highlands all show these characteristics, but the latter is almost biologically dead, due to acid-rain fallout.

Not all upland lakes, however, are oligotrophic: Lake Windermere in the Lake District is eutrophic. It is England's largest natural lake, 17 km/10½ miles long and 1 km/1½ miles wide, and because of its glacial origin the water is deep, reaching 67 m/220 ft in places. Several rivers draining agricultural land run into Windermere, carrying their nutrients, and although some areas of the shoreline lack vegetation, common reed has established wherever sediments have been allowed to settle in sheltered bays. Beneath the surface perfoliate pondweed with long leafy stems, the shorter shoreweed and Canadian pondweed grow and, where the water is not too deep, actually reach the surface forming green platforms. During summer swans and shelduck breed and although the attractively marked duck is familiar to birdwatchers on estuaries and sand-dunes, it also nests in woods, some distance from the water at the southern end of Lake Windermere – a habit that has fascinated ornithologists since the birds first bred in 1918.

black-headed gulls laughingly call to each other. Every March and April up to 6,000 pairs return to breed amongst the sedges and bogbean, which form the floating bog around this 81-ha/200-acre eutrophic lake. From March until the end of August the high-pitched laughing yelps deafen the visitor. In spring the males, who establish a territory, spend most of their time fighting off rivals with repeated stabs of the bill or threatening intruders by standing erect with necks outstretched to present a tall image.

Defence is generally interspersed with display. As a female lands within a male's territory, he immediately opens his wings, fans his tail and flicks his head from side to side. The female is nervous at first, but slowly she approaches and submissively lowers her head with the bill slightly inclined. Walking towards her, the male accepts her presence and their courtship continues with both birds tossing their heads in unison, until he leads his partner to the proposed nest site. Usually the female accepts the chosen site and both birds begin to build their nest, which is little more than a sparsely lined scrape shielded by vegetation.

Only one brood is reared in a season, but black-headed gulls are good parents, both sharing the duties of brooding, feeding and protecting the yellow-downed youngsters, until they fledge at around five weeks and disperse as autumn approaches.

One of the most interesting breeding ducks on this Cumbrian lake is the **red-breasted merganser** which first nested in the 1950s and is usually associated with remote lochs, lakes and the higher reaches of mountain rivers in Scotland and Wales.

In Ireland you are likely to see the merganser in winter, around Strangford Lough, Cork Harbour and the coast, but they breed well inland, to the north and west of an imaginary line running from west Cork to north Lough.

The generic name 'sawbill' is a descriptive term for certain ducks who are specialised feeders, diving for fish like grebes, and who prefer large, open expanses of water. In the British Isles these ducks, with long, tapering bill, ending in a curved hook, are represented by the smew, goosander and merganser. Unlike the mallard and other dabbling ducks the filtering lamellae along the edges of the mandibles are replaced by small sharp teeth which seize and grip the slippery prey. Whereas the smew is only a winter visitor to Britain and is most often seen on the reservoirs of south-east England (page 168) both the goosander and merganser are resident birds, but the goosander does not breed in Ireland and, as with the merganser, Scotland is its main breeding ground.

Early on an April morning, the water of Lake Windermere ripples in the breeze and the birches growing around the edge of the Lake are covered with catkins. A pair of red-breasted mergansers are fishing, each dive lasting for around twenty-five seconds. The fish they bring to the surface to swallow are 10–20 cm/4–8 in long. The male is instantly identified from the bank by his bottle-green head, twin crest of stiffened feathers, white collar and chestnut breast; only 50–58cm/20–23 in long, the duck is about the size of a mallard, but the slender red bill is unmistakable. The black upperparts have an iridescent sheen, with grey flanks and a dazzling white band on the wings is visible in flight. The female also sports a shaggy crest but the feathers match the chestnut brown of the rest of her head, which merges into the brown-grey neck without the demarcating white collar of the male.

With their long necks and slender bodies, their profiles are elegant and their ability to dive silently under the water and catch fish is marvellous to watch, bringing a magical touch to this spring morning on Lake Windermere. Many adult mergansers remain close to the coast where they overwinter, to breed in bays, inlets and estuaries, but this pair represent two of the increasing number which occupy territories on upland lakes, rivers and streams.

Over 2,000 pairs of red-breasted mergansers nest in the British Isles. The bird's range extended from Scotland into England and Wales nearly 40 years ago, providing excitement to birdwatchers, but it suffered increased persecution by fishermen, river owners and fish farmers, who claimed that, with the goosanders, the mergansers took too many valuable young fish.

Deep in the thick vegetation on the banks of a small island in Lake Windermere, the female merganser has built her nest using brambles and grass as extra cover. Sometimes the nests are under gorse and heather, or down rabbit burrows and in between exposed roots, but they are nearly always on the ground; whereas the similar **goosander** often nests in a hole in a tree (**133**) and even accepts specially designed nestboxes several metres off the ground.

North-west of Castle Douglas in Dumfries and Galloway, Loch Ken has been formed by the damming of the River Dee by the South of Scotland Electricity Board for hydro-electric power. The man-made loch is surrounded by woodland, open hills and farmland, and where the flood waters build up, marshland has formed producing a habitat important for waders and wildfowl, especially during the winter, when white-fronted and greylag geese flock to feed.

In summer the innumerable small bays of the Dee become nursery grounds for young goosander which breed along the river banks and the vegetated and wooded stretches of the loch. The adults, at 65 cm/26 in, are larger than mergansers but the plumage of the female goosander is very similar to that of the female merganser, although the upperparts are more of a bluish-grey, the chestnut head more vivid and the crest is so well developed that it flows backwards like a mane, rather than protruding like an unkempt thatch. The male has distinct differences, with a greenish-black head and neck, black back and grey upperparts; the underparts are pure white and, unlike the male merganser, it lacks the chestnut breast, which is a delicate shade of pink instead.

The first official record of goosander breeding in Britain is as recent as 1871 in Perthshire, but today over 1,250 pairs breed, having spread through Aberdeen, Angus, Selkirk and Dumfries with an estimated 900–950 pairs in Scotland each season and the remainder in Cumbria, Northumberland, Lancashire, Durham and, since 1968, various counties in Wales.

Their diving and feeding behaviour is very similar to the merganser but the size of the prey can be larger and sometimes frogs are taken to supplement the diet. It is their main nesting sites which set the goosander apart from the ground-nesting merganser. Early each morning at the beginning of the breeding season, paired goosanders fly over the copses and woods close to the loch or feeder rivers, looking for suitably cracked or hollowed trees where they can build a nest. They are never in a hurry to select the site and spend several mornings flying in a regular circuit before making a choice, which may be up to 1 km/⅝ mile away from the loch or river. If a nest site is chosen on the ground, the depression is lined with leaves and down, but in a hollow tree only a few wood chippings form the nest cup which is liberally lined with down. The down is used to cover the eggs when the female leaves the nest hole to feed.

For the first two days after hatching, the young remain inside the tree. Then the female stands at the base of the tree and calls her offspring to leave. Using the rough sides of the nest chamber for grip, they clamber to the entrance hole and one by one, responding to their mother's calls, they nervously launch themselves into space. Immediately the female goosander calls them together, and in a bewildered but organised troop, they are led to the water. There the ducklings hide in the marginal vegetation and seek additional protection by climbing under the wings of the female goosander, who is sometimes joined by her mate. More frequently she is left to raise the family single-handed. They remain together as a unit until autumn arrives, then disperse.

On many upland lakes during winter, gull roosts are a conspicuous feature. One of the largest is the huge gathering of **common gull (136)** at Ullswater, Cumbria, where thousands of these 41-cm/16-in grey-backed birds sit out in the middle of the lake forming a broad ribbon, nearly 1.6 km/1 mile long. In the daytime many of them can be seen feeding on the dry meadows of the Eden valley, but as dusk arrives it is best to position yourselves overlooking Ullswater because thousands of the gulls fly in from the eastern foothills and use the lake as their evening roost.

Despite their name and the fact that over 50,000 pairs breed in the British Isles, the gull is not as widespread as many other species of gull. The majority breed throughout Scotland and north-west Ireland, with isolated colonies in the Pennines, North Wales and Dungeness in Kent. As a breeding species the common gull is still absent from much of England, Wales and

Ireland. The winter influx of migrants from Europe, especially Scandinavia, tends to distort the population and distribution statistics. The difficulty is easy to appreciate since on Glad-house reservoir in Midlothian, for example, over 40,000 common gulls can be seen roosting.

Gulls are one of the most difficult groups of birds to identify, but the yellow-green bill and legs, together with the black wing tips marked with a white spot, distinguish this gull from the similar black-headed gull in winter plumage. They frequently fly with the herring gull, but they are smaller, with neater heads and narrower bill, lacking the red terminal spot on the lower mandible.

Common gulls nest in coastal and inland habitats; away from the coast, they prefer upland sites 500–1,000 m/1,640–3,281 ft above sea level, selecting heather-clad moorland slopes and especially the shores of upland lakes and islands in the middle of the water. Unlike the black-headed gulls, they do not breed in large colonies and many solitary pairs return to their breeding sites early in the New Year. During the breeding season the common gull once more becomes vocal, having spent the winter almost in silence. Both sexes have a shriller call than the herring gull and their mewing, whistling 'keeya-keeya-keeya' chorus is sometimes so high-pitched that the clamour becomes unbearable.

The simple scrape of a nest, lined with some grass or heather, usually contains three eggs before the end of April. Both sexes share in the incubation, which lasts up to four weeks. Even during the breeding season the common gull never quite forgets its scavenging and marauding habits and although the chicks are mainly fed on worms, molluscs, crustaceans and small fish caught from the lake, adults sometimes raid the nests of other ground-nesting upland birds, and eggs and fledglings feature on the young gulls' menu.

In spring around 500 pairs of wigeon and up to 6,000 pairs of teal remain in Britain to set up nesting territories, commonly in marshy, boggy upland country. **Wigeon (134)** in particular like to breed along upland rivers, tarns, oligotrophic lakes and the lochans of the Flow Country. The first breeding pair were discovered in 1834 in Sutherland, and the Highlands still remain the stronghold for breeding wigeon, although they have colonised suitable habitats throughout Scotland and even into upland Yorkshire. Only at Loch Leven and St Serf's Island does a large breeding colony break with tradition and nest at low altitude.

Whilst the air is still cold on a March morning, the shores of the upland lake are covered with a layer of thin ice. From a sheltered bay a few metres along the bank a clear 'whee-oo whee-oo' whistle breaks the silence and a superb male wigeon gives himself away, even though he is trying to conceal himself in the sedge tussocks. As our only grazing duck, wigeon mostly feed completely out of the water, but this male is uprooting plants in the shallows and eating any last year's seeds it can find whilst foraging through the sparse vegetation. With its short neck and squat appearance the wigeon is smaller than the familiar mallard, but its red-brown head and neck, capped with a golden yellow stripe from bill to the nape, make this skulking individual stand out like a Belisha beacon. Even the dull light does not prevent the pink breast, which merges into silvery-grey flanks, from looking stunning. The neat bill is tinged pale blue.

This lake and all the surrounding feeder streams, small islands around the margin and the moorland slopes under the bracken, will be searched thoroughly by the duck for a suitable nesting site. A shallow hollow is usually selected, well screened with vegetation and lined with grass and down. Seven or eight cream eggs are laid towards the end of April and early May.

In late May and early June it is worth returning to the upland lakes, because from the shelter of the heather and bracken you will obtain excellent views of the female wigeon with her ducklings, feeding in the shallows. Although the female performed all the incubation, once she takes the offspring to the water she is rejoined by the drake, so you will have the rare chance of seeing the whole family together with their variable plumages and markings.

On the upland lakes, meres and pools of the British Isles a small, 36-cm/14-in rapid-flying duck always livens up the habitat with its clear, whistling, 'kricc-kricc' note. This is the male **teal** with its beautiful chestnut-brown head and large green eye-patch which curves down to the nape, bordered on both margins by a creamy-yellow stripe. As it comes in to land on the water, look out for the diagnostic white belly which is completely hidden when on the surface of the lochan, showing only the light grey, black-flecked flanks and upperparts.

It is confusing that this attractive duck, which breeds on lowland lakes, streams or rivers, also commonly nests on upland moors, where small lakes, tarns, lochans and bogs with plenty of sedge and rush cover are among its favourite habitats. Even more confusing is that the teal is a highly mobile species, and although there are around 6,000 pairs breeding in the British Isles, including 1,500 pairs in Ireland, most of these resident individuals prefer to spend the winter around the coastline, dabbling for insects, seeds and aquatic vegetation on saltmarshes, mud flats, estuaries, drainage ditches and brackish pools. Since many thousands of European visitors join our own teal in the winter, huge populations build up and 75,000–100,000 of these ducks form rafts, all swimming closely together, and suggesting that our populations are much larger than they really are.

Numbers of teal steadily build up from August, when immigrant teal begin to arrive from Iceland, Holland, France and Spain, but in December hundreds congregate around Cork Harbour, Lough Neagh, the Shannon estuary and on the wetlands throughout Ireland, sometimes amounting to as many as 50,000. By January many begin to disperse, but those wintering along the Shannon generally remain until late March.

Because of the larger numbers during the winter, this is the season when birdwatchers generally watch teal. As you disturb a group feeding on a brackish ditch, they catapult from the water together with amazing speed and turn across the marsh, their green speculums flashing and their white bellies clearly visible as the flock twists and dives towards the mud flats. Teals can easily be mistaken for a flock of waders, which share the same habitats during the winter, but their agile, buoyant flight is almost unrivalled. As dusk falls, airborne teal return to the saltmarshes, their piping, bell-like calls interrupted only by the splash as they land, to feed once again in the pools before roosting above the high-tide level.

On their upland breeding grounds teal require tussocky vegetation at the very least, because in their lowland habitats, they always seek dense vegetation, although the available water can even be very shallow and small in area. The grass-lined hollow which forms the nest is well concealed, and similar to a garganey's. The 8–10 eggs are always laid during April and incubated by the female only. Whilst the female is incubating the male disappears to begin his moult, during which time he resembles the female in colour, but sometimes he returns to help rear the brood, once the ducklings have entered the water and begun to feed themselves.

Birdwatchers fortunate enough to spend time on the Ouse Washes or Orkney in March and April may have the luck to see the **pintail** which is perhaps our most elegant duck. The Ouse Washes are one of the major wintering grounds for the pintail in England, with a few pairs remaining to breed on the neighbouring marshland and eutrophic lakes of Cambridgeshire and East Anglia. In Ireland, between 4,000–7,000 immigrant pintails from Iceland and Russia overwinter at sites like the Wexford Slobs, North Bull and Rogerstown Estuary, but it is an extremely rare breeding bird. The undisturbed upland lochans, the oligotrophic wetlands called the Loons and Loch Isbister, on Mainland, Orkney, have become some of the best locations to observe at least six pairs of the total British breeding population. Hiking across the heather moorland towards the water, you might hear a soft 'kruck-kruck' springtime call of a male pintail carrying on the wind. The call is very similar to the teal's, but you are privileged to hear this sound, because at most times of the year the pintail is silent. As the breeding season approaches, the call of the drake becomes more frequent and the high-pitched, staccato 'quack' of the duck responds, sounding much like a soprano mallard duck.

It is difficult to believe that the familiar farmyard goose is a descendant of the **greylag goose (138)**. Although about 3,000 semi-domestic greylag geese now fly free and breed around natural lowland lakes, reservoirs, gravel pits and ornamental lakes of stately homes and parks, the true wild, indigenous greylags, which number 1,500–2,000 pairs, are confined to the Outer Hebrides and north-west Scotland. The largest colony is on Loch Druidibeg on South Uist, where the shallow water shows the typical stony shoreland and monotonous, sparse sedge and rush vegetation of an oligotrophic habitat. The entire loch is covered with tiny islands, on which most of the greylag geese nest, scraping out a hollow in the heather or dense grass and lining it with moss, dry grasses and soft down.

Mid-way through October our resident geese are joined by winter visitors from Iceland and the numbers peak to 90,000–100,000 birds which are best seen on the Solway Firth, the Lothians, Perth and other areas of Lowland Scotland. Instinct leads them to arable fields where they glean the barley grain from the stubble, moving on to the potato fields once the farmers have harvested their crops, and devouring all the left-over potatoes. Their robust heads and orange bills are constantly active, probing the soil and gobbling anything edible in their path. With their heads nearly always pointing downwards to feed, their white rumps and under-tail coverts are very noticeable; the rest of the upper plumage is dark grey and lighter grey underneath.

Conflict with the local farmers begins when the potato crop runs out, through to spring, when the geese leave for their breeding grounds. Hunger forces the thousands of geese to take off in their familiar V-formation to search for grass meadows and sprouting winter-sown cereals. Clearly the farmers should not be obliged to let their cattle graze on the spring grass alongside thousands of geese greedily depleting the precious crop, but unfortunately bird-scaring machines are only having a limited effect.

Towards the end of April, the farmers are relieved to see the winter-visiting greylags leave for their Icelandic breeding grounds – a sentiment shared by the Irish farmers, who watch

140
140 Red-throated divers are very easily disturbed from their nest, leaving the eggs open to predation.

nearly one thousand greylag geese depart from their fields for the Arctic Circle each spring. Curiously, over forty years ago up to 10,000 greylag geese used to overwinter in Ireland, but the numbers have fallen dramatically as the Scottish visitors increased. It seems very likely that one man's gain is another man's loss as the greylags themselves changed their migration routes over the decades.

Long before the Icelandic greylag geese reach their traditional nesting sites, our own greylags will be active on Loch Druidibeg: they claim territories by the end of February. The damp moorland in the immediate vicinity of the loch is as popular for the colony as the innumerable islands. Paired greylag are not very tolerant of neighbouring birds and excitable battles frequently occur between ganders. Even if the female on the nest is only passed too closely, she stretches her neck out in threatening defiance. Conversely neck-stretching in greylag geese is part of their courtship display. Between February and April, when the 4–9 whitish eggs are laid, the paired greylags stand facing each other, one bird slightly to the right of its partner, ready to begin the display ritual. The ceremony is called 'triumphing', because as the two birds extend their necks and lower their heads to the ground they exchange loud honking calls, continuing this behaviour each time they meet during the breeding season, when the female is not on the nest. Only the female incubates, but the gander keeps guard from a few metres away for the entire month his mate sits on the eggs, resuming his parental role once the grey-brown goslings leave the nest.

A few kilometres east of Glen Mor and the eastern shores of Loch Ness lies Loch Ruthven, running east–west, with tumbling streams draining into it from mountains 430 m/1,410 ft high on its southern shore and woodland stretching for much of the length of the loch on the northern shore. Most of the perimeter of Loch Ruthven is bare except for stones and mountain debris, but some of it has a growth of reeds and marginal vegetation. On this small loch, and other similar

141 The marginal nest of the rare Slavonian grebe is still susceptible to flooding.

stretches of water in Highland Scotland, the exotically plumaged **Slavonian grebe (141)** breeds.

Most Slavonian grebes breed in the Baltic, Scandinavia and Iceland and visit the British Isles in winter when they are seen around the coasts in sheltered bays and estuaries. In its winter plumage, which is far from exotic, this grebe can easily be overlooked. During late February and March the winter-visiting grebes return to their distant breeding territories and our own resident population of 50–75 pairs disperses to the shallow lochs and lochans in the Highlands. Very few bird-watchers are fortunate enough to see Slavonian grebes in their British nesting sites, but from February to April they have a partial moult and between mid-March and the beginning of April, when the grebes arrive in the uplands, their brilliant plumage is on display. Both sexes are identical with bright red eyes, glossy black head and back, contrasting with rich chestnut-brown breast and flanks with white belly. Perhaps the most attractive and certainly most ornate part of the 'breeding dress' are the bright orange-gold eye tufts, which extend towards the back of the head.

The sharp-pointed bill is used for catching prey, as with all grebes, but once Slavonian grebes have claimed their territory they defend it with aggressive behaviour and use their bill with alarming effect. They attack any bird, however large, resting on the waters, from below the surface, launching themselves torpedo-like into the unprotected underparts of the victim.

Once alone, the grebes perform their well-known courtship displays and, as with the great crested grebe which is the most frequently observed species (page 162), any ritual is performed to a strict sequence. Throughout the Highland summer but particularly as the pair bond is developing, both the Slavonian grebes belly-roll like playful otters, repeatedly flashing the white underparts to each other to strengthen relationships. This is usually followed by the famous penguin and weed-rush dance performed by most grebes, but not to the perfection of the Slavonian. Both grebes dive into the loch and re-surface holding strands of weed which dangle from their bills. As the

penguin dance begins, they rise out of the water on their tails, adopting a penguin posture, and approach each other face on until their chestnut breasts touch, and they shake their heads from side to side. Next moment, in a single, synchronised movement, they turn, stand shoulder to shoulder and the weed-rush is executed as the pair scuttle across the surface for many metres, still holding themselves like penguins and accompanying the move with excited trilling calls. They obviously enjoy this ceremony as much as it is significant for their successful breeding: it is repeated and performed effortlessly for up to fifteen minutes before nest-building begins.

Along the edge of the loch the grebes build several platforms of damp, rotting vegetation in the reeds and the birds climb out of the water and copulate on these rafts. Following several copulations, the pair slip into the water and after swimming from one to another, select one of these meeting platforms and convert it into a nest, by hollowing out the centre in what is nothing more than a floating pile of rotting aquatic plants. The female lays 3–5 white eggs and settles down to incubate them. Regular observation over a period of days reveals that her plumage is actually moulting during the incubation until she assumes a drab plumage without the breeding refinery. This strange Slavonian quirk is considered to be her defence mechanism, in order to camouflage her whilst on the nest rather than draw attention to the nest site, but it does not quite work: the male shares the incubation for the three weeks and he retains the breeding plumage until August – generally it is his gaudy markings which give away the location of the eggs and attract predatory crow and mink to rob the nest.

Once hatched the young grebes climb on to their parents' back in famous grebe style, with the female bearing the brunt of this taxi service, whilst the male is occupied fishing and bringing the catch back to the insatiable, zebra-striped chicks. Sometimes the Slavonian grebe is double-brooded, and it has the potential to rear ten chicks, but pike, gull, crow, heron, mink and collectors all take their toll and more frequently than not, a female Slavonian manages to rear only two chicks to the fledgling stage from her one brood. This is one of the reasons why only a maximum of 75 pairs exist, 80 years after the first British pair nested in Scotland in 1908.

It would take a lifetime to visit all the sea lochs, freshwater lochs, lochans, tarns, corries, river valleys, blanket bogs and mires of the Highlands. Despite their frequent remoteness and their often stark and barren appearance, many of the upland lakes and lochans reward you with the sight of a bird or several species which will remain in your memory for ever.

The elusive grey-headed, **black-throated diver** prefers the wilder deep lochs of the north-west Highlands and Outer Hebrides. Although it is a large bird, 58–73 cm/23–9 in long, with distinctive white stripes and patches on a black back, it is difficult to find. Loch Maree in the Benn Eighe Nature Reserve and the numerous lochs in the Inverpolly Nature Reserve are regular British sites. Alternatively, the extremely adventurous birdwatcher could visit North Uist (page 182) in the Outer Hebrides from April to late May; and a circuit of the larger lochs, including the RSPB reserve at Balranald, should guarantee a sight of around six of the 100 pairs in the British Isles.

Several inches shorter than the black-throated diver, but equally exciting, is the more common **red-throated diver** which, as its name suggests, displays a deep red bib **(139)** offset by a light grey head and a characteristic, slightly upturned bill. During the breeding season the sexes are identical: the upper body is grey-brown flecked with small white dots and the belly white dots and the belly is entirely white. During the winter month the plumage resembles that of a black-throated diver, with dark grey-brown upperparts, white underparts, head and neck, and the red triangular bib is absent. The best distinguishing feature at this time of year is the larger area of black on the crown and back of the neck of the black-throated diver, but it requires close examination to identify either species in their winter plumage.

Nearly twelve hundred pairs of red-throated diver breed in the British Isles but they are uncommon in Ireland, breeding in Donegal; the black-throated diver occurs only as a very rare winter visitor. All divers are amongst the most sensitive birds at the nest and the very fact that they search for the more remote, undisturbed lochs, indicates that they will leave their nest at the slightest disturbance. As fishermen, hikers and countrylovers seek to enjoy their hobbies in the more off-beat areas of Britain, they unknowingly flush these shy birds off their nests; although the eggs of the red-throated diver are olive green and well camouflaged with brown blotches, many are predated by crows, gulls and stoats when the sitting bird is forced away. Birdwatchers should always understand the behavioural habits of a species before attempting to obtain good views and a golden rule when birdwatching in 'diver's country' is to scan the immediate and distant lochs and pools regularly, to see whether a diver quietly slips off its nest. If it does you are duty bound to back-track and allow the incubating bird to return to its eggs as quickly as possible.

Having spent the winter off sheltered coastlines, the red-throated divers return to upland lakes, lochans and moorland pools each April. Spring always comes late in northern Britain, and early in the morning by a lake the air is still cool and a mist hangs like a veil across the water. At the edge of the lake the water appears calm, but an occasional fluttering breeze rustles the sedges, causing the mist to swirl like theatrical dry ice around their stems. The silence is broken by an eerie, prolonged mewing wail, followed by spine-chilling shrieks which echo round the lake. Heard for the first time, the mysterious, unnatural territorial and mating calls of the red-throated diver evoke an atmosphere of evil foreboding, as a strange, slender, almost reptile-like silhouette drifts out of the mist.

Red-throated divers are amongst the most primitive of all birds, with fossil records carbon-dated at forty million years old. Their very name suggests an ability to swim beneath the surface, and the red-throated diver hunts for fish at depths of 9 m/30 ft, capturing them with the dagger-shaped bill. The powerful webbed feet, which are set well back on the streamlined body, propel the bird along under the water, but they are virtually useless for walking on land, where their movement is laborious and ungainly. Divers only come ashore to breed and when you watch the red-throated diver dragging its almost tailless body across the shoreline, it is easy to understand why, once disturbed, they are reluctant to return to their nest to continue incubation.

Slowly the mist disperses on the lake and the visibility of the red-throated diver improves. The strange shape of the bird, with its long, muscular neck, holds your gaze, but suddenly it disappears before your eyes, with hardly a ripple, and remains submerged for over a minute. Physiologically the bird's circulatory system is adapted to store additional oxygen, which supplies the lungs during prolonged dives, and when the diver re-surfaces the distance covered during submergence is impressive. Completely unaware of your presence, the bird swims towards you, but on this occasion its body partially sinks below the water like a submarine and only the upper part of the

neck and head remain above water like a periscope. To be able to swim like this, the diver expels air from special internal air sacs which act as buoyancy tanks, and pulls its feathers close to the body, squeezing out surface air, so that the weight of its solid body causes controlled sinking.

Perhaps now sensing that somebody is watching it from the shore, the diver bobs to the surface and takes off on slender wings. The red-throated diver has the ability to launch into the air from even the most shallow of lochans, which is one reason why they are abundant on the Shetland Isles and Orkney where the dubh lochans and pools are small and shallow, whereas the black-throated diver, which needs more space and deeper lochs in order to get airborne, is absent from these islands.

Few birdwatchers ever see the red-throated diver's mating ritual, called the snake ceremony, performed, although the gutteral cooing call which accompanies it is frequently heard during spring around upland lakes. Both divers swim side by side, with their heads outstretched and open bills pointing downwards. As courtship progresses, the tails are kept well under the surface, and the rest of the body is held high in the water as the pair energetically propel themselves silently across the water like athletes dipping for the tape.

The nest is a heap of plant stems, moss and a few leaves built on the grass very close to the water's edge or on a small island. This habit is sometimes the downfall of the diver because if spring rains are heavy and flooding occurs, the nest and eggs are swamped; but if upland drainage schemes have been implemented or a drought sets in, the lake water-level can reduce drastically, so that both chicks and adults are faced with a longer and more perilous crawl to the water.

Towards the end of May or early June the two eggs are laid and most of the incubation is performed by the female over twenty-eight days. After hatching, the strange-looking chicks remain in the nest for the first twenty-four hours, then follow their parents to the water, sometimes hitching a lift on the adults' backs like grebes. Divers are excellent parents and remain on the lake feeding and protecting their family for several months, sometimes flying to larger lochs to capture food, which they bring back for the youngsters.

The versatility of the red-throated diver in being able to inhabit and breed on the smallest of upland lakes, lochans and moorland pools, has enabled their numbers to increase in recent years. They are tough resilient birds coping with some of the wildest, most inhospitable habitats in the British Isles, but their nervousness at the nest, leading to possible desertion, should always be respected.

With the arrival of winter, the red-throated and black-throated divers leave their upland breeding sites and with their offspring will be seen wintering at sea. For a short spell in autumn the mountain lakes have been important feeding and resting stations for passage migrants like osprey, harrier, tern and geese, but now they are sombre features of a desolate and bleak environment, appropriate to their Ice Age origin. Many of our upland lakes have been exploited by man, but others will, I hope, remain for ever untouched, far removed from the pressures to which their lowland counterparts are subjected, with pollution of the feeder streams and of the lakes themselves upsetting the natural ecological balance. Their beauty and commercial value has attracted fishermen, windsurfers, waterskiers and sailors to enjoy their pursuits and since so many of the lowland lakes have been lost during the last two hundred years, the birds have been forced to compete with man on those which remain.

PONDS

There can hardly be anyone interested in the countryside and wildlife who didn't have their childhood enthusiasm kindled by fishing for sticklebacks and tadpoles in their local pond. Because they are relatively shallow and have distinct margins, ponds are an easy habitat to study; and those found to be teeming with aquatic plants and mysterious animal life provide endless fascination.

To define a pond accurately is not straightforward. At what stage a lake silts up and becomes a pond, or the area of a pond is sufficiently large to be considered a small lake, is a matter of opinion and any definition designed to separate the two habitats is largely arbitrary. It is accepted that the majority of ponds are man-made, the most familiar being the village pond, dug where the water table lies close to the surface or where a natural hollow is fed by small streams, in order to provide a watering hole for local cattle and horses. A few, unusually deep ponds occur where there has been earth subsidence near the spring of a river, or where quarrying has caused a land slip which has filled with water.

For the purposes of this book, birdwatchers can consider a pond to be a small area of water which is not affected by wind producing choppy waves capable of damaging the banks. The stillness of the water favours the growth of surface water plants. Duckweeds are typical of most ponds, and because ponds are shallow and the water generally clear, light can easily penetrate to encourage plants to root in the mud at the bottom.

In the seventeenth century dewponds were frequently dug on chalk downlands to provide water for sheep. Shallow hollows with specially clay-lined bottoms, they were designed to catch as much rainfall draining from the surrounding land as possible and very rarely dried up.

Village ponds are frequently found at the main crossroads or on the main green of the village, because this was the centre of activity for many centuries. Ever since the Norman Conquest until the development of the railways, the most important travellers visiting towns and villages across the country were the drovers, who moved large herds of cattle from the mountains of Scotland and Wales to the English meat markets. When the drovers arrived in a village with their cattle, the first place they stopped was at the pond to water the livestock, and the villagers began to meet them there to discuss other business. Eventually tradesmen like bakers, food sellers, ale houses, blacksmiths and carpenters all set up around the village green and pond, which quickly developed as the area for the most regular and best trade and the focal point of village life.

In summer the vegetation associated with the pond grows in distinct zones, each with its own particular birdlife. The wealth of vegetation eventually brings the death sentence to the pond as, like the typical lowland lake, it slowly fills in from the edges. If they are to retain open water villages have to maintain and manage their ponds by periodically thinning out vegetation from the marsh and reed-swamp zones. With labour expensive and voluntary help increasingly more difficult to raise, hundreds of significant ponds have been lost as villages have voted to fill them in and save money.

We have already seen how important water is to birds every day, and ponds attract many species from long distances to drink, bathe or feed. The grass snake hunting for newts and frogs may attract the heron to make a fleeting early morning visit and the small fish might tempt kingfishers to feed if they are left undisturbed. In summer swallows and house martins dip over the surface for insects and to collect soft mud for their nests; and the marginal reeds provide shelter for reed bunting and pied wagtail. The submerged invertebrates provide food for moorhen, little grebe and mallard.

Having little fear of man, the **mallard (143)** greedily accepts bread and biscuit crumbs from young children standing round the edge of their local pond. It is the commonest and most widely distributed duck in the British Isles: 150,000–330,000 pairs breed and colonise a variety of habitats including lakes, reservoirs, gravel pits, rivers, canals, ditches, watercress beds, estuaries and saltmarshes.

Despite their exploitation of man-made habitats, mallards are truly wild birds, as will be appreciated by watching them on marshes. Late on a summer evening, the marsh with its dense screen of reeds and sedges appears almost deserted. Suddenly a flock of mallards make a rapid, noisy take-off from the reedbed. They fly strongly and always rise vertically from the water with rapid wingbeats, quacking loudly and banking sharply across the marsh. In this type of habitat the mallard is a different bird from those individuals of the village pond. The marsh becomes alive at dusk and mallards are ever wary of the hunting fox, as they dabble amongst the reeds and dense vegetation, but the village-pond mallard, although constantly wary, is much easier to examine.

At 50–65 cm/20–25 in, the mallard is the largest British duck. From September until the following July, when the bird is in breeding plumage, the drake, with yellow bill, bottle-green head, white dog-collar, chocolate-brown breast and grey-brown body, is very attractive. In contrast, the mottled yellow-brown duck is drab but perfectly patterned to sit undetected on her eggs; her bill is pale green. Both sexes show bright orange, webbed feet, and a beautiful violet-blue speculum edged with black and white on the wings, most noticeable when the ducks fly into land. Between high summer and early autumn, when the drake is in eclipse moult, it is only the yellow bill which helps birdwatchers confirm the male because in all other markings he resembles the female at this time and like her is better camouflaged from predators for the few weeks that he is flightless.

The familiar resonant 'quack-quack' is only uttered by the female. This simple call is given in many different ways, depending on whether the duck is communicating within a flock, calling her ducklings or about to take off. The drakes give a more subdued call mixed with whistles and grunts.

Throughout the year mallards occupy ponds but whether they breed near by depends on the richness of the surrounding vegetation. In the winter, when the weather becomes very severe, the ponds can become deserted as the ducks move to reservoirs, lakes and the coast. There they are joined by thousands of overwintering mallards from northern Europe, so the winter population of mallards frequently exceeds 350,000 birds, before thinning out as the breeding season arrives.

In the autumn the mallards begin to pair up and display but they still remain together in large flocks. October is the best month to watch these communal displays which always take place on the water, but if the pond is small, aggression sometimes gets out of hand. The drakes, resplendent in their breeding plumage, swim low in the water, flicking their heads and dipping their bills into the water, whilst revealing their black, curled tail feathers. As a duck approaches, the drakes respond and some of them rear out of the water, stretch their necks and whistle, while others raise their wings and swim around her.

The duck usually makes a choice from the drakes, depending on which male is displaying with the most vigour, but often as she makes her advances the other jilted birds object, and the proposed courtship develops into a brawl, as the males begin to quarrel amongst themselves, stabbing at each other with their bills and catching opponents by the necks. Frequently the female is forced to take flight, chased amorously by several of the drakes.

Eventually the duck is able to mate with the drake of her choice, when he separates himself from the rest of the group and she indicates her intentions by bobbing her head to one side as he swims close by. Mating is at its peak from November until February and as the drake mounts the duck, she is almost pushed completely under the water by his weight.

Ducks occupy their territories by March at the latest, and the nest is usually sited on the ground in dense reeds, brambles and nettles or sometimes in the crown of a pollarded tree a few metres off the ground. Because she is unable to carry material in her bill, the duck forms a hollow in the vegetation, and lines and surrounds it with any material she can pull from the immediate vicinity. Like the Canada goose (page 169), she finally lines the nest with down, pulled from her breast. This down is extremely important for both insulation and protection. After mating the drake leaves the female alone to incubate for about a month. During her twice-daily feeds, she pulls the down over the eggs to conceal them whilst she is away from the nest.

As the female incubates, the drake defends his territory from a distance, chasing away unmated males, but he is not averse to trying to mate with unattached females passing through. However, once the eggs hatch he leaves the rearing of the young entirely to his mate.

One of the delights of early spring is watching the female mallard hatch her eggs in the shelter of the pond's vegetation. For several hours she broods her beautiful brown and yellow ducklings until their down is fully dry then she leads them from the nest across the dangerous few metres of land to the water's edge. Often they follow in single file, softly 'peeping' all the time and constantly inquisitive as they lunge and stab at insects resting on leaves lining the route.

From a brood of ten ducklings, only 50 per cent reach flying stage, because herons, swans and coots sometimes attack and eat them, and in certain areas marsh harriers pluck them from the reeds. Mallards rearing young on the pond lose some ducklings to foxes, cats and rats; and in larger lakes and rivers, pike drag ducklings down from beneath the surface, and weirs and sluice gates suck inexperienced, stray ducklings to their deaths each season.

After breeding, adult mallards congregate in large flocks for their moult, frequently choosing the shelter of lakes and estuaries. In Ireland, large populations appear on Loughs Neagh, Corrib, Derravaragh and Iron, and the Wexford Slobs; in England more than 8,000 use the Humber estuary and thousands of others congregate on Abberton Reservoir (page 165) and the Ouse Washes (page 128).

If lowland farmers are without a natural pond on their land, they usually dig one out themselves at a suitable site to provide water for livestock, and left relatively undisturbed, farm ponds become important for many local birds. Wherever some vegetation is allowed to mature around part of the margins, moorhens will stay to breed; generally any farm with a pond and ditches bordering the fields, will have its resident moorhens.

When a small river or stream runs across the farmland and naturally fills and drains a pond, mallards almost certainly colonise and breed, but like the moorhen they do not tolerate exposed margins, and reeds are particularly important. Many of the farms surrounding my own market town have mature, well-vegetated ponds and because of the growth of reeds they are active in summer with foraging mallard, pied and yellow wagtail, reed bunting and sedge warbler; in the autumn and winter small flocks of snipe probe in the marshy shallows and flicker across the fields at dusk.

The main problem with farm ponds is the run-off from agricultural fertilisers which over-enriches the water and causes the algal bloom clouding, but on many of the clear un-polluted and well-vegetated farm ponds the little grebe or dabchick takes up residence.

The **little grebe (142)** or dabchick, is only 27 cm/10½ in long, and is the smallest grebe in Europe, occupying a wide range of habitats. In the British Isles it is found on lakes, streams, dykes, gravel pits, town ponds and even pools only a metre deep in alder carr, proving that it does not require a great amount of space. In Ireland it is the commonest grebe, breeding throughout the country, except in the mountains. Outside the breeding season, large numbers group at Lough Arrow, a 1,250-ha/3,088-acre lake in the north-west, and remain on view in open water more frequently than they do in spring and summer.

From February until July the little grebe is in breeding plumage and the sexes are identical. You need to scan the pond for a brown bird about the size of a man's clenched fist, which floats with the ducks and coots. The chestnut-brown cheeks and throat are very distinguishable through binoculars as is the yellow-white spot of the base of the bill, but after the moult in August the chestnut markings are lost and the usually dark brown plumage is much paler.

Timid by nature, the stumpy little grebe is difficult to see in summer, but where the reeds grow at the edge of the pond and the willows overhang low into the water, the grebe bobs to the surface. With a little jump and flick of its webbed feet, positioned just under the tail, it dives again and remains underwater for 15–25 seconds, searching for small fish, crustaceans, molluscs, insects and their larvae and tadpoles. Watching the grebe feed is fascinating: small prey is obviously eaten underwater, but fish are swallowed at the surface and sometimes insects are gleaned from floating water weed. Usually little grebes feed in pairs or entirely on their own. Because they are so skilled at diving, they use this as a method of escaping danger, rarely taking to the wing; sometimes they flutter across the surface using their feet to propel themselves over the water.

On winter days when the air is clear and the sun is out, the small ponds and lakes ring with the sound of little grebes calling to one another. They frequently remain in pairs throughout the winter and the duet of liquid, cascading, whinnying notes is very typical of occupied ponds from October until April. The little grebe's alarm note is a sharp 'whit-whit' call.

Compared with many other grebes the head feathers of the dabchick are not particularly striking, and their courtship

142 As well as being the smallest, the little grebe or dabchick is the most widespread species of the grebe in the British Isles.

143 The mallard is the most familiar duck in town and country.

display is unspectacular, although from March until April occupied territories are defended vigorously and clamorous disputes are regular. The breeding season is protracted and up to three broods can be raised from March until July. The nest is built by both birds amongst reeds at the margin of the pond or attached to the branches of willows trailing in the water, and is little more than a hollowed-out damp cradle. During April, 4–6 eggs are laid, and both parents incubate for just over three weeks, covering the eggs with water weed if they both leave to feed themselves.

Immediately upon hatching and drying, the striped buff and grey chicks swim and dive expertly, but for about nine weeks always remain close to an adult – generally the male, because the hen bird has begun to incubate her second clutch.

The oxygen content in the water has the most significant effect on the quality of the pond. The richest ponds are those fed by running streams carrying a high oxygen content, but the majority of village ponds are stagnant water: oxygen is only absorbed near the surface and by the photosynthesis of green plants in and around the pond. Furthermore if the pond is fully exposed to the sunlight, the warmed water is forced to release some of its oxygen into the atmosphere; village ponds in partial shade, although not so visually attractive, are richer in insect life and therefore birds, than those in full sunshine. The pond needs a healthy supply of vegetation to provide oxygen and food for herbivorous invertebrates, which form the main diet of many aquatic birds. The pond becomes choked with plants if not managed properly: although the surviving small ponds of our villages and countryside appear a natural and stable part of the environment, they are nearly all man-made and require management and conservation if they are to remain an attractive and important habitat for birds living close to man.

GRAVEL PITS

We know that many of our lowland lakes are artificial, created and shaped by the activities of man in the last 200 years. Many of the activities which have changed the face of our countryside arise from the building of towns, cities, industrial estates and motorways, which increasingly put a stranglehold on the green and pleasant land (Ch. 12). As the demand for more concrete increases, with new developments, ambitious housing plans and improved motorway systems, the need for the raw material of sand and gravel increases correspondingly. Ever since the First World War these industries have been expanding and today gravel pits are one of the most widespread forms of artificial lakes in Britain.

Gravel occurs naturally below the surface in certain regions of Britain. Although extraction causes destruction of a particular area, once the reserves are exhausted and the dredging equipment has been removed, the pits are usually flooded with water or fill naturally by seepage and precipitation, so creating a new habitat as the site returns to nature. The concrete which is partly made from the gravel to build something on an area of uncovered land eventually gives back a different area to wildlife in return. Over 50 per cent of the extraction pits are finally filled with water offering characteristics similar to reservoirs (page 164).

Each year, more than 1,618 ha/3,998 acres of land succumb to the sand and gravel industry and since 1975 an estimated 12,141 ha/30,000 acres of new, open water has become available for recreation and bird colonisation, which is encouraging when so many other wetlands and habitats are being destroyed. Wherever industrial and domestic growth is greatest, the extraction industry is frequently near by; 60 per cent of all gravel pits are found in the Midlands and southern England, and 50 per cent of all the water-filled pits occur south-east of a line from the Bristol Channel to Lincolnshire.

Around London, gravel pits are particularly common in parts of Middlesex, but a drive around the London orbital M25 now clearly reveals the numerous exhausted and active pits in Kent, Surrey and Hertfordshire, made possible by glacial drift conveniently close to London, where demand for concrete is greatest. These London fringe gravel pits are havens for winter wildfowl and the Wraysbury pits in particular have in recent years become renowned for the attractive winter-visiting smew (page 168). The interlinking M40 takes the motorist past old pits near Beaconsfield, Buckinghamshire, which are gradually being re-filled with corporation rubbish; and at Theale, near Reading, in the Thames Valley, extensive active and flooded gravel pits which were initially formed to provide concrete for the construction of the M4 occur on both sides of the motorway. Elsewhere gravel pits are found in Lowland Scotland, Wales, Northumberland, southern Yorkshire and along the valleys of the Ouse and Trent rivers, and many of them have become significant habitats for wildfowl, waders and other aquatic birds. In the Colne Valley, Hertfordshire, a series of sand and gravel pits which used to provide raw materials for building in London have become exhausted and the old pits are now full of water with reed swamp and marshland around part of their margins. Broad Colney Lakes, near St Albans and Stockers Lake, near Rickmansworth are two such pits which, with dense vegetation and willow and alders growing on some of the islands, have become wildlife sanctuaries in an area of high urbanisation.

Of course a recently excavated gravel pit with the banks stripped of vegetation and mobile, because of the shifting gravel, is not very attractive to birds, but since the 1960s when conservation societies explained to gravel contractors just how valuable their pits could be, many companies have become sympathetic. Following advice from naturalists, gravel pits are frequently dredged so that the banks have a gentle slope rather than inhospitable sheer sides, and the perimeter of the pits are no longer routinely circular, but are dug with a variable series of bays and inlets so that in spring, territorial male birds can happily occupy a stretch of water, without seeing, or being seen by, a rival bird a few bays further round. In this way the breeding populations of duck, grebe and coot have increased significantly in the last twenty or thirty years.

However, nature refuses to ignore even the most barren of habitats, and the margins and upper slopes of newly excavated gravel pits, with shallow feeding pools near by, provide the ideal conditions for the **little ringed plover** to nest (**145**). Although it is widespread in Europe, this plover is rare in Britain and chose a reservoir as its first British nesting site (page 164). By 1944 two pairs returned to the same reservoir, whilst others had colonised new suitable gravel and shingle sites, including one in Ashford, Kent.

By the early 1970s, the little ringed plover, having become more used to man, moved even closer to his company, and they now breed in the Surrey Docks and other dockland sites in East London. The British population was surveyed at 610 pairs in 1984, 287 of which were found south of Lincolnshire around water-filled gravel pits: for the first time those pairs found in the north outnumbered the southern population. With a 30 per cent national population increase since 1973, it is possible that the southern little ringed plovers have virtually saturated all available gravel habitats because on 110 sites there were 225 pairs. This significant population increase is largely a result of the rapid development of the gravel industry and its pits, where 75 per cent of the total population nest.

This bird might easily be confused with the common ringed plover (page 191), but at 15 cm/6 in the little ringed plover is smaller and has a trimmer build. The upper plumage is pale brown extending over the crown of the head, with a distinctive white collar and black breast band. Both species have predominantly white underparts but across the forehead and extending back from the base of the bill through the eye is another black band, which is more pronounced in the ringed plover. The little ringed plover has a vivid yellow ring around the perimeter of its eye, which is much paler in the male ringed plover during the breeding season. Whereas the ringed plover shows a distinctive orange-yellow bill with a black tip, the little-ringed plover has a black bill with a faint yellow tinge near the base, and there is a narrow white stripe running behind, adjacent to the black forehead stripe, which is absent in the ringed plover. The colour of the feet and legs are also different. Those of the little ringed plover are flesh-coloured whereas its larger cousin has orange-yellow legs, easily distinguished at reasonable distances. When the ringed plover takes off, clearly visible white wing bars allow it to be identified even at a distance, but the little ringed plover lacks these markings, and it is only when the bird flies away from you that its accurate identification can be confirmed.

Towards the middle of March and certainly by early April the little ringed plovers arrive on their inland sites. The pugnacious males arrive first and take up territories which provide a stretch of non-vegetated gravel and a shallow drinking and feeding pool close by. Look out for a territory-defending male performing his butterfly display flight, which takes place during April and involves the male slowly flying up and down his claimed stretch of gravel, constantly uttering a 'tree-tree-tree' trill. With all this activity the females are soon attracted as they begin to arrive and they land within a territory ready for the male to approach. The male bird stands in front of his intended mate, then crouches as he fans his tail suggestively. He repeats this several times until her interest is gained, then he leads her off to inspect several scrapes as possible nest sites. Whilst the female considers these proposed sites, the male bird behaves strangely, often marching up and down the gravel with his body held horizontally, and lifting his feet high off the ground like a soldier goose-stepping. Eventually the female decides on a site and indicating her satisfaction immediately crouches submissively as a sign to the male, who mates whilst standing on her back, quivering his wings at the same time.

The nest is marvellously camouflaged, but because of the bird's rarity should never be actively searched for. It is nothing more than a shallow scoop in the fine gravel with a few surrounding stones and plant material as a lining. The male formed this scrape before the female arrived on the territory, pressing his belly into the gravel and rotating, whilst kicking out material with his feet, creating showers of flying grit and gravel. Ironically, once the female has chosen one of his scrapes to lay her eggs, the male shows his pleasure by flicking small stones back towards her in the scrape.

Even if the gravel pits are not attractive habitats it is encouraging to know that so much publicity has been given to the rare nesting visitors and that many gravel contractors have responded by protecting the birds during the incubation period.

Fortunately, since gravel pits are on private land, human disturbance is confined to a minimum, but to prevent predation by gulls and crows, especially the ever-increasing magpie, some gravel companies are making sure that the nests are covered with wire-mesh cages, so that the plovers can pass through but the predators are kept out. Such future consideration and assistance from a commercial enterprise can only help to encourage this delightful plover to thrive and colonise even more new sites as they are developed.

The **common tern**, which is the most ubiquitous of the five British species, most frequently breeds around the coast, preferring exposed shingle beaches (page 190), but in recent years it has moved inland, encouraged by the availability of a habitat resembling a shingle beach away from the coast. Even at some of the London reservoirs the common tern now breeds on specially designed islands. As long as gravel and shingle occur without any plant cover, they will continue to extend their range inland. Within easy flying distance from the Norfolk coastline, where common terns regularly breed, are the flooded gravel pits called Lenwade Water, directly south of Blakeney. In recent years the terns have colonised these pits, which are managed by the Norfolk Naturalists' Trust to maintain the necessary conditions each season.

The majority of common terns overwinter off the coast of West Africa but return to our south coasts in early April, before dispersing to East Anglia, north-east Scotland, Shetland, Northern Ireland and various inland sites in south-east England. The 'kik-kik-kik' call as the terns arrive each spring is a welcome sound and with their flickering, graceful flight, grey and white plumage with black cap and long tail feathers they are also an attractive and elegant sight.

During the migration the common tern is easily confused with the similar-sized and marked arctic tern, but while both species have bright red legs and bills, the common tern has a black tip to its bill which is absent in the arctic tern and when they fly together on migration the arctic tern utters a 'keee-keee' note which helps to distinguish it, to the experienced ear.

Around the gravel pits, where gravel shores and islands are the main nesting sites, the common terns fly backwards and forwards, occasionally diving into the water for small fish with an audible splash. Their hovering, bouncing flight is a joy to watch and after a dive, during which they completely submerge, they re-surface and with a rapid shaking of their feathers soon take off again, to continue their hunting forays across the flooded pits, keenly looking for worms, freshwater invertebrates and fish.

Towards the end of May, three blotched eggs are laid in the shallow scrape which passes for the nest. Whilst the female tern broods the chicks, the male brings small fish to the nest, so reinforcing the pairing bond.

The pits at Lenwade Water also attract **sand martin (146)** which are summer visitors related to the more familiar house martins and swallows. Many of the gravel pits of Britain also contain large quantities of sand and as gravel is extracted, sand faces are exposed: here the sand martins nest in colonies. This 12-cm/4¾-in bird, with light-brown upperparts, white underparts and brown chest band, resembles the house martin in silhouette, but builds its nest in a chamber, situated at the end of a tunnel, rather than under the eaves of a house.

As the yellow coltsfoot begins to bloom, the first sand martins arrive, and during late March they are the only hirundines to have reached our shores from Africa. The first birds to arrive are experienced adults who made the same journey last year, and they search for soft sand and exposed faces of fine gravel. If the old face from last year still remains, the 'early birds' claim a suitable nest hole, but if only freshly exposed faces are available, the sand martins fly around the pits and carry out reconnaissance inspections, before disappearing over the water to hawk for insects.

A few days later, with the arrival of more birds, the gravel pits are alive with sand martins hovering at a sand face making new tunnels. The sand martins fly towards the sheer sand face and hover momentarily as they scrabble with their claws at the sand, eventually creating a small ledge, on which they perch. Once able to do this the sand martin faces the sand and repeatedly kicks backwards, sending out a constant hail of sand and grit until a tunnel begins to develop. The completed tunnel, up to 1 m/3¼ ft long and ending in a small chamber, takes up to three weeks to build; the sand martin always digs slightly uphill, so that the tunnel has natural drainage in case of flooding from rainfall, which drains rapidly through the sand and gravelly substrate. It lines the small chamber with dry

144

grass and feathers and on this meagre lining lays 4–6 white eggs in mid-April. This brood, which can be the first of three, is fledged by the end of May.

Sand martins have learnt to exploit other man-made habitats apart from gravel and sand pits and it is likely you will observe them nesting in railway and motorway cuttings, soft excavation heaps from the foundations of a large industrial site or even piles of pre-graded sand at a quarry. They are fascinating birds to watch, because they are gregarious at all times, even during migration and roosting, and the colony is constantly active. Each tunnel entrance is only a few metres apart, so hundreds of adults can be seen feeding their youngsters at once, and as they develop the juveniles become inquisitive and congregate to be fed at the tunnel entrance rather than remaining in the nest chamber, where it is cramped and dark. Both adults feed the young on an insect diet caught across the surface of the water-filled pit, and it is a marvellous summer evening when sand martins and swifts join to catch the midges, dancing just above the water.

Twenty days after being confined to the tunnel, the young, paler brown sand martins fledge and many of them take to the air for the first time together. The newly airborne youngsters

144 Skilfully landscaped and filled with water, disused gravel pits like this one at St Ives, Cambridgeshire, soon become a haven for birdlife.

are noisy and somewhat disruptive to the colony, sweeping across the sand face as their parents struggle to feed the second brood deep in the tunnel. Towards the end of August any non-breeding adults and the fledged broods congregate to form huge roosts, usually in the adjacent reed and bulrush beds, or any available scrub vegetation close by. After a succession of good breeding seasons, these roosts can number thousands of birds from neighbouring colonies, all congregating before they depart for Africa towards the middle of September.

Sadly the sand martin is no longer as common as it was twenty years ago and in many areas of Britain colonies which were large and regularly used have become deserted or hold less than ten pairs. It is not the loss of habitat that is responsible for the population crash (90 per cent in certain parts of the country), but a natural phenomenon in their wintering grounds. Like the whitethroat (page 82), sand martins winter in the Sahel region, south of the Sahara, which suffered two severe droughts in the autumns of 1968 and 1983.

Usually autumn rains in the Sahel provide plenty of insect life, and lush vegetation where the sand martins can find safe night roosts, but when both failed the sand martins starved in their thousands and many more were heavily predated. Those that managed to survive returned to Britain for our spring the following year, and our own recent spell of cold, wet and late springs caused further death or failed breeding seasons.

Clearly we have a responsibility towards the sand martins' survival, because their numbers can only increase whilst they breed in Britain; and we must also make sure that they are able to return to their wintering grounds. The International Council for Bird Preservation is trying to educate European countries who still shoot large numbers of migrating birds (page 133), including sand martins, during September to November; and the RSPB issued an information leaflet to sand and gravel pit owners in the spring of 1987, explaining the plight of the sand martin and how they could assist its recovery. Many pit owners responded, by planning early and providing a suitable sand face which the sand martins could use undisturbed until all broods had flown. The companies accepted that sand martins have been excavating nest holes in fine gravel and sand banks for millions of generations and that quarrying has only been active for about a century. If quarrying initially attracted the sand martins to venture closer to man, then at least man should try in return to get closer to an understanding of the sand martin and assist it during its hour of need.

Once the freshly exposed gravel settles and becomes colonised with plants, it is no longer suitable for species like the little ringed plover and common tern but many other species begin to thrive instead, encouraged by the cover of rosebay willowherb and brambles. This natural succession leads to the stabilising of the gravel and eventually scrub vegetation can survive, attracting whitethroat, willow warbler, yellow wagtail, reed bunting and yellowhammer.

When a pit becomes disused and water is pumped in, aquatic plants begin to colonise. Passing birds and the wind introduce the seeds of other plants and, since the supply of water pumped into many gravel pits originates from a nearby lake or river, fragments of water plants, capable of vegetative reproduction, are pumped in and eventually propagate. Canadian pondweed, water lilies and water crowfoot soon establish and release a supply of oxygen into the water, allowing microscopic invertebrates to survive and breed, which in turn provide a source of food for certain ducks.

Once reeds and mare's tail establish around the shallow of the flooded pit, the vegetation provides nesting sites for a further variety of birds and with the reassurance that they have protective cover, coot, moorhen, duck and grebe arrive to begin colonising the new aquatic habitat. Sticking to the feathers and webbed feet of some of these pioneer birds, the fertilised eggs of minnows, stickleback, roach, rudd and perch are introduced to the water and in a matter of years a healthy breeding stock of fish becomes established in gravel pits. This supply of food is exploited by heron, kingfisher, tufted duck, pochard, great crested grebe, smew and merganser, all of which visit gravel pits at different times of the year; and other vegetarian wildfowl arrive for the winter to browse and dabble on the vegetative bonanza. Canada and greylag geese, teal, wigeon, mallard and goldeneye are all winter visitors to many of the established flooded gravel pits of Britain.

One of the largest and nationally important flooded pits is the Cotswold Water Park, south of Cirencester in Gloucestershire. The lime-rich water is attractive to birds on passage migration and together with resident and summer breeding birds, over 120 species have been recorded, including rare birds like the marsh warbler and the strikingly marked, white-winged black tern which have been seen around the pits. The pits are also important because the entire area shows the typical stages of plant colonisation so well.

During winter the Cotswold Water Park, Ferry Meadows Country Park near Peterborough and hundreds of other flooded gravel pits across Britain attract large flocks of **tufted duck** from Iceland, Scandinavia and northern Russia: between December and late January, peak populations exceed 50,000 birds wintering on our lakes, reservoirs and gravel pits. The summer breeding population is much smaller, 5,000–7,000 pairs, but considering that the species first bred in Yorkshire in 1849 and another pair on Loch Leven in 1875, the increase in population within 140 years is incredible.

The gravel excavation industry is largely responsible for the breeding explosion of this duck, which prefers large areas of open water with vegetated islands where it can nest in safety; only the isolated pit is now without at least one breeding pair. At Loughs Neagh and Beg (page 146) in Northern Ireland as many as 1,000 pairs breed, with a further 200 pairs on Lower Lough Erne. On Loch of Harray on Orkney up to 2,500 pairs nest: the largest population of breeding tufted ducks in the British Isles.

The gravel pit throngs with ducks during the winter, mallard, wigeon, pochard and tufted ducks, all finding their own supply of food from the artificial supply of water.

As spring arrives, the pochards leave the gravel pit and disperse for their traditional, well-vegetated lake, because they have not yet adapted to breed around new gravel pits where vegetation is sparse; but the tufted duck has and the handsome black drake with white flanks and underparts swims in the shallows, his black crest drooping gracefully down the back of his head and the golden yellow eyes looking for a mate. The entire black plumage has a purple sheen as it catches the light. This is the breeding dress that was assumed after the late summer moult, so that even before Christmas tufted ducks are in breeding condition.

Uttering a low whistle, the male tufted duck tries to attract his partner and from the marginal reed mace beds, a raucous 'kurr-kurr' is followed by a dark brown duck, sliding into view. Her crest is shorter and her flanks are grey brown, but she also has the bright yellow eyes which are now fixed on the drake. Pointing his head upwards at an angle of 45° the drake whistles again, then reverts to a normal position. Having gained the attention of the female, he swims towards her, stretching his neck out and throwing it backwards like a pochard. This display is repeated several times and occasionally the drake gets so carried away that he rises out of the water on his legs, before resuming his surface position. In response, the duck dips her bill into the water and flicks droplets as she calls to encourage him and eventually he mates with her.

Tufted ducks prefer to nest at the edge of gravel pits in a clump of reeds, sedges or rushes and although pairs are formed towards the end of winter and early spring, nesting begins fairly late with some females still building the nest in May. The nest is a simple, grass-lined depression and the eggs are insulated with body down during the twenty-four day incubation, which the duck performs alone. Ducklings are escorted to the water within a few hours of hatching and are almost self-reliant, although the duck protects and broods them at night at first, before she too leaves them and undergoes her post-breeding moult. By the end of August, they are fledged and fly around the gravel pits, before dispersing to wintering grounds, which may be an adjacent pit or similar stretch of open water a few kilometres away, ready to be joined at the end of September by the first of the overseas tufted ducks.

Were it not for the gravel pits, the populations of **great crested grebe (147)** would not be as healthy as they are today. As with the little ringed plover, the populations of this large grebe increased during the second part of this century as the gravel extraction industry expanded. With its slender body, similar to the divers of upland lakes, long, thin, upright neck and grey-brown upperparts, the great crested grebe is familiar to most people walking near lakes, reservoirs and rivers. The bird remains around these habitats during the winter, when its plumage is basically grey on the upperparts and on the crown, with white face, neck and underparts, but in spring and summer the sexes are identical, and the gleaming white belly and front of the neck sparkles with water droplets in the sun. Few water birds are as striking as the great crested grebe in breeding plumage and about the time chiff-chaffs arrive from Africa, I always visit my nearest gravel pits to watch their display. Sometimes a March wind is whipping across the water but the grebes can be seen way out in the middle with their beautiful black, double-horned crests, well-developed chestnut and black tippets or frill on either side of the head, and resembling a bayonet in shape, a red and brown bill. During the nineteenth century it was fashionable for the middle classes to decorate their clothes, especially hats and dresses, with feathers, and the more colourful the better. It was cheap to decorate otherwise drab clothes with grebe feathers and when the craze developed into wearing complete 'grebe furs' the British population of great crested grebe nearly became extinct, falling to around thirty or forty birds in 1860. Fortunately by 1870 laws were enforced to protect it, but only just in time. It is a credit to the bird's resilience and adaptability, enabling it to exploit man-made lakes as well as natural waterways, that over 7,000 pairs now breed across the country.

On most days in March, gravel pits echo to the resonant croaking of the great crested grebe. Buoyantly swimming towards each other the pair of grebes raise their crests and fan their facial tippets as the gap between them closes. Then, in perfect harmony, the two birds start shaking their heads from side to side, starting with their bills pointing downwards, but continuing as the bills are raised vertically into the air. For three or four minutes this routine is performed, then one of the birds suddenly dives and disappears to begin what is called 'the discovery sequence'. Essentially it is a form of grebe hide-and-seek, with one of the pair remaining on the surface with all its feathers puffed out, whilst the other dives out of sight then tries to approach its mate from beneath the surface, creating the maximum surprise and excitement as it suddenly emerges alongside the floating bird.

After head shaking and the discovery, a short sequence of grebe tag begins, whereby one of the pair approaches its partner in head-shaking pose then at the last moment sinks into the water, turns and rushes away, only to turn around, glance at its partner and repeat the behaviour several times more. By this time the pair bond is well developed and the ritual reaches the highpoint of the entire ceremony called the weed dance, which is similar to that performed by the Slavonian grebe (page 153).

Moving towards each other with their necks upright and crests raised, they both suddenly dive, only to surface with

145

146

straggling water weed in their bills which they carry towards each other whilst swimming. At the last moment the pair rise out of the water so that their breasts touch and the surface beneath their feet is churning foam as they madly tread water to remain upright, shaking their heads rapidly from side to side whilst holding on to the weed. This ceremony terminates with a few mutually agreeable head shakes and bows. Only large open expanses of water are suitable for this elaborate display and during the last fifty years gravel pits have proved perfect.

The weed dance is normally followed by building the nest, which is anchored to reed stems so that it floats and can rise and fall with fluctuating water-levels. Upon completion of the

145 Little ringed plovers have taken advantage of the most barren of habitats, nesting along the margins of newly excavated pits.

146 Sand-martin tunnels are excavated in vertical sand faces, river banks or suitable cliff faces, where noisy colonies develop.

147 From near extinction levels in 1860 the great-crested grebe has benefited from gravel pits and reservoirs and is now a common breeding bird.

nest, mating takes place on top. Eventually up to six eggs are laid, which are incubated by both adults for twenty-eight days. The dark brown zebra-striped chicks leave the nest and ride about on their parents' backs; when one of the adults dives to find suitable invertebrate food, they rapidly scuttle to the warmth and security of the other surface-floating adult to await the food. As the young grow, they frequently divide into small groups with each adult looking after two or three grebelets but since they are double-brooded, very often the male looks after the family, whilst the female incubates the second clutch, or both roles can be equally shared.

Gravel pits are thus an extremely valuable, relatively new wetland habitat for birds and their significance in countryside which is continuously being urbanised should not be overlooked. Initially they may not be very attractive to look at, but with advice and conservation management in association with the landowners, many gravel pits have been landscaped and left to offer shelter and food for birds and recreation for man. As long as these two aspects continue and develop in sympathy with one another, gravel pits and the similar reservoirs will prove to be activities of man that lead to the conservation of birds.

RESERVOIRS

Man has altered wetland habitats by channelling rivers through concrete ducts, draining marshes and fenland and reclaiming flood meadows for arable pasture, so that today there is less freshwater than there was even 100 years ago. Even so, we all expect a freshwater supply in our homes, offices and factories, and this supply is stored in man-made reservoirs, industrial or drinking-water, designed and located so that they are fed by local rivers and streams. Since nearly every city and large town has reservoirs near by, stored water is found throughout the British Isles, especially in the heavily populated south-east of England, where demands are greatest. The birdlife of southern England has, therefore, been forced to become more dependent on gravel pits and reservoirs as drainage and disturbance of more natural wetlands has increased. Although species like the redshank, snipe and wigeon have declined as their marshland habitat has been destroyed, other species such as pochard, tufted duck and coot have benefited as their preferred open water habitat has increased with the increase of reservoirs.

Drinking-water reservoirs vary across the country. Some are huge valleys which have been dammed and flooded, like the Craig Goch Reservoir at Elan Valley in Wales; here the water is deep and lacks nutrients, with little freshwater life, apart from around the margins and near the surface. Other reservoirs are hollowed basins, completely concrete-lined, and their shores and margins are correspondingly barren with little value for plants and birds; this is the type of reservoir commonly built near populated areas. The third type of reservoir is the most valuable to wildlife: it is formed by building a concrete dam across a shallow, lowland valley and allowing the surrounding rivers and natural precipitation to drain into it. The 140-ha/ 346-acre reservoir called Rutland Water in Leicestershire is a good example of this type, and is extremely rich in birdlife with reeds and scrub vegetation around parts of the banks.

It is a bonus that many reservoirs are colonised by birds and other forms of wildlife because this is never considered when they are constructed. Reservoirs in upland Britain are colonised only by hardy species because the water draining through the local rocks and running into the reservoirs is generally acidic, so little plant or invertebrate life survives in the water and consequently, as with natural upland lakes, few birds colonise. An additional problem with many upland reservoirs is the constantly fluctuating water-levels as water is either drained out or pumped into the storage reservoir, exposing the lower banks for only short periods, and therefore preventing any plant colonisation which would attract certain birds.

The industrial reservoirs were mostly constructed 200 years ago, at the onset of the Industrial Revolution, which accelerated the need for water to power machinery. The canals of Britain also developed with the Industrial Revolution and barges were used to transport the increasing supplies of raw materials and machinery across Britain to new areas of industrial growth. This network of canals traversing the countryside required feeder reservoirs to keep their levels navigable and so a whole series of smaller reservoirs were built, of which the famous Tring Reservoirs (**148**) are an example, constructed initially to feed the Grand Union Canal which links London with Birmingham.

Dug in the nineteenth century from lime-rich damp meadows, the Tring Reservoirs cover 19 ha/47 acres of Hertfordshire countryside. They are so important for bird- and plant-life that they were designated a Nature Conservancy Council reserve 33 years ago. Around the margins the vegetation and reed growth is dense, so there is plenty of cover for nesting birds and because the reservoirs are fed by streams running over chalk, the water is rich in nutrients and fresh-water life.

Herons nest in the reedbeds and in spring dabchick, coot, moorhen, Canada geese and mute swans all go through their courtship displays and nest around the reservoirs. In winter large mixed flocks of ducks, including mallard, tufted duck, shoveler, pochard, wigeon and pintail congregate on the open water to feed, and a few Bewick's swans arrive from Russia. Black-headed and common gulls scavenge around the rubbish tips, sewage farms and countryside around Tring but return to the reservoirs to roost towards late afternoon.

Birdwatchers have always favoured these reservoirs during spring and autumn passage. In spring, look out for little ringed plover, which chose the shingle around the reservoir at Tring at low water as its first British nest site in 1938. They stop to feed alongside turnstone, godwit and sanderling before flying on to their breeding grounds. Regular spring birdwatching at Tring may reward you with a sight of the osprey on its way from Africa north to the Highlands and their traditional nesting sites (page 50). Later in May I have seen hobbies flying across the reservoirs and perching in the surrounding trees before they move on a few miles to nest on the Aylesbury plain, where they have reared young successfully for over fifteen years. As summer gives way to September, the autumn passage species rest at the reservoirs and waders like knot, little stint, wood sandpiper, green sandpiper and greenshank arrive to feed on the exposed mud. The Tring Reservoirs so regulate the Grand Union Canal that the water-levels are lowest in the autumn just before winter storms naturally raise the level, providing the perfect feeding station for waders on their way south to Africa and the Mediterranean for the winter.

Winter birdwatching around Tring Reservoirs is never without excitement and the surrounding alder, hawthorn and willow scrub attracts siskin, fieldfare, redwing, brambling and great grey shrike. Public hides and pathways provide a 3-km/1¾-mile nature trail and these reservoirs perfectly illustrate how some man-made habitats can be extremely valuable for birds and other wildlife.

With outbreaks of cholera and typhoid during the Victorian era, society came to accept the need for reserves of unpolluted drinking water and reservoirs were built nationwide. The majority of the major cities like Manchester, Glasgow and Sheffield either dammed natural lakes to raise their waterlevels or built dams and flooded huge valleys in the Pennines so that daily water supplies could be drawn.

Every day the equivalent of 136 l/30 gallons of water per person living in Britain is used, putting a huge demand on the reservoir network. The Thames supplies much of the water for London and the river is tapped above Teddington to fill a series of banked reservoirs, including the huge Queen Mary Reservoir at Staines, which is one of the largest earth-banked reservoirs in the country, covering 283 ha/699 acres and holding 36,000 million l/8,000 million gallons. In winter many ducks and coots form rafts on the water but the rarer goosander and black-necked grebe are also regular visitors.

As a breeding bird the **black-necked grebe** is extremely rare:

there are only 10–25 pairs, mostly confined to shallow freshwater lochs in Scotland. Over fifty years ago, hundreds of black-necked grebes bred as a single colony in Ireland, but the bird is now extinct there as a breeding species and is only seen as a very rare winter migrant.

The grebe is only 30 cm/12 in from beak to tail, and the sexes are similar, resembling the slightly larger Slavonian grebe (page 152). Few birdwatchers will be lucky enough to see the black-necked grebe in breeding plumage in Britain, and it is only during spring when the feathers are at their finest that the bird justifies its name. At a distance across the breeding loch the grebe appears all black, but when seen close to the 25-cm/9¾-inch-diameter nest, the bird's flanks can be seen to be distinctly chestnut, and as the adult slips on to the nest, the white underparts are clearly visible. The head, neck and wings are black and, radiating out from behind the bright red eyes, the distinguishing, wispy, golden-yellow ear tufts spread out like a fan.

Close to the Queen Mary Reservoir are the North and South Staines Reservoirs, covering 172 ha/425 acres, where thousands of pochard and tufted duck congregate each winter. Much of the water supply of north London is supplied from a group of reservoirs in the Lea Valley between Enfield Lock and Walthamstow and together with the reservoirs around Staines, they provide 1,416 ha/3,500 acres of open water in a series of man-made lakes, which are attractive to a wide range of birds throughout the year.

Throughout Britain, reservoirs vary tremendously. Many of them have a bottom formed of nothing but compressed soil which, after flooding, gradually becomes covered with silt, as debris is carried into the reservoir by feeder rivers. When this organic material decays, the silt layer increases until aquatic plants are able to root around the margin. Many reservoirs boast a healthy growth of water lilies and Canadian pondweed which themselves provide food and shelter for freshwater invertebrates like snails, dragonfly nymphs, water beetles and mayfly larvae, all of which form part of the diet of countless aquatic birds. Most reservoirs without plant and insect life will be used by birds for drinking and bathing, but wherever food supplies are rich, as in lowland valley reservoirs, many species of birds visit the habitat regularly and some stay to breed.

Huge rafts of ducks and coots on a reservoir indicate that it is rich in food. If winter populations exceed more than 1 per cent of the nationally known total for a particular species of duck, the reservoir is regarded as being of national importance to that species, which is one reason why Abberton Reservoir in Essex has become so popular with birdwatchers between September and March. With thousands of tufted duck, mallard and pochard and hundreds of goldeneye and shoveler, Abberton is the most important overwintering reservoir for wildfowl in Britain. The reservoir gains international importance because of the large numbers of teal and wigeon, which raft up on the water, accompanied by the rarer gadwall. At their maximum these eight species of duck account for more than 25,000 birds on the reservoir during the winter, to which can be added 5,000 coot and thousands of waders feeding on the meadows around the reservoir from late August to April.

Because Abberton is not far inland, the mud flats, salt-marshes and estuaries of the Essex coast are near by and any birdwatcher wanting a varied day's winter birdwatching should include this part of Essex in his itinerary. The possibility of seeing smew, goosander, Slavonian, red- and black-necked grebe and red-throated diver all in one day is almost impossible to accept, yet this is one reservoir where it can happen.

The Abberton Reservoir is the most reliable place to see some of the 6,000 **shoveler** population, having one of the largest gatherings of this species in Britain. As a breeding bird only about one thousand pairs nest in the British Isles, mostly confined to south-east England, and the bird is rare in Ireland, Scotland and Wales. It is interesting that our resident breeding shovelers migrate to France and southern Spain for the winter, leaving our shores between August and November, but they are replaced by shovelers from northern Europe and Russia which arrive from November onwards. Many reservoirs and lakes show their maximum shoveler counts during November because the populations are a mixture of British birds, which have not yet left, and the arriving European birds; but from December through to February, any shovelers seen in Britain are immigrants from colder climates.

At a distance many species of duck appear similar and their silhouettes confusing, but the 51-cm/20-in shoveller is unmistakable. No other duck has a bill longer than its head, or one which is flattened and spatulate like that of the shoveler. When seen close up this bill is even more incredible because the upper and lower mandibles cannot be completely closed together but are fringed with structures called lamellae. The specialised bill is highly adapted for filter feeding, so that the shoveler can collect large quantities of food in a single sweep, exploiting supplies of freshwater plankton unavailable to other ducks. The London reservoirs and the Ouse Washes are also favourite winter haunts for this bird, where they can be watched filter nibbling around the banks of the reservoirs and margins of shallow pools.

The drake shoveler is magnificent in spring plumage, and as the sun shines on the feathers the head is iridescent black-green, with dazzling white breast, chestnut-brown flanks and bright red legs. Binoculars reveal the black bill and bright yellow eyes, and when the bird takes to the air on rapidly beating wings, the beautiful green speculum flashes as the duck turns across the water. The female shows little of this splendour: she has the green speculum, but in other respects resembles a stocky, orange-brown billed, mallard duck, with mottled brown feathers.

On a nationwide basis it is difficult for birdwatchers to find worthwhile information about the reservoirs of Britain, but contacting your local water authority should be the first move in order to obtain details about access to private land or names of reservoirs within the water authority region with an ornithological interest. Over 70 per cent of our reservoirs have only average interest for birdwatchers because of their small-size oligotrophic conditions, poor marginal vegetation offering little cover for birds, or unfavourable sites in upland country. For birdwatching, the most productive reservoirs are found in south-west England, South Wales and southern and eastern England, especially around London. Birdwatching has become so intense on the London reservoirs that the Thames Water Authority has published a booklet, *Birdwatching at Reservoirs*,

148

148   Tring reservoirs in Hertfordshire were dug in the nineteenth century and although man-made, they have become a significant wildlife habitat, covering 19 ha/47 acres.

which gives useful information, including how to obtain an annual permit for access to a variety of their reservoirs.

The first reservoirs to be built around London were at Ruislip, Elstree and Brent, constructed towards the middle of the last century to support Tring, as a series of feeder reservoirs for the busy Grand Union Canal. Before their construction the only significant areas of water in London were the Serpentine in Hyde Park, Highgate Pond on Hampstead Heath and Pen Ponds on Richmond Common, but their total area was much smaller than any reservoir. Birds soon found the newly flooded reservoirs and because canal-feeder reservoirs do not supply drinking water, they are left open to the public, so birdwatchers also discovered their potential.

Brent Reservoir was completed in November 1835 and because of its shape, is known as the Welsh Harp. Surrounded by Kingsbury, Neasden and Hendon it soon became a wildlife oasis and birdwatchers of the last century recorded rarities like the Squacco heron, little bittern and Temminck's stint visiting the reservoir alongside countless rafts of wild duck. By 1913 the area surrounding Brent Reservoir was becoming urbanised: the North Circular Road was built in 1920, and by the 1970s over 60 per cent of the land surrounding the open water had been built upon, so the reservoir became an oasis in a concrete desert, with Wembley Stadium and the vast Brent Cross shopping centre overshadowing.

Today birdwatchers still visit the reservoir, but it has changed in 75 years. Tall buildings surround the water and dominate the skyline, and there is marshland on parts of the southern shore and scrub vegetation on the northern banks. Reed canary grass, common reed and bulrush form a partial fringe, providing shelter for nesting reed warbler, mallard, coot, moorhen, great-crested and little grebe and in the willow and hawthorn scrub, blackbird, song thrush, robin, hedgesparrow, great tit and willow warbler are frequently heard and seen.

The urban development and industrial growth around Brent Reservoir caused it to become polluted and on several occasions it has been drained, the concrete banks repaired and refilled with clean water. Rather than harming visiting birds, the maintenance of the reservoir has been beneficial, because the waters were restocked with healthy fish, and their breeding became more successful. The resulting fry attracted great crested grebes to colonise in larger numbers than before. Even more significant is the arrival of the common tern, which overwinters in southern Africa, but returns to Britain to nest each summer. The increase in small fish has attracted this bird to stay around the Brent Reservoir and the Welsh Harp Conservation Group have supplied floating gravel-filled rafts for the birds to nest on. In summer this species alone makes the reservoir worth a visit. It provides an excellent example of how we can encourage birds to colonise even the most urban man-made habitat, under sympathetic management.

As with other aquatic habitats, like the rivers and Broads, reservoirs have become popular for recreational sports, including water skiing and sailing, which are not really compatible with the requirements of birds or birdwatchers. At one time, drinking-water reservoirs offered no public access because of fears of structural damage and pollution, but permits were gradually issued to birdwatchers who, although considered somewhat eccentric, were accepted as not being harmful to the purity of the stored water. It was only after government pressure, following an increase in watersport interest, that water authorities began to open up their reservoir network to the public, and it was soon discovered that people paying for the privilege of enjoying their hobby did not pollute the water either.

The rapid increase in the number of human visitors to the reservoirs affected the bird populations, since few species accept the disturbance caused by sailing dinghies and speedboats, or people sitting conspicuously around the margins of the water, fishing for hours on end near reedbeds, where the birds once nested each year.

Birdwatchers and conservationists were faced with massive competition for the pleasure of visiting the reservoirs across Britain, and since fishing and sailing clubs are prepared to pay thousands of pounds annually to enjoy their recreation, water authorities are pleased to encourage their development. Birdwatchers have always paid small sums of money for permits which give them access to an ornithologically rich site, but since the hobby necessitates visiting a wide variety of habitats and locations in any one year, it is not really possible for birdwatchers to compete with revenue raised by sporting clubs who concentrate their activities on one reservoir or lake all year round.

Over a period of years, following pressure and awareness generated by conservation societies, the water authorities have realised that some recreation, although lucrative, does not encourage wildlife and conservation. Since their public image

149

149 With few natural enemies apart from man, Canada geese are long-lived, reaching twenty years. They have colonised reservoirs, gravel pits and both natural and ornamental lakes since their introduction from Canada 300 years ago. Plundering cereal and arable crops from farmland bordering wetlands, Canada geese have become unpopular with farmers and are frequently persecuted throughout the year, but nonetheless continue to breed successfully.

150 The male smew, with its unmistakable black and white plumage. The female smew has a chestnut cap and grey-black upperparts. Smews are winter visitors, favouring our southern reservoirs, especially Barn Elms and Brent, but they do not arrive until their Russian and Scandinavian breeding grounds have frozen up.

150

is important to them, many of the authorities have developed dual-interest reservoirs, where particular areas rich in wildlife are not open to disturbing water sports or fishing, and gradually birds have adapted, and colonised these quieter areas. By restricting boating and skiing to the deeper, open water, and preserving the shallows and vegetated areas for birds, many reservoirs are enjoyed and managed by compromise. At Brent, most of the recreational disturbance occurs at weekends, and in order to see the rafts of ducks, coots, grebes and waders which feed in the soft mud, you need to arrive early in the morning, before the first boats appear.

Together with London's Barn Elms Reservoir, where the duck first appeared in 1922, the Brent Reservoir has always been one of the top sites in Britain for the winter-visiting **smew**. The eastern end of the reservoir is the best place to see this attractive sawbill duck, where it feeds on shellfish in the shallow water, in groups of 10–30 birds. Like the shoveler, the smew cannot be mistaken for any other bird, despite sitting on the water with its head withdrawn between its shoulders like teal. The smew's rapid, twisting and turning flight, with regular descents to the water, mimics the agility of the teal, but its plumage is quite different (**150**).

In cold Septembers, the first of the smew arrive from northern Russia and Scandinavia, where they breed by lakes surrounded with trees. Like goldeneye and mandarin duck (page 36), they nest in hollow trees. The male is a striking bird, with a mainly white plumage and distinctive black eye-patches, which run forwards into the bill. The profile is characteristic: smews have small bills, straight foreheads and a rectangular-shaped head. Males show a distinctive white crest, with black markings, running around the nape; and with further black markings on the back, flanks and breast the male smew is very attractive.

Unlike the similar-sized neighbouring pochard on the reservoir, the smew very rarely includes vegetation in its diet. It dives beneath the choppy surface as a cold north wind cuts across the water and regularly remains submerged for fifteen seconds, but sometimes as long as forty-five seconds, hunting small fish and large freshwater insects and larvae. Birdwatchers should feel privileged when observing smews, because although they are regular winter visitors, Britain represents the edge of their overwintering range: only 100–150 birds turn up each year on reservoirs, gravel pits and estuaries, largely in south-east England and never missing out Barn Elms or Brent Reservoirs, where they are most commonly seen during January and February.

Depending on the weather, smew either stay on our reservoir network until May, or in mild winters leave in March for their northern breeding grounds, but in most years it is possible to watch the smew's courtship and pairing displays before they go.

Amongst a raft of mallards and coots a small group of smew paddle together. Look closely at the males, with their crests raised, their entire heads tilted backwards to the shoulders, and their bills pointing to the sky, as they move in on a solitary female. As they approach, their heads move sideways, left and right, then one of the males kicks down into the water and almost stands on the surface. This excited manoeuvre is followed by imitation drinking movements with the bill and head bobbing up and down, and the female responds with similar head movements.

The display and the female's response lasts for many minutes but the males make no further advance towards the female: all they do is maintain her interest. Suddenly the female does the chasing and rushes towards her chosen male with neck outstretched. Upon reaching him she bobs her head up and down in a deliberate arc, lowers her body in the water, and the male circles and copulates with her in a few seconds, leaving the other unsatisfied males to search for another mate elsewhere.

On most of the southern reservoirs, April brings a buzz of activity as migrating birds arrive or pass across the water, while overwintering ducks leave the reservoir and head for their breeding territories. Even though the increase in air temperature is barely discernible, the birds know that spring is waiting. Around the Dollis Brook inflow of the Brent, where scrub vegetation provides good cover, the departing fieldfares and redwings take their last meal in this country, before flying north to breed, but at the same time the song of a chiff-chaff and willow warbler uttered from the willow scrub announces the arrival of the summer visitors from Africa. A common sandpiper and yellow wagtail forage along the secluded edge of the reedbeds and the first swallows and sand martins arrive at the reservoir to drink and feed, adding their own special magic to a morning spent birdwatching on the reservoirs in early spring.

Migratory and passage birds find the London reservoirs very attractive as feeding and resting posts, where all around them sprawl concrete and tarmac. If you want to see wheatear arriving before they disperse to the downlands and uplands and the warblers before they disappear into dense scrub and woodland, visit one of the south-east reservoirs towards the end of April and into early May, especially after a cloudy night with drizzle and south-easterly wind: under these conditions thousands of migrants arrive, including small numbers of black tern which breed in Europe and only very rarely in Britain around the Ouse Washes.

For birdwatchers, our reservoirs are at their least productive during the summer, but by August they are once again the scene of activity as summer visitors stop off to feed on their journey south for the winter. After breeding elsewhere many of our ducks fly to reservoirs for their autumn moult. Mallard, gadwall, garganey, teal and shoveler may all be seen on different reservoirs and since 1972 gadwall, shoveler and goldeneye have all increased in numbers, colonising an increasing number of reservoirs around London and the south-east during winter. The ubiquitous flocks of coots gradually increase from late summer throughout autumn and at Barn Elms Reservoir up to 27,000 black-headed gulls fly in and roost each night throughout the winter, dispersing in the early morning to feed along the low-water line of the Thames and around the ponds and lakes of the London parks.

Birdwatchers in north-east London are fortunate to have Walthamstow Reservoirs on their doorsteps, where daily permits can be obtained at the entrance. The reservoirs are situated at the southern end of the Lea Valley and have been designated an SSSI by the Nature Conservancy Council because of their rich birdlife, mainly because there are over 100 pairs of heron which nest on tree-covered islands in the reservoirs south of Ferry Lane. Totally surrounded by Tottenham and Walthamstow, this is the fifth largest heronry in Britain – one of the marvels of urban bird colonisation.

Herons are large birds and visiting the reservoirs in April for the first time, it will take a while before you accept the constant observation of these birds flapping low over the houses as they satisfy the appetites of their young in the nests. Other large black birds flying across the network of reservoirs towards late afternoon and evening are cormorants which roost in other trees overlooking these man-made lakes in groups of 50–100 birds.

Walthamstow Reservoirs are important urban breeding sites for mallard, mute swan, tufted duck and pochard. In most seasons over twenty-five broods of tufted duck are successfully raised on the reservoirs and ten or twelve pairs of great crested grebe breed each year. In winter the 133 ha/328 acres of open water provide refuge for a mixed flock of up to 9,000 pochard and tufted ducks, many of which arrived in August to begin their moult, representing some of the largest flocks of these two species in Britain.

Wherever islands occur naturally in reservoirs or are provided artificially by conservation groups, the **Canada goose** soon begins to breed and Walthamstow is famous for its breeding population of this species. Other reservoirs have their own pairs, if willow scrub and alders are sufficiently dense to screen the nesting birds.

Introduced from America for the landed gentry and Charles II, 300 years ago, the large 90–100-cm/36–40-in bird escaped from the ornamental lake in St James's Park, London, and now breeds on lakes, gravel pits and reservoirs throughout the country; in Ireland it breeds mainly around Cork and Strangford Lough. Grazing quietly on the grass around the reservoir, it is easily recognised by its slender black neck and head, with white throat patches extending from the chin, down the sides of the head to beyond the eyes (**149**). Both sexes are identical with grey-brown upperparts, brown wings, black tail and brownish-white underparts. They are always reluctant to fly, preferring to amble down to the water for the occasional swim or to browse for aquatic plants, for they are entirely vegetarian, feeding on roots, stems and leaves or the seeds of grasses growing in adjacent meadows. For this reason they have become unpopular with farmers because sprouting cereal crops are just another form of grass to the geese and they graze the arable fields in the early morning, sometimes causing extensive damage.

Initially, because they were viewed as an introduced species, ornithologists took little interest in the Canada geese of ornamental lake and large pond, but nearly forty years ago, when the geese began to escape and colonise gravel pits and reservoirs along the Thames Valley, interest began to germinate. In 1953 the species was censused and 3,500 birds were officially recorded, but twenty-four years later the population had reached 19,500 birds, and it is now accepted as a wild breeding bird.

After three years a Canada goose is sexually mature and can breed. The frequently heard 'ah-honk' trumpeting call, uttered when several geese within a flock argue with each other, turns to an incessant bickering during the territorial and mating season: although they agree to nest in small communal groups, they are particular about distances between each nest, and a mated gander will not accept an unmated male too close to his partner. Like swans, they pair for life, and use the same nest site each year, with the female rebuilding the nest which is a hollow lined with reeds, grasses and leaves, with a central cup, thermally lined with feathers and down plucked from her own body.

If you have a colony of Canada geese on your local reservoir, it is likely that they can be watched all year round, because the adults are very sedentary, remaining within a 48-km/30-mile radius of their breeding territory. The only exception is a flock of Canada geese in north Yorkshire, who fly 300 miles north to the Beauly Firth near Inverness for their autumn moult. The 700 geese making the flight are all sexually immature birds, and so far no plausible reason has been found why this solitary group of birds instinctively fly to the shelter of the coastal mud flats for their moult, but cease to perform the moult migration once they establish breeding territories in north Yorkshire.

It is the diverse range and large numbers of birds that can be seen on reservoirs which make them popular with birdwatchers. The opportunities for observing courtship displays and feeding behaviour are an added bonus, and the possibility of a rare or unusual bird turning up unexpectedly is always exciting. Frequently the birds themselves are faced with challenges because the level of the water can fluctuate unpredictably: the floating nest of the great crested grebe anchored to reed stems and the nests of moorhens, coots and swans in the reedbeds and overhanging vegetation, can become isolated metres from the water and exposed to predation, or else completely flooded out. Ideal management and water regulation provides maximum high waters during the winter, which submerges all the summer and autumn vegetation, disperses the seeds and provides floating food for the dabbling ducks around the edges of the reservoir. In the spring some run-off or natural evaporation should expose areas of soft mud which is perfect feeding ground for the passage waders and will persuade resident snipe to remain around the reservoir and breed. Summer brings the greatest demand on the water supply and the level in the reservoir drops to meet this demand, with any luck avoiding the important few weeks when grebes and coots are brooding their clutches. If their nests become marooned by a sudden drop in water-level, many grebes, who are poor walkers on dry land, are unable to walk to the new low-water mark, which is why they require an almost constant water-level whilst incubating their eggs.

From August to October, further run-off re-exposes the marginal silt beds, and once again provides a feeding area for the autumn passage waders and allows new seeds to germinate which produce fresh plant growth, providing shelter for skulking birds in subsequent seasons. Blithfield in Staffordshire is a perfect example of a reservoir with large areas of exposed mud in autumn and as many as thirty species of wader have been recorded there because of this.

For many young birdwatchers, reservoirs will be where they cut their teeth on a hobby which may fascinate them for the rest of their lives. The first common sandpiper, knot and ringed plover may be seen from the concrete causeway of a London reservoir, or a red-breasted merganser distinguished from a goosander, with the assistance of a helpful birdwatcher sharing a welcome flask of coffee on a cold winter's afternoon. Starlings polka-dot the evening sky as they arrive at the reservoir to roost, their chatterings and cackles drowned by a jumbo-jet climbing out of Heathrow. At that moment you are reminded that these aquatic havens are man-made lakes, right in the middle of suburbia, but that does not stop the wildfowl arriving each autumn and winter, or the thousands of swifts which return early in May to scream across the water as they feed on insects, following their own long-distance flight from southern Africa. After a few days' recuperation, most of them disperse and on summer evenings, about an hour before sunset, they are seen performing their aerial acrobatics, together with the shrill scream, around the chimneys, towers and roof tops of towns and villages which form the cities and suburbs of Britain and Ireland.

CHAPTER 11

THE COAST

CLIFFS AND ROCKY SHORES

CLIFFS Although we call ourselves an island race, very few of us have actually spent time looking closely at the coastline and shores of our island. The British Isles consists of many hundreds of small islands and Britain alone has one of the most varied coastlines in Europe, covering at least 12,067 km/7,500 miles, with immense diversity of wildlife and habitat. Accurate figures for the length of the whole coastline of the British Isles are not known. England and Wales possess a coastline estimated at 4,500 km/2,796 miles, but adding the fjord-like Scottish and Irish coastlines to this figure would produce an astonishing total – for instance, a single island such as Mull has a coastline of over 480 km/300 miles.

Compared with Europe, our bird populations are exceptional only for our well-established sea-bird colonies where millions of birds breed. Internationally, the largely accessible cliffs of Britain and Ireland are known for their spectacular sea-bird nesting sites: almost 70 per cent of the world razorbill population nests along the coastline.

The success of our sea-bird colonies is mainly due to the nature of our rocky coasts, with their soaring cliffs and off-shore islands. The western coasts of Britain and Ireland are well known for their rugged, ancient, hard rocky cliffs; but most of us are familiar, too, with the less exposed coast of

152 An impressive rocky pinnacle off-shore from Handa Island provides an ideal nesting site for fulmar, kittiwake and guillemot.

151

151 Kittiwakes are true cliff-nesting gulls using small ledges on the most precarious rock faces. They breed after three years, remaining at sea for their first summer of life.

south-east England, with stretches of sand and shingle and expanses of saltmarsh and mud flats.

Geologically, the coastline of the British Isles is relatively young, shaped by the combined forces of deposition, erosion by the action of sea against the land and by wide-ranging sea levels immediately before and after the Ice Age.

The four great Ice Ages occurred during the Pleistocene era, which began about 1 million years ago and ended about 10,500 years ago, just before the Pre-Boreal period (page 14). The final great glaciation took place about 20,000 years ago and, as the ice came south from the polar regions, glaciers bulldozed valley floors to depths well below sea level. The seas actually froze and levels dropped 45 m/147½ ft below those of today, but when the glaciers finally melted and the seas thawed, the water rushed into the gouged valleys, forming the sea lochs of western Scotland and the firths of the east coast.

In East Anglia some of the small cliffs originated from boulder clay and mineral debris deposited by retreating glaciers which then became eroded; others on the east coast have formed the famous shingle banks of the north Norfolk coast (page 190). After the retreat of the glaciers of the last Ice Age, mineral debris was left deposited around Britain. Much of it remains inland, as a cover over underlying rocks, but some of it is constantly being transported around the coast of Britain by the tidal action.

The coastline is constantly changing and the power of the wind and sea can transform a sandy beach into a shingle one by depositing debris from further down the coast, or cause sheer cliffs to landslide into the sea, instantly forming a rocky shore. Storm waves on the Atlantic coast exert a pressure of thirty tonnes per square metre – a force that will eventually shift most obstacles. This is how some off-shore islands and rocky stacks are formed, especially if the substrate is soft. Such was the case with the chalk ridge that joined the Needles of the Isle of Wight to the Isle of Purbeck in Dorset. When this ridge was eventually destroyed the Isle of Wight and the straddled Needles became isolated.

Wave action slowly erodes a notch at any point of the coastline which, in time, extends to form a beach with a cliff. Where the land slopes gradually, these cliffs are not sheer, and at any point along the coast, future development of the cliffs depends on the hardness of the underlying rocks and subsequent wave action. Only the east coast of Britain, between the Thames and Humber Estuaries, has long stretches of coastline without cliffs: this is because the soft rocks of gravel and sand are unstable and are rapidly cut back by the sea.

Ideally, birdwatchers identify the type of cliff in a particular part of the country by the colour of the localised rock. There are the famous blinding white chalk cliffs of Kent, Sussex and east Yorkshire; the old red sandstone of South Wales, Devon, Caithness and around Moray Firth; and the dark brown basalt rock of Northern Ireland's Giant's Causeway, the islands of Skye, Eigg, Canna, Mull, Muck and the Farne Islands off the Northumberland coast. Then there is the grey gneiss of the Outer Hebrides, and the variable pink, red and blue-grey granite of the Cornish coast and the Scillies.

Limestone was formed about 100 million years ago from the shells of molluscs, common in the seas of the Cretaceous period. If you visit the limestone cliffs of Tenby in South Wales, the Great Orme in North Wales or Arnside Knott in Lancashire, you will see that such cliffs are havens for wild flowers as well as sea birds. Eighty-five bird species are found around the Great Orme, including breeding colonies of sea birds such as fulmar, kittiwake, razorbill, guillemot, chough, jackdaw and raven. Most limestone cliffs are equally rich in bird- and plantlife, and well worth scrutiny by the birdwatcher, who should be ready for the surprise of a rare or unusual bird, such as the peregrine, which frequently breeds on limestone cliffs in Wales.

One of the safest and most exciting methods of birdwatching around cliffs is on an organised boat trip, when the skipper sails his small vessel into the shadow of the towering cliff face. The deafening noise of the birds maintaining their territory has an almost physical impact.

Most of the cacophany of noise is from the throats of **kittiwakes**, who utter the wild call that gives them their name 'kitti-wa-a-k, kitti-wa-a-k', from nesting ledges and rock outcrops (**151**). They are attractive gulls and more sea-going than other species, expanding their breeding range everywhere; and if cliff faces are not available, they now use buildings or other man-made ledges.

The calls of the kittiwake are musical by comparison with the deep, growling, belching notes of **guillemots** and razorbills, standing on the cliff ledges like waiters dressed in traditional black and white. Whereas the kittiwakes build their nests on narrow ledges, the guillemots lay their single eggs on ledges which are too narrow to build a nest, so they don't bother. Only the unique, evolutionary design of the egg prevents it from rolling into the sea. The guillemot's egg is large, about 10–12 cm/4–4½ in long and tapered to resemble a pear, so that when it is knocked, as often happens on crowded ledges, it spins in a tight circle.

The **razorbill's** egg has a more usual shape and any similar knock would send it to its doom, so razorbills (**153**) have evolved to nest in crevices or hollows on the cliffs towards late April and early May. They are not as common as guillemots: the British population is around 160,000 pairs, a quarter of the guillemot breeding population.

Scanning the cliff face from an off-shore boat, it is easy to identify distinct zones on the cliff, which are colonised by species of sea bird according to their nesting requirements. We are fortunate to see large colonies of sea birds because the varied cliffs around Britain offer suitable nesting sites and are close to rich feeding grounds, which are fortuitously caused by the geographical position of Britain and Ireland. The warm waters of the Gulf Stream and North Atlantic Drift wash the coasts on the west and north of these islands. Cold currents moving south from the Arctic Circle meet these warmer currents and any overall mixing results in an area of upwelling where marine nutrients rise to the surface waters, providing food for plankton. This food supply is preyed upon by fish which themselves provide food for sea birds and man.

Look at the birds at all levels: the pale gulls, wafting like pieces of tissue paper on cliff-face breezes; the fulmars, effortlessly gliding across the cliff, then out to sea and back again; and comical puffins, razorbills and guillemots, constantly arriving and departing on rapidly beating wings. None of the ledges wide enough to hold an egg or nest is left unoccupied; any wider rock ledge with some earth cover is burrowed into by nesting puffins or cormorants, and shags adorn the broader ledges with their dilapidated nests made of coastal flotsam and jetsam (**156**).

Most sea cliffs around the British Isles have an average height of between 45–90 m/160–295 ft. The highest are in the islands off north Scotland: on St Kilda some of the granite cliffs tower 430 m/1,410 ft and on Foula in the Shetlands the old red sandstone cliffs rise 350 m/1,148ft. Mainland cliffs are not as tall, but impressive nevertheless: on the Sutherland coast the Torridonian sandstone cliffs at Clo Mor rise 210 m/689ft and the shale, sandstone and boulder clay Boulby Cliffs on the north Yorkshire coast drop 200 m/656 ft to the sea. In southern Ireland the Cliffs of Moher in Co. Clare drop 197 m/646 ft sheer into the Atlantic and extend along the coast for 8 km/5 miles, offering an impressive nesting site for all the common sea birds.

The toughest cliffs, resisting erosion, are those made of granite. Cornwall is supported by a backbone of granite which is exposed on the moors of Bodmin, Hensbarrow, Carnmenellis and West Penwith, where the granite also forms part of the sea cliffs. The ridge of granite reappears from the ocean floor 40 km/25 miles off-shore and south-west of the granite cliffs of Land's End, as the Isles of Scilly. This group of 145 rocks, only 5 of which are inhabited, is famous for its sea-bird colonies and rare migrants.

Cornwall has a complicated geological structure. Some of the most ancient rocks are the Pre-Cambrian rocks of the Lizard, composed of red and green serpentine which occurs nowhere else in Britain, apart from Anglesey and parts of Scotland. The Lower Predannack cliffs, south of Mullion, on the south-coast pathway, which are a nature reserve because of the diversity of flowers and birds found there, are a good example of this type of rock.

North-west of Boscastle, around Tintagel, the cliffs are among the finest in Cornwall with off-shore stacks, islands, headlands and coves. Further south, a band of slate extends on to the coastline, producing the magnificent cliff scenery of the Bedruthan Steps (157).

Birdwatching along the coastal footpath and cliffs of Cornwall, you will see breeding birds occupying specific regions of the coast. Fulmar and shag breed intermittently all along the coast from the extreme west to Henna Cliff in the north, but there are few cormorant. Guillemot, razorbill and puffin rarely breed north of Boscastle, but south and west of this area all these auks are common cliff birds. The Cornish stronghold for the kittiwake is on St Agnes Head. The discerning birdwatcher will see the rarer, more localised raven and peregrine which still breed on the cliffs, the latter feeding on feral pigeon, rock dove and the ubiquitous rock pipit and meadow pipit of the coastal grassland.

The cliffs of the south coast of Cornwall are not so rich in birds as those of the north and the best sites are undoubtedly on the west coast like Mullion Island, a Cornwall Naturalists' Trust reserve, breeding site for many great black-backed gull, herring gull, kittiwake and shag, together with a few cormorant, guillemot and razorbill. The largest breeding population of razorbill in Cornwall is on the Brisons off Cape Cornwall.

Cape Cornwall is the only official cape in England. In spring 1987 it was purchased by Heinz who gave the 26.3 ha/65 acres of land to the National Trust as a reserve. Sea birds breeding on the cliffs include kittiwake, shag, razorbill and guillemot, and already birdwatchers have recorded rare migrants such as the American redstart on the granite peninsula.

Another coastline, extending for 350 km/217 miles, composed of various rocks and rich in birds, is that of west Wales, where the old counties of Ceredigion, Pembroke and Carmarthen combine to form Dyfed. Some of the finest coastal scenery, much of it Pre-Cambrian and Cambrian rock, occurs on the Pembrokeshire Coast, between Cardigan and Tenby. Here the coastline of cliffs, rocky headlands and islands has become part of the Pembrokeshire Coast National Park. It is the most maritime and smallest national park, extending 58,276 ha/144,000 acres.

Across the huge ria (drowned river valley) of Milford Haven, on the south coast of the national park, are some of the finest limestone cliffs anywhere in the British Isles between Linney Head and Stackpole Head. They are frequently beaten by rough seas since they face south-west into the Atlantic and water surges into caves, booming loudly as sea is forced up blow-holes near the cliff edge, creating plumes of spray high into the air.

Birdwatchers visit this national park mainly for its sea birds and rare migrants, but the rugged cliffs are also the haunt of raven, peregrine and chough. Sixty pairs of chough breed on the west Wales coast, and the peninsula of Martin's Haven, near Marloes, is an ideal place to walk the cliff path and 'chough watch'. Peregrines have increased to around thirty breeding pairs. Other interesting species include isolated colonies of cliff-nesting swift and house martin; the latter species also nests on the red sandstone cliffs at Arbroath in Tayside, where it is considered a speciality. Only in these isolated colonies does the house martin still nest in its traditional manner, elsewhere preferring the eaves of houses.

The limestone cliffs of the Castlemartin peninsula, on the southern coastline of the Pembrokeshire park, are magnets for sea birds. At Green Bridge, Elegug Stacks and Stackpole Head, 750 pairs of kittiwake, 500 individual razorbills and a staggering 4,000 individual guillemots can be seen on the ledges, with a few shags and cormorants. The birdwatcher will find much to interest him at the Elegug Stacks, which are two limestone pillars rising from the sea within excellent viewing distance from the Flimston Cliffs.

Sea-bird colonies on cliffs are mesmerising places everywhere in the British Isles, but if I were allowed to visit only one site, it would have to be Bempton Cliffs on Yorkshire's east coast. The cliffs at 135 m/442 ft are the highest chalk cliffs in the country, dropping vertically into the North Sea. The 24.2-ha/60-acre site is part of Flamborough Head and is an RSPB reserve, claimed to be the largest breeding colony of sea birds on chalk in England.

It is the **gannets** (154) that make Bempton Cliffs so exciting; indeed, it is the only mainland gannetry in Britain. Numbers have built up since the 1920s to over 350 pairs nesting on the wide ledges, and this is the easiest place in Britain to watch them. From the top of the cliffs the gannets, white with black wing tips and pale yellow head, glide past at eye level. Their size is impressive: their narrow wings span 1.8 m/6 ft supporting a slender cigar-shaped body with tapering tail. They dive into the North Sea from heights of 30.4 m/100 ft, showing how perfectly evolved for fishing they are. As they begin to dive, watch how they plunge with wings partly closed to offer least resistance to the air. Just before the bird hits the sea, the wings close completely and the feathered torpedo slices into the sea in a plume of spray.

The most common bird on Flamborough Head is the kittiwake: over 80,000 pairs completely overshadow the 400 pairs of fulmar which use the cliff-face updraughts to perfection. The raucous wails of a thousand pairs of herring gull often drowns the gutteral calls of 14,000 guillemot, 3,500 razorbill and over 4,000 puffin which are crammed on to the

153

154

155

smallest ledges and crevices during the breeding season. Only by careful scanning will you be able to isolate the 20 or so pairs of shag, occupying caves near the foot of the cliffs.

Bempton Cliffs do not disappoint the birdwatcher during the autumn, when passage migrants like ring ousel, pied flycatcher and redstart fly through and Manx and sooty shearwater pass just off-shore. Winter brings the fieldfare, redwing, shorelark and snow bunting or the flitting short-eared owl, all adding to the 160 species recorded on the reserve.

ROCKY SHORES In north-west Europe rocky shores are the most common coastal habitat, found in Britain wherever

153 Seventy per cent of the world's razorbill population nests around the coastline of Britain. Here, with the nesting shags, a group of razorbills perch on cliffs with Bass Rock in the distance.

154 In flight, the gannet is spectacular with tapering body and swept-back wings, perfectly shaped for plunge diving.

155 Groups of eider duck often gather off shore. Two drakes accompany the females with their ducklings.

156 During the breeding season shags grow a distinctive head crest. They build large untidy nests and if approached quietly, the brilliant green eye becomes visible at close range.

high-impact erosion occurs, such as along the western and much of the northern coastlines. Only along the south shores of the North Sea are they scarce or absent. The effects of the Gulf Stream cause the marine life to be most diverse on the rocky shores of south-west Britain and western Ireland, which are bathed in the warm ocean current.

Most of the diverse flora and fauna of the rocky shore inhabit specific gulleys, crevices, pools and rocky platforms, and may be seen only with close examination at low tide. The animal life includes common sea urchin and the starfish, which feeds voraciously on the common mussels seen attached to nearly every rock at low tide. Acorn barnacles and star barnacle form a hard warty crust on the rocks and in the pools created by the sea, trapped in hollows, fish such as the sand gobby and common blenny survive until the tide flows back in.

The most familiar plants of rocky shores are the algae, represented commonly by the brown seaweeds and especially the wracks. These are tough seaweeds, tolerant of exposure to the air and sun, growing in distinct zones down the shore. At the top of the shore, sometimes exposed for several days during neap tides, is channelled wrack. Where the middle and upper shore regions meet, look out for spiral or flat wrack with characteristic orange nodules at the tip of the fronds. Further down, occupying the middle shore, two species of wrack, both with air-filled bladders, survive. Every youngster remembers squeezing the air out of these natural buoyancy tanks. Bladder wrack and knotted wrack are easy to distinguish at a casual glance. Bladder wrack has a central midrib to the frond whereas knotted wrack has no midrib and the frond is narrow. At the lowest part of the shore, festooning many of the rocks, is serrated wrack, distinguished by its flat frond with typical toothed or serrated margins.

These seaweeds, and many others, are significant for the birdwatcher. With each ebbing tide thousands of small crustaceans, such as sea slater, common sandhopper, shore hopper, skeleton shrimp and a burrowing amphipod called *Corophium volutator* are left behind on the shore. They cannot withstand exposure to the air and avoid desiccation by crawling under the fronds of the seaweeds, which retain enough moisture until the tide returns. Sandhoppers are nocturnal and prefer to shelter in the dark of the seaweed cover anyway. Here, too, other marine animals, such as molluscs and crabs, seek shelter. Consequently the seaweeds provide a varied and readily foraged supply of food for birds such as the turnstone, rock pipit and opportunist starling.

Depending where you birdwatch, the rocky shore will look different. These shores were originally created by geological upheavals before and after the Ice Ages, but more recent wear and erosion reveals the strength of the sea on the rocky shore. Depending on whether the local base rock is hard, soft, igneous or sedimentary, the rocky shores of Britain offer a variable resistance in the ceaseless battle between land and sea. Where the rocks are stratified, there are layers of different minerals of varying degrees of hardness; in sedimentary rocks, for example, the sea quickly wears away the soft strata, causing the harder rock to fall away and create boulders.

The beautiful horseshoe bay at Lulworth Cove in Dorset is a perfect example of how the erosion of the sea against cliffs can be selective. Here the sea had to penetrate the outer barrier of tough Portland limestone, but once this was done the softer chalk and clay behind were quickly 'eaten out' to open up the broad, sea-filled cove. Any boulders torn from cliffs lie strewn along the shore in jagged quarried piles, only to be worn down by constant wave action over hundreds of years.

Despite the huge food store amongst the seaweeds of rocky shores, shore birds are less common on this habitat than they are on estuarine mud and sand. Herring gulls (**201**), lesser and great black-backed gulls scream overhead, ready to scavenge crabs and small fish in the pools and the oystercatchers quickly prise whelks, limpets, periwinkles and mussels from the rocks at low tide. Towards late afternoon, if the tide is still low, herons fly from inland marshes to feed in the rock pools and in the channels between the submerged wrack-covered boulders.

Towards the end of summer and throughout autumn the rocky shores are at their most exciting for the birdwatcher. This is the time when passage migrants stop *en route* to fuel up; of these the **turnstone** is the best known. Turnstones do not breed in Britain but some breed in Scandinavia and visit our rocky shores in autumn to moult and feed before flying further south to winter in West Africa. Others of this species breed further north in Canada and Greenland, and these individuals remain along our rocky shores throughout our winter. As their name indicates, turnstones use their short beak to flick over stones and seaweed fronds, catching the crustaceans beneath, but their attractive black, white and chestnut plumage makes them well camouflaged against the seaweed and rocks.

A favourite feeding zone of the migrant **purple sandpiper** is amongst the rotting seaweed on the strandline of the rocky shore, especially on the north and west coasts of Scotland, but it also feeds within the breaking waves of the splash zone. Except when it is breeding, the bird is rarely seen away from rocky shores and during autumn migration mixes with turnstones on this habitat in flocks of several hundred.

Marvellous camouflage means that you will see this stocky, dark plumaged wader, with distinctive yellow legs, only if you thoroughly scan the shore. Occasionally purple sandpipers take to the air, before scuttling to the next group of boulders and seaweed, where they probe for small crabs, dog whelks, mussels and other small invertebrates.

The purple sandpiper very rarely breeds in Britain, usually nesting in Iceland and Norway, and returning to the coasts of Scotland to overwinter. Some individual birds flying south to overwinter in Europe may be seen further south in Britain, as they pass down the east and west coasts. In the Outer Hebrides during spring, large flocks of purple sandpiper congregate on the rocky shores before flying north to the Arctic Circle to breed.

Other waders you might see on rocky shores include knot, dunlin, common sandpiper, redshank and curlew. Spring and autumn prove the best seasons, as these birds use the shores then as resting and feeding stations. Of course birds of other habitats have learnt to use rocky shores as a source of easy food, and at the turn of the tide, as fish move back up the shoreline, shag, cormorant and grebe dive to plunder the returning fish. The most characteristic duck seen feeding on mussels around the seaweed-covered rocks is the eider (**155**); and where sea lettuce and the green seaweed *Enteromorpha intestinalis* grows, wigeon fly in to browse.

Rocky shores may not physically be the most obviously attractive habitat to view, but with their frequently accompanying cliffs and rugged promontories they have a beauty all of their own. The north-west coast of Scotland from Torridon to Durness is ragged, intersected with bays and rocky islets, and along its length sea lochs are gashed into the mountains, providing spectacular scenery. The northern tip of west Scotland forms Cape Wrath, a 110-m/360-ft red sandstone cliff, struggling to resist Arctic storms each winter. This seemingly endless, beautiful coast, is made up of some of Britain's oldest granite, thrown up by cataclysmic volcanic action, millions of years ago. These granite headlands, crags and shores have, for many thousands of years, resisted the pounding of the ocean and this fact, common to most of our rocky shores, makes birdwatching in this habitat even more fascinating.

157 Owned by the National Trust as part of the heritage coastline, the Bedruthan Steps is a magnificent stretch of cliff on the north Cornish coast.

OFF-SHORE ISLANDS

It is a poignant truth that the majority of us who live on mainland Britain have never visited the off-shore islands which make up our archipelago. Islands such as the Scillies, Orkneys, Shetlands, Outer and Inner Hebrides and Isle of Man are just names, creating mental images of lumps of rock with plenty of mist and rain. Visitors to southern Ireland often journey to Co. Kerry for the beauty of the famous lakes at Killarney and the equally famous Dingle Peninsula at Slea Head. Yet a few kilometres off the coast there are islands which are largely unvisited. Great Blasket Island off Slea Head is home to many types of sea bird; and the Skelligs are only a short boat ride into the Atlantic around Bolus Head from Ballingskelligs. These rocks, uninhabited apart from a monastery on Great Skellig, are home to 20,000 pairs of gannet on Little Skellig and large breeding populations of kittiwake, guillemot, petrel, shearwater and fulmar. The birds drift across the sea searching for fish just below the surface, occasionally sharing their feeding ground with basking sharks and porpoises.

The coastal islands of both the north and south of the British Isles were joined to the ancient landmass of Britain. After the Ice Ages, when glaciers gouged huge scars into the landmass, there followed a warmer period and the glaciers melted, causing the sea levels to rise dramatically and flood many coastal areas. The large majority of today's off-shore islands were at one time coastal hills and high ground, partly drowned as the glaciers melted. Some of these islands are grouped, such as the Orkneys and Shetlands, which were part of the Caithness plain before sea levels rose. But wherever they are, the islands are nature reserves in themselves for myriad birds and a variety of wildlife.

The majority of the small islands of Britain are so important for bird conservation that they are worthy of individual mention. Many are nature reserves owned by various county naturalists' trusts, the RSPB or the National Trust.

SKOMER It's an early morning start in June. A gentle swell licks across the bows of the lobster boat as it heads out to sea for an island, which, in the distance, resembles nothing more than a lump of black rock, interrupting the view to the horizon.

For a few kilometres, herring gulls follow the churning foam at the stern, but soon the gulls drift away and return to the harbour, only to be replaced by smaller black and white birds, skimming over the sea on unflapping, stiffly held wings. These Manx shearwaters breed on the island ahead, which is now only 1 km/½ mile away.

The small white flecks swirling around the island become recognisable as squadrons of sea birds. Fulmars on grey-white wings glide across the rock face and out to sea; shags, menacingly black and reptile-like, float on the surface of the sea beneath the cliffs, before diving for fish. High up on the ledges and crevices of the rock face guillemots and razorbills perch, and from the rabbit-grazed sward of turf on the island plateau puffins, with their brightly painted beaks, whirr out to sea for sand eels, and return to their disused rabbit burrows. Puffins spend the winter on the oceans, but in summer they return to this island to breed, as they have done for hundreds of years.

The cliffs are adorned with pink thrift and red campion, interspersed with washes of bluebell, white sea campion and stonecrop near the plateau. As the boat cautiously navigates into the shelter of the landing cove, an oystercatcher pipes alarmed from the shoreline.

The boat might be approaching any one of the many off-shore islands around our coast, but the unmistakable high-pitched 'kwee-ow' of a chough specifically identifies the island as Skomer. Only on this island and in a few other areas of west Wales, Holy Island off Anglesey and parts of west Scotland, is this scarlet-billed crow found nesting on the cliffs.

Skomer is 2 km/1¼ miles off the Marloes Peninsula of the Pembrokeshire coast and one of the finest sea-bird colonies in Britain. The island is a National Nature Reserve purchased by the NCC in 1959, and is the largest of the Pembrokeshire islands with an area of 294 ha/726 acres, 3 km/1¾ miles long and 2 km/1¼ miles wide north to south. The central plateau rises to a height of 78 m/256 ft and there are two bays, North and South Haven. The narrow strip of land connecting the two bays is where the largest puffin colony is found.

Skomer is a remarkable island, with a varied coastline offering steep terraced cliffs and boulder-laden slopes or gently sloping, sandy beaches. Most of the interior is moorland habitat, with bracken cover over three distinct shallow valleys with two main streams and several small rivulets. Flowers abound in spring and early summer, especially bluebells, scurvy grass and white sea campion.

It has the richest avifauna of all the Welsh islands, despite the fact that it receives the greatest number of human visitors, who arrive daily except on Mondays and Bank Holidays by boat from Martin's Haven. Well-marked nature trails guide visitors towards the birds without disturbing them and a maximum of 100 visitors per day observe storm petrel, puffin (**167**), guillemot, razorbill, fulmar, herring, lesser and great black-backed gull between April and September.

The high spot on Skomer is the Manx shearwater (**158**) population; with 80–100,000 pairs, it is the largest colony in the North Atlantic. Only a few of the birds are seen during daylight hours, which they spend skimming the waves far out at sea, or more commonly asleep in subterranean burrows. They are nocturnal and even a bright moon restricts their activity.

As dusk falls, the raucous sound from the gull colonies drops to a murmur and the distant stabs of light from the beams of lighthouses on Bardsey and St David's are just visible. Torch in hand, go to the old farm and take the main track eastwards. You will soon find dozens of birds caught in the beam of the torch, some flying crazily across the island, others coming in from the sea, and yet more emerging from nest burrows under your feet, where they awkwardly shuffle across the turf. Switch the torch off and sense the unforgettable experience of the hiss of hundreds of wings above your head, the rustling of bodies in the undergrowth and the ever-increasing babble as the birds call to each other with a mixture of shrieks, eerie caterwauling, crying and gurgling sounds which cease the moment first light appears on the horizon.

Few visitors to the island know that the **Manx shearwater** lays only a single egg, which is incubated in the burrow for over fifty days, followed by an incredible ten-week fledgling period. The juvenile bird leaves the nest and immediately makes a flight of 9,000 km/5,595 miles to winter off the south coast of

South America. It will make this journey instinctively many times: shearwaters can live over twenty years, and return to the same nesting colony year after year.

Rabbits have grazed the grass on Skomer producing areas of short turf, which is one of things that has attracted the **chough** to breed. This striking crow feeds on ants, which it probes for with red scimitar beak in the short turf (**159**), rather in the same way as green woodpeckers on our suburban lawns.

The highlight of a day on Skomer is watching a pair of choughs with their broad-fingered wings riding the up-currents of air moving off the cliff face. They twist and tumble with amazing skill, calling frequently and producing an aerial display seen in few other places in Britain.

SKOKHOLM Just over 3 km/1¾ miles south of Skomer lies Skokholm, where the red cliffs so noticeable on approach identify the rock as old red sandstone. With an area of 100 ha/247 acres it is well under half the size of Skomer. The island slopes from the higher western end with a height of 50 m/164 ft to the cliffs of 20 m/66 ft in the east.

Skokholm is flat-topped and the perimeter is mostly sheer cliff. There are two marshy areas but the soil is generally a light sand, mixed with bands of boulder clay, where tree mallow, rock samphire and various plantains grow.

Like Skomer, Skokholm is nationally known for its sea-bird colonies as well as for the site of the first British bird observatory established in 1933 by Ronald M. Lockley. Two significant differences between Skokholm and the neighbour-ing islands are the small populations of guillemot and the lack of kittiwake, a result of the slope of the sandstone cliffs which make the land inhospitable to these ledge-nesting species. The loss of these species is compensated for by over 6,000 pairs of storm petrel which, like the 36,000 pairs of Manx shearwater, hide in their burrows, cracks and crevices during the daytime. Puffin, numerous gull species and land birds such as lapwing and raven also breed on Skokholm.

The migrations of birds across Skokholm are well docu-mented and occur in spring and autumn. Spring migrants begin in March with black redstart, chiff-chaff and ring ousel, closely followed by sand martin and swallow. By April the majority of warblers are passing through such as willow warbler, whitethroat and grasshopper warbler. The swifts are the last to arrive, announcing the end of the spring migration towards late May. Reports of the bird observatory make compulsive reading for any birdwatcher: not only does it record rarities like melodious and icterine warblers, but it also vividly builds up a picture of bird migration from Africa and the Mediterranean across Britain.

In late August and September, the southerly movement of migrating birds includes pied and spotted flycatcher, common redstart, house martin and swallow. Late September is really the beginning of the autumn migration with thousands of birds heading south-east and by October the movement of migratory birds across Skokholm is magnificent.

GRASSHOLM The cone of rock 10 km/6 miles west of Skomer is called Grassholm. An RSPB reserve covering only 9 ha/22.2 acres, it is internationally important for its vast colony of gannet (28,000 pairs in 1984). This is the only gannetry in Wales; but more significantly it has become one of the outstanding ornithological sites in north-west Europe, as one of the three largest gannetries in the world.

Wandering gannets from other colonies, such as Little Skellig off Co. Kerry and Ailsa Craig in the Clyde, have contributed to an increase in bird population. As these other gannetries become overcrowded, exploratory flights are made to seek more suitable nesting roosts, hence Grassholm's expansion.

The birds on the island also flourish because access for humans is difficult and only possible during exceptionally calm weather. The gannets benefit from being undisturbed, as do other breeding birds like small colonies of guillemot and kittiwake on the north-facing cliffs. Razorbill, shag, herring gull and raven also nest elsewhere on the crags and among boulders.

RAMSEY This is one of the least known of the Pembrokeshire islands, 17.5 km/11 miles north of Skokholm and only 3 km/1¾ miles north to south. For much of its 264 ha/652 acres a plateau slopes on the east, with hills and rocks on the west.

Moorland heath covers the rock surface with a most beauti-ful display of flowers in summer. At the north of the island is the hill Carn Ysgubor, below which are cliffs, chasms and stony beaches.

Unfortunately Ramsey has brown rats, established since 1800. This is one of the reasons for the smaller colonies of breeding sea birds, which survive best on the high volcanic cliffs of the south-west. Guillemot, razorbill, shag, fulmar and kittiwake breed on the ledges and crags with a few Manx shearwater, which began to re-establish a decade ago.

Although Ramsey attracts fewer migrants, it is the jewel amongst Welsh islands for chough: up to a dozen pairs nest in the numerous caves and cliff crevices out of reach of the rats. Equally rewarding for birdwatchers are the several pairs of ground-nesting short-eared owl and the occasional pair of peregrine.

ANGLESEY Within the county of Gwynedd lies the off-shore island of Anglesey, separated from North Wales by the deep Menai Strait. It is such a large island with wide, flattened ridges and straight valleys that it possesses many habitats, such as lakes and sand-dunes (covered elsewhere). Here we only concern ourselves with two particular sites.

The first is the off-shore islands at Rhosneigr, on the west coast of Anglesey, which are not accessible, but from the beach at Rhosneigr it is possible to view the largest British colony of breeding roseate terns, about 100 pairs.

A visit to Anglesey must include some time spent at the second site, South Stacks Cliffs, an RSPB reserve of 315 ha/780 acres, about 5 km/3 miles west of Holyhead. The cliffs, which are at the southern end of Gogarth Bay, are Pre-Cambrian, rising 120 m/394 ft from the sea and they are the site of a significant sea-bird colony. Only a footbridge connects South Stacks Cliffs to the mainland.

The best time to observe thousands of nesting birds is between April and July, along the ledges between the light-house steps and Ellins Tower (which is the information centre). Over 1,500 guillemot crowd the cliffs, with lesser populations of razorbill, puffin, shag, kittiwake and fulmar.

Peregrine, raven and chough nest on the crags, too. It is fascinating to watch the ravens making egg-raiding sorties into the sea-bird colonies, when there is mobbing and clamouring until the raven departs. The choughs seem almost tame as they feed on the cliff-top turf near the RSPB car park.

Sea watching is recommended at South Stacks Cliffs. During the spring red-throated diver, Arctic and pomarine skua and scoter pass off-shore. During the autumn passage, migration is tremendously exciting: whimbrel, dotterel, greenshank, Leach's petrel and great skua all pass the cliffs together, and hen harrier and short-eared owl stop to feed.

ISLE OF MAN Like Anglesey, the Isle of Man is a large island with a variety of habitats. Two major plains occupy the interior: the northern plain is densely wooded with some gorse and heather moors whereas the southern plain is essentially upland country with numerous streams.

About 1.2 km/¾ mile off the south-west tip of the Isle of Man is a small island called the Calf of Man, covering just 242 ha/600 acres. It is jointly managed by the Manx Museum and Manx National Trust as an island for sea birds and a migration-recording observatory. Melodious, barred and icterine warbler are recorded, together with woodchat shrike, snow bunting and resident breeding chough, guillemot, razorbill, puffin and fulmar.

Spanish Head is also a Manx National Trust reserve, occupying 103 ha/256 acres of the south-west tip of the Isle of Man, a few kilometres south of Cregneish. The Calf of Sound separates it from the Calf of Man and the reserve has superb 122-m/400-ft-high cliffs. Here you will find the majority of typical sea birds, including kittiwake, fulmar and the auks; but short-eared owl, raven and chough also breed on the reserve.

AILSA CRAIG Just over 17 km/10½ miles west of Girvan in Strathclyde and 22.5 km/14 miles off the southern coast of Arran lies a small characteristic hump of granite rock called Ailsa Craig. It is the most important sea-bird island in the Clyde, with over 36,000 pairs of sea birds including a famous large gannetry situated on the 2.5-km/1½-mile-long west cliffs. Large breeding populations of kittiwake, gull, razorbill and guillemot breed together with puffin, fulmar and black guillemot.

The **black guillemot** is less widely distributed than the common guillemot and is best seen on the rocky coast and off-shore islands of north-west Britain. With bright red feet, distinct white wing patches and ebony black body, it sits in crevices and caves where it nests. During winter, its plumage changes: the majority of its body moults to white and its wings become almost totally black. Black guillemots are unique auks, because they still lay 2 eggs whereas the other species of auk have evolved to lay the single, specially shaped egg described on page 172.

Sharing the cliffs with the sea birds are nesting peregrine raven, twite, rock dove and rock pipit. Their presence makes a visit to this off-shore island even more worthwhile.

INNER HEBRIDES The islands of Rhum, Eigg, Canna and Muck are often referred to as the Small Islands; collectively they form the Inner Hebrides, south of Skye. Of these, the island of Rhum is an important sea-bird island.

Rhum is owned by the NCC and is a large island covering 10,684 ha/26,400 acres. A variety of rocks from granite to

158

159

160

158 Manx shearwaters only come ashore to nest in subterranean burrows.

159 A chough probes for ants in short, coastal turf. It is most likely to be seen around the coastline of Wales and associated off-shore islands.

160 Wherever the Arctic skua nests, surrounding breeding birds are at risk because it feeds on both eggs and young.

161 Using imported birds from Norway, a successful reintroduction programme of the white-tailed sea eagle has been carried out on Rhum in the Inner Hebrides.

162 Fulmars belong the the family of birds referred to as "tubenoses" because the nostrils open into a distinct tube visible on the beak's upper mandible.

Torridonian sandstone make its geology complex and the habitats include mountains, bogs and moorland, lakes, grassland, woodland, heath, sea cliffs and rock faces. Because of the habitat variety, the avifauna is rich, including breeding populations of golden eagle, merlin, peregrine, raven, red-throated diver and corncrake.

The cliffs of the south are the main breeding areas for the sea birds; here auk, kittiwake, fulmar, shag, herring and lesser black-backed gull nest. Arctic and common tern nest on the island; and the Manx shearwater colony (130,000 pairs) has adapted to nest away from the immediate coastline in burrows high on the mountain slopes of Askival (811 m/2,660 ft) and Hallival (720 m/2,362 ft) above sea level.

No visit to Rhum would be complete without looking for the rare **white-tailed sea eagle** (161). Until the beginning of this century the bird used to have regular eyries along the sea cliffs of this island and neighbouring Canna, Eigg and Skye. The last pair of sea eagles breeding in Britain was on Skye, but even these had gone by 1916, their native extinction caused largely by persecution by shepherds and farmers.

Whereas the osprey migrates regularly from one country to another, sea eagles do not wander and once the British birds were extinct, it was unlikely that natural recolonisation would occur from northern Europe. In 1975, the NCC, Scottish Wildlife Trust and RSPB joined forces to reintroduce the eagle to Rhum and young eagles from Norway were used for this experiment. Some of the birds died and the survivors, although happy in their new environment, failed to breed. It was 10 years after their initial introduction that a pair of adults reared 1 eaglet, and in 1986, after 82 eagles had been introduced for the experiment, 2 eaglets were successfully reared. In 1987 the breeding success was even greater with 2 pairs raising 3 juveniles between them.

It is now possible to see these magnificent birds flying along the cliffs of Rhum. The adults are unmistakable with a pure white, wedge-shaped tail and broad-fingered wings at the primaries. They are larger than golden eagles, but despite their size they are deftly acrobatic, snatching sea birds such as fulmar from the cliff face or plunging into the sea for fish or unsuspecting surface-feeding auk.

The eagles pair for life and lay two eggs in April in a nest of branches, usually high on a crag or cliff face. During spring birdwatchers will see the eagles spectacular courtship flights. High above the nesting ledge the pair of eagles spiral and soar, their silhouettes vulture-like when viewed from below. The male suddenly tucks its wings to the body and drops like a stone, diving at the female below him. She flicks over on her back and the talons of both birds lock in a vice-like grip as they whirl and tumble together towards the rocks. Their awareness of the rapidly approaching cliff face is acute, for at the last moment they separate, sometimes only metres from impact, before soaring to the heavens, to repeat their display.

The breeding experiment is now meeting with success, so it is only a matter of time before sightings of this bird along Rhum's coastline, west Highland cliffs and on the Outer Hebrides will be regular.

OUTER HEBRIDES AND ST KILDA Just off the north-west coast of Scotland lie the Outer Hebrides – a group of 120 islands, 14 of which are inhabited. The archipelago stretches for 240 km/150 miles from the Butt of Lewis in the north to the southern Barra Head. Locals call the chain of islands Long Island, which essentially comprises Lewis, Harris, North and South Uist, Benbecula and Barra. Associated islands include St Kilda, 72 km/45 miles to the west, the Flannan Islands and North Rona, 70 km/43 miles to the north. Collectively all the islands are known as the Western Islands. Some of these islands are made of rocks about 3,000 million years old but more recently the Ice Ages have sculptured the rock to its present-day form, so that most of the islands are less than 90 m/295 ft above sea level, although some of the mountains on Harris rise to 790 m/2,600 ft.

The Hebrides are a beautiful part of Britain with heather-covered, peaty moors, freshwater lochs transecting low-lying bogs, some rugged mountains and fertile machair, which are flat plains bordering on to dunes. The islands have markedly different east and west coasts: the east coasts have tall cliffs and sea lochs, while the west coasts are low-lying and flat, with broad white beaches. These beaches are made not of sand but of minute fragments of marine shells, forming extensive dune systems which are colonised by plants, eventually becoming the stable machair. The machair habitat is unique to west Scotland, the Shetlands and Orkneys; by far the best examples are on the Outer Hebrides such as North and South Uist.

The machair probably supports the largest numbers of breeding waders anywhere in Britain, including redshank, oystercatcher, ringed plover and dunlin. The rich wild flora attracts insects and provides seeds for birds such as skylark, corn bunting and twite.

The **twite** is a small finch (13.5 cm/5½ in) which was once widely distributed but is now largely restricted to north and west Scotland. Commonly found along the coast, it breeds on the machair during late May, sometimes rearing two broods. Superficially it resembles the linnet but is more brown overall with distinctive white wing bars; the cock birds have pink rumps which are displayed during courtship. Linnet-like twitterings are interspersed by the 'twaeet' call which gives it its name, and which it utters on the wing or when perched on fenceposts or boulders. During winter twites remain on the machair, surviving on the abundant seeds from the flowers which formed brilliant displays during July.

On the island of North Uist at Balranald the RSPB have a reserve covering 657 ha/1,625 acres. The habitat is a mixture of coastal lagoon with accompanying marsh and the machair which lies between the lagoon and the coastal dunes. The entire reserve provides an excellent introduction to the habitats of the Hebrides.

Spring and early autumn are the best seasons to visit the reserve. In April various waders nest in dense populations and lapwing, oystercatcher, dunlin, snipe and curlew call and display across the grassland. During the autumn migration, curlew, sandpiper, little stint and ruff, together with snow bunting, all pass across and rest on the island.

Balranald supports two rarities: the red-necked phalarope, which prefers to forage along the edge of lochs and marshes in the dense vegetation; and the corncrake, which has declined throughout Europe and is virtually extinct on mainland Britain. As many as 15 pairs nest on the reserve, which is one of the last remaining strongholds of this secretive bird. In most parts of Britain hay is cut during May for early silage and this interferes with the corncrake's nesting habits, for which dense cover is important. But in the Hebrides the grass is not cut until July, giving the corncrake a refuge, together with thick marsh vegetation, especially yellow iris, bordering the machair.

Machair habitat with associated birdlife is also found on South Uist, where the NCC reserve at Loch Druidibeg is worth visiting for the experience of an alternative Hebridean habitat: the peat moorland and lochs. The largest colony of native greylag geese (138) breed at the eastern end of this 16,777-ha/ 4,145-acre reserve which is largely moorland and marsh. Red-breasted merganser, red grouse, buzzard and merlin breed, and hen harrier often hunt the slopes.

Eighty km/50 miles west of Lewis is the island group of St Kilda comprising Hirta, Soay, Boreray and Dun. St Kilda is the most important sea-bird breeding site in Britain and the island group is a nature reserve covering 846 ha/2,090 acres, run by the National Trust for Scotland in association with the NCC.

Since the eighteenth century and probably long before, fulmars (162) have nested on St Kilda and today the islands still hold the largest colony of this bird in Britain. During the last century, the St Kildans exploited the fulmar for food, oil for their lamps, ointment for wounds and feather down for their beds, but today the birds are left in peace to breed since the only inhabitants are National Trust and military staff from the missile-tracking station on Hirta.

Birdwatchers visiting St Kilda never forget the gannetry on Boreray which with 50,000 pairs is the largest in the world. Approaching by boat, one sees a circling blizzard of birds around the rugged stacks and on Dun the puffin colony is spectacular, numbering a quarter of a million birds. At one time it was estimated that three million pairs of puffin bred on the St Kilda group; the St Kildans used to harvest 90,000 birds annually without affecting the following year's breeding success. Puffins normally commandeer rabbit burrows to use as breeding chambers but no rabbits are found on St Kilda, so the puffins excavate their own tunnels using their short stumpy legs with clawed feet as excellent shovels.

International birdwatchers rate St Kilda as one of the world's greatest bird-island groups. Manx shearwater, storm and Leach's petrel all breed on St Kilda in significant numbers, and the island even boasts its own sub-species of wren – the St Kilda wren, which is larger than the mainland species as well as being different in plumage and song. In winter, on-shore winds drive fish towards the stacks and large numbers of great northern divers arrive to feed. This large flotilla includes most of the British population and individuals from as far away as Greenland and northern Canada.

THE ORKNEY ISLANDS From John o'Groats looking north across the Pentland Firth, about 12.8 km/8 miles away are the Orkney Islands. These low-lying islands straggle north for 80.4 km/50 miles from Brough Ness on the southernmost tip of South Ronaldsay, to Dennis Head on North Ronaldsay. Seventy islands are positioned like stepping stones between the two Ronaldsays, but only twenty-one are inhabited; most people live on Main in the towns of Stromness and Kirkwall.

The coastlines on the western side of the islands have been cut by the sea into vertical cliffs, where there are some of the largest sea-bird colonies in Britain. The RSPB owns reserves on many of the islands, including Noup Cliffs in the north-west corner of Westray. Although the reserve only covers 14 ha/35 acres, sea-bird enthusiasts stare at the 2-km/1¼-mile stretch of sandstone cliffs in amazement. Here the horizontally strati-fied rocks provide perfect nest sites for thousands of birds, who are so densely packed that excessive jostling occurs and some juvenile birds are trampled to death. Well over 50,000 guille-mots (163) perch shoulder to shoulder, forming the largest colony in Britain, accompanied by 40,000 kittiwake,

also the largest colony in Britain. The scene is one of constant motion with birds flying in every direction, and the smell and whitewash of guano are unforgettable. Although there are large numbers of razorbill and fulmar there is only room for 400 pairs of puffin.

Behind the cliffs is a heathland habitat where Arctic skua (160) breed, providing interesting birdwatching when they rob the kittiwake colony for food. Typical heathland birds such as rock and meadow pipit and wheatear also breed here.

A few kilometres north-east of Westray, across the Papa Sound, lies Papa Westray; and at North Hill the RSPB have a 206-ha/509-acre reserve. The area is maritime heath, which, like machair on the Hebrides, is rich with flowers and, during the spring, alive with birds.

The largest UK colony of breeding Arctic terns (164) thrives here, numbering in excess of 6,000 birds. Many of the colony periodically take to the air to mob Arctic skuas, which breed close to the edge of the tern colony and maraud for easy food. Great skua, herring, common, great and lesser black-backed gull nest on the heathland, with dunlin and ringed plover as neighbours.

The most accessible and best-observed sea-bird colony is on Mainland at Marwick Head, 24 km/15 miles north of Stromness. The cliffs only occupy about 1.6 km/1 mile of coast but you will see all the typical cliff-face birds, along with rock dove, raven, jackdaw and peregrine. The 18.6-ha/46-acre reserve incorporates part of Mar Wick bay with associated wetland behind it; and on this damp grassland redshank, snipe, curlew and other waders court, display and breed.

To the east of Mainland, 5.5 km/3½ miles from Skaill, is the Copinsay group of islands including Corn Holm, Ward Holm and Black Holm, joined to the main island at low tide. The Horse of Copinsay is separated to the north by 1.6 km/1 mile of sea and most of the islands are little more than grass-covered cliffs. The entire island complex is an RSPB reserve covering 151 ha/375 acres and is an important site for all the sea birds such as guillemot, razorbill, fulmar, shag and cormorant, together with a few common and Arctic terns. Because of the islands' position on the east side of Orkney, rare migrants blown off course by easterly winds land to rest and feed. They include bluethroat, black redstart and red-backed shrike on a regular basis, making birdwatching on these small islands even more exciting and unpredictable. Few places in Britain are as breathtaking as the Orkney Islands early on a spring morning: lapwing and curlew call and display in flight, across the marshland snipe are drumming and a cock dunlin trills and whistles as he seeks a mate. These sights and sounds make the hills and moorland of Mainland Orkney some of the most thrilling in Britain.

THE SHETLANDS Birdwatchers with a sense of adventure are drawn to Shetland. One of the islands' attractions is the fact that they are the most northerly point of the UK, 160 km/100 miles north of John o'Groats, lying 6° south of the Arctic Circle. Shetland is a group of one hundred islands, fifteen of which are inhabited; the largest is Mainland with the only town of Lerwick.

Spring does not arrive in Shetland until mid-May, but when it does the wild flowers form an ever-changing carpet; and the birdlife is superb, although you will need to visit several islands to see all the Shetland species, probably at different seasons.

Shetland is attractive to birds for a variety of reasons. As with the west coast of Ireland, and much of the west coast of Britain, the Gulf Stream carries plankton and marine nutrients to the islands and provides a rich source of food for thousands of sea birds. In addition, since the islands are just outside the Arctic Circle, northern-breeding birds such as red-necked phalarope, red-throated diver and whimbrel choose to breed on some of the Shetlands regularly and nowhere else. As the Arctic summer quickly fades, many of the birds breeding north of Shetland fly south for the winter. Great northern diver, the elegant long-tailed duck and many other exciting species wing their way south to the islands and overwinter. In reverse, during the spring, northern-breeding birds like fieldfare and redwing pass across the Shetlands in thousands on their migration from southern Britain and Europe towards the breeding grounds in the Arctic Circle.

The most southerly of the Shetland Isles is Fair Isle. Covering 830 ha/2,050 acres, the island is made of soft red sandstone with cliffs rising to 200 m/656 ft, where all the usual sea birds breed on the ledges and crevices. Storm petrels nest in burrows and the few gannets which colonised in the mid-1970s have continued to increase, promising to become a large new gannetry in the future. Away from the cliffs are the rough grass hillsides; over a hundred pairs of arctic skua and up to fifty pairs of great skua nest on this open ground.

Great skuas (165) are large hefty birds 58 cm/17½ in long and possess aerial stamina. They are pirates, perfectly equipped to rob even larger birds, such as gannets, of their last meal, which they do by seizing the flying bird by the wing tip and forcing it down on to the sea. After surface harassment, the bird disgorges its fish and the skua grabs the easy meal. Wherever sea birds nest in the Shetlands, they are in danger of attacks from the great skua. Watching this bird pluck a young kittiwake from its nest or a ledge is one thing, but being on the receiving end of a nest-defending attack yourself is another; so beware if, during summer, you walk a few hundred metres into the hillsides on Fair Isle where the great skua nests and the aggressive dive-bombing begins. In a head-on stoop, the adult hits out with its webbed feet, striking the top of your head as it swoops past. Sometimes the skua lashes out with a stab of the beak instead. If attacked in this way, you will soon realise why Shetlanders call this bird 'the bonxie', which is a local term used to describe a bully.

There are two ornithological sites definitely worth a visit on Mainland, but these are at opposite ends of the island. In the south, 1 km/⅝ mile south-west of Scousburgh, is the Loch of Spiggie, the largest eutrophic loch in south Shetland. In the north, a dangerous tidal stretch of sea called Yell Sound separates Mainland from the island of Yell, and scattered in Yell Sound are of six small islands obviously called Yell Sound Islands, uninhabited except by sea birds.

You really need to visit the Loch of Spiggie with its bordering marshland in both spring and autumn to appreciate its glory. During the spring 50–80 **long-tailed duck** leave the sea to enter the loch for their pre-migration moult. Small and immaculate in appearance, the ducks change plumage dramatically from winter to summer; and because some are found around northern Scotland and the islands all year round, identification can be a problem for the uninitiated. Males are relatively easy to identify in summer, with dark brown back and neck and a white face; they have a characteristic, extremely long tail which represents about a quarter of the duck's body. Females lack this long tail, and have a white neck with brown cheek patches in summer, which match their brown body.

In winter the Loch of Spiggie is an important site for wildfowl.

163

163 Although courtship takes place on the sea, guillemots nest in huge cliff-breeding colonies.

164 The Arctic tern holds the world record for long-distance migration, flying 40,000 km/24,860 miles annually. It breeds in the north Atlantic and around the coasts of the Arctic ocean, and migrates to spend our winter in the Antarctic summer.

165 Great skuas are sturdy, fierce birds, who ferociously attack intruders entering their nesting areas, hitting out with their feet in a head-on swoop.

166 Gannet colony on Bass Rock in the Firth of Forth. The gannets build their own nests barely out of range of their neighbour's bills, so sometimes disputes occur.

Up to 300 whooper swans arrive to feed, mainly at the shallower north end. Tufted duck, pochard, wigeon and golden-eye overwinter here, and passage migrants like goosander, pintail and garganey 'bed and breakfast' on the loch before flying on.

Across the Yell Sound on the island of Yell itself, peat moorland, lochs and rugged cliffs occupy much of the 1,720-ha/4,250-acre RSPB reserve at Lumbister. Yell is not the most attractive of islands but the moors and lochs possess an audible magic produced by whimbrel and red-throated diver. Whimbrels (114) are one of our rarest breeding waders, confined to north-west Scotland, Orkneys and Shetlands. They prefer the high rolling moors and on Yell return to the heather at Lumbister towards late April. In the early morning the males fly high across the moor, moving in large circles on rapidly beating wings and uttering beautiful trills and ringing whistles. In contrast, the guttural cooing and mewing wail of the red-throated diver echoes down the lochs; the haunting moan is heard throughout the breeding season from late April and until the end of May.

The two eggs and chicks of the divers are predated by the Arctic and great skuas which nest on the moors, also attacking the nests of dunlin, golden plover, curlew and snipe. Merlin quarter the heather, preying on wheatear, twite, meadow pipit and skylark which nest on the slopes.

East of Yell and south of Unst is the famous island of Fetlar, the greenest and smallest of the northern Shetlands with an RSPB reserve covering 699 ha/1,727 acres. The island is accessible between April and August by boat from Lerwick, but on the reserve access is restricted during the breeding season from May to July.

Much of the island is moorland over serpentine rock which is a rare mineral found in neighbouring Unst and the Lizard in Cornwall. The moorland is the nesting habitat for whimbrel, curlew, golden plover and dunlin and since all these species have emotive calls, the atmosphere amongst the heather is memorable.

Higher up on the moorland slopes, Arctic and great skua nest and naturally cull the population of moorland waders. Up to twenty colonies of Arctic tern nest on the moors and, together with the skua, make the moorland of Fetlar of national importance. The wettest areas include the lochs and pools, where two-thirds of the entire British population of red-necked phalarope breed, using the water for feeding and display. Phalaropes can be watched around places like Loch Funzie without risk of disturbing the birds at the nest.

Red-necked phalaropes are small, neat waders and extremely colourful. The species has taken the right to sexual equality to the opposite extreme with a complete reversal of size, plumage and breeding role: the hen bird is marginally larger, but much more brightly coloured than the male, with reddish-brown neck and dark head. She totally dominates in courtship and pairing activity: after laying the eggs, she leaves the male to incubate them and rear the young, whilst she seeks another mate, produces a second clutch and finally leaves this second male to assume the role of parenthood.

The dotterel, which nests high on barren mountain tops in the Cairngorms and beyond in the Arctic Circle, is the only other wader which reverses the role of the sexes. As an evolutionary measure the development has some merit, because the female can concentrate on producing and laying eggs in an environment where the summer is short and predation is high.

The bird which undoubtedly put Fetlar on the national ornithological map is the **snowy owl (170)** which nested among rocks on the low slopes around Stackaberg. In the spring of 1967, RSPB Shetland Island Officer Bobby Tulloch saw on several occasions a female owl flying low across Fetlar. Whilst walking across the northern hills of the island on 7 June, he discovered the nest containing three eggs. This was the first record of snowy owls nesting in Britain.

Typically the owls nest in the Arctic wastes and tundra, but as the slopes of this windswept hill were covered in low-growing vegetation and the nest was sited in a grass patch amongst the stones, the owl was probably convinced that it was on normal breeding grounds. The view from the nest was panoramic, so the adults had ample warning of imminent danger and could easily see approaching prey.

In the Arctic tundra, lemmings form the staple diet of the snowy owl and the rise and fall in population of this rodent occurs every four years. During peak lemming years, snowy owls breed successfully with large broods, but in the troughs some snowy owls wander south, which is another possible explanation for the owls nesting on Fetlar. There are no lemmings on Fetlar, but rabbits became an excellent substitute and the snowy owls ruthlessly plundered other birds nesting close to Stackaberg. Food was easily obtainable: for a bird with a 1.5-m/5-ft wingspan, powerful talons and strong beak, even the Arctic skuas were defenceless against the snowy owl.

The 1967 nest eventually contained seven eggs and by August five owlets left the nest. The following year, the same pair of owls returned to breed, with an audience of many birdwatchers who had learnt of the breeding the year before. For the next seven years, the original pair reared eleven more young. During this period an additional female even arrived on Fetlar and laid eggs, but these were not fertile and failed to hatch.

But just as the snowy owl arrived unexpectedly to breed in 1967, so a twist of fate caused this phenomenon to end. After 1975 the old male failed to return. Being territorial it had chased all younger male owls from the island hillside and the remaining females were left without a partner. So ended a thrilling but short-lived phase of snowy owls breeding in Britain. Occasionally a few visiting birds turn up and some progeny of the original pair have lingered on, but there has been no pairing or rearing of young since 1975.

The most northerly point of the Shetlands and Britain is Hermaness on the island of Unst. At this point the cliffs are amongst the best in Britain, both for scenery and sea birds. Along the 3-km/1¾-mile stretch of cliffs sea birds throng and it is possible to look from above into a gannet colony of 5,000 birds on Muckle Flugga stack. Auk, kittiwake and fulmar cram the cliff ledges and on the neighbouring rough grassland over 800 pairs of great skua nest.

Hermaness is an NCC reserve and apart from cliffs, some of the 964 ha/2,382 acres include moorland and lochs where red-throated diver, whimbrel and dunlin nest. Those Shetland islands with a moorland or rough grass interior always attract nesting skuas and on Noss, off-shore from Mainland Lerwick, 200 pairs of great skua and 40 pairs of Arctic skua combine to harass the kittiwakes and gannets nesting in their thousands on the cliffs around Rumble Wick.

All the individual islands have their intrinsic beauty and magic, but Foula is something special – one of the most remote islands of Britain, with impressive scenery, a mystique of its own and huge colonies of sea birds.

An isolated island 24 km/15 miles west of Mainland, Foula covers 1,380 ha/3,409 acres. The old red sandstone cliffs on the west coast are sheer, rising 370 m/1,214 ft from the Atlantic at the Kame, making them the second-highest cliffs in the British Isles. These mighty bastions take the full force of Atlantic storms, yet offer refuge for cliff-nesting sea birds.

The highest density of sea birds anywhere in Shetland is to be found here on Foula. Sixteen species of sea bird nest on the island, with a grand total of over a quarter of a million individual birds, including 35,000 pairs of puffin and 42,000 pairs of fulmar, which first nested on the Shetlands here in 1878. Other important populations include 3,000 pairs of shag and the largest Shetland population of storm petrel, around 1,000 pairs. The smaller, rarer, enigmatic Leach's petrel nest on Foula; currently this is their only known site in Shetland. However, it has to be the vast great skua colony **(165)** (3,000 pairs) which remains foremost in the minds of visiting birdwatchers. As well as being the site for half of Shetlands' breeding population, the colony accounts for 30 per cent of those breeding in the northern hemisphere and is supplemented by nearly 300 pairs of Arctic skua. With this legion of aerial bandits it is a wonder that any other sea birds manage to raise their young.

ISLE OF MAY The southern coastline of Fife in east Scotland is washed by the tides of the Firth of Forth, which contains bird islands of national importance.

At the mouth of the Forth, just 8 km/5 miles south-east of Anstruther, the Isle of May (56.6 ha/140 acres) is one of the major migration spots on the east coast. Since 1934, a bird observatory on the island has recorded the passage of migratory birds crossing the North Sea and after strong easterly winds in bad weather during spring and autumn, vast numbers of exhausted birds settle on the island to recuperate. The more common species landing during the autumn include those which overwinter in Britain and Ireland; once after flying in poor visibility a thousand bramblings roosted and on a similar occasion the island was covered with 15,000 exhausted diminutive goldcrests. Rarer migrant visitors include gyrfalcon, sabine's gull, wryneck, scarlet rosefinch and lapland bunting.

The sea-bird colonies have shown a general increase in population, especially the puffins, with over 8,000 pairs occupying burrows right across the island, and 1,000 pairs of shag nesting low down the 54-m/177-ft cliffs; fulmar, kittiwake, guillemot and razorbill **(153)** all breed in expanding populations, too. Lesser black-backed and herring gulls breed but their numbers are controlled by wardens to allow further increases in the population of breeding common terns.

BASS ROCK Two km/1¼ miles off-shore from North Berwick on the southern shore of the Firth of Forth is Bass Rock, rising 90 m/295 ft from the sea and covering 10 ha/25 acres. It is the most accessible gannetry in Britain, with over 9,000 pairs breeding so densely that the cliffs are over-populated and nesting birds spread on to the slanting summit of the rock **(166)**. The views of the gannets from the boat when you arrive from North Berwick are mesmerising and once ashore it is possible to stand above the nesting birds and look down into the centre of the ever-active colony.

The association between the gannets and the island is so strong that it was named after the birds' scientific name, *Sula bassana*, although other birds such as puffin, guillemot, razorbill, shag, kittiwake and fulmar also nest in large numbers.

THE FARNE ISLANDS AND LINDISFARNE (HOLY ISLAND) Since the seventh century, birds have taken the protection offered by the Farne Islands and today nineteen species of sea bird are identified as breeding on the island group. There are twenty-eight islands, the largest being Inner Farne which covers 6.6 ha/16¼ acres, and they are all situated off the Northumberland coast, directly east from Bamburgh. The islands are owned by the National Trust and, although many are wardened to protect the birds, three – Inner Farne, Staple and Longstone – have public access.

From May to June, the sea-bird colonies are at their most active. All the species compete for cliff nest sites, utilising any space available. Among the earliest to nest are the shags, who build their untidy nests on the larger ledges, fiercely defending their territory from lesser black-backed (**168**) and herring gulls. Young shags nesting for the first year begin to build nests earlier than mature birds, in an attempt to claim the best ledges. It is comical to watch the older birds arriving at the scene and either throwing all the branches away or taking over the partially built nests from the younger birds.

Kittiwakes benefit from the aggressive nature of the ledge-policing shags by building their own nests on the smaller ledges amongst the shag colony. As a result they are left untouched by marauding gulls and stand a better chance of rearing their young. Kittiwakes' nests, about 30 cm/12 in in diameter (**151**), are fascinating structures built of mud, seaweed and ocean debris, all cemented together and to the ledge by large amounts of sticky droppings.

Where the soil is deep enough, **puffins** gain exclusive rights for their burrows – up to 15,000 pairs nest on Inner Farne, Staple, Brownsman and the Wideopens. Birdwatchers should keep to the pathways to avoid damaging the puffin colonies, because although their burrows extend 1.5 m/5 ft into the soil, they are only 30 cm/12 in or so beneath the surface: since the burrows form a labyrinth, any weight above them causes the roof to collapse. Young puffins remain underground for six weeks and are fed by both parents on sand eels, which they catch far out at sea. The small fish are held by their head in specialised grooves inside the puffin's beak, giving the bird a comical appearance (**167**). The young puffins grow fast, but their parents suddenly abandon them. Eventually pangs of hunger persuade them to leave the burrow and drop to the sea, where they begin to feed for themselves.

In a similar way, guillemots feed their chicks for about three weeks on spewed-up fish and on this protein-rich diet the chicks rapidly reach half the adult size. In the crepuscular hours, the adults encourage their young to leave the cliff and they plummet to the sea on well-feathered but ineffective wings. They are still reliant on their parents, but the floating juveniles quickly learn the art of fishing to supplement the food brought regularly by the adults.

There are no trees on the Farnes, but any low vegetation is used as nest sites by over 1,000 pairs of eider, which, being gentle birds, rely totally on their camouflage markings for protection from predating gulls. The grass swards and vegetated areas on Inner Farne and Brownsman provide ideal nest sites for common, sandwich and a few roseate tern, whereas Staple Island is a better site for the Arctic tern colonies. Arctic terns are particularly aggressive defenders of their nests and, even though those on Staple Island are more used to visitors than most, they attack and strike at the head with their extremely sharp beaks.

South of the Farne Islands, the rest of the east coast of Britain lacks notable off-shore islands. From the Wash, round the bulge of East Anglia, across the Thames Estuary and around the heel of Kent, cliff faces are largely absent. It follows that where there are no cliffs there will be no off-shore islands and – the Isle of Wight and Brownsea Island in Dorset excepted – it is not until the southern coastline of Devon, around Sidmouth that cliffs begin to reappear.

THE ISLES OF SCILLY No serious birdwatcher's life is complete until he has visited the Isles of Scilly, internationally famous for their birds. Over one hundred rocks, islets and islands make up the Scilly Isles but only five are inhabited and a further forty large enough to be colonised by plants and birds. All the islands are low lying (highest point 48 m/158 ft), with flat tops, formed by the shattered remains of a mass of granite forced from the bowels of the earth around 300 million years ago. Their extreme southerly location means that the islands are washed by the Gulf Stream, making the climate the mildest in Britain; frosts are very rare.

Apart from the inhabited islands of St Mary's, Tresco, St Agnes, St Martin's and Bryher, whose fertile pastures are cultivated, the majority of the Scillies are bare granite rocks with stunted heathland plants giving a sparse covering.

The numerous sand-dunes have their own abundant flora, including marram grass, sea bindweed, yellow horned poppy and garish pink, purple and dark yellow hottentot fig.

The Isles of Scilly are particularly important for birdlife and the sea birds are a special glory. On the inhabited islands, the breeding populations are small, but Annet, which has no access from April to August during peak breeding time, is one of the few places in southern Britain where storm petrel and Manx shearwater nest. Guillemot, razorbill and puffin also nest on the island but the best site for these latter species is the northern stack of Men-a-vaur, where kittiwake accompany them. Most of the outlying stacks and deserted islands hold colonies of sea birds. Although mainland Cornwall doesn't support breeding common tern, it nests on the Scillies, with several species of gull, cormorant and shag. The herring gulls are opportunists, never missing a chance to grab an easy meal from an oystercatcher after the wader has prised open a cockle. Watch the gull pick up a mollusc, fly above rocks and drop it to smash on to the rocks before swooping down to pick out the soft flesh. They can also be seen standing on soft sand when the tide is low and treading their webbed feet up and down: they have learnt that this brings marine worms to the surface.

The **cormorants** are interesting to watch, because they spend time in the water only when they are busy feeding; at all other times they prefer to sit in the warmth of the rocks. Sitting low in the water, they jack-knife and dive for prey which ranges from eels to flounders. A rasping tongue guides the wriggling fish to the back of the throat: the cusps of the tongue point backwards, forcing the fish in one direction. The prey head is swallowed first, and taken into the cormorant's gizzard, where it is ground to a pulp before digestion begins. Closely observe the cormorant colony and watch how cormorant chicks are only fed about twice a day. As the adult arrives, the chick sticks its head right inside its throat and with what look like violent thrusting movements encourages the parent to regurgitate a meal of partly digested fish (**169**).

Additional breeding birds include oystercatcher and ringed plover, land birds such as shoveler and teal around the freshwater ponds and great tit, blue tit, goldcrest, wren, linnet,

167

168

169

skylark, blackbird, song thrush and house sparrow inland. Interestingly, owls do not breed on the islands; neither do the corvids such as jackdaw, raven, rook or magpie. Other omissions from the smaller birds include blackcap, garden warbler, yellowhammer, bullfinch, and wheatear; and since there are few trees, crevice- and hole-nesting birds such as woodpecker, nuthatch and treecreeper are also absent.

What the islands lose in resident land-breeding birds, they certainly make up for in rare visitors, and it is these birds which attract armies of birdwatchers to the Scillies.

The autumn is the prime season – especially October, when gales blow migrating birds off their course on their journey to America or Asia. Many birds recorded in the Scillies have never been seen anywhere else in Britain; for example, the American purple gallinule, greater yellowleg, the American woodpecker, and the yellow-bellied sapsucker. The names are as incredible as the fact that the birds arrive in the first place, but without fail rarities land each autumn, as a result of freak weather conditions and the position of the island group. When depressions move east across the Atlantic, the small birds are sucked up in strong south-westerly winds towards the south of the ocean, and the first landfall is the Scillies.

During October and November, birds from the other side of the world – Asia and China – arrive mysteriously. Siberian yellow-browed warbler and Pallas's warbler, which usually overwinter in India and China, recently visited the Scillies.

In spring other unusual migrants arrive from Mediterranean climates. Little egret, squacco heron, bee-eater and woodchat shrike all overshoot their southern European summer breeding grounds and reach the Scilly Islands on strong southerly winds. Less colourful migrants like melodious warbler and wryneck regularly arrive and this unpredictable, bewitching influx of birds, together with the dramatic regular sea-bird colonies, makes a visit to the Isles of Scilly an unrivalled highlight of the birdwatcher's year.

Rocky islands are liberally dotted around our coastline. It is incredible that apart from Rockall in the Outer Hebrides, all the islands of Britain lie well within the Continental Shelf. Surely these off-shore islands should be explored, since they play an important part in nature conservation? How else will we ever confirm the importance of remote off-shore islands for migratory birds and discover other rocks like Cape Clear Island in Co. Cork, where as many as 40,000 sea birds an hour pass the island on certain days in autumn, accompanied by rare African and American vagrants? In 1959 a bird observatory was established at Cape Clear, and has been maintained by a team of knowledgeable amateur ornithologists ever since. We could learn much more about the movement of sea birds in the northern hemisphere by being more aware of island birdlife.

167 The colourful bill, here full of sand eels, has given the puffin its popular name of sea parrot. It is a true marine bird only coming ashore to breed in shallow burrows.

168 Lesser black-backed gulls are migratory birds, wintering around the coasts of north-west Africa, Spain and France, before returning to Britain from May onwards.

169 Hundreds or sometimes thousands of birds form the largest cormorant colonies, where the nests are built on cliff ledges, rocky outcrops and even in trees.

170 Female snowy owl. This species has bred in the Shetlands but is more likely to be seen as a rare winter visitor in northern Scotland and Ireland.

SHINGLE BEACHES

About one-third of the 11,000-km/6,840-mile coastline of England and Wales is fringed with shingle beaches; and wherever there are shingle beaches there will be found a secondary feature of such coastlines – the shingle bank. These transient, off-shore ridges of pebbles are found where a coastal headland juts out into the sea, creating a barrier; and they commonly occur at an estuary where combined forces of tidal current and wind cause the mobile shingle to form a wall of stone – sometimes causing the estuary and associated bays to be a navigational nightmare.

The shingle coast vividly reminds naturalists of the relentless power of the sea and wind: the wave-rounded pebbles are constantly battered by the sea into shelving beaches and the mobile shingle banks. With each wave breaking on the beach, the swash pushes the pebbles forwards, but the hidden, dangerous undertow associated with shingle coastlines drags the pebbles back into the sea as the backwash. There is a constant motion of pebbles being thrown on to the beach and being dragged back into the sea; and as the pebbles roll back into the sea, tidal currents move them horizontally along the coast before throwing them on to the beach yet again. This endless action causes the pebbles to be worn smooth as they travel up and down the beach and also along it, in a sideways motion known as long-shore drift. On the south coast, shingle drifts from west to east, but in Norfolk and Suffolk it moves from north to south.

There are various forms of shingle beaches – shingle spits, shingle bars, fringing shingle beaches and apposition shingle beaches: all are well represented around our coastline. The shingle which forms these beaches originates partly from cliff erosion, partly from boulder clay on the ocean floor, but mostly from glacial and gravel deposits swept away by rivers over thousands of years. The most famous shingle deposit is Chesil Beach in Dorset, believed to have been formed largely by a massive upwash of seabed deposits in the wake of the last Ice Age.

The shingle composition of Britain varies regionally. Along the south and east coasts it is mainly flint eroded from the chalk cliffs. On the west coast and the Scottish beaches, local rocks form a high percentage of the shingle and flint is almost absent. The commonest type of shingle beach in Britain is the fringing beach, comprising a shingle strip along the upper shore in contact with the mainland along its total length. This is the type of shingle beach found at Brighton and along much of the Sussex coast.

Shingle spits are fascinating structures, formed totally by long-shore drift at a point where the coastline suddenly changes direction. The shingle moving with the long-shore drift continues to be deposited along a distinct line from the original direction of the shore and forms a peninsula which grows out from the shore anchorage. Frequently the apical end of the spit turns landwards, forming a characteristic hook or even a succession of hooks, as at Blakeney Point in Norfolk. This shingle spit is one of Norfolk's oldest nature reserves and one of the key migration points in Britain, best visited in autumn. Rarities such as hoopoe, grey grey shrike, wryneck, bluethroat and red-rumped swallow are all recorded along this unique stretch of coastline, together with many other common species of birds. Large colonies of tern breed on the extremities of Blakeney Point and since they already have enough environ-

mental problems coping with the unstable shingle, you should observe them from a reasonable distance through binoculars. Most of the terns are sandwich and common, but the rare little tern is also found, together with several pairs of arctic tern. On the more stable areas of the spit breed oystercatcher and ringed plover, with redshank and black-headed gulls nesting where the shingle gives way to saltmarsh.

The most impressive shingle spit in Britain is Orford Ness in Suffolk, which stretches for over 18 km/11 miles. Originating at Aldeburgh over a thousand years ago, the ness has continued to elongate southwards, sometimes by a metre a month, blocking the River Alde's natural sea exit to the extent that it has been diverted to flow around the end of the spit.

Sometimes a shingle spit growing out from a fixed point on the coast curves back to the mainland and rejoins it miles down the coastline. This becomes a shingle bar: a beach running parallel to the shoreline at some distance away from it, joined to the mainland at both ends and frequently enclosing a brackish lagoon. The best example is the Fleet, a lagoon formed by Chesil Beach which is itself a shingle bar stretching along the Dorset coast for 30 km/19 miles from Bridport to Portland. At Portland the shingle ridge is vast, over 182 m/600 ft wide and 12 m/40 ft high.

The other type of shingle deposit is called the apposition beach, formed when mobile shingle, rather than drifting to form a spit, builds up in front of the beach. A series of off-shore gales pushes the shingle deposit out to sea, beyond the reach of the usual tides, eventually forming a parallel bank; as this process is repeated, an entire system of parallel ridges is formed a few metres off-shore. An extreme high tide, accompanied by the force of gales, moves the shingle ridges back on-shore, pushing the pebbles well above normal tidelines and forming large areas of stable shingle. Dungeness is the best example of an apposition beach in Britain, and the series of parallel ridges leading to its formation are easily visible. The beach is so stable that plants, such as gorse and broom, have readily colonised and it even supports a wood of holly.

The constant instability of the shingle habitat makes it generally inhospitable. Plants can only colonise the most stable of the shingle ridges; but where they survive, they provide a range of colour and interest. Many stable shingle beaches with a regular flora have been designated nature reserves, because they illustrate a unique adaptation between the plants and habitat.

A rich supply of food is necessary in any habitat before birds will colonise. Shingle beaches, with constant long-shore drift and lack of invertebrate food supply, are relatively barren places for birds. However, they are not without birdlife.

After stormy weather, when the sea has relentlessly pounded the pebbles, seaweeds, dead crabs, sea urchins, starfish and other marine life are frequently washed high up on the beach. This is the time to observe great black-backed gull, herring gull and other scavengers, such as carrion crow and jackdaw, picking over the organic detritus.

On most stretches of shingle coastline, man has built groynes and storm barriers to reduce the shingle drift. These structures provide perfect perches for fish-eating birds, such as cormorant and shag. Both birds have a dark blue-green plumage, long necks and an erect stance, but the cormorant has a white chin and face patches throughout the year and conspicuous white thigh patches in spring. The shag doesn't show these markings, but sports a distinctive forwardly curved head crest in summer and is overall slightly smaller than the cormorant. After feeding for fish, both on the surface and by diving for up to a minute, reaching depths of 16 m/52½ ft, the cormorants and shags frequently fly into the shore and perch on the beach groynes, holdings their wings outstretched to dry in the breeze and sun.

Wherever the shingle is piled in quantities likely to remain stable, plants begin to colonise the habitat. The pioneers include sea beet, which anchors into the shingle with a large tap root. Its leathery leaves eventually sprawl across the shingle, trapping the wind-blown debris which finally decays and forms humus containing the vital nutrients for growth. Sea-kale, sea sandwort, sea campion and sea pea are other localised colonisers of shingle which can withstand occasional burial and eventually assist in stabilising the higher reaches of the shingle.

Shingle plant succession is similar to that of sand-dunes (page 194), with the habitat sequence changing from mobile, bare shingle to grassland or dry heath, as at Dungeness, or scrub and saltmarsh as at Blakeney.

The stable plant-colonised areas of shingle provide a feeding area for birds, especially during autumn migration. Curled dock in seed during late summer and autumn is a source of food for greenfinch and yellowhammer; and pied wagtail, rarer shore lark and wheatear all search for food along the shingle strandline. Turnstone sometimes visit pebble beaches to forage for food; other passage migrants stopping to feed include sanderling, dunlin and ringed plover.

The **ringed plover** (**171**) is one of the few species which actually nests on shingle beaches. There are populations at Chesil Beach and along the north Norfolk coast at Blakeney, Snettisham and Titchwell. Inland-nesting birds frequent the shingle banks along many of the Scottish rivers such as in the Spey Valley, the flinty brecks of East Anglia and on the machair of the Outer Hebrides. The species is a solitary nester, although several pairs will nest along the same stretch of shingle. During the breeding season from April to June, it is easy not to notice the ringed plover because its sandy-coloured body gives it excellent camouflage against the pebbles.

Its brief courtship display is fascinating to watch: the cock bird crouches before the female, fans its tail, raises the feathers on its back, and half opens its wings. All this is performed in the shelter of the shingle ridges, near to the eventual nesting site. Four yellow-buff eggs, flecked with blue, brown and black spots, are laid in one of several scrapes made by the male, either in soft gravel and beach debris, or actually amongst the pebbles, in late April.

The perfect camouflage of the adults and eggs has led to a steady decline in the breeding populations of the ringed plover. Although there are still around 7,000 pairs in Britain, many of the eggs laid on shingle beaches do not hatch. The casual beach visitor, tourist, fisherman and even birdwatcher, walking along the shingle beach and not noticing the bird, flushes the female from the nest. She immediately makes distracting behaviour by fluttering low across the shingle and dragging or weakly flapping an imaginary broken wing. If the intruder does not quickly retreat from the area, the eggs rapidly cool and the embryos fail to develop. Human activities are responsible for many ringed plovers deserting their nests, and birdwatchers should be prepared to alter their route immediately they spot a distressed ringed plover on the beach.

Oystercatchers also nest on broad shingle beaches and spits, although increasingly they are becoming inland-nesting birds, with greater breeding success than individuals remaining on the coast. The noisy, piebald oystercatcher is unmistakable with pink legs, bright orange bill and red eye, making it unlike any other bird (**172**). During March and April – but on the shingle banks of the Scottish rivers as early as February – the male bird begins his courtship display: he runs rapidly towards the chosen hen with neck and tail outstretched, bill pointing down. With hunched shoulders, he bursts into a rapid piping call until the female responds to his advances. Sometimes they perform elaborate aerial displays during group courtships. Cock birds make attractive hovering flights, calling all the time to a partner on the ground: they fly energetically high into the air, then sweep low over the ground, swerving in large arcs across the display area. This type of flight is called the 'butterfly display'.

The oystercatcher nests in small colonies, spaced 300–400 m/984–1,312 ft apart. On the shingle banks, the nest is little more than a shallow depression, frequently lined with small pebbles, shells, twigs or seaweed. The three or four buff or olive-brown blotched eggs are laid towards the end of April or early May. The female performs most of the incubation.

Oystercatchers demonstrate the benefits of colonial nesting. The non-incubating bird of the pair frequently watches over its partner from a discreet distance, ready to raise the alarm, but often a single oystercatcher within a group assumes the role of 'look-out' and raises the alarm for all sitting birds with a loud piping call. If humans approach too close to the nest the sitting bird quickly leaves the eggs, running some distance across the shingle before taking flight. However, it is worth knowing that adult birds can defend their nest aggressively from the air and will circle round, calling vigorously and mobbing the intruder by striking with the bill.

The eggs and newly hatched chicks are frequent prey for gulls, crows and other predators, but when these marauders approach, the oystercatchers take to the air and battle with the attackers, striking the underparts of the predator with their long bill.

In Britain shingle is the most important nesting habitat for **little tern** (**173**). Strangely the bird prefers the less stable, non-vegetated shingle beaches, around high-water level. Flooding by storm tides and disturbance by humans annually interfere with the breeding success of the little tern, and other tern species are similarly affected. Consequently conservation measures have been imposed on all tern colonies. Britain probably has more breeding pairs of Sandwich tern, Arctic tern, little tern and roseate tern, than any other country in north-west Europe; and more than half of the 15,000 pairs of common tern breeding in Britain are found in England. The little tern is undoubtedly one of our rarest coastal breeding birds; there are around 2,000 pairs, mostly confined to south-east England and East Anglia. The 30 km/18½ miles of Chesil

171 One of the most attractive birds nesting on sand, gravel or shingle is the ringed plover, which has a clear flute-like song.

172 An oystercatcher on its eggs amongst the shingle. The arresting, loud, ringing whistle resembles the noise of a bosun's pipe, attracting the attention of birdwatchers and holidaymakers alike.

173 Because the sandy and shingle beaches favoured by little terns for nesting are often unwittingly disturbed by humans, breeding success is low.

Beach in Dorset support about 10 per cent of the breeding population of little tern.

The little tern lays two eggs at the end of May or early June in an unlined shingle depression. These are difficult to recognise, as they blend perfectly with the pebbles. In most reserves the area is fenced off and wardened to prevent human disturbance; at other reserves, varied conservation management has been necessary to preserve the populations.

Up to sixty pairs of little tern used to nest at Dungeness, relying on a large expanse of undisturbed shingle. However, commercial gravel extraction caused such disruption that only a few pairs remain on the coastal shingle. The best opportunity for seeing nesting little tern at Dungeness is now at Burrowes Pit within the RSPB reserve. Here specially created shingle islands provide sanctuary for a few pairs each season.

The RSPB reserve at Titchwell, Norfolk, also supports up to fifty pairs of breeding little tern. Most of Britain's population are along this coastline on managed reserves. There are significant breeding populations of little tern along the Norfolk coast at Scolt Head, Blakeney Point and the Stiffkey shoreline. These are also the sites for the largest tern, the sandwich tern.

The whole of the north Norfolk coast provides a fascinating study of the interaction of shingle, sand-dune and saltmarsh systems. Here mobile shingle becomes fixed by windblown sand, allowing plant colonisation and the formation of fringing dunes backed by saltmarsh. But for the little tern, stabilised shingle is unsatisfactory nesting ground. At Titchwell the RSPB manage the shingle banks by bulldozing away amassed sand and therefore maintaining bare shingle for the little terns.

You can easily recognise the little tern through binoculars by its small size (24 cm/9½ in), black cap with white forehead, yellow legs and a black-tipped yellow bill. The birds hover with rapidly beating wings, feeding close to the shore in channels or at the edge of the tide. They repeatedly plunge in and out of the sea, making sideways turns and backward twists in between catching small fish. Terns are always in a hurry, continuously uttering a piercing call until dusk, when they assemble to roost.

Colonies of common and Arctic tern also nest on shingle. In Britain the nesting sites of these birds overlap. Most common terns are found in four coastal sites: Strangford Lough in Northern Ireland, Shetland, Blakeney Point, Norfolk and Couquet Island, Northumberland, where over 1,000 pairs breed.

The Arctic tern, with a population of over 75,000 pairs, is the most common tern in Britain, but over 60,000 of the pairs are on the Orkney and Shetland Islands. The Farne Islands are one of the most southerly sites for large populations of Arctic tern (**164**) although a few pairs breed in Anglesey and north Norfolk. The Orkney island of Copinsay has a small colony nesting regularly and the largest British colony of 6,000 pairs is on Papa Westray. The Arctic tern is distinguishable from the common tern by its red beak without black tip.

Although shingle beaches, bars and spits represent one of the most inhospitable habitats in Britain for birds, it is important that their protection should be increased if the few species of birds they support – tern, ringed plover, oystercatcher and shelduck – are to be preserved. The human disturbance of this habitat is worst in southern Britain. Dungeness, which is still Europe's largest shingle ridge, supports a smaller variety of breeding birds today than it did in the early 1900s. At one time Kentish plover, stone curlew and various gulls nested on the broad apposition beach, but now these species have moved on because they could not tolerate the increase of disturbance: the extraction of gravel has changed the specialised structure of the habitat. Only on the areas managed as nature reserves are birds able to breed successfully each year. The RSPB reserve has nearly 1,000 pairs of black-headed gull, 70 pairs of herring gull, over 300 pairs of common tern and 170 pairs of Sandwich tern, which began to colonise in 1976. Dungeness remains significant for passage birds and it is a good site for birdwatchers to see unusual rarities. In spring wryneck, shore lark, bluethroat, firecrest and hosts of other migrants which are blown off their usual routes see the promontory of shingle from out at sea and fly in to rest and feed. Where the shingle has stabilised, grasses, heather, gorse and scrub vegetation provide seeds and insect food for these visitors. The plants also offer nesting sites for stonechat, meadow pipit and skylark; and rabbit burrows beneath coarse scrub are taken over in March and April by nesting shelduck.

In certain parts of the country, such as Essex, the shingle beaches are mixed with large quantities of marine shell fragments, especially cockle, and many of these beaches exhibit spits of similar structure. There are 360 ha/890 acres of protected nesting sites on spits at Bradwell, Foulness Point and Colne Point; and at the mouth of the National Nature Reserve at Hamford Water are the important shingle spits, Stone Point and Crabknowe Spit.

The Essex spits have become one of the major British breeding sites for ringed plover and little tern. There are over 300 pairs of ringed plover, representing around 5 per cent of the British total; and little tern are even more successful: in 1975 some 204 pairs bred on the spits whereas today over 420 pairs use these protected sites, representing about 20 per cent of the total breeding population. This is a far cry from the 20-km/12½-mile stretch of Essex sand and shingle from the Naze to St Osyth: once it was developed as seaside resorts this entire coast became sterile to birds.

Foulness Point is of national importance to ringed plover and little tern, but it is also home to half the Essex breeding population of common tern – as a result of an ironic twist of fate. When Foulness was being considered as a site for London's third airport, the Maplin Airport Authority created a man-made shell bank on Maplin Sands near Shoeburyness. Once the major threat to the wildlife of Essex was shelved, the artificial spit was left to develop into one of the most important nest sites for terns in the county.

The shingle bank is a unique and fascinating habitat, constantly changing as wave action continues to shift the shingle along our coastline. It is a coastal formation which we still need to learn much about, if conservation societies are to be able to maintain them as unique habitats for a few specialised and declining bird species.

SANDY BEACHES AND SAND-DUNES

We have already seen that rocky shores and cliffs dominate much of the western coastline of Britain and Ireland and that shingle beaches are most common along the southern and east coasts of England. As the cliffs, rocks and shingle are battered and eroded over the years by the sea, they gradually wear down into minute particles, forming sandy beaches, which are common along the low-lying parts of the south coast and also dotted around the entire coastline of Britain. Marine shells are also ground into fragments, adding to the sandy beach.

Thus sand is produced by the action of sea, which is also responsible for its dispersal by long-shore drift (page 190). If the swash of the tide up on to the shore is greater than the backwash, sand builds up to form a beach. Very often the backwash is stronger and the sand is transported along the coast, drifting around headlands until it reaches a bay where conditions are ideal for a beach to form. Sandy beaches are commercially important for the tourist industry and for this reason many local authorities build artificial barriers and groynes to prevent 'their' sand from drifting along the coast.

As with rocky shores, where seaweeds survive only at certain zones depending on exposure at low tide, the marine life living on sandy beaches has to be tolerant of adverse conditions. The sea brings plenty of food with each high tide, but at low tide the invertebrates, like worms, molluscs and crustaceans, become exposed to sun, drying effects of the wind and predation by birds. The easiest means of defence against these threats is to burrow beneath the sand, which is what the majority of invertebrates do in the intertidal zone (the area of sand exposed between high and low tides).

During the breeding season, very few birds remain on sandy beaches but in late autumn and winter they return, and they have learnt to exploit all the submerged invertebrates at low tide. Although nobody begrudges the holiday visitors their enjoyment, the birdwatcher stands a better chance of uninterrupted pleasure in the autumn and winter months when the people have gone and the birds fly back into this habitat to feed and roost.

At the highest point of the beach there will be a tideline, produced by the last high tide. Here the flotsam and seaweed lie stranded; sand hoppers and other crustaceans hide beneath the seaweed and provide food for ringed plovers, turnstones and even adventurous skylarks. Herring gulls roost on the beach and feed along the high-tideline; every holidaymaker has watched them scavenge for food and scraps left along the beach once the people have left. Right at the other extreme of the beach is the low-tide mark.

176 Once marram grass becomes established sand-dunes become more stable around the coastline.

174

175

174 Large flocks of knots pass across Britain in the spring and autumn as passage migrants, whilst a few remain in winter to feed on sandy beaches and mud banks where they probe for crustaceans, worms and molluscs.

175 In winter, when the sanderling is seen on most sandy shores in Britain, their plumage is pale grey above with black legs. In summer they breed in the high Arctic and they moult to reddish brown on the upperparts.

176

Other birds exploit this zone of gentle rushing water: **sanderlings** (175) are the most common, scurrying along the water's edge on blurred legs, probing for sand eels and submerged invertebrates. They may only be seen from late summer through to spring before they return to their Arctic Circle breeding grounds. This small wader (20 cm/8 in), with white and silver-grey plumage, dashes left and right at amazing speed. They may be distinguished from the more common knot and dunlin by their restless feeding and the fact that they form small flocks. The vast expanse of damp sand forming the intertidal region is where the majority of hidden food lies for waders such as knot, dunlin, curlew, whimbrel and bar-tailed godwit.

Dunlins (178) are some of the first birds to fly on to the damp, sandy beach as the tide ebbs, probing with their long, slightly decurved bills into the soft sand and leaving characteristic holes between their footprints as they work the beach for molluscs and crustaceans. Breeding in the uplands of Britain they are amongst the smallest of waders, visiting the coasts in autumn and winter, when their plumage is brown and white on the upperparts and greyish underneath.

The **knot** (174) is the largest of the small waders (25 cm/10 in) with a straight black bill and grey plumage with pale, streaked underparts and faint white wing bar. It is not easy to identify and can be confused with the sanderling. Waders are well known for causing the birdwatcher identification problems, so spend time studying them closely, especially in flight: sanderling and dunlin both have a conspicuous central black section to the tail, bordered with white, and the sanderling's wing bar is easy to see; whereas the knot lacks the black tail patch and the wing bar is hardly visible. Feeding on the exposed sand, knots congregate in vast flocks in winter, especially along the west and east coasts. They are nervous birds and, once disturbed, take to the air in unison with a roar of wing beats, flashing grey and white as they twist and turn across the beach and out across the bay before alighting as one at the opposite end.

Sandy beaches are less stable than shingle and the slightest breeze, 16 kmh/10 mph, will shift fine sand particles. It seems strange, therefore, that oystercatcher and ringed plover not only overcome the problems of nesting on unstable shingle but choose to nest on sandy beaches too. Perhaps this is because few other species of bird breed on the beaches and so competition for food and territory is reduced, which suits both birds. Both nests are shallow depressions in the sand around the spring high-tideline; and the eggs and chicks are perfectly camouflaged to prevent predation.

The black guillemot is a cliff and island bird, locally abundant in the north-west of Britain (page 180). In certain localities in this region, the bird also nests on sandy beaches, especially if there are sandy banks well above high tide, where crevices and hollows remain undisturbed by normal seas. Its favourite spots are amongst the pieces of driftwood or, more common still, inside old stone walls bordering the beach. Contact calls between adults and chicks make the nest sites easy to locate, but they must be watched from a discreet distance so that the feeding birds are not disturbed.

Wherever a large sandy beach is subjected to prevailing on-shore winds sand-dunes form. The constant wind causes the surface sand to creep forwards until it hits an obstruction such as flotsam and jetsam, driftwood or strandline vegetation, where it accumulates, especially on the lee side.

The strandline vegetation occupies the zone of the beach where the highest spring tides reach. It is dominated by annuals such as saltwort, sea rocket, Babington's orache and grass-leaved orache. The plant community is only temporary because eventually a storm or freak high tide washes it away, but whilst thriving the plants provide a natural, small barrier which restricts movement of the surface and wind-blown sand. Embryo dunes begin to form around these strandline plants and when they die in autumn the accumulated sand advances further inland. Around the roots and debris of the decaying annuals, perennial grasses, such as lyme grass and sand couch, establish and their roots begin to knit the surface of the mobile sand together; these grasses can even stand some immersion in saltwater during storm tides. Both grasses have long creeping rhizomes and are erect-growing, so when sand blows in and covers them, they grow up through the fresh sand, adding to the height of the dune.

The embryo dunes eventually develop into early foredunes where sand couch dominates and the sand builds up to a height of 1–2 m/ 3–6 ft immediately behind the annual strandline community. The foredune grasses only tolerate so much burial by sand and gradually as the foredunes rise, they become drier and less affected by saltwater. Once this happens, the main sand-dune grass, marram, begins to colonise; this is easily distinguished by its leaves, which are blue green on the upper surface with distinct ribs and grooves. Marram grass thrives in dry conditions and is very robust, growing rapidly even when partly covered by sand, withstanding 40–100 cm/ 12–39 in of sand deposition per year. The massive rhizomatous root system, which extends down to 1 m/ 3¼ ft below the surface, helps bind the sand, making it stable, but it also anchors the plant firmly so that the aerial parts can trap more sand. In Britain marram sand-dunes grow to around 20–25 m/65–80 ft. Providing mobile sand exists, marram will continue building dunes; it flourishes on a constant supply of new sand and, like cord grass on the mud flats, it is commercially planted in order to stabilise and develop new dune areas around our coastline.

One of the largest sand dunes in Britain, stretching for nearly 5 km/3 miles along the coast, is Newborough Warren, forming the southern corner of Anglesey. At low tide, Newborough perfectly illustrates the typical sand-dune development: and all the usual plants are present on the foredunes and there are fixed dunes which appear as a series of ridges. Walking from one of these ridges to another you will see the dune slacks in the hollows; these are damp throughout most of the year and certainly fill with rainwater in the autumn and winter.

Sand-dunes are not particularly rich in birds at any time of the year. But the flowers, which are numerous and varied, provide both insects and seeds in good quantities, attracting skylark, meadow pipit, linnet, whinchat and stonechat, some of which visit the dunes during the winter. Since small mammals like shrews and voles live on the fixed dunes the short-eared owl has learnt to hunt the habitat, especially during the autumn, when the bird moves down from its typical moorland habitat to remain around the coast and lowland farms. Flapping slowly on long narrow wings, the owl quarters the sand-dune, gliding periodically and dropping stone-like to catch its prey. The best time to see the short-eared owl is early evening, although it is one of the few owls which hunts in broad daylight.

Mature stable dunes eventually become colonised by scrub vegetation but dune-scrub is never very large in Britain and there are no areas where natural woodland has evolved. On the east coast, around Norfolk, sea buckthorn is the dominant shrub and the bright orange berries are stripped by fieldfare, redwing and other thrushes in winter. Elder, hawthorn, wild privet, dog rose and brambles form dune-scrub along different parts of the coast and provide nest sites for whitethroat, linnet, hedge sparrow, sedge warbler and yellowhammer. These species provide a regular source of food for the kestrel which, although typical of open farmland, has adapted to feed and breed near motorways, town centres and city parkland as well as hunting on sand-dunes.

Only two ducks commonly nest in sand-dunes: the eider and shelduck. Both are quick to chaperone their ducklings down to the sea or estuary backwater, within a few days of hatching.

The **shelduck** are usually paired in April, having gone through their courtship in March on the mud flats and marshes of the estuary. They build their nest in a rabbit burrow or under a bramble bush on the dunes: a basic structure comprising little more than a few strands of grass, blanketed with soft down plucked from the duck's plumage. Eight to ten yellow-white eggs are laid in the down and hatch within 30 days. The female only leaves the nest during the incubation period to feed with the drake; during this short break, she completely covers the eggs over with the down to prevent rapid cooling.

Amongst the gulls and terns, black-headed, herring, lesser and great black-backed gull, common, Arctic and Sandwich tern are all known to nest on the stable dunes in various-sized colonies. Sandwich terns nest so close together that the incubating bird is little more than stabbing distance away from its neighbour.

Sand-dunes are a natural habitat, very little influenced by man: British dune systems have reached their present form over the last thousand years. Exceptionally unstable, they can be destroyed by an overnight storm and eroded by the trampling of human feet. Most of the large dunes are maintained by a management system; they remain an interesting and essential feature of our coastline for birdwatcher and visitor alike.

ESTUARIES, MUD FLATS AND SALTMARSHES

It is a great advantage to the birdwatcher in Britain that he is never more than 112 km/70 miles from the sea, for during the year there are seasons when the density of birds along our coastline is greater than in any other habitat. Perhaps the greatest concentration of coastal birds occurs on the estuaries and neighbouring saltmarshes. Visitors to Morecambe Bay, for instance, can observe over 250,000 birds, during the winter, most of them waders, including knot, dunlin, sanderling and oystercatcher. Morecambe Bay is the huge estuary between Cumbria and Lancashire, formed from the combined estuaries of the Rivers Wyre, Lune, Kent and Leven. The bay covers over 260 sq. km/100 sq. miles and the vast tidal plain, rich with food supplies, is so attractive to waders and wildfowl that the area is a Mecca for birdwatchers throughout the year.

Estuaries, so often thought of as bleak, desolate places, have a magic all of their own and their formation makes them even more fascinating. Typically, they are formed where a large river meets the sea, thus causing the saltwater to be diluted by the inflow of freshwater from the river. The area where the saline and freshwater mix varies according to the tide level and the volume of freshwater released into the estuary. Sometimes the outflow of freshwater is so large that it actually flows over the top of the denser seawater on the incoming tide. However, in most British estuaries the wave and tidal flows are so strong that a thorough mixing of the two water types occurs and a gradual change from seawater to freshwater results. All plant and animal life surviving in an estuary, therefore, has to be tolerant of exposure to current action and variation and fluctuation in salinity levels.

Estuaries are affected by two daily tides, so there is constant water movement over the intertidal zone. This area is ever changing as suspended silt and debris, carried down by the river and by the incoming tide, are deposited. Although the erosion and deposition of stones, sand and mud is constant, salt-tolerant animals survive, providing a rich source of food for the birds.

The majority of our estuaries were created by the drowning of river valleys as sea levels rose over thousands of years. Occasionally they have been formed by land subsidence, but in all cases the lower estuary is flanked with broad mud flats and established saltmarshes, which are generally reclaimed from the sea by plant colonisation or formed by man and dissected by fast-flowing channels.

Estuaries themselves offer a region of sheltered water, so that as the tide returns, all fine sand and mud held in suspension is finally deposited. As the silt builds up the mud flats are colonised by saltmarsh plants, such as cord grass, which helps to stabilise the habitat. Cord grass has become established in Britain during the last century, and is the most successful pioneer coloniser of mud flats. It is a hybrid cross between an American and British species, with such a vigorous growth that it is used extensively in the process of reclaiming land from the sea. Throughout Britain and Ireland thousands of hectares of estuarine mud flats have been invaded by cord grass, some of it by natural colonisation, but in most cases by deliberate planting to assist reclamation of the intertidal zone.

Large areas of the Wash, Morecambe Bay, Solway Firth and Romney Marsh have been reclaimed from the sea, initially by employing cord grass. In south-east Ireland, near Wexford Harbour, over 10,000 ha/24,710 acres of mud flats were reclaimed in the middle of the last century, forming the North and South Slobs. These areas of alluvial mud are traversed by drainage channels and are used for arable crop and pasture land. They also happen to be the most important habitat for wildfowl in the Republic of Ireland, supporting over 15,000 birds in winter. In summer the slobs are visited by groups of little gulls and Tern Island gets its name from the largest breeding colony of roseate terns in Western Europe.

Once cord grass is established, further daily deposits of silt build up around the stems and leaves, so that eventually the plants are exposed to air for an increasing amount of time between each tide. Natural reclamation begins, and the mud flat eventually forms a saltmarsh habitat.

Estuarine mud flats are nearly always backed by saltmarshes and saltings, but throughout Britain and Ireland saltmarshes vary. Some, such as those surrounding the Dyfi estuary in Dyfed, south-west Wales, are grazed by sheep and cattle, and these grazed areas provide ideal wigeon-feeding grounds during winter. But few saltmarshes are grazed regularly: in most a natural succession of flowers occurs which begins with glasswort on the bare higher mud flats, where the minute seeds are favoured by teal. Teal in winter feed mainly on various seeds and their small beaks are adapted for this diet. They frequently feed at night and make maximum use of the low tides for feeding on the lower saltmarsh.

With each tidal flooding, the saltmarsh is covered with further silt deposits, until it rises to a level which can no longer be reached by the sea. Even though the soil remains heavily impregnated with salt, as the marsh becomes higher it dries out and grasses such as *Puccinellia* and creeping fescue colonise, providing nest sites for skylarks amd meadow pipit.

The highest zone of the saltmarsh, once it becomes permanently stable, is often claimed by man, who has built seawalls, allowing the marsh to be drained and used as pasture. This pasture provides ideal roosting sites for estuary birds at high tide and if you arrive at an estuary and find you have misjudged the tides, these pastures are the best alternative places to begin birdwatching.

Although estuaries and saltmarshes support huge populations of birds for roosting, moulting and feeding, especially during the winter season, they are not a primary nesting habitat in spring and summer. Birds are unable to nest on the intertidal mud flats and the lower marsh, where glasswort grows, because these zones are covered by neap tides each week. Vegetation on a saltmarsh is typically low growing, forcing birds to nest close to or actually on the ground. Only the middle and upper saltmarsh zones, which may remain unflooded for months, offer a habitat remotely suitable for breeding. The birds which manage to breed on the saltmarsh are mainly waders, passerines, ducks, gulls and terns. Gulls and terns nest in colonies, outnumbering any other breeding bird in this habitat.

In 1970, the British Trust for Ornithology launched the Birds of Estuary Enquiry which was organised to monitor and record the numbers of waders, wildfowl, and other types of bird using British and Irish estuaries. The results have been of great value to conservationists who realised that estuaries, which have always been under threat from industrial development, are significant and valuable habitats for birds. The Enquiry found that nationally the breeding birds of estuaries always

178 Like drifting clouds of smoke, flocks of dunlin wheel across estuaries and mudflats every winter.

177 Glistening in the morning sun at low tide, mudflats are feeding
ground for thousands of waders.

include skylark, redshank, meadow pipit, shelduck, oystercatcher, lapwing, reed bunting and mallard, and that these species and other breeding birds always choose to nest in distinct zones of the saltmarsh.

The colonial black-headed gull and common tern breed in any zone, apart from the lower marsh and areas disturbed by man. The monthly tide pattern on the marsh virtually determines the breeding success of the gulls, terns and waders. Generally these species lay an egg every other day and take up to eight days to complete their clutch. Although the incubation period varies, it is nearly always about four weeks, which means that from egg-laying to hatching is some five weeks: a period fractionally longer than the monthly interval between the high spring tides. Fortunately, during May and June, which are the peak nesting months, the high tides tend to be lower than during other months of the year. The birds nesting on the higher ground of the marsh normally survive, but it is common for freak high tides to swamp nest and eggs.

Only the redshank (**118**) is able to nest on the lower marsh with any success. This is because the chicks can float if the tide causes flooding. Normally the redshank nests along the edges of creeks, which offer higher ground than the surrounding marsh. Upon hatching, the downy redshank chicks are able to run about and also feed themselves. They remain close to the creeks with bank vegetation for cover, which is important because it is four weeks before they can fly away from danger.

The middle and upper marsh zones contain the majority of breeding birds, including the cuckoo, skylark and meadow pipit. On the saltmarshes of the east coast of England, the linnet is a common nesting bird of the upper marsh. Where there is grazing by cattle and sheep, numbers of all breeding species are reduced because grazing removes much of the groundcover. Strangely, though, some species prefer the grazed region of the upper saltmarsh: this is the best zone to look for yellow wagtail, lapwing and dunlin.

The upper marsh eventually gives way to firm, non-tidal land, which is colonised by rushes, reeds and other plants such as sea wormwood. Here, birds like the moorhen, reed warbler and sedgewarbler can commonly be seen or heard.

Many species of duck will breed along the edge of dykes on the firmer zones of the upper marsh, but only shelduck and mallard breed widely on estuaries. Shelducks are unique among estuary species because most of them nest well back from the saltmarsh. During March, shelducks congregate on the saltmarsh in mixed groups to begin their courtship display, and then disperse to seek dense vegetation inland, or rabbit burrows on sand-dunes, in which they build their nest. They only use the saltmarshes and tidal flats as sources of food and nurseries for the ducklings.

As with all habitats, it is the overall interaction between plant and animal species living within the habitat which makes it biologically healthy: whether plant or animal, one particular species is a source of food for another. Ecologically this is termed the food chain.

In an estuary the primary producers, or those species at the bottom of an overall food chain, are the green algae, one of which is the bright green *Enteromorpha*, which has tubular fronds. During late winter and between March and April there is a rapid growth of *Enteromorpha* in our estuaries and at low tide the green fronds are clearly visible, spreading across the surface of the mud flats. This algae provides one of the main sources of food for wigeon and Brent geese, which can be seen browsing on the algae mats at low tide from late autumn to early spring.

Langstone Harbour, near Portsmouth, Hampshire, is a vast area of mud flats, covering over 1,618 ha/4,000 acres. Here there are large areas of *Enteromorpha* which attract the Siberian, dark-bellied race of the Brent goose to overwinter there. The world population of Brent geese is estimated at 100,000 birds and most years over 7,000 of them feed on the mud flats in Langstone Harbour. These geese are also beginning to feed on the reclaimed pasture at Farlington Marshes, Langstone. They are becoming more approachable each season, so that it is now possible to stalk within 20 m/66 ft of the feeding birds.

To many people, estuaries appear to be no more than acres of oozing mud flats; there has even been the threat that London's third airport could be sited on a reclaimed area, viewed as a wet waste of space. Naturalists and birdwatchers know otherwise: acre for acre mud flats are far more productive than the deciduous woodland and even the fertilised agricultural land. Probably they are the most productive of all habitats.

This productivity is a result of the rich deposits of mineral nutrients, brought in by the tides and drained from the river. Any detritus (organic material from decomposing plants and animals) settles on to the surface of the mud. Within the estuarine food chain there are numerous mud-living invertebrates such as snails and marine worms, which feed almost entirely on this detritus; these invertebrates all withstand conditions of fluctuating salinity. Important species for waders include the ragworms and lugworms favoured by fishermen as bait, sandhoppers and the molluscs like common cockle, peppery furrow shell, spice shell and Baltic tellin.

The estuary birds have learnt to exploit this invertebrate food, most of which occurs in the top 4 cm/1½ in of mud. As the tide goes out, the waders feed on the exposed mud flats, moving down with the receding tide and gorging themselves on a food source of up to 70,000 mixed invertebrates per square metre of muddy sand.

For the majority of this huge invertebrate population the only defence against birds feeding is to burrow into the soft mud. The waders are perfectly adapted for this with their variably long probing bills and evolution has determined the species of prey each bird can feed upon. If you scan the mud flats with binoculars, you will see ringed plovers, with the shortest bill of all waders, feeding mainly on the surface, taking spire shell and some sandhoppers. Stint, lapwing and golden plover feed in a similar manner, walking in a jerky fashion or running like clockwork mice over the mud to grab food from the surface. Dunlin, knot and redshank, whose bills are 2.5–5 cm/1–2 in long, are able to probe into the top 40 mm/1½ in of mud and feed on worms, cockles, Baltic tellin and sandhoppers. It has been estimated that a single redshank consumes 40,000 sandhoppers per day. Only the curlew (bill length 12 cm/4¾ in), whimbrel (bill 8 cm/3¼ in) and black-tailed godwit (bill 10 cm/4 in) (117) are able to penetrate deep into the mud for lugworms, ragworms and bivalve molluscs which have retreated back into their burrows.

Apart from the ubiquitous waders, the shelduck is the other estuary species which exploits the mollusc food supply. It predates the spire shell from the surface as it walks over the mud, moving its head from side to side and sieving the shellfish from the silt; it also feeds on the sandhopper in the same way. This dabbling method of feeding is only used by the ducks when there are dense supplies of food.

Other estuarine ducks include the mallard, wigeon, shoveler and pintail, but the wigeon is the only species which typically feeds on the mud surface with shelduck. The wigeon is vegetarian and grazes *Enteromorpha* and sea lettuce from the exposed mud flats, whereas the other ducks prefer to feed in the shallow water covering the mud, even dipping their heads completely beneath the surface.

A day on an estuary and the surrounding mud flats and saltmarshes will keep the birdwatcher enthralled. The birds are always doing something interesting somewhere in the habitat, whatever the season. It is important to be aware of the tidal ebb and flow for the particular area, since this affects the feeding times of the waders. With increasing experience it is possible to find somewhere to set up position in the habitat and watch a particular species go through its daily feeding cycle.

At high tide, knots, for example, will be roosting on the upper shore, but as soon as the tide begins to ebb, they start to feed, moving down with the tide. When it is low water, some knots move on to exposed mussel beds, because their prey has burrowed deeper than 40 mm/1½ in on the exposed flats. With the return of the tide, the knots move back up the mud flats towards their original roost of high tide.

The waders with the longest bills – the curlew and godwit, for instance – always seem to leave their roost last. They seem to know that their main source of food, lugworms and ragworms, are further down the shore, and will remain underwater longest. If you observe carefully you will see that these long-billed waders are the most efficient feeders. They do not forage around or scuttle over the mud surface, burning up food reserves, but probe cautiously and effectively into the mud, and they seem to find food with each probe.

The redshanks generally begin to feed on the higher saltmarsh and then move down to the intertidal flats; whereas oystercatchers feed mainly on the mid-tidal zone and, when this area is covered by the flowing tide, fly into nearby fields to continue feeding.

In winter there are the familiar hordes of feeding waders and every day huge flocks of birds twist and turn across the pale sky. They are perfectly co-ordinated and each manoeuvre is in unison, even when coming into land. Frequently they sweep back and forth, low over the mud flats, before alighting as one. At high tide the estuary boasts an armada of various ducks; in particular at the Wash, Foulness and other south-eastern estuaries the dark-bellied Brent goose is a guaranteed delight to watch.

Towards the end of January in the estuaries of southern England some of the breeding species begin territorial and courtship display behaviour. Among the earliest is the redshank, which is a noisy, restless wader. During February the male bird begins its display flight, with quivering wings and musical song. It repeats this appealing flight across the marsh purely to attract a female into the air, who, once lured, will glide alongside the cock bird, calling in harmony, before gliding down to the ground. The display flight, carried out repeatedly, is one of the pleasures of the saltmarsh early in the year.

By the middle of February other estuary species are performing their display rituals, including the oystercatcher, ringed plover, goldeneye and mallard. The whole of the marsh reverberates with spring display calls and by April snipe bleat overhead and lapwings tumble and roll in the air across the reclaimed pasture of the saltmarsh.

Throughout April and into May some of our western estuaries, like those of the Solway, Ribble, Dee and Morecambe Bay, are visited by thousands of passage migrants: the sanderling, ringed plover and dunlin which breed in the short Arctic summer, but have wintered in Africa. They use our estuaries as fuelling stations, where they regain lost body weight and strength, before frantically moving on towards the Arctic tundra. Dunlin are particularly well known for calling whilst on migration, and just as the singing nightingale is the high spot of a summer night in an oakwood, the beautiful, plaintive trill of the dunlin is an emotive sound of the saltmarsh during May. As dusk falls, there is a frenzy of activity as dunlin flocks fly around the marsh like wisps of smoke (**178**), gathering more of their kind before heading north on their final journey to Iceland or Greenland to breed.

In late summer in the estuary the atmosphere changes. The redshank will still utter its alarm call as you pass by, but by mid-July many of the juvenile birds are on the wing, living independent lives and flying daily to the intertidal zones to feed. The adult birds are all in their summer plumage; to the observer they are at their most striking now. The oystercatchers, grouped at high-tide roost, make an impressive sight, with their flame-red eyes and orange bills contrasting with their black and white plumage.

During autumn, especially if we have an Indian summer and the temperature is equable, food supplies on the estuary are plentiful and most of the birds lead a lazy life. This is also the season of the main moult when all birds shed and replace feathers, and prefer to be free from disturbance.

Many of our large estuaries give shelter to moulting birds and two RSPB reserves are worthy of mention. Gayton Sands, on the north shore of the Dee estuary in Cheshire, is one of Britain's major sites for wintering waders: thousands of birds choose to moult there in the autumn. Near Snettisham, on the north Norfolk coast, a reserve covering 1,315 ha/3,250 acres is another significant moulting area for over 70,000 waders which roost on the mud flats, including grey plover, knot, dunlin, bar-tailed godwit, redshank and sanderling.

As November approaches, the adult moult finishes and seasonal storms persuade some birds to fly south to their wintering grounds around Morocco or in South Africa. Other species arrive from the Continent to spend winter in Britain, including godwit, knot, dunlin, wigeon, shelduck and various geese. From November, the estuaries have their maximum bird population, making it one of the best times of year to birdwatch; it is well worth visiting an estuary then, even if you do have to put up with adverse weather.

Estuaries and their associated mud flats are important to birds. Throughout the year they provide food and shelter for hundreds of thousands of individual birds and breeding sites for many others. In Britain there are 133 estuaries with over 1 sq. km/⅓ sq. mile of mud flats bordering the estuary. Including all the smaller estuaries it is estimated that there are over 2,500 sq. km/965 sq. miles of mud flats available for birds to feed on. In addition to this, there are the vast areas of saltmarsh which are equally important to coastal birds.

Birds have been using these estuaries and saltmarshes for longer than man has settled in Britain and the least we should do today is preserve them for future generations to enjoy and to enable the various species to continue feeding in relative security.

Few people would dispute the entrancing quality of the estuary at low tide, when the mud banks glisten with small rivulets in the afternoon sun and the bubbling call of the curlew floats across the marsh. Restless flocks of ringed plover and dunlin reel above the calm surface of the sea and finally alight to feed on the mud. Where a drainage creek runs out of the saltmarsh on to the tidal flats, a grey heron stands motionless, watching the tide; and way across the rippled mud on the far side of the intertidal basin, a small flock of Brent geese browse tranquilly on eelgrass. These are the sights and sounds associated with the estuary; observant study reveals that they are far from desolate places. As dusk falls, many of the birds have gone to roost, but the melancholy call of a single golden plover flying somewhere across the saltmarsh is a sound to be remembered and treasured; it would be a sad loss if it were to be replaced by the noise of industry or the shattering roar of intercontinental aircraft.

CHAPTER 12

CITY AND SUBURB

At four o'clock on a fresh mid-April morning, it is still dark, apart from the orange glow of the arching street lamps and the blinking coloured lights of an aircraft passing high overhead. The rhythmic chinking of glass moves from one doorstep to another as the local milkman begins his deliveries; the protesting snarl of a prowling cat and intermittent rumble of large lorries on the nearby road are the only sounds filling the air.

An hour before dawn breaks over these residential streets at just after six o'clock, a wren welcomes the fast-approaching new day with its rapid, piercing song. Twenty minutes later it is joined by the melancholy song of a robin singing from the top of a garden shrub. Just before sunrise the dawn chorus is at its best with blackbirds, song thrushes and blue tits all greeting the half-awake paper boy, who is completely unaware of the orchestra of sound around him, and in an unknown back garden the harsh, strident, full-spirited song of a cock mistle thrush echoes above the other birds. On a still morning such as this, the song of the mistle thrush carries for over 0.8 km/½ mile, usually from the upper branches of a tree.

With sunrise, the first few starlings appear from the east, flying out of London every morning at the same time ready to begin their noisy, suburban life before departing for the warmth of the city as dusk approaches. Their raucous cackling is not enough to spoil the song of a solitary chaffinch which begins to sing immediately the sun rises and is joined by distant woodpigeons and a single call of a jackdaw.

As I approach the edge of Perivale Wood from across the recreational ground, an ever-wary jay warns the entire wood of my arrival at one of the first nature reserves in Britain. Covering only 11 ha/27 acres and sandwiched between the Grand Union Canal on the northern boundary and the Central Line railway on its southern boundary, Perivale Wood was founded in 1885, and is still owned by the Selborne Society. In north London it represents one of a handful of woods of metropolitan importance – a perfect example of a clay soil oakwood, with hazel coppice, ash and wild service tree accompanying a spectacular display of bluebells in May; because of its value as a suburban ancient wood, access is restricted by permit from the Society.

The occasional person walking his dog knows of this small piece of woodland, but today as a kestrel flies off towards Sudbury golf course, the wood and I stand alone, ready to share the rich birdlife hidden in the undergrowth beneath the bare ash and oak branches.

Some of the early-arriving summer visitors are already here. Concealed in the canopy branches, a chiff-chaff calls continuously, whilst a blackcap which has probably overwintered in this southern, secluded wood, heralds another spring morning and will doubtless claim territory here, once a mate arrives. From deep inside the wood, the laughing call of a green woodpecker dominates all other sounds. Where the sun warms the southern edge of the wood, bright yellow lesser celandines are beginning to open; and later in the morning when the temperature rises, brimstone and speckled wood butterflies will dance along this margin, seeking nectar from any of the spring flowers.

Travelling by train on the Central Line into London, it is fascinating to birdwatch along the undisturbed wildlife corridor, until the train goes underground after White City. It is interesting to see all the different types of wildlife living so close to man: the sturdy rows of giant hogweed along the tracks at Perivale, the butterfly-laden buddleia bushes on the banks at Royal Oak and the common whitethroats which skulk each summer around the bramble bushes as the train approaches East Acton. Frequently in the evenings on the west-bound platform at White City, a song thrush sings loudly from the top of a sycamore tree.

Birdwatching does not need to stop the minute the countryside yields to buildings and man, because open countryside was there before development took place and, against all the odds, many plants and animals, including resilient birds, have managed to remain. In Greater London alone, over 100 species of birds nest, miraculously surviving despite the pressures imposed by man and 'city life', and they are well worth observing whenever the opportunity arises. Undoubtedly, though, urbanisation affects the rarer and less tolerant species more than the common and adaptable ones.

Many birds have positively benefited from the man-made environment: house sparrow, starling, pigeon, swift and house martin have all increased in numbers and expanded their ranges since man built cities and towns. Unfortunately, many of these are overlooked and some are classed as pests; but since 1980 attitudes of conservationists and naturalists have changed. It is no longer accepted that wildlife stops where the concrete starts, and there is an increasing number of urban wildlife groups, city ecology units and urban conservation societies. Most of the major cities have their wildlife advisory organisations who exchange ideas with the local authority's planning, parks and environmental departments and conservation is now as much a part of city life as country life. There is a genuine desire to encourage the wildlife, even though it was initially disturbed or destroyed by the building of the complex.

Within a 32-km/20-mile radius of St Paul's Cathedral, the suburbs of ever-expanding London include Heathrow Airport, Staines Reservoir, Brent Reservoir, Epping Forest, Rainham Marshes, Richmond Park and Perivale Wood, all of which act as islands for wildlife, where it can seek refuge against the urban sprawl all around. Other such islands in an urban environment include, from a bird's-eye view, small parks, gardens, allotments, golf courses, sports fields, rubbish tips, wasteland, copses, churchyards, canals, ponds and rivers – all far less hostile to many birds than the huge East Anglian prairie fields. These small, pocket sanctuaries within a conurbation are more productive for wildlife because the range of vegetation, providing food, shelter and potential breeding sites, is greater than on the larger agricultural area of land.

The growth of a built-up area is a complex process. Throughout history, towns have been built for various reasons and each generation of town-dweller has left its impression. When the Romans arrived, they occupied existing towns, but as a well-organised urban civilisation they brought new ideas and higher standards of living with them. Many towns became walled, to enclose markets, theatres and courts, automatically increasing the size of the town: urban life became firmly

179

established and has remained ever since. After the Norman invasion, towns developed as trading centres and market towns were built, attracting light industries like weaving, leatherworking and silversmithing, which set up around the town to supply the market traders. By the thirteenth century, coastal towns became important and expanded as maritime commerce developed. Between the thirteenth and seventeenth centuries, towns became more sprawling, with wide streets leading out of the centre into the suburbs, and it wasn't long before shops were built along these streets to serve the growing number of travellers passing through. Thus commercial buildings began to move out from the town centre and the whole town grew outwards.

The Industrial Revolution formed a new class of people called industrialists who became wealthy and their businesses prospered, causing cities like Sheffield and London to expand rapidly. It also initiated the movement of wealthy people out from the town and city centres, to live in the surrounding countryside or architecturally beautiful spa towns like Bath and Malvern. The working classes deserted the country and moved to live and work in the towns, in what became a massive upheaval in urban development. In 1800 nearly 70 per cent of the population were country dwellers, but 100 years later, after the Industrial Revolution, 80 per cent of the population lived in towns and that figure remains the same today for the population of the British Isles.

Following Victorian development of the railways, which encouraged the development of outer city suburbs, between 1925 and 1935 there was a further surge in the building of

179 Buckingham Palace gardens, Hyde Park and the Serpentine are important oases for birds in the middle of London.

suburban housing estates, forming outer suburbs to the central town, and in 1930 the first new industrial estate in Britain was built at Slough, with parkland and tracts of countryside in between the houses and factories. As the suburbs developed, so too did the allotments, small areas of wasteland, rubbish tips, cemeteries and reservoirs. The outer suburban rings of towns eventually join open countryside and green belt with occasional large and exclusive residences.

As the population increases, with a demand for housing, schools and areas of employment, the urban areas of Britain are forced to expand, and although green belt land is supposed to act as a buffer between urbanisation and open countryside, these boundaries are frequently pushed further and further out as the countryside is encroached upon by ring roads and satellite towns. Middlesex perfectly illustrates what has happened to London in the last forty years and this suburban sprawl is reflected in the majority of other towns and cities in Britain. Despite efforts to control the expansion of towns, man's need to build will never change so long as he requires a house in which to live and somewhere to earn a living. In these man-made habitats birds must find the variable 'wildlife islands': they will never defeat man's developments, so they are obliged to adapt to his ways in order to survive, because ultimately human populations determine which wildlife will survive in a world they have made their own.

BRICKS AND MORTAR

Throughout the cities of the world, pigeons and starlings are always found. In London, long before Nelson's Column existed, pigeons flocked in the streets, roosting on buildings and statues and settling in gardens in the suburbs. The variably coloured city **pigeon** is really a descendant of the rock dove which is now only found as a pure breeding wild bird on a few sea cliffs in north and west Scotland and along the Atlantic coastline of Ireland. It is not difficult to imagine how ancient cave-dwelling man probably shared the same caves as these rock doves and eventually captured breeding pairs to provide eggs and nestlings for food. This domestic association is responsible for the town pigeon living so freely amongst man today. Certainly the Romans kept and fattened rock doves for the table and after the Norman Conquest all manor houses and farmsteads had dove-cotes.

Whereas the wild rock dove has a distinct blue-grey upper plumage, with off-white underparts and white rump and is around 31 cm/13 in long with two large black wing bars, the domestic or town pigeon looks completely different. The rock dove nests and roosts on bleak cliff faces and the feral pigeon has adapted to the man-made cliffs provided by concrete buildings, where the window sills create ideal ledges for roosting. Hundreds of years ago, when pigeons first entered our cities and towns, by using these buildings they successfully exploited the conditions provided by man. Today they are one of the most ubiquitous urban birds, feeding, breeding and roosting amongst the bricks and mortar and surviving largely because town-dwellers and visitors like to feed them.

The negative side of feral pigeons is the way they deface and damage buildings and pavements with their droppings which amount to tons of guano each year. In the London borough of Westminster, the taxpayer foots an annual bill of £50,000 to clean up their whitewash; even the water in the fountains of Trafalgar Square has to be filtered to remove droppings and replaced with clean water every three weeks. In addition, a thick layer of droppings lines the communal breeding ledges and hollow eaves, which, together with carcasses of young unreared pigeons, can cause a health hazard by attracting mites and parasites into the roof spaces of city buildings; and the droppings harbour infectious fungal spores causing lung disease.

It is very difficult to control the pigeon population of our towns and cities while they remain popular with visitors, because the minute feeding is banned in one area, the opportunist pigeons fly somewhere else, foraging in the gutters and around the dustbins of restaurants and cafés until nature-loving humans start feeding them again.

The pre-roosting behaviour of **starlings** on fenland (page 132) is famous in London at St Paul's Cathedral, 10 Downing Street, the Foreign Office and the Odeon Cinema, Leicester Square, where many of the birds roost each night during autumn and winter. One of the largest roosts is Duck Island in St James's Park where several thousand congregate on the willow trees.

Just as the sun goes down on an autumn day, the starlings fly in towards London from the suburbs (**180**), where they have been feeding around the gardens and open spaces, in small groups. Starlings from the outer suburbs, some fourteen miles from the centre of London, pick up other birds from the inner suburbs and fly the final six miles as one enormous dark, flock, all screaming together and drowning the noise of the rush-hour traffic as they swoop towards their roost.

Urban roosting is a fairly new phenomenon: at the beginning of last century, the starling was not common in western England, Wales, Scotland or Ireland, and it was not until the end of the nineteenth century that starlings began to roost in London. Glasgow experienced the first town roost in 1875; a winter visit to Sauchiehall Street, Glasgow, reveals one of the largest urban roosts in Britain, where a large percentage of the 50,000 birds visiting the city all congregate. Similar numbers roost around Bradford each night throughout the autumn and winter; flocks of 15,000 birds occur over Birmingham (New Street), Newcastle and Bristol (Temple Meads) railway stations; and many conurbations have smaller gatherings throughout the year.

Like the pigeons, starlings are received with mixed feelings but so far no effective method has been discovered to limit the size of the roosts. Their behaviour probably started because man constructed the city in the first place. Offices, shops, people, cars and central-heating systems produce heat which is trapped in the brickwork of the concrete jungle, and during the daytime the buildings absorb the heat of the sun, releasing the stored heat at night. Starlings have learnt that towns and cities in winter are around 5°C warmer than the outlying country-side, providing a more comfortable roosting place. Ironically, as darkness falls on the commuters dashing to catch their trains into the suburbs, starlings are commuting from these very regions to roost the cold night away on a centrally heated window sill.

In Britain 4–7 million pairs of starling nest and a further 30 million birds from Europe join our residents each winter. Together with the house sparrow, they are amongst the best known of all birds, surviving alongside man and visiting our gardens regularly. Their black plumage, with iridescent green and purple sheen, is beautiful (**183**), but it changes slightly in autumn, when the breast feathers develop white tips which remain until they are shed in the following spring. Careful examination with binoculars reveals subtle differences in the sexes. During the winter the long, thin bill is dark brown, but in summer it turns yellow, and during the breeding season the bill of the male has a pale blue base, whereas in the female it is delicate pink. A more reliable method of spotting the differences is to look at the eyes of starlings: females throughout the year show a distinct brown ring around the iris, whereas in males this ring is absent. Other characteristics shared by both sexes include the stumpy tail and the comical, jerky, stiff-backed walk and the rapid and direct flight when the flock suddenly takes off over the roof tops to a communal perch on the telegraph wires.

Sociable by nature, starlings always feed together, and swaggering around the local park or back garden, they probe in the grass with half-open beaks, exposing a wide variety of food, including insects and larvae, spiders, worms, seeds and fruits. This omnivorous diet is one reason for the starling's population increase, because it means that they are able to survive in a variety of habitats, making use of whatever food is available. During spring and early summer their main diet is invertebrate prey and huge flocks amass on agricultural meadows, probing the grass for leatherjackets, caterpillars and insect fauna; after the breeding season and towards late summer, hedgerow and orchard fruits become the main diet and are replaced by seeds and household scraps during the winter.

As spring arrives the regular winter flocks begin to disperse, as pairs take up nesting territories, but sexually immature birds and unmated adults continue to form flocks throughout the summer, and since in starlings there is an unbalanced sex ratio of two males to one female, these summer flocks can remain quite large. The breeding season begins in April when the paired starlings move into woodland looking for natural tree holes as a nest site or seek holes in the roofs and eaves of houses, farm buildings or under the corrugated roofs of factory units. Wherever a cavity exists, large enough for the starling to squeeze through, the bird will rear its young, sometimes even in a nestbox.

Usually the male selects the nest site and begins to build the bulky, untidy nest of dry grass, leaves and small twigs. Most of the activity takes place during early morning, but towards the end of the afternoon a second flush of nesting activity occurs. Using a repetitive, serenading technique, sometimes from chimney pots and television aerials, the male attracts his mate into the nest chamber for her approval. Copulation frequently occurs near the nest, before the female begins her task of completing the structure by lining the cup with soft grass, feathers and oddments discarded by man, including cigarette butts, string, cellophane wrappings, elastic bands and pieces of material, illustrating just how closely the starling now lives with mankind.

Early in the morning before the streets are busy, a familiar sight in the city is that of **house sparrows (185)** enjoying an early morning bath, typically in a pool of water following heavy rainfall, at the base of a London plane tree. Their splashing and quivering is accompanied by an enthusiastic 'chirrup'. Later in the spring, a walk through any city or town park reveals another of their favourite pastimes – dust bathing in the tulip and wallflower beds or removing the petals from the yellow crocus under the trees. The sparrow only attacks the yellow flower crowns because it has learnt that they contain a richer, more palatable supply of nectar than the white or purple crocus which they invariably leave alone for man to enjoy.

Wherever there is human habitation, the house sparrow is now found, but originally it colonised the maquis and garigue scrubland habitats of the Mediterranean and North Africa where its short stout bill was ideal for feeding on grass seeds. As the wild grasslands became cultivated, the cereal crops provided a bumper supply of food and when farm buildings were constructed the house sparrow began its first association with man and his dwellings. Eventually farming encouraged the growth of neighbouring villages and finally towns, so the sparrow was able to leave the fields and follow man and his grain supply into an urban environment where it has suited it to remain. However, house sparrows have not fully lost their passion for grain, and each autumn, after the breeding season, they congregate in flocks and fly from suburbia to plunder the cereal crops all over the country. Sometimes they feed on spilt grain, but frequently they rob the ears of wheat before they are harvested, causing millions of pounds' worth of damage on a nationwide scale. With a population of 3–7 million pairs, even one third of the population devouring several grams of grain

each day causes significant damage and loss to the farmers.

The most isolated of farmsteads still has its small colony of house sparrows, but the majority are found around birdtables and buildings of villages, towns and cities. By their very character, they are always drawing attention to themselves and seem, despite their destructive nature towards crocus and cereals, to be accepted by urban man. In some towns the house sparrow becomes quite tame and in St James's Park, for instance, many feed out of the hands of regular visitors; but the majority of the population are wary of people, not allowing man to get too close.

For the city birdwatcher, house sparrows provide endless hours of fun. There are those who dare to eat a discarded British Rail sandwich on Euston station: the sparrows audaciously nesting in the wrought-iron gates of Buckingham Palace; and others at Admiralty Arch nesting in the galleon-bedecked lampposts, perching on the gunwales.

The detail of our common birds is frequently ignored. In spring plumage, the male house sparrow is a perfect example of an underrated attractive bird. The upperparts are an organised mixture of deep browns, edged with gold, and the underparts are greyish white, although beneath the beak is a black bib contrasting with the grey crown, bordered on the sides of the head by chestnut-brown stripes, running backwards from the eyes. During the winter much of these bold markings are lost, but by spring he is perfectly dressed to claim a territory, attract a mate and defend both against soliciting males. Throughout the year, the females retain their pale sandy-brown markings with buff underparts and although they lack the colourful headdress of the male, a pale straw-coloured band above each eye adds a touch of glamour.

From April onwards, courtship displays are commonplace, occurring on the ground, or the ledges and gutters of buildings. To begin with the sprightly cock bird chirrups loudly to attract attention from observing hen birds; then, with head and tail raised, and wings slightly drooped, he hops across to the female of his choice and continues to hop and chirrup around her. If she is keen on his advances, she responds by shivering her wings and lowering her body in submission.

House sparrows nest in any cavity and in the towns, man has provided the sparrow with drainpipes, hollow walls, spaces under the eaves, loose roof tiles and dense creepers growing up the side of buildings. Away from urbanisation, the house sparrow nests in haystacks, outbuildings and ivy-clad trees but, as its name suggests, the majority of house sparrows build their dome-shaped, untidy nest in the roof space of houses.

On the outskirts of a town, where crossroads and a long neglected pond mark the site of a once thriving village, a 12.5-cm/5-in bird, with dark blue back and white underparts, streaks through the air and disappears over the roof tops of the houses. From mid-April until the end of May, the aerial **house martins** arrive from Africa and become a part of town life across Britain and Ireland until they depart in early autumn. Sometimes confused with the swallow, the house martin is best identified by its shallow forked tail and flashing white rump, which is very noticeable in flight; once at rest it can be seen to lack the chestnut throat patch of the swallow. The sand martin (page 159), which apart from its brown plumage is very similar, arrives earlier in the spring, and after feeding over suburban

180

181

182

184

185

180 Towards dusk, as the sun sets, thousands of starlings fly in towards city centres from the suburbs.

181 Clearly displaying its feathered legs, a house martin collects mud from a puddle to build its nest.

182 Before they migrate south in autumn, house martins gather on south-easterly facing rooftops, which absorb the warmth of the sun.

183 The starling at the entrance to its nest inside a parkland statue typifies urban birdlife.

184 With their strong claws, swifts easily cling to brick walls near the nest site. Young birds are identified by their pale feather edges.

185 Never far from man and his buildings, the intelligent house sparrow has adapted to environmental changes and readily frequents gardens, parks and wasteland as well as city centres.

reservoirs, disappears to the quarries and gravel pits, whereas the house martins always head for the bricks and mortar of towns, cities and industrial estates.

Before man constructed buildings, house martins were cliff-nesting birds, but today only 1 per cent of our visitors still establish colonies on remote cliffs (page 173), quarry faces and steep river banks. The rest prefer a building in which to breed and up to 600,000 pairs rear their young in the heart of suburbia, or under the span of bridges, like the famous colony of over 400 nests at Atcham Bridge over the River Severn, near Shrewsbury.

High in the sky house martins twist and turn as they hawk for insects following their long and perilous migration: they are not as agile as swifts and less graceful than the swallow. Within a few days of reaching Britain, they congregate over the London reservoirs where insect life is abundant, and also eat small spiders floating on the air currents attached to gossamer threads which act as parachutes and control their descent. On warm days, insects are swept skywards on rising thermals and the house martins compete with town swifts for this aerial plankton, as it is called. Since Clean Air Acts were introduced, house martins have expanded their range from towns and urban fringes, right into the centre of cities where insect life survives once again. I have watched house martins building their nests under the eaves of the French Embassy in Knightsbridge, using Hyde Park as their main hunting air space.

The familiar quarter-globed nest, plastered to the eave of a building with a narrow entrance slit near the top, is made of mud, cemented together, and in place, by water. To construct this nest, the house martins become temporarily terrestrial to collect the supplies of building material. Once on the ground they are ungainly and waddle rather than walk, because they only regularly use their short, white feather-covered legs for perching or gripping the side of the nest, and they are unpractised at walking. In villages and farming communities, they collect mud from the edge of the local pond, or mud-churned gateways (181), but in suburbia, unless puddles by the side of the roads become available, they have to fly further afield to parks, sewage farms, building sites, river banks or large gardens to collect mud. To a certain extent, the availability of suitable soft mud and a water supply determines whether house martins colonise a suburban area, for many areas within towns and cities are without nesting colonies of house martins, even though ideally shaped eaves and soffits are available. The Knightsbridge house martins collect their supplies of mud from the shallow margins of the Serpentine in Hyde Park and Round Pond in Kensington Gardens. With the numerous pathways criss-crossing both these green city oases, there are always plenty of opportunities after a shower of rain for the birds to collect mud along the edges of these pedestrian tracks.

Starting the nest is the most difficult task. If the architecture or shape of the building frieze fail to provide the initial anchorage for the first beakfuls of mud, the house martins look for a suitable window hinge, or fixture used to attach external telephone cables. Eventually, about 2,800 beakfuls of mud later, the cement-like nest is completed and finally lined with feathers, straw and wispy seed capsules, caught on the wing. As it dries, the nest turns grey white, and the following season, if the nest needs repairing, it is easy to see by the colour changes where the old nest material remained and the new season's mud has been added.

House martins are social birds and their nests are built so close together that they frequently touch. When the first brood fledge, they remain united with their parents and even help with the feeding of the second and third broods. Watching a house martin colony can be very confusing, as a succession of mature-looking birds all fly in and feed juveniles in the same nest. Roosting is fun to watch, but cramped for the birds: the first-brood youngsters, the developing second brood and the adults frequently use the same nest to roost in; or in a real overcrowding emergency, they build a tenement nest near by for the airborne fledglings to use.

The feeble but pleasant-sounding twittering call of the house martin is uttered during flight, whilst the bird perches on telegraph wires, and always around the nest. Throughout September and early October, it becomes a common sound in suburbia. Gathering on south-easterly facing roof tops, where the tiles absorb the sun's rays from dawnbreak onwards, house martins perch and twitter (182) until instinct tells them to leave as one flock and head south for the winter, chasing the swifts which left our shores during mid-August.

Few birds have such an air of mystery about them as the **swift**, the most aerial of all known birds. Birdwatchers always feel a sense of magic when they arrive in Britain in May to scream about the roof tops and chimney pots of our towns and villages, and a sense of loss when they quickly depart for southern climates in August.

Because they never naturally rest at ground level, their shape may only be observed whilst they are flying. In silhouette, their long, sickle-curved wings, torpedo-shaped body and short, tapering, forked tail are unmistakable. Few people are lucky enough to see the plumage in close detail, since this requires observation at the nest, but it is uniformally dark, grey-brown, with a white chin patch and the eyes are a deep blue-black (184).

Swifts become sexually mature at around two years old and, unable to breed before this age, they spend their entire life on the wing, feeding, drinking and sleeping without their incredibly short legs ever touching the ground. In the event of their becoming accidentally grounded, these short legs and the length of their wings, formed by extremely long primary feathers, almost prevent the bird getting airborne again without human help. When ready to mate, courtship and copulation also take place on the wing. Usually mixed parties of swifts scythe through the air on rapidly flicking wings, twisting and turning between buildings, under telephone wires and between the traffic as part of their courtship ritual. You will need to follow these parties carefully with binoculars to see a male momentarily mount the back of a female in mid-air; with their wings pointing upwards in a V-shape and hanging like a sky-diver in mid-air, copulation takes place. The mating act takes only seconds, then the pair disengage and continue on their noisy flight. Alternatively, mating takes place at the nest site, following a preening session. Swifts pair for life, returning to the same nesting site every year. They do not remain together as a pair during winter, however, and migrate separately from Africa to Britain; they return to the nest site independently and mating follows the happy reunion at the site where they raised last year's young.

Swifts are so perfectly designed for life in the air that they are the fastest birds on earth: our European swift can reach 96 kmh/60 mph in straight flight. Their ability to fly at altitude is also legendary and there are fewer sights more typical of a warm summer night than a party of swifts spiralling ever upwards on the warm air currents, eventually disappearing as minute dots in the sky. They often feed at heights above 300 m /1,000 ft and, mastering the upper air waves, they regularly sky roost at 1,800 m/6,000 ft, sleeping together on the wing before descending to lower altitudes in the early morning to resume feeding. Sometimes aircraft pilots have seen swifts feeding at 3,000 m/10,000 ft, collecting aerial insects and floating spiders, all sharing the flight paths of intercontinental aircraft. They are selective about catching insects and only fly to areas where food is likely to be abundant. In suburbia the ideal places to watch swifts feeding are over reservoirs a few days after the birds reach our shores, and again on their migration south, near sewage farms and rivers, wherever insects like gnats, mosquitoes, midges and mayflies hover over the water and dance in their millions on the rising warm air at night.

Although the swift's beak looks small and pointed, the actual gape is vast and, when fully open, occupies the largest part of the face. Once it finds the aerial plankton, the swift collects food easily by flying backwards and forwards through the myriad insects with its mouth wide open. The beak acts as a scoop and directs the food into the throat pouch, which is a miniature form of the pelican's, and a food ball or bolus is created, measuring up to 1 cm/½ in in diameter, making the white chin patch distinct as an obvious bulge. The throat pouch is only used when food is being collected to feed nestlings: at all other times the trawled food is immediately swallowed. Each bolus contains 300–1,000 insects and is passed to a single swiftlet rather than shared between the brood. As the swiftlets develop, they compete for the food as it arrives, and as a result the smallest bird always takes longer to grow. Each day the brood of two or three young is fed about forty times by the pair, who bring over 20,000 insects to the nest, each one tracked down and caught by the adults. The peak feeding month is July, and the insects swallowed by the adults themselves, together with those taken to the nest, total over a million insects consumed by each family of swifts in this month alone. The breeding population of around 100,000 pairs is responsible for ridding the skies of an incredible number of insects during the few months they grace our shores.

The weather conditions determine the availability of insects. In good summers, when the temperatures remain above 10°C, swifts find plenty of food in the sky above our towns and villages, but in poor summers like those of 1986–8, when the cool and rainy periods were prolonged, flying insects become scarce and the adults are forced to fly tremendous distances to find sufficient food for their young: 800–1,300 km/500–800 miles per day is not unusual. Young swifts have their own in-built protection against shortage of food: as the supply of their specialised diet declines, their entire metabolism shows down and their breathing rate reduces, as does their pulse flow, which automatically causes the body temperature to fall, and the young swifts enter a state of almost suspended animation. Using this defence mechanism the young swifts save a large amount of energy and rely on their body fat. It is a process that no other species of bird has evolved. When food supplies return to normal, so does their metabolic level and a steady rate of growth can once more be achieved.

The swift uses any building with a small hole into the roof as a nest site but the entrance must be positioned so that the adults can fly in from below – momentarily pausing on the edge by clinging with their four, forward-pointing claws before shuffling inside – and suitable to drop straight out of into space, so that they can free fall for a split second before flicking their wings into action. Swift populations have increased as towns have developed, and some people even encourage them by fixing special nestboxes under their eaves. It is fascinating to examine a swift's nest, which in early years is a meagre cup-like structure, gaining size only after the pair return for several successful seasons: all the nesting material is caught on the wing, especially on blustery days, when dried grass, leaves, seed heads and feathers become airborne.

Although they are affected by air pollution, especially sulphur dioxide poisoning, swifts have successfully colonised parts of London ever since horse-drawn carriages attracted a plentiful supply of flies, and across the Serpentine, over Highgate Cemetery and the dome of St Paul's Cathedral, swifts are frequently seen each year. Other large cities have their regular colonies, one of the most famous of which twists, turns and defies gravity around the spires and towers of Oxford. Since many swifts live for ten or more years, traditional nest sites are returned to by generation after generation. It is awe-inspiring and certainly adds to the mystery of this high-speed bird, that during the ten years of its life, each swift flies a minimum of 2½ million miles. Even if town and city birds like the house sparrow and pigeon find it quieter once the 'screamers' leave in August, suburbia would be a far greyer place if they ever failed to perform their virtuoso aerial ballet across our summer skies.

GARDENS AND ORCHARDS

GARDENS A swift with its keen eyesight, flying over a town or city can easily see below the reservoirs and green patches which are the gardens, parks and churchyards (**179**); and other birds flying overhead have no difficulty in seeing trees, which line many of the streets and grow in the back gardens of homeowners. Out in the suburbs, these green patches become more frequent and finally merge in with the open country, where they act as wildlife corridor links, joining the town centre with the open countryside. Of course all urban and suburban areas vary: some are 'greener' than others and, depending upon the attitudes of local authorities, the numbers of parks, golf courses and tree-lined avenues fluctuate from borough to borough; but it is significant that, taken collectively, the majority of trees in suburban areas are found in back gardens – within Edinburgh, for instance, which covers 14,000 ha/34,600 acres, 84 per cent of all the trees are in people's gardens, and the remainder in churchyards, parks and playing fields. Our 16 million back gardens have therefore become important 'islands' for birds in suburbia, and the 80 per cent of the British population with regular access to a garden have a vital contribution to play towards the survival of the birds using them as refuges from the bricks and mortar. The trees and ornamental shrubbery, so lovingly planted by millions of keen amateur gardeners, attract species of birds, seeking food and shelter, which thousands of years ago were purely woodland species. As woodlands and copses were felled, their traditional habitats became scarce and overcrowded, so many birds evolved to survive in hedgerows and what became known as a 'garden' environment. Suburbs which are not plagued with feral cats often have more birds per hectare than nearby woodland, but the range of species is correspondingly smaller than in any of the countryside habitats.

Although man-made, historically reclaimed from ancient woodland, our gardens retain many of the characteristics of the woodland and birds exploit the rich, well-turned soil with its supply of invertebrates, the lawn which to them is similar to a woodland glade where worms can be caught, and the varied supply of plants, shrubs and trees, offering food, cover and breeding sites. Many woodland birds prefer the margins of the habitat, rather than the dense interior, and in a similar way, garden birds enjoy the open spaces between gardens which act perfectly as territory boundaries and provide good visibility: they can then see approaching predators, such as one of the country's six million domestic cats, which take the place of the weasels, stoats, squirrels and sparrowhawk of the woodland habitat.

The location of a garden, both geographically and within a conurbation, considerably affects how rapidly it becomes colonised with wildlife, and the difference in climate between the north and south of the British Isles should never be ignored. Gardens in industrialised polluted areas are less productive than those on the outskirts of the industrial town and a country cottage garden bordering woodland or open countryside is more rapidly colonised than a house in the middle of a new suburban estate. The house owner, whether a fanatically keen gardener or not, is the most important controlling factor of birdlife in the back garden, because just as the large open hedgeless, cereal fields of eastern England are barren of birdlife, so the person who regularly attacks their garden plot with herbicides, pesticides, weed killers, rake, hoe, shears and

186

187

lawn mower produces a perfectly manicured, but virtually sterile piece of land for birds and wildlife.

Right in the centre of cities and towns living accommodation is scarce, with narrow, small gardens, and even some of the most exclusive houses back on to a courtyard or mews, rather than a garden, but even here pots, urns, old sinks, concrete troughs, window boxes and balconies are crammed with flowers and herbs, illustrating man's desire to bring something of the countryside with him into the heart of the city. Although these houses are overshadowed and hemmed in by office blocks, department stores, hotels, hospitals and restaurants, if food is provided on a birdtable house sparrows, starlings, avenues and the mature limes, horse chestnuts, plane and monkey puzzle trees.

During the rapid building programmes before and after the Second World War, the semi-detached houses were built with small front gardens; many had fences and quite large rear gardens, with fruit trees, vegetable patches and flower borders, all totally enclosed with a privet hedge. This stereotype represents the largest part of suburbia, and now that the gardens have matured, they attract additional species of birds to those of the Victorian inner suburbs, including bullfinch, jackdaw and mistle thrush.

Wealthy Victorians delighted in the trappings of elaborate flowerbeds, terraced lawns and pathways where they could stroll, whereas the rural cottage garden of a poor countryman was almost entirely functional with some flowers interplanted among the crops which were essential to prevent him from starving. Today's suburban garden is probably a fusion of the two extremes, where exotic shrubs, roses, bulbs, perennials, vegetables and fruit all have their place; and even on estates, where it is rare to find two identical gardens, certain trends have developed. The garden boundaries tend to be lower, perhaps suggesting a more open, less private lifestyle; to save valuable time, lawns lack intricate curves; and shrubs are either evergreens or those requiring limited maintenance. The use of patio paving slabs saves gardening altogether, but provides extra song thrush anvils.

Out in the wooded suburbs, where houses tastefully blend with the countryside, tall oaks, beeches and silver birch surround gardens which are unregimented and full of varied shrubs. Here far more woodland birds are seen: treecreeper, great spotted woodpecker, coal tit and even nuthatch mix with all the species common to those gardens closer to the town centre.

Since I have an above-average-sized garden, but am a lazy gardener, the local birdlife probably celebrated on the day I moved in to occupy my house on the edge of a market town in north Buckinghamshire. My garden, like most of my neighbours', was cleared from ancient woodland which covered a vast tract of land from Oxfordshire through to Northamptonshire and was felled from 1623 onwards. It is completely walled, a trend favoured by the Georgians and mid-Victorians, and with the right care and attention could be transformed to an attractive garden. For the birds it already is, because they treat it like a local nature reserve, and, in turn, bring me hours of pleasure.

In summer the lawn is covered with blue speedwells, yellow dandelions and buttercups, with patches of white daisies. Early in the morning a green woodpecker regularly probes for ants and several jackdaws always fly across the roof tops and sit on my chimneys around breakfast time. Throughout the day blackbirds and songthrushes search for worms and snails and the courtyard birdtable with its paraphernalia of peanut feeders, half coconuts, suet, bird seed and household scraps is always a battlefield for blue tit, great tit, greenfinch, chaffinch, house sparrow, starling and robin. I only feed them during autumn and winter, and insist that they find their own natural food during the breeding season. Some years, in late February and March, especially when the weather resembles deep winter, rather than early spring, small greenfinch-like birds hang on the plastic orange peanut bags (**186**). These are the siskins of

186 Male siskin on a peanut bag. This garden feeding activity begins in February and peaks in March before the birds fly north to breed in Russia or Scandinavia.

187 This robin was attracted to breed in my garden by the removal of several bricks from an ivy-clad wall, so as to provide a suitable nest site.

188 The private life of the blue tit can be investigated by using a glass-backed nest box in the garden.

pigeons and occasional blue tits and blackbirds will use these 'isolated' feeding stations inside the enemy territory of the concrete jungle. In between the cobbles of the courtyard and crack of the patio paving stones, wind-dispersed groundsel seeds germinate and, straying from their favourite area of derelict land, goldfinches venture into the 'gardens' of town houses to tease out the seeds.

To the discriminating birdwatcher the gardens have distinct characteristics. Those of the Victorian terraces are small, with few trees or shrubs, and apart from the real town birds only collared doves, robins and dunnocks regularly visit them. The Victorians were also responsible for many of the tree-lined the coniferous woodlands, but for the last twenty-five years these yellow-green finches have been exploiting the peanut bags hung out for the tits in rural and suburban gardens; they always seem to prefer those in orange bags because they are easier to see from a distance. Normally, siskins are secretive birds and breed chiefly in the coniferous woods of Scotland, Wales and Ireland, but in winter they disperse throughout the country, and those which feed a few metres from my back door, could even be Continental winter immigrants. Whichever they are, this is the best opportunity I ever get of closely examining siskins.

Early in January 1986, 5 cm/2 in of snow fell and remained for around ten days as the temperature stayed well below freezing and many birds moved from the surrounding country-side, closer to the house to take advantage of the marginal temperature increase. At the bottom of my garden, before it joins a large playing field, two old apple trees and a pear tree shed the last of their crop from the upper branches, and redwings, fieldfares and mistle thrushes avidly fed on the pulp. The arrival of these species, which are not regular visitors to my garden, illustrates how gardens can be very rewarding habitats if food is available and weather conditions force truly wild birds closer to man, because their wild food supply is exhausted or hidden away beneath the snow. The fascination of garden birdwatching is that some species, like the lawn-probing blackbird, are permanently at home in the habitat, whereas for others, like the siskin, redwing and fieldfare, it is only a temporary refuge, making the garden unpredictable but all the more exciting throughout the year.

Similarly, in late summer, willow warblers and chiff-chaffs use my rose bushes, bramble patch and ornamental containers full of petunias as a feeding station on migration to Africa. Few gardens are sufficiently well-wooded to attract these leaf warblers as breeding birds, but many suburban gardens are seen as ideal places for a 'snack and rest' before moving on. Sadly most people with gardens miss or ignore all this action.

The back garden is the ideal place to begin birdwatching, by learning to identify by song and appearance all the birds which take up residence: 20–50 species are likely during a complete year, especially during the winter. Providing a supply of water is as important as food, because birds drink every day and like nothing more that a good bath in the summer, although blue tits with their winter diet of dry peanuts, drink far more in the winter.

Your own garden may be lacking in mature trees which offer natural nest-holes, but **blue tits (188)** are amongst the easiest of all the tit family to attract to artificial nestboxes. If it is impossible to fix the nestbox to a tree, then walls, fences or posts are suitable alternatives, as long as they are about 2.4 m/8 ft off the ground, in a quiet spot away from cats and where they receive some shade as well as sunlight, since there is always a possibility of nestlings overheating inside a confined nestbox in prolonged periods of sunshine.

The blue tits which are part of the oakwood birdlife (Ch. 2) have, for many generations, adapted to live in suburban gardens, but familiar as they are, much of their lifecycle remains a secret. In an attempt to learn more about their breeding behaviour, I have fitted one of my own nestboxes with a glass rear panel. The nestbox is mounted so that the glass panel backs on to a window of an out-building. From inside the building, shrouded with a black-out curtain so that the incoming birds cannot see me, I have been able to watch the secrets of nest-building; the male feeding the female with caterpillars, whilst she incubates the eleven eggs; and the sequence of the eggs hatching, to the day the attractive young blue tits struggle to leave the box via the small hole and fly into the garden for the first time. It has been used every season for five years.

If the birds see my garden as a reserve, they must accept that I also see it as my garden and expect some produce from it each year. So far, the way we share the plot appears to be mutually agreeable, but depending on how keen a gardener you are, your tolerance levels will differ. Insecticides are banned from my garden because the future of a blackbird dieting on poisoned caterpillars is not very promising, but in return I expect the birds to control insect pests. I enjoy the goldfinches feeding on the thistle heads in summer and nesting in the fork of a tall branch in the pear tree; and I enjoy watching even more the intoxicated blackbirds who have gorged themselves on fermenting plums under the trees in September. I tolerate and accept the bullfinches reducing my apple crop by destroying some buds each spring but get a little tired of seeing only purple and white crocus in bloom after the house sparrows have destroyed dozens of yellow ones. What an excuse I have for not labouring any more over peas or broccoli, after woodpigeons destroyed the crops in two successive years, partly encouraged by the fact that I refused to cover them in bird-snaring plastic netting! But I still harvest plenty of red currants and gooseberries, without the protection of nets, despite liberally sharing them with the birds, so this is some compensation. The constant clucking of young blackbirds using my herbaceous borders as a nursery in June is as welcome as the wheeling swifts which display above the house from April to 18 August, when they leave as regular as clockwork each year. Swallows nest above my car and re-spray the paintwork with their droppings throughout the summer, and the collared doves which perch and call in the ash tree outside my back door bring plaintive monotony and tranquillity to my garden at the same time.

Maybe being a lazy gardener and a birdwatcher has its advantages, but an efficient gardener would consider my system far from perfect. The perfection for me, however, is that in my garden I enjoy a particularly close and special relationship with the birds, especially the resident tame **robin**, who fiercely defends my garden as its territory from September, throughout Christmas, until the end of the following June. Apart from holly bushes, little dense cover is found in my garden for nest sites, but I do have ivy-clad walls, and the first year that I removed several bricks to create a cavity behind the ivy, the robins moved in; except for one year, when they decided that an old aluminium kettle in a mock-orange bush would make a change, they use the hole in the wall, screened with ivy (**187**).

Because British robins are so trusting of man and permanently occupy our gardens, they offer the birdwatcher a perfect opportunity to study the behaviour of one species very closely. Confusion can occur because the sexes are identically marked and it won't be long before you realise that the red breast, which is traditionally associated with peace and goodwill, is really intimidating war paint, as well as a sexual attractant. Early in September robins claim their territories in gardens, parks, cemeteries and woods. Although both sexes sing, the male is by far the more vocal and throughout December and early January its rich spring song increases to attract a mate. The melancholy song of robins is a continual sound of the countryside and garden throughout the year, especially at dusk, except for about five weeks in late summer: then they moult and skulk about in dense undergrowth whilst remaining completely silent, but they make up for this quiescent period with the approach of autumn. The autumn song, interspersed with frequent 'tic-tic' alarm notes, is rather weak when it begins in late August, but it is fully tuned and polished by Christmas. Robins are one of the few birds constantly singing in the colder months of the year and the same song carries on throughout the spring.

Whereas with most other birds, nest-building soon follows pair bonding, robins pair between December and March, but delay nest building, and after pairing they remain within their territory ignoring each other by mutual consent and singing only sporadically. In spring when the temperatures improve, garden robins respond with changes in behaviour and you will notice their upright, hopping gait, accompanied with numerous bows and flicks of the tail and wings. The female begins to collect nest material which consists of grass, dead leaves, hair and moss, and the nest is built in a variety of strange places, including garages, sheds, cupboards, discarded tins and letterboxes. In more natural environments rock crevices, hollow trees and dense bank vegetation are commonly used, but the habit of nesting in unusual sites is one of the reasons why the robin is so popular as a British bird.

As the female searches for nesting material, look out for the male encouraging her with his 'courtship feeding' whereby he brings insects and feeds her like a fledgling, so reinforcing the bond between them. The female stores this supply of food and draws upon it when she incubates the eggs for two weeks: although she leaves the nest momentarily to exercise and feed, her fat reserves allow her to return to the nest and eggs more quickly. Mating occurs at the same time as nest-building, and even in the garden is rarely seen because it is over so rapidly.

Once hatched, young robins have amazing appetites and the lives of both parents are dominated by feeding trips. After fifteen days, when the un-robin-like, brown speckled fledglings leave the nest, they weigh more then their parents. The fledglings' mottled plumage offers some protection by camouflage, but this is the most dangerous time of their lives as they learn to master flight, still relying on their parents for food. In the relative security of the back garden, up to a million robins are killed by cats each year. Survivors remain within a few kilometres of their birthplace.

Its beautiful song, dark plumage and bold behaviour, make the male **blackbird** (**197**) another suburban favourite. It is only in the last 150 years that the species has moved from its typical woodland habitat and shown a preference for gardens and parks; and only as recently as in the last fifty years have blackbirds colonised the larger towns and cities. Here they have adapted to live at higher densities than in the oakwood, and they have changed their nature too, frequently ignoring the presence of man wandering around the garden, although they still remain skittish, as a woodland glade species.

The cadence-filled song is heard from late February until the beginning of July, but apart from these tuneful notes, the blackbird has a wide range of calls which you will hear at some time during the year in the garden. If a cat or stranger walks down the path, it gives a strident 'pink-pink-pink-pink' warning note, but if really frightened, the alarm sound is a rapid, rattling call, usually uttered as the bird flies away over the garden fence. If the blackbird is in a nervous mood you will hear the repeated soft 'chook-chook' clucking call, which is

most common when the young have left the nest and are still unable to fly properly; but if the adult feels aggressive, it gives a high 'zee-zee' note, generally associated with territory infringement.

Blackbirds are regular visitors to my own garden. Running out from beneath the red-currant bushes, where he has been turning over dead leaves looking for insects, the male blackbird appears on the lawn. Striking in his jet-black plumage and bright orange bill, the blackbird runs across the grass and stops to give a sideways glance. This particular male has always allowed me to stand within 3.6 m/12 ft of him and as he cocks his head on one side, one yellow-rimmed eye watches me, whilst the other looks for danger.

A penchant for worms draws the male blackbird close to the spade on the rare occasions when I turn the soil, but the female keeps a safer distance rather than risk a brave approach, expecting me to throw worms to her. The only time the female blackbird almost treads on the spade is during the breeding season, when presumably the demand from hungry offspring overcomes her fear of man. Worms provide a large source of the moisture in a blackbird's diet and during rare summer droughts, when the worms burrow deeper in the soil and become difficult to reach, both adult and young blackbirds suffer; but the ability to survive on a varied diet is one of the reasons for the blackbird's colonisation success and during dry weather the aphids on my rose bushes, currant moth caterpillars on the gooseberry bushes and tadpoles in my neighbour's pond, all take the brunt of the blackbird's hunting forays.

Breeding activity starts in February, with the resident males proclaiming their territory and trying to attract the brown, speckled-breasted, pale-throated females to mate. Those birds fortunate enough to survive the winter reclaim the previous season's territory and even pair with their old mate. Once paired, the female begins to build the nest of grass and leaves, reinforced with mud, low down in a hedge or tree but sometimes in a man-made structure like a shed or coal bunker. The male occasionally helps in the construction of the nest, but as in so many species of birds, this domestic chore falls largely on the hen bird. Once she has completed the nest her attentions are turned to seducing the male and, with her tail held erect and beak pointing towards the sky, she runs across the edge of the lawn in front of her partner, uttering high-pitched calls of encouragement. With tail fanned and body feathers puffed out, the male responds, sometimes chasing the female noisily around the territory, but eventually she succumbs and the pair quickly mate.

In a good summer blackbirds successfully rear three broods, although many of the young birds die before the winter arrives and more fall victim to severe cold weather.

The British population of blackbirds is around seven million pairs with a few dispersing to Ireland and Europe, but the majority remaining sedentary all their lives. In winter the numbers are augmented by Continental visitors numbering thousands of birds, but these all leave by the following spring, leaving the resident population to their own gardens, churchyards, hedgerows and woodland, and causing the birdwatcher in suburbia to marvel at their ability to colonise successfully a habitat designed for the convenience of man alone.

One suburban species which would certainly not have survived our cold winters had man not provided seeds, coconut and apple, is the ring-neck **parakeet**, a tropical species which, having escaped from pet shops and aviculturists' collections, is now established in Greater London, Surrey, Sussex, Kent,

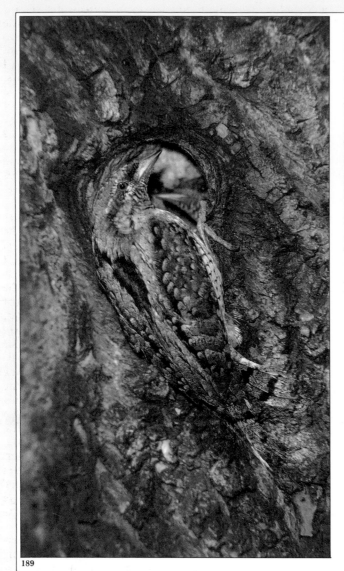

189

190

191

189 The mottled grey and brown plumage of the wryneck provides perfect camouflage against old tree-trunks.

190 The mistle thrush is absent from north-east Scotland and the Western Isles, but elsewhere is widespread wherever there are scattered trees.

Greater Manchester, Merseyside, South Wales and East Scotland. The 19-cm/7½-in bird breeds freely in many of these areas and as recently as September 1987 its range has extended to Poole in Dorset where male birds visit birdtables.

The parakeet's main body colour is greeny yellow, with a long pointed tail. The beak is crimson and the feet are yellow orange. The male is distinguished by a black throat-patch, and an attractive patch of blue shading the nape, with a rose-tinged collar giving the bird its name.

As long ago as 1855 the parrots were flying free in small numbers, having escaped from private collections, but by 1930 small flocks were visiting gardens adjacent to Epping Forest in Essex, and others appeared in Bedfordshire by 1936. Populations really began to expand from 1969–75, when parts of

Surrey, Kent and Sussex were colonised, with at least one nesting pair using the thatched roof of a farmhouse. The Surrey colonies seem to have fared particularly well during the last decade. Many of the free-flying parrots are non-breeding birds, but others are breeding successfully around Croydon, Esher, Beckenham and Bromley, and many suburban-living city-bound commuters regularly see the ring-necked parakeets when they leave early in the morning.

In late spring, when the yellow forsythia in my garden is past its best, on a warm April morning a small, 14-cm/ 5½-in, grey-brown backed bird, with streaked throat and white underparts, sits on the rotary clothes line halfway down the path. From a distance it might be confused with a hedgesparrow or stages, often involving twenty-four-hour periods of sustained flight, covering thousands of kilometres at a time. After the Sahara they fly to North Africa, stopping to rest and feed, before continuing to southern France and eventually Britain. May is perhaps the best month to look out for the spotted flycatcher, when they can be found occupying woodland glades, large parks with trees and mature gardens. They therefore tend to be restricted to the outer suburbs or the country garden, but up to 20,000 pairs breed throughout the British Isles, except for Shetland, making it far more common than the pied flycatcher of sessile oakwoods (page 24).

Once the flycatcher has claimed its territory it defends it and returns to a prime garden site each season as long as the birds survive; the weak trilling song of the displaying male frequently announces his return for another year.

Just as the pied flycatcher will use the articifial hole entrance of a nestbox in woodland, so the spotted flycatcher can be attracted to nest in gardens by putting up an open-fronted nestbox, used by robins. The nestbox should be fixed about 4 m/12 ft from the ground, preferably to a wall with ivy or virginia creeper festooning the brickwork which will cover the box, and the open front should be free of obstruction, so that the flycatchers have a clear flight path. One of the strangest nest sites I have seen was inside a coconut which had been sliced to remove one end and hung horizontally on wire for the blue tits in winter. When the flycatchers arrived in May, the husk was empty and provided a perfect suspended nest site which unfortunately was raided by grey squirrels just after the eggs hatched. Natural nest sites usually include holes in old walls or rocks, large cracks in tree trunks or clefts where a branch has broken away and, in gardens, cordoned fruit trees, especially pears horizontally trained along a brick wall (**191**). From the middle of May onwards spotted flycatchers lay their four or five eggs in the nest, which is built by the female out of dry grass, moss, wool and hair, all bound together with spiders' webs; and even when the flycatcher exhibits one of its strange habits of nesting inside disused nests of other species, the complete nest structure is built inside the platform.

Before they leave towards the end of August, spotted flycatchers generally have two broods and their success in rearing them depends on the availability of insect food. When temperatures are high and plenty of insects are flying, the familiar 'perch and dash' is the favoured technique, with large insects like hoverflies, craneflies and bluebottles being the main target, but if conditions become cool and insects cease to fly, the spotted flycatcher is forced to flit and dance amongst the tree tops, disturbing and catching any type of insect it can find to keep the hungry brood sustained. Like many insect-eating birds, it catches wasps and bumble bees, especially in early morning, when they are some of the first insects to be active. It removes the stings, by rubbing the insect's abdomen on a branch or post, before eating them or feeding them to the nestlings.

In most suburban and country gardens today, buddleia bushes thrive; these were introduced from China in the 1890s as an ornamental shrub and favoured by house owners, because their sweet scent and rich nectar attract peacock, tortoiseshell and red admiral butterflies into the garden right up until autumn approaches. Black- and yellow-banded hoverflies, honey bees and countless diptera become drunk on the long purple blooms which add rich colour to the shrub borders and provide a ready-made larder for the flycatcher. Although some ornithologists say that butterflies avoid the attack of the flycatcher by their wavering, erratic flight, those in my garden

191 Both adult spotted flycatchers feed the nestlings. While the female does most of the incubation, the male feeds her with insect delicacies so reinforcing the pair bond.

192 Waxwings are gregarious winter visitors and when hedgerow fruit becomes scarce they invade gardens to look for berries.

dunnock in colour, but its behaviour and profile makes the **spotted flycatcher** unmistakable. Using the rotary line and adjacent lilac bush as a perch, the flycatcher sits bolt upright, surveying the open space across the lawn to the flowerbeds. Without warning it darts high over the lawn, loops the loop and returns to the rotary line to resume its upright, watchful stance. The flycatcher is actually doing what its name suggests – plucking flies and other insects out of the air and returning to its perch to eat them and watch for the next passing prey.

Long after the chiff-chaffs, willow warblers, swallows and other summer visitors have arrived, this delightful, rather drab bird turns up from South Africa; many of our summer warblers overwinter south of the Sahara in West Africa and therefore do not have as far to fly. The long-distance migration is done in regularly fall victim to the bird towards the end of the summer. The sweet-pea trellis next to the buddleia is used as a perch and many of the butterflies and hoverflies hardly leave the blooms before the click of the snapping beak can be heard.

Garden birdwatching is absorbing throughout the year: residents like the blackbird and blue tit, with their singing or acrobatic ability, bring interest to nearly every garden, and the summer-visiting spotted flycatcher loops and darts across the quieter gardens, frustrating the unobservant gardener with its soft 'tzee' notes delivered inconspicuously from a high branch.

If your garden is in eastern England, and especially if you are near the coast, you may be lucky to have one of the rarest winter visitors to Britain feeding close to the house. The **waxwing** is a beautifully marked bird about the size of a starling (18 cm/7 in) and breeds in the taiga which is the sub-Arctic, marshy, coniferous and birch-forested area of Scandinavia and northern Russia. They appear in Britain, infrequently and unpredictably, but once seen they are never forgotten, with their pink-brown underparts and brown back, together with grey rump and tail which gradually shades to black with a distinct yellow tip. The under-tail coverts are rich chestnut brown, as is the forehead, which shades into pinkish brown towards the crown where the feathers extend into an attractive, distinctive crest. Waxwings compel you to examine them closely with binoculars. The head is intricately marked with a black chin-patch and eye-stripe, which begins on top of the beak and extends to behind the crest, and there are white markings below the eye and near the base of the lower mandible. The wings are mainly black, with white patches and margins, and the name is derived from the secondaries, which have red tips resembling sealing wax.

This is one of the species which serious birdwatchers, called 'twitchers' or 'birders', travel from all over the country to observe and from its magnificent plumage it is easy to see why. Often it is one of these birdwatchers watching the Norfolk coastline in winter who first observes the waxwings flying overhead, their long pointed wings and characteristic, square-shaped tail being sufficient to activate the grapevine. The birds are rarely vocal but a feeble, high-pitched trill supports its Russian name of 'reedpipe bird' and is further evidence that the waxwings have arrived,

In their breeding habitats waxwings feed on an insectivorous diet, which is chiefly mosquitoes, but it is their passion for autumn berries, especially rowan or mountain ash, which causes them to leave the inhospitable taiga and disperse across Europe. Whilst breeding, waxwings keep in small flocks after the young have fledged, but in late summer these family flocks unite and begin feeding on local berries, the supply of which can rapidly become exhausted. From late September and throughout October the large waxwing flocks reach southern Finland, but it may be as late as December, if the berry crop in northern Finland was sufficiently good to keep the birds there. Totally dependent on the crops of berries, the waxwings move further south all the time, and some even reach Italy and Greece by Christmas, but generally it is between December and February when they arrive in Britain.

Feeding in your back garden, waxwings give the impression of being extremely tame, but the reason why they move from the coast into towns and suburbia is that earlier migrants like redwings and fieldfares have plundered all the berries in the countryside; so the waxwings visit churchyards looking for juniper berries and back gardens for cotoneaster, pyracantha and rowan berries. Cotoneaster berries attracted a flock of more than 400 waxwings to feed on a roadside bank in Aberdeen, one December morning in 1970, immediately after crossing the North Sea. An invasion arriving in Britain varies from half a dozen birds to over ten thousand in the winter of 1965–6, which coincidentally followed a poor berry crop throughout Scandinavia. During the 1965 invasion, only isolated pockets of Britain were fortunate to receive large numbers of waxwings at once, and the thousand early arrivals which converged on Lincolnshire soon dispersed as they moved across the country. The further west they fly the smaller the flocks become, but flocks of over one hundred birds are sometimes recorded in Ireland; good years for Britain's bird-watchers included 1930–1 and 1956–7. In 1987 in Norfolk at least five were seen towards late January on the main road near Cromer, feeding on bright red viburnum berries, and an additional six birds were seen in Sheringham: not even the Arctic conditions and 1.8 m/6 ft snow drifts covering much of Norfolk at the time were enough to keep the birdwatchers away.

If you are one of the chosen few to have waxwings feeding in your garden, savour the moment, because it is a chance in a lifetime to watch individuals in the flock stretching and straining for a prized berry. Despite their size, they are enchanting acrobats, hanging upside down and fluttering around a berry cluster or enjoying a piece of apple hung in the tree (**192**). With this temptation, the waxwings sometimes remain in the vicinity of a garden for over a week, but those that survive our winter will have left by the end of April, to return to their breeding grounds in the sub-Arctic forests in the far north.

ORCHARDS The berries the waxwings so eagerly devour are only the wild fruits of the countryside, or those of cultivated garden shrubs, but for centuries man has grown his own fruit. The hard and bitter crab apple was the only native apple, growing wild in woodlands and hedges, before the Romans introduced the first cultivated apple in the first century BC. The first commercial orchards had their origins in Norman Britain when monks grew apples and kept bees to help raise funds for their monasteries and abbeys and many of the ancient strains of fruit popular in the thirteenth century are recorded in ancient monastic tomes.

During the Industrial Revolution as the population grew, so did the demand for fruit, and apple, pear, cherry and plum orchards became a familiar part of the country, frequently adjacent to farmyards but also attached to large country estates. The Victorian railway network, offering cheap, efficient transport from the orchards to towns and cities, caused further expansion of the fruit-growing industry and commercial orchards moved further out into the country, especially to the south and south-west where warmer climates improved the chances of the fruit ripening. At one time, Kent produced 25 per cent of all Britain's eating apples and almost the same proportion of cherries; Worcestershire was equally famous for apples, pears and plums, where they grew on well-drained soils, protected from late frosts which are fatal for newly set fruit.

Ancient orchards were managed differently from the modern-day commercial orchard. Tall, wizened and gnarled trees, with sheep, pigs and chickens feeding on the grass beneath, are rare wildlife havens of antiquity, for today popular strains of trees are grafted on to dwarf root stock which grow to a maximum of 2.4 m/8 ft tall, for easy picking; they bear fruit when they are only three years old, with continuous production for several decades. The old-style orchard trees, full of holes in damaged trunks, provided nest sites for tree sparrow, starling, blue tit, and owl.

The woodpecker-like **wryneck (189)** was common during Victorian times in south-east England, with orchard tree holes being its favourite nesting habitat. Even forty years ago, wrynecks were widespread in traditional orchards, but since these have been grubbed out and replaced with dwarf, slender and smooth-trunked trees, the wryneck has become virtually extinct as a breeding bird. The exceptions are a few isolated colonies in south-eastern orchards and in recent years Scandinavian immigrants have begun to colonise the central Scottish Highlands, where it was absent in its heyday anyway. Most birdwatchers see this species on migration on the east coast from August to October, but a few may see it in an old orchard feeding on ants in the grass.

In rural areas and the outer suburban regions, where there are larger houses, small orchards can still be found which are not highly commercial ventures, but are haphazardly managed to produce enough fruit for the house owner, and in good seasons, a surplus supply to sell on the roadside or to the local greengrocers. Other gardens of houses built in the 1940s always had several fruit trees planted, which will now be mature and bark-encrusted after over forty years of growth. These are the sheltered sanctuaries where sprigs of parasitic mistletoe grow, after a bird has transferred the seed into a crevice in the bark of an apple tree whilst wiping its beak. The hoary boughs are laden with blossom in May, bees drone as they collect the plentiful supply of pollen and, where branches have broken away or natural holes occur, blue tits and great tits build their nests. Goldfinches, so typically birds of wasteland and scrubland in late summer and autumn, build their nests high in the outer branches of apple and pear trees, whereas the less popular bullfinch rarely nests in the orchard but visits it in early spring. A solitary bird can remove twenty-five buds a minute, and between them a pair can strip out thousands of precious buds in a day's feeding. It is probably because man desires weed-free orchards and arable land and has removed food providing hedgerows that the bullfinch has to supplement its winter diet of seeds with succulent buds, because herbicides have drastically reduced the amount of weed seeds the bullfinch can feed upon during the winter and hungry wild birds soon search for alternative food, else they die.

In the least disturbed and most overgrown of country garden orchards, the shy hawfinch nests, building a platform of twigs within the branches of old pear or apple trees, and preferring to use its massive bill on cherry stones. Only a lucky few gardeners see this bird close to their house, since the majority of the breeding population hides away in mixed woodland where beech and hornbeams grow (page 30). However, the equally elusive, sparrow-sized, lesser spotted woodpecker frequently drills its nest under a branch of an old apple tree and its high-pitched call and weak drumming on a dead branch are as often heard in an old orchard as they are in deciduous woodland and copses.

Fruit is a significant part of the diet of many birds, especially in winter, when most of the berries are fully ripe but the **mistle thrush**, with its grey-brown upper plumage and buff-white belly covered in dark spots, is particularly fond of apples, plums and cherries, which tempt it into the orchard during summer. At 27 cm/10½ in it is the largest British thrush but it is not so familiar as the song thrush (page 23). The total breeding population is around 500,000 pairs, spread across the British Isles, but it is rare in the Outer Hebrides and totally absent from Orkney and Shetland. At one time the mistle thrush was only a southern bird but it seems that with the expansion of the fruit-growing industry, it followed the orchards and today the large, quiet traditional orchards and fruit trees in suburban gardens are still the favourite haunts. It considers mistletoe berries a real delicacy, hence the bird's name, and in winter this is the fruit which draws the mistle thrush into the orchard, long before it roams the surrounding countryside for rowan and hawthorn berries, and steals holly, yew and ivy berries from village and town churchyards. It also enjoys worms and insects, feeding on garden lawns, but preferring the longer, more neglected grass of the orchard where it forages close to the trees, ever watchful of all that is around it: although they are more bold than the song thrush, with an air of assertiveness, they are constantly wary of danger especially from hunting sparrowhawks.

Whilst birdwatching in the different habitats throughout Britain, you will gradually learn how attractive the songs of the thrush family are, from the piping whistle of the ring ousel on the moorlands and warbling call of the redstart in the sessile oakwoods to the pure melodious and melancholy songs of the song thrush and robin in the back garden or woodland glade. The mistle thrush has a more restricted song than the aptly named song thrush, but the loud, clear, full song delivered from January to June carries a long way and the quality and richness more than make up for any indication of monotony.

From the far end of the orchard the loud rattling alarm call of the mistle thrush carries through the trees. One of the pair dives from a branch towards the ground, only to rise from the thick patch of grass and perch on an apple tree, where it continues its alarm note. The cause of this commotion is a stoat, which slinks out of the grass, turns to look at the thrush and then leaps away at speed towards the old stone boundary wall. Once satisfied that the danger has gone, the pair of mistle thrushes continue with their courtship, which involves much splaying of tails to reveal the white feathers on the outer margins, and the female often flicks and quivers her wings. Towards the end of the breeding season, in March, the mistle thrushes were in family groups, but in October and November these flocks dispersed. This particular pair claimed their orchard territory long before Christmas and, as February faded, the female had already begun constructing her nest, high in a fork of one of the apple trees about 7 m/20 ft up **(190)**. Dry grass, roots and moss form the main structure of the deep, well-built nest and mud is used for bonding the layers together, but unlike that of the song thrush it is lined with grass rather than mud.

During the whole nesting period mistle thrushes defend their nest fearlessly, attacking magpies, jays, cats and humans who approach too closely. This behaviour remains constant during the second brood and when the fledglings are first out of the nest.

Despite this aggressive but laudible behaviour in defence of their nest and young, the mistle thrush is still popular with man, who seems willing to share some of his fruit crop in exchange for the company of this attractive thrush. It also colonises recreation fields, golf courses and large open parks.

PARKS

Fortunately many of Britain's cities and towns can claim to have at least one park and some can actually boast several extensive parks, which are not only visited by hundreds of people at weekends, but are also extremely rich in birdlife. One such is Longmoor, an area of wetland and surrounding heathland in Sutton Park, near Birmingham; another is Richmond Park where 1,011 ha/2,500 acres of rough grassland and woodland form the largest 'green wildlife island' in London, totally isolated from open countryside by suburbia. Many much smaller parks dotted around the country are a mixture of mature trees, hawthorn bushes and brambles, contrasting with ornamental shrubs and managed flowerbeds. Birds survive in these parks and there is proof that even with regular human visitors a municipal amenity area can be an important bird sanctuary. Local authority parks departments have been advised by conservation societies that dead timber and rotting leaves are not unbearable eyesores but invaluable sources of food, offering potential nest sites for birds like green woodpecker, nuthatch, treecreeper, dunnock and great tit, which are as much at home in parkland as they are in their more natural habitat.

Parkland was developed as early as the seventeenth and eighteenth centuries, when it was considered stylish to create a sophisticated rural atmosphere in the centre of a city or town. Charles I and Charles II were particularly active in this ambition, although they preferred to create classical public open spaces like St James's Park and Covent Garden, which eventually led to the creation of imposing Georgian squares. It was the Victorians with their enjoyment of visible affluence who designed and created many of the present-day parks, purchasing land and converting it into public gardens for the working classes who were allowed to lose themselves in a world of peace and green plants before returning to the grime and drudgery of work and the reality of their poverty.

In Victorian times the gardens were always perfectly maintained, to the point of being clinical habitats with no wild area where wildlife could survive. To a certain extent these attitudes prevailed until 1939, with municipal gardeners and park keepers restoring concrete pathways and weeding every flowerbed. After the Second World War, manpower was directed to other jobs and, due to rising labour costs, methods of maintenance changed towards the use of herbicides and insecticides, which kept the weeds controlled, but prevented natural wildlife colonisation. Fortunately, today parks have become more natural. Hyde Park and Holland Park are both examples of parks in which areas have been handed back to nature with a minimum amount of park keeping and disturbance, enabling birds to feed and nest happily in the town. As with every habitat created by man, and even those altered by him, the way in which the park is managed determines the plants and animals which are to be found there, although the position and size of the park and amount of leaf cover are also critical factors. Wandsworth Common, in south London, and Linn Park, Glasgow, are two examples where parks authorities promote wildlife and the growth of natural plants and consequently both have a varied birdlife. But for every single park which is managed sympathetically to encourage wildlife colonisation, there are many more still maintained as an assemblage of foreign plants and shrubs where all leaves are removed and burnt, rotten branches are automatically considered a public danger and are lopped off, and dead wood on the ground is immediately cleared up. These parks have a poor leaf-litter invertebrate fauna and few British broad-leaf trees, and as a result warblers and blue tits find them largely inhospitable. Conversely the dense evergreen foliage popularised in these parks attracts song thrush, blackbird and greenfinch to breed and the ubiquitous privet hedge is a favourite with nesting dunnock.

Birdwatchers should not ignore their local parks. Wherever there is a patch of green in suburbia, species move in to colonise and some of the rarities and unusual species found in the open country turn up in urban parks when they are least expected, especially if a supply of water is available. Unexpected bonuses include the hand-tame nuthatches in Kew Gardens and the nocturnal hunting tawny owl, but even the repetitive, descending trill of the chaffinch, heard drifting across the park in summer is worth attention.

Chaffinches begin singing in February and their song is familiar not only in parks and gardens but also in hedgerows, broad-leaf woods, especially oak (page 18), and scrubland. In winter when they flock with greenfinches and yellowhammers on farmland, feeding on spilt grain, they are silent. They are our most common finch and one of the most numerous birds: 5–7 million pairs nest throughout the British Isles except Shetland, and they are very localised in the Hebrides.

The male chaffinch, which gives his presence away with a 'pink-pink' call, is a beautiful bird in breeding plumage (**193**) with a dusky-pink breast and darker pink back, blue-grey head and nape and black-brown wings marked with white on the shoulder. The upper tail feathers match the wings but their outer edges are white. All the white markings show up well, either when the bird is at rest or in flight. The female shows the double white wing-bar markings, but she is otherwise marked for camouflage on the nest, with a mixture of soft brown and beige plumage with paler underparts. Both sexes have an attractive moss-green rump which is identifiable as they fly away from you in an undulating movement. This feature distinguishes them from the similarly marked brambling, with whom they fly in beechwoods during the winter (page 32).

In most parks in February, you will hear resident male chaffinches announcing their territories by singing from a song-perch high in the trees. The song occasionally stops as both birds chase each other through the trees in courtship flight, with the male pausing periodically to fan his tail and flutter his wings suggestively. In early April the female builds one of the neatest and most beautiful nests of all British birds. She weaves grass and rootlets together, adds copious supplies of moss, lines the cup with feathers and hair, then decorates it with lichen or silver-birch bark, as if putting the finishing touches to a wedding cake. The completed nest is rivalled only by the mossy, lichen dome of the long-tailed tit (page 75). The female chaffinch incubates her five eggs in May, whilst the male feeds her on small snails and seeds. During summer the invertebrate content of the adult's diet is particularly high for a finch, but the slender beak is perfectly shaped for both an insect and seed diet. The nestlings are fed exclusively on insects immediately after hatching, for instant protein, and gradually weaned by both adults on to a mixed diet which they maintain once they become independent.

Parkland birds are soon identified as those who prefer trees and shrubs to nest in and open grassland to feed on, but if mature hedgerows and small copses stretch across the park as well, listen out for the **turtle dove (194)**, which arrives from Africa at about the time the chaffinches are egg-laying and incubating. Because they prefer warm, dry habitats, turtle doves favour woodland margins, orchards and churchyards, but their liking for fumitory and other wild-flower seeds has encouraged them to colonise the more natural, sympathetically managed park where weedkillers are rarely used. Within these four habitats, a total of over 100,000 pairs breed, mostly confined to eastern England, with small colonies in the West Country and east Wales and rare sightings in Scotland and Ireland.

Sitting on top of a telegraph pole along the margin of the park, the 27-cm/10½-in dove makes its soft 'turr, turr, turr' call, a familiar summer sound, then suddenly it takes off, climbs rapidly on quick-flicking wings and glides back down in a circle towards the pole with its tail fanned on the descent. Its mate is perched in the tree near by and together they take off, flying fast across the park in a twisting flight until they disappear into a distant hedgerow where they are building the frail nest, forming a scanty platform of twigs. They use a variety of hedgerow shrubs, like hawthorn and elder, and the nest is always low down, sometimes only a few metres above the ground; here the two eggs are laid in May. Like all doves and pigeons, the young, or squabs, are fed on regurgitated pigeon's milk (page 35) which is rich in protein. They fledge within three weeks, enabling the parents to rear a further two or three broods, if the season is warm, before migrating south in August.

Turtle doves are probably the most attractively marked of their family with distinct chestnut upperparts covered in black patches and a pink-tinged breast with black and white neck-patches. They are a pleasure to watch in parkland on a warm summer's day. They are not guaranteed in all town parks, but then neither is any species of bird, since habitat conditions and natural distribution make some birds common in a particular town or area, but rare and retiring elsewhere. Some towns, like Watford, have excellent parks on their doorstep: in Cassiobury Park, on the banks of the River Gade, turtle dove regularly breed, together with stock dove, collared dove, cuckoo, kestrel, mallard, great spotted woodpecker, nuthatch, treecreeper, blackcap, willow warbler and many more species. Clearly the diverse range of birds demands an equally wide range of habitats which, with a mixture of woodland, scrub, wetland and rough parkland this excellently managed park offers; yet it is only 17 km/10½ miles from St Paul's Cathedral. The more urban and suburban parks of this nature that man is prepared to create, the closer birds and other wildlife will move to the town centre for him to enjoy.

193

193 Chaffinches are the commonest finch in the British Isles, as much at home in deciduous woods as they are in parks and gardens.

194

194 The lazy, soporific, purring call of the turtle dove is one of the memorable bird calls of summer.

CHURCHYARDS AND CEMETERIES

Throughout the British Isles, towns and cities expand from year to year and encroach on the countryside, which has already suffered from intensive farming methods, industrial growth and the development of roads, such as the new Okehampton by-pass, through areas of outstanding natural beauty and National Parks, built purely for convenience without considering the wild, beautiful and ever-decreasing countryside. The countless thousands of ancient churchyards in the British Isles are therefore especially sacred. Separated from the twentieth century by an old stone wall, yew hedge, or fence, they are fascinating as pieces of land left largely unspoilt, a virtual museum of what the countryside used to be like.

Churchyards are found in every habitat, from rocky seashore and moorland to chalk downland, heathland and deciduous wood, and as centuries have passed they have become important unofficial nature reserves, many of them encompassing a variety of habitats inside their boundaries. Within half an acre of one Dyfed churchyard, there is grassland-heath, scrubland, woodland copses, wetland and river, all with their corresponding variety of wildlife. With 10,000 churches and over 40 cathedrals built in medieval times alone, each with their own churchyard, today there is about 8,000 ha/20,000 acres of quiet birdwatching countryside to be explored, often right in the middle of suburbia. Here churchyards offer a haven for wildlife surrounded by factories, houses and shopping centres, providing a sharp contrast with their surroundings. Birdwatchers who visit churchyards regularly have in the past been rewarded by the sight of crossbill, black redstart, waxwing and, in one Suffolk churchyard, the rare nutcracker, which is exclusively a bird of passage. In Witton Cemetery in Birmingham and churchyards in Shropshire and Norfolk, grey partridges actually nest and feed, seeking a retreat from the countryside, where intensive agricultural methods have caused their decline (page 82).

To capture the New Year beauty of churchyards, they are best visited a few weeks after Christmas when early hazel catkins and snowdrops are blooming. Much later in the year barn owls can be seen floating over the grass of some West Country churchyards hunting for shrews and voles in the long grass. The atmosphere in Martyr Worthy churchyard in Hampshire is indescribable as two nightingales duet into the night with the River Itchen meandering along close by.

The Saxons from the sixth century onwards built most of the original rural churches, but by 1086 many of these wooden buildings had been replaced by thousands of stone churches, built near the village centre. A boundary marks the hallowed burial ground, which has been reclaimed from the surrounding meadowland and which today, although managed to control the plant growth, has never been sprayed or fertilised; many country and suburban churches are surrounded by relic ancient haymeadows, containing hundreds of wild flowers.

Unfortunately some churchyards are being tidied up: ground is levelled and grave mounds, headstones and kerbs are removed because the modern gang mower cannot easily cope with these obstructions. The oasis habitat and ancient flowers are being destroyed by weedkillers, threatening in time the very essence of the churchyard itself. Mercifully the majority of ancient churchyards are being managed sympathetically and motor mowers are used only in some areas, and the scythe used wherever possible. By delaying the cut to the end of June, it is possible to keep an attractive sward of grass, and the abundant insect life feeding, breeding and sheltering in the grass attracts many birds into the churchyard. Song thrush, robin, starling, pied wagtail and great tit are all regular visitors, and wherever meadow ants build their colonies, the green woodpecker flies in to feed. The blackbird remains one of the most common churchyard birds: perhaps it sees the habitat as a particularly quiet garden, where it is already twice as common than in its traditional woodlands.

Throughout the centuries rich parishioners donated and planted trees in their churchyards, and cypresses, rhododendrons and laurels were mixed with native oak, beech, lime, elm and holly. Traditional rookeries in churchyard elms used to be a regular sight in Britain, but with the loss of these trees, the rooks have transferred to the upper branches of beech and lime, although stock dove, tawny owl and great spotted woodpecker all nest in suitable lower branches and decaying trunks. Lower still, in the thick scrub, bullfinch, blackcap and chaffinch nest. The ancient, gnarled yews, typical of most churchyards, are the favourite nest sites for goldcrest, coal tit, mistle thrush and green finch.

Out of the lichen-encrusted churchyard wall, a wren whirrs away up into the yew tree to forage for insects for its brood. Each year somewhere in this hollow wall, wren, blue tit and spotted flycatcher build their nests, the latter using the grave headstones as feeding perches, and they all successfully raise their broods away from the dangers of suburbia. Churches themselves vary: whereas Norman and Saxon churchyards are more interesting for those birds which prefer to nest in holes in walls, the intricate architecture of Gothic and Renaissance churches provides more nesting sites than earlier churches and certainly than those built more recently. In the towers and spires, around the grotesque gargoyles, and wherever a stone ledge, cranny or architrave allows, pigeon, starling, house sparrow and house martin nest. Many of the bell towers today have grilles over their sound windows to prevent kestrel, barn owl and jackdaw from nesting, but some vergers are sympathetic towards these visitors; in other cases the grilles eventually rust away and shortage of funds prevents their being replaced. In these innumerable cases the wily jackdaw is never slow in taking advantage of a noisy but protected nest site, and it is commonly seen around the spires and bell towers of town and country churches.

Flying around the impressive spire of the Church of St John the Baptist in Burford, Oxfordshire, a flock of **jackdaws** barrage the air with their high-pitched, metallic 'tchack' calls. On rapidly beating wings, they survey the surrounding village but prefer to glide, soar and dive around the church, occasionally disappearing inside the spire where they nest. Jackdaw flocks range in size from a dozen to over a thousand but outside the breeding season are sometimes mixed with rooks, starlings and gulls. Even in the breeding season, which begins in mid-April, after a courtship which involves the male strutting about with his crown feathers and wings raised, jackdaws are colonial birds. They seek tree holes (**198**), rabbit burrows, cavities in cliff faces, chimneys, empty buildings and churches, where they build nests of twigs and grass, thickly lining the cup with softer grass, wool and hair. Like the rooks, jackdaws return to traditional nest sites each year, adding new material to the original nest annually, until it eventually becomes a massive, untidy structure, which alone is a good reason for many churches taking preventive action to stop jackdaws nesting in their tower.

As the jackdaw hunts for insects, larvae, worms , snails and seeds, the churchyard birdwatcher gets the best opportunity to see its black plumage with silver-grey cheeks and nape, and binoculars reveal the blue and green gloss on the head, wings and tail, and the alert blue-grey eye, short pointed bill and powerful black legs. Compared to the rook and carrion crow, the jackdaw is small and is not so common: there are only around half a million pairs in the British Isles and it is rarest in north-west Scotland.

The young, slightly browner jackdaws grow healthy on their high-protein diet and after fledging, they form family flocks and learn to gyrate and twist around the church and village buildings, flying out into the surrounding countryside to search for invertebrates on arable land. Throughout the winter jackdaws feed in flocks on open grassland and farmland, removing a large number of agricultural pests from the soil, but as spring approaches they disperse and head for their traditional breeding site and favourite, hospitable churchyard.

The cool porches of many churches have their resident sparrows and in a few rural parishes swallows still nest on the darkened beams. The lychgate, the roofed gate at the entrance of many churchyards, is another favourite nesting site where spotted flycatchers and blue tits build their nests if the swallows have not got there first.

Whereas in the nineteenth century the rural churchyards of small towns and villages always seemed to be able to cope with the burial of the deceased, those situated in cities could not: in highly populated and industrialised areas, when cholera epidemics began, 50,000 people died in London alone each year, and local churchyards, which were really village churchyards swallowed up by London's growth, became overcrowded and a serious health hazard. The same problem was occurring all over Britain and the first cemetery, officially recognised as a burial ground away from the church, was opened in Norwich in 1819, followed by the establishment of separate protestant and catholic cemeteries in Belfast. Other major cities followed suit, before London, after an Act of Parliament in 1832, opened Kensal Green Cemetery, in what was then a small suburban village of London. Thereafter Victorians dealt with the building of cemeteries with the same enthusiasm as that with which they approached parks, public gardens, railway networks, and water supplies: by 1841, there was a ring of cemeteries around London at Highgate, Tower Hamlets, Brompton, Abney Park, Nunhead and Norwood, all situated in rural settings or private grounds, away from the city centre. Because competition between cemetery-building companies became severe, cemeteries had to be designed in an appealing way to encourage people to want to be buried there; consequently, like the gardens of the aristocracy, the cemeteries were laid out with lawns, pathways and herbaceous beds, and planted with foreign shrubs and evergreens, designed to give the cemetery an atmosphere of peace. These cemeteries were popular in their day and were run as a prosperous business with dozens of staff to maintain the gardens alone, but slowly their popularity became their downfall, as they began to fill up and spare burial land became more difficult to acquire. The trees and dense shrubbery grew and required further, regular maintenance and as the tree seeds produced seedlings and began colonising areas still set aside for burial, it became obvious that without an increase in labour forces these cemeteries could become overgrown and wild places.

The two world wars were finally responsible for the neglect of these cemeteries, because with no regular gardeners, the plantlife took over. Today Highgate, Tower Hamlets, Nunhead and Abney Park in north London are completely wild sites, where nature has turned the marble and granite monuments and tombstones into an ivy-clad haven for birds and wildlife. Sycamore, ash and birch saplings have grown into bird-sheltering undergrowth and woodland flowers thrive.

The extremely varied birdlife in these cemeteries is similar to that of a town or city park (page 218) but suburban birds have colonised too. Early in the morning the cemetery air is filled with the flutey song of blackbird, song thrush and robin and wherever the brambles, nettles and elderberry form an advancing jungle, the diminutive wren scolds any live human visitor. Later in the day starlings, feral- and woodpigeons feed amongst the tombstones and in summer, swift and house martin have learnt to swoop for the insects rising on the air currents from the grassy expanses.

Nunhead Cemetery, covering more than 24 ha/60 acres, has some areas of mature woodland, where native trees stand alongside imported turkey oak, cypress and ginkgo. Here in summer, chiff-chaffs nest close to the city of London and as dusk falls over this delightful wilderness, the wavering call of a suburban tawny owl floats across the cemetery. Many of these cemeteries have their own specialities: black redstarts (page 226) have nested at Brompton Cemetery and the songs of blackcap, chiff-chaff and robin mix with the attractive descending warbles and trills of the willow warbler in the spinneys of Abney Park Cemetery.

Victorian cemeteries in their time were considered attractive, inviting places in which to be buried, but today for the city and town wildlife they are even more attractive and important for the survival of many species. Many of them are publicly owned and others are managed by conservation groups, like the Friends of the Highgate Cemetery who control the rapid colonisation of sycamore and birch to make sure that other less robust shrubs and plants, important for birds, are able to grow. Highgate is open to the public and any birdwatcher visiting London should make a point of seeing this spectacle where the impenetrable jungle, which had choked the resting place of 166,000 people, has been skilfully cleared, thinned and landscaped, after forty years of neglect. More than one hundred wild flower species now colonise the cemetery, and the birds still have their ivy, brambles, hawthorns and evergreens, providing shelter, food and breeding sites; since the controlled management, the breeding populations have actually increased.

Whether a large, neglected or conservation-managed cemetery, an oasis in the middle of cities and urban encroachment, or a small country churchyard filled with shrubs, wild flowers and grasses, where the organ and chiming bells seem to mix perfectly with singing hedge sparrows and chaffinches, sacred grounds need preserving. Many of them cannot be managed solely for wildlife, but most parishioners and church councils

196

197

198

196 The familiar song of the chiff-chaff has become a regular sound in overgrown churchyards.

197 Familiar to both yards and gardens, adult male blackbirds are characterised by their orange bill and yellow eye-ring. Young

males retain a black bill for their first winter.

198 Jackdaws like derelict buildings and churches around which they constantly fly, but their favourite nest site is a hole in a tree.

195 Churchyards have increasingly become important sanctuaries for urban birdlife including the greenfinch and bluetit.

are willing to encourage wildlife in their churchyards, especially as increased public awareness towards conservation in churchyards has reassured them that wildlife conservation does not mean a totally unruly wild churchyard, and that selective pruning of trees and shrubs at the right time of year and the retention of wild corners with brambles and nettles will encourage hedge sparrow, goldfinch, yellowhammer and even whitethroat to stay and breed.

Churchyard and Victorian cemetery conservation has become even more popular during the last ten years and as the habitats of the British Isles and the birdlife they contain are under constant threat, often with the full awareness of the Government, these places of human rest may become more important for birds and other wildlife, as they become valuable living sanctuaries too.

WASTELAND AND RUBBISH TIPS

WASTELAND In 1699 the Oxford ragwort was brought to Oxford Botanic Gardens from Mount Etna in Sicily. The wind-blown seeds took a century to colonise the city walls, and in one 'giant leap' for plantlife reached the track of the Great Western Railway, which was opened between Oxford and London in 1838. Once established on the clinker, which was similar to the volcanic ash of Mount Etna, its dispersal was phenomenal, reaching London in 1867, Edinburgh in 1954 and Belfast in 1964; and today Oxford ragwort is a primary indicator of wasteland, acting like a beacon to birds although the cannibar moth caterpillars which feed on its leaves are poisonous, and regurgitated by any species of bird making its first attempt to eat them.

Even the most urban person knows the yellow flower, because wherever you live, there is a patch of wasteland – an abandoned industrial site, an old builders' yard, a one-time corporation car park or a piece of no-man's land between houses where people walk their dogs and illegally dump garden and household rubbish. Such areas are considered by society to be neglected and derelict waste ground, an untidy area of the landscape best ignored. Even the latin name of the colonising Oxford ragwort, *Senecio squalidus*, suggests these areas are unkept and squalid; but for each one of the 10,000–160,000 wind-dispersed seeds the plant produces annually, they are important sites. And as pressure on the more attractive countryside grows, conservation societies are campaigning that wasteland should not be misused or over-developed, because it represents a unique, important habitat which, properly maintained, could become an area of value to local inhabitants and wildlife right in the middle of the country's conurbations.

We have seen how cities and towns continually grow at their edges where new houses and offices are built, but at the same time some areas of the original city centre fall into disrepair and derelict wasteland develops. Some areas of wasteland in London and other cities developed as a result of the vast Victorian railway network being modernised and streamlined to make it more efficient; British Rail own countless disused railway sidings, depots and goods yards, which have remained idle since steam trains were phased out in the 1960s and today are some of the largest areas of undisturbed wasteland. Much of this land is valuable building land and British Rail are gradually realising their assets by selling some of it to property developers and construction companies, for luxury houses, offices and business premises, so delaying encroachment and reducing development pressure on the outer suburbs and green-belt areas for a little longer. Paradoxically, however, development of inner-city and town wasteland is destroying some of the few wildlife havens found in the concrete jungles, and urban wildlife trusts, conservation societies and even a few enthusiastic individuals are campaigning to buy or protect certain prime wasteland sites in an attempt to 'green' the cities. As recently as February 1987, there was the well-publicised case of Lester Holloway, a sixteen-year-old schoolboy who saved a piece of wasteland from destruction in the heartland of Shepherd's Bush. The area, because of its proximity to the prison, is called the Scrubs and includes Scrubs Wood. Owned by British Rail, it was about to be changed into a depot for Channel Trust Trains. Having birdwatched on the wasteland for twelve years, Lester Holloway realised its conservation value: on the 1.6-km/1-mile stretch of threatened land he had recorded 350 plant species, 20 butterfly species, foxes, lizards, hedgehogs and rabbits, all breeding, and 26 species of birds, including rare winter migrants like the waxwing (page 216). After compiling a report, lobbying his local MP, involving the London Wildlife Trust and gaining the support of the local Tenants' Association, he persuaded the Channel Tunnel Consortium, British Rail and the Government that the Scrubs could well be one of 'London's best undiscovered nature reserves' and on this piece of land at least, no further work will be considered without the involvement of Hammersmith and Ealing Councils and the London Wildlife Trust.

Mankind has always created waste and wasteland in the course of progress, whether building bigger and better houses, or the mining of fossil fuels and mineral reserves. Before the Industrial Revolution any exploitation of the earth's natural resources was on a reduced scale and abandoned mining sites, for example, soon became recolonised by natural vegetation, healing the scars on the surface. However, from 1800, the Industrial Revolution demanded huge supplies of coal to smelt iron, slate, quarried stone and clay for bricks, with the result that spoil heaps, worked-out quarries and industrial waste tips occurred across the country at a rate faster than nature could claim them back. The Industrial Revolution created wasteland in specific areas of Britain, but man's continued progress during the twentieth century has vastly increased the production of wasteland, which can be categorised either as damaged land or dormant land.

Damaged land is more difficult to convert to productive land because it includes the wasteland of the manufacturing, chemical and building industries; the sand and gravel pits of the south east (page 158); the clay-brick pits of Bedfordshire; snow-like, china-clay heaps of Cornwall; and the coal mines, quarries and clinker waste of Wales and the industrial North. Together with all the non-combustible, non-decomposable waste from chemical factories, metal industries and ash from coal-fuelled power stations, the damaged wasteland, which is infertile and toxic (often shaped like miniature mountain ranges), presents a long-term problem. Remarkably, even on these inhospitable scars, some birds colonise: starlings build nests within cavities of shale piles and meadow pipits make use of any piece of scrubland. Disused Welsh quarries offer man-made nesting ledges for a few pairs of chough and the occasional kestrel finds a suitable nesting site on industrial spoil heaps, where it can catch pied wagtails foraging for insect food.

Dormant land is simply wasteland which has been temporarily forgotten, and in some cases was created by the decline of certain industries as product demands and methods of manufacture changed or progressed. When manufacturing industries collapse, so do the service industries, including those involved with transportation. Across Britain there are at least 4,856 ha/12,000 acres of disused railway land; because North Sea Gas was piped on to the supplier direct, the gas industry was left with obsolete sites; and the dock authorities have their own derelict sites, although these are recently becoming prime housing areas of the future.

Collectively wasteland occupies an immense area, about 101 million ha/2½ million acres or almost 5 per cent of the total land surface of Great Britain, with an estimated 100,000

199

199 Easily overlooked, the female black redstart builds her nest on wasteland, railway yards, gasworks and factory sites.

200 One of the most attractive sites on derelict land is the goldfinch pulling seeds from a thistle head.

200

ha/250,000 acres confined to our towns and cities alone. Now that public awareness has been stimulated into appreciating the potential of this land, man has a chance to take the opportunity to reclaim some of it for valuable urban development and preserve the rest for the benefit of wildlife.

Much of the wasteland still found in London is a result of the Second World War, and although some has been reclaimed and built upon, pockets of 'green bombsites' still remain. Birds and other wildlife thrive on these bombsites and they must be thoughtfully developed or preserved in the future.

When, in December 1987, His Royal Highness, the Prince of Wales, made his headline-hitting speech to the Royal Institute of British Architects, condemning the designs and styles of buildings erected on bombsites in London, he was probably not aware of the feeling of support from the man in the street and certainly many conservationists. Like the conservationists, he was concerned that unsympathetic building development, can destroy an area even further, rendering it as much of a barren landscape as it was beforehand. Man has already made two attempts around St Paul's Cathedral. Following the destruction

by the Great Fire of London in 1666, buildings were replaced with larger constructions built of stone, which presented an alien habitat for wildlife typical of parts of today's towns and cities. When these buildings were destroyed during the Second World War, some were replaced with concrete and glass monstrosities, but other bombsite land remains so far undeveloped. The decision just after the war to demolish half-standing buildings for safety reasons left piles of rubble and derelict wasteland which has been untouched ever since, and nature was grateful to take over land unwanted by man.

One of the plants that thrives on this rubble is willowherb. Since each mature plant produces around 80,000 seeds, dispersed on the wind by a feathery wind-sail, it was not long before all the London bombsites were covered in drifts of cerise pink, interspersed with the bright yellow of Oxford ragwort and golden rod. Other plants soon colonised, and evening primrose, which produces up to 30,000 seeds a plant and can remain dormant for forty years before germinating, bloomed across London on the wasteland. Today it is possible to walk on to a small bombsite just off Ludgate Hill, in sight of St Paul's

Cathedral, where on this temporary car park, evening primroses grow on brickwork and blackbird, blue tit and dunnock (hedge sparrow) find suitable nest sites each year.

Perhaps the most common and well-known shrub of bomb sites and other wasteland is buddleia. The wind-dispersed seeds thrive on the barren soil of bombsites and the lime and cement mortar exposed on derelict walls; consequently this native of China now forms dense thickets and sprouts from old walls on all types of wasteland across Britain and Ireland. As wasteland becomes colonised with flowers and shrubs, the insect life increases, attracting the birds, and even while London was being bombed, feral pigeons and house sparrows were beginning to consider the newly created derelict land as possible breeding sites.

The biggest excitement for war-time naturalists was the breeding of a summer visitor called the **black redstart (199)** which used the bombsites as its favourite nesting habitat. There are earlier records of breeding success elsewhere in Britain between 1845 and 1909, and several pairs nested on Sussex cliffs in 1923, but the first pair nesting in London was recorded in 1926, at the Wembley Palace of Engineering, which hosted the Empire Exhibition between 1924–5. When the exhibition was over, many of the buildings were left empty, and from 1926 at least three pairs used the Palace of Engineering as their nest site, until 1941. Other early London nestings include one in 1927 when a pair quite sensibly used the British Museum of Natural History; in 1933 a fearless pair used the Woolwich Arsenal; an academic pair chose the University of London Senate House in 1939; and in May 1940, a divine pair nested in the surrounds of Westminster Abbey. The formation of the bombsites four months later led to their greatest expansion throughout London in future years, and in 1942 they were breeding in the bombed-out Cripplegate region of London.

Perhaps not as colourful as the more common redstart of sessile oakwoods (page 24), the male black redstart, at 14 cm/5½ in is the same size, and when fully mature is still an attractive bird. The upperparts are dark grey, turning to sooty black with age, and the crown, face and breast are particularly dark, with much paler grey underparts; the tail, which is constantly flicked, is typically a deep chestnut red, with a darker central stripe running its length and the under-tail coverts are white. When the male is perched, you can see white wing patches, which are completely absent on the female, who is brownish grey on the upperparts and lighter grey beneath. The fledglings are similarly marked except they are speckled.

Since the breeding population in Britain is still only around one hundred pairs, with 33 per cent still around London, the black redstart is a Schedule I protected species. The real reason for its scarcity is that we are geographically on the northern limit of its natural range. In Europe they are common birds, replacing our robin as the species which tolerates man; they favour moving close to habitation, breeding in the back gardens of towns and villages in Holland and Germany, and in the Mediterranean they feed regularly around the flower-adorned patios and balconies. Throughout its breeding range in Europe and Asia, the black redstart's natural nest sites are rocky, scree-covered mountainside, where it nests in crevices between the crags and boulders. Perhaps because the crumbling buildings and piles of rubble on London's bombsites were so similar to their natural breeding sites, they were able to capitalise on these newly made habitats – although this theory doesn't explain why they chose the City bombsites first.

After the war, black redstarts expanded their range in Britain, spreading to over eleven counties. Today they are still largely confined to man-made sites in the south-east, East Anglia and around Birmingham, with Yorkshire being the most northern county. When some of the bombsites were reclaimed during the 1960s, the black redstarts moved on to other derelict and wasteland sites, and their main breeding grounds now include gasworks, disused railway yards, power stations and industrial sites, where they search for holes in masonry, high ledges or clefts behind rafters and pipes.

Birdwatching for black redstarts can be frustrating because even though you may be at a known site, they are difficult to spot. Males arrive in March and April, and the loud territorial call is a twittering warble, followed by a rapid-firing rattle, which they utter between arrival and June.

Eighteen days after hatching, during which time both adults feed the young on an insect diet, the fledglings leave the nest, allowing the parents to begin their second brood; and towards August the young birds begin moving south, followed in September and October by the adults, who have fed up for the flight on berries, caterpillars, beetles and other small invertebrates, gleaned from around the wasteland.

The black redstart never seems to choose the more attractive parts of the urban environment and even though its strong, purposeful song heard on a summer's day is frequently drowned by industrial and city noise, any bird that made use of the bombsites so successfully should be given the opportunity of protection on wasteland sites elsewhere.

Every birdwatcher has their favourite piece of wasteland other than bombsites: a piece of forgotten land, perhaps with an area of hawthorn, sycamore and ash scrub covering rusting, discarded tins, fridges, old bicycles and other inorganic junk like television sets, where willow warblers call from the scrub each summer and wild flowers from all over the world choose to grow in an unorganised exotic garden.

As the established plants produce seeds, seed-eating birds quickly arrive and linnet, greenfinch and goldfinch feed avidly on the rich and varied supply. From the far side of the piece of wasteland a flock of small (12 cm/4¾ in) birds, uttering a canary-like twittering song, fly towards you in undulating, dancing movements. They circle a small clump of willow scrub, and as they turn, a whitish rump similar to that of a brambling (page 32) or bullfinch (page 83) is visible; but when they land on a mixed patch of groundsel and ragwort, broad yellow bands across their wings and an attractive red, white and black patterned head, clearly identify them as **goldfinches (200)**. At rest, the black tail and wings are easy to see, as are the small white markings on the ends of the wing feathers, but these are only present during spring and early summer and are gradually worn away as the season progresses. With their buff backs, shoulders, flanks and neat bibs, these goldfinches make an attractive sight on small patches of wasteland, which is one of their favourite habitats. Their 'tswitt-wit-wit' song is heard from March until July, sometimes as they fly overhead, or from a perch, like the stem of a thistle or teasel which commonly grow on wasteland.

Their population and distribution in the British Isles seem to fluctuate but around 300,000 pairs nest, mainly in southern England; they are rare in many parts of Scotland and totally absent from the Highlands, which indicates that their distribution is perhaps climatically controlled, because plenty of ideal habitat exists in the north.

You will also identify goldfinches away from wasteland, since they like scrubland, sand-dunes and saltmarshes, country-roadside verges and allotments, wherever there is a supply of suitable seeds. Most often they feed on thistles, their primary seed source, and their long, thin, tweezer-like bill mandibles are perfect for extracting the seeds from inside the barb- and spine-protected seed heads. They are sensible birds, however, and although they eat thistle seeds from June until late autumn, they attack the seed heads on the ground and other loose seeds first, leaving those on the taller stems of the plants until winter, when snow covers over the ground level supply.

Its specially designed and operated bill allows the goldfinch to be the only bird capable of extracting the seeds from deep inside teasel flower heads. Males, with their slightly longer bills, find this even easier than the female birds: watching them flitting from stem to stem and perching agilely on the large dead flower heads is one of the pleasures of wasteland bird-watching. Look closely, too, as they feed on the seeds of small thistles and burdock, because they use their feet in a unique manner, pulling a seed head and stem with their bills towards them, then placing it under their feet like a clamp whilst they extract the seeds.

You may be fortunate enough to have goldfinches nesting in your suburban garden but the male is usually heard displaying in quieter hedgerows, scrubland and waste ground in April. Their territories are small, and being gregarious, several pairs often nest close together in loose colonies. The slow-flapping, wavering song flight with fanned tail is designed to show off the large, striking, gold wing bars to their best advantage. Once a male is secured, the female builds the nest, collecting dead grass, rootlets, hair and wool and she lines it with hair and the soft pappuses of seeds, collecting the material from all over the wasteland. The male makes each journey with the female, but only perches and watches her, never assisting with the carrying of nesting material.

During May four to six eggs are laid in the deep, cupped nest and incubated by the female only for two weeks, during which time the male feeds her at the nest, so that she only needs to leave to drink and exercise; but once the eggs are hatched the male assumes a parental role and helps to feed the brood on a regurgitated mixture of seeds and a few insects, frequently collected a good distance away from the nest. When the breeding season ends, like so many other finches, goldfinches form family flocks called 'charms' and move about the country-side, visiting scrub and wasteland where food is most plentiful. This behaviour also teaches the young birds where good supplies of seeds can be found in the future. Typically, goldfinches are considered resident birds; in fact some remain in Britain throughout the year, but 75 per cent of our summer population, including first-year birds, migrate to wintering grounds in Belgium, Holland, France, Spain and Portugal. Sadly many fall victim to the gun (page 133) or cagebird trapper during their journey south.

The metropolis of London has great wasteland birdwatching potential. Abandoned dockland wharves, south of Tower Bridge at Deptford and at the Isle of Dogs, with their adjoining railway yards, offer rich pickings, with cormorants drying their wings on wooden jetty posts and capstans, and city kestrels nesting in the disused warehouses. To the wasteland birdwatcher, there is little to compare with the fascination of the derelict land further down the Thames, at Canning Town, where ramshackle factories, warehouses and gasometers surround scrub vegetation: here meadow pipit, grey wagtail, red-legged partridge and pheasant breed, and heron and kingfisher fish in overgrown creeks, portraying city wasteland at its best. Throughout London and into its suburbs, there are patches of wasteland left and forgotten, some covering many hectares and others small islands liberally spaced between buildings and discovered by the adventurous few. For the birdwatchers who know them they are unpretentious yet magical places, with goldfinches dancing from thistle to thistle and skylarks hovering overhead. Their future is important for our city and suburban birdlife, so let us hope that many of them, abandoned and forgotten, will remain undisturbed to provide sanctuary for wildlife.

RUBBISH TIPS Towards late afternoon on a warm day in summer, mixed flocks of gulls wheel overhead and starlings catch hundreds of insects as they rise above the ground. A vixen leads her cubs in broad daylight into the shelter of some willow scrub and a heron flies away with what looks like a rat in its bill, landing several hundred metres away in front of a colourful display of sunflowers. Strange-named plants like fat-hen and shepherd's purse are growing commonly and here and there hemp forms healthy plants after months of growth. Five hours later as dusk falls, the quietness is broken by scurrying, chirping colonies of African house crickets and noctule bats flit across the darkening sky.

This is not some strange semi-tropical habitat, but the perimeter of one of Britain's numerous open rubbish tips where the hemp or cannabis grows from seeds discarded with the rest of the dirt from the budgerigar's seed tray and the crickets survive because of the build-up of heat, stored in the decomposing rubbish. Here they scavenge and feed alongside cockroaches and with the bluebottles, houseflies, midges and millions of springtails, attract feeding bats at night and numerous birds during the daytime.

Every year, on average, each person disposes of at least 317.5 kg/700 lb of rubbish, amounting collectively to 700 million paper bags and nearly 400 million aerosol cans annually! Population growth and urban expansion, especially since the nineteenth century, have caused a huge increase in household and domestic refuse, which has to be disposed of by local authorities and requires large areas of land to accommodate it. Since we are all responsible for creating the refuse we must accept that county councils have an ongoing problem and sometimes have to utilise empty gravel and clay pits or disused quarries as controlled-tipping or land-filling sites, rather than site rubbish tips on the outskirts of towns or convert productive agricultural land into open tips. Sometimes this might even mean the loss of an industrial wildlife oasis, but the demand on land for refuse disposal is so great that sacrifices have to be accepted, especially as the alternative has already meant that heathland, saltmarshes and bogland, which are far richer in natural wildlife in the first place, are being destroyed or are under threat from other commercial, urban and industrial pressure.

In controlled-tipping disposal, the refuse is covered periodically in shallow layers of soil which helps to stifle the offensive smells and untidy appearance of open tips, but many councils have converted to more modern and socially acceptable disposal methods whereby rubbish is deposited on huge conveyor belts, selectively sieved and sorted into combustible and non-combustible material, the glass is removed, a huge electromagnet extracts valuable ferrous metals and the remainder is incinerated at around 1000°C. Sometimes organic material is removed before incineration to produce organic compost which eventually produces fertiliser with a commercial value.

On old-style open and controlled-tipping refuse sites the rubbish, organic waste and garden material, which is largely

201 Feeding on fish offal around a canning factory herring gulls are true scavengers and regularly visit rubbish tips well inland in search of food.

grass cuttings, attracts a wide range of birds, other animal life and plants. Situated away from houses and public buildings, these rubbish tips are ornithological islands, with conditions unlike the surrounding land and with a different and concentrated supply of food, often attracting birds in greater numbers and variety of species than are found on the surrounding land for miles around.

On open tips across the country grey and yellow wagtails feed in the water-filled lorry tracks and actually nest; oystercatchers have been known to raise broods on some Essex rubbish tips, and wherever a stable corner of the tip has been covered with soil, and scrub has colonised, meadow pipit, linnet, and greenfinch arrive to feed. Magpies are regular visitors to the more rural rubbish tips, where they turn over the garbage and catch the occasional mouse, vole and young rat.

The **carrion crow**, as it name suggests, is a far more widespread scavenging member of the crow family, frequently visiting tips early in the morning before the vehicles arrive and snapping up the crickets as well as eating household scraps, which supplement its main diet of soil invertebrates.

Away from the rubbish tips, the carrion crow feeds on dead sheep and lambs in upland country (page 96), but in lowland Britain it is responsible for removing more carrion, killed on the roads, than most other species of bird. Its 45-cm/18-in long dark body, with bristle-like feathers around the base of its bill, is well known to all birdwatchers. Carrion crows are solitary birds or move around in pairs, but on rubbish tips non-breeding birds can turn up in large numbers: 250 individuals have been recorded at large tips around London, replacing the ravens and red kites which scavenged in medieval times.

Unlike the rook, which looks similar, carrion crows are solitary nesters and they defend their territories vigorously, building the large twig nest in a hedgerow or copse tree, and lining the deep cup with sheep's wool. Four greenish-blue eggs are laid in April, and incubated for nearly three weeks by the female only. Thereafter both adults feed the youngsters for a further five weeks before they fledge and form family parties until the young decide to disperse to find their own feeding territories. Carrion crows have learnt that there are better scavenging conditions in towns than the countryside and by using the rubbish tips as a regular, easy source of food, they thrive particularly well.

The much smaller, more attractive jackdaw (page 220) also feeds on rubbish tips, where it searches for the plumes of smoke rising from the smouldering rubbish, and flies backwards and forwards through it performing its 'smoke-bath' routine; it also displays this ritual around the chimney pots of suburbia. Since it is nearly always followed by a bout of preening, the smoke bath is thought to be a preliminary stage in plumage maintenance and perhaps after feeding on rubbish tips it is also an effective fumigation control.

Because rubbish tips are not the most popular of birdwatching habitats, it is possible that many interesting species turn up and leave completely undetected. Whooper swans, for instance, have been seen on rubbish tips in southern Ireland. Gulls are by far the most common visitors. Over 5,000 herring gulls regularly visit the two tips in Dublin Bay and since the nineteenth century gulls have replaced crows as the main scavengers of the larger cities. At one time they were regarded as sea birds, but they have become urbanised, moving into the rubbish tips where the regular and varied supply of food has caused them to neglect the coast for this unsavoury inland and man-made habitat. The great black-backed gull was almost entirely a coastal bird and now it is often seen feeding on inland rubbish tips: the lesser black-backed gull used to be only a summer visitor to Britain and, although it is not such an ardent scavenger, many of them now overwinter in certain areas, because of the rubbish-tip food supplies. Black-headed gulls (page 148) nested in London as long ago as 1946 and have scavenged for food alongside man ever since; they are just as likely to be seen following a dustcart on a rubbish tip as they are following the plough on arable land.

The **herring gull** has become the most regular visitor to rubbish tips, both on the coast and inland, and in the last few decades its British breeding population has more than doubled, partly due to the everlasting supply of edible waste on rubbish tips. The herring gull has extended its range far inland, even changing its nesting habits from 1940 onwards to suit its more urban lifestyle, by using the ledges and balconies of town and city buildings as man-made cliffs to raise its broods. As long ago as 1960, herring gulls were nesting in London and every summer on buildings in Cardiff, Newport, Gloucester, Bristol and other major conurbations, herring gulls build their nests and rely on corporation rubbish tips as a main supply of food.

Overhead a large flock of herring gulls scream their raucous 'kee-u-kee' calls as, with a few black-headed gulls, they glide above the fluttering rubbish. Turning at the far corner of the pit, they begin their noisy patrol and fly past once again. Suddenly they become agitated as a dustcart rumbles into view, leaving a rising cloud of dust in its wake, before finally reaching the tipping area. Unloading yet another landslide of rubbish, with a crunching of gears the empty lorry rattles away into the distance, and before it has gone 100 m/330 ft, the herring gulls descend in a frenzied, scuffling throng and are the first birds to examine the pickings of the first delivery of the day.

Away from rubbish tips, herring gulls feed on live fish and fish offal (**201**), crustaceans, worms, insects, roots, grass, potatoes and fruit. The gull is so omnivorous that it is perhaps rivalled only by man, so it is appropriate that much of its diet is obtained from man's rubbish and his discarded food. Given the chance, herring gulls also kill any small animal or bird they can, including the nestlings of other gulls, and are useful disposers of roadside carrion too.

Only thirty years ago the gull was still looked upon with some affection as the species which welcomed the visitor to holiday resorts with its yelps and loud chattering noises, but now that its population has increased to around 300,000 pairs and today lives so close to man far inland, its scavenging behaviour and constant noise have made it far less popular. Every birdwatcher knows the 55–60-cm/22–24-in adult herring gull (**201**) with its grey back, white underparts and black wing tips, edged with white. The pink legs and yellow bill are further characteristic features and the mottled brown juveniles are easily distinguishable for the first three years when they lack the grey and white markings.

During winter they are often seen flying and roosting in large flocks, when our resident birds are joined by visitors from northern Europe, to feed around the coastline, harbours, seaside towns and inland reservoirs, lakes and farmland, where they search for meadows and arable fields. In the spring the birds disperse and return to breeding sites around the coasts of Britain and Ireland. Many of the nests are isolated on steep cliffs and rocky stacks and ledges but where space allows, such as on shingle banks, saltmarshes and sand-dunes, they form colonies where the males perform their noisy, boisterous courtship ritual.

Both adults build the large nest, in a hollow in the sparse vegetation. It is surrounded by grass, heather, seaweed, sticks and tideline debris ready for the three olive, dark-blotched eggs which are laid between May and June. Despite their camouflage, the eggs are often predated by great black-backed gulls, therefore the adult herring gulls watch closely over them during the twenty-seven day incubation period and maintain this vigilance whilst the vulnerable chicks are in the nest for a further thirty days.

Watching herring gulls around the coast, dropping shellfish on to rocks so as to be able to feed on the soft flesh inside, and diving after fish on the returning tide, is enjoyable but their increase in population and their change in habits have brought their problems. Because they now favour feeding on rubbish tips, they spend hours treading in rotting refuse and their feet and plumage become impregnated with bacteria, which multiply in the warm rubbish and are transferred with the gulls' droppings. Health problems could possibly arise if large numbers of the gulls fed on rubbish tips one day and then transferred to drinking-water reservoirs the next, taking contamination with them. Although around London the open-reservoir water is purified before it is isolated in covered tanks and then piped to the customer's domestic taps, pure-water storage reservoirs are particularly at risk in certain parts of the country.

Methods are now being used to scare herring gulls away from some rubbish tips and reservoirs, but it is unlikely that these birds will ever completely ignore a supply of food they have found so useful. From the birdwatcher's point of view, rubbish tips offer gull rarities as well as pest species like the herring gull: for instance, Iceland and white-winged glaucous gulls are nearly always seen around this man-made habitat.

The birdlife of wasteland and rubbish tips has adapted to live close to man, but its future is under threat from him because economic pressures require every hectare of land to be used to maximum effect and, in lowland areas in particular, land is so valuable that even small areas of wasteland left forgotten for over forty years are considered to be potential building land with a commercial price. Consequently many of these wildlife havens are gradually being developed. As disposal methods for human rubbish changes, the open tips and controlled-tipping type of rubbish tips will be replaced, with the result that any birds who have learnt to exploit these habitats will be required to find their environmental niche elsewhere.

SEWAGE FARMS AND WATERCRESS BEDS

SEWAGE FARMS Thousands of years ago man used springs, streams and rivers for his water supply, both for drinking and domestic purposes. As populations increased and settlements developed, the demand on water supplies increased and, during the sixteenth and seventeenth centuries natural freshwater supplies became contaminated by overcrowded cities and towns, up or down river, and the gutters little more than open sewers; totally unsanitary living conditions prevailed and the River Thames, for instance, was used as the city drain and water supply. It was not until the Victorians were struck by epidemics of cholera and typhus, which are both transmitted by water, that it was decided that two separate supply systems were needed, one for drinking, cleaning and washing, the other for used water which flowed into a disposal system which became the sewer system we use today. The Victorians constructed large drinking-water reservoirs, separate from the header reservoirs used to supply the canal systems; one of the first of these in London, at Stoke Newington, was built in 1834. At the same time, the sewer system was developed, taking all liquid waste and channelling it to be discharged into rivers, miles from any town, or directing it to sewage farms which were built across the country.

The Victorian sewage works were sited on the outskirts of towns, away from habitation, and as towns and cities have grown over the years, the sewage works have always been left isolated with fields and hedgerows all around them, both for sanitary and health reasons because of the disposal methods used, and to screen their presence from society. Across the country these sewage farms vary in their methods of sewage disposal and their potential as bird habitats; the availability of scrubland, hedgerows, trees and open fields near by causes a sewage farm to support more birds than one without these additional habitats.

Sewage farms get their name from the early methods of disposal used at the beginning of this century, when the sewage was contained in shallow lagoons, eventually flooded on to surrounding land which had retaining embankments, and regularly ploughed in, which is why the farms were surrounded by fields. Before the sewage was ploughed into the ground it was often flooded with a thin layer of water for a few days, which encouraged invertebrate life to breed in the organically rich shallow wetland. The soil also became heavily populated with earthworms and since many of these old sewage farms were sited in river valleys, which migratory birds use as route markers, it was not long before spring and autumn migrants discovered the abundant food supply. Birdwatchers soon discovered the variety of birds which turned up at these sewage farms, which in their own way became legendary. Because of the large surrounding wetlands, migratory waders visited in their hundreds. Ringed plover and dunlin were the most common species, accompanied by common sandpiper, wood sandpiper, green sandpiper, greenshank, lapwing, snipe and redshank, which all probed and pecked for 'migration fuel' in the shallow mud and water. Rarer species like little stint, blacktailed godwit and curlew sandpiper would be seen and when it became known that these elusive birds occurred in larger numbers on the farms than on marshes and coastal mud flats, birdwatchers from all over Britain visited their local sewage farms at weekends.

The shallow lagoons were equally suitable for dabbling ducks; shoveler, mallard and teal would also be regular visitors and during their passage, common and black tern would fly down to feed. In summer all old-style sewage farms would have their flocks of swallow, sand and house martin patrolling the lagoons and flooded fields to catch the emerging insects. If ever birds learnt to exploit a man-made habitat, the old-style sewage farm was the prime example.

However, the majority of old sewage farms have been modernised since the last war. The large open fields became unacceptable to new public health standards and inefficient as a method of treating the increasing sewage coming from ever-expanding towns and cities. Few waders and ducks visit the restyled, compact sewage works without the shallow open lagoons or irrigation fields, but other types of birds, especially passerines, which have learnt to exploit the new sewage filtration systems, gather at these sites.

Untreated sewage now enters modern sewage works via the main sewer inlet, whence by gravity it flows into detritus tanks or balancing tanks, where heavy grit settles out. Free from grit, the sewage passes into at least four primary sedimentation tanks, where heavy sludge settles out and is siphoned off by pumps into the drying beds or open storage vessels. This isolated sludge is collected and treated elsewhere. The liquid sewage meanwhile is piped from the sedimentation tanks on to circular biological filters which are built at ground level; these are probably the one aspect of sewage works recognised by the majority of casual observers. They are called percolating filters because they are filled with clinker and granite chippings and covered with special bacteria and fungi, which biologically break down and oxidise the liquid sewage dispersed from a rotating perforated arm or boom above the clinker.

In modern sewage works, the circular percolating filters, which vary in number, are the most important part of the works for birdlife. Starling and pied wagtail perch on the rotating booms and dart down to catch insects settling on the clinker beds beneath. They have become adept at knowing just how long they can remain on the clinker before the boom returns, showering them in pre-treated liquid sewage.

Because the **pied wagtail (202)** favours damp ground near ponds, rivers and muddy farmyards and is mainly insectivorous, it has become common around sewage works and is gradually becoming a regular suburban species.

Walking quickly on the clinker of the filters, the wagtail suddenly dashes forward and captures an insect, its long tail bobbing continuously. It is a dapper bird, with bold black and white plumage and a trim 18-cm/7-in body always on the move. You can always hear its loud 'chisick' contact call and it frequently performs aerial, flycatcher-like movements around sewage works to catch the rising insects.

With the arrival of April the male pied wagtail begins to occupy his breeding territory, and from a wall or one of the sewage works' buildings delivers a beautiful courtship warbling song which soon gives way to aerial chases. The male noisily pursues the female who has a slightly greyer plumage and lighter crown, until she alights some distance from him. He approaches her by an indirect route and fans his tail whilst quivering his wings; as he gets closer, he bobs his head, finally throwing it back to show off his black throat patch as a final sexual gesture. If the female accepts his advances, the two birds fly around their territory for a few days, strengthening the pair bond, and eventually the female begins to build the nest in a crevice in a wall, hollow pipe, outbuilding, disused piece of farm machinery or tree covered in ivy.

In most years two broods are raised but by July the breeding is over and many wagtails form flocks around the sewage works, school playing fields or other open spaces. This flocking behaviour is performed mainly by young birds in southern England and a larger percentage of adults in the north. It occurs in August and September and demonstrates the partial migratory behaviour of the pied wagtail: these groups fly south to France, Spain and Morocco for the winter, whereas others remain and survive on insects caught along river margins and on sewage-work filter beds. Except in particularly hard winters, the rotating booms never freeze over and insects and organic matter can always be found and so overwintering pied wagtails are able to exploit this source of food.

Overwintering wagtails roost communally, frequently using scrub vegetation or reedbeds, but in recent years more of them are following the example of urban starlings, and roosting in city trees or on the ledges of buildings in London, Bristol, Leicester, Liverpool and Birmingham. Over a thousand birds perch on a factory roof at Sparkhill, Birmingham; and in Dublin's O'Connell Street a further thousand pied wagtails roost in the plane trees, chattering into the darkness as they enjoy the extra warmth of the city streets.

Even though the present-day sewage treatment plant is not such an outstanding habitat for birds as the old-style sewage farms, it is still a worthwhile birdwatching habitat. Throughout the year pied wagtails and starlings feed around the primary sedimentation tanks and are joined in winter by chaffinch, gull and carrion crow. The small worms, midges and insects on the charcoal attract summer yellow wagtail, resident pied wagtail, meadow pipit, dunnock and even chiff-chaff to congregate around the percolating filter beds.

At some sewage works, before the purified liquid is discharged into the local watercourse, it is piped from the percolating filters on to an adjacent grassland irrigation region and, by a system of sluices and channels, is rotated over a series of fields. These plots are the only large areas of wetland habitat on modern works. The underlying soil is extremely rich and fertilised, and each year sedges, rushes and lush vegetation grow, providing nesting sites for sedge warbler, reed bunting, redshank and snipe. It also has the advantage that it does not freeze solid during the winter and because of this, and the supply of food, these irrigation plots provide excellent birdwatching, especially for waders and wildfowl. Mallards and teal are regular visitors and snipe, lapwing, curlew and water rail can be seen on these marshy fields during the winter.

Sewage works provide insects and seeds for the opportunist bird fauna and the adjacent man-made wetland in some districts provides a perfect breeding area. They are particularly valuable if the rivers and marshland in the local countryside have disappeared because of increased urbanisation.

WATERCRESS BEDS Some of the sewage purification works in my own area still retain the irrigation grassland plots, even though other mechanical methods are available, and sometimes on these fields during the winter, **water pipits** feed. Typically they are not a British bird, inhabiting marshy Alpine pastures in Europe, but in severe winters a few turn up in Britain and search for regular supplies of insects.

Contrasting markedly with sewage works, their other favourite overwintering habitat are watercress beds which occur mainly in southern England, especially on the fast-flowing chalk streams in Hertfordshire, Berkshire, Hampshire and Wiltshire. Because cress beds are fed by chalk water springs which remain at an even temperature throughout the year and rarely freeze up, clear water is always running through the watercress and water pipits have learnt they can always find insect larvae, such as bloodworms (which are the larvae of non-biting midges), daphnia, freshwater shrimps and water louse, in much the same way as the sewage percolating filters provide constant insects and seeds during the winter. Meadow pipits (page 72) feed by cress beds all year round and are very similar in appearance, but it is the behaviour of the water pipit which distinguishes it: they are nervous and wary birds and you will have difficulty getting close to them before they call and fly away. Some of the best-known sites for these birds are the Beddington Sewage Works and River Wandle in Surrey, where they are required to run the gauntlet of hunting kestrels and short-eared owls; the cress beds of the River Gade and Colne Valley in Hertfordshire; and around Cassiobury Park (page 219).

Birdwatchers spending time around coastal habitats and inland reservoirs during winter are also likely to see water pipits because, although 90 per cent of those visiting Britain spend their time at sewage works and cress beds, they can be found at any unfrozen 'water system' where invertebrate food is available.

At any one time of the year pied wagtails represent 50–80 per cent of all the birds visiting sewage works, but they are by no means confined to this habitat; they are also one of the most common birds found around watercress farms, and are often joined by grey wagtails who feed and nest in the lush vegetation near by.

Cress beds, from the birds' point of view, are nothing more than permanently wet habitats where they can drink and find regular supplies of food. Some species like moorhen and dabchick have been known to breed amongst the cress, but the beds are commercial sites with a certain amount of human disturbance and birds associated with towns or park wetlands are the species most likely to be seen around cress farms during the summer. Both mallards and blackbirds are regular visitors and sometimes damage the watercress by dislodging plants in their search for insects and larvae.

During severe winter weather, cress beds become very important sites of refuge for water rail, snipe, woodcock, redwing, fieldfare, meadow pipit and both resident wagtails; and if the cold snap is prolonged, rarities like bittern turn up, along with other species on migration, including spotted crake, ruff and curlew sandpiper.

Because of their value as bird wintering grounds, disused cress beds are purchased by county naturalists' trusts as reserves. The shallow, spring-fed lagoons are maintained, and the surrounding marshland vegetation is left to encourage breeding and roosting birds throughout the year. Some of these reserves now have over forty species of breeding bird recorded, which is a positive indication of the importance and value of watercress beds as an aquatic, man-made habitat.

202

202 The pied wagtail is a regular visitor to sewage farms, watercress beds and other aquatic habitats because of the rich supply of invertebrates

LINEAR HABITATS

LINEAR HABITATS Many of the habitats in this chapter are so completely man-orientated that they cannot even be referred to as semi-natural habitats. There is another fascinating group of habitats which have appeared as artificial ecosystems, purely as a result of man's developments. Because of their unique shape they are collectively referred to by biologists as linear habitats, with an indefinite length, but uniform width. Such habitats include canals, railway embankments, motorway and road verges. Although no single one of them can be considered nationally significant, collectively and within a particular region of the British Isles they have a wildlife importance and conservational value, because they occupy such a large area of the countryside. Many of these habitats are strictly out of bounds to all but official maintenance staff, but because of their undisturbed nature, they provide refuge for an ever-increasing number of birds, mammals, insects and flowers, which cannot practically be conserved, and perhaps do not require any real conservation management because their very ecological niche gives them all the protection they need. Voles, shrews and whitethroats surviving on a busy motorway embankment, with established scrub and tall grass providing shelter and food, do not really need any help from man; these verges were initially designed for landscape and aesthetic reasons, and any attempt to manage them as nature reserves for the future would be both difficult and expensive, especially when compared with their overall conservation value.

CANALS Few waterways were created by man, but the canals completely owe their existence to his efforts. The Romans dug Britain's first canal, called the Fossdyke, more than 1,500 years ago, and it is still being used along its length from Lincoln to the River Trent. Most of the tranquil stretches of canal, which criss-cross the countryside and blend in as part of the natural landscape, were built in the heydey of canals from 1760 to 1830. At this time, the railways had not been constructed, but the growth of industry around the country demanded that raw materials and merchandise were delivered around the major towns and cities, and horse-drawn trucks and sailing ships, hugging the coastline, were both too slow and unreliable in their deliveries, as the Industrial Revolution established. In 1755 the short Sankey Brook canal was cut between the Lancashire coalfields of St Helen's to Warrington on Mersey-side, proving conclusively how a single horse could tow a loaded barge, with a greater load of coal than sixty horse-drawn carts could manage, to its destination in far less time. The extremely rich, entrepreneurial Duke of Bridgewater immediately saw the potential of canals and hired his private engineer, James Brindley, to connect his coal mines at Worsley, with Manchester by a 11.2-km/7-mile canal. This Bridgewater Canal was completed in 1761 and launched the era of the canals, when a network of these inland waterways linked one part of industrial and commercial Britain with another, cutting the cost of transportation by up to 80 per cent, and in its own way, changing the lifestyle and face of Britain for ever.

By 1830, more than 6,500 km/4,000 miles of navigable waterways had been built and, using the famous system of locks, transport was possible even against the gradient of the land. But the commercial heyday of canals was short-lived, because in the 1830s and 1840s the Victorians built the railway system across Britain and the steam train replaced the horse-drawn barges; by the beginning of this century, canal traffic had obviously declined and financially was no longer a viable means of transport. As a result, small arms of the canal system began to deteriorate and eventually traffic ceased altogether. After the Second World War most of the existing 8,000 km/5,000 miles of canals were nationalised and became controlled by the Ministry of Transport, but following an Act of Parliament in 1962, the British Waterways Board took control of the canals and have maintained them ever since. Although there is hardly any commercial traffic, their value remains with the increase in pleasure-boating which, at least, keeps many stretches in working order. Other stretches of the canal system have long been choked with invading aquatic plants and wherever natural succession has continued, they have dried up, following invasion by willow and alder scrub, so that lengths of canal have become wildlife havens.

Although they resemble long straight rivers, the canals' structure is quite different and determines the wildlife, to a large extent. Rivers have variable depths along their lengths, with rapid-flowing shallows and deep calmer pools, but canals were dug with a uniform profile and are deep in the central navigational channel, shelving to the margins which are frequently retained by steel or concrete banks. Where these are absent, however, marginal vegetation grows, offering shelter to a variety of birds but under constant threat from the wash from pleasure-boat traffic.

For the birdwatcher the potential of canals (**204**) varies according to the amount of recreational disturbance, so although it is possible to enjoy good birdwatching along a stretch of navigable canal, the most productive canals are the quieter, neglected 'side cuts' where the marginal vegetation is dense and established. Here common reeds grow with bulrushes, and beautiful yellow flag add their splash of colour.

These emergent plants with most of their foliage above the water surface provide nesting cover for birds. The moorhen, so common on farm and village ponds, rivers and streams, forages through this jungle, occasionally announcing its presence with its loud 'curruc' call. The reedbeds encourage the little grebe or dabchick (page 156) but whenever you see reed warblers, you can assume that you have found a length of quiet canal which will be rich in birdlife. Apart from the cuckoo, seeking out the reed warblers nesting in the marginal stems, sedge warblers and reed buntings colonise this type of canal and normally keep well away from those stretches used by pleasure boats.

The marginal plants give way to lush tow-path vegetation, including willowherbs, nettles and tall grasses, but eventually, further back from the edge of the canal, sallow willow, hawthorn and wetland scrub plants colonise. Left undisturbed, they attract their own range of birds, including the common and lesser whitethroat, linnet and yellowhammer. There are always plenty of insects near unpolluted canals – mayflies, dragonflies, alderflies and mosquitoes all breed in the water – and throughout the summer screaming parties of swifts and quieter swallows and house martins dip across the canal to catch their prey. They nest in the nearby towns, reminding you that these disused canals were once built to transport material and goods from one urban area to another. Only a few centuries ago all these birds would use the canals for food and breeding sites, accepting the slow-moving horse-drawn barges, but today they colonise only the more peaceful backwaters away from heavy boat traffic.

Today canals still have their commercial value. Many are used purely for leisure activities, others have been turned into managed nature reserves and some still remain neglected and derelict, especially those passing through industrial areas, where they become filled with rubbish and polluted by chemicals. The British Waterways Board is gradually reclaiming many of the old canals it controls, some for continued boating recreation, but others as good examples of a linear habitat nature reserve. They are fertile habitats and once clean, flowing water is restored, the natural vegetation soon colonises and the birdlife arrives, looking for the increased volume of invertebrate life. If the boating speed limit of 6.4 kph/4 mph were regularly observed, many more recreational canals would develop a strong marginal vegetation, and they too would become a more interesting habitat. On the Basingstoke Canal, rare aquatic plants, invertebrate life and birds survived, and when the canal was cleared, many of the plants were transferred to the adjacent 'flashes', which were the reservoirs used to top up the canal systems during their working days. The canal was dredged, cleaned and refilled and the flashes were soon colonised by the rare plants and invertebrates, so now pleasure boats use stretches of the open canal system and naturalists can enjoy Basingstoke Canal Flashes Nature Reserve, which is so successful that it is an official SSSI, with appropriate flora and fauna to match. The canal network of Britain offers many similar untapped examples where nature reserves could be created from disused canal cuttings and the public could enjoy their recreational activities. If the British Waterways Board uses its skills and draws upon the resources and expertise of conservation societies, the potential for birds and wildlife to live alongside a public amenity is particularly exciting for the future.

RAILWAY EMBANKMENTS (203)

RAILWAY EMBANKMENTS (203) As the age of the canal died, so the railway era was born. Most of the railway links between cities and the industrial centres were built during the 1830s and 1840s, following the successful opening of the Stockton and Darlington Railway in 1825 by George Stephenson, which was the first passenger route in the world. Built using little more than the nineteenth-century muscle power of the navvies, a vast network of lines ran across the country. At the time steam-engine power was limited, so the railway lines had to be built on the flat wherever possible; therefore in upland country, huge sweeping curves of track were laid to follow the contours of the land and avoid deep valleys. Today some of these routes, which took a long time to lay, offer spectacular views of mountainous and moorland Britain. Gradually the power of locomotives improved and the increase in passenger traffic demanded that railway tracks were laid more rapidly, so more direct routes were built, involving viaducts, bridges, tunnels and hillside cuttings and forming the basis of British Rail's Intercity network. Many of the routes remained scenically breathtaking and travelling on the Skipton, Carnforth, Ulverston and Whitehaven line you can use your carriage as a comfortable bird-hide, as you cross Morecambe Bay. From high on the viaducts the views across the mud flats are excellent, with thousands of waders and wildfowl feeding on the mud as the sun glints on the pools of water. If you were to try to approach them on foot from the headland, they would take off the minute you appeared on the horizon, but they accept the regular passing of trains and carry on feeding regardless. At Leighton Moss Reserve, where bitterns breed in the reedbeds, they even 'boom' their courtship reply to the horn of the diesel train passing at dusk and in the morning.

Once rail links connected the major cities, the railway companies built tracks into rural areas between 1850 and the 1860s. They were immediately supported in preference to the horse-drawn carriage, but by 1918, when Britain was criss-crossed with railway tracks, cars and trams provided alternative means of transport and the roads were being seen as the next major development. The last major line construction was in 1900 with the opening of a mainline from London, Marylebone, to Nottingham, Sheffield and Manchester. After the Second World War, the railway companies were in financial trouble and many of the tracks needed repair, and in 1948, when they were nationalised, British Rail took on 30,600 km/19,000 miles of track. The car took away valuable business, and the more profitable lines were forever subsidising the rural line networks. In 1962, when British Rail made an £87 million loss, Dr Richard Beeching, head of British Rail, began to prune the service, closing non-profitable country lines and stations to reduce losses. His investigations led to the famous Beeching Report of 1963 which was responsible for a massive reduction in services between 1952 and 1967, as a result of which only 17,700 km/11,000 miles of track were left in operation. All across the country Victorian railway tracks and stations were closed and forgotten. British Rail has sold some of the land, especially to the farmers whose property the track bed runs across, but the farmers have not gone to the expense of flattening the embankments and they still remain as part of the 30,000 ha/75,000 acres of 'railway land' across the countryside.

The deserted tracks did not scar the country for long. Even one hundred years ago they were rich in plant and animal life, which soon took over again once the trains had gone. Apart from taking up some of the 12,900 km/8,000 miles of closed track, British Rail left the track beds to nature and many areas which are inaccessible have become unofficial nature reserves with rabbits and foxes breeding alongside each other and lizards and grass snakes basking on the clinker.

Even when the railways were active the embankments received the minimum of management, except for hand mowing three times a year to produce a short grassland, which reduced the risk of fire caused by sparks from steam engines. In 1965 as a cost-cutting operation, this management was discontinued and the short turf soon changed to tall grassland. The coarser grasses provided excellent cover for voles, field mice and shrews, which were soon discovered by kestrels, which is one of the reasons why this falcon is still seen hovering over this habitat today. With continued lack of disturbance and management, since their closure many disused railway embankments have become colonised with brambles, wild dog rose and hawthorn, providing an important supply of autumn fruit for blackbird, fieldfare and thrush, similar to the hedgerow, acting as roadside larders. Railways have always been less comprehensive than the road and lane network, but their embankments were always more undisturbed and managed sparingly; the plants and animals which occupied them a century ago and have colonised them since are still underresearched.

The traveller's loss, as railway lines closed, has been the naturalist's gain, since many track beds have officially and unofficially become footpaths and even bicycle routes. No birdwatcher lives far from a disused track, such was the latticing complexity of the Victorian network, and a special map was published in 1982 by HMSO showing all the disused railways in England and Wales. The birdwatcher who studies it and understands the contours of Ordnance Survey maps will soon realise what birdlife is likely to be seen from a particular railway bed, crossing heathland and open grassland, skirting woodland or hugging the coastline. In their own way, because of the method of construction, the railway bed and route it takes will be different in nature from that of the immediate countryside. The high sloping embankments exposed to the sun or breeze are dry and well drained, whereas a cutting, where flooding is possible, is often a damp stretch of the track bed. Within this varying linear habitat, 5.5 m/18 ft wide and many kilometres long, the flora and birdlife changes regularly according to conditions on the track and in the surrounding countryside.

The track beds are free from the effects of the herbicides and fertilisers of the surrounding farmland, and are colonised by more species of wildlife than motorways, because they have an older history and the habitat is therefore more established; they have become the richest tangled ribbon of green in Britain. Scurrying down the embankment on to the deserted line you arrive in a special birdwatching world. Even though a century ago their creation destroyed habitats, they are now valuable places for goldfinches feeding on the numerous thistles growing in the clinker and green woodpeckers searching for ants' nests in the dry grassy embankments. Where the wayfaring trees, elder and gorse bloom in summer, turtle dove, bullfinch, chaffinch and long-tailed tits feed and build their nests. Disused tracks bordering lakes and wetlands are excellent vantage points from which to watch for common sandpipers and mallards and in certain parts of Britain where the railway was routed around ravines and cliffs, buzzards (**206**) and ravens give themselves away with their characteristic calls. The disused railway tracks are particularly productive birdwatching spots when migratory birds follow their routes, using the ready supply of insects and berries as sustaining fuel.

Providing the journey is in daylight, when making a long-distance train journey in what is a mobile hide it is worth using maps to pick out official nature reserves, including some of those owned by British Rail and leased to wildlife trusts, or some of the twenty-three separate reserves given to conservation societies for their management and protection.

As you edge around Poole Harbour oystercatchers, redshanks, curlews and shelducks are visible, probing and filtering through the sticky mud; and fallow deer and buzzards can be seen as the train passes through the New Forest; in winter, short-eared owls (**207**) hunt along the rough grass corridor of the embankments and stare at you from wooden fenceposts along the route. Often the view is improved as the train takes an embankment raised above the level of the surrounding countryside, and as you pass one of the numerous isolated farm buildings, you might see swallows disappearing inside to feed a hungry brood, or a song thrush using a trackside pile of clinker as an anvil to crack open a snail shell.

Since many of our habitats are decreasing in size and wildlife value because of commercial pressures, both active and disused railway lines are vital green corridors for birds moving across the country. It is therefore important that stretches of disused railway track are protected and converted to nature reserves, rather than used for dumping rubbish, because if public interest can be increased and more awareness generated towards the value of wildlife conservation of man-made habitats, at least as a nation we will be able to say, 'We are getting there.'

ROADSIDE AND MOTORWAY VERGES In the constant evolution of transport systems in Britain, without doubt the most significant change to man's mobility was brought about by the invention of the car and its development to its present-day power and design. The car has brought individuals freedom to travel virtually anywhere they wish, and it is a luxury that few people would contemplate being without. But as the car has dominated twentieth-century travel so the roadways have had to be developed and repaired, in order to cope with the millions of cars, buses and lorries which now use them every day. Britain's roads have always been evolving, from the drover's tracks, the country lane and main A-road to the motorways first built in 1958, which virtually replaced the railway links from one town or city to another. Whether it is a straight A-road originating from some of the 13,000 km/8,000 miles built by the Romans, or one of the multi-laned motorways which lie over countless ancient footpaths and cost £12 million per mile to build, every road has verges, which collectively cover over 210,000 ha/520,000 acres, with those associated with motorways occupying 5,000 ha/12,400 acres. Although close to persistent traffic, which is only a few metres from their edges, the grass verges of Britain's roads and motorways have become important wildlife habitats colonised by plants, birds, mammals, insects and reptiles. They which are undisturbed by man and survive in what have become unofficial nature reserves, moving from one area of the country to another along these grassy linear highways.

Roadside verges are perhaps the most familiar because they are more common. Most include a belt of grass, sometimes periodically cut but frequently left to grow tall because of local authority maintenance reductions, and backed by a hedgerow or belt of trees, screening the road from the countryside on the other side. Birdlife along the road verge is therefore a mixture of grassland or meadow birds and hedgerow species. Starlings are always seen probing the grass verge for invertebrates and sparrows collect nesting material from the side of the road, where they also pick up gravel and grit to aid digestion. Crows and rooks are frequently seen doing exactly the same on motorways, where they tempt fate by remaining in the middle of a lane until the last moment – although young and inexperienced birds sometimes misjudge.

Passing traffic is the main problem for survival in the roadside verge and thousands of birds and mammals are killed this way each year, but none of this carrion is wasted since magpies and carrion crows always remove the corpses in between the flow of traffic.

Long-distance motorway driving is often considered to be the most monotonous form of travel, but for the naturalist and birdwatcher the journey is enhanced by observing the changing habits of the surrounding countryside. Britain's motorways rarely pass through the same habitat for more than 40km/25 miles and often the changes in both habitat and geology occur more frequently. Motoring along the M3 from London to Basingstoke, for instance, the predominant habitat on the London Clay is deciduous wood – especially oak, which abruptly changes to heathland plants, such as heather and gorse, with birch scrub, immediately the motorway reaches the sandy soils of Bagshot and Chertsey.

For a short distance near Hook in Hampshire, the M3 passes through countryside formed on London Clay again, and the habitat noticeably changes to oakwood before the motorway reaches the Hampshire chalk and beech and ashwoods replace the oak trees. Within this 56km/35-mile journey along the M3 the observant motorist passes through three distinct habitats.

203

203 Criss-crossing the countryside, disused railway tracks offer sanctuary to a wide range of birds.

Most other motorways thread their way through an equally diverse ecology, although the motorway verges which have been created and planted by man are frequently of uniform appearance, until local plants begin to colonise. Observing the changes in habitat and wild flowers growing on the embankments breaks the monotony of motorway driving and research shows that rather than distracting the motorist, it actually makes the driving safer.

Motorway verges represent the best-known and most-unexplored land of today and these verges are only infrequently cut and disturbed. The wild flowers, which are the first things to colonise a new motorway verge, are specific species: chalkland flowers colonise motorways running through downland,

whereas on sandy soils, heath bedstraw and harebell are found. The salt that motorway service vehicles liberally dispense on the motorways at the first signs of snow and ice accumulates at the motorway edges, and where it is washed into the drainage pebbles, saltmarsh plants have colonised, miles away from the coast. No motorway has yet been designated a nationally important wildlife site but, collectively, the verges and embankments are extremely important as sanctuaries for wildlife species, many of which are losing their habitats elsewhere. Motorway and roadside verges provide refuge for over 600 species of flowering plant which have attracted 25 species of butterfly, 6 bumble bee species and myriad other insects. Half our mammal species, 6 reptiles and over 40 species of birds have been recorded along these linear nature reserves.

The grasses grow long and shed their seeds in summer providing food for linnets and seeds of bramble, dispersed by

204

205

206

207

204 Canada geese on the Kennet and Avon canal. Wherever the bankside vegetation is lush and disturbance from boats is minimal, canals are potential bird habitats ready for colonisation.

205 Kestrels are commonly seen feeding over motorway embankments and are as successful on this linear habitat as they are in open countryside.

206 Birdwatching from a moving railway carriage adds a new dimension to the hobby. Sometimes buzzards can be seen wherever tracks cross moors and hug mountainsides.

207 Short-eared owls can be watched in winter from the train as it passes rough grassland around the New Forest and elsewhere.

birds years ago, have grown into bramble thickets where whitethroat, blackbird and dunnock build their nests. The greenfinch is particularly well known for changing the appearance of motorway verges. Since this bird and other finches are mainly berry and seed eaters, they are responsible for dispersing hawthorn seeds along Britain's motorway network, especially the M4, M40 and M25. The service station has become exploited by house sparrow, starling, pigeon and chaffinch, all foraging around the wastebins for discarded bread and fruit, and many of them are bold enough to sit around parked cars begging for food.

The noise of the motorways has been accepted by all the birds and animals colonising the grass verges and their acceptance of man's presence is really their success. Deep in the unsprayed, uncut and undisturbed grass, field mice and voles live their lives, much as they did in the ancient fields that covered the land after the forests were felled centuries ago. They live almost unnoticed – except by one bird hovering on the wind, poised ready for the kill: the kestrel, who knows just when to dive.

The **kestrel** still nests on windswept moors and rocky crags (**205**), but if ever a bird has learnt to exploit a man-made environment and survive, in the last few decades the kestrel can claim the prize. It is now our commonest bird of prey and the quivering wings and fanned tail are a regular sight as the bird hovers over suburban parks, wasteland, most of our motorways as well as open country. It has accepted man and come right into the heart of his cities, even taking household scraps from suburban and town gardens, although it still prefers to hunt for voles, mice, small birds, beetles and worms in more open habitats. Perhaps its most independent streak is shown by its habit of nesting in cities: in London, 340 pairs are known to breed regularly, using ledges and windowboxes of buildings such as Guy's Hospital, the Law Courts in the Strand and the Natural History Museum.

High above the M25 surrounding London, a kestrel hovers 60 m/200 ft above the ground. Its head is absolutely still, but its eyes are fixed on a patch of grass which twitched a few seconds ago. With exceptional eyesight the kestrel can spot any such movement and having seen it many times before, it knows that a small mammal is foraging around for its own food. Occasionally the kestrel flicks its wings just enough to maintain its position; even in a high wind it masters the air currents perfectly, keeping its head motionless, watching and waiting.

Suddenly the kestrel stoops, only to break into a second perfectly executed hover 20 m/66 ft above the ground; then it drops like a stone and with outstretched talons catches the field vole, which dies instantly from the impact.

With its prey gripped firmly by the talons, the kestrel almost immediately flies to a feeding perch where the prey is torn apart by the strong hooked beak. Since kestrels now regularly hunt the exposed motorway and roadside verges, it is easy to watch their behaviour of food mantling. Just after the kill for a few seconds before take-off, kestrels spread their wings and tail and screen their food like an opened umbrella. This mantling is performed to prevent any other watchful large bird such as a carrion crow from stealing the kill, before the kestrel flies to its perch.

At 34 cm/13½ in this male kestrel, with his blue-grey head and upper tail, is slightly smaller than the female, who lacks the blue-grey plumage. As it perches on a nearby fence to eat its prey, you can see the light chestnut upperparts, liberally

dotted with black markings and there is a black band at the extreme end of the tail. From motorway bridges crossing rural sections of the motorway you can often watch kestrels hunting and sometimes you will observe the female with her uniform brown plumage, streaked and barred with reddish-brown markings.

Only during the breeding season are both birds regularly seen together, and during spring the shrill 'kee-kee-kee' calls of the pair performing their exciting, skilful courtship display are heard. It is only during the soaring display flight that the kestrel may be mistaken for the sparrowhawk: both soar in the breeding season and both species have a long tail. However, the kestrel's wings are long and pointed, whereas those of the sparrowhawk are broad and rounded at the ends, normally seen when the bird flies low over hedges in search of food. Between April and May up to five eggs are laid in a hole in a tree, or in an abandoned crow or pigeon's nest, since they never build their own nest. For a month the female incubates the eggs, occasionally assisted by the male, and both parents feed the grey downy young on insects and meat. They develop rapidly and fledge after twenty-eight days.

Because of pesticide poisoning the kestrel population dropped in the 1940s but some survived and as certain toxic chemicals were outlawed, they fought back, adapted to changing habitats and found roadside and motorway hunting a perfect substitute for open countryside living.

Towards late summer the young kestrels disperse, sometimes as far as southern Europe, where they spend the winter. The surviving birds return in spring to join the resident population of kestrels which have often overwintered on salt-marshes, where food remains plentiful. Most young kestrels return the following year to breed within a few kilometres of their own birthplace.

Despite a wide range of prey, food supplies become scarce for the kestrel during winter, and the resident birds expand their hunting territories, ousting weaker neighbouring kestrels or trespassers. This is one of the best times of year to see hunting kestrels regularly spaced out along motorways and vigilantly maintaining their source of food.

Today this small falcon has a healthy breeding population with no threat of extinction, although huge volumes of traffic certainly cause pollution to the kestrel's chosen habitat. Nobody knows what long-term effect lead pollution and exhaust fumes have on motorway wildlife, although the greatest lead pollution occurs within a region barely 50 metres/164 feet of the side of the road surface where the kestrel hunts daily.

In Britain there are more than 25 million registered drivers with 2 million new cars purchased each year; increasing demand for a more efficient widespread road network in the twenty-first century. Building new roads will unavoidably destroy some habitats but the increase in road verges will, if suitably managed, provide new wildlife havens. Already certain County Council Highway Departments have recognised the importance of this man-made habitat, and with the co-operation of their County Naturalists' Trust, they have designated many Roadside Verge Nature Reserves, (RVNRs). In Worcestershire alone there are over eighty such reserves managed to protect wildlife and motorist. No herbicides or pesticides are used and controlled mowing is performed to maintain the visibility at junctions for the motorist. Large-scale mowing occurs in the autumn, rather than summer, to allow plants to form their seed heads and by varied and controlled cutting, a range of different height, grassland habitats, is created across the width of the verge, attracting a wider range of animal life.

Motorways are here to stay and the present government is planning a massive development programme to meet demands of the increasing road traffic. At least a journey down a motorway can be a little more interesting with the knowledge that you are travelling along one of Britain's nature reserves, totally created by man and suitably colonised by birds.

CHAPTER 13

HABITAT MANAGEMENT AND

In Chapter 1 we saw how Neolithic man began clearing virgin woodland for his own benefit, creating open spaces for cultivation. So began man's interference with the environment, which over thousands of years, together with the forces of nature, brought changes to the countryside, forming the different habitats of Great Britain and Ireland.

We have seen how changes to the countryside have, in the last century, been so numerous and rapid that the ancient natural habitats of Britain are now confined to isolated relics in an urban and industrial wilderness. Struggling to survive in these pockets of refuge, birds and other forms of wildlife try to adapt and are pushed ever nearer to the limits of their survival.

When agricultural, forestry or industrial developments destroy an ancient wood, they remove not only ancient flora and fauna which have taken hundreds of thousands of years to evolve, but an irreplaceable record of people's lives and crafts. Likewise old hay meadows, chalk downland, moorland, heaths and even saltmarshes contain similar information about the past. Many of these living museums have suffered the same fate and can never be recreated.

The open countryside between the encroaching cities and towns has been plundered, often in an insidious manner; for instance, where a few acres of damp meadow have been drained, ploughed and fertilised with corresponding disturbance to the wild flowers, butterflies and birds. Village ponds have been filled in and hundreds of miles of hedgerows are grubbed out annually. These changes are frequently mourned only at county level, rarely becoming national headlines. Yet, added together we now know these losses represent an alarming destruction of Britain's countryside. Today rural Britain has been completely transformed and while farming, industry and urbanisation have triumphed, the effect on wildlife has been catastrophic.

Despite their unrivalled ability to disperse, birds have not escaped the effects of habitat destruction. As upland moors have been converted to forestry plantations or ploughed for agriculture, merlin, black grouse and hen harrier populations have declined; similarly black-tailed godwit, bittern and marsh harrier, which are dependent on marshland or reedbeds for survival, breed in diminishing numbers as their habitats have been drained and ploughed. As man increased his ability to change the appearance of the countryside, the habitat losses became so rapid that birds faced a problem of where to escape to, and in Britain forty-six species now form an endangered or 'red list', as designated by the International Council for Bird Preservation (ICBP). Twenty-eight of these species are classified as 'vulnerable', which means that although their numbers are stable or possibly increasing, the populations are confined to isolated areas and the loss of any one of these habitats would result in a severe drop in the overall population. The Slavonian grebe (page 152) and Dartford warbler (page 62) are perfect examples of this category.

The most endangered species are the five which belong to the 'threatened' category: red-backed shrike, wryneck, dotterel, roseate tern and bittern. They occur in such depleted populations that unless something is done very soon to stop the decline, they will become extinct as breeding birds. Habitat loss is responsible for the bittern's decline, but regional climatic changes since the 1920s have largely caused the decline of red-backed shrike and wryneck which, in Britain, were at the northernmost limits of their European breeding range. Climatic changes cannot be altered and as these changes have occurred, ornithologists have been obliged to accept that certain birds have become rarer. All that man can do is provide suitably managed sites where these declining species can survive, even if they eventually become extinct because of natural climatic changes.

The ICBP consider four British birds to be 'declining', including the merlin (page 107) and corncrake (page 146). Their numbers are falling so low that soon they will be viewed as 'vulnerable' or 'threatened'. The Kentish plover and white-tailed sea eagle are two of the five species which are viewed as 'extinct' as true breeding birds in the British Isles, although as mentioned in Ch. 11, re-introduction programmes from Norway resulted in the white-tailed sea eagle breeding again in 1985, not having bred here since the beginning of the century.

The decline of bird species is not just taking place in the British Isles: the same reasons and causes in every country have currently put 10 per cent of the world's birds under threat. The value of protecting birds in Britain is undermined if they are threatened elsewhere and of the 208 regular breeding birds in Britain, 56 are summer migrants. They fly to us from developing countries, where their habitats are being destroyed on a large scale, but they are also shot and trapped for sport, food and the pet-trade as they migrate across Europe (page 133) and many millions of birds are lost annually in this way. Thus today's conservationists are faced with a huge problem. Often in order to conserve what we in Britain consider to be our wildlife, we need to think and strategise on a worldwide basis.

The roseate tern is the latest addition to Britain's 'threatened' category, and is our rarest seabird. As summer visitors, arriving in April, the adults and juveniles depart to overwinter in West Africa. The decline in birds returning to the British Isles in 1984 was so severe that it led to an investigation: it was discovered that large numbers were being killed or trapped in Ghana. The ICBP and RSPB reacted quickly to protect the roseate tern on a global scale and an education programme, supported by the government of Ghana, is now in operation to inform the local inhabitants about their environment and to make them aware of the worldwide effects on the roseate tern, if they continue to hunt what they consider to be their local birds.

Local conservation in the future has got to be viewed as conserving for the world. To many people the future of a bird's life is irrelevant: a common argument is that, with so many people starving and struggling to live, why are the lives of a few birds important? But conservationists, politicians and mankind need to concentrate on one basic fact: there will be no future for humans unless world development programmes incorporate the basic needs for wild plants and animals. Conservation must be viewed as a priority in any future attempts to solve social, economic and environmental problems of the world; no longer can it be considered a low priority.

THE FUTURE OF BIRD CONSERVATION

208

208 7000 years ago the peatlands of the Flow Country were covered in birch and pine trees. Here a greenshank incubates its eggs in our last primeval habitat next to a pine stump preserved in the peat for several thousand years. In 1980 man and private forestry came to the Flows and now their future is threatened. Already 130 pairs of greenshank have been banished by the new forests. Is the future of all our birdlife and habitats now similarly in the balance?

This book exposes the threats to British birds, but it must also alert every conservationist in the country: the 3 million paid-up conservationists in Britain must be prepared to do more than just part with membership money and believe they are contributing to wildlife and habitat protection. Their subscriptions are of vital importance if this work is to be continued, but paying lip-service to a good cause is no longer enough. Conservationists have got to change both in their own attitudes and in their overall awareness of environmental problems. I would not wish to decry the valuable work all the major conservation societies have already achieved, with the help of their members and staff, but it has to be said that there are definite areas of failure. If the conservation lobby fails now as, nationally and internationally, we sit on the knife-edge of

unalterable change, we will have only ourselves to blame, and an impoverished legacy to pass on to our children and future generations.

Conservationists have largely failed to communicate effectively their environmental awareness. Television programmes have provided acclaimed wildlife documentaries since the day Heinz Sielmanns' woodpecker film put BBC's *Look* series on the map, achieving excellent viewer appreciation figures second only to the Coronation. Years later, Sir David Attenborough's *Life on Earth* won an audience of 14 million people – only just below the wedding of the Prince and Princess of Wales. Books on natural history continue to gain in popularity. Thus environmental issues have been exposed to the population of the British Isles for years. Yet, if the message has been received, any acceptance of it and action which should have followed has been poor, which indicates either that conservationists are failing to communicate with society or that society is generally apathetic and does not respond.

Eighty per cent of the population of the British Isles (56 million people in 1988) live in urban surroundings and although the interest in nature conservation appears considerable on the surface, there are many town folk who are totally unaware of how or where their fruit, vegetables and bread grow or come from. Even though these people are aware of environmental issues covered by the media and probably belong to at least one conservation society, urbanisation on today's scale has detached them from the countryside and stifled any feeling of dependence upon nature. Intellectually, an education programme is necessary so that everybody realises that conservation is inter-related with the issues of providing food supplies and even employment.

Many other people in Britain, perhaps as a result of television exposure, accept that conservation on a worldwide basis is important, but believe that Britain's plants and animals are relatively unimportant. The plight of the loggerhead turtles in Turkey, or the fact that tropical rain forests are being destroyed at the rate of 12 ha/30 acres per minute, are accepted as worthy causes for campaign and support, but Britain's habitats are sometimes viewed as insignificant. The truth is that habitats in Britain are not insignificant and many species have their greatest populations in the British Isles. Seventy per cent of both the world's gannets and razorbills have their strongholds in Britain. Whereas in Europe the populations of golden eagle and peregrine have declined, our own populations have remained constant as a result of protection and now represent a vital proportion of the total European population. Although bluebells grow elsewhere in Europe, they only form their blue-scented carpets in British woodlands and are therefore worth protecting, especially as visitors from across the world come to see them.

It is my view that there are problems to overcome at the grassroots of conservation in Britain. It is laudable to be aware of world conservation problems, but far greater awareness is needed about the problems on our own doorstep which possibly have worldwide implications. Successive governments, industrialists and farmers have not considered the consequences of the environmental changes they have implemented or performed during their own lifetimes and if conservationists and the general public had lobbied more effectively, or had been more aware of what was happening, they would surely have campaigned against or stopped the tide of destruction.

To improve conservation in Britain and protect the remaining habitats, conservation must be supported by the majority and will need to become more persistent to immediately stop destruction, since there will always be disagreement and competition for land between conservationists, landowners and landusers. Conservation must be shown to be relevant to everybody now, not just as a cause pursued by a minority 'green' political party or 3 million committed conservationists – still very much a minority in population terms. Majority support will only come about if the importance of conservation is heard, understood and seen as relevant to all social classes and age groups, and not just to elitist sections of the community.

Some recent research statistics by the Royal Society for Nature Conservation reveal some interesting facts about people's awareness of conservation and their priorities. The survey was performed on a sample of the general public and trust members. Only 7 per cent of the general public knew something about the RSNC and of these only 25 per cent could name their own local trust or Urban Wildlife Trust. More alarming still is that 40 per cent of county trust members knew little or nothing about RSNC, with 12 per cent being totally unaware that their trust was part of the RSNC. This means that at county level in Britain, there is a vast unawareness of the fact that forty-eight county trusts collectively manage the wildlife conservation of the United Kingdom which are co-ordinated and advised by the RSNC. Far too many trust members are insufficiently informed to realise the involvement of the RSNC or that it even exists. Thus the 180,000 members of the county Nature Conservation Trusts are seen in perspective. The trusts own or manage 1,680 reserves, but how many more could be controlled by them if local conservation was taken more seriously by a better informed membership.

The survey further revealed that 'the general public are most concerned with various forms of pollution and less worried about countryside matters. The dumping of nuclear waste is the single most important issue'.

All trust members come from a very small segment of the total population. Nearly 50 per cent are over 55 years old and only 16 per cent under 34. Every member is important to a local conservation trust, but the question must be asked whether the trusts are either appealing directly to the wrong section of the community or failing to attract the age group which can be physically more active in conservation and can offer years of service. In contrast the junior section of the RSPB has over 100,000 members under 15 years of age and clearly are aware that everything depends on the younger element of society. The schoolchildren of today are the birdwatchers and conservationists of tomorrow and any long-term change in conservation attitudes must come from educating young people now.

The RSNC survey admits that it and the trusts are less well known than other nature conservation organisations and that people are confused about their identity – if they know of them at all.

The county Nature Conservation Trusts are important for the overall conservation of Britain's habitats, but the RSNC survey clearly reveals the need to improve their image, nature conservation awareness and membership recruitment. To a certain extent, conservation achievements can be gained at national and international levels only if we have a uniformly credible and successful local conservation movement first.

The 1987 RSNC survey of attitudes to nature conservation revealed that 78 per cent of trust members come from higher socio-economic groups and 39 per cent were qualified at degree level. Consequently within their ranks they have potential leaders and committee members to launch a reform in county conservation. Conservation should always be promoted as exciting, but practical and relevant to all society; it cannot be promoted solely by enthusiasm. The issues of conservation, whether at county level or international level, are not always straightforward and because of their diversity, committees are necessary to solve the problems. Since committee members never carry out a reform, but only initiate it, active members of conservation bodies must be prepared to stand up and be counted and promote new ideas and campaigns.

This is where ardent conservationists are important and their success will depend on their powers of oratory and persuasiveness, backed by the expertise of the committee. The launch of any campaign is critical for its success, which is why today's active conservationists need to be aware of their local environment, that of the nation and the current international disasters. If the campaign is launched too early, the impetus may wane and the impact lose effectiveness. If, however, a campaign is launched too late, the very habitat or species it sets out to protect may already be destroyed.

During 1987 and 1988 numerous environmental issues reared their heads, requiring immediate responses from conservation bodies. Awareness was created and campaigns to reinforce the issues will continue throughout 1989 and, if necessary, for years to come; and timing was critical for each campaign.

Much of upland Britain and certainly the Flow Country of Caithness and Sutherland have been destroyed by forestry plantations – many of which were privately owned by celebrity high-income earners, receiving 60 per cent tax relief on their forestry investment. Chancellor Nigel Lawson, in his Budget speech in March 1988, removed forestry from the tax system and conservationists celebrated the news because they considered that this would effectively reduce the scale of afforestation in Britain. However the celebrations were short-lived. Not many people are aware that a week after the Budget huge grant increases for planting conifers were announced, indicating that the Government aimed to continue supporting the destructive spread of conifers and that the forestry lobby had been exerting pressure and influence to preserve their industry. The new grants covered more than 60 per cent of the costs incurred in conifer planting, so grant aid for afforesting 25 acres increased from £100 per acre to almost £250 per acre, whether 25 acres or 4,000 acres are planted. Clearly the intentions remain as they were before the Budget, to promote afforestation at the expense of wildlife and the environment, employing a grant scheme rather than a system of tax concession.

Certain areas of upland Britain and certainly the Flow Country will be closely monitored because they have been designated as being of world importance by the International Council for the Conservation of Nature. They have approached the Government, asking it to protect parts of the Flow Country under the World Heritage Convention. If the Government fails to respond, the European Commission, requiring an environmental assessment of all projects likely to damage important habitats, may be obliged to intervene.

The conservationists of Britain need to be aware of our latest forestry situations and campaign against them because the European Commission alone should not have to force the Government and the Forestry Commission into protecting Britain's wildlife. Such heritage is the responsibility of us all and nobody can justify an attitude of indifference.

If this lobby does not materialise and become active, conservation will fail miserably when faced with severe pressure from economic needs. Two issues in 1988 perfectly highlighted the need for public conservation awareness and immediate co-ordinated and planned action.

In January 1988 the national press leaked the information that the Government planned to sell off some of Britain's National Nature Reserves (NNR) as part of its privatisation scheme. The fifty-five reserves owned by the Nature Conservancy Council (NCC) are under threat by the proposed government sell-off scheme, which immediately devalues the work of the NCC in securing valuable land for the benefit of wildlife and the enjoyment of the population.

Many other NNRs are only partly owned by the NCC or leased and held under management agreements. However, 25 per cent of the NNR landholding is threatened, which immediately poses serious problems for conservationists. They face the task of persuading the Government that it has a duty to protect Britain's national heritage and should not relinquish its responsibility for maintaining conservation of the prime wildlife habitats through the NCC.

If the sell-off takes place, financially it would be impossible for the county Nature Conservation Trusts, the National Trust and other voluntary conservation bodies to buy all, or even part of the NNR holding. Without government grants it would also be impossible for independent societies to find the resources to manage these valuable sites properly, and the delicate natural balance of the habitat would be threatened.

The Department of the Environment argues that if voluntary bodies cannot manage these prime national sites, they should be offered to private companies and individual buyers. The conservation lobby need to be astute in their campaign to save the NNRs. If these sites still carry the restrictive covenants necessary to guarantee their protection, it is unlikely that they will pose an attractive, worthwhile proposition to purchasers. If they are stripped of their covenants, they are likely to be doomed by commercial exploitation.

The Secretary of State for the Environment, Nicholas Ridley, remains unmoved by all noises of disapproval. He puts the future responsibility on the NCC by saying, 'I have asked the NCC to examine its portfolio and consider whether there is greater scope for both future and existing resources to be kept in private ownership with appropriate conservation safeguards.'

The second conservation issue of 1988 was the Environment Secretary's plans to build more houses in the already overpopulated south-east of England. He generously conceded to the retention of the green-belt land surrounding London, but instead targeted the green land and open fields beyond, in the protected pastures of the Home Counties. Mr Ridley proposed the building of a further 600,000 houses in this area within the next decade and asked Berkshire alone to accommodate 43,000 more houses by 1996, which was 7,000 more properties than the ceiling set by Berkshire County Council.

Already the Government has faced battles in the Commons from among its own ranks, campaigning strongly against plans which further threaten any area of the British Isles gradually becoming more devoid of open countryside and wildlife habitats. It is equally important, however, that the Government hears protests from the electorate at local level and from all those people who consider the countryside of the south-east to be already stretched to its limits.

These topical issues are just two of the many about which conservationists need to campaign and create public awareness. Birds and wildlife generally have been pushed to their survival limits for years and, if they could, would scream out for mankind to consider the remaining countryside and habitats from their point of view. Such a reappraisal of values is the only sensible way forward.

Just as the environment is ever changing, so are attitudes towards conservation, and no doubt in the next few years conservationists will be confronting many other issues and developments.

Because of all the current pressures on the habitats of the British Isles and those proposals which look set to continue threatening the environment, conservationists are obliged to accept that some campaigns require more immediate action than others. One such campaign concerns our estuaries. Technologists are looking towards the tides around the British

209

coastline as a potential source of energy which can be harnessed without producing any polluting residues. The proposal is to increase tidal-power generation to supply electricity to the national grid, which would be achieved by building porous barriers or barrages across estuaries. Unfortunately, in the basin of the estuary these barrages would inevitably alter the tidal flow, especially on the ebb tide. Water would be retained longer in the estuary basin and the balanced chemical nature of the water would be altered, reducing salinity and increasing levels of pollutants, so affecting the ecology of the estuary. Feeding grounds of coastal birds, especially the waders, would be restricted and since 25 per cent of all Western Europe's waders overwinter on the estuaries and marshes of Britain, millions of birds would be forced to find somewhere else to feed – or die. As many as thirty of the estuaries around our coastline are threatened for one reason or another.

Such threats, looming on the horizon, must be given priority by conservationists, necessitating an approach of conserving entire habitats rather than single species of plant or animal. If the NNRs do fall into private ownership, one of the priorities must be a massive acquisition of land throughout the country which will fully protect not only the priority sites such as the SSSIs but also numerous other 'lesser' sites. These areas might not be national major environmental habitats, but are important at county level and represent important tracts of countryside for local populations. Taken collectively, such sites are extremely significant for their flora and fauna and some might eventually aspire to SSSI or NNR status. There are, of course, countless other sites which have not as yet been professionally surveyed or evaluated by conservationists and a system must be established whereby funds are generated to finance these surveys and enable necessary purchases to be made quickly. Government capitation for environmental issues has always been meagre compared to those sums made available for defence, education, transport and even health. Despite the recent reduction in government agricultural grants for drainage schemes, which will help conservation, and the increase in the NCC's grant from £22.7 million in 1985–6 to £32.1 million in 1986–7, which has enabled the NCC to protect more SSSIs, more money is urgently required.

Only when governments are prepared to accept that conservation problems are as significant as those of defence and other issues will realistic funds be made available to protect effectively all the necessary sites and manage them satisfactorily. Since it is unlikely that the Government's derisory conservation budgets are going to improve overnight, the onus is on the independent societies somehow to raise more funds. A major problem is that nobody has so far found a way of making vast profits from good conservation, but there are untapped resources which could bring in revenue. If as many sites as possible are to be protected the population of today must realise they need to pay for the countryside of tomorrow. Only a handful of societies make any public entry charge to their nature reserves. Admittedly the NCC cannot realistically charge for entry into the NNRs purchased by the taxpayer, but perhaps the time has come for all other societies to charge for entry to their reserves purely to raise funds to buy more land and important sites more quickly. Mankind thinks nothing of parting with the price of a gin and tonic each day just to lie on a sunbed whilst on holiday. It is therefore realistic to assume that when the public visit a particular nature reserve, they would be prepared to part with a similar sum, if they realised the significance for the future. If every existing conservation society member pooled £1 annually for site purchase conservationists could begin to make further inroads into habitat protection; but how much more could be achieved by charging all visitors to reserves?

Once a reserve is purchased all the management programmes which need to be implemented to constantly maintain the varied habitats cost money. The National Trust charges non-members to visit its properties and reserves and visitors are always willing to contribute to maintenance costs in this way. All reserves, especially if they involve traditional management schemes like coppicing, controlled flooding or grazing, need to be regularly managed otherwise they will deteriorate or revert to a different habitat and lose their specific wildlife value. It is easy to see how funds are spent on the basic management of maintaining footpaths, repairing fences or building reception centres, as well as training wardens and generally running the reserve, but the objective must be to convince the public that any money used has been well spent.

Throughout the British Isles agricultural, industrial and commercial developments have occurred which have destroyed the countryside, often with the aid of public funds. No longer should the individual allow his or her money to be spent in such a way, especially when it could so easily be directed towards conservation. The increase in public support for preserving the environment indicates that, given a chance to vote, individuals would prefer their taxes to be spent conserving rather than destroying.

Birds may not appear initially to be that important within the complexity of the universe, but they have been on this planet longer than mankind and a world without them would be a poorer place. If they finally disappeared it would mean all the habitats had become barren, so by making sure that birds continue to survive, significant steps will have been taken to preserve our many complex habitats, ensuring that our planet remains an habitable place.

RECOMMENDED SITES

The following list of recommended sites, including sites of national significance, has been compiled in order to help and encourage readers to observe birds in their natural habitat. The sites are grouped according to the habitat they represent, although some sites offer more than one kind of habitat.

Each site has been given a four-figure reference, using Ordnance Survey maps in the 1:50,000 Landranger Series. Great Britain is divided into 100-kilometre grid squares, each of which receives two letters as shown. The 100-kilometre squares are subdivided into 10-kilometre squares, numbered from the south-west corner of the square, in an easterly and northerly direction. Handa Island (NC 1348) is located in the 100-kilometre square NC, at the intersection of 1.3 kilometres

east and 4.8 kilometres north. Each reference pin-points the site precisely but in the case of vast areas such as National Parks the reference only locate parts of the habitat. Equally map references for rivers only pin-point part of the course, which may run through several counties, and vary in nature, with corresponding birdlife through each one. Suburban birdlife can be discovered in any of the market towns and cities of the British Isles.

Certain islands are marked on the map but are not included in the gazetteer simply because they are individually mentioned in the main text. Irish sites have not been given map references because the O.S. Landranger series of maps are not used in Ireland, so the county and position on the adjacent map will have to suffice.

Deciduous Woodland

1. Killarney Oakwoods (Kerry). Ancient Sessile oakwoods with conifer plantations surrounded by highest mountains in Ireland. The adjacent lakes attract large numbers of wintering wildfowl.
2. Glengariff Wood (Cork). A beautiful sessile oakwood, good for jays and warblers including blackcap and wood warbler.
3. Glen of the Downs Reserve (Wicklow). Mixed deciduous woodland with nesting warblers and redstarts.
4. Belvoir Park Forest (Down). South of Belfast, thirty-five breeding species have been recorded in this wood, including chiff-chaff, sparrowhawk and jay.
5. (Also coniferous) Castlecaldwell Forest (Fermanagh). Willow, alder and conifers dominate this RSPB reserve at the western end of Lower Lough Erne. Long-eared owl, and sparrowhawk can be seen with sandwich tern and tufted duck on the lough.
6. (Also coniferous) Lough Navan Forest (Fermanagh). Crossbills breed in this forest, together with warblers and jays. Hen harriers are often seen too.
7. Wistmans Wood (Devon) SX6177. A unique stunted pedunculate oakwood on the west-facing side of the Dart Valley, Dartmoor.
8. (Also coniferous) Yarner Wood (Devon) SX7878. Sessile oak, rowan, holly and birch mixed with conifer plantations. The wood lies along the valleys of the Yarner and Woodstock streams and pied flycatcher and wood warbler frequently breed.
9. Savernake Forest (Wiltshire) SU2266. Ancient oak and beech forest used for royal hunts until the 16th century. Rich in a wide variety of woodland birds.
10. New Forest (Hampshire) SU2806. 100 square miles of deciduous woodland, heath and wetland. Hawfinch, wood warbler, redstart, green and great spotted woodpeckers, tawny owl and honey buzzard are among the breeding birds.
11. Blean Wood (Kent) TR1161. Oak mixed with beech, hornbeam, ash and sweet chestnut. A good range of woodland birdlife is present.
12. Epping Forest (Essex) TQ4198. Ancient woodland, chiefly pollarded beech and hornbeam. Redpoll, redstart, hawfinch, willow warbler and blackcap are among the breeding species.
13. Burnham Beeches (Buckinghamshire) SU9585. Ancient pollarded beech mixed with oak. A wide variety of woodland birds breed including nuthatch, treecreeper and chiffchaff.
14. Flitwick Moor (Bedfordshire) TL0435. Ninety species of bird have been recorded in this mosaic of alder carr and birch scrub, including water-rail and grasshopper warbler.
15. Wyre Forest (Worcestershire) SO7576. Ancient oakwood with areas of old coppice. Redstarts, pied flycatchers and woodcock all breed.

16. Colt Park Wood (Yorkshire) SD7777. Ungrazed ash woodland growing on limestone pavement with interesting flora.
17. Roudsea Wood (Cumbria) SD3382. Ash and oak growing on limestone rich in flowers and birds including sparrowhawk, tawny owl, blackcap and garden warbler.
18. Morrone Birkwoods (Grampian) NO1390. Good example of Scottish birchwood mixed with juniper.
19. Craigellachie (Highland South) NH8812. Both downy and silver birch grow in one of the largest birchwoods in Speyside. The wood is alive with birdsong in summer including willow warbler and spotted flycatcher.
20. Mound Alderwoods (Highland North) NH7996. Alder carr bordering Loch Fleet, offering a wide variety of birds.
21. Rassal Ashwood (Highland North) NG8443. The most northerly ashwood in Britain, with typical birdlife.
22. Coed Cymerau Isaf (Gwynedd) SH6942. One of the most important oak woodlands inside the Snowdonia National Park, with redstarts and pied flycatchers breeding.
23. Gwenffrwd – Dinas (Dyfed) SN7847. Two large blocks of sessile oakwoods, with frequent sightings of red kite.
24. Cwm Clydach (Gwent) SO2112. Beech trees growing at the Western limit of their natural range mixed with some ash, wych elm and sessile oak.
25. Forest of Dean (Gloucestershire) SO6008. Mixed deciduous woodland with breeding buzzards, ravens, nightjars, wood warblers, hawfinches, woodlarks, redstarts and pied flycatchers.

Coniferous Woodland

26. Black Wood of Rannoch (Tayside) NN5755. An important remnant of the ancient Caledonian pine and birch forest with trees up to 250 years old. Capercaillie, Scottish crossbill, siskin and tree pipit all breed.
27. Glenmore Forest (Highland South) NH9709. Remnants of ancient Caledonian pine survive amongst commercial Scots pine and sitka spruce. Crested tit, Scottish crossbill and capercaillies all breed.
28. Rothiemurchus Forest (Highland South) NH9110. Fine stands of native Caledonian pine with breeding crested tit, crossbill and tree pipit.
29. Loch Garten (Highland South) NH9718. A remnant of Caledonian pine forest owned by the RSPB and famous for its Ospreys. In summer up to sixty species of bird breed in the forest including Scottish crossbill and crested tit. The new RSPB reserve, Abernethy Forest Estate, is adjacent and covers 8498 ha/21,000 acres, including native Caledonian pine.
30. Culbin Forest (Grampian) NH9861. A large area of conifer plantations growing on sand and famous for crested tit, goldcrest and capercaillie.

31. Strathfarrar (Highland South) NH2737. The pinewoods of this glen provide some of the finest remnants of the ancient Forest of Caledon with Scottish crossbill and crested tit breeding.
32. Glen Affric (Highland South) NH2424. One of the most attractive reserves in Scotland with ancient Caledonian pines combining with hills, lochs and waterfalls. Black grouse and capercaillie breed.

Heaths and Breckland

33. The Lizard (Cornwall) SW7018. Much of the West Lizard is formed of serpentine rock and the entire area offers maritime heathland and coastal cliffs.
34. St Agnes Head (Cornwall) SW7051. Interesting maritime heathland with fine cliffs attracting rock doves and ravens.
35. Aylesbeare Common (Devon) SY0589. One of the best heathland areas in south east Devon owned by RSPB. Stonechats, nightjars and Dartford warblers all breed.
36. Arne (Dorset) SY9888. Outstanding heathland bordering oak and birch woodland, mudflats and saltmarsh and owned by RSPB. The best place in Britain to see the rare Dartford Warbler.
37. Studland Heath (Dorset) SZ0284. A National Nature Reserve comprising heathland and sand-dunes. Typical heathland birds including linnet, yellowhammer, nightjar and hobby breed.
38. Frensham, Thursley and Hankley Commons (Surrey) SU9040. The most interesting heathland remaining in Surrey; partly afforested with conifer. Birdlife includes nightjar, whinchat, stonechat, hobby and lesser whitethroat.
39. Chobham Common (Surrey) SU9764. Wet and dry heathland with breeding woodlark, nightjar, whinchat and stonechat.
40. Chailey Common (Sussex) TQ3821. Wet and dry heath with birch scrub attracting a variety of birds.
41. Cavenham Heath (Suffolk) TL7573. Breckland heath mixed with woodland and fen. Stone curlew, woodlark, grasshopper warbler and linnet.
42. Weeting Heath (Norfolk) TL7588. Typical Breckland heath with stone curlew and wheatear breeding and crossbill nest in the old pine trees.
43. Thetford Heath (Suffolk) TL8782. Breckland heath with conifer plantations. Stonechat, whinchat, tree pipit and crossbill breed and in winter great grey shrike occur annually.
44. Wangford Glebe (Suffolk) TL7583. The last remnant of genuine sandy Breckland with interesting range of plants and animals.
45. (Also deciduous woodland) Cannock Chase (Staffordshire) SJ9784. A large mosaic of heathland, woodland and bog which is designated an Area of Outstanding Natural Beauty. Heathland, scrub and woodland birds breed here, including 66 per cent of the Midlands nightjar population.

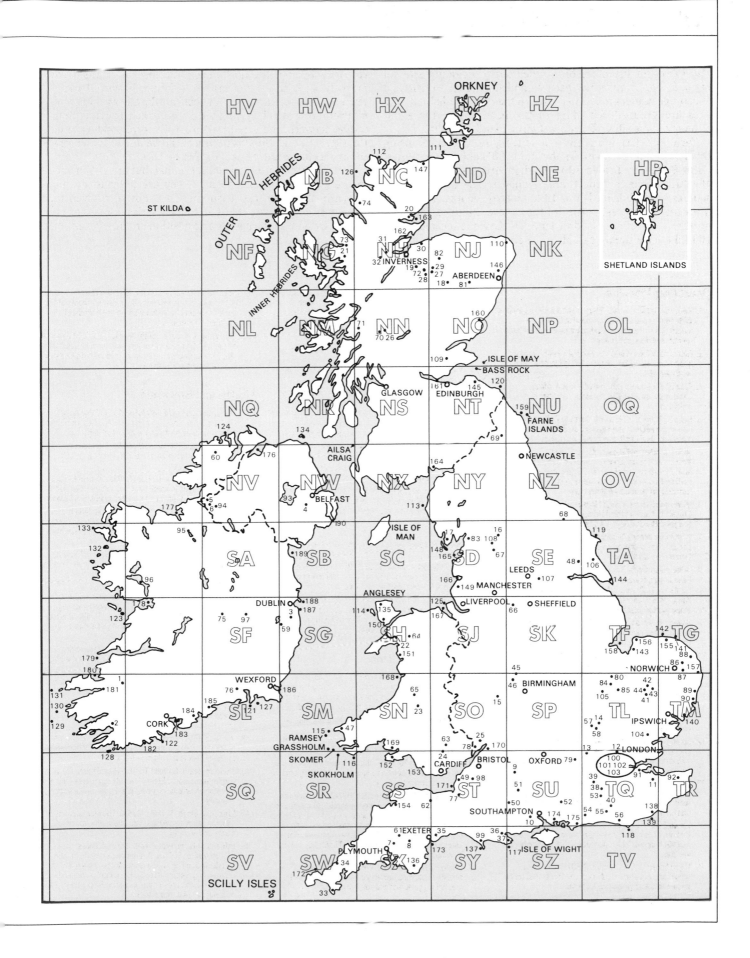

46. (Also deciduous woodland) Highgate Common (Staffordshire) SQ8490. Open heathland and birch scrubland attracting yellowhammer, linnet, woodpeckers and warblers.

47. St David's Head (Dyfed) SM7428. Extensive area of maritime heath with high seacliffs offering typical heathland birds, chough and raven.

48. Skipwith Common (Yorkshire) SE6537. One of the largest lowland heaths in northern England with breeding nightjar stonechat, whinchat, linnet and grasshopper warbler.

Downs and Scrubland

49. Brean Down (Somerset) ST2958. An important limestone down for migrating birds. With the adjacent cliffs a wide range of clifftop, grassland and scrubland birds breed.

50. Wylye Down (Wiltshire) SU0036. An area of rich grass downland which is an NCC reserve.

51. Pewsey Downs (Wiltshire) SU1163. A magnificent stretch of open chalk downland managed by the NCC and rich in downland birds and flowers.

52. (Also deciduous woodland) Old Winchester Hill (Hampshire) SU6421. Chalk downland mixed with deciduous woodland; hawthorn and juniper scrub. All three native woodpeckers, kestrels and numerous warblers occur.

53. (Also deciduous woodland) Box Hill (Surrey) TQ1751. A dramatic area of chalk downland and scrub with box and yew trees. Typical down and scrubland birds breed despite frequent human visitors.

54. Levin Down (Sussex) SU8813. Juniper grows on this south facing chalk downland and scrubland birds are common.

55. Ditchling Beacon (Sussex) TQ3213. A steep scarp of the South Downs with magnificent views and numerous scrubland birds.

56. Cuckmere Haven and Severn Sisters Country Park (Sussex) TV5199. An outstanding area of clifftop downland, chalkland estuary and sheer white cliffs. Meadow pipit, skylark, common whitethroat and stonechat breed, but the entire area is excellent for observing migrating birds in spring and autumn.

57. Ivinghoe Beacon (Buckinghamshire) SP9616. Chalk grassland hills overlooking the Vale of Aylesbury. The typical scrub vegetation attracts numerous breeding birds.

58. (Also deciduous woodland) Totternhoe Knolls (Bedfordshire) SP9821. The mixture of chalk grassland, scrub and beech woods attract a wide range of birds including woodpeckers, warblers and tree pipit.

Mountains or Moorland

59. Wicklow Mountains (Wicklow). Largest area of high moorland and mountains in Ireland. Ring ousel, red grouse and hen harrier occur.

60. Glenveagh National Park (Donegal). Mountainous country with woodland and lakes. Merlin, peregrine, raven, golden plover and ring ousel breed.

61. Dartmoor National Park (Devon) SX6773. 94,500 hectares/233,509 acres of moorland with granite tors and wooded valleys. Stonechat, whinchat, meadow pipit, ring ousel, golden plover, curlew and snipe are among the breeding birds.

62. (Also deciduous woodland) Exmoor National Park (Devon and Somerset) ST9040. The park is a mixture of moorland, heathland, coastal cliffs and woodland and dipper, raven, buzzard, merlin, curlew and wheatear are typical birds of the habitat mosaic covering 68,635 hectares/169,597 acres.

63. Brecon Beacons National Park (Powys) SO9920. Heather moors, wooded valleys and upland streams covering 134,421 hectares/332,154 acres provide a variety of habitats for typical upland birds.

64. Snowdonia National Park (Gwynedd) SH6154. A great diversity of birds including ring ousel, merlin and hen harrier are seen within the mountain, moorland and valley habitats covering 218,455 hectares/539,802 acres.

65. Cors Caron (Dyfed) SN6963. Formerly called Cors Tregaron, this is one of the best upland peat bogs of Britain. Red Kite, curlew, redshank, merlin and hen harrier are often seen.

66. The Peak National Park (Derbyshire) SK2066. Spectacular upland moors and bogs covering 140,378 hectares/346, 874 acres where dunlin, curlew and red grouse are among the breeding birds.

67. Yorkshire Dales National Park (Yorkshire) SD8473. This park covering 176,113 hectares/435,175 acres contains some of Britain's most spectacular scenery. Buzzards, raven, ring ousel, peregrine and short-eared owl are frequently seen.

68. North York Moors National Park (Yorkshire) SE6092. Some of the best red grouse moors in Britain occur within this 138,050 hectare/341,121 acre park.

69. (Also deciduous woodland) Northumberland National Park (Northumberland) NU9027. Large area of conifer plantations (Kielder Forest) are mixed within 113,110 hectares/279,494 acres of upland country where dipper, golden plover, dunlin and merlin breed.

70. Rannoch Moor (Tayside) NN4053. A mosaic of bogs, peat moorland and lochs with a variety of moorland birds.

71. Glencoe (Highland South) NN1556. Spectacular, steep-sided mountains offering shelter to golden eagle and peregrine, whereas ptarmigan and golden plover breed on the moors.

72. Cairngorms (Highland South) NJ0101. High granite peaks and plateaux where golden eagle, ptarmigan, dotterel and greenshank breed.

73. Torridon (Highland South) NG9059. This mountainous wilderness offers some of Scotland's finest scenery, where golden plover, ring ousel, wheatear, golden eagle and peregrine breed.

74. Inverpolly (Highland North) NC1312. A vast mountainous area, interspersed with moorland, bogs and lochs. One hundred and four species of bird have been observed including golden plover, greenshank, black-throated diver, goosander and ptarmigan.

Rivers or Flood Meadow

75. River Shannon (Tipperary) Longest river in British Isles with excellent flood meadows between Portumna and Lanesborough. At the tributary of River Suck with Shannon, 14,000 wigeon, 2,000 black-tailed godwit and 300 white-fronted geese congregate in winter.

76. River Suir (Waterford) Callows at Coolfin and Portlaw provide feeding grounds for 200 greylag geese, swans and ducks in winter.

77. Somerset Levels (Somerset) ST3625. The flooding of several rivers onto neighbouring low lying grassland provides winter feeding grounds for wigeon, golden plover and dunlin. In spring lapwing, redshank, snipe and curlew breed.

78. River Wye (Gwent) SO5401. A spectacular river gorge running through some of the most ancient woodland in Britain. Riverside birds are complemented by woodland species.

79. River Thames (Buckinghamshire ref.) SU7984. Along its length from Gloucestershire to the estuary in the North Sea, the Thames offers varied birdwatching as it flows through different habitats.

80. Ouse Washes (Cambridgeshire) TL4786. The largest flooded freshwater meadows in Britain visited by 3,000 Bewick's swan and 30,000 wigeon each winter. Black-tailed godwit, ruff, redshank and snipe breed each year.

81. River Dee (Grampian) NO1391. One of Scotland's productive salmon rivers with mixed woodland on its banks. Shingle banks are found along the river coarse and common sandpipers, grey wagtail and oystercatcher are among the breeding birds.

82. (Also coniferous woodland) River Spey (Highland South) NO0124. This river runs through one of the most visited regions of Scotland. Spey Valley includes Loch Garten, ancient Caledonian forests and the margins of the Cairngorms reserve so that scenery and birdlife are both varied. The Spey's floodplain near Kingussie forms Insh Marshes, an RSPB reserve, where greylag geese feed in winter and wood sandpipers and goldeneye breed.

Marshlands, Fens and Broads

83. Leighton Moss (Lancashire) SD4875. This freshwater marsh has areas of open water together with dense reedbeds and alder-willow carr. Bittern, gadwall, garganey, bearded tit, and grasshopper warbler are some of the breeding birds. Excellent for wintering wildfowl.

84. Woodwalton Fen (Cambridgeshire) TL2384. One of Britain's major relict fens covering 205 hectares/506 acres with waterfilled dykes, reedbeds, and alder carr. Insect, birdlife and flora are extremely varied.

85. Wicken Fen (Cambridgeshire) TL5670. Relict fenland with a mere surrounded by reeds and marshland. Snipe, redshank, reed warbler and reed bunting all breed regularly and in summer Cetti's and Savi's warbler and marsh harrier occur.

86. Hoveton Great Broad Nature Trail (Norfolk) TG3215. Accessible only by boat, the trail overlooks fenland, alder carr and Broadland and provides a good introduction to the wildlife of the habitat.

87. Strumpshaw Fen (Norfolk) TG3406. With reedbeds, alder-willow carr, open water and grazing marshes all within 247 hectares/610 acres, birdwatching is superb. Cetti's, Savi's, grasshopper and reed warbler are seen together with marsh harrier, bearded tit, water rail, kingfisher, snipe and yellow wagtail.

88. Hickling Broad (Norfolk) TG4121. Access is by permit only, but this broadland reserve protects one of the largest areas of open water surrounded by reedbeds and wet woodland. Bittern, bearded tit, Savi's, grasshopper, reed and sedge warbler are among the breeding birds.

89. Walberswick (Suffolk) TM4974. Reedbeds, marshland and scrub vegetation provide shelter for bitterns, marsh harrier, bearded tits, water-rail and grasshopper warbler. In spring and autumn passage migration is interesting.

90. Minsmere (Suffolk) TM4767. Perhaps the most famous RSPB reserve, with reedbeds, lagoons, dunes and alder-willow carr attracting avocet, little tern, bittern, marsh harrier, water rail and Savi's warbler amongst many other species.

91. (Also deciduous woodland) North Kent Marshes (Kent) TQ7976. These large marshes lie in the Thames estuary and the varied habitat attracts many winter visitors including white-fronted geese, Bewick's swan, smew, scaup, hen harrier, short-eared owl and even Lapland bunting.

92. Stodmarsh (Kent) TR2260. One of the best wetlands in Britain especially for breeding Savi's and Cetti's warblers. Carganey, shoveler and teal breed and osprey and black tern seen on migration.

Lakes, Gravel Pits or Reservoirs

93. Lough Neagh (Armagh and Fermanagh). The largest freshwater lake in the British Isles with several islands and various marginal habitats. Internationally important wintering populations of whooper and Bewick's swans, teal, shoveler, pintail, tufted duck, pochard and goldeneye occur on the lake.

94. Lough Erne (Fermanagh). With an indented shoreline and wooded islands, this large lake has distinct upper and lower basins. There is an RSPB reserve at Castle Caldwell and the lough is the main Irish breeding site for common scoters.

95. Lough Gara (Sligo/Roscommon). Two lakes are connected by a narrow channel. Lesser black-backed gulls breed and winter wildfowl populations are high, including white-fronted geese.

96. Lough Corrib (Galway). This large lake has an area of marshland at the southern end and many islands, attracting breeding gulls. Each autumn around 22,000 pochard and 12,000 coots gather on the lake.

97. Westmeath Lakes (Westmeath). Lough Derravaragh is one of the most significant of a series of shallow lakes covering 1,400 hectares/3,459 acres. Overwintering wildfowl include 6,000 pochards, 3,000 coots and 2,000 shovelers.

98. Chew Valley Lake (Avon/Somerset) ST5761. Covering 656 hectares/1,620 acres, this large reservoir attracts breeding garganey, gadwall, ruddy duck and sedge warbler. Overwintering wildfowl include Bewick's swan, pintail, goldeneye and smew.

99. Radipole Lake (Dorset) SY6779. An extensive freshwater lake with reedbeds and scrub margins. Cetti's warbler, kingfisher, water-rail, bearded tit and lesser whitethroat breed and passage migration is interesting in spring/autumn.

100. Barn Elms Reservoir (London) TQ2377. The reservoir is an SSSI with permit access. Residents include great-crested grebe, tufted duck, mallard and coot. In winter gulls, cormorant, gadwall, wigeon and grey wagtail are common and passage migrants include black tern and common sandpiper.

101. Queen Mary Reservoir (Ashford, Middlesex) TQ0770. An important site for wintering wildfowl and migrant species. Great crested and black-necked grebe are often seen, whereas gadwall, goldeneye and goosander are frequent visitors.

102. Staines Reservoirs (Staines, Middlesex) TQ0573. Good birdwatching is obtained from the central causeway between Staines North and South reservoirs. Both are SSSIs. Large populations of wintering pochard and tufted duck, together with wigeon, teal, goosander and goldeneye occur annually.

103. Lee Valley/Walthamstow Reservoirs (London) TQ3790. This group of reservoirs is rich in birdlife including a large heronry. Mute swan, Canada geese, mallard, pochard and tufted duck breed. Thirty species of waders have been recorded on migration including green sandpiper.

104. Abberton Reservoir (Essex) TL9718. The best known reservoir in eastern England with goldeneye, goosander, teal, pintail and wigeon guaranteed.

105. Grafham Water (Cambridgeshire) TL1568. Sheltered creeks, surrounding woodland and grassland make this reservoir attractive for wintering teal, shoveler, wigeon, gadwall and pochard. Waders and terns occur on spring and autumn migration.

106. Hornsea Mere (Humberside) TA1947. A natural lake surrounded by alder-willow carr and reedbeds and rich in both wintering and breeding birds. Sedge warbler, corn bunting, shoveler and gadwall are some of the breeding species.

107. Fairburn Ings (Yorkshire) SE4627. An RSPB reserve formed by mining subsidence. Greenshank, spotted redshank, ruff and green sandpiper occur as passage migrants; whooper swans overwinter and lapwing, snipe and redshank breed.

108. Malham Tarn (Yorkshire) SD8967. An important upland lake with surrounding bog and fen. Common sandpipers, curlews, redshanks and golden plover all breed nearby.

109. Loch Leven (Tayside) NO1501. The largest natural eutrophic lake in the country: 1600 hectares/3900 acres. Numerous islands, including St Serfs have breeding mallards and tufted ducks. Wintering wildfowl include pink-footed geese, goldeneye, goosander, wigeon and shoveler. Passage migration is interesting.

110. Loch of Strathbeg (Grampian) NK0759. Covering 222 hectares/550 acres, the loch is Britain's largest dune-slack lake, attracting spring and autumn migrants and wintering wildfowl. Greylag and pink-footed geese populations are significant.

Sea Cliffs

111. Dunnet Head (Highland) NK1973. Cliffs topped with moorland. Fulmar, kittiwake, black and common guillemots, razorbill and puffin all breed.

112. Clo Mor (Highland) NC2571. Huge seabird colonies breed on mainland Britain's highest sea cliffs including all the auks, fulmar, peregrine and rock dove.

113. St Bees Head (Cumbria) NX9511. Magnificent sheer sandstone cliffs with large seabird colonies including all auks, kittiwake, fulmar and herring gull.

114. South Stack (Gwynedd) SH2082. An RSPB reserve at the western tip of Holy Island, Anglesey where guillemot, razorbill, puffin, cormorant, shag, kittiwake, fulmar and a few chough breed.

115. St Davids Head (Dyfed) SM7428. The high cliffs are well known for chough, raven and rock pipit.

116. Pembrokeshire Coastal Path (Dyfed) SN1646–1707. Between Cardigan and Tenby the coastline comprises outstanding seacliffs with fulmar, guillemot, razorbill, kittiwake, shag and various gulls breeding.

117. Purbeck Cliffs (Dorset) SY9078. Good seabird colonies breed on this fine stretch of limestone cliffs.

118. Beachy Head (Sussex) TV5895. These famous cliffs provide one of the best migration viewpoints on the south coast with birds ranging from pomarine skuas to black-throated divers.

119. Bempton Cliffs (Yorkshire) TA1973. These sheer, spectacular cliffs are an RSPB reserve with thousands of auks breeding, together with 500 pairs of gannets and over 65,000 pairs of kittiwakes.

120. St Abbs Head (Borders) NT9168. 12km/8 miles of cliffs with vast seabird colonies, including 10,000 guillemots alongside razorbill, fulmar and kittiwake.

121. Hook Head (Wexford). A rocky, exposed headland, outstanding for watching migrants and vagrants. The most easterly breeding site for chough on the south coast of Ireland.

122. Old Head of Kinsale (Cork). Cliffs and sea-stacks form this rugged headland where razorbill, guillemot and kittiwake breed.

123. Cliffs of Moher (Clare). Dramatic cliffs facing the Atlantic where puffin, razorbill, guillemot and kittiwake all breed.

124. Horn Head (Donegal). Reputedly the finest headland in Ireland where sheer cliffs rise 200 metres/656 feet and provide crevices for Ireland's largest razorbill colony alongside puffins and guillemots.

Off-shore Islands

125. Hilbre Islands (Merseyside) SJ1888. Located in the mouth of the Dee estuary, the islands are a birdwatcher's paradise because of the thousands of waders and rare migrants.

126. Handa (Highland) NC1348. Owned by the RSPB, this uninhabited island with high cliffs has a rough grassland interior with lochans. Thirty species of bird breed, including great and Arctic skuas, eider and red-throated diver.

127. Saltee Islands (Wexford). These two uninhabited islands provide the only large seabird colonies in SE Ireland. Gannet, shag, cormorants and kittiwake all breed and spring and autumn passage migration is rewarding.

128. Cape Clear Island (Cork). The high cliffs and boggy interior of this island attract black guillemot, chough and skuas to breed. It is famous for large autumn seabird movements, especially great shearwaters.

129. The Skelligs (Kerry). The islands comprise three precipitous rocks off Bolus Head. Little Skellig has Ireland's largest gannet colony together with guillemot and kittiwake.

130. Puffin Island (Kerry). This uninhabited island lies on the northern side of St Finan's Bay. Thousands of puffins, together with large numbers of manx shearwater and storm petrel breed.

131. Blasket Islands (Kerry) Famous for seabird colonies, these exposed islands off Slea Head have difficult access. Manx shearwaters, puffins, razorbills and storm petrels breed.

132. Clare Island (Mayo). The interior of this exposed island off Clew Bay is rolling moorland where corncrake breed, but the cliffs attract guillemot, razorbill and chough.

133. Inishkea Islands (Mayo). Both these low-lying islands are uninhabited and lie off the Mullet Peninsula. 60 per cent of the Irish wintering barnacle geese, congregate on the islands.

134. Rathlin Island (Antrim). Lying barely 4 km/2.5 miles off the Antrim coast, the high cliffs and stacks attract large seabird colonies, especially razorbill, guillemot and kittiwake. Breeding chough are also found.

Shingle Beaches

135. Cemlyn (Gwynedd) SH3393. This shingle bank is a storm beach where sandwich, common and arctic terns breed with oystercatcher and red-breasted merganser.

136. Slapton Sands (Devon) SX8243. The most south westerly shingle beach in Britain with adjacent Slapton Ley lagoon. Spring and autumn passage migration is good and 10,000 gulls winter roost on the shingle.

137. Chesil Beach (Dorset) SY6280. One of the largest shingle beaches in Britain where little tern and ringed plover breed.

138. Rye Harbour (Sussex) TQ9418. This shingle foreshore and bordering saltmarsh with lagoons has a spectacular birdlife including little and common tern, oystercatcher, redshank, black-headed gull and ringed plover.

139. Dungeness (Kent) TR0619. One of the largest shingle ridges in Europe with up to fifty species breeding in the RSPB reserve. Passage migration is interesting including wryneck, black-tern and bluethroat.

140. Orfordness (Suffolk) TM4348. A huge shingle spit where lesser-black backed and herring gull breed. Wildfowl congregate in autumn and winter on the saltmarsh.

141. Blakeney Point (Norfolk) TG0046. The shingle spit and sand-dunes of the point form a National Trust reserve. Sandwich, common and little tern breed together with oystercatcher and ringed plover. Passage migration is rewarding including many rarities.

142. (Also sand-dunes) Scolt Head (Norfolk) TF7944. This NCC reserve can only be reached by boat, but the shingle and dunes provide interesting birdwatching especially for terns.

143. (Also estuary) Snettisham (Norfolk) TF6433. The shingle banks border mudflats and have resulted from the extraction industry. Common tern, oystercatcher and ringed plover breed, but wildfowl numbers are impressive in winter.

144. Spurn Peninsula (Yorkshire) TA4115. This narrow shingle spine is one of the best places in Europe for watching passage migrants including rarities.

Sand-dunes

145. Aberlady Bay (Lothian) NT4680. This open bay with sand dunes and saltmarsh is an important site for resident and migrant birds with 228 species recorded and 55 species breeding including eider duck.

146. Sands of Forvie (Grampian) NK0227. Shelduck breed on the dunes together with the largest population of eider. Four species of tern nest on the remoter dunes and wildfowl roost on the neighbouring Ythan Estuary in winter.

147. Invernaver (Highland North) NC6960. The sand dunes merge into moorland behind, so typical sand dune birds breed alongside snipe and greenshank.

148. Isle of Walney (Cumbria) SD2162. Lying in the mouth of Morecambe Bay this narrow island is home to breeding eider, arctic and sandwich tern, oystercatcher and shelduck.

149. Ainsdale Dunes (Lancashire) SD2910. Vast sand-dunes managed as an NCC reserve with typical dune birdlife and interesting flora, amphibians and reptiles.

150. Newborough Warren (Gwynedd) SH4063. Excellent sand-dunes managed as an NCC reserve with herring and lesser black-backed gulls breeding alongside meadow pipit, skylark and curlew.

151. Morfa Harlech (Gwynedd) SH5835. Sand-dunes, saltmarsh and mudflats form a National Nature Reserve with wildfowl in winter and curlew, lapwing, redshank and shelduck breeding.

152. Oxwich (Glamorgan) SS5086. A well organised nature trail reveals all the typical flora and fauna including wintering wildfowl and waders.

153. Kenfig Dunes (Glamorgan) SS8081. A superb dune system with freshwater pools, attract breeding sedge and grasshopper warbler and passage waders including greenshank, sanderling and whimbrel.

154. Braunton Burrows (Devon) SS4635. One of the largest dune systems in Britain and managed as an NCC reserve. Flora and fauna are typical of sand-dunes.

155. Holkham Dunes (Norfolk) TF8944. Extensive sand-dunes with pine trees, bordering mudflats. Autumn and spring passage migration is impressive including rarities, and white-fronted geese arrive in winter to roost and feed.

156. Holme Dunes (Norfolk) TF7044. These sand-dunes are attractive to passage migrants and with residents, over 280 species have been recorded including rare, barred and icterine warblers.

Estuaries or Mudflats

157. Breydon Water (Norfolk) TG4705. Mudflats and marshland attract black-tern and spoonbill on migration; and white-fronted Brent and pink-footed geese often visit this large inland estuary.

158. The Wash (Lincolnshire) TF5040. Extensive mudflats fringed with saltmarsh are exposed at low tide and one of the most important sites in Britain for wintering waders and wildfowl.

159. Lindisfarne – Holy Island (Northumberland) NU1042. Mudflats covering 3,200 hectares 8,000 acres attract wigeon and the largest wintering flock of light-bellied Brent geese, outside Ireland.

160. Montrose Basin (Tayside) NO6957. Huge mudflats are exposed at low tied and dunlin, knott, oystercatcher, curlew and redshank are among the seasonal waders.

161. Inner Moray Firth (Highland North) NH6949. The Beauly Firth area has large mudflats and saltmarshes and wildfowl and waders are numerous. Merganser and goosander can be seen off-shore.

162. Cromarty Firth (Highland North) NH7873. The Nigg and Udale Bay reserves represent the most important wintering site for wildfowl and waders in N.E. Scotland. 10,000 greylag geese roost on the estuary.

163. Loch Fleet (Highland North) NH7796. At low tide huge mudflats are exposed for feeding waders and wildfowl. Goldeneye, common scoter, eider and long-tailed duck overwinter.

164. Caerlaverock (Dumfries & Galloway) NY0365. The mudflats are huge but extremely dangerous providing sanctuary for the entire wintering population of Spitzbergen barnacle geese and around 15,000 oystercatchers during October.

165. Morecambe Bay (Lancashire) SD4666. Situated between Cumbria and Lancashire this huge estuary covering 2485 hectares/6140 acres, provides fascinating birdwatching throughout the year. The premier site in winter to see waders in vast numbers.

166. Ribble Estuary (Lancashire) SD4026. The extensive mudflats and huge saltmarshes make this estuary attractive to a wide range of waders and wildfowl including the largest roost of wintering pink-footed geese in N.W. England.

167. Dee Estuary (Cheshire) SJ2577. The mixture of sand, mudflats and saltmarshes make this wide estuary important for wildfowl. Twenty-two of the twenty-seven British species occur here and in winter, over 140,000 waders; over 10 per cent of the British population roost.

168. Dovey Estuary/Aberdyfi (Dyfed) SN6595. This National Nature Reserve is one of the most important wildfowl sanctuaries in Wales. Ringed plover, sanderling, dunlin and oystercatcher are among the waders seen.

169. Burry Inlet (Glamorgan) SS9750. Formed by the broad estuary of the River Loughor, the sandflats and saltmarsh attract large flocks of wintering oystercatcher and wildfowl.

170. Slimbridge/Severn Estuary (Gloucestershire) SO7205. On the south eastern bank of the Severn Estuary is Slimbridge, the headquarters reserve of the Wildfowl Trust. 404 hectares/1000 acres of mudflats and marsh attract white-fronted geese, Bewick's swan, wigeon, pintail and shoveler each winter.

171. Bridgwater Bay (Avon and Somerset) ST2746. On the south side of the Bristol Channel, the shallow bay has huge mudflats which are famous for whimbrel in spring and thousands of mallard, shelduck and wigeon in winter.

172. Hayle Estuary (Cornwall) SW5537. Large flocks of great black-backed, lesser black-backed, black-headed and herring gulls occur here in winter, together with a wide variety of wildfowl. Bar-tailed godwit, green sandpiper and spotted redshank are among the more unusual waders.

173. Exe Estuary (Devon) SX9878. This vast estuary forms one of the most important wader and wildfowl wintering sites on the south west peninsula. Dark-bellied Brent geese, wigeon and dunlin occur in large flocks.

174. Farlington Marshes and Langstone Harbour (Hampshire) SU6804 and 6904. Farlington marshes are an important wetland on the south coast at the head of Langstone Harbour. Brent geese regularly overwinter in the harbour alongside shelduck. Over 40 species of wader have been recorded.

175. Pagham Harbour (Sussex) SZ8796. A small but accessible reserve of mudflats and saltmarsh with numerous waders and wildfowl.

176. Lough Foyle (Donegal/Derry). Extensive mudflats are best observed between Muff and Roe estuaries where wigeon and other wildfowl overwinter.

177. Sligo Bay (Sligo). The rivers Ballysadare, Drumcliff and Garavague flow into this estuary where vast mudflats attract barnacle and Brent geese, wigeon and bar-tailed godwit.

178. Galway Bay (Galway). This vast bay on Ireland's west coast is one of the best sites for wintering wildfowl and waders. Nimmo's Pier at the Claddagh is ideal for watching divers, waders and gulls, including glaucus gull.

179. Shannon Estuary (Clare, Limmerick, Kerry). At low tide enormous mudflats are exposed attracting thousands of birds. At Fergus estuary 16,000 black-tailed godwits feed in spring and at the same site in winter 33,000 dunlin roost.

180. Tralee Bay (Kerry). The best areas of mudflat and saltmarsh are near Derrymore Island and Bannow Harbour. Brent geese, wigeon and common scoter congregate in winter.

181. Castlemaine Harbour (Kerry). Saltmarsh and mudflats surround this large estuary where thousands of Brent geese, pintail, wigeon and shoveler overwinter.

182. Clonakilty Bay (Cork). Two inlets flow into this sandy bay which is good for passage waders and overwintering black-tailed godwits.

183. Cork Harbour (Cork). The River Lee and several smaller rivers flow into this large estuary where good views of overwintering wildfowl and waders can be secured at Glanmire and Carrigaline.

184. Ballymacoda (Cork). This is the estuary of Womanagh River with surrounding mudflats and saltmarshes. Golden plover, black-tailed godwits and lapwing are often seen.

185. Dungarven Bay (Waterford). Extensive mudflats and saltmarshes attracts numerous waders and Brent geese.

186. Wexford Harbour and Slobs (Wexford). The River Slaney runs into the broad sandy estuary and behind the sea walls of the harbour are North and South Slobs. Large populations of wintering wildfowl graze these reclaimed meadows including over 5000 Greenland white-fronted geese.

187. North Bull (Dublin). One of the most important wetlands in Ireland for vast populations of wildfowl and waders including dunlin, knot and purple sandpipers. The saltmarsh and mudflats act as a high tide wader roost for Dublin Bay.

188. Rogerstown Estuary (Dublin). A broad estuary with mudflats and sand-spits. Brent, barnacle and greylag geese overwinter together with wigeon and the estuary is good for passage waders.

189. Dundalk Bay (Louth) Thousands of oystercatchers and bar-tailed godwits winter on this broad shallow estuary with extensive mudflats. South Marsh and Lurgan green are the main high-tide roosts.

190. Strangford Lough (Down). The mudflats of this virtually land-locked inlet are extensive and the northern area around Newtonards offers good birdwatching. Whooper swan, Brent geese, wigeon and knot occur in large numbers.

INDEX of BIRDS and GENERAL INDEX

Numbers in italics refer to illustrations, Numbers in bold refer to main entries

GENERAL INDEX